2000

D0981958

John L. Lewis

A BIOGRAPHY

John L. Lewis

A BIOGRAPHY

MELVYN DUBOFSKY
and WARREN VAN TINE

Quadrangle/The New York Times Book Co.

Designed by Beth Tondreau

Library of Congress Cataloging in Publication Data

Dubofsky, Melvyn, 1934-
  John L. Lewis.

  Bibliography: p.
  Includes index.
  1. Lewis, John Llewellyn, 1880-1969.
2. Trade-unions—United States—Officials and employees—Biography. 3. United Mine Workers of America—History. I. Van Tine, Warren R., joint author.
HD6509.L4D8 1977   331.88'0924 [B]   76-50819
ISBN 0-8129-0673-X

Contents

(Illustrations follow pages 150, 334 and 440.)

Acknowledgments

As with most works of scholarship, this book could not have been completed without the assistance of numerous individuals and institutions. Simply listing their names and contributions in an obligatory acknowledgment scarcely seems adequate compensation for the services they provided us.

Fellowships and grants-in-aid from the Research Foundation of the State University of New York and The Ohio State University Graduate School enabled us to launch the initial research for the project beginning in 1971. The National Endowment for the Humanities generously awarded one of the authors (Melvyn Dubofsky) a Senior Fellowship for the year 1973-1974 that enabled him to devote his full time to research and writing.

Arnold Miller, president of the United Mine Workers of America, Tom Bethel, a union staff official, and Edgar James, then also on the UMWA staff, kindly allowed us to examine the UMWA's archives, including the office files of John L. Lewis, before they had been catalogued and could be opened for general use. They also permitted us to move about union headquarters freely and to use the union's Xerox machines to duplicate important documents from the files.

David Dubinsky, Jacob Potofsky, A. H. Raskin, Rex Lauck, John Owens, George DeNucci, and Len DeCaux all graciously shared their memories of John L. Lewis and the American labor movement with us, and in most cases permitted us to tape-record their reminiscences.

Mrs. Doris Bell, John L. Lewis's sister-in-law, was an untiring correspondent whose letters provided information about the Lewis family and John L. Lewis's private life not available elsewhere.

So many individuals and institutions made our work easier that it is almost impossible to thank them all. But let us try. Joseph Howerton and the staff of the Social and Economic Branch of the National Archives and the Federal Records Center, Suitland, Maryland, led us through the government's voluminous collection of documents concerning John L. Lewis, the coal miners, and the labor movement from 1919 through 1952. Jonathan Grossman, the Department of Labor historian, permitted us to use his office's index to the files of the United States viii • ACKNOWLEDGMENTS

Mediation and Conciliation Service and he also obtained permission for us to examine those files. The staffs of the following presidential libraries offered us unstinting service and discovered and photocopied many a rare document for us: the Franklin D. Roosevelt, Herbert Hoover, Harry S. Truman, and Dwight D. Eisenhower Libraries. Ron Filippelli of the Pennsylvania State University Labor Archives permitted us to use his institution's oral history collections as well as its other labor movement records. Philip Mason and Dennis East of the Archives of Labor History and Urban Affairs, Wayne State University, helped us find relevant materials in their vast holdings on the CIO and the modern American labor movement. Richard Strassberg of the Martin Catherwood Library at the New York State School of Industrial and Labor Relations provided assistance at crucial moments. A. D. Mastrogiuseppe, Jr., Assistant Curator of the Western Historical Collections at the University of Colorado Libraries, photocopied large parts of the Josephine Roche papers for our use. The Ohio, Illinois, and especially Iowa historical societies provided material on coal miners and coal unionism. Ms. Lida L. Greene, Librarian of the Iowa State Historical Department, helped us track down obscure facts about Lewis's Iowa years and sent us rare family photographs. Finally, the staffs of the Library of Congress, the Columbia University Oral History Collection, the University of West Virginia Library, the Catholic University of America Archives, the Archives of Ohio University, the Manuscript Division, Alderson Library, University of Virginia, the State Historical Society of Wisconsin, and the Lilly Library, Indiana University, unfailingly responded positively to all our requests for material.

Equally important in our work was the assistance, advice, and criticism of fellow historians and scholars. Their contributions make this truly a collaborative project. Neil Basen, a graduate student in history at the State University of Iowa, energetically tracked down hints about Lewis's Iowa boyhood and early manhood as well as offered sound counsel concerning the relationship between Lewis and Herbert Hoover during the 1920s. Sidney Fine of the University of Michigan carefully read the chapters on the 1930s, CIO, and the New Deal and patiently corrected some of our errors and improved our understanding of that turbulent decade in American history. Ellis Hawley of the University of Iowa did the same for the chapters on the 1920s and the relationship between Lewis and the Republicans. Nelson Lichtenstein of The Ohio State University shared with us his singular knowledge of government-labor relations during World War II and read carefully the chapters that cover those years. David Brody of the University of California, Davis, and David Montgomery of the University of Pittsburgh read the entire manuscript. In reading such a lengthy manuscript with patience and care and never seeming hectoring in their criticism, much of which was sharp but all of which was constructive, Professors Brody and Montgomery proved that a community of scholars indeed exists. To all these friends and fellow historians, we apologize for errors that we may have let go uncorrected in the text and assure them that even where we did not follow their suggestions (which was rare), we appreciated their criticism.

Without our editor at Quadrangle, Emanuel Geltman, who prodded and pushed us constantly as well as polished our prose, this book might still be only a dream.

Last, to the generations of men and women whose collective sufferings and struggles made John L. Lewis a powerful labor leader, and who made the actual history we have written about—to them, above all, should go the primary credit for *John L. Lewis: A Biography.*

Melvyn Dubofsky
Binghamton, New York
September 17, 1976

Warren R. Van Tine
Columbus, Ohio
September 17, 1976

Prologue

On December 30, 1969, Joseph A. "Jock" Yablonski, his wife, and his daughter retired for the night in their house in Clarksville, Pennsylvania. Situated in the southwestern part of the state—amidst the soft-coal fields and coke ovens, whose owners and workers had waged among the most violent labor conflicts in United States history—the Yablonski residence still wore the raiments of the Christmas season. Having celebrated the birthday of their "saviour" and enjoyed a family reunion, the Yablonskis looked forward to an exciting new year.

"Jock," long a loyal, unquestioning lieutenant in the efficient force that controlled the United Mine Workers of America, had turned against his boss. Originally coming to office in the era of John L. Lewis, Yablonski dutifully served Lewis's successors: Thomas Kennedy (1960-1963) and William A. "Tony" Boyle (1963-1973). Prodded by a growing discontent in the coalfields toward Boyle's stewardship of union affairs, Yablonski now planned to challenge the UMW's incumbent leadership—to lead a rank-and-file coal miners' rebellion against an increasingly bureaucratic, distant, and corrupt union machine. Having lost a bid for the UMW presidency in a rigged election held only three weeks earlier, "Jock" Yablonski intended to carry his struggle against Boyle to the United States Department of Labor and the federal courts. In the end, he expected justice and victory to be his, if not peace and good will to all men.

But "Jock" Yablonski never saw the new year. The evening of December 30, three strangers arrived in Clarksville: Paul Gilly, Aubran "Buddy" Martin, and Claude Vealey. Parking their car near the Yablonski home, they slashed all the telephone wires leading to the residence, and then they entered. "I stood at Joseph Yablonski's bedroom door with the carbine," Vealey later confessed to the FBI.

> Paul Gilly was standing beside me. Buddy and I were to shoot simultaneously. Buddy opened the door to the bedroom and fired two shots into Margaret [*sic*]* Yablonski, who was lying in bed.

---

*The daughter's name was actually Charlotte; Margaret was the wife.

I aimed the carbine at the Yablonskis, who had awakened. Mrs. Yablonski laid in bed and was screaming and Mr. Yablonski was getting up. I tried to fire the carbine and it did not work. . . .

Paul Gilly took the weapon from me . . . and tried to fire but the gun jammed. Buddy Martin came over, stepped just inside the door and fired four times, emptying his gun at the Yablonskis.

After Buddy fired, the woman made no further sounds and I could hear Yablonski gurgling. I took the weapon from Buddy, the 38. caliber revolver, fully loaded it again, walked into the Yablonski's bedroom and stood at the foot of the bed near the dresser and fired two shots at Joseph Yablonski.

When I fired, Yablonski had fallen to a sitting position on the floor. . . .

I then walked into the daughter's room, saw that she was not moving in her bed . . . and returned to where Buddy and Paul were. We went downstairs, put our shoes back on in the hallway, went out the same way we came in and returned to the car and drove out of Clarksville, Pa.

Five days passed before a son, Kenneth Yablonski, visited his parents' home on January 5 and discovered the three bodies. Kenneth and his brother, Joseph "Chip" Yablonski, Jr., immediately conjectured that the UMW leadership had ordered their father's murder. Who else had a plausible motive? Yet the murders of the wife and daughter seemed senseless. Perhaps the murders were all the acts of a madman or -men; such tragedies had happened before and would happen again.

But the murderers were not madmen. They were amateur, incompetent hired killers who killed three people at a cut-rate price: $5,100 (split three ways). Their amateurism and incompetency showed in the trail of clues they left behind—clues that led law officers directly to them.

The arrests and confessions of Vealey, Gilly, and Martin only lifted the curtain on the Yablonski tragedy. As their story went, the trail of murder ran from Clarksville to the district offices of the UMW in Kentucky-Tennessee to international union headquarters in Washington, D.C. By early 1972 a member of the union's international executive board and a Tennessee district president had been implicated in the murder plot. Their subsequent trials and testimonies linked "Tony" Boyle to the murders, and on September 5, 1973, federal officials arrested the deposed UMW president and charged him with conspiracy to murder the Yablonskis. After a year and a half of legal proceedings delayed by various appeals and Boyle's parlous health, a jury convicted him of planning and ordering the Yablonski murders. And in September 1975 a judge sentenced Boyle to prison.

While the law pursued the murderers, "Jock" Yablonski's sons, UMW insurgents, and outside reformers struggled to oust Boyle and the incumbent union leadership. With assistance from the federal courts and the Labor Department, they won the right to hold a new union election. And Arnold Miller, as presidential candidate heading the insurgent slate, won the December 1972 election. On December 22, 1972, three years after the Yablonski murders, a new UMW administration promised to implement the reforms that had precipitated a triple murder. The insurgents-turned-incumbents pledged to restore the UMW to its rightful possessors—the members, to break down the bureaucratic distance between leaders and led, and to end the practice of "unionism as usual."

Only six months before the murders of the Yablonskis, the man whose name is most indelibly linked to the UMW died peaceably, a victim of the infirmities of old age. On June 11, 1969, John Llewelyn Lewis, the man who had ruled the miners' union from 1919 until his retirement in 1960, the man who had built the CIO and organized mass-production workers during the 1930s, the man who for three decades had defied presidents and challenged congressmen, the twentieth century's preeminent American labor leader, passed away in his eighty-ninth year. He was fortunate that his death removed him from implication by the public in the Yablonski murders.

Yet one must ask: Was John L. Lewis's final, lasting legacy to the coal miners and the American nation a trade union so corrupt and amoral that it resorted to murder to silence its critics? Is it true, as one critic of the UMW has written, that "the conduct and policies of John Llewelyn Lewis had led directly to the miseries of the United Mine Workers of America in the decade of the 1970s"? What, indeed, is John L. Lewis to be remembered for? Leading the mass of American workers during the 1930s from industrial thralldom to freedom? Acting as the lone labor leader to challenge, from 1939 to 1960, the emerging "imperial presidency" that led, inexorably, to Richard M. Nixon and Watergate? Or being the union president who built a labor machine based on collaboration with employers, on corruption, and on murder?

The story of John L. Lewis, in many of its most salient aspects, can be likened to a prism that refracts and magnifies the history of the American nation and its workers in the twentieth century. His life and career are paradigmatic of the forces that pushed Americans ahead from Woodrow Wilson's New Freedom to Franklin Roosevelt's New Deal, into two world wars and a cold war, from a Great Depression to unprecedented affluence, and from national self-assurance to self-doubt. Lewis's active years as a labor leader, moreover, paralleled the rise of the American working class and its labor movement from the background to the forefront of national political and economic struggle. For more than five decades, from 1908 to 1960, Lewis's career in trade unionism reflected oscillations in the American labor movement—rose and fell with the mobilization and demobilization of workers as an independent political and economic force.

When Lewis began his career as a trade unionist, in 1908, the American labor movement had just ended its initial and most substantial era of growth; yet trade unionism accounted for less than 10% of the nonagricultural labor force, lacked mass membership and power in the enterprises most characteristic of modern industrialism, and scarcely exercised effective national political influence. When Lewis retired in 1960, American trade unionism represented 25% of the nonagricultural labor force, claimed its greatest membership in the mass-production, basic industries, and exerted wide-ranging influence on Capitol Hill and in the White House. In the events and developments that propelled the labor movement from the fringes of the economy to its core, that built its membership from just over

1 million to more than 15 million, and that transformed it from political impotency to unprecedented power, Lewis could claim preeminence. If Samuel Gompers, from 1886 to 1917, fathered the child that grew into the American labor movement, John L. Lewis, during the 1930s, built Gompers's puny adolescent into a lusty movement, the industrial world's most effective instrument for collective bargaining. But Lewis's life illuminates more than the rise of the American labor movement. It exposes several of the dominant themes and tendencies of United States history.

First, Lewis's career is a case study in the myth of the self-made man. From obscure origins as the child of penurious immigrant parents, John L. Lewis rose to fame, power, and wealth. By the mid-1930s, he had become the most powerful labor leader in American history—the first trade unionist to be considered a potential presidential candidate. He conferred with presidents, intimidated congressmen, and interacted with Washington's high society. Individualism and possessiveness personified America's self-made men; Lewis fit the pattern. Self-assertion, pretentiousness, fondness for worldly goods, and social climbing characterized much of Lewis's personal behavior. Paradoxically, however, without the collective strength and solidarity of common folk, Lewis could never have satisfied his more personal, selfish ambitions. For he built his career, his fame, and his power as the leader of a movement founded on collectivism and solidarity. No better example exists of the inherent tension between the self-made man and the society that created him than the life and career of John L. Lewis.

Second, the story of Lewis reveals how trade union leadership evolved from a calling to a career, its exemplars from missionaries to professionals. The first and perhaps second generation of American trade union leaders sacrificed personal security, comfort, and even health to build a labor movement that would, in the future, produce a freer, more equal, perhaps utopian society. Some of their inheritors used the labor movement for personal and organizational aggrandizement. As unions grew larger, more stable, and more powerful, their leaders acquired job security, lush perquisites, and professional life-styles. Organization and personal aggrandizement proceeded hand-in-glove. Lewis's career exemplified that transformation in the American labor movement, as he alternately played the missionary and the professional, the charismatic leader and the rational bureaucrat.

Linked to the transformation of the labor leader's perception of his role was a change in the relationship between trade unions and employers. At their birth and during their formative years, trade unions were protest organizations that represented the workers' claims to economic and political power. Their raison d'être was to protect the workers' interests in an inevitable conflict between employees and employers, labor and capital. Ineluctably, almost imperceptibly over time, however, trade union behavior shifted away from protest and conflict toward collaboration and accommodation between labor and capital. Founded to fight employers in the interest of workers, unions sometimes came to serve capitalism in search of labor peace, higher productivity, and social harmony. No twentieth-century American labor leader preached class struggle more loudly than John L. Lewis—nor practiced class collaboration more cunningly.

As significant as the shifting relationship between labor and capital was the relationship between individuals and the state, voluntary associations, and coercive public power. During the 1920s (unsuccessfully) and the 1930s (successfully), Lewis sought to use the power of the federal government to strengthen trade unionism and conquer intransigent antiunion employers. At the height of the New Deal, Lewis linked the fortunes of the coal miners' union and the CIO inextricably to the policies and goals of the Roosevelt administration; the prerogatives of trade unions and the power of the state often seemed indistinguishable. By the end of the 1930s, however, Lewis began to question what he now characterized as an omnipotent, imperial state. As federal actions impinged increasingly on the behavior of individuals and voluntary associations (trade unions most notably), Lewis feared that American liberties would shrink. The omnipotent state and personal liberty, Lewis asserted, were in conflict. Indeed, by the 1940s, Lewis's rhetoric portended an inevitable battle between free men and a coercive state that transcended the irrepressible war between labor and capital.

Related directly to Lewis's fear of the omnipotent state was his perception of the United States' proper role in world affairs. Traumatized by his experiences as a Wilsonian during World War I, Lewis came to believe that the United States could serve the world best by minding its own business. Together with many other prominent Americans frequently dismissed as isolationists, Lewis saw the United States as the globe's brightest symbol of liberty. But he argued that the nation could promote liberty elsewhere only through exemplary domestic behavior, not persistent overseas intervention. Not only would an adventurous, interventionist foreign policy fail to promote freedom abroad or protect national security; it would inevitably create an "imperial presidency," circumscribe individual liberties, and replace the American republic with a vulgar empire. Yet, paradoxically, Lewis, after 1945 demanded that the government forcefully resist Soviet expansion, and supported the cold war at home and abroad.

Finally, Lewis's life and career expose the inseparable relationship between means and ends. Himself a practitioner of the theory that power is the only morality, Lewis used every instrument at his command to accumulate power. Brutality, bullying, deceit, and bluff were all means Lewis used to achieve his ends. Many even have asserted that Lewis's policies as union leader led inexorably to the Yablonski murders, that his favorite means necessarily produced warped ends, and that evil can never create good.

Because Lewis's life and career illuminate the themes cited above and formed a vital component in the "organizational revolution" at the heart of twentieth-century United States history, a detailed examination of them should help us comprehend better where the nation stands today and in what future direction it might move. Lewis's role as a powerful labor leader also reveals the tensions inherent in voluntaristic institutions between democratic ideals and the oligarchic imperative associated with modern bureaucracy. A biography of Lewis is thus not only a dramatic and intrinsically exciting individual life story; it is also, and more importantly, a description of the salient social and economic forces that have shaped modern America and an examination of the emergence of a professional, rational, bureaucratic labor movement.

As historians, we are, to be sure, most interested in those aspects of John L. Lewis's life that illuminate recent American history. Necessarily, that implies more attention to his career than his life, to his public behavior than his private actions. It also goes without saying that documentation concerning Lewis's public career is more extensive and, in most instances, more reliable.

The focus of our biography—Lewis's public behavior—notwithstanding, we seek, wherever possible and whenever the evidence allows, to explore the darker recesses of his personal, private, and family life. But here a few caveats are in order. Despite the trendiness of psychohistory and psychobiography, we have eschewed formal, structured psychoanalysis of our subject. Let us explain why. As C. Vann Woodward has observed, the historian, unlike the psychiatrist, can seldom, indeed usually never, explore the behavior of his subject at a mother's breast, in the bedroom, and in the bathroom. Those influences that psychiatry deems most essential to understanding human behavior are simply beyond the reach of even the most sophisticated historical research techniques. True, as Erik Erikson has proved, some historical personalities lend themselves to psycho-analysis. Lewis, we assert, does *not* lend himself to the Eriksonian method.

Lewis's public fame and his manipulation of publicity notwithstanding, he was the most inaccessible of individuals. No private diaries, corpus of family letters, or personal reminiscences survive (or in fact ever existed) for Lewis and his family. He had many acquaintances, few friends and confidants. What little the recollec-tions of his acquaintances reveal about his private life tends to be contradictory or unverifiable. Born and raised in obscurity, Lewis emerged from a sociocultural milieu impenetrable to historians. We simply cannot generalize about or draw valid hypotheses concerning his personality formation during infancy, childhood, and adolescence. Maintaining few written records of his thoughts and deeds, totally lacking in friends, and committed to shielding his family from view, Lewis, as a private person, remains hidden from even the most diligent historians. Once, when an inquisitive reporter sought to explore the motives behind an action taken by Lewis, the labor leader responded: "Questions as to motive will be purely speculative. Some philosopher has said the pursuit of motives is the most elusive task in all the world."

Being rather more immodest and speculative than Lewis was in his answer to the reporter's question, we two historians do indeed probe the motives that led our subject to behave as he did. More immodest still, we even draw conclusions and make inferences about Lewis's personality, private behavior, and family relation-ships, despite, what is for historians, a lack of reliable sources.

That, however, is *not* the core of our biographical method. Rather, we prefer to focus on behavior and action, to examine, as far as the evidence allows, what Lewis actually said and did as well as the consequences of his words and deeds. Though we occasionally draw inferences about his personality and motivation, we prefer to allow trained psychiatrists and dedicated psychohistorians, amateur or otherwise, to use our findings, however crudely empirical, to formulate their own more learned analyses of the Lewis pysche. Indeed, we encourage them to do so and hope that our contribution eases their task.

Having made our position and approach clear, we claim one more virtue for our biography. All previous books, essays, and sketches of John L. Lewis, whether hagiographical or critical, relied on considerable hearsay, gossip, and conjecture. They failed, by and large, to distinguish fact from myth, reality from illusion. We sought to break that tradition, for it is our belief that John L. Lewis, the victorious commander in the American labor civil war of the 1930s, as much as Oliver Cromwell, deserves a detailed and accurate portrait—warts and all.

I.
From Obscurity to Power,
1880-1919

CHAPTER 1
Obscure Origins, 1880 -1908

Mention Iowa, and the American commonly thinks of rolling prairie, corn, and hogs—a state populated and exemplified by prosperous farmers. "It was sublime!" exclaimed a fictional nineteenth-century prairie pioneer upon his first glimpse of the Iowa landscape. "Bird, flower, grass, cloud, wind and the immense expanse of sunny prairie, swelling up into undulations like a woman's breast turgid with milk for a hungry race." On the "great green sea" that was Iowa in the 1840s, farmers, by 1890, had built, in the words of prairie agriculture's historian, "one of the most prosperous agricultural economies the world had ever seen . . . where each year the rains, the summer heat, and productive soils produced the broad-leafed fields of dark green."[1]

Mention South Wales, and the American typically imagines coal, slag heaps, soot, and green valleys turned gray by modern industry's voracious appetite for energy. One thinks of tired, bent, crippled men, young and old, emerging from coal pits at day's end covered from forehead to shoetops with black dust. Exhausted, the men silently walk home to "long rows of bare slate-roofed cottages crawling in parallel rows up the sides of denuded valleys." There—in the nightmare landscape in which Welsh miners passed their lives between pit and chapel—darkness, danger, and death stalked.[2]

Prosperous Iowa and bleak South Wales scarcely seem linked by any common threads of history. Yet in reality the experience of immigration tied together the two disparate landscapes. Sometime in the late 1870s, most probably in 1876, John Watkins, his wife Sarah, and their children settled in the town of Lucas in Lucas County, south-central Iowa. Most likely in that same year, Thomas H. Lewis also arrived in Lucas County. Watkins, then fifty-two years old, and Lewis, twenty-three years old, had left South Wales within a year of each other (1869 and 1870, respectively) to seek better lives overseas. Unrelated and unknown to each other in the old country, Watkins and Lewis linked their lives and families in the new land. In 1878, Thomas H. Lewis married eighteen-year-old Ann Louisa Watkins, the Watkins's eldest child still residing at home. And on Lincoln's

3

birthday, February 12, 1880, Thomas H. and Ann Louisa Watkins Lewis celebrated the birth of their first child, a boy named John Llewelyn.[3]

What circumstances had brought the Watkinses and Lewises halfway around the
globe from South Wales to south-central Iowa? And what were they doing in
Lucas County in 1876? It is easier to explain why they left South Wales than how
they arrived in Iowa. After 1850, the Industrial Revolution rapidly transformed
South Wales. Long an isolated, primitive region of small, self-sufficient dairy and
vegetable peasant farmers insulated from the vicissitudes of the commercial grain
markets, Wales in the late Victorian era became a primary source of the highest
grade "steam coal" and an ideal location for the expanding British iron and steel
industry. Industrialism reshaped the Welsh countryside and its social structure.
Population growth, indigenous and migratory, caused proletarians to outnumber
peasant farmers. The spread of a cash economy and a substantial rise in land rents
compelled many small farmers to become part-time coal miners and drove their
male children into full-time work in the pits or iron and steel mills. Enmeshed ever
more deeply in the British and world capitalist economy of the late nineteenth
century, the Welsh fell victim to capitalism's recurrent crises. Irregular employment, fluctuating prices, low wages, and dangerous work annually drove thousands of Welsh to emigrate overseas—to Australasia, Canada, and, mostly, the
United States.[4] John Watkins and Thomas Lewis were among the numerous
natives of South Wales who sought a better life abroad.

Yet John Watkins and Thomas Lewis claimed different family origins and came
to Lucas in different fashions. Neither Watkins nor Lewis was a typical immigrant.
Watkins, who sailed from Swansea with his family in 1869, was older than the
ordinary emigrant (forty-six in 1869, an advanced age for a nineteenth-century
workingman). Lewis, who departed from Wales the following year, was younger
(sixteen years of age) than the typical male emigrant without family members
already settled overseas. And whereas the Watkins family journeyed directly to the
United States, Lewis sailed for Australia. One Welshman thus eventually reached
Iowa from the east and the other from the west.[5]

What the Watkins family and the young Lewis did between their departures
from Wales in 1869-1870 and their arrivals in Iowa in 1876 remains obscure. For
John Watkins, who had been a coal miner in Wales, life in the new world probably
consisted of a persistent migration from one raw coal camp to another in search of
steady work, better conditions, and higher wages. During the 1870s America's
coal industry grew rapidly, and skilled Welsh miners were in great demand. Tom
Lewis, the son of a small Welsh farmer and himself a part-time coal miner as an
adolescent, probably chose Australia in search of land and a rural life. His
ambitions apparently frustrated in that British dominion, young Lewis took ship
for San Francisco. Precisely when he arrived on the West Coast is unknown,
though it could not have been before late in 1872. His life in the United States
during the next four years also appears obscure. According to an obituary printed

in the *United Mine Workers Journal* (1919), Tom Lewis participated in the "gold rush" that opened up the Black Hills of South Dakota in 1876. The same obituary alleges that he also worked in the coal mines of Ohio, Indiana, and Illinois in the late 1870s. Given the lack of solid evidence on Tom Lewis's peregrinations, however, it seems logical to assume that he traveled directly from the Black Hills to south-central Iowa, a more natural route than a detour back east through Ohio, Indiana, and Illinois. And there in Lucas County, Tom met the Watkins family and his future wife, Ann Louisa.[6]

Here a brief digression on the Welsh origins of John Llewelyn Lewis is in order, especially considering how successfully he subsequently masked the character of his ancestors. Beyond the facts that John Watkins was a coal miner and that he left Wales in 1869, little is known of the Watkins clan, and John L. Lewis did nothing to trace that lineage. About Thomas Lewis we know a bit more. Contrary to images of John L. Lewis as the descendant of a long line of coal miners, his father was perhaps the first member of the Lewis clan to work in the pits. His great grandfather John L. (Llewelyn?) Lewis worked the Golden Grove Farm on Goppa Mountain near Pontardulais, fathered several children, and died when comparatively young. A son, Thomas, and his wife, Gwenllian, took over the farm and eked out a hard living. Thomas and Gwenllian Lewis, the parents of four boys— Thomas, Henry, Llewelyn, and William—died toward midcentury and were buried at the Goppa Fach cemetery, Pontardulais. The family farm apparently could not support four sons, and Thomas (John L.'s father) entered the mines developed near his birthplace shortly before emigrating. Henry subsequently also emigrated to the United States, Llewelyn went to Italy, and William worked in South Wales as a tinplate millman. As late as 1937, a relative, Tom Lewis, a coal miner and local union official, still occupied Golden Cottage, the ancestral farmhouse.*[7]

About Lewis's maternal ancestors more is known. John Watkins married above his station. Sarah, his wife, was the eldest daughter of John Jeremiah, the first surveyor and chief mining engineer for the Powell firm, later the Powell-Dufryn Coal Company. The Powells belonged to the Welsh elite, became business barons in the coal and iron industries, and assimilated the customs and conventions of the English ruling class. The Jeremiahs also assimilated themselves to their English masters; all John's children, except for Sarah, rose in the social order. A grandson, Richard Jeremiah, entered the lower gentry and served as a justice of the peace and president of a county agricultural society. A granddaughter, Martha Edmunds, married into the clergy. It was the Jeremiah family line, certainly more prominent and prestigious than the Watkins's or Lewis's, that John L. Lewis later in his own life sought to establish, trace, and honor.[8]

---

*John L. Lewis knew so little about his family lineage that in 1922 he mistakenly identified Henry and Llewelyn as his maternal grandmother's brothers.[9]

*　　*　　*

Still, one may rightly inquire, what forces brought such Welsh immigrants as John Watkins and Tom Lewis, the former a coal miner and the latter torn between mining and farming, to south-central Iowa, not to the coalfields of Pennsylvania, Ohio, or Indiana, where most Welshmen dug black diamonds? First, Lucas County, Iowa, in 1876 resembled coal mining areas back east. The county, in fact, resembled the Missouri hill country just to its south more than the gently rolling Iowa prairie, and its most precious natural resource was a black mineral (coal), not black soil. Indeed, in the Lucas of 1880 and the neighboring hamlet of Cleveland, where Lewis was born and lived as an infant, miners and laborers far outnumbered farmers. According to the 1880 federal census, Lucas had 247 wage workers and only 7 farmers, and Cleveland numbered 125 wage earners (at least 105 of whom listed themselves as miners) to 1 farmer. Not only did wage workers in general and coal miners in particular dominate the local social structure; the vast majority of local residents apparently bore Welsh surnames. Lucas-Cleveland, Iowa, in 1880, then,　was essentially a Welsh immigrant coal mining community.*10

Coal was first discovered in the Lucas area early in 1876, probably near the village of Cleveland. Not until the discovery of coal did the area experience substantial population growth. Although local businessmen developed several mines between 1876 and 1880, only one, the Whitebreast Coal and Mining Company,** located on Whitebreast Creek, a mile east and south of Lucas, proved a success. Its development begun on May 1, 1876, the Whitebreast mine shipped its first coal in October of the same year, and by 1881 it employed 300 miners underground and 60 craftsmen and general laborers on the surface. From April 1880 to January 1881, the mine produced between 9,069 and 16,667 tons monthly, with production peaking in the late fall; it disbursed a monthly payroll of between $11,531.07 and $23,310.23. The company sold most of its coal directly to railroads, and seldom had an excess to sell to local consumers for domestic heating purposes.11

Undoubtedly, Watkins and Lewis arrived in Lucas in 1876 to develop the Whitebreast mine and work in it. For it was a common practice among mine owners to recruit experienced British miners through extensive advertising in immigrant newspapers and labor journals. It was also customary for miners in newly developed western regions to receive premium wages as an inducement to leave more settled areas.

The type of society and culture that the Welsh immigrant miners established in

---

*Much of central and south-central Iowa from 1880 to 1914 had a flourishing coal mining industry. In an area from Des Moines approximately fifty miles to the east and to the south, coal miners were almost as numerous as farmers. It was in this region that John L. Lewis passed his first twenty years.

**This was not simply a small local enterprise. The owners were sufficiently wealthy and successful in the coal business to operate another mine under the same corporate name in the more productive Illinois coalfields.

Lucas seems beyond historical reconstruction. Certainly a substantial number continued to communicate in the Welsh language, for, according to the 1880 census data, many of them, like John L. Lewis's grandmother, Sarah, reported themselves as illiterate in English. When the folklorist George Korson prepared a children's biography of John L. Lewis, the subject cooperated with the author in an attempt to recreate the milieu of his childhood. For Korson, Lewis recalled an immigrant community in which organized song festivals in the Welsh language— eisteddfodau—served as the most popular and cherished group activity. Such festivals were, to be sure, characteristic of first-generation Welsh immigrant life in the United States; but Lewis's reminiscences about life in Lucas are suspect.[12] His family left there while John was still an infant, and when they returned later in the century, the community was no longer predominantly Welsh in character.

The chapel was as important as the pit in the lives of Lucas's Welsh immigrants. Welsh miners founded two of the earliest churches in the towns of Lucas and Cleveland. In 1878 Cleveland's residents formed a society of the Congregational Church and erected a place of worship. Two years earlier another immigrant Welsh group in the town of Lucas had formed a branch of the Reform Church of the Latter Day Saints of Jesus Christ (Mormon). The American environment had thus produced a strange transformation in the religious beliefs and affiliations of Welsh miners and their families. In the old country, the workers were primarily members of the dissenting sects, ordinarily Baptist, Methodist, and Primitive Methodist; in Lucas, Iowa, they affiliated with Congregationalism and, more remarkably, a schismatic Mormon sect.

In the link between Welsh immigrants and Mormonism hangs a strange tale concerning John L. Lewis. According to the 1881 county history, one of the founders of the Mormon church in Lucas was John Watkins, John L. Lewis's grandfather. It seems unlikely that Thomas Lewis, if either a Congregationalist, a typical Welsh dissenter, or, less likely, a nonbeliever, would have courted a Mormon's daughter, especially one who took her father's faith seriously. In the late nineteenth century other Christian church groups ostracized Mormons, and Mormons scarcely associated with "heathens." Is it then possible that John L. Lewis was raised in a Mormon household and that his subsequent rejection of the faith of his mother, whether for theological or opportunistic reasons, explained his lifelong adult silence on all matters of religious preference and church affiliation? It is a question well worth posing, as one with a Mormon background would not have risen far in a labor movement dominated by evangelical Christians, Roman Catholics, or outspoken nonbelievers.[13] His mother's Mormonism may also help explain Lewis's distaste for all alcoholic beverages and his generally prudish sexual life as an adult. Perhaps, also, Mormonism influenced Lewis's strange amalgam of individualism (possessive materialism) and communitarianism (trade unionism), a world view Mormons shared especially with Jews.

The 1881 county history records no evidence of any Welsh cultural activities or institutions other than the two churches. That may have resulted from the ethnocentrism of the history's American-born, socially respectable, elitist compilers; or, indeed, it may have reflected social reality in Lucas. Where the truth lies, we may never know. Suffice it to say that by the end of the century, when John L. Lewis resided in the area as a young man, few traces survived of an earlier vibrant Welsh immigrant culture.

Frankly, the influence of any sort of immigrant culture or religion on John L. Lewis during his formative years remains obscure, as does most information about his preadult life. About all that we can say with reasonable certainty is that John spent his infancy in the Lucas-Cleveland area. Beyond that, the most ordinary aspects of his early life remain forever hidden. No photographs or portraits of his maternal grandparents survive. The only surviving photographs of his parents date from the mid- or late 1890s and are formal, posed studio portraits. In them, one sees Thomas H. Lewis in the pose of a prosperous, respectable citizen approaching middle age. Dressed in a well-tailored dark vested suit, white shirt, and full four-in-hand tie, he is well groomed, with neat, evenly parted short hair and a full mustache that hides his entire upper lip and most of the lower one. Apparently a large man with broad shoulders, an ample chest, and full stomach, Thomas H. Lewis in the 1890s chose to have himself photographed in the conventional sober style of the time. In the bulk of his body, the straight, direct line of his nose, the imposing eyebrows, the sharp eyes, and the prosperous yet conventional garb, Thomas H. Lewis resembles nothing so much as his own son John L. as photographed in the 1920s and 1930s. Ann Louisa Lewis, by contrast, seems more serene if equally respectable in appearance. Also dressed in a dark-hued conventional outfit for the photographer, Ann Louisa appeared less concerned about having every hair on her head in place, and her softer features suggest a dreamer or romantic rather than an ideal mate for her more conventional husband.

Although we now know that John L. Lewis was born and lived the first fifteen months of his existence in Cleveland, not Lucas, we don't know whether he was delivered by a doctor, a midwife, or a family member (the 1880 census indicates no doctor in Lucas or Cleveland). His parents resided in a single-family dwelling, but we don't know whether they owned it or rented it from the Whitebreast Company. Cleveland, named after the Ohio city, was founded in 1878 as a completely company-owned, -planned, and -developed town. Company control was so complete that rules forbade the sale of liquor on any town property. Yet evidence suggests that by 1881 most miners owned their homes. Lewis, however, asserted in 1940 and also 1941 that he had been born in a company house.[14]

The family milieu in which Lewis formed his first images of external reality also seems impenetrable. One suspects, but there is no proof, that his parents and grandparents spoke Welsh more often than English among themselves and their friends. (As late as 1900 his father remained an alien.)[15] Tom Lewis worked a long day in the mines, from sunup to sundown, and probably returned home too exhausted to spend much time with his only child. But in 1880 he was unemployed for three months—likely the late spring slow season for coal mining—and may have then showered attention and affection on the infant John L. Ann Louisa, apparently a gregarious, generous, and affectionate young woman with deep-red long hair remained at home. In a mining town, few opportunities except for domestic service attracted females outside the home. Ann Louisa also likely spent much time with her own mother, who lived only a mile away in Lucas.[16]

More than affection likely bound daughter to mother. Grandmother Sarah Watkins was, in 1880, fifty-one years of age—a woman who had borne twelve children, less than half of whom had survived infancy and childhood. Perhaps old and worn beyond her years, Sarah had to care for a household consisting of her coal mining husband; an eighteen-year-old son who also mined; a five-year-old daughter; an eleven-year-old adopted son (put to work in the mines); and four male boarders, three of whom were crippled. Sarah certainly needed Ann Louisa's assistance to care for such a ménage. It is thus quite likely that John L. Lewis as an infant encountered death (conversation about Sarah's deceased children and the parents of the Watkins's adopted son). He also saw human frailty revealed in the crippled bodies of the three boarders. In a sense, the Watkins's household and its Lewis appendage resembled a modified extended family, but it is questionable how much security, comfort, and affection such a network provided its members.[17]

John L., his mother, and his grandmother spent most of their time at home. The men, when employed (usually nine months of the year), occupied themselves beneath the ground. Aside from home and work, Lucas-Cleveland offered few diversions to its residents. The thirsty Cleveland dweller could escape to one of the two saloons in Lucas. But for Welsh chapel types, whether Congregationalist or Mormon, saloons were forbidden territory. Cleveland boasted one general store, patronized primarily by miners; and Lucas, as befit a town three times larger (981 to 380 residents), possessed a larger business district. Children of school age could attend either of the one-room ungraded schools taught by the two local teachers, one in Lucas and the other in Cleveland. For their parents, church services and socials beckoned. Coal miners had one other diversion—and a notable one. The largest single structure in Cleveland, a two-story hall, the lower floor of which served as the schoolhouse, was built and financed by the miners. Yet the impressive building did not signify a work force far advanced in the mechanics of trade unionism or collective action. Not until February 1881 did the local miners establish an aid society to assist members in distress (by then mutual-benefit societies had had a long tradition among British workers), and the Miners' Hall still lacked a library or reading room—features prominent in almost all late nineteenth-century union facilities.[18]

Lucas, however, claimed a branch of the era's preeminent national labor organization: the Knights of Labor, Local Assembly No. 850. Probably founded in 1878 or 1879, L.A. 850 was led in 1880 by one Daniel W. Jones, most likely a Welshman. Between February 1881 and May 1882, the records of the Knights of

Labor indicate no affiliate in Lucas. L.A. 850 either discontinued paying dues to national headquarters or went out of existence, perhaps to be replaced by the miners' benefit society founded in Cleveland in February 1881.[19]

During the period in which L.A. 850 became moribund, Tom Lewis moved his family away from Lucas, for in July 1882 a second son, Thomas A., was born, in Beacon, Iowa, a small town about seventy miles northeast of Lucas. Only a couple of miles from Oskaloosa, Beacon appeared, according to an 1889 Rand-McNally map of Iowa, to be surrounded with small towns whose names were redolent of Welsh anthracite patches in northeastern Pennsylvania. Moreover, Mahaska County, in which Beacon was situated, was one of Iowa's primary coal producing centers.[20]

During the Lewis family's absence, L.A. 850 rejuvenated itself, becoming by July 1882 the largest Knights of Labor local assembly in Iowa. Perhaps their organization's rejuvenation and size led the local coal miners to engage in the almost legendary protracted strike against the Whitebreast Coal Company. This was the labor conflict that the legend of John L. Lewis, as repeated in nearly every biography and sketch of the man, tells us that Thomas H. Lewis led—refusing to surrender and consequently suffering blacklisting as a result of his radical militancy. Yet precisely when the strike occurred, what caused it, how long it lasted, and how it was ended remain unknown. Neither the records of the Knights of Labor, the United States Bureau of Labor Statistics reports on strikes in the United States, nor state of Iowa official sources report a strike in Lucas-Cleveland in the year 1882. And the one local newspaper, the Chariton *Democrat-Leader*, whose issues for 1882 survive, contains no references to a strike in Lucas or Cleveland.[21]

But the *Democrat-Leader* does report singularly interesting news about Lucas coal miners in the year 1882. In 1880 the mine labor force had been all white and mostly Welsh immigrant in composition. By March 1882 Afro-Americans were at work in Cleveland's mines. What brought the blacks to the Lucas area, how many there were, and how long they remained cannot be discovered from the available evidence. That blacks were working in the area's mines prior to any strike is certain, and that they were employed in the Whitebreast mine is even more certain, for in May 1882 the *Democrat-Leader* reported the death of a Negro miner in the Whitebreast shaft. It also seems reasonable to assume that the local white miners perceived the blacks as a threat to their economic security and wage levels, which is perhaps why mine owners employed Afro-Americans. In fact, by October 1882 racial antagonism in Lucas seemed so intense that the *Democrat-Leader* reported,

> it seems to be the war of the races. . . . the determination seems to be that the "negroes must go." We have talked with a number of the white miners, and they tell us that the conduct of the colored men is such that it is impossible for the two races to live there in peace or safety, and as the white men are largely in the majority, it would be only natural that they should remain, and the negroes go. It would not be surprising to hear of a deadly encounter, and if it comes, it will no doubt be a bloody one.[22]

Despite the Chariton newspaper's warning of an impending race war in Lucas, no such untoward event occurred. Nor apparently did local miners strike against the Whitebreast Coal Company. On all fronts, withdrawal seemed to characterize the behavior of the miners. Their Knights of Labor local assembly collapsed when the national organization in the course of the year 1882 suspended sixty-four members of L.A. 850 and expelled another sixty-seven.[23] Unable to force the black workers to leave Lucas, to alter company labor policy, or to salvage their labor organization, white miners like Tom Lewis may have simply decided to seek work elsewhere. For we do know that late in 1882 the senior Lewis, after a brief return to Lucas-Cleveland, again moved his family away from the area.

The year 1882, then, jolted the infant John L. Lewis with several shocks. First, his mother gave birth to a second child, Thomas A., a sibling rival for parental affection. Second, John observed his father's behavior during a crisis, one that may have been precipitated by racial conflict, and that also likely heightened tension in the household. Third, twice in the same year, John was wrenched away from the familial and physical world that had sheltered and nurtured him since birth. For the next fifteen years, as John passed from childhood to adolescence to early adulthood, his family moved persistently among the towns and cities of central and southern Iowa.

John L. Lewis's life between the ages of three and seventeen seems almost a closed book. The few references that Lewis made about those years to associates, journalists, and biographers cannot be verified through historical sources. A diligent search of various Iowa records—city directories, state censuses, school records, and vital statistics—failed to uncover any trace of the Lewis family's peregrinations.[24]

What can be pieced together from a variety of diffuse sources reveals a pattern common for late nineteenth-century working-class families, particularly families of coal miners. Perhaps the most typical feature of working-class life was spatial mobility; families seldom remained permanently in the same home or neighborhood and moved in amazing numbers from city to city and state to state. Upwardly mobile workers sought better neighborhoods; frustrated workers fled the rent collector and sought better jobs elsewhere. And coal miners, of course, necessarily moved when the mine in which they worked was depleted. The fact that the Lewis family moved repeatedly between 1882 and 1897 did not distinguish it from other American working-class families.[25]

The economics of Iowa coal mining also explain the persistent residential mobility of the Lewis family. In Mahaska County, where the family dwelled more than once after departing Cleveland, work was good, although, according to one report, "the operators rule, as it were with martial law and to the extent that the men dare not even express their opinion, should they differ from those of their employers." In Lucas, the operators not only ruled with an iron hand but, according to the same source, "every thing is lovely and the goose hangs high. The wages per ton are just what the operators are a mind to make it, and the men have to submit to just such treatment as the company, through their bosses see fit to deal out to them regardless of justice." The Des Moines district, however, where the Lewises lived much of the time between 1888 and 1897, was booming by 1887, and miners earned decent wages with steady work. Moreover, by January 1887, Des Moines area miners seemed sufficiently organized to act collectively to resist a wage cut.[26]

With several exceptions, the sort of work Thomas Lewis did and his family's place of residence between 1883 and 1897 appear obscure. At the birth of their third child, George (1885), the Lewises resided either in Cedar Mines, Monroe County, a small town east of Lucas, or in Cedar, Mahaska County, a more substantial coal mining region. Still later, when John was old enough to do the family shopping (certainly by 1889),* the Lewises lived in Oswalt, about twenty-five miles northeast of Des Moines. Oswalt was so small that John did the family shopping in Colfax, a mile south, a larger though still small Iowa farm town that he reached by train. From Oswalt the family moved to Oskaloosa, a small city by national standards yet large for south-central Iowa.[27]

One must wonder what sort of employment other than coal mining Tom Lewis found in such small towns. Could he have been a farm laborer as well as a miner? To be sure, his Welsh origins were agrarian, and he undoubtedly had worked on the Lewis family farm. Moreover, larger Iowa farms customarily needed steady, if not year-round, laborers, and smaller farms always needed hired hands during the cultivating, haying, and harvesting cycles. Demand for coal miners declined precisely when the need for farm labor rose. This was also the sort of work that younger male children, John L. and Thomas A., for example, might be expected to share in at an early age.[28]

By the mid-1890s, the Lewises had apparently settled in Iowa's largest city and its capital, Des Moines. There the senior Lewis claimed to have been employed by the city police department, and an 1894 studio photograph does show Thomas H. Lewis and two mates posed in Des Moines policemen's uniforms. Coal mines also operated just outside the city, and it is possible the father still took occasional employment in the pits. John L. Lewis, when revising his own official autobiography in 1964, asserted that he had attended high school for three and a half years, obtaining all but his diploma. If he indeed attended high school, it would have been in Des Moines, where he also sold newspapers to supplement the family's income, defended his younger brothers in street fights, and played amateur baseball. By then, 1894-1897, John had developed into a strapping working-class lad of more than average height—extremely broad in the shoulders, wide in the girth, and with a handsome face topped with stunning and wavy auburn hair.[29]

What else can be said about the Lewis family between 1883 and 1897?

*Alma Dennis (Dennie) Lewis was born in Colfax on January 22, 1889. *UMWJ*, Feb. 1, 1962, p. 6.

Working-class families, especially among coal miners, tended to be larger than those of the upper classes. To this rule the Lewises proved no exception. Between 1882, when John's first brother, Thomas, was born, and 1894, Ann Louisa Lewis gave birth to six other children, four of whom survived infancy (George, b. 1885; Alma D. (Dennie), b. 1889; Howard, b. 1891; and Hattie, b. 1894). Spaced approximately two years apart, the births represented maximum fertility for Ann Louisa and suggest that the deceased infants were born either between Thomas and George (1882-1885), George and Alma D. (1885-1889), Howard and Hattie (1891-1894), or after 1894. The birth pattern also indicates that throughout the years during which the Lewises moved persistently, Ann Louisa always had an infant at her breast or underfoot. Without help from the older children, all of whom were male prior to the birth of Hattie, Ann Louisa would have faced a staggering household burden.[30]

One can only imagine the domestic routine in such a home and in an environment such as Iowa's—blazing hot in the summer and freezing cold in the winter. The typical coal miner's home was no more than a shack rented from the local coal company. Framed in clapboard and roofed with tar paper, it lacked central heating, indoor plumbing, and electricity. Water would be drawn from an outside well, and family members would relieve themselves at a primitive outdoor privy. A coal-burning cookstove heated the home in winter, boiled its water, and cooked its food; in summer it probably made the kitchen-living area the most uncomfortable in the home. When Tom Lewis was fortunate enough to work in the mines, his wife, Ann Louisa, would have to rise before dawn, start a fire in the stove, and prepare breakfast and a dinner pail for her spouse. As dawn broke and the senior Lewis departed for another day's work, Ann Louisa would awaken the older children, cook their breakfasts, and prepare them for school. Later but still early in the morning, she would tend to her preschool age children. Part of the late morning and early afternoon, she might have free time to visit neighbors, shop at the local store, wash, sew, or simply relax. Before long, however, Ann Louisa would have to prepare for the return home of children and husband. Water had to be drawn from the well, heated on the stove, and set in a metal washbasin so that Tom Lewis could bathe and remove the coal dust from his body. Supper, meantime, had to be prepared, cooked, and served. After supper, the household had to be tidied and the next day's supply of water and coal brought into the kitchen. Family members would then straggle off to bed (the growing family probably never shared more than two bedrooms).[31]

The impact of family expansion and household routine on John L. Lewis can only be surmised. At first, the presence of male siblings probably produced rivalry, not burdens, for John was too young to assist his mother in household chores. Never especially close to his first brother, Thomas, John developed an intense relationship with the next four children—George, Dennie, Howard, and Hattie. One might assume from this pattern of sibling relationships that by Dennie's birth in 1889, John had begun to assume responsibilities in the household that grew greater after the subsequent births of Howard and Hattie. Certainly, during his adult years, John L. Lewis evinced singular concern for his siblings' welfare, protecting them from their own foibles, employing them in good jobs, and even providing them with homes.

What else might reasonably be said about John L. Lewis's childhood and adolescence? We might surmise that his connection with Welsh culture and language became attenuated. The Lewises lived in towns and cities not dominated by Welsh immigrants and used the language of their English-speaking neighbors; the children chose as playmates typical American-born Iowans. For John L. Lewis this meant a childhood and adolescence that separated him from the culture of his parents, introduced him fully to American mores, and transformed him by age seventeen into an acculturated second-generation American.[32]

Whatever the Lewis family did between 1883 and 1897, they returned to Lucas County in the latter year. By then, however, the area's character had been altered. No longer did coal dominate the local economy; nor did the Welsh far outnumber other groups. The number of producing coal mines had increased, but by 1900 farmers clearly surpassed miners in local number and significance. Lucas scarcely included any miners among its residents as recorded on the 1900 federal manuscript census, and Cleveland, despite a substantial number of miners, was no longer a company town or the residence solely of miners and their families.[33]

The factors that brought the Lewis family back to Lucas are unclear. Perhaps Ann Louisa desired to be close to her parents, both of whom were by then octogenarians, and to enable John and Sarah Watkins to see more of their grandchildren. Perhaps Tom Lewis had lost his job in Des Moines and chosen to move his family into his father-in-law's home in Cleveland (owned free and clear by the Watkinses) while he and his older boys sought work in the coal mines, which were likely to expand production as the national economy boomed after four years of severe depression. Perhaps a new opportunity beckoned Thomas Lewis back to Lucas County.

Again the absence of records and sources makes it impossible to draw firm conclusions about the Lewis's life from 1897 to 1901. The only firm surviving evidence raises more questions than it answers. The 1900 federal census lists the Thomas H. Lewis family as residents on a farm in Whitebreast Township (the rural section beyond Cleveland); the senior Lewis reported his occupation as farmer, and the three oldest boys—John, Thomas A., and George—were listed as farm laborers. And Tom Lewis rented the farm.*[34] Because the census was taken in June, it might present a misleading picture of life for the Lewis family. Many

---

*Because the manuscript agricultural schedule for 1900 remains closed, no information is available on the size of the farm; its value; or the number and type of buildings, machines, livestock, and primary crops.

American coal miners of that era dug coal during the winter and farmed during the warmer months. Why not the Lewises?

Several scraps of evidence link John L. Lewis to the mines. Writing to Lewis in 1966, an old acquaintance from Lucas enclosed a photograph of the old Big Hill Mine, where, he observed, Lewis had mined coal as a young man.[35] The Lewis Papers at the State Historical Society of Wisconsin also contain photographs of the mines Lewis worked in as a young man and references to his days in the pits. Equally interesting, former United Mine Workers president John P. White asserted in a speech delivered on John L. Lewis Day in Lucas County on June 1, 1924, "that Mr. Lewis was the first recording secretary of the first local union organized in Lucas County." And the *United Mine Workers Journal*, in August 1941, printed a photograph of the original 1901 charter of Local Union No. 1933 of Chariton, Iowa (the Lucas County seat), which listed John L. Lewis as its secretary.[36]

Aside from farming and working in the mines from 1897 to 1901, John L. Lewis apparently performed as an amateur actor in talent shows at the Lucas Opera House. He also managed the facility and brought in traveling companies to perform *Uncle Tom's Cabin*, *St. Elmo*, *East Lynn*, and medicine shows.[37]

By the age of twenty-one, then, John L. Lewis had experienced a varied existence. He had lived in hamlets, small towns, and Iowa's largest city; attended one-room ungraded rural schools and an urban secondary school; peddled newspapers on city streets, worked the soil, dug coal, performed in amateur theatricals, managed a small-town theater, and served as a trade union officer. He seemed a young man of many talents and interests, a typical small-town striver, yet a person whose future promised no spectacular accomplishments. In 1901, however, a restless aspect of John's personality would also reveal itself.

For most of his formative years John L. Lewis had been saddled with unchildly responsibilities. As the oldest child in a large but poor family, he had had to assist his mother with the housework, tend the younger children when asked, and do a variety of chores. In adolescence he had worked first part-time and then full-time in order to supplement family income. But by 1901 he could more freely and easily choose his own path in life. Though Ann Louisa bore another child, a son, Raymond, in October 1900, the youngest daughter, Hattie, though now in school, was also old enough (seven) to assist with household chores. The older boys, Tom and George, could work full-time and add substantially to family income.

In finally choosing to exercise his independence, John L. Lewis made the break with his family as complete as possible. Not only did he depart the household; he left for the mountainous West and remained away for five years. More surprising than his flight from the family and pursuit of personal autonomy was his relinquishment of the union post to which he had just been elected. In seeking a new future, John L. Lewis had apparently rejected a career in trade unionism.

Precisely what Lewis did in the West remains subject to doubt. At various times he claimed to have worked in gold, silver, lead, and copper mines from Montana in the north to Mexico in the south. It would not have been surprising if he had also labored on railroad and general construction gangs. He also hinted that he had been a member of the Western Federation of Miners, the most militant labor union of its era (1893-1907), though no records prove or disprove the claim. Yet when reminiscing about his western experiences among family members, Lewis—a niece, Myrta Nickey, recalls—never spoke about work in the hard-rock mines. Instead he told colorful stories about his many "business" ventures.[38]

A plethora of tales have accumulated concerning Lewis's western hegira, most of which are recorded in Saul Alinsky's biography of the labor leader and most of which are unverifiable. The most dramatic story concerns Lewis's involvement in the 1903 disaster at the Union Pacific Railroad Company's coal mine in Hanna, Wyoming. Passing through the area by chance, Lewis arrived in time to assist a rescue team in carrying out the torn, charred bodies of 234 miners.* "The descent into the mine that had become a charnel house was for Lewis a descent into hell," writes Alinsky, "but what ripped his emotions to shreds was the sight of the numb, mute faces of the wives now suddenly widows of the men they loved. It was at Hanna, Wyoming, that John L. Lewis was baptized in his own tears."[39] Dramatic? Certainly! True?

How important those five years were in shaping Lewis's life and in what ways they might have we will also probably never know. "I would say," Lewis allegedly told Alinsky, "that those five years of my life did more to shape my feelings and my understanding of how people behave than anything else in my experience. Those five years were probably one of the most important parts of my life."[40] If so, they scarcely helped Lewis in forging a permanent, secure identity or purpose in life. He returned to Lucas at the end of 1905 no surer of what he wanted to do in the future than when he had left, no wealthier, if perhaps wiser, and scarcely a success. And now he was in his mid-twenties, an age at which most successful men had chosen their occupations, professions, or careers.

Back in Lucas among family and acquaintances, John settled into his prewestern routine. He entered the mines again, and later claimed that in 1906 members of the Lucas County miners' union chose him as their delegate to that year's United Mine Workers convention. If Lewis played an active role at the convention, or even attended it as a delegate, no records disclose his contribution to the miners' cause. Once again, moreover, work in the mines and election to union office failed to convince Lewis that his future lay in the labor movement.

John still toyed with amateur theatricals and managed the local "opera house."

*Cecil Carnes and Saul Alinsky in their biographies of Lewis date the disaster in 1905, spell the town as Hannah, and list the number of dead as 236 (Alinsky) and 400 (Carnes). For correct date and data, see *UMWJ*, July 2, 1903.

He also joined the Lucas Lodge (Good Shepherd Lodge No. 414) of the Masons (of its sixty-three recorded members in 1907 few bore obvious Welsh surnames), and in 1907 he was elected junior warden (his future father-in-law, Dr. John C. Bell, was the lodge's highest officer). Indeed, in 1907, as John L. Lewis associated himself with Lucas's solid citizens, ventured into a business partnership, and participated in town politics, he appeared more the striving bourgeois citizen than the emerging proletarian leader.[41]

The year, 1907, also saw John L. Lewis take a wife. On June 5, he married Myrta Edith Bell, the oldest child in a family of seven children ranging in age from seven to twenty-seven. The Bells had moved to Lucas from Ohio between 1884 and 1887. The head of the family, John C. Bell, practiced medicine and was a graduate of the College of Physicians and Surgeons, Keokuk, Iowa, which he attended in 1882 and 1883. Before attending the Iowa school, Dr. Bell had probably served a three-year practical apprenticeship with his father, a doctor back in Ohio.* Dr. Bell received a license to practice medicine from the state of Iowa in 1890 and belonged to the American Medical Association. He also earned enough income to purchase a home (mortgaged) and to send his oldest children, Myrta and her sister Florence, to Drake University in Des Moines for summer sessions. Dr. Bell was one of Lucas's most respected citizens—a member of the prestigious Presbyterian church, and the leader of the most influential men's club, the Masons.[42]

On the surface, the Bells appeared to be everything the Lewises were not. They traced their lineage back to the colonial era, claimed superior educations, practiced prestigious professions (medicine for the father and teaching for the eldest daughters), and belonged to what passed for a Lucas elite. Marriage into the Bell family represented for John L. Lewis a firm step up the American social ladder.

But why did Myrta, throughout her life exceedingly concerned about social status, choose to marry a coal miner and the son of immigrant parents? The best we can do is make educated guesses. Eligible males may have been scarce in a town the size of Lucas and especially for a young woman (not so young, however, in terms of a first marriage) as demure, reserved, and withdrawn as was Myrta Bell. For such a woman, most of whose peers had probably already married, John L. Lewis may have seemed a prize well worth the pursuit. He was handsome, outgoing, obviously talented, and patently ambitious. By 1907 he had outgrown life as a coal miner and proved it, as we will see, by his other activities. Perhaps it is best to consider the union of John L. Lewis and Myrta E. Bell as a marriage of convenience and mutual advantage.

Theirs was not a tempestuous or passionate courtship of two love-struck post-adolescents. If John L. Lewis was only a year or two older than the typical male at first marriage, Myrta Bell was fully five years older at first marriage than the typical female. By age twenty-seven, John had experienced many environments and forms of work; he was a mature adult who had fashioned his own identity.

*A graduation and degree requirement.

Myrta too, by age twenty-seven, after more than seven years of teaching experience, was a mature, self-sufficient adult.

The marriage of two such mature individuals renders suspect the myths that have flowered concerning Myrta's influence on John L. Lewis. According to Alinsky and other biographers, Myrta "organized Lewis's reading habits and introduced him to Dickens and to Homer and other classics. She encouraged his interests, guided him, and loved him. Myrta Bell was to become the most important single force in the life of John L. Lewis." She also, it has been alleged, taught her husband diction, voice inflection, and effective speech mannerisms.*[43]

The facts of John L. Lewis's life before marriage suggest otherwise. In 1907 he was not putty in his wife's hands, a malleable material that could be shaped in any form Myrta desired. Rather, he was an individual who had completed all but the final term of secondary school (quite an accomplishment for the 1890s), practiced his speech and language on the stage of the Lucas Opera House (where he also became acquainted with the classics and not-so-classics), and knew that impressive classical allusions could be drawn from *Bartlett's Familiar Quotations* and the even-more-familiar Bible. Later in life he evinced no deep interest in literary classics, preferring instead military history, western adventures, formula mysteries, and what became his favorite magazine in the 1950s and 1960s, *American Heritage*, a popularized, easy-to-read version of the national past.[44]

If John L. Lewis remained malleable in 1907, it was by his own choice and his continuing failure to select a "career." Indeed, in his pursuit of occupational success, 1907 dealt Lewis two more severe blows. First, local voters rejected his bid for the Lucas mayoralty,** more probably a loss of prestige rather than material benefits.[45] Second, and more important, Lewis failed in business. Sometime in 1907 he and a man named Brown opened a grain and feed business in Lucas. Their venture was ill timed, for 1907 was a year of bank failures, a national financial panic, and an ensuing economic recession. Brown and Lewis, who apparently supplied first-quality hay to dealers elsewhere, could not collect from their customers. Lewis, in fact, tried for nearly six years, from September 1907 to March 1913, to collect from one customer, A. L. Deibel, of Little Rock, Arkansas. At first, Lewis's letters demanding payment were plaintive. In August 1908 he pleaded for the smallest remittance. The next month, Lewis implored Deibel, "I am sorely in need of money and will take it as a great favor. If you can't spare so much, please send what you can." And a month later, he beseeched, "Why don't you try and come across with a small amount?" At that time, it might be remarked

*Myrta's formal education was not that superior to her husband's. She graduated from high school but was not a college graduate. She only attended the 1898 and 1899 summer sessions at Drake University, probably to satisfy state certification requirements for school teachers.

**Alinsky alleges that Lewis's father-in-law, Dr. Bell, fought his son-in-law's candidacy. See also Doris P. Bell (Myrta's sister-in-law) to Melvyn Dubofsky, Jan. 13, 1976, for a similar story.

Lewis's signature lacked the grand flourishes associated with it during his reign as powerful labor leader. Five years later, in 1913, when Lewis had found steady employment and a career in trade unionism, his demands for payment from Deibel no longer sounded plaintive. Now he threatened legal action. "Right is right and nothing else," Lewis wrote on March 5, 1913, to Deibel's lawyer in his last letter on the subject. "I sold him the hay in good faith. He sold the hay and received cash therefore. He has profited at my expense. I submit that this is unfair."[46]

A failure in politics and business less than a year after his marriage, John L. Lewis seemingly had reached a career dead end. Restlessness, frustration, or a combination of both led Lewis to make the biggest decision of his life. In the spring of 1908, he chose to pursue a career in trade unionism, a choice from which he never thereafter deviated and which, within a decade, brought him unalloyed success.

Sometime between April 4 and June 25, 1908, John L. and Myrta E. Lewis left Lucas, Iowa, for Panama, Illinois—a company town recently developed in the central Illinois coalfields. A short time later, John's parents, his five brothers, and his two sisters also moved to Panama. There the Lewis men began to cement the first blocks in the magnificent union edifice that John L. Lewis intended to construct for American coal miners.

CHAPTER 2

The Road to Power, 1908-1919

The young man who arrived in Panama, Illinois, in the early summer of 1908 resembled and differed from the typical American coal miner. Twenty-eight-year-old John L. Lewis was the son and grandson of coal miners. Like the children of most miners, he had experienced an unsettled childhood and youth as the Lewis family moved frequently from one small Iowa town to another. And like other miners' sons, the young Lewis had left the household from 1901 through 1905 to seek work far from home, in his case in the coal and nonferrous mines of the Rocky Mountain West.

Why, then, did the young husband of a thoroughly middle-class, status-conscious wife choose to move from a small Iowa village to a newly developed, raw west-central Illinois company town? Why did Lewis, the frustrated politician-businessman and sometime-thespian, return to the pits and seek a career in the labor movement? To these questions we will probably never find fully satisfactory answers. Yet the available facts enable us to draw several logical inferences and, more important, to dispute myths that have evolved concerning Lewis's early union career.

Legend suggests that Lewis carefully and consciously plotted his move to the Illinois coalfields in order to better his chances of rising in the UMW hierarchy. It also implies that no miner from a Welsh community in Iowa could muster sufficient support within the UMW to win national office. But Illinois was, by 1908, the largest single district (No. 12) in the miners' union and a state with diverse ethnic groups among its coal diggers. Once in Illinois, the ambitious Lewis could gain experience in dealing with non-Welsh miners and build a substantial union electoral machine.[1] This legend contains a grain of truth—but only a grain.

More prosaic reasons probably best explain Lewis's selection of Panama. First, and perhaps foremost, the Lewises moved as an extended family group. John's parents, as well as his five brothers and a sister, accompanied John and Myrta. Finding employment for a male family group of six miners was no mean task, especially in the recession year of 1908, when coal mine employment declined.

Panama provided a solution, for it was the sit
Indeed, prior to the sinking of a shaft in 190€
(named for the creek on which the town was sit
the Lewises moved there in the summer of 19(
1 was the largest in Montgomery County a
thirty-first-largest producer in the state. Begin
Shoal Creek Mine had 230 a year later, 375 b
was the mine large and expanding; it also pro
1907 through 1910, the mine operated from a
maximum of 273. In 1909, an era still domi
Shoal Creek's coal was mined by machine—
and guaranteed high daily earnings for the ty

Geography also played a part in Lewis's migration decision. The main railroad lines east from Lucas provided excellent service to Springfield, Illinois, the state capital and, in 1908, itself a coal mining community situated about thirty-five to forty miles north of Panama. Springfield, moreover, was the headquarters city for District 12 and a vortex of UMW political machinations. Panama also lay just east of—a short carriage trip away from—the most organized and militant county of coal miners in the state: Macoupin, with such famous mining towns as Mount Olive (where Mary "Mother" Jones was buried), Benld, and Gillespie.

Although economics and geography best explain the Lewis family's move to Panama, John's desire for a career in trade unionism had some influence. Yet Lewis would not have settled in Illinois, as Saul Alinsky suggests, in order to improve his political prospects in the union,* for that state was a bitter cockpit of intraunion politics, one in which candidates eager to establish their claim to rule the roost regularly annihilated each other. When Lewis arrived in Illinois, District 12 numbered many prominent union politicians, among whom the most notable were John H. Walker, Frank Hayes, Duncan MacDonald, Frank Farrington, Adolph Germer, and William Sneed, to name just a few. Lewis was scarcely in a position to challenge any of them for power, and he did not do so. Instead, he attached himself to some of the more prominent figures in the union and used their influence to gain preferment.

Panama, to be sure, introduced Lewis to a variety of ethnic types. A county history published in 1918 observed of the village: "It is a mining town of some 1,500 population, largely composed of those of foreign birth, who do not as yet assimilate well with our native people." Scattered bits of evidence indicate that Italian immigrants may have been the dominant ethnic group.[3]

The Lewis family, however, was not in Panama to learn from the immigrants; it was there to use them. In Lucas, the Lewises had been only one among many

---

*Iowa may have been a secondary coal producing state, but the man with whom Lewis would be closely associated in his rise to power and who was president of the UMW from 1911 through 1917, John P. White, was an Iowan. Mining coal in Iowa and serving the UMW in an outlying district did not disbar a man from the union presidency.

lsewhere they might have been one among a majority of English-speaking families. But in Panama they were a tightly knit English-speaking Protestant background set down amidst a mass of non-English-speaking immigrants. And the UMW then was run by men of British origins and Protestant connections; even the Irish Catholic union leader proved the exception at the uppermost levels of the union hierarchy. In the world of union politics, new immigrants deferred to English-speaking leaders, who, in turn, appointed the immigrants to UMW positions they might never have won in contested elections.[4]

Beyond jobs in an expanding coal mine and the chance to serve as English-speaking leaders to an immigrant population, Panama had little to offer the Lewis family, especially Myrta. Lucas, too, might have once seemed a dismal coal mining village, but by 1908 it had an "Opera House," a library, a flourishing lodge of Masons, and Myrta's father, Dr. Bell, town elder and leader. All Panama offered, aside from its coal mine, was a post office, a bank, a lumberyard, several stores, and, in the words of the county history, "several places where booze may illegally be obtained, interfering to some extent with the security and stability of the town and clouding the future prospects for growth and permanency."[5] Panama apparently failed to provide the Lewises with a home of their own. The records available at the county courthouse in Hillsboro indicate that the family owned no property in Montgomery County at any time during the years 1908-1918. Because a part of Panama lay in an adjoining county, where records are unavailable, it is possible that the Lewises did own property. More likely, however, as was typical in a new mining village that would not have existed except for coal, John and Myrta lived in a company house, as did the other family members.

Life in Panama did not separate John and Myrta from their family and friends in Iowa. They visited regularly with the Bell family and probably also with John's maternal grandparents. Such trips were especially frequent during the summer months, when coal mines cut production and travel was easier. John and Myrta maintained their links to Lucas well into the mid-1920s and only severed them completely after the death of Myrta's father in the mid-1930s.

The six Lewis men (Raymond was too young) wasted no time entering union and town politics. Within a year of their arrival, John's brother, Thomas, served as a Panama police magistrate, and John had been elected president of UMWA Local 1475, which, by the end of 1910, was among the ten largest locals in the state of Illinois.[6] From that beginning the Lewis family extended its reach ever deeper into union, town, and state politics. When John resigned his local union presidency in 1911 for a more prestigious position in the labor movement, a younger brother succeeded him in office. As John thrived as a trade unionist, his younger brothers also pursued successful careers. The police magistracy proved only a start for Tom. In June 1916 he was elected president of Local 1475 and, most remarkably, at the same time also apparently acted as manager of the Shoal Creek Coal

Company's Mine No. 1. The next year, in July 1917, he assumed office as a state mine inspector, one of the ripest political plums available to UMW members. Younger brother Dennie (Alma D.), in 1916, became financial secretary of the Panama local, a position he retained until conscripted for military service during World War I.

Not only did Thomas A. Lewis see nothing peculiar in serving simultaneously as local union president and manager of the mine in which the union members labored; he and the other Lewis men enriched themselves at the expense of the union treasury. Long after John L. had severed his official connection with Panama Local 1475, the officials of District 12, at the urging of several discontented Panama miners, investigated the Lewis family's stewardship. The two auditors appointed by the state officials uncovered a pattern of corruption and embezzlement whereby Tom and Dennie Lewis as well as their father, Thomas H., maintained a dual set of books, issued illegal checks, and forged checks to double the expenditures legally approved by the local union. Between September 1916 and July 1918, the auditors estimated, Thomas A. and Thomas H. Lewis tapped the local treasury for $631.66 and Dennie for $255.71. The auditors described the Panama scandal as "one of the widest conspiracy cases in the United Mine Workers on record."[7]

The Lewis brothers had been extremely blunt in building their union machine. A former associate who later turned against them testified to how the Lewises recruited him. "[Tom A. Lewis said:] use common sense and cooperate . . . they [the Lewises] were running the town and that it was useless to buck the machine that he may as well do as they said." Upon taking Tom's advice, the informer became the next "elected" president of Local 1475.

Throughout the crisis engendered by the scandal, which did not erupt until 1918, a UMW election year, the Lewis family stood together. Brother George W. offered the local full restitution for the embezzlements of his father and two brothers—and he made good on the offer. John, then acting vice-president of the UMW and engaged in his first race for national elective office, never once criticized his kin publicly. (If he did so privately, no evidence exists to prove it.) He insulated himself from connection with the scandal and never suffered from its impact. Much as Lewis's union rivals used the Panama case to smear John in 1918, 1920, and later, they totally failed to associate the eldest Lewis brother in any way with the misdoings.[8]

Indeed, by 1918 John L. Lewis had become too adept a bureaucrat and wily a union politician to involve himself in cheap financial chicanery, or if he did so, to keep written records of the transactions. As we have seen, John lost no time in becoming president of Local 1475. He lost less time entering district and international union politics, where he quickly showed a talent for choosing winners. In Illinois he immediately associated himself with John H. Walker, a popular union leader of Scots extraction and a socialist who was then president of District 12, later would serve as president of the state federation of labor, and was admired by

A. F. of L. president Samuel Gompers. During the 1909 UMW election John threw the support and the votes of his large Panama local to the winning slate: Tom Lewis of Ohio District 6 for president and William Green (also of District 6) for secretary-treasurer. A year later he campaigned for John P. White against the incumbent Lewis and reendorsed Green; again Lewis was on the winning side.[9]

Whenever possible, Lewis used the influence, votes, and power he controlled in the large union local to inveigle patronage appointments from UMW superiors rather than run for office and face a union electorate. He pursued the course recommended by New York City Tammany Hall boss George Washington Plunkitt. Like Plunkitt, Lewis built a political machine from the bottom up. Beginning with the support of family members, as also did Plunkitt, Lewis gained control of a large local union (comparable to a city ward) and then used his local power to gain preferment from district and international union officials (the counterparts of city district leaders and bosses). The rules of urban machine politics, as applied by Plunkitt, proved equally germane to the universe of American trade unions.

Lewis's first union appointment resulted from his efforts on behalf of John Walker and William Green in 1909. One of the worst mine disasters in state history occurred that autumn in the small northern Illinois town of Cherry, a tragedy that erased the lives of almost the entire local adult male population. In the aftermath of the disaster, District 12 intensified its lobbying campaign in Springfield for improved mine safety laws, and John Walker chose Lewis as one of his new lobbyists, appointing him a District 12 legislative agent. In his new position, one that brought him to Springfield often, John ingratiated himself further with Walker and established links to state politicians.

Previous biographers have emphasized that the Illinois state legislature enacted more stringent mine safety legislation after Lewis's appointment as lobbyist.[10] Yet whatever effect Lewis had as a lobbyist scarcely equalled the pressure legislators experienced as a consequence of the Cherry disaster and of the ensuing outcry for protective legislation generated in newspapers and among reformers. Moreover, there is no evidence either in the *United Mine Workers Journal*, District 12 publications, or the state legislative journal that Lewis exerted extraordinary influence in promoting more stringent mine safety legislation.

Lewis continued to involve himself deeply in UMW politics. UMW elections were customarily sordid affairs in which charges and countercharges of fraud flew about recklessly and in which electoral results seldom passed unchallenged. As William Green reminded Lewis on December 21, 1910, there was a distinct possibility that the national UMW convention scheduled for January 1911 would declare President John White's recent victory fraudulent. "I say this," wrote Green, "because as you well know the cry of fraud will be raised and every method resorted to in order to continue control of the organization. It is highly important that our friends prepare for this contest and try to have the local unions represented by men who will not permit such action to be taken."[11] Lewis thus saw to it that he represented Panama Local 1475 at the 1911 convention.

Although he remained largely in the background as a convention delegate, the few times Lewis took the floor revealed his political acumen. First he moved that William Green be seated as a delegate when challenges arose disputing the secretary-treasurer's credentials. Later, toward the end of the convention, Lewis again demanded the floor, this time to defend Samuel Gompers against the allegations of a black UMW delegate who accused the A. F. of L. leader of charging that Negroes were not far enough removed from slavery and barbarism to act as good union men.[12]

As the 1911 convention ended, Lewis could take pride in what he had accomplished in a brief Illinois union career. John Walker, one of the state's most popular labor leaders, admired Lewis, and the UMW's highest elected officers, White and Green, owed him a political debt. Moreover, Lewis's defense of Gompers during the convention did not pass unnoticed.

By the spring of 1911 Lewis could also take pride in the growth of his family. Early in 1910, a daughter, Mary Margaret, was born to the Lewises, and only a year later, on April 14, 1911, a second daughter, Kathryn, blessed the Lewis household. From his marriage in 1907 until Kathryn was six months old, John acted the proper family man. Aside from brief trips to district headquarters in Springfield, he remained at home with Myrta. A growing family, however, suggested to a man as ambitious as John that it was time to seek a position more important and more remunerative than that of a common coal miner, local union president, or state legislative agent. And for a person as cunning as Lewis, opportunities in the labor movement beckoned.

In the autumn of 1911 Lewis obtained the position he wanted. Gompers needed a special agent to represent the A. F. of L. in the territory of New Mexico, where organized labor was actively campaigning for the adoption of a "progressive" state constitution with some of the most advanced protective labor provisions in the nation. Lewis seemed an ideal job candidate; he came from the nation's largest union, he had worked in the coal and metals mines of the American West, and he had some experience as a lobbyist. He also came highly recommended. John P. White informed Gompers that in Lewis, he would "secure the services of a valuable young man, who is well balanced in every respect and has a large grasp upon the affairs of the organized labor movement." Endorsements from John Walker and William Green also supported Lewis's candidacy.[13] And Gompers certainly remembered that Lewis had defended him at the 1911 UMW convention.

On October 21, 1911, Gompers offered Lewis a three-month appointment as a special A. F. of L. organizer in Santa Fe, New Mexico, with the promise that a permanent position would follow. Two days later, Lewis accepted the appointment and promised to arrive in Santa Fe on the twenty-fifth. Gompers granted his new agent a salary of $5.00 per day for a six-day week, hotel expenses not to exceed $2.50 daily, and full railroad expenses; Lewis also received a $150.00 advance.[14]

Lewis's new position represented a substantial improvement in material status. His $5.00 daily wage was more than even the most skilled miner could earn in 1911, and considerably more than local union officials received. The A. F. of L. job also included steady employment—a prospect beyond the reach of most American wage earners in 1911, especially coal miners. Lewis's basic annual salary (he soon received the permanent appointment which he held for six years) of $1,560.00 was nearly double that of the average wage earner and, with expenses added, amounted to a sizeable annual income. The appointment, moreover, brought Lewis into contact with the most influential single man in the labor movement, Gompers, and with a host of trade union officials across the nation.

Lewis's new position also entailed sacrifices, the most obvious of which were his family and home lives. From his initial assignment in New Mexico in October 1911 until his resignation from the A. F. of L. in February 1917, Lewis seldom had the opportunity to be at home with his wife and young daughters. Two travel diaries, for 1912 and 1915, capture the flavor of Lewis's routine as an organizer and establish beyond doubt the absence of "normal" family life.[15]

After completing his initial New Mexico assignment successfully in December 1911, Gompers dispatched Lewis to West Virginia to work among coal miners.[16] He remained in West Virginia until February 16, 1912, not returning home to Panama until March 4. Thus he was away from home for 133 consecutive days, after which he spent a week with his family before again taking to the road. In March and April 1912, Lewis traveled to Saint Louis, Washington, Pittsburgh, Wheeling, and the coal mining districts of West Virginia. The first week in May found him in Washington, whence he went to New Orleans and to Alexandria, Louisiana, before returning to Washington on May 13. Not until May 19 would he return to Panama—this time after an absence of 70 consecutive days—for a two-week visit. Lewis spent most of June and July speaking in the coal mining districts of Illinois and Indiana and conferring with union officials in Indianapolis —national headquarters for the UMW as well as several other major trade unions. In those two months, as well as in August, he was occasionally to visit home for a day or two. But after spending Labor Day weekend in Panama, Lewis departed for Pittsburgh and spent the remainder of the year, except for four days, away from home. September found him working the Pittsburgh-Wheeling-Cleveland area, from which he returned home on October 2. Four days later Lewis departed by train for Denver en route to New Mexico, where he stayed the remainder of the year.

Assuming that Lewis's travel diary is accurate, during the year 1912 he spent a maximum of twenty-nine or thirty days at home with family in Panama. For this sacrifice he received the salary of $1,560.00 plus expenses of $3,173.11. Away from home, he apparently traveled and lived comfortably.

The year 1915 found Lewis even more peripatetic than 1912. He worked the

Pittsburgh area—including parts of Ohio and West Virginia—traveling constantly from one industrial community to another. But now, at least, he had more opportunity to be with his wife and young daughters, for John brought Myrta and the children to Pittsburgh, where he established a new household for the family. Yet Myrta was never completely content in Pittsburgh. Separated from her family and friends, she was married to a man who in 1915 still remained away from home for more than half the year. Each summer, fatigued by the heat and humidity of Pittsburgh and beset by loneliness, Myrta would take the children with her back to Lucas to visit the Bell family. In Lucas, Myrta and the children would occupy a small house owned by her father next to Dr. Bell's personal residence. Lewis occasionally visited his wife and children in Lucas (also his own parents and siblings in Panama) but devoted most of the summer of 1915 to organizing workers in the Pittsburgh region. And 1915 also saw Lewis's travel expenses rise by approximately 20 to 25%, bringing them to almost $4,000.[17]

Some years later Lewis would express what it meant to be a labor organizer in the early decades of the twentieth century. During the 1919 UMW convention Lewis sought to still complaints about the manner in which the union appointed its organizers. "The life of an organizer is not a bed of roses," he told the delegates.

> Our field workers are laboring in fields remote from their homes in the non-union or partially organized sections, where we demand their constant attention to their duty and the application of their entire time to the work of organizing the unorganized. They are privileged to return home at stated intervals to visit their families and renew their home associations, but are asked to spend no unnecessary time in such a manner.

And so, Lewis proceeded, the corps of organizers constantly changes as some men discover how unsatisfactory is such an employment and such a life.[18]

He might also have mentioned that organizers spent more time on passenger trains—day coaches as well as Pullmans, the primary means of intercity and interstate travel before World War I—than actually organizing workers. Trips between distant cities consumed more than a day, and shorter trips between adjacent cities sometimes took the better part of a day. Once in town the organizer ordinarily found himself in sleazy hotels, greasy-spoon restaurants, and working-class taverns—the type of resorts most convenient to a community's industrial section and its inhabitants. The pay may have been good and the employment steady, but the organizer's life was tightly circumscribed by the imperatives of travel and the kind of social amenities available in industrial communities. For the family man, given the conventions of early twentieth-century married life, the role of trade union organizer meant anguish about fulfilling responsibilities. Unlike the Jet Age businessman or labor leader who might return home the same evening after a long day far out of town, the pre-World War I labor organizer, like a traveling salesman, seemed forever on the road.

Yet Lewis retained his position as an A. F. of L. organizer for a full six years, a period when he was regularly absent from home and during which his daughters grew from infancy to childhood. While Lewis traveled, Myrta bore the full responsibility for raising the girls, a task rendered more onerous by a brief residency in Pittsburgh, away from family and friends. Not until Mary Margaret and Kathryn were of school age would John rejoin the household on a regular basis and then move it to Springfield on a street occupied by other members of the extended Lewis family.

What precisely did Lewis do during his years as an A. F. of L. organizer? What did he gain by sacrificing home, family, and local and district union offices? How did his association with Gompers affect his subsequent rise to power in the UMW?

Lewis's employment with the A. F. of L. had many advantages for a man eager to rise in the labor movement. First, it enabled Lewis to escape temporarily from the savage political infighting that in the UMW ruined the prospects of many rising young labor leaders. Yet organizing for the A. F. of L. allowed Lewis to maintain his contacts among coal miners and indeed to win new friends and allies in such outlying coalfields as there were in West Virginia, Alabama, and New Mexico. Second, Lewis considerably widened his contacts within the labor movement. A typical week in 1912 saw him confer regularly in Indianapolis with Frank Duffy, secretary-treasurer of the United Brotherhood of Carpenters and Joiners; address local machinists; and speak to "scab" mechanics.[19] He also gained first-hand knowledge of the jurisdictional conflicts that plagued A. F. of L. affiliates and consumed so much of Gompers's time. Third, Lewis benefited tangibly from his association with Gompers, whose influence and patronage within the labor movement were unrivaled. Fourth, Lewis learned how to deal with and serve important political leaders and the vital role of state and national politics to organized labor. In short, Lewis's employment with the federation proved an ideal apprenticeship in labor movement bureaucracy and politics.

Organizing for the A. F. of L. in the years before World War I also had its heartaches and frustrations. Nothing depressed Lewis more than his lack of success in organizing mass-production workers in the Pittsburgh-Wheeling-Cleveland industrial triangle. When he was not mediating jurisdictional disputes, circulating among coal miners, or addressing union gatherings, Lewis devoted his time to trying to organize glassworkers, steelworkers, and electrical industry employees in Pennsylvania, West Virginia, and Ohio. He achieved some success among the more skilled glassblowers and pottery workers but failed miserably, as did a host of other organizers, in attempting to bring trade unionism to steelworkers.

For over six weeks, from late August to early October 1915, Lewis involved himself in an intensive organizing campaign among employees of the Westinghouse Electric Company at its Turtle Creek plant in East Pittsburgh.[20] After weeks of proselytizing among workers and addressing huge mass meetings, Lewis had to concede failure. On September 30, the Westinghouse workers, by a margin of 7,073 to 2,495, voted not to strike and to accept the company's terms. Years afterward Lewis wrote to a friend that "it does not seem very long since you and I labored together in our great enterprise in the Turtle Creek Valley of Pennsylvania. I laugh again as I recall the morning on which we had our bonfire which consumed the debris of our projected strike."[21]

His failures as an organizer notwithstanding, Lewis had several substantial triumphs during his A. F. of L. years. Success, of course, crowned his first assignment for the federation when New Mexico voters adopted the labor-endorsed state constitution. Lewis proved so skillful politically in New Mexico that during the 1912 presidential election, the chairman of the Democratic National Committee asked Gompers to assign Lewis to campaign in the Southwest on behalf of Woodrow Wilson.[22] Thus the first tangible evidence of Lewis's politics places him among the Wilsonian Democrats.

Wilson's victory in 1912 involved the A. F. of L. and Lewis more deeply in Democratic and national politics. The A. F. of L. in particular and workingmen in general formed an important element in the Wilsonian coalition and, as such, were regularly consulted by the new administration on a variety of matters. In 1916, for example, President Wilson through Secretary of Labor William B. Wilson sounded out Gompers for labor's reaction to Judge John H. Clark of Cleveland as a possible successor to Charles Evans Hughes on the Supreme Court. Gompers immediately asked Lewis, then in Washington for the dedication of the new A. F. of L. building, to depart for Cleveland in order to investigate Clark's qualifications. Although Gompers's personal secretary believed Lewis to be overwhelmed by the magnitude of the request, he carried out his assignment with dispatch. A month later, Lewis returned an extremely negative report on Clark, who was not appointed to the Supreme Court. Later that same year Gompers asked Lewis to check the credentials of a possible appointee to the federal court for the Western District of Missouri. This time Lewis, whom Gompers now referred to as one of his organization's "most trusted representatives," submitted a favorable recommendation.[23] Although the available evidence is scanty, it seems certain that Lewis did considerable political work for Gompers and the A. F. of L.

Gompers considered Lewis an able organizer qualified for highly confidential assignments. But precisely how close a relationship the sage old fox of the labor movement and the rising young lion established is open to question. For several reasons, it is unlikely that Gompers and Lewis maintained the father-son, teacher-student relationship that Alinsky's biography suggests.[24] First, Lewis's peregrinations, as recorded in his travel diaries, left him as little time to be with Gompers as to be with his wife and children. Meeting together only once every several months, and sometimes less frequently, and then only on official A. F. of L. business, Lewis and Gompers had little opportunity or reason to form a deep personal relationship. Nor did Lewis have much occasion to chaperone Gompers during the latter's recurrent bouts with the bottle. Indeed their relationship was so distant in some respects that once in 1917 Gompers apparently confused John L. with a different Lewis.[25] And as far as learning from the old master was concerned, the same limitations apply. They were simply not together enough; Lewis was too egotistical to play the willing pupil to any teacher; and Lewis learned more than enough about the labor movement from six years of fieldwork.

Yet Lewis perhaps had a closer relationship to Gompers than most A. F. of L. organizers. The old man referred to the younger man in salutations as "Dear Friend John" or "My Dear Lewis." Gompers several times asked Lewis to travel with him, and Lewis accompanied Gompers, at the latter's invitation, on a speaking tour of Indiana and Illinois in 1916. The A. F. of L. president also assigned Lewis to especially delicate and confidential tasks—the political work noted above as well as a special assignment for two months with President John P. White of the UMW.[26] But one might also argue that this relationship was founded on strict business and political considerations.

In the years during which Lewis served the A. F. of L., the United Mine Workers formed the largest single bloc of votes within the federation. The first Secretary of Labor, William B. Wilson, was an ex-UMW official and a supporter of John White. For Gompers, ever the pragmatic labor politician, it paid to cultivate the mine workers' union. Lewis came to the A. F. of L. with the most important credentials: the blessings of John White, William Green, and John Walker. Considering the tight network of relationships built among present and former UMW officials, Lewis's place on the A. F. of L. payroll added to Gompers's influence with Labor Secretary Wilson. John White and the UMW also benefited from the Lewis appointment. The miners' union remained during the years 1911-1916 an organization wracked by factionalism. For those in command, it always paid to have friends in Washington among A. F. of L. and government officials. A kind word from Gompers, a firm decision by the A. F. of L. executive council, a patronage job from William B. Wilson could strengthen UMW incumbents and weaken insurgents. Gompers and Lewis thus formed a relationship based on business, not pleasure; union politics, not friendship; and one that would later ease Lewis's rise to power in the UMW.

Throughout his A. F. of L. years, Lewis never neglected the coal miners and their union. He spent considerable time in the mining districts of West Virginia and quite regularly circulated among the miners of Illinois and Indiana. A. F. of L. business also took him frequently to Indianapolis—national headquarters city for the UMW. Lewis, moreover, continued to meddle in internal UMW politics. In February 1912, only four months after assuming his A. F. of L. position, Lewis published a pseudonymous broadside aimed at his UMW enemies. Signing himself "Juvenal Gordon," the actual author used a literary style and phrases indelibly associated with John L. Lewis. "Gordon" accused former UMW president Tom Lewis and perennial District 12 candidate, Duncan MacDonald of enriching themselves at union expense. "Darkness would be on the face of the earth and the voice of the organization, like that of Rachel in the Wilderness, would be heard in wails and lamentation," if the Tom Lewises and Duncan MacDonalds held office. "Jowl by cheek," "Gordon" charged, did MacDonald "sit at luxury-laden tables with the dissolute sons and the butterfly daughters of the idle and vicious rich, with captains of industry and malefactors of great wealth. Royally was he entertained. . . . Merrily he tripped through Folly's halls." In 1912, John L. Lewis, already the master of sarcasm, invective, and the purple passage, posed as the ally of UMW radicals, combating class collaborationist officials who supped at capitalist tables. "Yours for the ultimate and complete economic emancipation of the downtrodden proletariat and the triumph of working class principles," pledged "Juvenal Gordon."[27]

Lewis did more than compose pseudonymous leaflets criticizing his union enemies for class collaboration. He also engaged in electoral shenanigans worthy of the most cunning big-city boss. These political tricks, furthermore, revealed how shallow were Lewis's personal loyalties. John H. Walker, who had given Lewis his initial boost up the union ladder, was the first to experience Lewis's ingratitude. In 1915 Walker challenged White for the union presidency, and in the ensuing bitter campaign for votes, Lewis backed the incumbent White. Lewis contributed to the corrupt world of UMW politics a series of forged telegrams, purportedly sent by Walker, appealing to employers for financial support in the race against White. Lewis knew in 1915, as he had known in 1912, that the most deadly charge one could make against a miners' union official was class collaboration; nothing angered the rank and file so much as the thought of being "sold out." Whatever the exact effect of Lewis's forged telegrams (which Walker did not learn the truth about for several years), White triumphed, and Lewis received his reward.[28]

On the last day of December 1915, Gompers assigned Lewis to assist President White of the UMW in thwarting union militants and insurgents. White promptly put Lewis to work. At the UMW convention, which met in Indianapolis from January 18 to February 1, 1916, Lewis played a decisive role. He served as chairman of the resolutions committee, and he also presided during the debate over the committee on officers' reports; these were posts that gave him substantial authority during heated floor debates. Lewis proved a strong, decisive convention chairman—one who was well versed in parliamentary procedure and adept at avoiding the personal, ad hominem type of argument common at UMW conventions. Committed to defending the White administration, Lewis spoke as a realist on all intraunion and external political issues. On policy resolutions that ranged from old-age pensions to union solidarity to hostility to the National Guard to racialism in the labor movement, Lewis pleaded for moderation; in his words not swapping horses while in midstream and thus disturbing the equanimity of the present union situation.

His reaction to a resolution introduced by black delegates to deny UMW funds to other unions that refused to admit Negroes disclosed lucidly Lewis's desire to balance the needs of black coal miners against the racialism then so prevalent in the labor movement. Lewis assured his union's delegates that their "colored" brothers agreed with him that the UMW could not deny assistance to another trade union in need "because they have failed to mould their laws exactly in compliance with our wishes." Lewis, in fact, grew perfervid in his defense of trade union autonomy. "Every organization," he shouted, "has a right to frame its own policy without regard or consideration of the opinions of members of other organizations, and nobody guards that right any more jealously than we do." Asked by a black delegate the equity of assisting labor unions that bar members solely because of color, Lewis switched his line of argument from principles to pragmatic considerations. "We feel that although some organizations do not grant us justice in this matter," as "our colored brothers say, we could not take the position that women or children should suffer or that labor should lose in a contest of an industrial character because we could not be included in that proposition." Class should transcend race for UMW members, Lewis argued, although in other unions, unfortunately, racialism might prevail.[29]

The 1916 convention also found Lewis in open conflict with the union insurgents who would oppose him during the next decade. But in 1916 he fought them not in his own right, but in the interest of John White. In a long and bitter debate concerning Alex Howat—the rambunctious, argumentative, and tempestuous Kansas District 14 president and a man with whom Lewis's own early union presidency would be tightly entwined—Lewis used his position as convention chairman to make rulings in favor of White and William Green and against Howat's supporters. Earlier in the convention Lewis clashed with Adolph Germer, an Illinois insurgent, prominent socialist, and polemicist. Just as Lewis, in 1912, had accused his enemies of tapping the union treasury to enrich themselves, Germer suggested that the White administration was profligate and demanded that a special committee of three travel in all UMW districts seeking evidence of financial peculations. Commanding that Germer supply evidence or shut up, Lewis reminded the Illinois delegate of the latter's own alleged extravagance with union money and warned: "I feel it is well if you seek to pick the mote out of your neighbor's eye first to clear your own."[30] Lewis's performance during the 1916 convention won for him the sobriquet "Old Iron Jaw."

On every score the 1916 convention, so ably chaired by Lewis, sustained the White administration. By then, Lewis had linked his future to White, who wasted no time in showering good fortune on his younger supporter. In the summer of 1916, White appointed Lewis to the wage scale committee charged with negotiating a new contract for District 5 miners in western Pennsylvania. In the last week of July Lewis served as chairman of a special convention that reorganized District 5, bringing to the district presidency Philip Murray, a man with whom Lewis would be associated for the next quarter of a century and the man who would become Lewis's most loyal union lieutenant.

Obviously satisfied by his rising stature in the UMW, Lewis, in 1916, for the first time in his career ran as a candidate in an international election, seeking election as a UMW delegate to the 1917 A. F. of L. convention (the union was entitled to five). That contest tells us a good deal about Lewis's standing among coal miners. Two or three years earlier he was probably unknown to most UMW members; by December 1916, however, John L. Lewis had received a year's publicity in the union journal and visibility as chairman of that year's convention. He was also clearly a favorite of President White, no mean consideration in union elections. Thirty-eight men, including the most prominent and respected leaders of the UMW, contested for the five delegate positions. Only eight candidates received more votes than Lewis, but their margins were enormous: White and Frank Hayes polled over 100,000 votes; John Mitchell and William Green received over 90,000; and John Walker, then Lewis's most bitter enemy, garnered 85,359 to Lewis's 48,672.5. Frank Farrington, who would challenge Lewis for control of the union in the 1920s, also outpolled Lewis by a wide margin. Yet those whom Lewis bested included such prominent union men as Alex Howat, Tom Kennedy, Phil Murray, William Mitch, and Robert Harlin. The final results revealed, then, that Lewis, although not the most popular of candidates, had considerable rank-and-file support.[31]

Lewis's role in the 1916 UMW international elections produced a plethora of rumors. White won reelection by less than 9,000 votes out of almost 200,000 cast in a hotly contested race with John Walker (52% to 48%). Walker, a man consumed by his desire to obtain the union presidency and one unable to concede that he might lose a fair election, saw conspiracies everywhere. Given the Byzantine nature of UMW elections and the power exercised by incumbent administrations, White undoubtedly used chicanery and patronage to hold his office. But Walker preferred to believe that he was a victim of conspiracy and that the prime conspirator was his former Illinois ally, John L. Lewis. In November 1916, Walker complained to Gompers that Lewis had been abusing his A. F. of L. position by campaigning for White among coal miners. Lewis immediately denied Walker's allegations, complaining that it was a case of the pot calling the kettle black. In a letter to Gompers dripping with sarcasm, Lewis alleged that Walker, in fact, had sought the former's support in the union election; Lewis then asked: "Is it possible that . . . Walker is considering this matter with the biased judgment of one frantically scrambling for office and has worked himself into a mental attitude wherein he believes that all who are not 'electioneering for him' are 'electioneering against him'?" Lewis swore that he had abided by and would continue to abide by the A. F. of L. policy concerning noninterference in the internal affairs of affiliates, and he suggested that his desire to do so "will, of course, be greatly strengthened by the knowledge that my ever vigilant friend, Mr. Walker, with his sensitive ear attuned to catch the slightest discordant note, stands ready at all times to aid and assist by keeping a constant super-vision over me."[32]

Lewis's denials and sarcasm notwithstanding, circumstantial evidence suggests that Lewis was active in the 1916 union election. It is scarcely likely that he polled almost 50,000 votes without some effort on his own behalf; and it is even less likely that he failed to influence the substantial bloc of votes cast by his old Panama local. White's action soon after his reelection also gives the lie to Lewis's denials. On January 23, 1917, White appointed Lewis international statistician for the UMW, a post that was customarily a sinecure but one for which White and Lewis now had different plans.[33] Lewis thus formally entered the UMW hierarchy in the same manner he earlier had joined the A. F. of L.—by patronage appointment.

Lewis assumed the statistician's post on February 1, 1917, a particularly opportune moment in trade union history. Since the initial upsurge of modern American trade unionism in the years 1897-1903, the labor movement—the UMW included—had lost momentum. Employer resistance, judicial decisions, and economic recessions retarded the further growth of trade unionism. Between 1904 and 1915, the membership of the A. F. of L. and the UMW grew more slowly than during the previous decade.[34] The coal miners fastened their union more securely in the states composing the Central Competitive Field (western Pennsylvania, Ohio, Indiana, and Illinois) and in several outlying western states (Iowa, Missouri, Kansas, and Oklahoma) but experienced much less success in the southern Appalachian states of West Virginia, Virginia, Maryland, Kentucky, Tennessee, and Alabama. A recession beginning in 1913 and deepening into a depression by early 1915 threatened to deal trade unionism further setbacks. But the European war, which had erupted in late summer 1914, stimulated the American economy. Production boomed, factories and mines operated overtime, workers enjoyed a sellers' market, and trade unionism advanced aggressively.

As 1916 passed into 1917, the pace of labor militancy quickened. Millions of workers walked off their jobs. Scarcely an industry or a region remained untouched by labor discontent. After the United States entered the war in April 1917, industrial turmoil worsened. The nine months beginning in April saw more strikes than during any previous full year in American history, and 1918 witnessed an even more fevered wave of strikes. In the two years 1917-1918, the UMW added more members, absolutely and relatively, than it had from 1904 through 1916. By Armistice Day, 1918, the UMW claimed over 400,000 members and was by far the nation's largest single trade union.

Not only did American workers grow militant and their unions flourish; harassed employers improved working conditions, and the federal government showered its benevolence on American labor. Wages rose appreciably, though not always quite as rapidly as prices, and the eight-hour day became common. The mine workers for the first time began to win substantial collective bargaining agreements in the southern Appalachian fields and in some of the other outlying districts. Before, but especially after, the nation entered the war in April 1917, the Wilson administration wooed labor leaders. Federal officials, including the president, promised to promote "legitimate" trade unionism (meaning the A. F. of L. variety) if trade unionists endorsed the war effort. And in 1918 the government made good on many of its promises. Never before had organized labor in America appeared so successful, nor had it wielded so much influence in "official" Washington. Lewis and the mine workers, moreover, were at the center of the wartime labor vortex.[35]

Lewis's travel diary for 1917 and reports in the UMW *Journal* indicated his widening role in the miners' union. In 1917 Lewis still spent more time on the road than at home and slept more often in hotel rooms and Pullman berths than in his own bedroom. But his train travels now took him on a different circuit, in which he did new things. He traveled more frequently between Springfield, Illinois (his new family residence) and UMW headquarters in Indianapolis and also often visited New York City and Washington, D.C. His trips to coal mining districts involved UMW, not A. F. of L., business, and they concerned collective bargaining more than public speaking. By mid-1917 Lewis served as a key UMW negotiator and Washington lobbyist. In February and March, he reorganized District 15 (Colorado) and then negotiated a generous contract with one of the larger Colorado mining companies. April brought him to New York to participate in the most important union business: the renegotiation of the Central Competitive Field contract. June 1917 saw Lewis and Frank Hayes win a new and better union contract for the District 17 miners of the New River and Winding Gulf regions of West Virginia. And in August, Lewis negotiated a contract for Alabama District 20 coal diggers. Between his collective bargaining sessions, Lewis represented the union in Washington. In late June, he attended wartime coal conferences among UMW officials, coal operators, and federal authorities and also testified before a Senate committee. During the Washington conferences, called by the government to elicit support for the war effort among mine operators and UMW leaders, Lewis ridiculed the suggestion that a coal production committee whose members lacked knowledge of the industry should determine prices, wages, and working conditions. It is useless to talk of patriotism and government control to miners, Lewis asserted, "when they are compelled to remain idle owing to the lack of cars to carry the coal they produce." In the event, however, Lewis cooperated in federal efforts to regulate production and labor relations in the coal industry. Thus, in September and October, he returned to Washington for a series of conferences with coal operators and federal officials that resulted in a revised Central Competitive Field agreement that, as a consequence of wartime inflation, increased miners' wages substantially. Throughout 1917 Lewis labored to make himself indispensable to fellow union officials, coal miners, operators, and government leaders.[36]

John White granted Lewis a singular opportunity to publicize his accomplishments and to trumpet his name within the union. In late summer 1917 Lewis became business manager of the UMW *Journal* as well as international statistician. As administrator of the union paper, Lewis followed precedent; wherever possible, he featured the accomplishments of the incumbent officers and his own "prominent" role in bringing them about. The *Journal*, after all, existed more to convey the union leaders' position on issues than to enlighten coal miners—and John L. Lewis would not break precedent.

The year 1917 saw Lewis apparently involved in less honorable sorts of business, union and otherwise. A travel diary entry for August 17 reads cryptically: "This date lost $1470.00 in stud at Willard. Wentz room. Peabody, Chase, Dick Williams." How could Lewis afford to lose $1,470, more than half his then current union salary, in a single evening? Was the Peabody mentioned a member of the great midwestern coal mining family? If so, what led a union official to participate in a high-stake poker game with coal operators?

Another name that would plague Lewis throughout his career first appeared in 1917. According to Robert Harlin (president of UMW District 10, Washington), who participated with Lewis in the March 1917 Colorado negotiations, a Mr. Hamilton, a prominent Pennsylvania coal operator and agent of eastern financial interests, joined in the bargaining sessions and assisted the UMW.[37] What a financier-employer was doing for the union in March 1917 nobody then asked. But the Mr. Hamilton that Harlin cited must certainly have been one Al Hamilton, a Pittsburgh resident with interests in coal mines, steel, and business journalism, who was an associate and friend to Lewis; indeed the two men did numerous favors for each other.[38]

By the end of 1918 union rivals charged that Lewis's relationship with Hamilton was the axis around which union corruption revolved. Hamilton, it was asserted, for a price, either protected mine operators from the union or assisted Lewis in obtaining union contracts. Lewis, it was implied, shared equally in the payments Hamilton secured, a lucrative arrangement for both men.[39]

Additional circumstantial evidence linked Lewis to Hamilton and also to a pattern of union intrigue. Hamilton, among his other interests, published at various times the *Coal Trade Bulletin* and *Labor World* of Pittsburgh and the *American Miner* in Indianapolis. Lewis used these trade journals to leak vital union and industry information, to libel his rivals, and to promote his own ambitions.[40] Moreover, one K. C. Adams, sometime-editor of *Labor World* and *American Miner*, was a good friend of Hamilton's and an even better and closer friend to Lewis. The Adams-Lewis association included the former's eventual editorship of the UMW *Journal* and his employment as a confidential union lobbyist and public relations agent in Washington. By 1917, then, Lewis was deeply involved with the shady entrepreneurial characters and the peculiar style of collective bargaining that would shadow his entire trade union career.

Lewis's growing influence in the labor movement in the summer of 1917 also followed more conventional lines. In June, along with such prominent UMW figures as John White, Frank Hayes, William Green, and John Mitchell, Lewis served as a member of the wartime coal production committee's labor delegation. And Lewis used his influence with Gompers to win patronage jobs for several of his supporters in the UMW.[41] Even greater gains awaited Lewis—not, however, before family tragedy intervened.

Since the birth of his first daughter in 1910, Lewis had been most prominent in the family by his absence from home. The year 1917 proved no exception to the rule. The months of June, July, and August saw him at home infrequently and then most often only for a day. When he finally rejoined his family for an extended visit, it was the result of personal tragedy. As was her custom in the late summer, Myrta had returned to Lucas with the children, where the first week in September, Mary Margaret became seriously ill with typhoid fever. By September 6, Lewis's seven-year-old firstborn child had died, and on September 8, she was buried in Lucas.[42]

The impact of Mary Margaret's death on the Lewis household remains shrouded in mystery. In the biographical data that Lewis, his younger brother Dennie, and his daughter Kathryn later fed to inquisitive journalists and putative biographers, accurate facts were rarely given concerning either the birth or death of Mary Margaret.* That the death of her firstborn daughter profoundly affected and depressed Myrta Lewis has been attested to by a sister-in-law, who also recalls that John was grief-stricken by the tragedy. Six-year-old Kathryn probably experienced a loss as great, or greater, than her mother's. The passing of Mary Margaret must also have been related to John and Myrta's decision to have another child, for only fourteen months later, on November 25, 1918, the Lewis household increased again to four members with the birth of a son, John L. Jr.[43]

Unlike the female members of his family, John could compensate for his daughter's death by immersing himself more deeply in union affairs. On September 18, 1917, less than two weeks after the funeral, Lewis returned to UMW headquarters in Indianapolis and spent most of the next six weeks there and in Washington. Those six weeks proved a decisive period in Lewis's emergence as president of the mine workers. Political bargaining in Washington among Gompers, Labor Secretary William B. Wilson, and President Woodrow Wilson led to John P. White's appointment as a permanent member of the wartime Federal Fuel Board and labor adviser to fuel administrator Harry A. Garfield. White promptly resigned his UMW presidency and, under the union's constitution, Vice-President Frank Hayes automatically succeeded to the highest office. White and Hayes, in turn, appointed Lewis acting vice-president, a position that required international executive board confirmation. Contrary to John Brophy's assertion that members of the IEB opposed Lewis's appointment, the board approved his promotion

*Saul Alinsky, in his biography of Lewis, mistakenly places Mary Margaret's death in 1921. He probably culled the information from Cecil Carnes' earlier and totally inaccurate biography of Lewis, which also cites the death as occurring in 1921 and was probably, in turn, the source for the information in James Wechsler's unflattering *Labor Baron*. Other biographies and sketches simply fail to mention either Mary Margaret's birth or death.

unanimously, prompting Lewis to scribble these words in his travel diary for Thursday, October 15, 1917, the day White announced his own resignation: "Our ship made port today."[44] Indeed it had, for without once winning election to an international union office, Lewis had become the UMW's second-ranking official.

As vice-president, Lewis had wider latitude for action than the post customarily allowed. President Hayes proved himself ineffective and addicted to alcohol. Lewis gladly filled the administrative vacuum. It was Lewis who most often represented the union during delicate negotiations with coal operators and federal officials. And it was Lewis, not Hayes, to whom Gompers turned when he wanted a prominent labor leader, one who "was true blue," to guide a party of British trade unionists visiting the United States to promote Allied wartime unity.[45] As Hayes sank deeper into his drinking habit and fell victim to despondency, Lewis, in effect, ruled the UMW. Always the opportunist, however, Lewis bided his time before seeking the presidency in his own right.

Despite Hayes's alcoholism, he remained a popular figure among the rank and file, and Lewis knew it. Thus in the 1918 union election, Lewis chose to remain as Hayes's running mate—an especially wise choice, as Lewis obtained only fifteen nominations for the presidency from union locals compared to Hayes's 714 and John Walker's 295. In the vice-presidential race Lewis had a clear field, receiving 773 nominations to his closest contender's 89. In fact, Walker's running mate in the election, Thomas Kennedy, chosen to add anthracite voting strength to the ticket (Kennedy was a leader in Anthracite District 7 of northeastern Pennsylvania), obtained only 23 nominations and, as Lewis gloated, not one in "Illinois, Indiana, Ohio, Western and Central Pennsylvania and all of the Southwestern districts and the Northwestern fields, including Alabama, Tennessee, Kentucky, and West Virginia, although my erstwhile friend, Mr. Walker, had made all possible efforts to secure the nominations for him in Illinois."[46] In the event, the Hayes-Lewis ticket swept the field.

Less than a year after his successful race for the vice-presidency, Lewis became the UMW's acting president, once again achieving high union office without contesting an election. In one of many letters written during the 1918 campaign filled with paranoid charges of corruption and conspiracy, John Walker accurately prophesied the future. "Just as soon as the election is over," he wrote a friend on December 4, 1918,

> if by any hook or crook they [Lewis, K.C. Adams, Al Hamilton] can steal it, I expect they will depose him [Hayes]. Lewis will go in the position and another henchman of Al Hamilton's will be appointed Vice-President, and the organization will then be completely in control of the most unscrupulous, corruptionists that ever represented crooks, trying to destroy the labor movement and prevent the progress of common humanity.[47]

Aside from Walker's comments about crime and corruption, the remainder of his prophecy came true. In the spring of 1919 Hayes traveled to Europe on a joint

A. F. of L.-UMW mission to discuss postwar reconstruction with British and continental labor leaders, leaving Lewis home to serve as the UMW's acting president. In Europe, Hayes's alcoholism worsened. After his return to the United States in midsummer 1919, Hayes proved unable physically to administer the union. Lewis thus ran the UMW unofficially until January 1, 1920, when Hayes, citing ill health, formally resigned from office. Lewis then became acting president and promptly appointed Philip Murray as acting vice-president.[48] Murray was a longtime Pittsburgh area associate and acquaintance of Al Hamilton. Was there an element of reality in Walker's paranoia? Did Lewis succeed to the union presidency as the result of an elaborate and dirty conspiracy?

Walker's allegations preceded Lewis's emergence as president of the UMW. After Lewis's triumph, other rumors concerning the methods he used to obtain power circulated among coal miners. As late as 1937, Frank Farrington, in a letter to a United States senator, alleged that Lewis's "progress to the top was infested with gross intrigue, base ingratitude and plotting so foul that no honorable man would employ nor [sic] profit from."[49] In this letter, otherwise more notable for its inaccuracies and malicious gossip than its truth, Farrington raised one question never satisfactorily answered: Why did Frank Hayes, "penniless, and without any prospect whatever, for other employment . . . though less than 40 years of age, retire from a high and important position, which was eminently satisfactory to him and the attainment of which was a realization of his life's ambitions?"

Farrington provided no answer. But fourteen years later, in 1951, James Lord, once a UMW official and later head of the A. F. of L.'s mining department, supplied an answer to Adolph Germer. Lord, by then an old man living in Colorado, sent Germer a six-page crudely printed letter in pencil in which he analyzed Lewis's sudden rise to power in 1917-1918.[50] According to Lord, Lewis initially enticed William Green, a man said to resemble a Baptist minister more than a labor leader, with an attractive prostitute with whom Green spent a weekend at the Gayoso Hotel in French Lick, Indiana. Lewis obtained a photostatic copy of the hotel's register, which he used to eliminate Green as a rival for the union presidency. With Green eliminated, Lewis's agents encouraged Hayes, who found the presidency too burdensome, to resort to drink for escape. Rendered physically and mentally incompetent by alcoholism, Hayes, in the summer of 1919, agreed to resign in return for a promise by Lewis to support Hayes for the remainder of his life. Lord even claimed that John P. White had supplied him with a copy of the Gayoso register a year before the latter's death. "Outside of dates," swore Lord, "this is an exact chronicle."

Lord's story seems truly incredible—outlandish to say the least. Yet why should an elderly man, no longer Lewis's union rival nor in a position to humble the UMW president, lie? Had Lord told his tale in 1919, during the 1920s, or even during the 1930s, when numerous rivals challenged Lewis for union supremacy and a myriad of enemies sought to discredit him, it might readily be cast aside as mere malicious gossip. But by 1951, for both Lord and Germer, the old struggles with Lewis had receded, and both men could recall the past with equanimity. Lord's painfully composed letter appears much more the product of an old man seeking to set the record straight than a screed comparable to Farrington's 1937 epistle. Indeed, Lord resolves the two most puzzling features of Lewis's rise to the UMW presidency: why Frank Hayes, after 1919, publicly supported Lewis and remained on the UMW payroll, and why the more prominent and popular William Green stepped aside for Lewis. Yet Lord's story, however true it rings or logical it appears, lacks corroborating evidence.

Lewis may indeed have achieved his position using the methods suggested by Walker, Farrington, and Lord. But he had also proved himself by 1919 an exceedingly able union official, one who in many respects was a far better administrator than his predecessors or contemporaries. During the war years no other UMW official proved so adept at negotiating union contracts in hitherto nonunion districts or at improving existing contracts. No other union official had superior contacts in Washington or presented more effectively the union's case before government agencies and administrators—certainly not Frank Hayes or William Green. During the January 1918 UMW convention, the first one at which Lewis served as an international officer, he gave a virtuoso performance. His reports to the delegates were remarkable for their detailed statistics, thorough content, and complete knowledge of the economics of coal and the risks of mining. Despite considerable rank-and-file hostility to the Washington Agreement of October 1917, which increased miners' wages substantially but penalized them monetarily for unauthorized strikes, Lewis masterfully elicited overwhelming delegate support for the UMW administration. During a debate with Alex Howat Lewis demonstrated why he got along so famously with mine operators and government officials. Referring to the Washington Agreement, he observed: "It is a purely business proposition; it is devoid of all sentiment."[51] And for the next forty years, at one convention after another, Lewis would place business before sentiment, immediate achievements ahead of ultimate ideals.

Lewis may have used cunning and even corruption to fight his way to the top, but he also earned his command of the UMW. In 1919 the miners' union had no more impressive figure. Gompers looked to Lewis as one of the nation's most responsible trade unionists and implored him to serve as labor representative to President Wilson's 1919 Industrial Conference.[52] No UMW leader handled raucus convention delegates more diplomatically and more authoritatively. Nor could any union member match Lewis's oratory. By 1919 he had already mastered two different but equally effective styles of public speaking. When emotion and sentiment were needed, Lewis had at his command an ample supply of carefully prepared and rehearsed* biblical and Shakespearean allusions that enthralled union delegates. At those moments his youthful experience on the stage of the

*Manuscript copies of Lewis's later radio speeches indicate that he carefully chose the striking phrases associated with his rhetoric and that he tried them out before small, private audiences before using them on the radio or at conventions.

Lucas "Opera House," however crude and amateurish, served Lewis well. Never at a loss for words, even during the most tempestuous debates, he mastered the caustic comment and the ad hominem argument. He also changed pace with consummate skill. When the time came to defend a new contract or to analyze the economics of coal mining, rather than to cut down a union rival, Lewis marshaled facts and figures with the best of economists. Indeed, early on he used eminent economists for advice, and during the war years he built a relationship with the academic economist and reformer W. Jett Lauck that over the next three decades would influence all the UMW's economic proposals. Scarcely pausing for breath, Lewis could change from the dramatic orator to the professional technocrat. By 1919 Lewis had learned how to discard allies and cultivate rivals. He felt no qualms about destroying John Walker's power in the UMW, and he acted with alacrity in recruiting Walker's running mate in 1918, Tom Kennedy, as a member of the Lewis team. Depending on the occasion, Lewis applied lessons drawn from the Old Testament, Shakespeare, and Machiavelli; he mixed charity with vengeance; he cajoled and he roared; he played the lion and the fox.

Yet Lewis did not reach the top without personal sacrifice. For almost nine years he lacked a close family life. His firstborn child, who died at the age of seven, probably spent at most a year of her short life in her father's presence, and his younger daughter, Kathryn, later intensely possessive of her father, had an early childhood equally devoid of a paternal presence. On the road and in strange towns, Pullmans, and hotel rooms, where Lewis spent most of his time between 1911 and 1919, he enjoyed few of the diversions popular among his traveling trade union contemporaries. The saloon, the ball park, and the opposite sex failed to attract a vigorous, physically handsome man then in the prime of his life. All Lewis's energies, all his desires, seemed to be sublimated in a single-minded drive to dominate the mine workers' union and become the most influential figure in the American labor movement.*

Travel, family tragedy, and an apparently lonely existence left few overt scars on John L. Lewis. In 1919 he seemed a vibrant, tireless, and attractive man, a perfect specimen of robust good health. Wavy dark auburn hair topped a leonine face that featured penetrating blue eyes, a fine aquiline nose, a firm full mouth, and remarkably bushy eyebrows that lent Lewis a singularly sensuous and mysterious appearance. The most conventional, conservative dark blue and gray suits draped broad shoulders, an immense chest, and stout legs. Not quite six feet in height but in excess of 200 pounds, John L. Lewis's body showed the first signs of corpulence but not the least indication of age. A powerful trade union had found a leader of commanding physical stature.

By midsummer 1919, Lewis had achieved a part of his great ambitions. He was acting president of the nation's largest and, perhaps, most militant trade union.

---

*The few surviving samples of family correspondence, rare indeed, suggest Lewis's inability to express personal sentiments or convey human feelings in written language. His language was intended for the bargaining table and the public platform, not the family or even friends.

With 400,000 members and union contracts covering coalfields from Alabama to Montana and from northeastern Pennsylvania to Washington State, the UMW seemed a labor colossus able to paralyze the American economy. Coal powered railroads and the merchant marine, supplied almost all the nation's electric energy, fed iron and steel furnaces, and heated the vast majority of homes. A coal strike would indeed be a national emergency.

CHAPTER 3

The Testing and the Triumph 1919-1920

World War I ripped apart the fabric of the Western World. Bolshevik revolutionaries ruled Russia; the German Empire, scarcely half a century old in 1919, stood in ruins; the ancient Hapsburg Empire, and its more recent offspring, the dual monarchy of Austria-Hungary, had vanished, the victim of wartime defeat and Czech, Serbian, Croatian, Rumanian, and Bulgarian nationalists. In 1919 Communists seized power in Bavaria and Hungary, and in the streets of Berlin militant German leftists, the Spartacists, fought pitched battles with returned troops and city police backed by a reformist Social Democratic government. On the plains of western Russia and eastern Poland, Leon Trotsky's Red Army waged full-scale war with Polish nationalist forces. In Italy workers seized factories, and in Great Britain, the Labour party, which had replaced the Liberals as the nation's second party, proclaimed its program for a postwar socialist order. Wherever one looked in 1919, one witnessed radical turmoil and masses in motion. A new world seemed to be in the making.

In the United States, too, workers and their spokesmen dreamed of a new, better, and more equal society. In the midst of the war, Sidney Hillman, immigrant leader of the men's clothing workers, proclaimed labor's new goals. "What labor is demanding all over the world today," he asserted, "is not a few material things like more dollars and fewer hours of work, but a right to a voice in the conduct of industry." By 1918 Hillman was fired by messianic dreams, as he related to his daughter: "Messiah is arriving. He may be with us any minute—one can hear the footsteps of the Deliverer—if only he listens intently. Labor will rule and the World will be free."[1]

Whether divinely or mundanely inspired, American workers in the year 1919 acted vigorously to reshape society. The year began with a general strike in Seattle, where for five days in February the city's workers paralyzed local industry and services except for those items deemed essential to life and health. Exercising administrative skill and common sense, Seattle's workers ruled the city with minimal disorder.

The Seattle General Strike initiated an unprecedented wave of labor unrest. Over 4 million workers struck in 1919, a number never before reached and not to be exceeded until 1946. Workers demanded shorter hours, higher wages, and freedom for all wartime political prisoners. In Boston, early in September, even the police walked off the job, and later that month over 300,000 iron- and steelworkers left work in the first mass strike to affect that giant industry. Railroad workers, who remained on the job in 1919, nonetheless demanded nationalization of the railroads. As working-class militancy surged, union membership by year's end soared to over 5 million.

Working-class politics also revealed a new face in 1919. In Illinois so-called labor progressives under the leadership of Chicagoan John Fitzpatrick formed a citywide labor party, then a statewide organization, and finally the National Labor party to participate in the 1920 presidential election. Similar labor party movements sprouted in industrial centers across the nation, while immigrant workers swelled the ranks of the Socialist party's foreign language federations, which ultimately broke with reformist socialism and united with other Bolshevik sympathizers to form an American Communist movement.[2]

American radicals in the year 1919 awaited an imminent revolution; conservatives, equally sensitive to the possibilities of revolution, sought to thwart radicalism. Regardless of former political loyalties and traditions, Democrats and Republicans united to combat radicalism. A Democratic president, Woodrow Wilson, and a Democratic attorney general, A. Mitchell Palmer, used federal coercion to extirpate radical influences from American society. Their anxieties and fears were fully shared by the man who in 1920 would be the Republican presidential candidate. "I am really more anxious about the tranquillity of our country," wrote Warren G. Harding in the autumn of 1919,

> than I am about personal or party success. I really think we are facing a desperate situation. It looks to me as if we are coming to a crisis in the conflict between the radical labor leaders and the capitalistic system under which we have developed this republic. . . . I think the situation has to be met and met with exceptionable [sic] courage.

Much to Harding's subsequent relief, the Wilson administration proved courageous in combating organized labor, causing the Ohio Republican to concede that President Wilson, "in spite of his illness . . . may be considerably more sane than some of us have been willing to believe."[3]

Harding's anxieties had been triggered in October 1919 by an impending national strike of soft-coal miners. Long one of the most militant affiliates of the

A. F. of L. and a union with a substantial socialist membership, the United Mine Workers could scarcely remain immune to the labor unrest sweeping the nation. Moreover, internal union politics and external economic conditions further stimulated militancy among coal miners. Wartime increases in wage rates never equaled price inflation, and after the basic Washington wage award of October 1917, coal miners' wages fell further behind prices. Increased coal production, owing to the demands of war and then to the immediate needs of postwar Europe, guaranteed miners steadier employment and greater job security than normal. Protected by the marketplace on one hand and federal benevolence on the other, the mine workers' union grew during the war years, building its membership and widening the geographical scope of its collective bargaining agreements.

Internally, however, the union had problems. Its president, Frank Hayes, lacked the authority and the ability to run the organization. Almost as soon as he had been elected president in December 1918, Hayes found himself under attack by a number of putative successors, among whom the most prominent and dangerous were Frank Farrington of Illinois, Robert Harlin of Washington, and Alex Howat of Kansas. Furthermore, Hayes's vice-president, John L. Lewis, schemed to grasp the union power steadily slipping through Hayes's palsied fingers. The various pretenders to Hayes's UMW throne maneuvered to enlarge their union constituencies and in doing so promised rank-and-file miners higher wages, shorter hours, and greater union influence in the industry.

The UMW, however, faced an anomaly, for the 1917 Washington Agreement bound the union not to renegotiate the basic contract before the war officially ended or April 1, 1920, whichever came first. Although an armistice had been signed in November 1918, the victorious allies in September 1919 had yet to implement final peace terms, nor could one be certain when the United States would ratify a peace treaty. Legally, then, the coal miners' union was caught in a dilemma: If, in 1919, neither the operators nor the Federal Fuel Administration voluntarily met the UMW's wage demands and a strike ensued, it would pit the miners not simply against their employers, but also against the federal government, which was a party to the 1917 agreement.

Political realities notwithstanding, union leaders and their rivals had to satisfy the rank and file's insistence on higher wages. Thus, in March 1919, President Hayes convened a National Policy Committee meeting at the union's Indianapolis headquarters to discuss the possible termination of the Washington wage agreement and the restoration of peacetime labor conditions. During the policy committee's sessions, the more militant demands carried, as aspiring union politicos outdid each other in bidding for rank-and-file support. Among the more important union goals set in March were the achievement of a six-hour day and five-day week, the nationalization and democratic management of all the coal mines in the United States, and the appointment of an officers' committee to draft a bill for presentation to Congress providing for nationalization of the coal mines. The means to achieve such ambitious aims, however, were left ambiguous.

Unsure as to when a peace treaty would be ratified and the union would be free to negotiate a new agreement, Hayes and the policy committee equivocated. Militant demands had been enunciated, their achievement had been declared a basic union goal. But, concluded President Hayes, the basic agreement "shall not be disturbed until a special International Convention is held."[4] Whether such a convention would be called before or after the formal ratification of a peace treaty was left open.

In the late winter, spring, and summer of 1919, while a myriad of strikes fanned the flames of labor discontent, UMW leaders restrained dissatisfaction among coal miners. Drinking more heavily, President Hayes rapidly lost control of affairs and was only too glad in the spring of 1919 to travel to Europe as part of a government-sponsored labor mission. Farrington, Howat, and Harlin, meantime, returned to their respective district headquarters to solidify their local strength, search for political allies elsewhere in the union, and plan for the December 1920 UMW election. And John L. Lewis administered the daily affairs of the UMW at headquarters in Indianapolis.

Lewis's new role, heightened status, and increased income was reflected in the way he lived. For the first time in almost a decade, he spent considerable time with his family.[5] Indeed, for the first time since they left Lucas, John and Myrta had a real home of their own. Lewis in 1917 had purchased a large (the largest on the street) and typically midwestern Victorian-style three-story frame house on a wide, tree-lined street in a respectable Springfield, Illinois, neighborhood. He also purchased two other houses in the same neighborhood for his parents and sisters. John's younger brothers simultaneously established households in Springfield, thus reuniting the Lewis clan. The move had made it possible for Mary Margaret and Kathryn to attend the Springfield public schools regularly and for Myrta to enjoy the company and assistance of her in-laws while John was away from home.

Lewis's desire to become a homeowner, to assist his parents, and to be close to his brothers and sisters is certainly understandable. His decision to reside in Springfield rather than Indianapolis makes less sense. His 1919 travel diary suggests Lewis's greater attention to family affairs. Seldom before the coal strike crisis of October-November was he away from home for extended periods of time. In fact, the diary records constant trips between office and home, Indianapolis and Springfield, Why, then, did Lewis reside in Springfield, when he administered the UMW from Indianapolis? Why did a man who apparently felt guilty about his absences from the family in the years 1911-1918 and about the death of the firstborn child, endure regular train trips between two cities and lonely nights in hotel rooms in preference to being at home with Myrta and the children? What aspect of Lewis's personality demanded such an existence? Successful politicians, businessmen, and union leaders necessarily sacrificed many of the customary obligations of family life to the exigencies of the "job." But that scarcely explains why Lewis voluntarily chose to establish his home in a city distant from his central place of "business." Perhaps during his years as an organizer he had grown accustomed to absence from the family; perhaps Myrta's oppressively bourgeois character, her accumulation of fragile antiques, and her excessive cleanliness irritated him;* perhaps he feared, owing to guilt about his daughter's childhood death, that if home and office were in the same city, he might tend to spend more time with his family at the cost of his union career and soaring ambition.

Whatever the conscious or unconscious motivations, Lewis drew a sharp line between home and career, family and business. It was as if the two aspects of Lewis's life required totally different personalities and to intermingle them would diminish his dual roles as father-husband and union leader. The union role necessitated public presence, cunning, excessive selfishness, and low ethics; proper family life demanded privacy, personal warmth, cooperative effort, and a firm moral code. Only by keeping the two roles in separate, even airtight, compartments could Lewis play them simultaneously and successfully.

The manner in which Lewis reorganized his life-style in 1919 also had enormous impact on his future family and union relations. Kathryn now saw her father more regularly. One could imagine that when Lewis was at home he tried to compensate for past neglect of his surviving daughter; one can also surmise that Kathryn became intensively possessive of her father and that his still-frequent departures from home upset her. This singular relationship between father and daughter to which the elder carried guilt and the younger brought possessiveness in the 1930s and 1940s caused no end of trouble for Lewis.[6]

And what of his infant son, John Jr., born in November 1918? Obviously the son accepted his father as a regular presence in the home whose absences were no more common than his appearances. Yet the intensity of the relationship between father and daughter must have increasingly irked John Jr., who built a circumspect relationship with his father and ultimately elected to follow the profession of his maternal grandfather, medicine, whereas Kathryn chose a trade union career.[7]

Family tragedy also once again stalked Lewis's rise in the union hierarchy. His appointment as acting vice-president had been preceded only a month earlier by his daughter's death; a month before he assumed command of the UMW from a debilitated Frank Hayes, his father, Thomas, died on February 27, 1919.

During the summer of 1919, with formal ratification of the peace terms no closer to achievement than the previous winter, coal miners chafed at the restraints under which they labored. Consumer prices soared while wages remained frozen at levels fixed in October 1917. Miners, moreover, were still bound by the wartime penalty clause in their contract, which penalized them financially for wildcat

---

*The inventory of Lewis's estate suggests that he parted with most of the antiques—particularly the smaller items such as plates and spoons—after Myrta's death in 1942.

walkouts. Yet despite legal restraints and the penalty clause, miners, especially in Illinois and Kansas, spontaneously laid down their tools. Union left-wingers and ambitious office seekers eager to ride rank-and-file militancy into high office, encouraged "spontaneous" strikes. In Illinois, the union district in which socialists were most influential, Frank Farrington, the district president and a man of vaunting ambition, witnessed local rebellions against the wartime contract. In Kansas, another state noted for its radical union tradition, district President Alex Howat, more famous for his fiery rhetoric and emotional rebelliousness than his intelligence or administrative ability, proved eager to lead insurgent coal miners.

That summer Lewis commanded a powerful but undisciplined union army. If coal miners failed to improve their working conditions either through collective bargaining or government award, they threatened to strike under insurgent commanders. Unless Lewis acted decisively, his troops might desert him and follow his union rivals. With Lewis's claim to the union presidency resting on the shakiest foundation, he could ill afford a substantial challenge. If he lost control of the miners and failed to improve their contract, the odds favored Lewis's defeat in the December 1920 UMW election. Indeed, Lewis's political enemies believed that they had placed the acting president in an impossible predicament. In a public newsletter and a subsequent private interview with a Bureau of Investigation secret agent, K.C. Adams analyzed political machinations inside the UMW. Lewis's enemies, observed Adams, "sought to build a sentiment among the men for wage increases, reduction in hours and other betterments so unreasonable in makeup that Lewis's failure to achieve them in wage negotiations with the operators would sound the death knell of his political future."[8] If, as expected, collective bargaining collapsed and the miners walked out, Lewis would be compelled to support coal miners in a conflict involving the federal government as well as the mine owners. Just as the operators would reject the UMW's "exorbitant" demands, so, too, would the federal government smash an "illegal" strike. Boxed in on all sides Lewis was doomed to certain defeat in the upcoming union election. At least, so plotted Farrington, Howat, Robert Harlin, John Walker, and other rivals of John L. Lewis.

In this difficult and dangerous situation Lewis established his claim to union leadership. First, he drove a wedge between his union opponents; next he directed a strike against mine owners and federal officials (in the process forcing the government to break the strike, thus shifting blame for its failure); and finally, he won for coal miners substantial improvements in their basic contract. His handling of the 1919 strike led many coal miners to agree with K. C. Adams that "no other leader in their ranks possesses the daring and ability of Lewis."[9]

Well aware that he would lose control of the UMW and popularity among coal miners unless the 1917 agreement was revised, Lewis induced the union's executive board to call the special convention recommended by the March policy committee report. On September 9, 1919, over two thousand UMW delegates gathered in Cleveland, Ohio, to discuss their union's future. This was the first convention at which Lewis presided as the UMW's chief officer, and it proved the stormiest in many years. Debate and discussion focused primarily on the issue of winning a new contract for miners and authorizing UMW officials to call a strike. A wealth of other issues, however, also embroiled the convention and caused problems for Lewis. Ethnic and racial tensions aggravated the customary conflict between district officers and international officials over district autonomy. And candidates for the UMW presidency used the special convention to maneuver for power.

From the convention's opening moments to its adjournment two weeks later, on September 23, Lewis resisted challenges to his authority. It was no simple task to control upwards of two thousand rebellious coal miners, most of whom were union militants and few of whom felt any special loyalty to John L. Lewis. To repudiate the militants would be to risk outright defeat; to accept completely their demands would strip Lewis of much of his authority and endanger his chances for election. On the one hand, then, Lewis had to address the militant spirit stirring the delegates; on the other hand, he had to discipline it. This meant tolerating small tactical losses in order to achieve ultimate strategic advantages.

As soon as the convention opened, an insurgent delegate from Illinois District 12, one Gomer Davis, Welshman and constant thorn in Lewis's side, moved that the number of delegate votes necessary for a roll call be reduced from 500, as recommended by the Rules Committee, to 250. Following an acerbic but brief personal exchange between Lewis and Davis, the delegates, by a substantial majority, passed the Davis proposal.[10] Other resolutions passed by large majorities also disclosed the appeal of radicalism to delegates. One resolution, taking note of the English "Triple Alliance,"* asked UMW officials to confer with their counterparts in the railroad unions for the purpose of formulating a similar American alliance. A second resolution demanded the creation of a labor party and required UMW officers to convene a meeting of trade unions, the Non-Partisan League, cooperative movements, and farmers' organizations. In reacting to the latter resolution Lewis revealed his intrinsic caution. "The chair will rule," he advised, "that the adoption of this resolution is simply a declaration of principle and in conformity with the constitution does not bind or tie up the political rights or transgress the inherent political freedom of any individual member."[11]

On the issue for which the convention was specifically called into session— contract negotiations—Lewis also mixed militancy with caution. In his formal presidential report to the delegates, Lewis declared that the union should not be penalized for the Senate's failure to ratify the peace treaty.** Because the coal miners for over two years had demonstrated their good faith and met their moral

---

*The coalition among coal miners, trnasport workers, and longshoremen formed shortly before World War I that threatened British capitalism.

**The Senate never ratified the Treaty of Versailles. Not until July 2, 1921, did the United States formally end World War I.

responsibilities and since the actual fighting had been over for a year, Lewis recommended that the convention rule the 1917 Washington Agreement officially terminated no later than November 1, 1919. If mine operators refused to re-negotiate the Central Competitive Field contract on the terms demanded by miners, Lewis recommended a national bituminous strike. To satisfy the militants further, he suggested that the next contract eliminate the wartime automatic penalty clause. Other aspects of his report, however, disclosed caution. Lewis explained that he had delayed wage negotiations until the fall in order to conduct them at the most propitious time—a period when coal production rose, demand increased, and miners had steadier work. Circumspection also led Lewis to temporize on the policy committee's call for nationalization. Because the question was so complicated and fraught with grave implications, union officers, he asserted, lacked the time to prepare a proper plan for congressional action. Yet Lewis dared not repudiate nationalization in 1919; instead, he advised the delegates that their union would obtain material from England including copies of the mine nationalization legislation introduced in Parliament.[12]

The convention granted Lewis full authority in contract negotiations. As proposed by the Scale Committee, the body charged with drawing up all union contract demands, the delegates voted to ask for a 60% wage increase applied to day labor, tonnage rates, yardage, and dead work.* They also demanded the six-hour day at the face,** the five-day week, and the abolition of the automatic penalty clause. If these demands could not be achieved through collective bargaining, the delegates authorized Lewis to call a general strike of all bituminous miners in the United States on November 1, 1919.[13]

On nonwage issues Lewis fought a daily battle with union insurgents, especially on the questions of local unions' right to strike and the appointment of union organizers by the president. The most heated debate during the convention and the sharpest challenge to Lewis's authority concerned the right of a group of Illinois insurgents to be seated as delegates. Lewis's response proved his political acuity. During the summer of 1919 over thirty local unions in Illinois had declared strikes in violation of the contract and in disregard of orders from district President Frank Farrington. Lewis immediately backed Farrington and authorized the Illinois official to revoke the charters of all dissident locals, which Farrington did. The suspended locals, however, sent delegates to the Cleveland convention hoping that union militants would repudiate Farrington and Lewis. As they expected, the Illinois insurgents found an influential advocate in Alex Howat. Howat, like Farrington eager to succeed Lewis as president, intended to use the case of the contested Illinois delegates to strengthen his appeal as the union's most militant leader. Howat thus challenged Farrington as well as Lewis, which pleased the

*Work inside the mines that produced no coal but was essential for its production.
**American miners were traditionally paid, not from the time they entered the mine (portal to portal, see p. 421), but for the time spent at the workplace in the mine, sometimes an hour's walk underground.

acting UMW president. In order to maintain his own authority in Illinois, Farrington allied with Lewis at the special convention and, in so doing, assisted Lewis in
thrashing Howat, whose resolution to seat the Illinois rebels was defeated by 1,704
to 288 votes.[14] In one stroke, then, Lewis trounced one rival for office and
simultaneously set him in direct conflict with a second contender for the UMW
presidency.

Lewis's handling of the appointments issue again demonstrated a keen political
touch. Customarily the UMW president appointed organizers and auditors, and
just as traditionally various union districts demanded the right to elect such
officers. The battle was no mere tempest in a teapot. For the working coal miner,
who could not be sure of a job from one day to the next, appointment as a union
auditor or organizer was a lush and secure patronage plum. For the UMW
president it was a means to build a political machine and to extend his influence
directly into the coalfields. In brief, the appointments issue set district officials
against international officers. Most of the district officials who demanded the
election of organizers and auditors were left-wingers, English-speaking, Protes-
tants, and centered in Illinois and Indiana. Lewis realized this, and he also knew
that the UMW had a substantial non-English-speaking and nonwhite membership,
one that was a rising proportion of total membership. "Out of all the thousands of
foreign-speaking men in Illinois," Lewis reminded the delegates, "the chair
knows of but one foreign-speaking man among the sixteen members of the
executive board. . . . In Ohio, Indiana, western Pennsylvania and numerous
other districts . . . we find no foreign-speaking men represented on district
executive boards." To make the point clearer, he stressed: "We have scores of
men of the colored race who are entitled to representation and who believe that
under an elective system they would be denied representation."[15]

Foreign-speaking and nonwhite delegates took the convention floor to validate
Lewis's assertion. A black delegate from Illinois asserted that the election of
officers "would mean closing forever the door of opportunity in the face of colored
men in the miners' union." The only way people of his race could obtain an
education in unionism, he added, was through the appointment process. An
Italian-speaking delegate argued that only through the appointment of non-
English-speaking organizers could the great mass of unorganized immigrant
miners be brought into the union. The debate further revealed that black and
foreign-language union members had their own racial and ethnic caucuses with
which a leader as astute as Lewis could ally.[16]

The 1919 convention established a pattern in UMW politics that would be
repeated over the next decade with only minor variations. Tactics first used by
Lewis to divide and conquer his rivals in 1919 would be refined and applied more
thoroughly at subsequent conventions. And the more Lewis thrashed his rivals, the
more tumultuous conventions became. Even in September 1919 the convention
literally stalled, owing to the level of shouting, heckling, and general commotion.
Lewis warned the delegates in 1919, as he would at later conventions, of the

financial cost of disorder. "It costs the miners of the United States and Canada about $30,000 a day to operate this convention—on a six-hour basis that is $5000 an hour. If you waste an hour you are wasting $5000 that the miners are paying."[17] Ever the practical man, Lewis could think of no argument against unlimited debate more convincing than the economic one; to Lewis in 1919, and later, it was money, and money alone, that moved the world.

Convention delegates also learned from their president's formal report and his comments during floor debate much about the tactics that he would use to solidify his control of the union—some would say to build a union autocracy. Explaining that the union constitution meant what he said it did, Lewis justified his purge of the elected officers in District 18, British Columbia, and his establishment there of a provisional administration governed by the international. "There must be no compromise," he insisted, "with any element of our membership that seeks to compete . . . with the United Mine Workers of America." Since the Canadian officers had affiliated District 18 with the "One Big Union" movement, an organization founded on the "daydreams of visionaries" and hostile to the "legitimate trades union movement," Lewis had no choice but to remove them. Similarly, convention resolutions and constitutional obligations compelled him to appropriate union funds for the publication of the UMW *Journal* and its free distribution to all union members. Naturally, only the constitutional obligation and the economics of mass printing, not the opportunity to spread his name and accomplishments before all coal miners and prospective voters, determined Lewis's policy on the free distribution of the journal.[18]

Only three days after the special convention adjourned, representatives of the union and the mine operators from the Central Competitive Field met in Buffalo, New York. The union-management negotiations, which began in Buffalo on September 26 and resumed in Philadelphia on October 9, were doomed to failure. On the one side, UMW representatives had been instructed to seek wage and hour demands which were absolutely unacceptable to the operators; on the other side, the operators felt no compulsion to bargain seriously. In late September and early October 1919, the union remained bound to the terms of the wartime contract, and the mine owners, moreover, expected the federal government to enforce that agreement. Lewis thus used the negotiations more to demonstrate the recalcitrance and miserliness of the operators than to achieve his union's demands. Phrases associated with the Lewis of the 1930s and 1940s already fell from his lips in 1919. Sarcastically referring to the attitude of the operators, who refused to renegotiate wage scales, Lewis dripped with venom: "during this crisis from out of Macedonia comes the cry: 'We gentlemen stand here with spotless robes and white mantles and are ready to negotiate a wage scale . . .'—except as affects our mines." "In God's name," he pleaded, "we expect some consideration to be given those 452,000 human souls [the miners] who are asking for bread and have been given a stone."[19]

The breakdown of collective bargaining thrust the federal government into the situation just as the mine owners expected. As soon as he learned that negotiations between the union and the operators had stalemated, Secretary of Labor William B. Wilson wired John L. Lewis and the chairman of the operators' negotiating committee, Thomas T. Brewster, to meet jointly in his Washington office. Wilson also requested that Lewis postpone any strike order until after the Washington conference.[20] In their response to Wilson's request, the union and the operators exposed their basic strategy. Replying for the Central Competitive Field operators, Brewster agreed to confer with the secretary and the UMW provided: (1) the union promised to respect the existing contract to its legal termination; (2) the union rescinded the existing strike order effective November 1 and allowed miners to work pending negotiations; and (3) the present eight-hour day, six-day week remained in effect. The mine owners in the outlying districts supported Brewster, informing Secretary Wilson: "The operators are depending on you using your influence to avert . . . a catastrophe, *by compelling an observance of the existing contract*" (Italics ours).[21] For the union, Lewis could scarcely promise to rescind the strike order, especially when the operators had refused to bargain about material issues. To cancel the strike not only would have left the miners impotent to redress their grievances; it would have rendered Lewis's position in the UMW politically untenable. Yet to reject federal overtures, would leave the UMW at the mercy of employers supported by federal power.

As November 1, the date set for the strike, approached, the mine owners looked to the government as a strikebreaking agency while union officers sought to neutralize federal intervention. The disputants thus cooperated in Labor Secretary Wilson's last-minute efforts to avert a conflict. From October 21 to October 24 union and management representatives met with Secretary Wilson in Washington, where the sessions were off the record and discussion was not even transcribed. The operators refused to negotiate unless the UMW rescinded its strike order, and union officials felt such negotiations to be pointless if miners surrendered their only effective weapon. In a final effort to block a strike, Secretary Wilson read a letter from President Wilson appealing to the miners and operators to settle their differences peacefully or "to refer the matters in dispute to a board of arbitration for determination, and to continue the operation of the mines, pending the decision of the board." The operators grasped the president's solution, for it compelled the UMW to withdraw its strike order. Placed in a dilemma by the president's letter, union officials agreed to reopen negotiations but refused to call off the strike or accept binding arbitration. At that, the operators walked out of the conference, terminated all bargaining, and expected that the federal government would smash a miners' strike.[22]

The next day, October 25, President Wilson's associates played the operators' trump card. In a public statement demanding that the union rescind its strike order prepared by Joseph Tumulty and Walker D. Hines for the bedridden Wilson, the president labeled the impending miners' walkout as "not only unjustifiable but unlawful."[23]

Lewis learned of the president's statement while on his way home to Springfield. Intercepted by reporters at a train stop in Bloomington, Illinois, Lewis was asked to respond to Wilson's plea. "I am an American, free born, with all the pride of my heritage," he replied with customary aplomb.

> I love my country with its institutions and traditions. With Abraham Lincoln I thank God that we have a country where men may strike. May the power of my government never be used to throttle and crush the efforts of the toilers to improve their material welfare and elevate the standards of their civilization.

The reporters who interviewed Lewis in the parlor car claimed to find him perusing the *Iliad* and *Odyssey*. Amazed to discover a labor leader reading classical literature, the journalists probed for an explanation. Lewis responded: "The world is about the same now as it was then."[24] This offhand reference to continuities and cycles in human history reflected, more than the reporters then realized, Lewis's essential view of human nature and social dynamics.

Lewis's reaction to the president's statement expressed another salient aspect of the man's personality. On October 26, 1919, as he would do numerous times in the future when faced with serious crises, Lewis withdrew into total isolation, cutting himself off from friends, associates, and public. Arriving home in Springfield late on the twenty-sixth, he shut off all external communications and left word with the swarm of reporters still pursuing him that he was not to be disturbed before 11:00 A.M. the next day.[25]

In the privacy of his home, Lewis decided not to retract the UMW's strike order. To be sure, he had no choice in the matter. Coal miners had waited too long for wage increases to defer them pending arbitration, a process the results of which were not guaranteed. Moreover, in the year 1919—with millions of workers on strike, and rebellion in the air—one could scarcely expect militant coal miners to behave as the president and the mine operators desired. Not surprisingly, the UMW's executive board, meeting on October 29, rejected Woodrow Wilson's plea and resolved to call the miners out on November 1.

That same day, October 29, a letter from Joe Tumulty, President Wilson's secretary, to William B. Wilson suggested Lewis's and the coal miners' dilemma. Learning of the UMW executive board's decision and still unalterably opposed to a strike, Tumulty stated why he thought the union and the miners must defer to federal wishes. "I am sure," he wrote, "that many of the miners would rather accept the peaceful process of settlement . . . than go to war against the Government of the United States."[26] Suddenly an economic struggle between workers and employers had been transformed into a political conflict between labor and the state; a private battle in which compromise was ordinarily the rule had become a public crisis in which the rule of law had to prevail. This change in the terms of battle boded ill for Lewis and the coal miners.

Lewis soon received the bad news. On October 31, Attorney General A. Mitchell Palmer applied in federal district court in Indianapolis for an injunction against the strike. Without hesitation, Judge A. B. Anderson issued an ex parte temporary restraining order against the UMW and set November 8 for a full hearing. Anderson's injunction indicated the lengths to which federal authorities were willing to go in order to avert a coal strike. Almost a full year after World War I had ended, the Attorney General applied for injunctive relief on the basis of a wartime statute, the Lever Act, which prohibited conspiracies by two or more individuals to restrict the distribution or production of food or fuel. It was not originally intended to restrain trade union efforts to improve working conditions. That same day, October 31, the federal government put its troops on alert in the West Virginia coalfields and dispatched Bureau of Investigation secret agents to Indianapolis.[27]

Actually, federal officials expected not to use the full panoply of coercive weapons at their command. An injunction had been secured, federal troops placed on alert, and secret agents dispatched primarily to frighten union leaders into accepting federal arbitration. Even before resorting to these weapons, cabinet members urged Samuel Gompers to intercede with Lewis, which the A. F. of L. leader did. Writing to Lewis on October 29, Gompers pleaded: "I urge that the situation be courageously faced and an endeavor made by all means to avert the strike if possible, or at least postpone it pending the opportunity for negotiating an agreement." The same day Palmer sought his injunction, he also assured Gompers that if the UMW postponed the strike, President Wilson would appoint a five-man commission to adjust the dispute and render an award retroactive to November 1, 1919. At the end of the strike's first week, Palmer still promised to delay legal action—that is, the full hearing before Judge Anderson—if Lewis called off the strike.[28]

The pressure federal officials placed on Lewis was revealed in a letter Gompers wrote to the UMW leader on December 30, 1920. Gompers and Lewis had been quarreling about the former's role in the 1919 strike, with Lewis accusing the A. F. of L. president of having served as a lackey for A. Mitchell Palmer. An angry Gompers responded that during a crucial phone conversation with Lewis on November 7, 1919, he had said:

Now, I may say this, John: No matter how you may be beset by detectives and the wires and telephones tapped, we asked the Attorney General and received his assur-

ance that whatever you may say to me over the phone will not at any time be used
against you or others in any attempted proceedings or in any other way, so that you can
talk freely upon the subject.[29]

Lewis had plotted his strike strategy weeks before the walkout. In October, K.
C. Adams had assured subscribers to his news service that "government persua-
sion or interference will not deter Lewis. He is possessed of a spinal column of
iron. He will never weaken until the rank and file cry out 'Enough'." Such
sentiments endeared Lewis to union militants and undercut the appeal of union
rivals. But he also offered mine operators and federal officials good reasons to deal
with him instead of other union leaders. "Lewis is not a socialist, bolshevist, labor
party man or government ownership advocate," assured K. C. Adams. "He has
never been a blind follower of any alleged reform or reformer. He does not belong
to the 'whoop 'em up' variety of labor leader. . . . There never was at the head of
any labor organization a man so thoroughly soaked in practicality." A month later
Adams repeated the same line in a private interview with a Justice Department
undercover agent.[30]

Militancy for the miners, pragmatism and conservatism for employers and
government officials—that was the Lewis formula in 1919. In the future also he
would portray himself as a conservative counterweight to more radical labor
leaders and rebellious rank and filers. In return for thwarting radical influences,
Lewis, however, expected to receive personal advantages and substantial material
gains for the men he represented.

Thus a peculiar ritual was acted out during the 1919 coal strike. In an economic
struggle transformed into a political conflict, mine operators sat in the audience as
union leaders and public officials played their assigned roles. The highest federal
officials threatened repression in order to terminate a strike that they declared a
national emergency; John L. Lewis acted militantly and obdurately in order to
wrest economic concessions otherwise unobtainable.

The basic disparity in power between coal miners and government quickly
emerged. The miners held one weapon: the power to strike and thus eventually to
paralyze a society dependent upon coal for heat, energy, and transportation. But
even that weapon's effectiveness was diluted because not all miners were union
members, nor did all mines operate under union contract. The government's
weapons were many and less diluted. Courts stood ready to serve injunctions;
troops prepared to assist operators to reopen their mines with strikebreakers; spies
infiltrated all levels of the union, tapped phones, and intercepted cables; immigration authorities threatened to deport alien UMW members and strikers; and
newspapers and magazines, supplied with artfully leaked information concerning
the strike, fueled a blatant antiunion propaganda campaign.[31]

On November 8, Lewis experienced the first heavy blow in the government's
effort to end the strike. Judge Anderson issued a temporary mandatory injunction
that gave officers of the UMW until 6:00 P.M. on November 11 to withdraw and

cancel their original strike order. Anderson's injunction barred all aspects of strike action, and it named eighty-four UMW international and district officers. It was the most sweeping injunction issued against a major union since the Pullman Boycott of 1894, when federal court orders had effectively thwarted the strike of Eugene V. Debs's American Railway Union and resulted in Debs's imprisonment for civil contempt, a sentence sanctioned in 1895 by the United States Supreme Court.

Other aspects of the 1919 crisis resembled 1894. During the Pullman Boycott the A. F. of L. executive council convened at Debs's request and considered a sympathetic general strike, which Gompers opposed. In November 1919 the A. F. of L. executive council assembled to weigh American labor's response to a blatantly antilabor legal injunction. This time, however, the strike leader, John L. Lewis, did not request the meeting; and now, the executive council and Gompers pledged to support the miners, whose leaders they asked to disregard Judge Anderson's "unconstitutional" injunction. Lewis, in fact, did not even learn about the A. F. of L.'s action until a day later, and when asked by reporters to comment, he said cryptically, "Very interesting."[32] Gompers, evidence suggests, recommended that Lewis risk imprisonment in order to bring to a culmination the issue of government by injunction. Relating this story years later, Lewis smiled as he said to Adolph Germer, "I told Gompers, 'Why don't you go to jail.' "[33] Lewis indeed called Gompers's bluff, for the A. F. of L. sanctioned no general strike.

Faced with the prospect of swift legal action and the imprisonment of all the UMW's officials unless the strike was canceled, Lewis convened an emergency meeting of his union's executive board in Indianapolis on November 10. For hours, with scarcely an interruption, the board members discussed how to respond to Anderson's injunction. Press reports hinted that Farrington and Howat led a more militant faction that preferred to defy the injunction and challenge the government, but that conservative influences seemed likely to dominate. The reporters proved prescient, for at 4:10 A.M. on November 11, the executive board, at Lewis's behest, voted to comply with the injunction under protest.[34]

Although Lewis canceled the strike, miners, with few exceptions, stayed home. Which is probably what Lewis expected, and which, as he desired, compelled the government to make the next move in the crisis. Himself a politician, Lewis knew what to expect from federal officeholders. Elected public officials, like union officials, sought votes and rarely alienated potential constituents. Considering how important organized labor had been to the Democratic party in 1912 and 1916, Lewis rightly suspected that Wilsonians would hesitate before breaking a strike. To a degree, he was correct.

Labor Secretary Wilson made a final effort to effect a compromise solution. His department's Bureau of Labor Statistics prepared a careful study of the relation between prices and wages in three key coal mining towns that concluded that between December 1914 and June 1919, prices had risen about 80% and miners' wages only about 48%, with prices rising perhaps another 5% between June and

December 1919. Thus the commissioner of labor statistics recommended that miners' wages be increased 31.61%, which meant 27.12 cents a ton for contract miners and $1.58 daily for day workers (31.61% for yardage and deadwork).[35] Armed with this information, Secretary Wilson, at a conference between UMW officials and mine operators on November 14, made the following proposals. He agreed with the operators that the UMW's demand for a 60% wage increase and a six-hour day was "impossible," but he declared the operators' contention that because the peace treaty had not been ratified, the 1917 contract remained in effect, equally illogical. "I want to say to you," Wilson told the operators, "that the people of the United States are not Shylocks. They are not insisting upon the collection of the technical provisions of the bond when the condition under which the bond was made have been materially changed." With these remarks, the Secretary of Labor laid the foundation for an agreement based on the Bureau of Labor Statistics' proposal for a 31% wage increase.[36]

But just as Lewis recognized the realities of national politics, so, too, did the mine operators. If Democratic officials weighed organized labor's political influence, they also evaluated the sentiments of the vast majority of nonunion voters. To accept William B. Wilson's recommendation of a 31% wage increase implied a substantial rise in the selling price of coal. Because the cost of coal in 1919 bulked large in the typical householder's budget, especially during the winter months, a government-authorized rise in retail prices might cost the Democrats votes. Several federal officials certainly believed so. Federal fuel administrator Harry A. Garfield, whose agency was reestablished to deal with the crisis, using his own set of price-wage figures, calculated that miners' wages had fallen only 14% behind prices and that operators could make up the difference without raising prices.[37] Garfield's opinion aided the operators, for it undercut Secretary Wilson's contentions as well as the 20% increase the operators had already offered the miners. Better yet for the operators, President Wilson supported his fuel administrator, the practical effect of which was to give Garfield, in the words of Labor Secretary Wilson's advisers, "veto power over any results arrived at in the negotiations between the Secretary of Labor and the operators and miners."[38]

This, indeed, being the case, after two weeks of negotiations in Washington in which the UMW agreed to bargain on the basis of a 31% wage increase and the operators refused to offer more than 14%, the union representatives and the operators ended their conferences on November 28 no nearer agreement than at the start.[39] Most miners still remained at home; coal production had not yet reached 50% of prestrike levels; UMW officials faced the prospect of being cited for contempt; and federal officials played consumer politics. Attorney General Palmer suggested that the public support Dr. Garfield, reject the UMW leaders' unlawful strike, and "refuse to be stampeded by threats of lack of fuel into concessions which will insure unreasonably high prices in all commodities for at least three years to come."[40]

With negotiations having collapsed again, federal officials hastened to act decisively. The government offered the operators up to 100,000 federal troops to protect those miners willing to resume coal production and declared martial law in Wyoming. Justice Department agents and Immigration Service officials intensified their repressive tactics, and on December 3, Judge Anderson cited eighty-four UMW officers for contempt of court, placing all international, district, and local officers in Indiana under arrest until $5,000 bonds were provided for local officials and $10,000 for the others. As Lewis later reported to his union members, by the first week in December 1919, the federal government had determined to end the strike.[41]

But once again Democrats preferred compromise to repression. On December 6, an ailing President Wilson, in a move designed by cabinet members, invited Lewis and William Green to Washington to confer with Palmer and Tumulty. Wilson's advisers warned Lewis that the government would yield only to superior forces. Yet they also stressed that the president had authorized them to pledge that if the miners returned to work on the basis of an immediate 14% wage increase pending hearings by a presidentially appointed bituminous commission, Wilson would guarantee just and fair consideration of the miners' demands for wage increases, shorter hours, and improved working conditions.[42]

With the new federal proposal in hand, Lewis and Green returned to Indianapolis for a special meeting of the district presidents, the UMW executive board, and the union Scale Committee. To help Lewis make the case for President Wilson's proposal, Labor Secretary Wilson wired the UMW leader on December 8, urging him to accept the proposed terms because the strike "threatens the very foundation of our social life." Secretary Wilson asked Lewis to read the telegram to the UMW board members, and he also released it to the press.[43] For three days the union officials debated the government's proposal, and in the end, they decided unanimously that "while protesting in our hearts against what we believed to be the unjust attitude of the government, we decided to submit to the inevitable." On December 11, Lewis formally asked the strikers to return to work with the knowledge that they had won an immediate 14% increase in wages and that the president's commission would undoubtedly, within sixty days, hand down a retroactive award substantially increasing wages, lowering hours, and improving conditions. To insure that the leaders' decision satisfied the membership, Lewis scheduled a reconvened international convention for January 1920 to vote on the proposed settlement.[44]

Years later Lewis would be criticized for selling the miners out in 1919 and particularly for his comment on December 7, when he recommended the strike's termination: "I will not fight my government, the greatest government on earth."[45] Radicals and Communists especially asserted that Lewis's weakness in 1919, when the UMW was powerful and miners exceedingly militant, presaged the union's rapid decline in the 1920s. Had he defied the injunction, rejected the president's proposals, gone to jail, become a martyr to labor's cause, goes the radicals' version of UMW history, the history of American labor during the 1920s might have been far different. Bayonets could not dig coal, nor would soldiers risk their lives beneath the ground doing work with which they were unfamiliar and for which they were unskilled. Had the miners remained on strike, the government would have forced the operators to concede to union demands, and the UMW and organized labor in America would have entered the 1920s a rising instead of declining power in society. Perhaps, perhaps!

Lewis, it might be argued, had a far better case than his critics. First, he could cite the actual cost of Eugene Debs's labor martyrdom in 1894: a lost strike and a dying union. When the American Railway Union's officials went to prison in 1894, their cause collapsed. As Lewis told his union's reconvened convention in January 1920: "What would it have availed to have a convention with every officer incarcerated and any other men who assumed to take our places as officers finding themselves confronted with the same obstacles?"[46] Second, all of the UMW radicals shared Lewis's perception of reality in December 1919; John Brophy, Frank Farrington, Alex Howat, and Robert Harlin all signed the call for the strike's termination, and not one voted against the December 10 decision.

Other factors buttressed Lewis's position. Never did the strikers curtail all coal production, and anywhere from one-quarter to one-third of the nation's coal was produced in nonunion mines. Before the strike was officially ended, coal production approached 50% of normal levels and, depending on one's predilections, could be compared to a glass half full or half empty. Miners may indeed have been militant in 1919; but they were also deeply patriotic, and once the strike became a conflict between union and government and its political, as distinct from economic, ramifications intensified, union leaders realized that many miners might return to work. For most miners distinguished between the state and capital, public officials and private employers, and they expected equity from the federal government. And the federal government offered the miners carrots—sweet ones at that—as well as sticks. Yet if the carrots lacked sweetness, the sticks were more than weighty. No one enjoys dwelling within sight of armed troops nor living under constant surveillance with mail intercepted and phones tapped nor fearing summary deportation nor enduring constant legal process. That would have been the fate of coal miners and their leaders had the strike continued. Even after the strike ended the UMW remained judicially interdicted. Alex Howat was imprisoned for contempt of Anderson's injunction because he refused to call off strikes in Kansas unrelated to the 1919 general strike. Even Lewis's intercession with Attorney General Palmer brought no relief to Howat, who remained in prison.[47] In fact, the case against the UMW in Judge Anderson's court dragged on until December 1920, and despite the expenditure of vast sums of money and the retention of Charles Evans Hughes as the union's attorney, Anderson refused to reconsider his original decision applying the wartime Lever Act to a peacetime labor dispute.[48]

Lewis did what he had to do in December 1919, what circumstances and the realities of power demanded. Had he been more radical and less conservative, more idealistic and less opportunistic, he probably would have acted similarly. No UMW official was more sincerely radical and intrinsically idealistic in 1919 than John Brophy of central Pennsylvania, in the 1920s one of Lewis's most acerbic and bitter union critics; but he never criticized Lewis's tactics, strategy, and decisions during the 1919 crisis. Ultimately the 1920 reconvened convention and the presidential commission's arbitration award justified Lewis's decision to terminate the strike.

Lewis, however, could not rest once the immediate crisis passed. Throughout the last weeks of December 1919, he bargained with Attorney General Palmer concerning the UMW's legal plight and Howat's imprisonment. Simultaneously he prepared for the reconvened union convention, scheduled to open in Columbus, Ohio, on January 5, 1920, and to present the UMW's wage claims to President Wilson's Bituminous Coal Commission. All this occurred, moreover, while Lewis's rivals—Howat, Farrington, and Harlin—struggled for power within the UMW.

As over 1,900 UMW delegates convened in Columbus during the first week of January 1920, the battle lines within the UMW hardened. For three days the delegates vigorously debated Lewis's decision to terminate the 1919 strike under the proposed arbitration agreement. Acting President Lewis, pleading for coopera- tion with the government, regularly took umbrage at delegates who fired what he characterized as "insulting questions" at the chair. Harlin and Farrington led the opposition, which impugned Lewis's courage, implied that the UMW leader had practiced "class collaboration," and called upon the delegates to reject President Wilson's "compulsory" arbitration commission. The opposition busily built its platform for the December 1920 UMW election in which Harlin, Howat, Farring- ton, and John Walker would unite to challenge Lewis.

By January 1920, however, Lewis had created a smooth-running union machine. His loyal lieutenant, Phil Murray, delivered the votes of western Pennsylvania's miners; Van Bittner led a West Virginia delegation loyal to Lewis; Tom Kennedy, two years previously John Walker's ally and running mate, had joined the Lewis team and brought with him the support of northeastern Pennsyl- vania's anthracite miners; and Secretary-Treasurer William Green provided legiti- macy and strength in Ohio's vital District 6.

What his political machine could not provide was partially compensated for by Lewis's brilliant rhetoric. In a major speech defending the strike's termination and the acceptance of President Wilson's settlement terms, Lewis overwhelmed the delegates with emotionalism, sarcasm, anecdotalism, and patriotism. To those delegates who impugned his courage, Lewis had ready ripostes. Rebuking an Irish-American militant, Lewis observed: "I happen to know that while Mike is a stern and unyielding exponent of Irish freedom that he does his fighting for Ireland in America. Even though the Irish people may be compelled by force of circumstances and the rule of the British Empire to continue their fight for an additional 700 years, you will still find Mike in America.'' To a second delegate who suggested that UMW officials were bourgeois, Lewis sneered: ''I have no doubt that Delegate Lynal is a braver man than I am, because he is brave enough to go without a collar and I am not.'' And to those delegates who demanded more audacity from their leaders, Lewis rejoined: ''It would be a great deal like the engineer of the express who said to the bull that stood in the track, 'I admire your courage, old man, but I doubt your judgment'.''

Disposing of his critics with sarcasm and anecdote, he appealed to the delegates to understand the plight of a union leader. ''We have felt the weight of our burden,'' sighed Lewis. ''We have paced the floor at night into the wee small hours of the morning, when the men and women of our organizations were peacefully sleeping in their beds wondering what we could do.'' And what did we leaders receive for our pains? The most terrible attacks, hate letter after hate letter, threats upon our lives. ''We were insulted in conference, we were insulted in the streets, we were insulted on trains and in hotels. Ye gods! Such concentrated fury was never visited upon any helpless set of men in such an unjustifiable way!'' Referring to a newspaper cartoon, Lewis said: ''Not satisfied with putting my head on the serpent, they placed my name at the top so the people might not be mistaken in thinking John L. Lewis was a reptile and the heel of the public should be placed on his head.''

Lewis also appealed to the delegates' common sense and patriotism. He reminded them that, as a result of his leadership in the 1919 conflict, the ''lamentations of no widow can be heard . . . and the wails of no fatherless child can assail our ears.'' And, finally, wrapping the American flag around his immense chest, he informed the delegates, ''We are Americans. I shall never lead any organization but an American organization. . . . I think we have the greatest nation of any on earth; I think we have the greatest people of any in the world. I am proud of the traditions of our country.''[49]

Swayed by Lewis's rhetoric and held in line by Murray, Bittner, and Kennedy, the convention delegates overwhelmingly approved their leader's handling of the 1919 strike. By a vote of 1,639 to 231 the UMW voted to accept President Wilson's settlement terms and to abide by the award of the Bituminous Coal Commission.[50] Lewis had survived the first major crisis of his union career and could look forward with optimism to the December 1920 UMW election.

For an American labor leader in 1920, however, things were never so simple as they seemed at first glance. With the assistance of Labor Secretary Wilson, Lewis won a substantial wage package from the coal commission in February 1920; tonnage men, the bulk of the miners and union members, received an increase of 27%, and day men gained a 20% raise.[51] But the award caused as many problems as it solved and nearly precipitated a new crisis in the union. The daymen, who already earned less than the tonnage miners, rebelled at a settlement that left them even further behind. With good reason, then, many of the daymen, especially in the always-rebellious Illinois District 12, engaged in spontaneous walkouts in violation of the new contract in order to win more substantial wage benefits.

Not just miners rebelled at the terms of the commission's award. In Alabama and parts of West Virginia, mine owners refused to accept the commission's terms, defied the federal government, and broke off relations with the UMW. In those two states the union became involved in authorized strikes that hemorrhaged the UMW's treasury. And in Howat's Kansas District 14, Lewis faced scattered local strikes in violation not only of the federal award but also of state antistrike law. The triumphs Lewis had won at Columbus and afterwards from the Bituminous Coal Commission now seemed fragile indeed, and that fragility endangered his prospects for election as UMW president.

Throughout the summer of 1920, as Lewis attempted to steer the UMW through the poststrike crises, his union rivals organized for the approaching election. In July and August Lewis engaged in newspaper recriminations with Howat and Farrington marked by insults, rumors of corruption, and slander.[52] Howat and Farrington continuously agitated among miners dissatisfied with the February 1920 wage award and endorsed the spontaneous walkouts in violation of contract in Illinois and Kansas.

Harassed on one side by President Wilson, who demanded that miners respect the federal award, and attacked from the other side by rivals and miners, who demanded more, Lewis skillfully undercut the appeal of the Howats and Farringtons. He quieted the insurgent miners in Illinois, who returned to work on the basis of promised new wage negotiations. These occurred in Cleveland that August, and in them Lewis won a $1.50 daily wage increase for the Illinois district that later covered the entire Central Competitive Field and also the outlying districts. As a result of the increase, UMW dayworkers had won a basic wage of $7.50, by far the highest in the history of American coal miners and a rate for which Lewis took full credit.[53]

Lewis's triumphs at the bargaining table brought no surcease from internal UMW politics. His rivals, who asserted that they wanted to "get honest, competent men put in charge of our organization," found no dirty trick or canard untried in their campaign against Lewis.[54] They resurrected and exaggerated the 1917 Panama scandal, even charging that the Lewis family had enriched themselves at the expense of widows and orphans. John Walker, generally the kindest and most generous of men, referred to Lewis as without "a drop of red blood in his veins. He is a sneak, a treacherous hound in my judgment, cowardly, every atom of him." And Walker once again implied that the UMW was controlled by Al Hamilton of Pittsburgh, whose crowd would go to any extremes, including murder, to prevent their candidates from being defeated in the union election.[55]

Lewis's union enemies selected their candidates for office wisely. For president they offered Robert Harlin of Washington State, a man with few known enemies and one widely associated with the popular demand for nationalization of the mines; for vice-president, they ran Alex Howat, well known for his enemies within the union but more admired among the rank and file for his courage and militancy. Frank Farrington chose not to run because he realized that his personal integrity was suspect among large sectors of the union membership. John Walker, whose rectitude could scarcely be challenged, campaigned for Harlin and Howat from the sidelines because of his previous electoral defeats and his separation from the UMW since 1917. The machinations of these men led Lewis in October 1920 to write to an old friend as follows: "I am kept so busy with my enemies that I scarcely have any time to give my friends. We have, of course, a tremendous fight in our organization between the orderly, constructive element and the disorderly destructive element. I am undaunted in the fight, however, and expect the ship of state to maintain its stability and remain afloat."[56]

Lewis's optimism flowed from his control of the levers of union powers. For every dirty trick his rivals played, Lewis could counter with an ingenious, if usually strained, interpretation of UMW law. In the miners' union, unlike the federal government or American state governments, the constitution meant what the president said it did, and the only court of appeal was the international executive board, more often than not simply the president's own hand-picked tribunal (some would say "kangaroo court").[57] Lewis first exercised his power of constitutional interpretation to eliminate rivals for office. For example, in the spring of 1920 Lewis ruled John Walker ineligible to stand for election as a UMW delegate to the A. F. of L. convention because Walker was an officer of the Illinois State Federation of Labor and hence not a UMW member. An acrimonious exchange of correspondence between the two labor leaders, in which both cited the UMW constitution and union precedent, revealed that Walker had the better constitutional case; but Lewis had the power, and he exercised it to remove Walker's name from the slate.[58]

Successful in eliminating one opponent, Lewis became more audacious. In the fall of 1920 he attempted to rule Robert Harlin's candidacy for the presidency illegitimate. Citing a clause in the UMW constitution that required a candidate for office to have had five years practical experience as a miner, Lewis declared Harlin ineligible because the latter had entered the United States in 1907, been elected to union office in 1910, and thus had at most three years practical work as a miner. This time, however, Lewis's tactic failed, and its failure illuminated his audacity. Harlin remained a candidate for president partly because, as the author of the constitutional clause in question, his interpretation of its meaning was hard to challenge and partly because he could prove that he had worked as a miner in England for almost two decades before emigrating.[59]

What he could not accomplish with constitutional interpretations, Lewis achieved with publicity and money. The union journal, edited by Ellis Searles, Lewis's handpicked editor, denied space to the rival slate for office, banned all "political" news from its columns, and advertised the union leadership's contributions to the welfare of coal miners.⁶⁰ Finally, the union's organizers, appointed and paid by Lewis, served their master loyally.

The role played by organizers during the election campaign became Harlin's ultimate charge against the Lewis administration. Simultaneously with the bitter UMW election, the union waged a labor conflict with recalcitrant Alabama mine owners who refused to accept the federal settlement. The struggle in Alabama caused the wholesale eviction of striking miners and widespread economic misery. The Alabama strike and lesser conflicts in West Virginia also played havoc with the UMW's finances, and Secretary-Treasurer Green displayed the cautious bureaucrat's reluctance to part with precious funds. Lewis, however, backed Van Bittner, whom he had dispatched to Alabama to run the strike with money and organizers. Harlin nevertheless sought to use the suffering endured by union miners in Alabama and West Virginia to boost his candidacy for the presidency. Only three days before the election, Harlin publicly released a telegram from Farrington in which the latter charged that Lewis was lavishly financing campaign workers

> while striking miners of West Virginia and Alabama are crying for bread which can not be furnished them. . . . It is a shame that the funds of our union should be expended with such reckless random [sic] for campaign purposes while they who are fighting to establish the standard of the United Mine Workers in nonunion fields are unable to secure even the meager support of our International union.⁶¹

Harlin's politics in this instance were transparent. He expected Farrington's charges to add votes in districts where he already had strength and to win support among southern Appalachian miners, among whom he had no following.

But Lewis had built his union machine too well for his enemies to wreck. Not only did he have firm allies inside the UMW; influential public officials and the most prominent mine owners preferred Lewis to his rivals. Phil Murray secured western Pennsylvania; Tom Kennedy did likewise for anthracite; Ohio District 6 fell in line; the Alabama and West Virginia miners showed their appreciation for Lewis's financial and moral support; and William Mitch, of Indiana, a recent addition to the team, provided Lewis with a slender electoral ·majority in the Hoosier state.⁶² The final results gave Lewis a better than 60,000-vote margin over Harlin, though Murray beat Howat by only 11,000 votes. Except for Illinois, long the core of anti-Lewis sentiment, the administration slate carried the vital Central Competitive Field and the southern Appalachian area, the most productive coal mining regions. The opposition's electoral strength centered in the outlying western United States and Canadian districts, areas of lesser importance in the industry and in union affairs.⁶³

In January 1921, Lewis had finally attained the UMW presidency in his own right. An imposing public figure, he possessed a voice that more than matched his physical stature. Having mastered the imperatives of public speaking in the premicrophone age, Lewis's voice alternately bellowed and modulated, crooned and cursed. He charmed and cajoled his audiences, entertained and taught them, agitated and pacified them. So fine was his voice modulation, so smoothly could Lewis change moods, that listeners became hypnotized by him and cheered platitudes, inappropriate classical allusions, and outright solecisms. For Lewis, speech was an instrument to sway audiences, not enlighten them. And he used that instrument impressively.

The union Lewis commanded was also imposing. No other labor organization in the United States was as large or as publicized. The only industrial union that functioned in a major industry, the UMW was a power in the land. In 1921 coal reigned supreme as a source of energy, and miners possessed the potential power to paralyze society through a strike. As a consequence, Lewis stood in the front rank of labor leaders; only Gompers had greater public recognition and, perhaps, esteem. But the old man, who led a federation of autonomous affiliates, lacked the economic power wielded by the younger man, who commanded an army of over 400,000 militant coal miners. The 1920s seemed full of promise for John L. Lewis.

II.
Trade Union President, 1920-1932

CHAPTER 4
A President and His Union,
March 1921-March 1923

John L. Lewis's first two years as president of the United Mine Workers of America glowed with success. Republican leaders wooed him, businessmen flattered him, and editorialists praised him. In 1921 Lewis even challenged Gompers for the presidency of the A. F. of L. Despite a postwar economic depression (1920-1921) that sapped union strength and deflated wages, Lewis preserved the UMW as the nation's largest trade union and, during a five-month national coal strike in 1922, preserved the high wages miners had won during and just after World War I.

Beneath the glittering surfaces of Lewis's success, however, lay a foundation of dross. Fundamental flaws in the economy of coal, the structure of the UMW, and the character of John L. Lewis soon appeared. The 1921 depression, from which the nation rapidly recovered, presaged the future for coal miners and their union. And the UMW's apparent victory in the 1922 coal strike actually undermined the stability of the mine workers' union. Lewis's own inexplicable oscillations between moderation and radicalism, "business unionism" and "reform unionism," class struggle and class collaboration exposed a pattern of sheer opportunism that threatened the UMW. Whether these flaws were inherent in Lewis's character or necessitated by the times, intrinsic to the labor leader or precipitated by the American 1920s, would be revealed through the history of the UMW during the prosperity decade.

By the end of the 1920s Lewis had become famous as the nation's most eminent labor Republican. Read most biographies of Lewis, glance at his associates' reminiscences, speak to former trade unionists or public officials who knew him, and a consensus emerges that identifies John L. Lewis as a lifelong Republican. Every commentator cites Lewis's political behavior from roughly 1920 to 1933 to prove his Republicanism. Yet closer analysis suggests that Lewis's relationship with the GOP flowed from his perception of political reality in the 1920s, not from personal conviction, and that even during the Republican heyday Lewis's ties to party leaders and presidents were more strained than cordial.

Lewis carried to the 1920s, as did Herbert Hoover, a tradition of Wilsonianism. For almost eight years, from Woodrow Wilson's initial bid for the presidency in 1912 until the coal strike of 1919, Lewis had cooperated politically with Democratic leaders. Wilsonianism, however, collapsed in the wake of postwar disillusionment, and Lewis had better reasons than most citizens to turn against Wilson and the Democrats. The government's role in the 1919 coal strike, especially the policies implemented by the Justice and War departments, rankled the UMW leader and remained a persistent sore point. But Lewis did not campaign actively for Warren G. Harding in 1920; nor did he play a substantial role in national Republican politics. He wired Harding only once to congratulate the Republican candidate for a speech delivered in Terre Haute, Indiana—one that Lewis promised would be circulated widely in the Illinois coalfields.[1]

Harding's brief tenure in office provided Lewis no obvious role or influence. The labor leader received only one recorded recommendation for appointment as Secretary of Labor, and Lewis himself recommended no candidates for that post or any other cabinet position. Republicans, nevertheless, recognized Lewis's stature as head of the nation's largest trade union and, together with Gompers, usually invited him to serve on honorific committees that required broad-based public membership. In March 1921 Harding asked Lewis to serve on a special committee to consider medical care and vocational training for disabled veterans, and in October 1921 he asked him to serve on the advisory commission to the Washington Conference on Limitation of Armaments.[2]

One federal committee on which Lewis served revealed his differences with the Republican leadership and suggests the continuity of his beliefs on government involvement in economic affairs from the 1920s through the New Deal of the 1930s. By the autumn of 1921 economic decline and high unemployment had become critical political issues. Urged to act by Secretary of Commerce Herbert Hoover, President Harding, in September, invited representatives of industry, labor, and the public to Washington the following month for a special conference on unemployment. Hoover, the mastermind of the conference, planned to prove the Republican administration's determination to reduce unemployment. Absolutely opposed to direct federal subsidization of the unemployed, Hoover preferred to rely on a combination of voluntary action by industrialists to increase private investment (and hence employment) and state and municipal spending for public works. Applauded by industrialists, public representatives, and editorialists, Hoover's program to combat unemployment received an unenthusiastic response from labor's delegates, including John L. Lewis.[3]

Publicly, Lewis advocated direct government credits to the unemployed, the creation of a compulsory employer-financed unemployment insurance system, and nationalization or stringent government control of coal mining. Responding to employer demands for wage deflation as the solution to unemployment, Lewis observed that he would gladly accept "wage deflation" if business tolerated "profit deflation." "It is the duty of employers," he intoned, "to let the public know the real truth, that excessive profits and not labor costs are responsible for the maintenance of unwarranted prices." During private sessions Lewis apparently broached more far-reaching proposals for direct federal intervention in the economy—suggestions so radical that years later Herbert Hoover and his industrialist friend complimented each other for secrecy that enhanced Lewis's reputation as a responsible labor leader.[4]

If President Harding's conference on unemployment disclosed some of the issues that divided Lewis and Republican leaders, the bituminous and anthracite strikes that erupted in 1922, 1923, 1925, and 1927-1928 inflicted deeper sores on the political relationship. The marginal role that Lewis played in national politics in 1921 and 1922 continued after Harding's death in 1923.

Labor politics offered Lewis a more attractive arena in which to exercise his talent and ambition. The presidency of the UMW afforded him potential control of the largest single bloc of votes cast at A. F. of L. conventions and great influence with Gompers. But a precedent set in the prewar years awarded the UMW's seat on the A. F. of L. executive council to the union's secretary-treasurer, not its president.[5] Hence William Green, not John L. Lewis, sat on American labor's most prestigious executive committee. Lewis might have demanded Green's seat, but such a request would have precipitated an open break with Green, a popular figure in the UMW, when Lewis's grip on the presidency was shaky. Political realities foreclosed Lewis from demanding a seat on the executive council. As much an egotist as a realist, Lewis instead chose to gamble recklessly, to contest Gompers for the presidency of the A. F. of L.

The militancy that had stirred American workers since 1916 had not abated in 1921. Many of the larger national trade unions, the coal miners among them, still demanded the creation of an independent labor party and the nationalization of such vital industries as railroads and mining. Since organized labor's setbacks in 1919, Gompers, however, had drifted toward a conservative position—one more consonant with his prewar membership in the National Civic Federation, his integration into the Wilson Democratic administration, and his wartime declaration of loyalty to the American system. Many of the younger, radical members of the A. F. of L. chafed under Gompers's leadership and desired more militant officers.

In May and June 1921 John L. Lewis presented himself as a radical alternative to Samuel Gompers. Playing a cautious political game, Lewis privately sought the A. F. of L. presidency and publicly issued disclaimers of such an intention. Writing to UMW Indiana District 11 official William Mitch on May 25, 1921, Lewis declared:

With respect to the Presidency of the American Federation of Labor, I am not in any way a candidate for the place and have not in any manner authorized my name to be used. While you may know, I have been for some period of time rather out of sympathy with the policies of President Gompers, yet the matter presents a number of difficult equations which are worthy of consideration.[6]

Lewis's letter to Mitch had been occasioned by newspaper publicity and rumors that he intended to seek the presidency. Socialists inside the labor movement and social reformers outside were exhilarated by such rumors. In May, Basil Manly, an ex-staff member of the United States Commission on Industrial Relations and a prominent left-wing reformer, urged Lewis to challenge Gompers and provided him with a breakdown of the prospective vote at the A. F. of L. convention that showed Lewis winning 22,951 delegate votes with only 19,507 necessary for election. Yet Lewis procrastinated, writing to Manly on May 28:

I do not care to be in any sense considered as a candidate for the place but, of course, I am not unaware that my failure to deny the newspaper reports has caused considerable uneasiness in certain quarters and has likewise aroused some degree of enthusiasm among my personal friends. Under present circumstances, I think the matter can well be held in abeyance until my arrival in Denver during the convention.[7]

Three days later, in a letter to his friend K. C. Adams marked personal, Lewis unburdened himself more fully. "I am not in any sense a candidate for the position," he assured "Dear friend Kacy," and

I have not in the least degree, solicited the support of any individual nor authorized the use of my name by anyone. Of course, if circumstances should so shape things around that the Presidency of the A. F. of L. were handed on a silver platter one would have to give the subject deserving consideration, but in my humble judgment this is not likely to happen for a number of very substantial reasons. I am not unaware, of course, that my failure to deny that I was a candidate has given growth to the so-called boom but I am deriving quite a lot of quiet satisfaction from the fact that I know many people who are now nightly afflicted with fears and apprehensions. A denial of my candidacy at the present time would, of course, be equal to the application of ice cold bandages to their fevered brows and I am simply withholding any announcement that would reduce their relatively high temperature.[8]

Why Lewis revealed personal motivations to K. C. Adams seems inexplicable. Adams, after all, made his way in the world by leaking inside information to subscribers to his *American Miner* and various other newsletters; he was a purveyor par excellence of rumor and gossip, the more slanderous the better. One must conclude that despite Lewis's warning to Adams that "these rather rambling observations are . . . for your private consumption and not in your capacity as purveyor of information to an awaiting world," he knew what to expect from

Adams, who was the perfect person to raise the fever of Lewis's enemies. The letter to Adams disclosed another unflattering attribute of Lewis's character: his eagerness to inflict pain on rivals. Years later, labor economist and public official Isadore Lubin remembered Lewis remarking during an afternoon of private negotiations: " 'Lubin, you don't know how much I enjoy seeing you try to walk on eggs.' . . . When we left, he [Lewis] said he would compromise and go along with us, but he loved to see people suffer.'' Or as labor reporter Edwin A. Lahey said: "John L. Lewis bleeds lemon juice. He'd cut his mother's throat.''9

Until the A. F. of L. convention opened in Denver, Colorado, on June 21, Lewis remained silent and allowed rumors to circulate. Sometime during that period, however, Lewis decided that he could indeed defeat Gompers, for on June 20, 1921, he publicly declared his candidacy for the A. F. of L. presidency. By then, he had also chosen a political strategy. Counting on the substantial bloc of votes cast by eight UMW delegates, Lewis planned to add the support of those unions committed to nationalization, such as the railway brotherhoods and machinists; and those unions represented by socialists, such as the ladies' garment workers, brewery workers, and his old Indianapolis friends the carpenters, whose leaders detested Gompers. To solidify left-wing support, Lewis endorsed nationalization of the railroads and coal mines and also the establishment of federal old-age pensions and unemployment insurance. Moreover, he coordinated his campaigning at the convention, a process the *New York Times* described in a report of June 21 as "hot electioneering,'' through two UMW left-wingers, John Brophy and Adolph Germer.10 Germer, a longtime Socialist party of America leader with close ties to New York City immigrant socialists, was assigned to keep in line the votes of the International Ladies' Garment Workers Union delegation. When Lewis learned that the ILGWU executive board had instructed its delegation to support Gompers, he directed Germer immediately to press Lewis's candidacy with ILGWU President Benjamin Schlesinger.11

Lewis's candidacy posed the first effective threat since the 1890s to Gompers's command of the A. F. of L. Gompers thus used all his political wiles to thwart his opponent. First, he and his lieutenants hinted to convention delegates that the antilabor Hearst papers were behind Lewis's challenge. Second, Gompers used his patronage power within the labor movement and among Washington party politicians to hold wavering delegates in line. Third, and most important, Gompers split the UMW's own delegation. Three bitter enemies of Lewis—Frank Farrington, Alex Howat, and John Walker—were among the eight UMW delegates at Denver, and Gompers won the support of all three, a fact that undermined support for Lewis among many uncommitted delegates. Prior to the balloting Walker, on June 23, published an interview in the *Denver Post* that assailed Lewis's character and that, in fact, was prepared by one of Gompers's own secretaries. Walker so detested Lewis that he perceived the A. F. of L. election as just another conspiracy hatched by Mr. Hamilton of Pittsburgh, "the crooked 'go-between' between the crooks in . . . the Miners' union and the corruptionists among the coal operators,'' to extend their control to the A. F. of L.[12] Despite entreaties from Brophy and Tom Kennedy asserting that Lewis stood for the UMW's policies of nationalization and welfare legislation, personal animosities prevailed over miners' principles. The three UMW delegates, two of whom claimed to personify the radicalism and militancy of the rank and file, preferred Gompers, the candidate of labor conservatism, to Lewis, the putative radical challenger.[13] Yet the difference between Gompers and Lewis was perhaps more apparent than real, and the *New York Times* may have been correct when, on June 23, it commented editorially that both Lewis and Gompers were "labor conservatives," although the former was "an unknown quantity."[14]

The split in the UMW delegation, the ILGWU's majority vote for Gompers, and the incumbent president's fine-tuned political machine defeated Lewis. He polled only one-third of the total vote cast, losing most of the railway department support he had counted on and picking up most of his votes from the machinists' union, the carpenters, and the dwindling band of socialists. In defeat, Lewis appeared magnanimous, at least publicly, thanking the delegates who had voted for him and applauding the independence and integrity of those who had originally promised their support but then exercised the privilege of changing their minds.[15] Two weeks later, he assured Van Bittner: "I am, in a measure, rather glad I was not elected to succeed President Gompers, as there is, of course, ample work for me to do in our own organization."[16] Gompers returned the magnanimity, as befit a man who still had to deal with the leader of the largest affiliate in the A. F. of L. In September Gompers asked Lewis to accompany him on the train trip from Indianapolis to Washington for President Harding's unemployment conference.[17]

If Lewis proved charitable in defeat, he nevertheless harbored resentment against Walker, Farrington, and Howat. Before the decade ended, he would remove all three from the UMW; but in 1921 Lewis had more immediate objectives in mind. He went to his union convention in late September determined to bind future UMW delegations to A. F. of L. conventions to the unit rule. Mixing personal animosity with principled argument, Lewis slashed away at Farrington et al. In his formal presidential report, Lewis characterized his foes as peevish, selfish, irascible, disgruntled, and farcical. Striking an old refrain, he observed that "it is a manifest absurdity for us to pay $50,000 a year for the privilege of sending eight delegates and then have the influence of the organization curtailed and its voting strength neutralized." Later in open debate with Farrington, Lewis denied that personal bitterness prompted his desire for the unit rule. How, he asked delegates, could they allow their representatives to support a man—Gompers— who opposed nationalization, government old-age pensions, unemployment insurance, and health and accident benefits? Personal privilege was irrelevant, Lewis asserted. We do not send men to A. F. of L. conventions to represent personal privileges or enjoy them; "we are sending those men to represent the United Mine Workers of America and conform themselves to its principles. It would indeed be passing strange if we could not presume to issue instructions to a delegate. . . . *We pay them*" (italics added). Responding to Lewis's logic and influence, the convention delegates by voice vote amended the UMW constitution to bind A. F. of L. delegates to the unit rule.[18]

What had been the result of Lewis's bid for the A. F. of L. presidency, and why had Lewis challenged Gompers in 1921? Answers to those questions do not come easily, but enough information is now available to dismiss conventional misconceptions concerning that event in Lewis's career. Lewis's assertion during a conversation with Alinsky that he never electioneered for a single delegate vote at the A. F. of L. convention is plainly untrue.[19] Suggestions that Lewis made the race as a publicity gambit, motivated principally by the maxim: "He who tooteth not his own horn the same shall not be tooted," are equally unlikely.[20] Not that Lewis was averse to publicity. Rather, he was too opportunistic and egotistic to risk a resounding personal defeat for a few newspaper lines. His defeat, moreover, had negative organizational as well as personal ramifications; it widened rifts within the UMW and stimulated new threats to Lewis's still-insecure tenure as union president. Only the conviction that he had a real chance to win, that Basil Manly's vote projection of early May reflected actual delegate sentiments, explains Lewis's decision to declare his candidacy publicly and to electioneer in Denver.

But why would he trade the presidency of the largest and most powerful trade union in the nation, a position he had just won, for the A. F. of L. presidency? Prestige, it must be noted, was a consideration never absent from Lewis's calculations. He was a striver, a climber, a man driven by ambition and perhaps eager to compensate for his lowly social origins by achieving parity with America's economic and political elite. Interestingly, on his passports during the 1920s Lewis listed his occupation as "executive," not labor leader or trade union official. The presidency of the A. F. of L., a post that involved considerable honorific association with presidents, governors, and even chambers of commerce, conferred more prestige and status on its occupant than the leadership of the UMW. It is also conceivable that in June 1921 Lewis had premonitions of the UMW's bleak future. The presidency of the A. F. of L., in that case, offered him a chance to escape from a future fraught with internecine union struggles and economic tragedy for American coal miners.

From 1910 to 1920, the bituminous coal industry had experienced extraordinary economic growth, reaching a productive peak in 1918. High wartime prices and an insatiable market for coal brought marginal mines into operation and led operators to develop properties in previously underdeveloped regions, especially in the southern Appalachians. The coal strike of 1919—which reduced stockpiles—and the economic needs of postwar Europe prevented a collapse in the market for American bituminous. But after the British authorities disciplined their rebellious coal miners and production recovered on the Continent, foreign demand for

American coal diminished. Overproduction glutted domestic markets and the soft coal industry in the United States slumped, a decline aggravated by the postwar depression of 1920-1921.

In late summer 1921 a special investigator for the Department of Labor feared an impending crisis in soft coal. Production in 1921, he cautioned, was unlikely to exceed 400 million tons, the lowest total in twelve years, "while production capacity is the greatest in the history of the coal industry." Production had already fallen almost 25% from 1920 levels, and because the great coal consuming industries—iron, steel, and the railroads especially—were then operating at only 25 to 50% of their capacity, the reserve stocks of coal above ground had soared during the summer of 1921. Consequently, most bituminous mines operated in August between 30% and 50% of capacity, adding thousands of coal miners to the rapidly rising rolls of the unemployed. The plight of the coal industry, the Labor Department agent concluded, was "a staggering fact sufficient to stagnate the 'Micawber' expectations of those who imagine that the pendulum of prosperity will soon swing the industries of the country back to the normal pace of past progress."[21]

The economics of coal posed a myriad of problems for the UMW. Operators beset on the one hand by high wages and on the other by falling prices for their product sought to stimulate per capita productivity either through intensive labor discipline or the substitution of machines for men. In either case they discharged miners. Even more threatening to the UMW was the operators' desire to escape the union and the growth of productivity in nonunion mines in West Virginia, Kentucky, and Alabama.

Even with prices falling the relatively high cost of coal led such major coal consumers as the railroads, the steel industry, and public utilities to introduce more efficient methods of fuel consumption. Efficiency in fuel consumption caused a long-term decline in the demand for soft coal that was aggravated further by the competition of oil and natural gas for the domestic heating and light industrial markets. In August 1921, John L. Lewis would have to have been blind to miss seeing the economic disease that blighted bituminous: too many mines and too many miners producing too much coal.

Events in Alabama and southern West Virginia delivered the initial shocks to the UMW. Alabama coal operators had refused in November 1919 to accept President Wilson's compromise settlement and subsequently proved equally adamant in declining to implement the award of the president's coal commission. Instead, they slashed wages to prewar levels, endured UMW-sanctioned strikes, and smashed the union. Lewis's unswerving support failed to save from extinction Alabama UMW District 20.[22]

During the war years the UMW, for the first time, had succeeded in organizing the Fairmont and Kanawha coalfields in northern and central West Virginia; but union organizers had had little success in the southwestern counties of Logan, Mingo, and McDowell, which lay just across the Tug River from eastern Kentucky and notorious Harlan County. In the immediate postwar years some of the nation's largest coal companies, including subsidiaries of U.S. Steel, the Consolidation Coal Company, and the Island Creek Company, developed properties in southwestern West Virginia primarily to escape high union wages and restrictive work rules. The mines of Logan, Mingo, and McDowell counties captured markets from the unionized operators of the Central Competitive Field.[23]

Financed by UMW headquarters, the leaders of West Virginia District 17, C. Frank Keeney and Fred Mooney, determined to unionize Mingo and Logan counties. Their resolute effort to organize the nonunion mines met with equal determination by nonunion employers to keep the UMW out and resulted in what a contemporary journalist entitled as a *Civil War in West Virginia*.

Logan and Mingo counties shared traditions of violence that antedated the industrial age and its labor conflicts. Inhabited primarily by mountain folk of old English stock, the two counties, which were isolated from the remainder of the state and the nation by their forbidding mountainous terrain, had a history of clan feuds associated with the fabled Hatfields and McCoys—mountaineer families whose gun battles have become staples of American folklore.

Historically, violence in Mingo and Logan counties had been personal and familial; with the emergence of coal mining as the major local industry, economic, class, and racial tensions superseded personal animosities as the causes of violence. Nonunion operators resorted to physical force to fight the UMW, and local union sympathizers turned to the rifle and the dynamite stick to combat strikebreakers and open-shop mines. The two counties teemed with private gunmen, whom the county sheriffs cloaked with the authority of law. As legally appointed deputies, although paid by the coal companies, the private detectives terrorized local union members, their families, and labor sympathizers. UMW organizers who entered Logan or Mingo County risked physical beatings and summary executions. For their part, union advocates used the weapons every family in the region possessed to attack company gunmen.[24]

As conditions deteriorated in Logan and Mingo counties, the union miners of northern and central West Virginia acted to "liberate" their beleaguered comrades. In late August 1921 approximately 6,000 armed union miners and sympathizers marched southwest from the Kanawha Valley to Logan County, where 2,000 well-armed private detectives and county deputies awaited them. At Blair Mountain the two armies exchanged thousands of rounds of gunfire. Fullscale war seemed imminent. On August 30, 1921, the governor of West Virginia declaring that citizens of his state were engaged in an insurrection that he could not suppress, asked President Harding to intervene. The president immediately issued a proclamation commanding the persons engaged in the alleged insurrection to disperse and retire to their homes on or before September 1. To enforce his proclamation, Harding dispatched Billy Mitchell's 88th light bombing squadron and a force of

2,150 regular army troops to West Virginia, although by September 3 and 4, most of the union men had returned home. The only human casualties in the encounter between the United States Army and the UMW in West Virginia were three officers and one enlisted man, who lost their lives when the army plane carrying them back to their post crashed.[25] Military intervention temporarily curbed violence in Logan and Mingo counties; it also terminated the UMW's effort to organize the region's coal mines.

The Harding administration, which had used force to suppress union "lawbreakers," refused to punish local officials who violated the miners' constitutional rights. The United States attorney for West Virginia, Elliott Northcott, advised Washington that coal company officials and Logan and Mingo county officials, not coal miners or union leaders, were primarily responsible for the violation of state and federal laws. "As United States Attorney," wrote Northcott,

> I am convinced that a condition exists in Logan County that is not compatible with the principles upon which this Government rests and there exists a conspiracy to suppress and intimidate citizens of the United States in the free exercise of privileges secured to them by the constitution and laws of the United States, and that some action should be taken to punish the conspirators and put an end to the conspiracy.

According to Northcott, the Logan coal companies financed County Sheriff Don Chafin's elaborate "private police system" and autocratic political machine; in return, the sheriff protected the mine owners against unionization. In both Mingo and Logan counties, reported Northcott, local officials purged democracy and trade unionism, preferring the profits that flowed to them from nonunion coal and cheap labor.[26]

Legal actions initiated by nonunion coal operators also crippled the UMW. Ever since the union signed its first contract in 1898 with employers in the Central Competitive Field, open-shop operators had charged that the agreement included an unwritten clause in which the UMW promised to organize all the nation's mines. In seeking to validate its pledge, the UMW, nonunion operators alleged, was engaged in a "criminal conspiracy" to restrain trade by denying nonunion miners the right to work. That had been one of the claims made by West Virginia operators in the *Hitchman* v. *Mitchell* case (which the Supreme Court decided against the union in 1917), which paralyzed the UMW's prewar organizing campaign in Appalachia.[27] After the war ended and domestic normality resumed, West Virginia operators returned to the legal offensive. From Judge A. B. Anderson's federal district court in Indiana and in numerous state courts in West Virginia, the operators secured injunctions that prohibited UMW organizers from approaching nonunion mining properties or proselytizing among nonunion miners. By the early 1920s, in most parts of southwestern West Virginia and eastern

Kentucky, judges had ruled it a crime, punishable by civil and criminal contempt, for the UMW to attempt to organize nonunion mines.[28]

Where miners already belonged to the union and mines operated under union contract, employers found other legal weapons to use against the UMW. An Arkansas coal company—the Coronado Company—which had been the victim of a UMW strike and ensuing property damage, brought suit not against individual miners charged with criminal action, but against the UMW, which, the owners charged in court, should be held responsible for violence and property losses during strikes it sanctioned. The Coronado Company asked the courts to hold the union responsible for the company's financial losses and to assess treble damages. The case, which the UMW fought all the way to the Supreme Court, imperiled the union's existence. If the UMW could be held financially liable for strike damages, coal operators could "tax" the union out of existence. In a politic ruling, the Supreme Court denied the Coronado Company its full damage claims, thus saving the UMW a huge financial penalty; but the court majority implied that where sufficient evidence existed a trade union could be held liable for the actions of individual members or strikers even when they acted without explicit union orders. Not only did the Supreme Court in the Coronado case decisions of 1922 and 1925 raise a potential legal threat against trade unions; it also declared that strikes aimed at organizing nonunion mines interfered with the movement of coal in interstate commerce and hence could be enjoined under the terms of the Sherman Antitrust Act, thus further crippling any chance the UMW had to organize nonunion Appalachian mines.[29]

Even when the coal miners' union won favorable decisions in court, it suffered grievous losses. In 1920 the UMW expended over $150,000 in legal expenses; the following year the cost of legal assistance soared to almost $460,000; and in 1922 the union expended nearly $223,000 for attorneys and legal costs. Only once during the entire decade of the 1920s did the UMW's legal costs drop substantially below $100,000 annually.[30]

Legal battles and the costs of the West Virginia organizing campaign left the UMW in parlous financial condition. In June 1921 Secretary-Treasurer William Green informed Lewis that for the period February-May 1921, union expenses exceeded revenues by $108,627 and that the organization had only a bare minimum left in its Indiana bank checking account. Worse yet, most of the UMW's recent expenditures had been financed by a special assessment of nearly $700,000, of which little remained to be collected. Moreover, added Green, the depression in the mining industry had caused union membership to fall to its lowest level in over a year.[31]

Green's report only hinted at the union's economic predicament. From 1920 through 1922, three years during which a nationally sanctioned coal strike occurred only in the last year, the UMW expended more than $2 million annually on strike relief. In 1920 strike payments represented 54.3% of all union expenses; the next year, 52.6%; and in 1922, 54.0%.[32]

His union's financial plight vexed Lewis. He had increased his salary once from $3,000 to $5,000, and in 1921 he proposed that it be raised to $8,000. Lewis had implemented or recommended similar salary increases of almost 200% over a two-year period for other international officials. With the UMW's expenses now exceeding its revenues, Lewis's salary requests seemed excessive, and he knew it. But rather than reduce the salaries of union officials or postpone recommending a second round of increases to the 1921 convention, Lewis cut the union's field staff drastically and on June 28, 1921, suggested (in reality, commanded) that every international officer and field worker donate their July salary to the union.[33]

Financial difficulties seemed minor compared to the other problems Lewis faced as union leader. More immediately threatening was the depression in soft coal and the bituminous operators' insistence on wage reductions. Unionized employers asserted that high wages made it impossible for them to compete successfully for markets with nonunion operators and that they must have the right to negotiate competitive state or district contracts in place of the basic Central Competitive Field agreement. Yet union miners, unable to live adequately on current earnings, resisted wage reductions. Lewis found himself caught between harassed operators and a restive union rank and file; no policy could satisfy both groups simultaneously, yet Lewis, as union president, was compelled to act.

To compound Lewis's predicament, federal authorities shared the coal operators' perception of economic realities. The Labor Department agent who in August 1921 analyzed the economics of soft coal saw only one solution to a depressed market: The union and the operators must voluntarily reduce "inflated" wage rates before April 1, 1922. Unless the UMW accepted wage deflation, he warned, nonunion coal production would rise, union miners would be discharged, and unemployment would worsen.[34] Commerce Secretary Herbert Hoover, who sought to avert a prospective national coal strike in 1922 by negotiations or compulsory arbitration, agreed that high wages for union miners caused irregular employment and that, in his words, "we are . . . in a most vicious circle of trying to support an overplus of mines and miners at a cost . . . to the public." Hoover suggested that wage reductions would solve part of the problem by inducing surplus miners to seek work elsewhere, stabilizing employment for the remaining union miners, and reducing the cost of coal for consumers. Consequently, Hoover believed that an "impartial" arbitration board would favor substantial wage reductions, which was why unionized operators reluctantly acceded to the Commerce Secretary's peace overtures; but Lewis and the UMW adamantly rejected arbitration. Unsuccessful in his union-management diplomacy in October 1921, Hoover warned that "both sides are setting the stage for an irreparable conflict . . . and I am impressed with the fact that we stand in considerable national danger."[35]

Precisely how Lewis personally felt about government diagnoses of the ills that beset soft coal is impossible to discern. As the elected leader of the mine workers, however, he refused to defer to the wishes of Hoover and President Harding for industrial peace in the coal industry. Had he tolerated wage reductions or compulsory arbitration, he would have precipitated open revolt in the UMW. Any action by Lewis that threatened the material status of his rank and file endangered his tenure as union president.

In September-October 1921, when UMW delegates met in regular convention, and in February 1922, when they reconvened in special session to consider contract demands for the upcoming negotiations, militancy prevailed. By overwhelming majorities, convention delegates favored nationalization of the coal mines and the creation of an independent national labor party. In February 1922 the UMW delegates stripped equivocal language and compromise proposals from the Scale Committee's recommended contract demands. Delegates substituted insistence on the six-hour day underground for the committee's proposed eight-hour day and the word *demand* for *recommend* in asking for weekly wages and abolition of the wartime strike penalty clause.[36] Lewis found himself under constant attack by militant delegates who, for example, rejected by a substantial majority their president's proposal for substantial salary increases.[37] Farrington, Harlin, Howat, and Walker sparked the anti-Lewis floor sentiment and almost stole the convention from Lewis's control.* On one key vote during the 1922 reconvened session that cut to the heart of Lewis's power in the union, he won only 51.5% of the delegate votes and gained his slender majority primarily because of the patronage and funds he controlled as president.[38]

On nearly all matters concerning negotiations with employers for a new agreement in 1922, the UMW rank and file held Lewis captive. In other words, if he acceded either to wage reductions or binding arbitration, he would lose his influence with the membership. While a prisoner of his rank and file, when conflict came, Lewis artfully could play a role that he relished: commanding general of a union army engaged in total war during which any criticism of his leadership could be characterized as treason.

With the national coal strike now inevitable, Lewis acted as the personification of labor militancy. On February 1, in a letter sent to the officers of sixteen railway unions, he invited them to meet with UMW officials in order to plan a common front against employers' demands for wage cuts. A worried *New York Times* editor wrote the next day: "President Lewis's proposal that the railway workers unite with the mine workers contains a menace such as never before raised its head in this country."[39] And on February 21-22—at a meeting in Chicago attended by fifteen railway unions, including the four largest, and UMW officials—those in attendance agreed to unite miners, railway workers, and longshoremen (shades of

*See Chapter 6, pp. 116-121.

the British Triple Alliance) "for closer cooperation of our forces which will operate to more effectively protect the union workers in wage struggles." Lewis, who dominated the meeting, served as its chief speaker, and hogged its press releases, outlined no precise program of allied labor action. He even denied that plans had been set for a sympathetic rail strike on April 1 to coincide with the UMW walkout.[40]

What, then, was Lewis up to? His prestrike strategy encompassed three immediate objectives. First, the proposed American "Triple Alliance" and the fighting rhetoric that accompanied it stimulated morale among UMW militants and assured them that Lewis intended no surrender to the mine operators. Second, the possibility of the railway unions uniting with the coal miners might impress employers with the futility of a coal strike and cause them to accede to the UMW's primary demands before the April 1 negotiating deadline. Third, the threat of joint strike action by what newspapers estimated as an alliance of over 2 million union workers was intended to trouble Washington officials, specifically Hoover and Harding, who, in their anxiety to avert industrial crisis, would urge operators to meet the union's demands.

Yet when the *New York Times* observed editorially on February 3 that Lewis "may just be bluffing," the editors were more astute than they realized. Later in the month the paper's editors proved even more perceptive, when they noted that the February 22 Chicago agreement "is a rather dry sop to the radical workers in the mines," and prophesied the UMW's future with startling clairvoyance. "Coal overproduction," *Times* editors suggested, "doubtless induces a feeling that the miners' cause is lost."[41]

Bluff was indeed intrinsic to Lewis's strike strategy, but coal operators and government officials refused to be misled. On April 1, 1922, he thus led the largest single coal miners' strike in United States history. Not only did all the miners in the unionized bituminous fields walk out. Many of the major nonunion fields—especia..ly Somerset, Fayette, and Westmoreland counties in Pennsylvania—also struck, as did the 155,000 anthracite miners of northeastern Pennsylvania, whose contract had also expired on March 31. Over 600,000 coal miners left work on April 1 or shortly afterward in a struggle that determined the future of the UMW for the next decade.

Bluff, militancy, and florid language punctuated Lewis's behavior during the strike's early stages. Called before the House Labor Committee on Monday, April 3, Lewis read a four-hour statement, in which he used the threat of mine nationalization and government operation of the industry as a club to pressure the operators into agreement. Lewis made a distinction without a difference between government ownership of the mines and nationalization—he asserted that nationalization implied cartelization and government regulation of a private industry—and that his proposal would ensure greater earnings for the miner, legitimate profits for the operator, and cheaper coal for the consumer. "There seems to be no hope," he stressed, "except through nationalization. No remedy has been offered by the operators and in default of any other remedy the mine workers seriously suggest that the Government take over and operate the mines.''[42]

As the strike wore on, Lewis continued to threaten operators with government control. In June, the editor and public relations expert of the union journal, Ellis Searles, published an article in the *Review of Reviews* that argued that, owing to the managerial deficiencies of mine operators, Congress must regulate the bituminous industry as it did transportation and that a government commission of mines comparable to the Interstate Commerce Commission be immediately established.[43]

Lewis's threats may have impressed the miners and the public—but not the operators. A Republican administration and a Republican Congress were unlikely to enact radical legislation; and an administration in which one of the most influential cabinet members, Secretary of the Treasury Andrew Mellon, was himself a major investor in bituminous mines would scarcely assist the UMW. Although the Harding administration's reaction to the crisis in coal, as expressed primarily by Commerce Secretary Hoover, favored neither miners nor operators, it was a neutrality that, in effect, benefited employers. The president, Hoover, and Labor Secretary James J. Davis considered themselves conscientious public servants whose primary duty was to insure consumers an adequate supply of coal at equitable prices. President Harding, especially, thought that the coal miners shared administration concern for the public welfare and that only autocratic and radical union leaders favored a strike—to say the least, a most peculiar reading of UMW political reality.[44]

From the day the coal strike began to the moment it ended, the Harding administration maneuvered to insure the public an adequate supply of coal. It acted on the initial assumption that the industry's surplus capacity and production from nonunion mines would offset any loss of output resulting from the strike.[45] To insure that nonunion operators earned no windfall profits, Hoover urged them to sell their coal at prices no higher than those established by the fuel administration in 1919. Lewis complained bitterly to Hoover about the latter's efforts to insure a sufficient supply of nonunion coal, and he warned the commerce secretary that such a policy endangered union coal operators (as well as the UMW), who would never regain markets lost to nonunion competitors. But Hoover and Lewis simply talked past each other, using the same English language to convey contradictory interpretations of reality. In a letter to Lewis, the commerce secretary assured the union leader that the government was absolutely neutral in the conflict. "The administration," Hoover pledged, "is not injecting itself into the strike; it is trying to protect the general public from the results of the strike."[46]

Fortunately for the miners, Lewis had a better grip on the economics of coal than Harding or Hoover. Fortunately for Lewis, the miners showed more determination and solidarity than operators or federal officials expected. Throughout April, May, and June the strikers held fast. They paralyzed production in the Central Competitive Field and kept it to a trickle in the hitherto nonunion fields of

Pennsylvania and West Virginia. Faced with legal injunctions, arrogant company guards, and summary evictions from company housing, the strikers in the non-union fields carried on. During the spring, summer, and autumn, UMW-financed and administered tent colonies sheltered thousands of strikers. As coal inventories disappeared and nonunion production failed to satisfy current demand, a major winter fuel crisis loomed.

One tragic event illustrated the lengths to which some coal miners would go in order to secure their aims. It also made inevitable federal intervention in the strike. In 1922 Illinois, District 12 was the UMW's best organized and most militant district. In most Illinois mining communities, nonunion operators were anathemas, and strikebreakers occupied a lower rung on the moral order than Satan.

Yet it was in Illinois that a marginal coal operator, William J. Lester, sought to operate a tiny strip mine just outside the union stronghold of Herrin in "Bloody" Williamson County. Hiring members of a Chicago steam shovel workers' union and protecting them with heavily armed guards, he intended to resume production at his strip mine and sell his coal at strike-inflated price levels.[47]

As tensions rose in the Herrin area and gun battles erupted between union miners and company guards, a local UMW official, on June 18, wired Lewis for advice. What should local strikers do, he asked, about a mine resuming production with workers holding union cards? The next day, June 19, Lewis replied by wire that the steam shovel union had been suspended from the A. F. of L., that it was an illegitimate union, and that "representatives of our organization are justified in treating this crowd as an outlaw organization and in viewing its members in the same light as they do any common strike-breakers."

Two days later, on June 21, the clash everyone expected erupted. A large force of armed union men and local sympathizers surrounded the Lester mine, placed the strikebreakers and guards under siege, and demanded their surrender. Outnumbered and outgunned, Lester's men raised the white flag. As the triumphant union men marched their prisoners toward Herrin, their emotions and hatred for the strikebreakers got the better of them. Suddenly the captors began to assault and shoot their prisoners, chasing some of them through a local woods as if they were wild dogs. They stomped wounded men and shot defenseless victims. Angry union men even prevented bystanders from aiding or comforting the dying. When the rampage finally ended, nineteen prisoners lay dead, all of them slain brutally; the next morning Americans read in their newspapers about the "Herrin Massacre."

For three months the 1922 miners' strike had been peaceful. Newspapers neglected it; Washington pursued a hands-off policy. But after Herrin, the coal strike received banner headlines. Editorialists, clergymen, and ordinary citizens demanded retribution, usually called justice, for the perpetrators of the "massacre," commonly identified with the UMW and Lewis's telegram of June 18.

Republicans and Democrats arose in Congress to denounce those responsible for the "massacre," criticize the UMW, and condemn the strikers.[48]

Lewis promptly denied that either the UMW or his own telegram of June 18 had caused the "massacre." Asserting that the union refuses to condone lawlessness and deploring the tragedy, he implied that the "sinister influences" of thousands of detectives and "Secret Service operatives" had precipitated the bloodshed. A year later, in July 1923, during a private conference with agents of President Coolidge, Lewis offered a revised explanation of the "massacre." He stressed Lester's repudiation of a union agreement and observed that the autocratic behavior of private gunmen had brought local passions to a white heat. Lewis neither condoned nor excused the brutal murders at Herrin but instead asked federal officials to comprehend the incident in light of its full circumstances, remembering that "in the past there had been numerous instances of miners killed by armed guards and gun men employed by operators, all without protest from the public." Moreover, he added, "it was not the duty of the union to apprehend the murderers or to find out who was responsible for the murders. This was a matter for public authority." Finally, Lewis hinted that "communist agitators" had instigated the violence.[49]

The Harding administration no longer could proclaim its neutrality. John L. Lewis could no longer stoke the strikers' militancy. A new round of tripartite negotiations among union representatives, mine operators, and federal officials was in the offing.

By June 1922 the shortage of coal had passed from a potential crisis to a real one; soaring prices for the scarce commodity stirred consumer resentment and induced northern operators to offer a settlement to the union; moreover, an impending strike on the nation's railroads scheduled for July 1 threatened to remove nonunion coal from the market. Something had to be done—and quickly.

During the last week in June, Lewis, Labor Secretary Davis, Commerce Secretary Hoover, President Harding, and selected operators conferred informally. Lewis stressed the necessity of a national or Central Competitive Field agreement for the union; operators emphasized their need for contract (wage) flexibility, competitiveness with nonunion mines, and, hence, local (district and state) contracts with the union. Although the gap between the union position and that of the operators remained unbridgeable, Harding invited UMW officials as well as anthracite and bituminous operators to the White House for a conference on Saturday morning, July 1. Harding's conference made no progress when Lewis refused to discuss separate district agreements.[50]

Unable to bring union and operators together, Harding, on July 9, broached his own strike solution, one obviously concocted by Hoover. The president proposed that miners resume work immediately at the March 31 wage level pending the appointment and decision of a federal arbitration commission that would fix permanent wage levels. The commission, consisting of three men appointed by the union, three by the operators, and five by the government, would establish a temporary wage scale to prevail from August 10 until March 31, 1923. The part of the proposed solution most dear to Hoover required an exhaustive federal inquiry into coal mining aimed at a complete reorganization of the industry.[51]

Neither operators nor union leaders at first understood what Harding's plan entailed. The promise of an arbitration award attracted the interest of the operators; the suggestion of a national agreement and a reorganization of the industry intrigued Lewis. A few days later, however, at a lengthy meeting of the UMW's Policy Committee on July 15, members found substantial loopholes in the president's plan. Harding had linked fact-finding and arbitration; the union position, as defined by Lewis, favored a full inquiry into all aspects of the coal industry but rejected arbitration and any change in wages or conditions prior to the completion of the federal investigation. More important to Lewis and his union, Harding's plan excluded some union operators. Lewis thus informed the president that the UMW Policy Committee had decided to reject his settlement proposal.[52]

Lewis's message confirmed Harding's belief that the union was more recalcitrant than the operators and that it was responsible for protracting the strike. Hoover undoubtedly shared the president's sentiments, for in an unsigned and uninitialed memorandum concerning the July 9 settlement proposed (one which he obviously had prepared), the commerce secretary included the words: "Order men to return to work."[53] Which is almost what the president did on July 17, during a conference with mine operators, when he advised them to resume production regardless of the UMW and offered federal troops to protect company property. Indeed, the next day, July 18, he wired the governors of all coal-producing states ordering them to protect coal mines and advising them that federal troops had been placed on the alert for strike duty.[54]

Just as Lewis had originally hoped to bluff the operators into submission and the government into complicity with the union, Harding intended to bluff the strikers, if not their leaders, into returning to the pits. Threatened by nonunion labor on the one hand and military intervention on the other, the strikers, Harding calculated, would surrender. But just as mine operators had called Lewis's bluff, the union called Harding's, and the president was scarcely prepared in July 1922 to use regular army troops to break a strike (especially one led by a putative Republican union president).

Harding's proposal of July 9 and his statements of July 17 and 18 scarcely stimulated coal production. Operators in the well-organized northern districts and governors in those states would not resume production on a nonunion basis and risk open, violent confrontations with strikers. Simultaneously, the railroad shopmen's strike, which began on July 1, reduced shipments from the nonunion mines. Coal disappeared from the marketplace, and with summer ending, its price soared. Mine owners could now afford union wages and earn substantial profits, which is precisely what Lewis expected.

By the end of the first week in August, the outlines of a strike settlement emerged. "Matters are such," Lewis wrote on August 4, "that the present situation cannot endure indefinitely and I expect the coal operators to capitulate in the near future at least in substantial numbers. The strike is won in so far as wages are concerned and it only remains to devise some procedure which will enable us to realize upon our victory."[55] Lewis's beliefs were apparently based on a secret understanding he had reached at a conference in Pittsburgh with operators from the Central Competitive Field. Whatever the precise details of the secret Pittsburgh agreement, the conference revealed to Lewis divisions among the mine operators, which he relied on to achieve his goals.[56] The Pittsburgh meeting was followed by bargaining sessions beginning in Cleveland on August 7. Operators representing Districts 2 and 5 in Pennsylvania and District 6 in Ohio joined Lewis in Cleveland; the Illinois and Indiana operators' associations boycotted the sessions.

Lewis's bargaining strategy was simple, and, as usual, his was the only voice that spoke for the union. Once a number of mines resumed production under union contract, he reasoned, the recalcitrant operators, fearful of losing markets and profits to their competitors, would also sign with the UMW. By August 15 Lewis won a tactical victory: Operators controlling about 60 million tons of production and employing 100,000 miners in seven states contracted with the union on the basis of the status quo ante. During the next four weeks, other northern and western operators rushed to sign up with the union, until by mid-September, Lewis had reached agreements covering nearly all the prestrike union mines. "It was a triumph of comparative unity," wrote Heber Blankenhorn, "over inherent disorganization."[57]

Lewis celebrated the settlement as a great victory for the UMW. In a period of wage deflation and labor intensification, he had preserved 1920 wage rates and job conditions until April 1, 1923. Whereas employer resistance and federal repression crushed the railroad shopmen's strike, Lewis steered his union ship to a safe shore. "The miners may well be termed," he proclaimed, "the shock troops of the American labor movement, and this controversy their industrial Verdun."[58]

Lewis certainly did not realize the irony inherent in his victory proclamation. The French had indeed held the Germans at Verdun in 1916—but at what enormous cost: a loss of human lives that sparked widespread mutinies among the troops and antiwar demonstrations throughout France. Without allies, especially the United States after April 1917, France's "victory" at Verdun would at best have been Pyrrhic. The coal miners' triumph in 1922 also came at enormous cost; but the UMW, unlike France, lacked powerful allies within the American labor movement who could provide fresh men, money, and material.

The preservation of existing wage rates in the 1922 agreement notwithstanding, Lewis's and his union's losses were many. For the first time since 1898, the UMW failed to sign the operators of the Central Competitive Field to a single agreement. If all the mine owners accepted similar terms, they nevertheless signed individually or by district association, one of the issues that originally caused the strike. That, however, was the least of the union's losses. Nonunion production in West Virginia, Kentucky, and Alabama remained untouched and thus free to chip away further at the markets for union coal. And the nonunion miners of Somerset, Fayette, and Westmoreland counties, Pennsylvania, who had joined the strike, resisted to the bitter end, and refused to return to work when the August agreements excluded them were in the end deserted by the union. Not only did Lewis exclude former nonunion miners from the strike settlement; he denied financial assistance to miners who remained on strike after mid-September.[59] The reason was quite simple: Lewis lacked the resources to subsidize a protracted strike in Pennsylvania's nonunion fields.

By the summer of 1921, as we have seen, the UMW's expenses exceeded its revenues—a financial situation worsened by the 1922 strike. In order to meet strike expenses, which exceeded $1 million, union officers sold $550,000 worth of UMW securities, borrowed $50,000 from the Brotherhood of Locomotive Firemen, and, in a singularly strange deal, borrowed another $200,000 from the Harriman National Bank of New York* on the personal notes of William Green and John L. Lewis.

Paradoxically, one of the nation's great capitalist families, the Harrimans, saved the UMW from bankruptcy in 1922 and was not bashful about its assistance to the union. One of the bank's directors commented: "If they [Lewis and Green] should come into this office in need of $5,000,000 they could have it within an hour . . . we deem it our duty to help them." And bank president Joseph W. Harriman added: "The United Mine Workers of America do banking business here, and have done so for some time. Their business with us has always been conducted along business lines."[60]

The 1922 settlement divided rather than united the UMW. In the wake of Lewis's strike "victory," mutinies erupted among the rank and file. The aftermath of the strike also demonstrated the hollowness of Lewis's militancy. Before the miners walked out, he had raised publicly the specter of a labor triple alliance among coal miners, railroad workers, and longshoremen. After the miners returned to the pits but while the railroad shopmen remained on strike against the most notorious federal antilabor injunction in history, Lewis repudiated sympathetic strikes in support of the shopmen. Learning that Gompers and the A. F. of L. executive council might be considering a general strike, Lewis wired William Green on September 11: "I do not know whether there is any foundation for such talk but suggest to you it is my judgment any serious contemplation of such policy is in error."[61]

Lewis rejected militancy and labor solidarity within the miners' union when it concerned action, not words. Many of the operators who signed with the union in August and September ran nonunion as well as union mines. John Brophy of District 2 maintained that strikers should not return to work until their employers signed for *all* their properties, including those that had been hitherto nonunion. But Lewis insisted otherwise, for in his eagerness to weaken operator resistance at

*See next chapter for Lewis's relationship with the Harriman family.

the Cleveland conference, he promised mine owners that he would not demand agreements covering their nonunion properties. And when union members, on their own volition, as happened in District 2, refused to return to work until their employers also signed for nonunion mines, Lewis ordered them back.[62]

For most of September Lewis and John Brophy, in private conferences and correspondence, argued the issue back and forth. Lewis pleaded sanctity of contract—the necessity to respect the agreements he had signed for the union in Cleveland; Brophy stressed union solidarity and the dangers inherent in allowing operators to run nonunion as well as union mines. In the end Brophy capitulated to Lewis's persistence, refusing to admit the equity of Lewis's policy but ordering men in union mines back to work. "Their loyalty to their fellow workers [non-union strikers]," Brophy lamented to Lewis, "is a splendid exhibition of sacrifice and solidarity and [it] is very unfortunate that their efforts are going to be vain [sic]."[63]

Lewis's mismanagement of the 1922 strike and settlement, his critics then and later asserted, matched his betrayal of the miners during the 1919 strike. By ordering union men back to work before nonunion strikers achieved recognition, Lewis, his enemies maintained, had broken union solidarity. "Why a man so forceful and astute as Lewis was in many ways, should have made this colossal blunder can only be explained," surmised Brophy, "by some fatal defect in his character."[64] The "colossal" blunder of deserting the nonunion miners in 1922, hindsight would prove, guaranteed the collapse of the UMW later in the 1920s by leaving the coal industry a house divided.

Such criticism of Lewis and his policies would have been just had he been negotiating from a position of strength. The solidarity and militancy exhibited by coal miners during the strike of 1922 was indeed remarkable. But so was the resistance of the largest mine operators. The 1922 strike scarcely touched the nonunion fields of West Virginia, Kentucky, and Alabama; in Pennsylvania's nonunion fields, operators, led by the steel industry and its captive mines, refused to recognize the union; and in the outlying western fields of Kansas, Oklahoma, and Washington, among others, antilabor laws and governors partially broke the strike. The federal government in 1922, as in 1919, Lewis realized, would not allow the strike to reach a point that threatened a consumer crisis, and the Harding administration was less sympathetic to labor than Wilson's.* Herbert Hoover's and Warren G. Harding's determination to be neutral in the struggle and to be guided only by the public interest translated for Lewis into a simple statement that, in the event of a crisis, federal officials would break the strike, as they did during the 1922 railroad conflict. Beset by external economic and political liabilities, Lewis commanded an organization split internally. As he informed Adolph

*At one point during the Cleveland conferences, Harding threatened to punish Lewis if he did not accept the operators' proposals. See George G. Moore to John L. Lewis, July 12, 1944, United Mine Workers Archives, Lewis File.

Germer early in August, during the strike he had had to overcome "opposition from people within our ranks" as well as "tremendous obstacles" externally.[65]

All such obstacles, furthermore, had to be surmounted when the UMW lacked funds; without the sale of union-held securities and the loans extended by other labor organizations and the Harriman National Bank, Lewis might have been impotent to bargain with employers in 1922. He had only to look to Britain, where coal miners experienced an equally bleak postwar economic situation and where the once mighty miners' union had been shattered economically by employers allied to a Tory government, to see portents of the UMW's future. Because Lewis understood that too many miners were producing too much coal and that the American labor movement was growing weaker, he was pleased to come away from the 1922 strike with the preservation of the status quo ante. For Lewis the 1922 settlement represented a substantial victory against overwhelming odds; for the UMW and the coal miners, however, it presaged decline.

The 1922 coal strike revealed further flaws in Lewis's strength. Soon after the strike ended, Congress, at the urging of the Harding administration, established the United States Coal Commission to make an intensive investigation of the economics of coal mining and to recommend a reorganization of the industry and its union-management relations. Militants in the UMW naïvely expected that such a federal commission might assist them in a campaign to nationalize the coal industry. The commission appointed by the Harding administration, however, proved more to the liking of the operators than the union. Not a single representative or ally of the UMW sat on the commission; and, although none of the seven members directly represented the coal industry, none could be considered antipathetic to the operators, though more than one was antiunion.[66]

From such a commission Lewis expected little—and he received it. The union cooperated with the commission, and its assistance made possible the most complete study of the American coal industry ever published. The commission's final report portrayed graphically the utter disorganization of bituminous mining and the appalling conditions under which most miners worked and lived. It also lauded the substantial contribution unionization had made to the miners' welfare. But the commission's final recommendations proved even more disappointing than Britains's recent experience with royal coal commissions. Where the British Sankey Commission pointedly recommended a complete reorganization of coal mining—almost nationalization—which the Tory government had refused to implement, the United States Coal Commission submitted recommendations that were, in the words of one scholar, "vague, platitudinous, and occasionally even meaningless." Its recommendations, on the one hand, recognized the contribution of national agreements to labor stability; yet, on the other hand, they sanctioned district, state, and local agreements. Commissioners, on the one hand, applauded the UMW's contributions to labor peace and the miners' welfare; but, on the other hand, they endorsed nonunion mines as a necessary restraint to a potential union monopoly and restraint of free competition in coal.[67] Such trivial recommendations received the fate they deserved from operators, union, and government, absolute neglect.

The commission, or at least its chairman and secretary, however, played a role in averting a soft-coal strike in 1923 and settling an anthracite strike the same year.* Exhausted by the long 1922 struggle, neither mine operators nor union coal miners wished to repeat that experience in April 1923. Although northern operators still desired wage reductions and the option to sign local contracts with the unions, they were not prepared to fight for their claims.[68] When, early in January 1923, John Hays Hammond suggested that the mine owners sign a new one-year agreement maintaining current wages and conditions until April 1, 1924, the operators, after ritualistic resistance, submitted to Hammond's request and the UMW's demands. On January 4, 1923, at a conference at the Waldorf-Astoria Hotel in New York City, operators representing mining interests in Ohio, Illinois, and Indiana signed a new contract similar to the one due to expire on April 1, 1923, and continuing a $7.50 wage for dayworkers and a rate of $1.08 a ton for contract miners. Although the agreement was expected eventually to spread to all the unionized mines in the north and the west, the UMW once again had failed to reestablish the traditional Central Competitive Field basic contract.[69]

If economic circumstances and political realities made Lewis an opportunist in his negotiations with mine owners during and after the 1922 strike, his manipulation of the mine nationalization question disclosed what John Brophy called "some fatal defect in his character." Ever since 1916, UMW conventions had voted in favor of nationalization of the nation's coal mines, and John L. Lewis had approved nationalization in principle, raising only pragmatic, political reservations. Yet when John Brophy sought in April 1921 to have material printed in the UMW *Journal* that discussed District 2's plan for nationalization, editor Ellis Searles responded: "I do not believe it to be the mission of the United Mine Workers' Journal to publish propaganda. . . . There is another reason why I believe it would be unwise to publish the 'Miners' Program' in the Journal," he commented, "and that is, that it appears to be . . . a denunciation of the policies of the Union. . . . The Journal['s] . . . columns should not be used for the purpose of attacking its [UMW] policies."[70] A most peculiar response indeed, considering that Searles was John L. Lewis's mouthpiece, that nationalization was official UMW policy, and that Lewis had even sanctioned it in principle. Stranger things were to follow.

At the September-October 1921 UMW convention, delegates adopted, without

*See Chapter 5, pp. 103-105.

a dissenting vote, a resolution endorsing nationalization of the mines. In response to President Lewis's comments about the complexities of the issue, however, the delegates accepted his suggestion that the union appoint a mine nationalization committee. On October 5, the last day of the convention, John Brophy submitted a memorandum that Lewis approved granting the following duties and powers to the nationalization committee: (1) it was to devise a practical policy of nationalization; (2) it would make occasional reports prior to its final completed nationalization treatise; (3) the international union would bear the committee's expenses; and (4) the committee would complete its work promptly. Lewis requested only that the committee, once established, do nothing publicly that might create the impression that nationalization was a scale (contract) demand on the operators or release publicity prior to the 1922 labor-management negotiations.[71] Two days later, October 7, in a letter officially appointing Brophy; Christ J. Golden, president of District 9, in a Pennsylvania anthracite area; and William Mitch, secretary-treasury of District 11 (Indiana) as the Nationalization Research Committee, Lewis charged them with ''formulating a detailed practical policy to bring about the nationalization of the coal mines and to aid in the dissemination of information among our members and the public and the crystallization of sentiment for the attainment of such end.'' He further assured his three appointees that he ''will be glad to co-operate with each of you gentlemen in the fullest possible way.''[72]

Lewis's promise of complete cooperation proved misleading. Ellis Searles closed the *Journal*'s columns to proponents of nationalization, and Lewis never overruled his subordinate's editorial policies. Denied access to the union's journal, members of the nationalization committee also had to go outside the UMW for information, materials, and even funds. Brophy, for example, contacted prominent members of the Socialist party, the Workers' Education Bureau, the Bureau of Industrial Research, and the League for Industrial Democracy (left-wing reform groups located in New York City), including Norman Thomas, Roger Baldwin, Herbert Croly, Mrs. Willard Straight, Heber Blankenhorn, and Arthur Gleason. From March through September 1922, Brophy, Golden, and Mitch were so busy with the strike that they relied for information almost completely on the New York leftists. The New Yorkers were not entirely disinterested parties; the Thomases, Baldwins, Blankenhorns, and others intended to use their relationship with the UMW nationalization committee as the entering wedge in an effort to move the American labor movement to the left. But their interest in the mine workers enabled Brophy to publicize nationalization in the pages of the *New Republic* and *Nation*.[73]

Never personally enthusiastic about nationalization, Lewis grew more leery as New York intellectuals poked their fingers into his union pie. Early in January 1923 he informed Brophy that the union had yet to discuss or approve a specific nationalization plan, that it was thus misleading for the committee to release information in the name of the UMW, and, finally, that it would be unwise for committee members to appear before the United States Coal Commission. On January 21, at a three-hour meeting with members of the nationalization committee, Lewis berated them for their contacts with leftists and their efforts to publicize nationalization outside the UMW. Lewis's criticism led Christ Golden to resign.[74] Shortly afterward Lewis had Ellis Searles unleash a newspaper blast at the Bureau of Industrial Research and League for Industrial Democracy. Typically, Searles accused Brophy's friends of being "Greenwich Village reds" seeking to "butt in on the affairs of the miners' union" and of being "parlor coal diggers, who might better be designated as gold diggers, [and] represent nothing." Searles's press release of January 28 was a long-delayed reaction to Christ Golden's speech favoring nationalization at the annual dinner of the League for Industrial Democracy on December 29, 1922.[75] So scurrilous was the UMW editor that Norman Thomas, on January 29, addressed an open letter to John L. Lewis in which the Socialist leader caught the essence of the UMW president's position on nationalization. "To favor nationalization but to forbid public discussion of concrete plans," Thomas wrote, "reminds me of the old nursery rhyme:

> Mother may I go out to swim?
> Yes, my darling daughter,
> Hang your clothes on a hickory limb
> But don't go near the water."[76]

A day after the appearance of Thomas's letter, Lewis disclosed his utter opportunism. Writing to William Mitch, Lewis asserted that in his October 7, 1922, letter appointing the nationalization committee, he had never meant to suggest that committee members were free to publicize their plans before the mine workers had approved them. Having denied the committee the right to disseminate information among coal miners through the union journal, Lewis now informed Mitch that the committee lacked the right to crystallize sentiment for nationalization among the general public.[77] More the union politician than Brophy or Golden, Mitch took his cue from Lewis and urged Brophy not to follow Golden's example of resignation. When Brophy did, in fact, resign on February 5, 1923, Mitch, echoing Lewis's line, reminded Brophy that publicizing the issue outside the UMW had been wrong, that a Republican administration in power made nationalization inopportune, and that even in Europe, nationalization was no longer a "live issue." Mitch apparently sent copies of his correspondence with Brophy to Lewis, who remarked: "I . . . think it indicates excellent judgment." Controversies concerning the UMW should not be aired publicly, wrote Lewis on February 10, 1923. Outsiders, especially from New York, must not intercede in union affairs, and the nationalization question should be laid to rest.[78] Since the nationalization committee had argued its case publicly and established contact with left-wing intellectuals outside the union, Brophy was correct when he wrote to Mitch on

February 13 that "it was evident during our conference with John Lewis at New York that the activity of the Nationalization Committee was very objectionable to him."[79]

With mine nationalization a dead issue by mid-February 1923, the possibility of a soft-coal strike in 1923 ended by the agreement of January 24, and the UMW not scheduled to hold another convention until January 1924, Lewis took a well-earned vacation. Since his elevation to the acting union presidency late in the summer of 1919 he had scarcely had a moment's leisure. When he was not struggling to defend the UMW against operators, government officials, and antilabor judges, he was busy combating union rivals and asserting the international union's claim to hegemony over the separate, and ostensibly autonomous, districts. On February 24, 1923, putting all that behind him, he and Myrta sailed from New York on board the S. S. *Celtic* for a six-week combined vacation-business trip to Great Britain.[80]

Lewis left Philip Murray in charge of the UMW. A letter from Murray to Lewis dated March 15, 1923, in which the acting union president tried to humor his "boss," reveals better than any other extant document Lewis's conception of how best to run an efficient trade union. Murray, to be sure, advised the Lewises not to rush home, to rest fully while they had the opportunity, for they were unlikely to have another one soon. "The only thing that your friends in the office and I fear," wrote Murray jocularly, "is the possibility of your returning home with spats, cane, and a monocle." Murray's strained humor also cut to the heart of Lewis's conception of union politics. Our friends in charge of the constitutional department, joked Murray, "have been making rulings having for their purpose the preservation of the principles as laid down by yourself. It goes without saying that these rulings not only protect the interests of the organization, but also protect our friends." All joshing aside, Murray assured his absent chief that UMW affairs were running smoothly and that "if any of these district officers peep their heads up, I will do just as you would do,—kick them out of the organization, then revoke their charters." Finally, Murray expressed what he considered to be his boss's estimate of such militants as John Brophy. "Your close-up of British nationalization," he suggested to Lewis, "will give you an appreciation of the *nuts* who are leading the movement for nationalization on this side of the ocean" (our italics).[81]

CHAPTER 5

Emerging Labor Statesman, 1923-1924

By the spring of 1923 John L. Lewis had traveled far from his obscure origins. His parents had left Wales in 1869 and 1870 as part of the post-Civil War wave of British emigrants who took advantage of reduced steamship rates and steerage passage to better their fortunes overseas. A half-century later John Lewis reversed the route of his parents; but he traveled first class, saw his name in the society column of the *New York Times* listed with other illustrious citizens, and, on his passport, described his occupation as: *executive*.[1]

Lewis's passport photograph suggested material success. His hair gleamed a fine, rich auburn, his eyes shone clear blue, his face appeared unlined. The good life provided by the perquisites of a trade union presidency was apparent in the folds of fat that enveloped his face and neck. With his hair parted neatly in the center, Herbert Hoover style, he looked the typical middle-aged corporation executive or public official. Next to him, his wife, Myrta, seemed diminutive and demure; she also appeared ten years his senior.

A career in trade unionism had thus far been good to Lewis. As a third-generation UMW official he could treat the labor movement as a career, not a calling or a mission. First-generation union leaders in the United Mine Workers and elsewhere received minimal salaries, bare expenses, little secretarial assistance, and no security of tenure; in most cases, they fell from office as easily as autumn leaves. Its second-generation leaders typically bettered themselves through the labor movement. John Mitchell of the UMW gained national repute, hobnobbed with the business elite, counted prominent politicians among his friends, and, at his death, left behind a not inconsequential estate. Mitchell's successors in the presidential office also improved themselves materially. Tom Lewis became a well-paid official of a West Virginia mine owners' association, and John P. White served first as a federal official and then as a business executive. By the time John L. Lewis entered office his predecessors had established a pattern of union careerism. Presidents were well paid, received elastic expense arrangements, employed extensive secretarial staffs, and traveled first-class. They attended formal dinners in tails and white ties.[2] If they had not in fact been admitted to full membership in the corporate-political elite, they tried to imitate its life-style.

Union business still took Lewis away from home—the three-story house he maintained on West Lawrence Avenue in Springfield, Illinois. The journey between his home and UMW headquarters in Indianapolis became routine in the 1920s. Yet it was now not unusual for Lewis to bring office secretaries home with him so that official business could be transacted in Springfield as well as Indianapolis. Collective bargaining and political lobbying carried Lewis on a travel circuit among the cities of New York, Philadelphia, and Washington, where he stayed at the finest hotels: the Ambassador, Roosevelt, and Waldorf-Astoria in New York; the Bellevue-Stratford in Philadelphia; and the Willard in Washington. His wife often accompanied him, as did other members of his immediate family, especially his closest brother, George W. During the summer, daughter Kathryn traveled with her father frequently, though the child of the family, John L. Jr., usually remained at home.

Family support proved essential to Lewis's existence. Most family members cared for each other in time of trouble, and aunts and uncles tended Kathryn and John Jr. when John L. and Myrta traveled during the school year. Most members of the Lewis-Bell clan earned their livelihoods directly or indirectly through the UMW. Those family members Lewis did not place directly on the union payroll obtained positions through union influence. Brother Dennie's job with the State Mine Inspection Department resulted from the mine workers' political influence in Illinois. And brother-in-law Floyd C. Bell became cashier of a bank in Indianapolis that Lewis served as president.

The Lewis family during the 1920s developed a distinctly haut bourgeois life-style. Photographs of John L. Lewis (and they were becoming increasingly numerous by this time) show him in the finest tailored and conservatively cut dark business suits with vest, gold chain, tightly starched white collar, and silk tie. Myrta dressed demurely but stylishly and in winter wore a luxurious mink coat.[3] During the 1930s the socially prominent Gardner Jackson and his wife considered Myrta Lewis the most tastefully dressed person that they knew.[4] In August 1920 Lewis purchased headstones for the graves of his daughter, Mary Margaret, and his father, which cost $1,000—one-third the sum of his annual salary. The gravestones were inscribed simply with the names, birthdates, and death dates of the deceased—nothing more.[5] Lewis also began to purchase and drive expensive Cadillac roadsters, as union leaders together with other Americans entered the automotive age. Lewis's 1926 travel diary, for example, contrasts starkly with his earlier ones. Where heretofore the diaries recorded the costs of constant railroad travel and Pullman berths, the 1926 book consisted entirely of entries estimating the cost of fuel, tires, and tune-ups for Lewis's Cadillac. In the 1920s Myrta developed her life-long passion: the acquisition of expensive and delicate antiques. Beginning with the Lewis's 1923 visit to Britain and the purchase of seventeenth- and eighteenth-century English antiques in Swansea and Cardiff, Myrta dealt regularly with antique dealers on two continents. In 1928, when coal miners were fortunate to average $30.00 a week in wages, Myrta spent $35.00 for one English sterling silver soup ladle (nineteenth century) and $16.50 for one "fine old spoon." Later she accumulated Waterford compotes, French porcelain, Chippendale furniture, and Oriental rugs. Incomplete family account books suggest that the Lewis family spent thousands of dollars during the 1920s and 1930s for Myrta's acquisitions. The Gardner Jacksons, themselves antique lovers from the more traditional upper-class American elite, were immensely impressed by Myrta Lewis's "exquisite taste" in Colonial antiques, with which, during the 1930s, she decorated the Lewis's homes in Alexandria, Virginia.[6]

While Myrta collected expensive old furniture and china, John accumulated prestigious country club memberships. On December 1, 1922, he became a lifetime member of the Congressional Country Club in Washington, his membership certificate signed by the club's president, Herbert Hoover. And in 1926 the directors admitted him to a lifetime membership in the Army, Navy, and Marine Corps Country Club (also in Washington).[7] Lewis, however, was neither a golfer nor a social drinker, and his country club memberships obviously were primarily for the status they conferred, not the leisure activities they offered. Lewis's primary outdoor interests were deep-sea fishing off the Florida coast and hiking and trail riding in the high mountains of Colorado and Wyoming. Later in life, when his income made it possible, he purchased a vacation home on Pine Island off the Florida Gulf Coast and became a regular summer visitor to a resort in the Jackson Hole area of Wyoming that catered to wealthy business executives.

Outside the large family circle to which he was close and devoted, Lewis lacked intimate friends. Phil Murray, who served him faithfully and well for a quarter of a century, never entered John L. Lewis's charmed social circle. Lee Pressman subsequently observed that to the best of his knowledge the Lewis's and the Murray's never once met socially for dinner, a party, or a nonofficial occasion.[8] The diaries and correspondence of other Lewis associates in the UMW and CIO suggest a similar social distance between them and their "boss." Like a corporate executive patronizing his "employees," the best that Lewis could do was to take Murray, Kennedy, and Lauck on a fishing trip for a day. When Lewis was in Indianapolis during the period 1920-1933, he seldom spent time away from the office with fellow members of the UMW. Instead, he joined a steady evening poker game that included "Big Bill" Hutcheson, president of the carpenters' union; Dan Tobin, president of the Teamsters; and officials from other unions with Indianapolis headquarters. Lewis's attitude toward colleagues is best revealed in a story told by R. J. Thomas, who, in 1937, had just been elected president of the United Auto Workers. Immediately after the election, Lewis advised Thomas: "Well, look. I think it's all right for a man in your position now to have some recreation but don't let them [UAW associates] get too close to you. By coming close to you they will become contemptuous and they won't give you the proper respect. If you plan poker, and you live out in Detroit, play with your neighbors or somebody. Don't play with anybody in your official capacity."[9]

Lewis followed his own rules of social etiquette religiously. He kept fellow officers of the UMW at a distance, practiced regal aloofness, and acted in the union as a king to his court. Lewis reserved his friendship for business executives, high public officials, and members of the hereditary American elite. They dined with the Lewises on a reciprocal basis, and he charmed them with well-told stories and stimulating conversation. The Herbert Hoovers, the Gardner Jacksons, the Harrimans, the Cyrus Chings, corporation executives in general—they were the type of people John L. Lewis cultivated. Cyrus Ching, a United States Rubber Company executive and later a prominent federal labor mediator, described Lewis as "a brilliant conversationalist," the "soul of courtesy . . . a typical Southern gentleman." Nonflamboyant in private conversation, Lewis, according to Ching, had a dry, keen sense of humor, one that enabled him and George Love, a leading coal company executive, to swap stories for seven consecutive hours as Ching laughed ceaselessly.[10]

During the 1920s Lewis established a particularly close business and personal relationship with the Harriman family. Not only did Jacob Harriman, president of the Harriman National Bank, extend a substantial line of credit to the UMW during the 1922 strike; he also personally phoned President Harding to plead the union's case. Lewis, for his part, deposited UMW funds in Harriman's bank and sought to obtain other union business for his banker friend. Harriman regularly extended credit simply on the basis of Lewis's personal signature without collateral. For example, W. Jett Lauck, the UMW's economic adviser and Lewis's personal tax and real estate consultant, financed his own many—and mostly unsuccessful— real estate ventures through loans obtained from the Harriman National Bank on the signatures of Lewis and Phil Murray. Averell Harriman occasionally invited Lewis to polo matches in which the former played. And Lewis, the trade union leader and miners' spokesman, felt no embarrassment appearing at the matches attended largely by members of New York's "400."[11]

Later in the 1930s, when Jacob Harriman ran afoul of the law as a result of his bank's practices before and during the Great Depression, Lewis came to his aid. His bank ruined, his health shattered, his trial for fraud scheduled to open in federal court, Harriman, in May 1934, pleaded with Lewis to appear for him as a character witness. Writing to Lewis from Doctor's Hospital in New York, Harriman lamented: "My good name is in jeopardy and I am *fighting for my life*. And as you, too, are a good fighter you will appreciate my position and I leave it all to you!" Lewis proved a loyal friend, not only testifying in court himself but also urging William Green to bear witness concerning Harriman's good character. Lewis also visited Harriman in the hospital, a visit that Harriman wrote "built me up—my months back have been filled with heart-breaking cracks—but I'm keeping my head up and am fighting back as you told me to. . . . God bless you for your kindness—and I shall never forget it.''[12] Thus did Lewis pay off his debt to the man who, in the 1920s, assisted the UMW financially, provided liberal loans to Lewis's friends, and, in 1924, promoted John L. Lewis's candidacy for the Republican vice-presidency.

Lewis's relationship to the world of banking went considerably beyond his acquaintance with Jacob Harriman. In September 1923 Lewis agreed to become president of the United Labor Bank and Trust Company of Indianapolis, Indiana (capitalized at nearly $1 million) and demanded ''a salary commensurate with the character of the institution and the degree of responsibility involved.'' He also suggested that the bank's organizers appoint his brother-in-law Floyd C. Bell cashier and a member of the board of directors at a starting salary of $4,000 to $5,000 per annum, to rise when business increases. In his letter of acceptance, Lewis enclosed two separate personal checks for $1,100 in payment for ten shares of bank stock each for himself and Floyd Bell in order to qualify them for their executive positions.[13]

The reasons for establishing a labor bank and appointing Lewis as its president seem obvious. Three of the largest labor unions in the nation—the miners, the teamsters, and the carpenters—and many smaller ones had their national head-quarters in Indianapolis. Unions, moreover, maintained an enormous cash flow as dues receipts trickled in and benefits poured out. A bank fortunate enough to become a depository for union funds gained substantial economic advantages, which is what the directors of the United Labor Bank likely expected from Lewis's presidency. The bank did, to be sure, become a depository for substantial UMW funds; but, in the absence of complete financial records, one cannot know to what extent it was patronized by other Indianapolis unions. Lewis's bank presidency during the 1920s and his business relationship with Harriman served as an apprenticeship for his subsequent banking enterprises in Washington and his financial manipulations with entrepreneur Cyrus Eaton.

Lewis not only assimilated a haut bourgeois life-style from his associations with the nation's economic and political elite; he also absorbed their ideological values and their imperious business practices. A man who had flirted with radicals and radicalism from 1917 to 1922, became by 1923 ''the scourge of the reds.'' The elected leader of a putative union democracy, he increasingly practiced autocracy in his administration of the UMW.

At the height of the red scare, 1918-1919, Lewis and his union were among its most notable objects. By 1923, however, as fear of radicalism abated, Lewis entered the battle against the red and the rebellious. In January 1923, the UMW international executive board officially condemned bolshevism and radicalism. In June of the same year, during the annual Tri-District (anthracite) convention in Scranton, Pennsylvania, Lewis, finding himself under attack by union militants led by one Rinaldo Cappellini, resorted to red-baiting. Aware that William Z.

Foster's* son-in-law, Joseph Manley, was among the observers at the convention, Lewis launched a tirade against communism, calling Foster, Manley, and their ilk "industrial buzzards" and ordering them to go to their "beloved Russia." Verbally rebuking the three Communists in attendance, Lewis shouted, "And now I ask you that you remove your carcasses without the door." Whereupon enraged supporters of Lewis severely beat Manley and an associate just outside the convention hall. The little diversion left Lewis in complete command of the convention. The insurgent Cappellini later received what had become traditional Lewis treatment for opportunistic union rebels: a well-paid position on the international payroll.[14]

Scranton only began Lewis's private little red scare. In September 1923 Ellis Searles prepared a UMW "White Paper" on the Bolshevik threat to the American labor movement, which was subsequently printed as an official United States Senate document. In the paper, Searles alleged that Soviet Russia was financing a campaign led by William Z. Foster and his Trade Union Educational League (TUEL) to disrupt responsible trade unions, subvert the A. F. of L., and capture American labor for bolshevism. Substituting fiction for fact wherever necessary, Searles charged that Communists had instigated the 1919 steel strike, the 1922 bituminous and railway shopmen's strikes, and the "Herrin Massacre."[15] Years later a prominent businessman wrote to Lewis: "No one seems to recall that you alone for ten years were the only bulwark against Communism penetrating the United States, when it was a true menace . . . and . . . that you were the obstacle to the recognition of Russia."[16] Other anti-Soviet businessmen probably appreciated Lewis's sentiments on the Russian question, as did Herbert Hoover and the Republican party hierarchy.

Correspondence between Lewis and Jett Lauck suggests, however, that Lewis's aversion to Soviet Russia was opportunistic rather than principled. In 1926 Lauck desired to visit Soviet Russia as part of an American trade union delegation and recommended Lewis to the trip's sponsors as a natural labor delegate. Lewis was intrigued with the prospect of visiting Russia and the esteem that he might gain as head (a position Lauck promised him) of the American delegation. But he wondered: "On the face of it I scarcely like to identify myself with an expedition which might be believed by many to be the forerunner of an attempt to bring the Russian situation to the forefront in this country." And after further thought about the domestic implications of an association with such an expedition, he informed Lauck: "advise your friends who are interested in the Russian matter that I cannot, under any circumstances, participate in the venture and would deprecate the use of my name in any form in connection therewith."[17]

Lewis's opportunism should not be confused with indecisiveness, as his administration of the UMW proved. Despite the intense criticism from insurgents that he endured from 1920 to 1926, Lewis ran the union as he pleased. Secretary-

*The nation's leading trade union Communist during the 1920s.

Treasurer William Green, the only official whose tenure in office preceded that of Lewis, lacked the power to challenge the union president. On two separate occasions in 1923 and 1924 when Green acted in accord with the union constitution, past practices, and precedents, Lewis berated him. In May 1923 Lewis curtly informed Green, "I would be very glad to have you accommodate your bookkeeping arrangements . . . so as to square with the rulings of the President's office." Green promised to conform with Lewis's wishes. In 1924, when Green again cited past union precedent and procedure as a basis for his action, Lewis raised the superior standard of presidential authority and interpretation.[18]

Lewis's management of union finances offered abundant evidence of his cavalier approach to authority. Between 1922 and August 1924, Lewis authorized Ellis Searles to spend more than $19,000 in union funds, of which over $12,000 was expended in the form of bribes to obtain information or influence people in the interest of the UMW. None of Searles's expenditures was billed or receipted, nor was Secretary-Treasurer Green allowed to record them in the union's books. When Green complained of such unethical practices, Lewis replied: "I have discussed the matter with him [Searles] and am entirely satisfied that his expenditures were legitimate and that the organization received full value therefrom." When Green refused to accept Lewis's explanation and demanded a personal meeting with the president, Lewis again asserted that he possessed the authority to sanction Searles's activities for the union. Yet Lewis, always eager to avoid written records of activities such as Searles's, notifed Green: "I see no reason . . . to discuss the matter through the instrumentality of correspondence. I will be glad to discuss the matter with you personally at any time."[19] No record exists of a Green-Lewis conference on the matter; nor is there any indication that Lewis ever altered his conception of how union funds might be spent.

The union journal, as edited by Searles, also remained the exclusive property of Lewis. Not even district officers could get their material printed without Searles's permission, and Lewis relied on the editor to exercise his judgment in the UMW president's interests. When William Mitch, secretary of Indiana District 11 and by 1923 a firm Lewis supporter, pleaded with the president to order Searles to publish articles written by Mitch, the Indiana official got nowhere. Lewis referred him back to Searles, and the editor announced that *Journal* policy foreclosed its use

> for the purpose of promoting or propagating political or socialistic doctrines for any political party or organization, nor can they be used for the purpose of denouncing or attacking any action or activity of the Government except in cases where such action or activity appears to be detrimental to the welfare of the United Mine Workers of America. . . . The Journal is published for trade union purposes, and not as a political forum.

A frustrated Mitch simply let the whole matter drop.[20] Considering Mitch's treatment in the matter, one can surmise how Searles treated Lewis's declared rivals and critics and why union insurgents found it so difficult to maintain contact with the rank and file.

In some instances power inadvertently fell into Lewis's lap. Ironically, during the 1920s union failures enhanced Lewis's authority. Union stability insured district vitality; and prosperous, successful districts zealously guarded their autonomy against international incursions. When union districts declined, whether because of internal factionalism, incompetent officials, or employer resistance, their autonomy vanished. District 17, in West Virginia, for example, never recovered from the "civil war" of 1921, the ensuing arrests and indictments of its leaders, and the various legal suits in which it was entangled. By 1924, district officials faced financial ruin as creditors demanded payment on loans extended to the West Virginia organization. Unable to pay their debts or even meet current operating expenses, President Frank Keeney, Secretary-Treasurer Fred Mooney, and all the other West Virginia union officials, in mid-June 1924, filed an appeal asking the international executive board to assume the administration of District 17. Effective June 16, Lewis suspended the autonomy of District 17, appointed Percy Tetlow its new president, and assigned Van Bittner to administer the unionized northern half of the district.[21] The previous summer, the Nova Scotia Canada district had lost its autonomy as a consequence of political divisions within the district between Communists and anti-Communists.[22] Before the decade ended, other outlying union districts would lose their autonomy, or whatever had remained of it, as Lewis's direct control of UMW affairs would widen immeasurably.

The years 1923-1924, however, were not without frustrations for Lewis. As an anonymous union poet wrote of his president in April 1923:

> Troubles the test of you
> Seeking the best of you
> A hard man to deal with
> but when
> The battle is done
> And the struggle is won
> You'll find he's the maker
> Of men.[23]

Most of Lewis's problems flowed from the economics of the coal industry and his negotiations with operators. His ability to influence the economics of coal mining and the attitude of employers was far less than his authority to control the UMW. Soft-coal mining remained an economically prostrate industry throughout the prosperity decade. And hard-coal, or anthracite, mining, the one stable element in the industry, carried its own burdens for Lewis and his union.

The economics of anthracite differed from that of bituminous. A handful of companies controlled by coal-carrying railroads dominated hard coal—an industry limited geographically to three counties in northeastern Pennsylvania. Not only did competition among operators scarcely exist; the market for anthracite was far more stable than that for bituminous. Hard coal, unlike soft coal, was used primarily for domestic purposes, heating homes in the Northeast. Consequently, the demand for anthracite fluctuated more in relation to the thermometer than to the barometer of industrial activity, as did bituminous. Anthracite had its own problems. By the 1920s its era of growth terminated as new homes increasingly used natural gas and fuel oil for domestic heat. Furthermore, rises in the market price for hard coal threatened to induce more homeowners to invest in transforming coal-burning furnaces into ones that consumed gas or oil.

On the surface, anthracite was the one secure element in the UMW situation. Almost all the miners were union members, some 155,000 in all, and scarcely any nonunion hard coal entered the market. As union membership slipped elsewhere, hard-coal miners became an increasingly large proportion of UMW membership. They also formed a solid bloc of voting support for Lewis at UMW conventions; and, not infrequently, the votes from the three anthracite districts (numbers 1, 7, and 9) provided the UMW administration with its margin of victory. Lewis thus could scarcely neglect the interests of anthracite miners; nor could he leave them insecure and less well paid than soft-coal miners.

General labor peace had prevailed in the anthracite region since the strike of 1902 and the award of President Theodore Roosevelt's Anthracite Strike Commission until the summer of 1922, when the hard-coal miners struck for five months. In 1923 conditions remained much as they had been ever since the basic settlement of 1902, for the 1922 strike had been ended on the basis of the status quo antebellum leaving its causes unresolved. In anthracite, unlike bituminous, the union lacked both closed-shop contracts and the dues checkoff. Wage rates varied considerably even among union miners, and dayworkers earned from $4.20 to $5.60 daily compared to the $7.50 minimum in unionized soft coal.[24]

In 1923 anthracite operators still fought most of Lewis's demands. Higher wages implied increased prices for anthracite, a price Lewis felt consumers should pay, given the risks of coal mining, but one that operators were convinced would impel consumers to substitute gas or oil for coal. Unwilling to cut profits or lose customers, the operators balked at wage increases. They resisted the closed shop and the dues checkoff even more strongly. Although the operators customarily deducted the cost of mining equipment, house rentals, and company store purchases directly from the miners' regular paychecks, they refused to do the same for union dues, asserting that the checkoff infringed on the constitutional right of free contract. They also feared that to concede the closed shop and the checkoff in the anthracite mines would undermine the open-shop on the railroads, which they also operated. On the issue most important to union officials—union security—and the one most important to miners—higher wages—little room for compromise existed, and a hard-coal strike seemed likely when the 1922 agreement expired on September 1, 1923.[25]

An autumn hard-coal strike posed inescapable political ramifications. Unless householders in the Northeast could obtain coal before Election Day in November, they might vote against incumbent Republicans. Consequently, the Coolidge administration and the various state governments in the northeastern anthracite-consuming states sought to pressure the operators and the union into agreement, with Coolidge and Governor Gifford Pinchot of Pennsylvania assuming the lead. Coolidge requested the United States Coal Commission to speed its investigations of the industry and come up with a settlement satisfactory to operators and miners; Pinchot urged the operators to raise wages and provide union security through a voluntary dues checkoff.[26]

Negotiations between Lewis and the operators dragged on through July and August 1923 without success. When federal officials suggested arbitration of the issues in dispute, a procedure acceptable to the employers, Lewis observed that "arbitration . . . gave too much power to one man, and the history of such arbitrations showed that they usually resulted in a compromise not based on justice and equity, but on the line of least resistance." Lewis also rejected federal objections to his insistence that operators hire only union members. To government agents who asserted that the closed shop would create a monopoly in violation of the antitrust laws, Lewis responded that the union was incapable of achieving an actual monopoly of labor and that "if a monopoly in fact there was no objection to it because it was not unlawful. He said that lawyers must be members of the bar and that the legal profession was just as much a monopoly as the occupation of a miner, should a requirement be made that all miners must be members of the United Mine Workers."[27] On the last day of July, after a month of fruitless negotiations in Atlantic City, Lewis wrote to his friend K. C. Adams: "The anthracite wage negotiations are completely wrecked, but I still find myself able to sleep at night. In the event that the anthracite operators or the government officials . . . finally come to the conclusion that it is desirable to make a new agreement in . . . anthracite, they will find us willing to listen to anything they have to say."[28]

But during the month of August operators and public officials had nothing new to say or propose. New York City, where the negotiators moved, proved no more conducive to compromise than Atlantic City had been, although Lewis was privately more conciliatory than his public recalcitrance indicated. More concerned about union stability than about improving conditions for the miners, Lewis, before and during the 1923 negotiations, proposed that the operators sign a long-term contract (three or four years) maintaining current conditions. The operators, however, preferred not to bind themselves for an extended period, during which the market outlook for their product seemed bleak.[29] Yet the more rapidly fall and the November elections approached, the more eager public officials became to formulate a settlement, especially as the union issued orders to the anthracite miners to strike beginning September 1.

The UMW strike order precipitated a final frantic round of negotiations among union officials, operators, the United States Coal Commission, President Coolidge, and Governor Pinchot. The site of the bargaining moved from New York to Philadelphia and, finally, to Harrisburg, Pennsylvania. In his new style, Lewis left New York on August 27 with his wife, two children, brother George, personal secretary, and entire office staff to establish headquarters at the Bellevue-Stratford Hotel in Philadelphia. Falling victim to a cold, Lewis, ever concerned about his health, remained in his hotel room while Philip Murray represented the union in the bargaining conferences, at Pinchot's Harrisburg executive office, that brought a settlement.[30]

After a strike that lasted only five and a half days, Governor Pinchot, on September 7, announced the terms of his compromise settlement. The new two-year anthracite agreement included a 10% wage increase for day and tonnage miners; a voluntary system of dues checkoff in which union delegates, not management, collected the money; and the promise of only marginal increases in the retail price of anthracite.[31]

Although an apparent triumph for Lewis, the UMW, and the hard-coal miners, the 1923 agreement, in fact, left unresolved the primary causes of the short strike. Operators still rejected the closed shop; nor had they agreed to equalize wages; and despite the 10% wage increase, anthracite miners still earned less on an hourly basis than their brothers in bituminous or than other industrial laborers whose work was safer. Another strike, this time a longer and more costly one for the union and the miners, would have to be waged to resolve the outstanding grievances.

Meantime the crisis in soft coal, which first emerged during the depression of 1920-1921, had worsened rather than abated by 1923. More than ever it was now apparent that the bituminous industry alone could not solve the problem of too many miners in too many mines producing too much coal. Nonunion fields, moreover, continued to capture markets from the higher-cost unionized fields. Because wages represented almost 70% of the cost of coal production, union contracts that required high daily and tonnage rates placed organized mines at a competitive disadvantage compared to nonunion mines, which could adjust their wage levels to price fluctuations for coal. But even nonunion mines and nonunion miners suffered from the industry's surplus capacity. In one major nonunion West Virginia field, in November 1923, a month of high demand, over one-third of the mines were idle, and the others operated only two and a half to three days a week. By the end of March 1924, as the demand for coal diminished with the approach of warmer weather, over half the field's mines closed down, and the others ran only two days a week.[32] Despite high basic daily wages ($7.50) and tonnage rates ($1.08), union miners could scarcely sustain themselves and their families. Irregularity of employment reduced annual wages for northern bituminous miners down to the level of $750.00 to $1,500.00, yet the Bureau of Labor Statistics estimated an income of $2,500.00 as the minimum necessary to sustain a family of four at a basic health and decency level.[33]

Lewis saw no easy escape from the dilemma of bituminous coal. To continue current labor practices meant further competitive losses to nonunion operators, higher unemployment in the union fields, and a declining UMW membership. The alternative of bringing supply into closer accord with demand for coal also posed a threat to the union. Reduced supply could be achieved only by shutting down at least one-third of the operating mines—those considered to be marginal or high cost—and hence causing considerable unemployment among coal miners. Whichever alternative Lewis chose, the result would be a reduced membership for the UMW.

Lewis personally preferred a total reorganization of the soft-coal industry. He and his economic adviser, W. Jett Lauck, throughout the 1920s corresponded about and discussed privately their plans to stabilize the coal industry by consolidating production into fewer, more efficient units; restricting competition in marketing and pricing; and liberating the coal industry from the antitrust laws. The Lauck-Lewis program for coal proposed to reward employers who provided miners with steady work by requiring operators whose mines had irregular employment patterns to pay substantial financial penalties into an unemployment insurance fund. Theoretically, more efficient production by fewer and larger firms would enable operators to pay higher wages, offer steadier work, protect profit levels, and insure consumers against sharp price rises. Lewis's and Lauck's proposals to stabilize the coal industry required an active role by the federal government never before contemplated in peacetime. On the one hand, federal officials had to allow operators to divide markets and fix prices, in violation of antitrust legislation; on the other hand, the federal government had to act positively to protect union operators from nonunion competitors and use its power to protect the UMW in the nonunion fields.[34]

Some operators in the northern fields favored Lewis's program for soft coal, and almost all northern operators desired protection against Appalachian nonunion competitors. As one central Pennsylvania operator wrote to Lewis in July 1923: "Many operators—both 'outlaws' [nonunion] and inlaws—are wishing more power to your union."[35] But no prominent federal officials, among whom the most significant was Herbert Hoover, desired to implement the UMW program, for it implied far too much government regulation of a private enterprise. Hoover, like Lewis, wanted to stabilize the bituminous coal industry, encourage economic consolidation, stimulate efficiency, and reduce competition; but the commerce secretary also wanted to restrain union power by protecting the nonunion mines.[36]

Aware that the UMW lacked the strength in 1923 to endure another national coal strike and that such a conflict would likely destroy both the UMW and the unionized operators, Lewis worked behind the scenes with friends in industry and government to avert a walkout.[37] Two Pennsylvania operators—F. E. Herriman, president of the Clearfield Bituminous Coal Corporation, a New York Central Railroad subsidiary; and Rembrandt Peale, chairman of President Wilson's Bituminous Coal Commission—acted in December 1923 as private intermediaries for Lewis in discussions with northern operators about a new contract with the union. Herriman reported to Lewis that operators of a "substantial tonnage" were in accord with their ideas and opinions, and Lewis, in turn, thanked Herriman for the "efficient manner in which you are handling the subject."[38] That same month Lewis met Herbert Hoover, two prominent New York City financiers, and chief Associated Press correspondent Melville Stone at a private dinner arranged by George G. Moore, a utilities and coal capitalist, in the latter's suite at the Ambassador Hotel in New York. For two hours Lewis and Hoover discussed the economics of soft coal and the best way to avert a strike in 1924. Both men agreed that only a protracted period of industrial peace could save the soft-coal industry from economic ruin by offering the larger, more efficient operators a chance to drive marginal competitors out of business.[39]

In the final weeks of December 1923 and throughout January 1924, Lewis and Hoover worked feverishly to arrange a new agreement between coal operators and the union. Lewis cultivated his supporters among the employers and also won union endorsement for his aims; Hoover urged recalcitrant western Pennsylvania operators, especially those associated with the industrial empire of his cabinet colleague Andrew Mellon, to bargain with the UMW.

As the conference in Jacksonville, Florida—which had been provided for in the January 1923 agreement—approached in February 1924, Lewis's and Hoover's industrial diplomacy appeared successful. On February 4, Lewis reported to the commerce secretary that at the recently adjourned UMW convention, despite being "somewhat hampered by the ultra-radical influence which hovered around the . . . convention [we put through our program] without amendment of any character." What the convention in fact did was to authorize Lewis "to secure the best agreement obtainable from the operators in the Central Competitive Field on the basis of no reduction in wages" for a four-year period (April 1, 1924, to March 31, 1928), said agreement to be subject to membership ratification. Hoover did his part, obtaining commitments from western Pennsylvania operators to join the bargaining in Jacksonville.[40] And on the eve of the Jacksonville conference, the *Financial World* of New York observed: "Capital can doff its hat to him [Lewis] in admiration and deep in its heart wish there were more like him, for it is the kind of leadership based upon the mutuality of understanding. Lewis is capable of appreciating there must be an amicable partnership between capital and labor to secure the maximum advantage for each of them."[41]

Jacksonville worked out precisely as Hoover and Lewis had planned. A week after the conference opened on February 19, operators and union negotiators reached agreement on a new three-year contract that preserved existing terms, provisions, and conditions. That same day the UMW's International Policy

Committee approved the agreement and recommended that it be applied to all the outlying union districts.[42] And the next day Hoover advised President Coolidge to compliment Michael Gallagher, chairman of the coal operators' committee, and John L. Lewis for carrying through "the undertakings that each of them made with me [Hoover] in December last" and for maintaining constructive peace in the industry. On February 20, the commerce secretary also informed Lewis that "I believe you have worked out one of the most statesmanlike labor settlements in many years." To which President Coolidge added a week later that Lewis had taken "a long step toward the establishment of permanently better understanding between employers and employees." Lewis, in return, thanked federal officials for their substantial assistance in arranging a satisfactory settlement.[43]

Publicly, thereafter, Lewis and Hoover seemed to form a mutual admiration society. The union leader echoed the federal official's political philosophy. "I am not one," proclaimed Lewis, "who believe[s] that enactment of arbitrary legislation will prove to be a panacea for every maladministration of industry or that economic law can be set aside by the sweep of a legislative pen." Referring specifically to the coal industry, Lewis added: "We must give economic laws free play. . . . It is the survival of the fittest. Many are going to be hurt, but the rule must be the greatest good for the greatest number." In gratitude for such statements, Hoover voiced his opinion that "Mr. Lewis is more than a successful battle leader. He has a sound conception of statesmanship of long-view interest to the people and the industry he serves."[44]

Privately, however, Lewis and Hoover failed to agree in March and April 1924 concerning the commerce secretary's more detailed plans for economic stabilization of bituminous coal mining. Despite Lewis's paeans to private enterprise, the free market, and the law of supply and demand, he realized that the UMW could survive only through federal regulation of the coal industry. Hoover, on the contrary, preferred government to stimulate private enterprise, not control it.[45] Soon the two leaders would be in open conflict over the meaning and implementation of the Jacksonville Agreement. But in the spring of 1924 the future of bituminous coal appeared sufficiently secure for the Commerce Department to observe in its annual report: "The coal industry is now on the road to stabilization. . . . The gradual elimination of high-cost, fly-by-night mines is bringing about a greater degree of concentration of labor upon a smaller number of mines, the increase in days of employment per annum, and thus a larger annual return to the workers."[46]

By the summer of 1924, Lewis's power in the UMW and his influence outside had peaked. When nominations came due in August for election to international union office, not a single challenger for the presidency emerged; not even Alex Howat dared challenge Lewis. Yet secure as Lewis's position seemed, he still evinced signs of paranoia. "My leisure moments have been very few of late as is usually the case," he apologized to K. C. Adams, "my friends always suffer in order that I can devote myself to the affairs of the organization and give some attention to my several enemies."[47]

Politically, Lewis acted as the nation's most successful and eminent labor Republican. In April, Jacob Harriman laid before President Coolidge John L. Lewis's claim to the Republican vice-presidential nomination. During the summer Republican officials appointed Lewis a member of the Advisory Committee of the Republican National Committee, and Lewis privately and publicly endorsed the incumbent President, largely because, as he wrote to K. C. Adams, "I judge that President Coolidge will be re-elected."[48] After Coolidge's reelection a prominent mine operator, speaking for himself and several bankers and steelmen associated with the Mellon interests, asked Lewis if he would be interested in becoming secretary of labor. And delegates to the 1924 A. F. of L. convention endorsed Lewis for the secretaryship. But the UMW president played coy, discouraging an open interest in the cabinet office.[49] Lewis's coyness probably flowed from his realization that he lacked effective influence with the Coolidge administration.

For Lewis's political influence was more apparent than real. Nothing illustrated his marginal role in the Republican party better than the elevation of A. B. Anderson from the district bench in Indiana to the United States Circuit Court of Appeals. This was the same Judge Anderson who had handed down the notorious injunction against the UMW in the 1919 coal strike and similar injunctions against union organizing in West Virginia. A promotion for Anderson was certainly not to Lewis's liking, and he intervened with the Coolidge administration to stop the appointment. Too wise to argue personal grievances, Lewis suggested political expediency, implying that the promotion of Anderson might harm Coolidge in the 1924 Indiana primary and general elections. Senior Senator James Watson of Indiana, however, advised the president to discount Lewis's objections. "I do not share the alarm expressed by Lewis," wrote Watson, "because in the first place seventy percent of the miners in my state are Socialists and Democrats, and the others vote the Republican ticket all the while. This has been so for years and will be so this fall." Lewis's objections to Anderson thus proved unavailing, though the president, for expedient political reasons, postponed appointing the Indiana judge to the court of appeals until after the national election.[50]

If Lewis had limited political influence, his standing among some coal operators remained remarkably high. Several of the union operators in the fall of 1924 considered establishing a powerful new owners' association, with Lewis as its chief executive officer. One operator, who originally broached the suggestion to Lewis at Jacksonville in February 1924, still felt in November that Lewis would be the ideal man to head an operators' association. On November 18, 1924, Joseph Pursglove, a Cleveland operator, asked Lewis directly if he would accept such a position. "I do not think it appropriate," replied Lewis on November 27, "that I should have anything to do with the formation of a coal operators' association and naturally am not open to suggestions for employment by such an organization."[51]

As the year 1924 ended, Lewis was about to win his final major trade union triumph of the 1920s. Shortly after the A. F. of L. convention adjourned in late November 1924, the aging Samuel Gompers took seriously ill. On December 3, the A. F. of L. president died, and with him ended an era in American labor history. With the A. F. of L. presidency now apparently more readily within his grasp than it had been in 1921, Lewis instead urged William Green's claim to the position. Why? To begin with, Lewis probably realized that the most influential members of the A. F. of L. executive council, as imperious in their behavior as he was, preferred not to have another strong executive succeed Gompers. A steady poker partner of Dan Tobin and Bill Hutcheson, two of the three most influential A. F. of L. members, Lewis obviously knew that they would not tolerate him as their putative superior in the labor movement. And all the members of the executive council apparently shared the estimate of Lewis held by Gompers's longtime personal secretary, Florence Thorne: "Lewis was impatient with differences of opinion, and he wanted to tell people what to do rather than argue it out with them."[52]

Green, however, appeared a perfect candidate. Already a member of the executive council, he represented the nation's largest trade union. Where Lewis was imperious in his relations with others, Green was deferential; where Lewis ignored the opinions of others, Green always preferred to compromise rather than carry his own position.

Green's triumph also served Lewis's aims in two important respects. First, it removed a troublesome official presence from the UMW. Alone among international officials in the years 1919-1924, Green had challenged Lewis's interpretations of the union constitution and his administrative practices. Second, Lewis assumed that Green would simply act as a surrogate president of the A. F. of L. Despite their past differences concerning UMW policy, Green, in the end, had always deferred to Lewis, and Lewis saw no reason why such a relationship should not persist. An entrepreneur friend of Lewis's once referred to Green and Murray as Lewis's "pair of canaries."[53] Just as rumors had circulated in 1919 and afterward that Lewis had used a sexual scandal involving Green to remove the latter as a challenger for the UMW presidency, stories passed among A. F. of L. executive council members that sexual improprieties by their new president placed him in Lewis's power.[54] Whatever the truth of the matter, there is little doubt that Lewis expected Green to be his man and that until the dramatic break between Lewis and the A. F. of L. in the years 1935-1937, Green did indeed serve the interests of the UMW president.

With Green rising to the A. F. of L. presidency, Lewis could appoint his own secretary-treasurer, and he chose Thomas Kennedy, of District 7 in Pennsylvania, whose appointment solidified Lewis's strength in the anthracite districts.*[55] For

---

*Kennedy was the first man from the anthracite region ever to serve as an international executive officer.

the next seventeen years, until Lewis and Murray split in 1941, Lewis, Murray, and Kennedy formed the unshakable triumvirate that dominated the United Mine Workers. And when Lewis finally retired as union president in 1960, Kennedy succeeded him.

As 1924 ended, then, John L. Lewis stood on the top of the trade union world. He and his handpicked associates ruled the United Mine Workers, and a Lewis man headed the A. F. of L. In fact, the final results of the 1924 UMW election gave Lewis a more than two-to-one victory over an obscure left-wing opponent, George Voyzey.*[56] The Jacksonville agreement of February 1924 seemingly protected the UMW in its northern strongholds for a three-year period and maintained high wage levels for union miners. His standing with the Coolidge administration, just returned to office by a landslide margin of victory, was unsurpassed among trade unionists. Herbert Hoover, the strong man of the cabinet, served, so Lewis thought, as a transmission belt for the UMW president's ideas. Financial journals, bankers, and many northern coal operators praised Lewis as a labor statesman—the one American labor leader who grasped the reciprocal relationship between capital and labor and who devoted himself to harmonious labor relations. So prominent a public figure had Lewis become that the citizens of Lucas County, Iowa, invited their most famous native son home in the summer of 1924 to join them in a gala celebration in the county seat of Chariton on John L. Lewis Day.[57]

---

*Critics of Lewis suggest that the one-third of the total vote credited to the unknown Voyzey indicated the depty of resentment that rank-and-file miners felt toward their leader. It also revealed the persistence of radicalism within the UMW.

CHAPTER 6

Union Tyrant:
Mastering the Opposition,
1921-1927

The United Mine Workers, like most American trade unions, had originated as a confederation of autonomous local and regional organizations. For most of the UMW's first three decades, 1890-1920, the union had functioned as a decentralized institution in which effective administrative authority existed at the district level. However much international officials, the president included, dominated the process of collective bargaining, they nevertheless were as much the servants as the masters of district officials. The most powerful district presidents chaired the union's major policy committees and established the bargaining parameters within which the president negotiated with employers. Moreover, electoral coalitions among the largest northern districts determined the fate of international officers, which is why in the UMW, as in most American trade unions before World War I, the president lacked secure power. Even John L. Lewis, during his first two years in office, maintained his authority by the barest majority.

If Lewis inherited a decentralized union structure, he grappled with a complex national economy. Not only did the largest coal companies operate mines in several union districts; improved means of transportation, as noted in previous chapters, widened the scope of competition for markets among producers. More than ever before, nonunion coal competed with union coal and wage bargains struck in the Central Competitive Field affected the outlying districts. The slightest alteration in working practices or conditions in one district threatened the markets and profit margins of all other union districts. As long as district officials retained the authority to negotiate about working conditions not covered by the CCF agreement, neither unionized operators nor international officials could relax. If Illinois District 12 officials, for example, authorized the introduction of labor-saving machinery or of more intensive work practices, operators in that district might capture markets from Indiana, Ohio, and western Pennsylvania producers and, consequently, weaken the UMW in those contiguous regions.

The dialectical relationship between a decentralized union and a national economy created inherent ironies. When the autonomous districts flourished, as did District 12 from 1910 to 1930, the power of the international union over its members proved diluted. International, or presidential, authority waxed only insofar as district power waned. But the districts would only relinquish or diminish their autonomy if faced with financial or structural ruin. In other words, the power of the international and of John L. Lewis expanded as the districts lost members, income, and power. Ironically, then, Lewis achieved undiluted authority to negotiate binding national agreements with employers only as the number of union members he represented declined at a rapidly accelerating rate. Put simply, Lewis's personal power in the UMW during the 1920s rose in proportion to the decline in his union's actual strength and influence. That for John L. Lewis was the cruelest of ironies: to struggle so hard and so ruthlessly for union power, only to clutch the shattered shell of a labor organization.

Lewis approached internal organizational problems in much the same opportunistic manner as he dealt with the union's external relationships. Personal alliances were broken as easily as they were formed. The antired hysteria that won for Lewis the plaudits of businessmen and Republican politicians could also be used—and effectively, at that—to tarnish the luster of union opponents. Less principled rivals could be captured with the lure of an international sinecure; unintelligent or politically clumsy opponents could be ridiculed and led to destroy themselves; the principled and the adroit could be ruthlessly purged and even physically abused. Because Lewis's internal rivals were more divided among themselves than his external "opponents" in business and politics, he functioned more ruthlessly within the union than outside, and his sheer opportunism combined with political cunning produced success rather than failure.

Lewis had been president of the UMW less than a year when his opponents formed an anti-Lewis coalition. Elected president in December 1920, Lewis would preside over his first convention in September 1921, the initial opportunity for his rivals to challenge Lewis's authority in the UMW. It was an opportunity, moreover, eagerly awaited by his challengers, among whom the most notable and influential were Frank Farrington and John Walker of District 12 (Illinois) and Alex Howat of District 14 (Kansas). Walker personified the union's old guard socialists, men of high principle and rectitude. Howat, at his best, exemplified the militancy, flavor, and courage of rank-and-file miners. Farrington, in contrast, copied Lewis's opportunistic and entrepreneurial style of union leadership; the District 12 president allied himself to Illinois Republicans, nestled up to the coal operators, and simply envied Lewis's place in the union. United solely by their hostility to Lewis, whatever its motivation, these men in 1921 represented powerful tendencies in the UMW.

As early as March 1921 Howat schemed both to end Farrington's control of District 12 and Lewis's authority in the international. Allying with the old socialist UMW faction, Howat claimed to represent the rank and file against the autocratic Farrington and Lewis. So bitter was his enmity to Lewis that Howat even considered forming a rival miners' union if he lost his fight to defeat the president at the 1921 UMW convention.[1]

While Howat plotted to unseat Farrington and Lewis, the latter two trade unionists carried on their own personal war. For a brief time in 1919 and 1920 Lewis and Farrington had been allied, as the UMW's then acting president sustained the District 12 president in the latter's struggle against insurgent Illinois miners. By early 1921, however, the terms of battle had been reversed, as Lewis now supported Illinois insurgents who accused Farrington of misspending $27,000 in district funds. Farrington's alleged misappropriation of union funds resulted in a correspondence with Lewis that—had it not been so serious—would have been laughable. "It was with rare pleasure," Lewis informed Farrington on February 25, 1921, that he had read the Illinois official's letter, which fairly scintillated with wit and humor and which "would justify one designating it as a literary gem. There are, of course, some rude individuals who have no appreciation of the poetry of literature who would probably designate your effort as being of a ponderous and labored nature. Far be it from me, however, to nip budding genius in the bud by any such depressing observations." In a more serious vein, Lewis referred to the main item of contention, Farrington's failure to itemize $27,000 in union expenditures, and observed: "I have a fairly accurate memory for such things and might even surprise you if I took time to chronicle some of the things which I have not forgotten. For instance, I never forget a friend and I find it equally as difficult to forget a foe."

Not to be outdone in rhetorical venom, Farrington replied on March 8: "My dear President, I trust you will not take offense because I state that your letter is worthy of a vainglorious egotistical ass. . . . I am constrained to believe that of late you must be reading 'Deadwood Dick' 'Ruthless Robin' or something of that kind, instead of devoting your time to a study of the problems of the struggling masses." In response, Lewis took a blue pencil and wrote across the face of the letter, "Yapping, Bombast & Drivel," signed it Lewis, and returned it to Farrington.[2]

Lewis derived great pleasure from the Byzantine nature of UMW politics. While Farrington, Howat, and Walker, among others, opposed him, Lewis watched them battle among themselves in Illinois and intensified the District 12 struggle by issuing rulings that aided the Illinois insurgents. Lewis also used the splits among his rivals to attack them before they struck him. And he selected the clumsiest of his foes—Howat—to eliminate first.

For several reasons Howat appeared the most vulnerable of Lewis's rivals. First, he led a smaller, weaker UMW district, one that had fewer than 12,000 members and depended on support from the international and bargaining gains won in the Central Competitive Field negotiations. Second, Howat had few sympathizers, if any, among the coal operators and numerous enemies among Kansas and federal government officials. Third, few of Howat's allies in the UMW trusted him, partly because of his weakness for alcohol and partly because he tended to act before he thought.

Howat's battles with operators, public officials, and John L. Lewis were of long standing. During the 1919 coal strike Howat had been the one district president who declined to respect Lewis's agreement with President Wilson and who, in the event, served time in prison.* His bumptious behavior in Kansas, especially his endorsement of wildcat miners' strikes frequently in violation of contract, led Howat into persistent conflict with operators, Kansas public officials, and Lewis. So common were miners' walkouts in Kansas that the state, during the postwar wave of antiradical hysteria, passed an industrial court law that effectively outlawed strikes and mandated compulsory arbitration of labor disputes—a policy that was an anathema to the entire American labor movement, Lewis included.

Despite the Kansas law that banned strikes and a 1920 contract between District 14 and the Southwestern Coal Operators' Association that the UMW guaranteed, Howat, as district president, endorsed local strikes in violation of state law and sometimes union contract. This meant that District 14 was constantly involved in litigation in Kansas courts and that Kansas operators regularly threatened to sue the UMW for not compelling Howat to implement contract terms. Howat, moreover, proved unable to distinguish between strikes for good cause and those without reason, between walkouts banned by a law that the UMW challenged in court and those forbidden by a labor contract that the UMW pledged to enforce. Whatever the reason for a local strike, Howat posed as the defender of the rank and file and, if need be, as an imprisoned martyr to its cause. He transformed all disputes between miners and operators into a clash between the union and the unjust Kansas industrial court law, between freedom and tyranny. Lewis, on the contrary, distinguished between strikes banned by law and by contract, and he used that distinction to destroy Howat and to seize control of District 14.[3]

One clause in the contract between UMW District 14 and the Southwestern Coal Operators' Association forbid all strikes until the issues in dispute had been adjudicated by a joint union-management committee. Only if that joint committee failed to resolve the issues could a strike be declared with international union sanction. Despite that clause, Howat had endorsed strikes at two small Kansas

*See Chapter 3, pp. 59-61.

strip mines, which together employed fewer than forty miners, that occurred in violation of the contract. The operators of the Dean and the Reliance mines had altered work rules without previous union approval; but, instead of taking an apparently justified grievance to a joint committee for resolution, the miners had walked off the job with Howat's sanction. Their strike violated a union contract, and, incidentally, a state law.

Lewis promptly took advantage of Howat's tactical blunder. At the mid-August 1921 UMW international executive board session, Lewis called Howat to testify about the Kansas mine disputes. Rumors immediately surfaced in the press that Howat faced suspension and that the IEB planned to assume control of the Kansas district. Speaking for Lewis, William Green denied publicly that the executive board had considered Howat's suspension.[4] The following month, however, at the 1921 UMW convention in Indianapolis, Lewis gave the lie to Green's public denial.

The 1921 UMW convention constituted the first significant challenge to Lewis's tenure as union president. For two weeks, from September 20 to October 5, 1921, over 2,000 delegates debated Lewis's internal union policies and struggled for mastery within the UMW. As delegates argued about the relative authority of district versus international officials, about the sanctity of contract versus the rights of working miners, debate turned angry, words spilled over into physical force, and violence loomed. So bitter and tumultuous did the convention become in its closing moments that Lewis warned the delegates that "when this convention passes upon a proposition by majority vote, then all men will understand that that will be the will of this organization, and the fact that some delegate may arise in the aisle and beat his breast like a tom-tom in the wilds of Africa will not change that decision. I don't want any more brave and bold delegates to come charging down this aisle." In what by then had become his typical mode of argument, Lewis requested the delegates to proceed dispassionately and to remember that each roll call vote cost the union $40,000 or more.[5]

The tempestuous behavior of delegates to the 1921 convention flowed from the strength of Lewis's opponents and the importance of the issues debated. The year 1921 witnessed the consummation of a working alliance among Howat, Farrington, Walker, and Robert Harlin. Had they been able to add John Brophy and William Mitch to their coalition, they might well have defeated Lewis on a climactic roll call vote that determined Howat's future. But Lewis proved sufficiently adept in September 1921 to curry favor among Brophy, Mitch, and other UMW left-wingers by satisfying their desire for nationalization of the coal mines.* Lewis also proved an expert at framing the convention debate in terms that buttressed his own position.

Lewis first tangled with Frank Farrington. The District 12 president, raising the standard of "district autonomy" to defend his unaccounted expenditure of

*See Chapter 4, pp. 90-92.

$27,000, argued that districts should be free to operate as they pleased and that ever since the birth of the UMW "districts have jealously, religiously and consistently insisted upon the right of self-government." Lewis's demand that District 12 account for its expenditures was, Farrington asserted, "a flagrant, arbitrary, arrogant invasion of district autonomy."[6] To this line of argument, Lewis had a ready riposte. Lecturing delegates that the United States had waged a costly war over the autonomous right of the separate states to enslave human beings, Lewis asked: "Is the United Mine Workers of America now going to be involved in a question of state's rights?" To allow districts to go their own way, suggested Lewis, would precipitate a process of union disintegration as subdistricts and then locals challenged superior authority on the basis of autonomy. Moreover, to carry the principle of autonomy to its logical conclusion would vitiate the trade union principle that an injury to one is the concern of all. United we stand, divided we fall, implored Lewis.[7]

Lewis realized that he commanded general delegate support against Farrington because few miners, radicals especially, sanctioned the manner in which Farrington administered District 12. If John L. Lewis, in 1921, was on his way to becoming a big-time union autocrat, Frank Farrington was already a practiced small-time dictator.

After defeating Farrington's challenge, Lewis turned to the more serious and divisive Howat-Kansas question. If Farrington matched Lewis in egotism, intrigue, and opportunism, Howat far surpassed both in appealing to rank-and-file delegates and coal miners. Where Lewis and Farrington ingratiated themselves with operators and politicians, Howat gloried in the role of class warrior, the man who would risk prison before selling out workers to their employers or public officials. Where Farrington used the principle of district autonomy to excuse misallocation of union funds, Howat spoke in favor of union solidarity and warned delegates that to surrender the rights and traditions of Kansas miners ultimately threatened the security of miners everywhere. Howat assured the convention that he had sanctioned the Dean and Reliance strikes, because employers had unilaterally altered work traditions, and unless the coal miners' prerogatives were defended in Kansas, operators would also change customs in Oklahoma, Illinois, Iowa, and other districts. Which policy was preferable, he asked the convention, Lewis's collaboration with operators or Howat's own defense of the coal miners' rights? Howat promised to fight to the last drop of his blood to compel the Kansas operators to respect coal miners' customs and prerogatives.[8]

Lewis refused to debate Howat about coal miners' customs or prerogatives. Instead he instructed delegates that the union protected its members best through the instrument of a binding contract with employers and that Howat's methods in Kansas violated the sanctity of contract. If Kansas tactics spread elsewhere, Lewis implied, operators would sign no contracts with the UMW, and miners would one day "have no pledges to conform to." The issue in Kansas, concluded Lewis, was not the conditions of employment, but "a question of honor and a question of whether you are going to meet your obligations or repudiate them.'' Unless miners met their obligations, he advised, the UMW had no future. On that note, and after four days of noisy, raucous debate, Lewis closed discussion on the Kansas affair and asked delegates to cast their votes for or against the executive board's decision to suspend Howat and the officers of District 14 for refusing to order striking miners back to work.[9]

The ensuing roll call vote disclosed how well Lewis had estimated his own strength. Delegates from only four out of twenty-seven union districts cast a majority of their votes against the suspension of Howat, and of the four districts, only Illinois 12 represented substantial size and influence. Lewis amassed over 60% (60.7% to be precise) of the delegate votes, a remarkable triumph when one considers the coalition formed by Howat, Farrington, Walker, and Harlin.[10]

Howat, to be sure, vowed to fight his suspension and the convention decision and, with the undivided support of Farrington's Illinois miners, never to surrender to Lewis. Lewis, on his part, wasted no time in acting, removing Howat and his fellow district leaders from office on October 12 and replacing them with personally appointed provisional officers under his own control. Thus did "provisionalism" win its first major victory in the UMW, as a doubly victimized Howat (he was imprisoned as well for violating the Kansas industrial court law) hurled his imprecations at Lewis, whom, he said, could "go to hell."[11] Much to Howat's satisfaction and Lewis's chagrin, however, the convention vote and the executive board action of October 12 aggravated rather than terminated the Kansas affair.

Howat's suspension once again stimulated Lewis's union rivals to build an antiadministration coalition. District 12 leaders immediately pledged Howat financial and moral support, and four of them visited the Kansan in prison.[12]

Van Bittner, whom Lewis had dispatched to Kansas to assume control of District 14, reported back in early November concerning the complicated local situation and how he was using every weapon at the international's disposal to adjust matters satisfactorily and see to it that "the influence of our friend, Howat and his regime has gone forever." Among the weapons at Bittner's disposal was the international payroll, which he used to employ Kansas miners who agreed to defend Lewis's action locally. Bittner also prevailed upon the presidents of the surrounding Oklahoma-Arkansas-Texas, Iowa, and Missouri districts to endorse the Lewis policy and to refuse to accept transfer cards from Kansas miners. (Unable to obtain transfer cards, Kansas miners would either have to return to the local pits or go jobless.) Two acts, however, Bittner rejected. First, he declined to use force to seize district headquarters from the Howat supporters who had refused to relinquish its possession; and second, he refused to go to court to obtain the same result.[13]

Howat found sympathizers outside the UMW as well as within. In what could only be termed a glaring rebuke to Lewis, Gompers and the A. F. of L. executive council sustained Howat's position in the intraunion dispute. In December 1921 Lewis and four other UMW delegates appeared before the A. F. of L. executive council to ask for its support in the struggle against Howat. Lewis assumed that Gompers would defend sanctity of contract and repudiate Howat's threat to establish a dual union, the worst sin in the American trade union decalogue. Much to Lewis's surprise, Gompers asserted that Howat deserved commendation for fighting an unjust Kansas law, one that mandated compulsory arbitration—a practice repudiated by the A. F. of L. It is hard to believe, despite what the A. F. of L.'s official historian, Philip Taft, writes, that Gompers and fellow council members were ignorant of the distinction between the walkouts in violation of union contract that caused Howat's suspension and strikes directed against the industrial court law. It is more likely, Taft's disclaimers notwithstanding, that the Kansas controversy provided Gompers with an opportunity to rebuke Lewis for his disloyalty at the June 1921 A. F. of L. convention.[14] Whatever the real reason for the A. F. of L.'s decision, and personal pique seems a more likely explanation than trade union principles, Howat received aid from an unexpected source, assistance that he wasted through further foolish actions.

In a step in violation of a specific clause in the UMW constitution, Howat went to court seeking an injunction to restrain Lewis from suspending District 14 officials. Foreclosed by law from judicial relief in Kansas, Howat took his case to a Missouri circuit court where, on January 14, 1922, the judge ruled that because Howat had violated both union law and a legal contract with coal operators, the international executive board had been justified in suspending him from office. "No man or set of men," declared the Missouri judge, "can violate and defy the Kansas laws and at the same time get relief from the courts of equity of a sister state."[15]

Frustrated in court, Howat again appealed to the UMW rank and file. The union constitution provided an administrative appeals process that Howat ignored because of Lewis's domination of the UMW hierarchy. Instead he intended to carry his grievance directly to the membership when the union met again in special convention in February 1922. Howat believed, with good reason, that at the reconvened convention additional district leaders and delegates would vote in his favor. Clearly, if Lewis's suspension of Howat went unrepudiated, then other district presidents might in the future be vulnerable to similar autocratic punishment. That, at least, was how Howat assumed other district officials would interpret Lewis's action; and, in the event, he was not far from wrong.

When the UMW delegates reconvened in Indianapolis on February 14, 1922, they found themselves once again confronted with the Lewis-Howat conflict instead of the impending struggle between miners and operators. A convention called solely to discuss collective bargaining and strike plans spent almost all its time debating the Kansas controversy.

In the interim between October 1921, when the original convention had adjourned, and February, when it reconvened, Howat had gathered substantial additional delegate support, so much so that Lewis allowed Howat to address the convention although the Kansas insurgent lacked convention credentials. In his speech to the delegates, Howat acted the militant. He explained that the Kansas difficulties arose from his stouthearted opposition to an unjust state labor law that imposed tyranny on coal miners, and that he considered "it an honor to be condemned and vilified by the corporation press of this country." Unless the delegates endorsed his appeal, Howat warned, "in time to come this is going to be a one-man organization."[16]

Lewis, too, proved true to tradition in defending himself against Howat's charges. If Howat proved his courage by fighting capitalist employers and politicians, Lewis demonstrated his own fearlessness against dangerous enemies. "Day by day, mail after mail," he intoned dramatically, "I have been receiving letters telling me that if I presumed to preside over this convention, telling me that unless I resigned as President of the United Mine Workers it had been decreed in secret conclave I would die." Against this "organized plot of terrorism," Lewis swore that he would stand fast. Having proclaimed his own courage, Lewis appealed to the delegates' sense of solidarity and union loyalty. On the eve of an impending conflict with employers, Lewis warned, the union "army is now asked to halt and wash out its dirty linen. To stay the advance, to stay the preparation while the generals of the army undertake to demonstrate to their forces as to who is the greatest scoundrel. What a sight under these circumstances! . . . Are you going to stop now," he asked, "and become embroiled in a controversy that will only serve to expose your weaknesses to your foes?"[17]

Lewis's plea to the delegates for solidarity went unanswered. For five days they indeed proceeded to wash their dirty linen in public, to shout, and to slug each other. Allan Haywood, then an anti-Lewis delegate from Illinois, at one point charged the press table, cursed, and threatened reporters. Howat's disputed Kansas delegation raced up and down the aisles creating a tumult as it instigated other delegates to heckle Lewis and Vice-President Murray.[18]

Such bedlam led the octogenarian Mother Jones, an honorary delegate, to plead for harmony. Beseeching the delegates to do the impossible, she implored them to "muzzle up now" and support the officers that they had elected but also to honor Howat, the type of man the nation needed "to fight the battles of the workers." Recalling the legacy of another Kansas rebel, John Brown, Mother Jones proclaimed that "in the years to come there will be another monument built to the memory of a man from Kansas, and that will be built to the memory of Alex Howat."[19]

Whether Mother Jones' impassioned plea for harmony aided Howat or Lewis more was hard to tell from the results of the raucous roll call vote that followed. Balloting on the question of whether or not to reconsider the suspension of Howat, the UMW delegates divided right down the middle. Howat retained his voting strength in the Illinois delegation, by far the largest at the convention (it cast 952 votes for Howat, 25 for Lewis), and picked up support from John Brophy in District 2 and in the southwestern (Oklahoma-Arkansas-Texas) and western (Montana, Wyoming, and Washington) delegations. Lewis won his largest majorities in two of the anthracite districts, the declining southern Appalachian districts, and Kansas, whose official delegation he now controlled. Out of the 4,028 votes cast, Lewis secured a bare majority of 51.5% to his opponent's 48.5% Considering that many of the votes were cast by phantom Appalachian locals; Kansas delegates representing the international administration, not local miners; and delegates on the international payroll, one can perceive how tenuous was Lewis's control of the UMW in February 1922. A handful of votes cast the other way might have ended Lewis's power in the union; and had his opponents been united in a positive alliance rather than a negative coalition of convenience, they might indeed have won enough votes to handcuff Lewis.[20]

The closeness of the vote explains the bitterness that preceded it and the tumult that followed. Lewis, as customary in a time of crisis, withdrew into a shell. Instead of acting as convention chairman during the roll call or even casting his own delegate vote, he spent most of the decisive day at his office clearing away routine work. The vote itself failed to quiet the acrimony in union ranks, as the convention adjourned on February 18, in the words of one newspaper report, "amid wild disorder, with hundreds of delegates howling like madmen, bewailing the defeat of Alexander Howat." Howat, moreover, refused to accept defeat, vowing that "they can't keep me down . . . I am in the fight to a finish. John Lewis will never get away with this deal that he has handed me." To which Frank Farrington added: "Lewis is a dead bird now, and has come a cropper."[21]

Howat returned to Kansas to fight, and Farrington offered him the funds. But their struggle proved fruitless. Lewis simply waited on Howat's administrative incompetence. The funds from Illinois intended to subsidize strikers in Kansas only enriched Howat's cronies. Among the items purchased by his supporters in Kansas with Farrington's funds was an enormous amount of candy, causing Lewis "to wonder what they did with nearly 14 tons of candy."[22]

But a sweet tooth was the least of the Howat camp's problems. Lewis kept affairs in the Southwest tightly in his grip and again sent Van Bittner from western Pennsylvania to Kansas in order to quell the insurgent forces. As usual, international funds and patronage flowed to anti-Howat men in the southwestern coalfields. The more frustrated Howat became, the more he erred in his policies. Unable to regain electoral control of District 14, he actually established a dual organization, which in March 1923 enrolled strikebreakers during an authorized walkout. Such actions even alienated Howat sympathizers. The strange thing is, Van Bittner wrote to Phil Murray, "that if we had arranged this trap for Howat to fall into, we could not have done a neater job, as everybody realizes the fact that there is not much credit coming to a man who would organize a bunch of scabs and take them into a local union, and leave fifty men who are on strike out in the cold."[23] Howat's clumsiness notwithstanding, he remained a threat to Lewis's union power throughout the 1920s because he served the purposes of other influential Lewis rivals.

The year 1922 was not only the year that saw the resolution of the Howat-Kansas struggle and the combined bituminous-anthracite strike; it was also an election year for the UMW, and Lewis's foes were busy organizing their alliances and counteralliances. Farrington continued to engage in an acrimonious correspondence with Lewis and to lay various Byzantine political schemes. Pennsylvania insurgents, unhappy with the terms of the emerging 1922 bituminous settlement, planned to nominate an anti-Lewis ticket for union office. And Lewis proved that his own political flair exceeded that of his rivals.

Aside from Farrington, the central figures in the 1922 union election were Tom Stiles, an editor and publicist for District 2; Powers Hapgood, a young Harvard graduate, son of a socially prominent Indianapolis family, full-time coal miner, and leader of the nonunion Somerset County, Pennsylvania, strikes; and John Brophy, president of District 2. The three Pennsylvanians were united by radicalism, commitment to union democracy, and personal rectitude. Eager to build an anti-Lewis coalition, Hapgood and Stiles wired Brophy, who was in Cleveland for the 1922 negotiations with operators, for his advice. "International officers will have no opposition in coming election as it is impossible to defeat any of them," advised Brophy by return wire. "It is your duty to use every effort to cooperate with present international officials in the prosecution of this strike. It is no time for men to talk about naming a ticket." Only later did Hapgood and Stiles learn that their telegram to Brophy had been intercepted by a Lewis agent, who dispatched the return telegram signed Brophy. The Lewis tactic only reinforced Hapgood's determination to defeat the UMW president; but, unlike Lewis, who would shake hands with the devil if it served his purposes, the university-educated coal miner refused to ally with Farrington in a common anti-Lewis front.[24] Thus divided among themselves, Lewis enemies suffered an ignominious defeat in the union election.

Although opposition to Lewis inside the UMW intensified after the 1922 election, his rivals continued to slay each other. The rising dissatisfaction among coal miners with Lewis's union policies prompted William Z. Foster, a leader of the American Communist party and founder of the Trade Union Educational League, the party's labor arm, to seek support among UMW members. Committed to boring from within existing trade unions and antipathetic to all forms of dualism, Foster's TUEL sought to create "progressive" cells, or blocs, that would eventually capture control of "legitimate" unions. For Foster, the UMW seemed the most desirable of targets; it was not only, in 1923, still the nation's largest union, but it also had a tradition of rank-and-file militancy and political radicalism. Militants and radicals, moreover, chafed under the cautious but autocratic Lewis leadership. To seize on rank-and-file dissatisfaction with Lewis, Foster called a meeting of the Progressive International Conference of the United Mine Workers of America to convene in Pittsburgh on June 2 and 3, 1923.[25] Foster's venture into the arcane world of coal miners' politics, as we will see, inadvertently assisted John L. Lewis in the latter's struggle to achieve hegemony within the UMW.

For every anti-Lewis union leader Foster attracted, he repelled one. Of the UMW officials Foster vexed, none was angrier than Frank Farrington. A conservative by instinct and a Republican by choice, Farrington presided over the most radical of all the union districts. Customarily criticized by such socialists as Adolph Germer, John Walker, and Duncan MacDonald, Farrington now worried about Communist influence in Illinois. Consequently, he realized the impossibility of fighting Lewis and the Communists simultaneously, and he chose to make peace with the lesser of the evils: John L. Lewis. On May 21, 1923, Farrington informed Lewis that unless "real believers" in the UMW united, destructive elements will gain control and "the Red Flag will be our standard, or else demoralization and division in the ranks . . . will prevail."[26] Further correspondence in late May and personal conferences early in June produced a Lewis-Farrington coalition aimed against union radicals, all of whom were labeled Communists. Farrington kept a pleased Samuel Gompers informed of the new twist in internal coal miners' politics, and he culminated his coalition of conservatives on June 13, 1923, by repudiating his previous link with Howat, who had attended Foster's Pittsburgh conference.[27]

The Pittsburgh conference also split Lewis's Pennsylvania critics. Among the participants at the conference were Powers Hapgood and a second delegate from District 2, both of whom attended without the approval of district President Brophy. Although the Pittsburgh conferees had resolved to work within the UMW and to reject dual unionism, Brophy, like Lewis, distrusted all Communists and considered them, by definition, to be dual unionists.[28] He also suspected that Lewis would characterize all participants in the Pittsburgh conference as dual unionists, apply constitutional sanctions against them, and thus split and scatter progressive miners. That prospect combined with Brophy's utter weariness from six years of ceaseless intraunion strife motivated him to resign from District 2 leadership.[29]

Brophy proved a good prophet indeed, for on July 11, 1923, Lewis ordered him to discharge Hapgood and the other District 2 delegate in attendance at Pittsburgh from union office because they, along with all other participants in the progressive conference had "treacherously consort[ed] with the avowed enemies of our organization and participate[d] with them in their sinister and reprehensible activities."[30] Pessimism overwhelmed Brophy, who had decided as a member of the IEB to fight Lewis's expulsion of alleged "dual unionists" but who nevertheless believed that in a year or two Lewis would crush all Communists and radicals inside the UMW.[31]

Lewis revealed his intent to be unrelenting in his handling of union radicals in a letter to Adolph Germer written in August 1923. (Germer, then in California, had criticized Lewis for his hysterical red-baiting.) "To those of us who are still on the firing line and are compelled to daily endure the verbal bombardment of those in opposition to the legitimate aims of the United Mine Workers," wrote Lewis, "there is little time and less disposition to stop and quibble over the niceties of speech and the manifold variations of the English language."[32]

Lewis's opportunism enabled him to be more flexible and generous than his sometimes self-righteous and dedicated radical critics. In the same letter to Germer that Lewis filled with venom, he added the warmest personal and human touches, praising the motives of his critic and wishing "that the passing years . . . leave their mark upon you but lightly." He also offered the father of his bitter enemy Powers Hapgood a directorship of the bank in Indianapolis that Lewis headed, and hypocritically informed the senior Hapgood that his son should feel free to fight the UMW president, who "expects it and claims to desire it."[33]

Red-baiting Hapgood, Howat, and other UMW men who attended the Pittsburgh progressive conference temporarily left many of Lewis's rivals in a state of shock. But they recovered quickly and reorganized themselves to provide a substantial challenge to Lewis's union leadership at the January-February 1924 coal miners' convention. Behaving as opportunistically as their hated opponent, the insurgent miners formed an alliance of traditional UMW left-wingers, Communists, and anti-Lewis conservatives. Early in the convention this alliance won a majority voice vote repudiating Lewis's right to appoint union organizers and field officials. Whereas in the past insurgents customarily demanded roll call votes after suffering defeats in viva voce balloting, Lewis in 1924 resorted to the roll call device and caused a convention uproar when he announced that his power to appoint officials had been upheld by a vote of 2,236 to 2,106. For the next hour the insurgents kept the auditorium in an uproar as they whistled, stamped their feet, demanded a recount, raced up and down the aisles, and engaged in fistfights.[34]

The 1924 mine workers' convention ended as tumultuously as it had begun. Lewis adjourned the session on Saturday, February 2, amid wild disorder as rival factions struggled for physical possession of the platform. Defeated in yet another delegate vote, Alex Howat leaped to the stage only to be thrown off bodily; for the next fifteen minutes his supporters labored unsuccessfully to push Howat back up on the platform while Lewis men formed a solid wall of opposition. In a final gesture to demonstrate his authority in the union, Lewis called his wife to his side for an impromptu reception on the auditorium's stage.[35]

Lewis analyzed the 1924 convention's meaning with customary exaggeration. The United Mine Workers had been targeted for subversion, he asserted, by the "gray wolves of a pernicious philosophy. . . . Gathered here [Indianapolis] were Foster, Meyerscough, Howat, Dunne, Hamilton* and others of their ilk with

---

*Foster, Dunne, and Hamilton were prominent members of the American Communist party. Meyerscough was a Communist coal miner and was a delegate from western Pennsylvania.

ample funds at their disposal to carry out their preconceived plans for the destruction of the largest unit of American labor . . . it behooves our citizenship to recognize the menace of such sinister influences and to place the heel of their disapproval upon its serpent head.'' The delegates' heels had stamped out Howat, and with his destruction, implied Lewis, the forces of conservative trade unionism had vanquished destructive Communistic influences among mine workers.[36] Once again red-baiting proved Lewis's tactic for all seasons and all places.

Never again after 1924 would Lewis preside at a UMW convention during which a substantial number of delegates challenged his power. Other threats to Lewis's hegemony in the union would arise—and for many of the same reasons—but they would pose far less danger to his rule. Indeed, as we will see, each effort by insurgents to curtail Lewis's power resulted, ironically, in the expansion of the UMW president's authority. By 1930, Lewis would fashion a union whose constitution granted the chief executive autocratic power.

In the mid-1920s only one UMW district—No. 12 in Illinois—remained partially independent of Lewis. After Howat's defeat at the 1924 convention, the authority of the international union ran unchallenged throughout the Southwest. John Brophy's resignation as president of District 2 in 1923 led to his replacement by men much more susceptible to Lewis's influence. Frank Farrington, of Illinois, stood as the solitary obstacle to undiluted union power for John L. Lewis. If Frank Farrington could be made to disappear, reasoned Lewis, District 12 would become more amenable to international union discipline.

Farrington, however, could scarcely be red-baited or accused of promoting dual unionism. After all, he had allied with Lewis in 1923 to save the UMW from the "Reds," and no more conservative or business-oriented trade unionist existed anywhere in the American labor movement. Unable to use his customary ploys, Lewis resorted to even more devious tactics.

The precise mechanics of Lewis's plan to purge Farrington remain something of a mystery. Certain facts, however, may be inferred from the actual course of events. Like Lewis, Farrington enjoyed the good life—fine clothes, fast cars, ample food, and association with corporate executives—and needed the income to buy it. Like Lewis, he also desired union power, a prospect beyond his reach by 1925-1926. Unable to replace Lewis as UMW president, Farrington elected the good life. Before Lewis nearly every top UMW official had eventually entered the employ of the coal operators as a labor relations executive with a high salary. Farrington proved true to that old UMW tradition by signing a contract, in July 1926, with the largest coal operator in Illinois—Stuyvesant "Jack" Peabody, of the Peabody Coal Company—to serve as labor adviser for a three-year period beginning January 1, 1927, at an annual salary of $25,000 (three times Lewis's and five times his own union salary). The contract, signed on July 1, 1926, included a pledge from Farrington disclaiming all future office in District 12.

Under the terms of the then-secret contract, Farrington would have his money, Peabody under-the-table influence in District 12, and Lewis one less union rival.[37]

With the contract in his pocket and his future financially secure, Farrington left for a grand tour of Europe that included the French Riviera, most of Italy, Switzerland, Austria, Germany, Brussels, Paris, and London. While abroad, however, Farrington unexpectedly decided that he would take the money from Peabody and still serve as District 12 president. "The more I think of it," he wrote to "Jack" Peabody on August 1, "the more firmly I am convinced that I can do the operators more good by continuing as president of the Illinois miners and I wish you would not make known the fact that I have signed a contract to work for you until we can talk it over."[38]

Farrington's repudiation of his pledge to resign from union office led to a strange denouement for the Illinoisan. John L. Lewis, who had the most to lose from Farrington's change of mind, in late August made public the terms of the secret contract and demanded that Farrington either resign as president of District 12 or that the Illinois district executive board dismiss him from office. On August 30 Farrington resigned his district presidency and went to work for Peabody coal as its labor consultant.[39] Thus did Lewis remove his District 12 rival and forever taint his reputation among coal miners.

What remains unexplained in this peculiar affair is how Lewis obtained copies of the secret contract and the Farrington-Peabody correspondence. Peabody later claimed that his Chicago office had been burglarized and that the thieves provided Lewis with the compromising documents.[40] That, of course, was a possibility, but scarcely a probability. The real explanation lies in the relationship among Lewis, Peabody, and Farrington, in which the former two outsmarted the latter.* Peabody's desire to gain influence among union officials was quite natural, but one might assume that an operator as large and important as Peabody would seek bigger game than Farrington—only a district official. One might logically infer that Lewis prompted Peabody to offer Farrington the original contract that included Farrington's resignation as District 12 president in return for the maintenance of harmonious relations between the Peabody Coal Company and the UMW.[41] And finally, one may surmise that when Farrington repudiated an essential part of the agreement, an action that displeased Lewis, "Jack" Peabody personally provided Lewis with copies of the contract and the correspondence. In fact, the burglary story falls of its own weight. If Lewis had really been ignorant of the secret Peabody-Farrington arrangement, he would have had no reason to hire burglars or to have expected them to discover compromising documents in the company's offices. Lewis, in short, proved a far more skilled class collaborationist than Farrington. Lewis had engineered Farrington into a cul-de-sac in which the

*"Jack" Peabody may have been the same "Peabody" involved with Lewis in the 1917 poker game at the Willard Hotel. See p. 36.

District 12 president could preserve the secrecy of his original agreement with Peabody only by first resigning from union office.

With Farrington's reputation forever tarnished among coal miners, not a single district official threatened Lewis's authority. Had collective bargaining triumphs coincided with Lewis's political successes, his power might have gone unchallenged. But just as Lewis vanquished one union rival after another, the UMW lost one contract after another, and its membership and income declined sharply.* Union setbacks prompted old and new critics of Lewis's leadership to seek a change in the administration of the UMW.

A group of trade union radicals and their sympathizers began to meet together in the summer of 1926 to discuss plans to revitalize the UMW. At a meeting at John Brophy's home in Clearfield, Pennsylvania, during the July 4 weekend, Powers Hapgood; Albert Coyle, left-wing editor of the Locomotive Engineers' *Journal*; and Art Shields, a Communist journalist, discussed a plan to defeat Lewis in the December UMW election. "We haven't gone very far yet," wrote Hapgood on July 5 "but we have hopes."[42]

In the days and weeks that followed, Hapgood served as a link between Brophy and such Communists as Jay Lovestone and William Z. Foster, who were eager to put a ticket into the field against Lewis. At Hapgood's insistence, the Communists agreed to withdraw their own candidates if Brophy sought the UMW presidency.[43] In August Brophy took the leap, issuing an open letter criticizing Lewis's administration of the UMW and promising to organize the nonunion fields and, as his later campaign literature would stress, "Save the Union."[44] Despite Brophy's later disclaimers about his relationship with trade union Communists in 1926, there is no doubt that he allied with Communists against Lewis.[45] And well he should have, for both the Communists and Brophy criticized Lewis for similar reasons and sought similar objectives; the heart of Brophy's campaign policy encompassed aggressive organizing in the nonunion fields, nationalization of the coal mines, and the creation of a labor party—goals in harmony with Communist policy.

Lewis could not and did not fight Brophy on the issues. By 1926 he had few organizing triumphs to proclaim and no intelligent miners' leader dared publicly repudiate nationalization or a labor party. Instead, Lewis resorted to time-tested tactics. Searles closed the columns of the union journal to any news of the Brophy campaign; a host of minor officials appointed by Lewis and paid from the international treasury campaigned for him in the far-flung union districts; and, finally, Lewis red-baited Brophy, whose alliance with the Communists made him an easy target for Lewis's antiradical rhetoric. As usual, Lewis reduced every question to personalities and conspiracies.

*See next chapter.

Once again a purloined letter figured prominently in Lewis's strategy, this time correspondence between Albert Coyle and Powers Hapgood that discussed the Communist role in Brophy's campaign. Setting the stage well by saving the Coyle-Hapgood letter for the October 1926 A. F. of L. convention in Detroit, Lewis appeared on the platform as the central character in a trade union drama that pitted Americans against "Reds." Reading from the Coyle-Hapgood letter, which discussed several prominent Communists, Lewis pointed his finger at the convention gallery and at W. Z. Foster, "the arch priest of communism in the United States," who made annual visits to Russia to make his reports and receive his orders. "Never has a convention of the American Federation of Labor," reported the *New York Times*, "witnessed such an excoriating attack on communist attempts to 'bore from within and seize, control, and wreck the American labor movement' as marked today's session."[46] Two days later, when Brophy denied that he and Hapgood had ever received the Coyle letter and stated that Lewis was using immoral tactics to discredit his candidacy, the *Times* buried Brophy's statement on page seven under a microscopic headline.[47] Lewis's tactics proved so successful that even the officers of District 2, Brophy's former close friends and associates, repudiated their former president for allying with such "disreputable individuals" as Albert Coyle and Jay Lovestone.[48]

Lewis's campaign tactics not only assured his victory by a wide margin over Brophy, a triumph Brophy and his supporters later claimed was stolen at the ballot box,[49] but they once again divided the leftist opposition internally. In the spring of 1927, Hapgood, reflecting on what had happened to the insurgent campaign, lamented: What if the communists were friendly? "Must they always be told to go to hell and their cooperation refused in certain things in which every honest progressive believes merely because we differ from them in ultimate revolutionary ideology?"[50]

Fresh from his victory over Brophy, Lewis turned the 1927 UMW convention into a complete rout of union progressives. Among other actions, the convention that opened on January 25 and lasted for just a week raised President Lewis's salary by 50% to $12,000, barred Communists from union membership, and eliminated from the constitution's preamble the phrase that miners were entitled to the "full social value of their product" and substituted instead the words: "an equitable share of the fruits of their labor."[51] Other convention actions exemplified Lewis's unchallenged authority. For the first time since the UMW was founded in 1890, the president's report to the delegates, in effect the union chief's "state of the union address," was most notable for its brevity and lack of substantive information. Delegates ceded the IEB the right to levy assessments on union members without time limit—a right never before granted the international officials.[52] Lewis, his fellow officers, and a majority of the delegates scrubbed the

UMW clean of all taint of radicalism. Lewis repudiated nationalization of the coal mines and praised Hoover's program of voluntarism as the solution to the coal industry's ailments. The Resolutions Committee recommended against the recognition of Soviet Russia because of its desire to subvert American trade unions and the American government, and Secretary-Treasurer Tom Kennedy delivered a long, virulent anti-Communist tirade. By a large majority the delegates resolved to endorse the A. F. of L.'s nonpartisan political policy of rewarding labor's friends and punishing its enemies.[53] So complete was Lewis's domination of the convention that a new rule denied delegates the right to amend a report or resolution until after it had been voted on.[54] In other words, insurgent delegates could revise official recommendations only if delegates first rejected them by majority vote. But insurgents were so scarce at the 1927 convention that for the first time in Lewis's tenure as president, they lacked the strength to obtain roll call votes on crucial questions.

Lewis's behavior as convention chairman personified his autocratic power. To delegates who questioned him about Howat's status in the union, Lewis replied: "It does not make any difference what you think. The chair has ruled." When Howat himself asked for the right to speak, Lewis responded: "You will not, and you will sit down."[55] When several delegates asked why the union had never released the full tabulation on its 1926 election, Lewis asserted that he did not feel like spending $10,000 just to please one Communist miner (John Watt). In the same speech, he referred twice to "John Brophy and all his slimy friends."[56] Shortly afterward, when Powers Hapgood asserted his right to be seated and speak as a delegate, Lewis ruled that Hapgood was not a member of the union and added: "Any man who thinks he can abuse the privilege of the convention and come here and defy the chairman . . . or the convention rules is merely a fool." Then, turning directly to Hapgood, Lewis observed: "If I hear another word from you you will be ejected from the convention and conducted to the street."[57] Lewis reserved his choicest rhetoric for Brophy, who had had the temerity to seek the union presidency. Because Brophy was also rash enough to criticize Lewis's policies and state that the union had lost power and members, Lewis accused him of having committed treason by providing the operators with information detrimental to the coal miners. "In the days when people were besieged in a walled city and a soldier got upon the top of the wall and called to the enemy that the people were weak," Lewis narrated, "they merely took his life and threw him off the wall to the dogs below. Here in these modern days we tolerate the lamentations of the timid and we even tolerate at times the words of a traitor . . . [but] I say . . . that the man who stands upon this platform and mouths mutterings of consolation to the enemies of this Union is nothing more nor less than a traitor."[58]

During the convention and immediately afterward, Lewis carried the internal struggle directly against his critics. Lewis sympathizers entered Hapgood's hotel room during the convention and brutally beat the young insurgent. To Brophy's demand for a full tabulation of the 1926 union election results, Lewis responded that Brophy was simply pursuing the policy set by William Z. Foster and the Communists. Any union members sympathetic to Brophy or the "Save the Union Campaign," which survived Brophy's electoral defeat, found themselves labeled as "Reds" and expelled from the UMW as dual unionists.[59] When the most committed "Save the Unionists" arrived in Pittsburgh in September 1928 to hold a meeting, 200 loyal UMW members denied the insurgents access to their meeting hall, fought with them in the streets, and killed one radical and injured five others. The police arrived in time to arrest over 122 men, nearly all union radicals.[60] Earlier, Brophy and Hapgood both personally experienced the wrath of Lewis. In May 1928 Lewis ordered the Nanty-Glo Pennsylvania union local to which Brophy belonged to expel the union critic for acting as dual unionist.[61] Hapgood in 1928 and 1929 found it almost impossible to obtain employment as a miner. Unwilling to work in nonunion pits, Hapgood was denied a union card wherever he went.[62] Wherever "Save the Unionists" met, Lewis agents arrived to disrupt them, for as one loyalist observed: "It just takes some one to carry the battle to them and they wilt." By July 1928 any UMW member who failed to follow the Lewis line faced expulsion. In the language of the Bible, to which coal miners customarily alluded, "Those who are not with us are against us." Or in the more piquant words of Indiana district president William Mitch, who had just expelled a number of local insurgents: "They are not Save the Unionists; they are wreck the unionists."[63]

By the year 1928, then, Lewis had perfected the instruments of his union power: press, purse, and patronage. Ellis Searles edited the UMW *Journal* to suit Lewis. In the columns of the *Journal* only the UMW president won victories for the coal miners. Setbacks to the union cause appeared in print only when they could be used to cite opponents of Lewis for treason to the UMW. Granted the right by the 1927 convention to assess dues without fixed time limits, Lewis had won the additional financial resources needed to assure international union dominance over the scattered districts. William Green had long since departed as secretary-treasurer, and his successor, the deferential Tom Kennedy, lacked the will to challenge Lewis's cavalier style of spending union funds. At the 1927 convention, moreover, for the only time during the decade of the 1920s, no substantial group of delegates disputed Lewis's right to appoint international organizers, auditors, and fieldworkers—the men responsible for carrying Lewis's influence to the rank and file; the issue never even came to a vote.

The perfect union autocrat by 1928, Lewis, ironically, saw his external influence in ruins. Everywhere he turned in that final year of America's prosperity, Lewis was at a loss. His corporate and Republican party allies deserted him by the droves. Operators, who had once praised him as a labor statesman and even weighed hiring him as director of an employers' association, now refused to deal with the man or his union. Politicians, who hitherto had sought his advice and encouraged his political ambitions, now rejected Lewis's proposals to save the coal industry; and Herbert Hoover refused even to consider him for appointment as secretary of labor. It is to this aspect of Lewis's failure as union leader in the 1920s that we now must turn our attention.

CHAPTER 7

The Collapse of the Union, 1925-1928

Within the UMW during the 1920s, John L. Lewis marched from triumph to triumph. Inheriting an organization of cantankerous and ambitious individuals in which no president except John Mitchell had held office securely (after 1905 even Mitchell experienced unrelenting criticism), Lewis tamed or purged the union insurgents. Beginning with the narrowest of victories over his foes at the 1921 and 1924 union conventions, Lewis by 1927 firmly controlled the UMW. Indeed, by 1928 not a single influential union rival threatened Lewis. Alex Howat, Frank Farrington, John Brophy, Powers Hapgood, and scores of other critics had been ousted from the UMW. Among the old Illinois District 12 socialists, Adolph Germer had temporarily left the labor movement; Duncan Macdonald operated a bookstore in Springfield; and John Walker, occupied as president of the Illinois State Federation of Labor, played no role in the UMW. Served obediently by Philip Murray and Tom Kennedy and dictator to an international executive board composed of deferential district representatives, Lewis ruled his union domain unchallenged.

If Lewis had had the time or inclination to defend his autocratic union policies, he undoubtedly would have asserted that only a strong, centralized union, commanded by a resolute and omnipotent field general, could safeguard the life of the working miner. Coal industry executives, to be sure, functioned in a hierarchical corporate structure in which, theoretically, authority flowed down from staff officers of corporate headquarters to line officers in the coalfields. Separate mining properties in different coalfields operated under a common, centralized company policy. Hence no union whose power was diluted by autonomous districts commanded by independent officers could contend successfully with its more centralized and authoritarian corporate foes. More to the point, the ultimate test of a union's service to its members came during industrial conflicts, which union metaphors, without exception, likened to war. No military battle could be waged by armies whose line officers disobeyed staff orders and whose field units failed to coordinate their battle plans. To prepare the UMW better for its struggles against operators, to coordinate strike plans, and to discipline field officers, John L. Lewis eliminated district autonomy and punished disobedient subordinates. He sought unrestrained union power not to inflate his own ego or status, but to defend common miners better against powerful, autocratic employers. Had he chosen to explain analytically his calculated diminution of "union democracy" between 1921 and 1927, that is undoubtedly how John L. Lewis would have rationalized his behavior as union president.

During the 1920s, however, Lewis could scarcely defend his autocratic practices in such terms. For as he extended his authority within the UMW by purging his opponents, the union collapsed externally. The stronger Lewis became as a union official, the weaker his organization grew in dealing with coal operators. Autocratic authority for the UMW president failed to ameliorate the persistent crisis in bituminous coal.

By the late 1920s the bituminous coal industry was a disaster area. Domestic production of bituminous (between 30% and 40% of the world's entire output) declined steadily, falling in 1927 nearly 60 million tons below the 1920 level. So, too, did the size of the labor force, dropping between 1920 and 1927 from over 700,000 miners to approximately 575,000. Yet a persistent surplus of labor forced the typical miner to work only 142 to 220 days a year, ordinarily closer to the lower figure. This meant that despite the high minimum daily union wage of $7.50 hundreds of thousands of coal miners earned less than an adequate annual income.[1]

Four states—West Virginia, Pennsylvania, Illinois, and Kentucky—produced about 70% of the United States' supply of soft coal, and in three of those states the UMW had been shattered by the end of 1925. Only Illinois—a state with relatively large, mechanized, efficient mines and with markets partially protected by economic geography—remained a union stronghold. Unionized operators in Pennsylvania, Ohio, and, to a lesser extent, Indiana could not compete successfully for markets with nonunion operators in Kentucky, West Virginia, or their own states. Consequently, union operators either went out of business or hired nonunion miners.[2]

The UMW's financial records, officers' reports, and convention proceedings attest to the organization's decay. After the 1924 convention, the president, the vice-president, and the secretary-treasurer, in their reports to the next three conventions (1927, 1930, 1932), kept silent about membership trends. Rather than reveal the precise statistics of decline in membership, the officers preferred such glittering generalities as Lewis's remarks to the 1927 convention: "Internal affairs . . . are in satisfactory condition. . . . the great majority of membership is loyal to its declared policies and established principles. . . . it still remains unshaken in a splendid state of complete stability."[3] To maintain the fiction of a large, healthy union, the UMW continued, even after its membership had fallen below 100,000, to pay per capita dues to the A. F. of L. on a paper membership in excess of 400,000.[4] Millions of dollars of union funds expended to fight nonunion employers and relieve out-of-work miners failed to retard the UMW's decline. In 1927 the union expended over $1,500,000 on relief, and the following year over $3 million. So little remained in the UMW treasury afterward that in the two succeeding depression years of 1929-1930, when coal miners desperately needed relief, the union spent a total of $38,500 on aid to the unemployed.[5]

In February 1924, President Coolidge, Commerce Secretary Hoover, the nation's press, and especially the financial journals had hailed John L. Lewis as a labor statesman. Such praise had been occasioned by the Jacksonville agreement of 1924, the instrument of labor-management peace in the soft-coal industry that, by outlawing strikes for three years and maintaining then-current high wage rates, would grant the industry breathing space from strife and enable it to eliminate inefficient high-cost mines, excess miners, and managerial chaos. Theoretically, then, everyone benefited from the Jacksonville agreement. Union operators were freed from annual strikes or the threat of them; the UMW won long-term security in its CCF strongholds; and consumers gained a steady supply of "cheap" coal.

Economic realities promptly dashed the hopes of northern operators, UMW leaders, and federal officials for industrial peace and stability in the soft-coal industry. Bound by the terms of the Jacksonville agreement to high wages for a period of three years, union producers lost sales to operators who paid wages 30% to 50% lower than the union scale. Companies that met the price of competition from nonunion mines often did so only at the cost of losing money. By the summer of 1924 soft-coal operators, especially in Pennsylvania and Ohio, where the competition for markets was fiercest, began to demand revisions in the Jacksonville wage scale. "Some operators," Lewis informed K. C. Adams in August, "are still muttering about the necessity of modifying the Jacksonville agreement. I shall do my best to prevent their dreams in this respect from coming true." On the surface, at least, Lewis remained calm and even optimistic, assuring Adams that the union's organizing campaign in northern Western Virginia was progressing well, that the situation in the southern part of the state had not worsened, and that union miners in southwestern Kentucky loyally refused to return to the mines for wages below scale.[6]

Lewis, however, had little reason for his optimism. By November 1924 the unionized northern operators were livid with rage about the terms of the Jacksonville agreement. On November 18, Joseph Pursglove of the Pursglove Coal Mining Company, lamented to John L. Lewis: "Something must be done or all the men who are operating union coal mines are going bankrupt. . . . All the union operators are in a bad shape financially and it certainly will not be a good thing for the industry as a whole . . . for these men to go bankrupt."[7]

By early 1925 the union operators' desire for a general downward revision of the wage scales spread west into Indiana and Illinois and affected federal officials. Commerce Secretary Hoover, an architect of the Jacksonville agreement, allegedly informed Lewis at a conference in mid-February 1925 that the union wage scale was "uneconomic." Such advice was neither pleasing nor news to Lewis who, according to *Cushing's Survey*, a business newsletter, bluntly informed Hoover: "You got me into this mess; it's up to you to help me out. You dictated the Jacksonville scale; it's up to you to end it."[8]

But there seemed to be no alternative to the Jacksonville agreement for either Lewis or Hoover. How, asked *Cushing's Survey* on February 19, could Hoover offer the operators a compromise "without handing to them a club and extending to them an invitation to beat Mr. Lewis' brains." Lewis, to be sure, could not confess his own weakness, request a wage revision, and suffer repudiation by his rank and file. Nor could Hoover repudiate the Jacksonville scale without harming his own and party's political credibility among coal miners and other organized workers.[9] Lewis thus reaffirmed to operators his determination not to revise the Jacksonville scale, and Hoover remained silent.

Union operators had only one choice under the circumstances, and they took it. On March 10, 1925, Secretary of Labor James Davis reported to President Coolidge that mine operators had started to transfer many of their operations to nonunion properties, that employers in the outlying districts had openly repudiated the Jacksonville agreement and cut wages 25% to 40%, and that most union mines might close after April 1. The operator's intention, concluded Davis, was to starve the miners and their union into submission to a reduced wage scale.[10]

Lewis paradoxically, expected, even looked forward to, some of the ills that beset the soft-coal industry. A gambler by instinct, he had decided to suffer small immediate losses in order eventually to enjoy immense gains. The Jacksonville Agreement, he believed, would drive hundreds of inefficient mines and perhaps 200,000 surplus miners out of the trade. Even the Illinois operators believed Lewis sincere in his desire, reported the chief of the Commerce Department's Coal Division, "that more men . . . be driven out of the industry before prosperity can be restored."[11] Temporarily, Lewis's courageous public commitment to a high wage scale pleased rank-and-file miners even as they lost their jobs. "Before we started this fight," Lewis told a *New York Sun* reporter in May 1925, "we measured our own strength and that of our opponents. We expect losses, perhaps heavy losses, but we are confident of victory in the end."[12]

Lewis's gamble depended for success on two variables he failed to control. First, he assumed that the more efficient unionized northern mines, as a consequence of their higher productivity and lower unit labor costs, could easily compete for markets with nonunion properties that he believed to be inefficient and labor intensive. Second, he expected the federal government to enable union operators to share information about costs, prices, and markets without fear of persecution under antitrust laws; he also assumed that the ICC would revise freight rates to favor union over nonunion coal. And he expected the Coolidge administration to defend the UMW. From its position of strength in the large mechanized northern mines, the UMW would appear so powerful, Lewis informed the *Sun* reporter, "that there will be no coal miner in the country willing to stay outside the union ranks."[13] But outside of Illinois few northern union mines could compete with their nonunion Appalachian competitors, and federal officials seemed more concerned about consumers and coal operators than the needs of the United Mine Workers. For Hoover, Davis, and Coolidge, indeed for almost all federal officials, the nonunion mines served to insure consumers a steady supply of coal and acted as a restraint on potential union monopoly.[14]

Events in West Virginia and western Pennsylvania soon ruined Lewis's strategy. The UMW president had committed all his organization's dwindling resources into a struggle to retain the northern West Virginia coalfields for the union. Men, such as Van Bittner; money; and even assistance from the A. F. of L. proved of no avail. "I came from Morgantown to Fairmont this P.M.," a West Virginia UMW leader wrote to William Green on January 31, 1925, "and the searchlights on towers along the Monongahela was penetrating the darkness with their sun like rays. Machine guns are mounted in these towers and their brown muzzles command a view of the surrounding community. To tell you the truth Bill I dread to see the leaves come out if this situation does not improve, because it seems that disaster impends on every hand."[15] But disaster had already befallen the West Virginia coal miners, whose union membership had declined in two years from 75,000 to 10,000—7,500 of whom survived on union benefits.[16] A similar collapse in union membership followed in western Pennsylvania, where the two largest companies—Consolidation Coal and Pittsburgh Coal—repudiated the Jacksonville agreement, cut wages across the board, and broke off relations with the UMW. From these two giant companies, the open shop spread across the Pennsylvania coalfields, leaving the UMW by the fall of 1925 with a corporal's guard of members in the state.[17]

Lewis reacted to his lost gamble and the collapse of his union by publishing a book, *The Miner's Fight for American Standards*. Published in the early summer of 1925, the book distilled Lewis's knowledge of the coal industry, revealed his values, and promoted his solution to the ills of soft coal. Nothing in the book would have surprised coal miners or operators—it was not written for them. Instead, it was intended to win public favor for Lewis's program and influence federal officials to rescue the union from its economic predicament. Not surprisingly, Lewis personally sent a copy to Herbert Hoover.[18]

Fifteen years later, in 1940, flushed with success from his reorganization of unionism in the coal industry and the CIO's triumphs in mass-production industries, Lewis allegedly said: "Would that mine enemy had written a book."[19] Although Lewis might have uttered these words about his authorship of *The Miner's Fight*, it is unlikely he did so. When some of the more hyperbolic rhetoric is stripped away from the book, its statements about the economics of coal, the function of the labor movement, the role of government and the nature of "American civilization" accord with Lewis's basic values.

The extent to which Lewis himself wrote any large portion of the volume remains subject to doubt. Throughout his career in the labor movement, Lewis relied on a stable of ghostwriters to prepare his speeches, essays, and, one might assume, book. Three men in particular—Ellis Searles, K. C. Adams, and W. Jett Lauck—composed the bulk of the material that appeared under Lewis's name. Lauck, a noted economist, experienced Washington lobbyist, and well-paid UMW consultant, probably wrote the sections of *The Miner's Fight* that analyzed the economic relationship between the soft-coal and railroad industries. K. C. Adams, union publicist par excellence filled the book with its purple passages. But the tone was vintage Lewis.

The book can only be understood in relation to the collapse of the Jacksonville agreement and the dominant values of Calvin Coolidge's America. It was, to be sure, a propaganda piece for middle-class Americans who believed with their president that the business of America was business and with Congressman Bruce Barton—founder of Madison Avenue's Barton, Batton, Dustine, and Osborne— that Jesus and his apostles had been history's greatest sales force. The book assured its readers that the United Mine Workers was neither new nor revolutionary—that it was an American institution founded on American characteristics. "When the United Mine Workers of America declares that it will take no backward step,* this great union," proclaimed Lewis, "speaks in unison with the heart beats of America, and puts into economic language the very essence of the American spirit." Free enterprise, he reassured citizens vexed by trade unionism, guarantees the ultimate prosperity of all by encouraging each man to better his own condition. Trade unions and corporations serve the system as phenomena of capitalism that share an economic aim: *gain*. Lewis asked every thinking businessman and American to support the UMW "because it proposes to allow natural economic laws free play in the production and distribution of coal." The Jacksonville agreement, Lewis suggested, had subjected the mining industry to "the law of supply and demand" and thus was working an economic cure through elimination of marginal mines.[20]

Having assured citizens of the UMW's conservatism, Americanism, and commitment to classical economics, Lewis turned to the book's real subject matters: the preservation of the Jacksonville agreement, the maintenance of high wage rates, and the total unionization of the coal industry. This part of the work, most likely written by Jett Lauck and more in tune with Franklin D. Roosevelt's than Herbert Hoover's beliefs, actually rejected classical economics and its most important tenet: the law of supply and demand. Now Lewis informed readers that

---

*The policy of adamantly refusing to revise downward the wage rates set by the Jacksonville agreement.

free competition in the marketplace must not be allowed to drive down wage rates and that any voluntary reduction in union rates would only induce further cuts in nonunion mines, igniting a cycle of ever-decreasing wages. The American system, proclaimed Lewis, was based on expensive labor, not cheap labor—labor that could earn enough to purchase the products of American industry and provide the economy with an immense domestic market untroubled by the vagaries of international trade. "Those who seek to cheapen coal by cheapening men," he wrote, "seek to reverse the evolution of American industry. It cannot be done." Wage reductions, he concluded, not only would harm the domestic economy; they would also retard the process of reorganization in the coal industry by allowing marginal high-cost, low-wage mines to remain in production.[21]

Not a fool, Lewis realized that his commitment to high wages depended on total unionization of the industry; unless all miners received the same scale, low-wage nonunion mines would continue to eliminate union producers from the marketplace. Hence the UMW president demanded that the federal government join with the miners' union in extending the protection of the American Constitution and American law to the remotest corners of the country—especially West Virginia, Kentucky, Alabama, and western Pennsylvania—because "what Lincoln once said of the nation applies with poignant force to the coal industry today: It cannot live 'half slave [nonunion] and half free'."[22]

Because Lewis desperately needed Hoover's support, he filled his little book with concepts dear to the heart of the commerce secretary. The UMW, Lewis promised Hoover, "is as practical as the most efficient business man or production engineer, and its atmosphere is fatal to glittering generalities." Employers and unions must cooperate voluntarily, suggested Lewis, to eliminate the inefficient and unscientific, to discharge their social duties successfully, and to provide profits without exploitation. Only when "cooperative capitalism" replaced "competitive capitalism" would the nation's basic industries achieve stability and dependability. Lewis, like Hoover, looked forward to the day when businessmen, federal officials and trade unionists could function cooperatively and use their ingenuity and modern science to create a harmonious corporate society based on high wages, mass consumption, and steady profits.[23]

From certain ideas that he expounded so forcefully in his 1925 book Lewis never retreated. American civilization, he always believed, was founded on high wages achieved by substituting capital for labor, machinery for human hands. A high-wage, mass-consumption economy, in turn, necessitated total unionization of the labor force. Unscrupulous employers, Lewis knew, abounded and were quick to cut wages in order to increase their profits. Only if "responsible" employers, public officials, and labor leaders allied to promote trade unionism throughout the economy could twentieth-century enlightened capitalism be safeguarded from retrograde nineteenth-century capitalism. And by 1925 he realized that an active federal government was mandatory.

Much to Lewis's chagrin, his book and his ideas met a hostile response. The critic of archaic capitalism found himself accused of being an antiquarian labor leader. "Lewis," wrote the author of a special *New York Times* feature on labor leaders after Gompers in June, 1925, "though only 45 years old, represents the older type of labor executive, autocratic, more aggressive than penetrating, unreceptive to the newer principles, a protagonist of simple unionism." Two months later an editorialist in the same paper, oblivious to the message in *The Miner's Fight*, accused Lewis of lacking the statesmanship and economic acumen of Sidney Hillman, president of the Amalgamated Clothing Workers of America, whose union pioneered joint planning with men's clothing manufacturers. "The United Mine Workers," noted the editorial, "make no effort to join with the employers in a joint responsible undertaking. . . . They bluster and threaten and stay outside the circle of broader industrial planning and technique."[24]

Still worse, Hoover kept silent about *The Miner's Fight*, federal authorities failed to guarantee the Jacksonville agreement, and the United Mine Workers continued to decay.

Unable to sustain his cause through propaganda, Lewis resorted to threats of economic warfare. On June 30, 1925, speaking to delegates to the tri-district anthracite convention, he accused the Pennsylvania Railroad, the Consolidation Coal Company, the Pittsburgh Coal Company, and the combined Rockefeller-Mellon interests of a conspiracy to break the Jacksonville agreement. To rousing applause from the audience, he threatened a national coal strike unless operators implemented the 1924 agreement. While Lewis threatened a strike in bituminous, delegates to the tri-district convention set the stage for a walkout in anthracite by demanding that in upcoming negotiations with employers the union seek wage increases of $1 a day for daymen and 10% for tonnage miners, the equalization of working conditions, and full recognition of the union through the checkoff of dues at the company offices.[25]

By the summer of 1925 anthracite remained the UMW's only stronghold outside of Illinois. UMW Secretary-Treasurer Tom Kennedy insured that Districts 7 and 9 hewed to the Lewis line, and Rinaldo Cappellini, once a young insurgent, brought hitherto rebellious District 1 into line.

Lewis, most concerned with the collapse of his union in the soft-coal fields, plotted to use its strength in anthracite to pressure federal officials. A strike by hard-coal miners, he assumed would create a crisis in the densely populated northeastern states, which relied on anthracite for domestic heat, and cause problems for incumbent politicians, mostly Republican, at the November elections. Although Lewis apparently offered the anthracite operators a long-term contract that preserved existing conditions provided they introduced the checkoff (a demand that cost no money), he was not unhappy when employers rejected his proposal.[26]

For almost two months, beginning on July 9, a joint conference of operators and miners negotiated in Atlantic City. While John bargained with the employers, Myrta and the children enjoyed the sand, sun, and seawater. By early August, when federal mediators joined the deadlocked conference, Lewis's strategy had emerged. Because anthracite operators refused to accept any of the union's demands and insisted that they be submitted to binding arbitration, Lewis prepared for a long strike. Simultaneously he demanded that federal officials act against soft-coal operators who had violated the Jacksonville agreement. Lewis thought it only fair that the same federal influence applied to secure the original 1924 agreement be exerted to have it respected. Demanding federal intervention in soft coal, Lewis rejected it in anthracite. We can take care of ourselves in hard coal, he told an Associated Press executive, who then informed Hoover confidentially: "If it [the Coolidge administration] wants ring side seats we will be glad to provide them when the fight starts."[27]

Lewis explained to the Associated Press executive why he had no interest in arbitration, whether proposed by operators or federal officials. "It is only offered us," he said, "where we are weak. It is never offered us where we are strong. It was offered Judge Gary by President Wilson in the steel strike of '19 and Gary hasn't accepted yet. Why should we accept it where we are strong?" Always, added Lewis, the federal government rushed in when the union was strong, seeking arbitration and urging compromise. The intervention of four cabinet heads in 1924 produced the Jacksonville agreement instead of a bituminous strike. What might have happened in the 1924 elections, asked Lewis, had a national coal strike occurred? Yet after the election when operators began to repudiate the agreement, what did the administration do? Nothing, answered Lewis. And nothing more would happen, he asserted, until the suffering caused by a strike created sufficient public clamor to precipitate federal intervention.[28]

In that frame of mind, Lewis departed Atlantic City in mid-August for headquarters in his favorite Philadelphia hotel, the Bellevue-Stratford, a site closer to the anthracite fields. For another two weeks he went through the motions of seeking labor peace; but on August 24, he advised K. C. Adams: "The region will shut down on September 1st."[29] And so it did, as 150,000 hard-coal miners answered their union's strike call and began what would be the longest strike in the history of the anthracite industry.[30] As no hint of a settlement emerged during the walkout's first two weeks and federal officials worried about its ramifications, Lewis made it clear that the federal government could not influence the anthracite negotiations unless it entered them with its hands cleansed by the act of publicly reprimanding those bituminous operators who had violated the Jacksonville agreement.[31]

The start of the long strike in anthracite introduced one of the most arduous periods in Lewis's tenure as UMW president. After his wife and children returned home to Springfield in September for the opening of a new school year, Lewis remained in the East and resumed a travel schedule reminiscent of his days as an A. F. of L. organizer.

Wherever Lewis went in these months, reporters, government informants and controversy followed. When he and Phil Murray appeared in Fairmont, West Virginia, on September 25 to assist Van Bittner's organizing campaign among the district's nonunion miners, the UMW president was met with fifteen separate state and federal injunctions intended to restrain Lewis and his union from organizing nonunion mines and picketing the property of the Consolidation Coal Company, one of the major violators of the Jacksonville agreement. The most sweeping of the injunctions was handed down by a state court that acted on the plaintiffs' allegations that pickets shouted, barked like dogs, hissed, and called working miners scabs, yellow dogs, and other dirty names, all the while singing the following chorus:

> Shoot them in the head,
> Shoot them in the feet,
> Shoot them in the dinner bucket;
> How are they going to eat?

The next day, a short time after being served with forty-one fresh injunctions, Lewis addressed an audience estimated at between 25,000 and 30,000 miners and their families. Introducing the featured speaker, Bittner remarked that injunctions were like "leaves of grass in the lives of labor leaders," and Lewis pledged that the coal companies could not print enough injunctions to drive the union out of West Virginia. Lewis also used the mass meeting and the publicity that it generated to remind federal officials of their obligation to the UMW. The industry has a right to expect, he observed, "that the moral influence and power of those same government officials" who promoted the Jacksonville agreement "be utilized to preserve the integrity of the agreement and to maintain . . . the tranquility of the coal industry."[32]

Hoover now clearly feared that the UMW president desired to drag the administration into the bituminous controversy. "Mr. Lewis's personal attitude toward you is not cordial," one colleague informed Hoover. "He evidently expected that you would urge the operators to observe the Jacksonville agreement. He feels that a statement by you at the proper time would have made it impossible for them to break the agreement."[33] In fact Lewis expected that Hoover and President Coolidge would urge Treasury Secretary Andrew Mellon, whose brother's company, Pittsburgh Coal, had initiated the repudiation of the 1924 agreement in western Pennsylvania, to act in the matter. But no one in the Coolidge administration intended to satisfy Lewis.[34]

Confronted by a stalemate in anthracite, where the operators still demanded arbitration, and stymied in Washington, Lewis made public his case for federal intervention in bituminous. On November 22 he released to the press a letter addressed to President Coolidge demanding that the administration enforce the Jacksonville agreement. The letter appeared in the newspapers before Coolidge received it, an act Lewis must consciously have taken in order to irritate federal authorities and deflate their self-esteem.[35]

Lewis's action stimulated cabinet discussion among Hoover, Mellon, and Davis, and President Coolidge. The results of the cabinet meetings and official correspondence scarcely gratified Lewis. Although Hoover apparently informed Lewis privately and in advance of the intended federal response, it did little to assuage Lewis's resentment of the government's reply. As drafted by Hoover and amended by Davis for Coolidge's signature, the official federal reply to Lewis's letter of November 22 denied that the administration had been a party to the Jacksonville agreement. It deplored any breach of contract by operators but observed that "the government not being a party to contracts has no status in enforcement." Yet the government paradoxically warned Lewis that if his union struck to enforce contracts, it would violate a binding agreement and "be a fatal blow at most collective bargaining." Federal officials suggested that Lewis take his grievance to court, the only institution mandated to enforce contracts; if the UMW failed to receive legal satisfaction, Hoover would then recommend that Congress pass legislation making such contracts enforceable; and, finally, Hoover personally insisted that the UMW accept arbitration to settle the anthracite dispute. Hoover honestly but wrongly believed that Lewis would support the proposals because "he has a sense of responsibility of his group to these questions."[36]

Lewis's frustration now broke through as he remarked to a newspaperman about President Coolidge's forthcoming statement: "No man can rebuke me with impunity." Though perhaps only the reaction of a tired man and hardly a threat to the president, the comment disclosed Lewis's deep feelings of hurt. Aware that the Coolidge administration had not *signed* the Jacksonville agreement, Lewis nevertheless asserted that federal influence had made it possible and that he knew "better than any other person how the agreement was made." Hoover's suggestion that Lewis go to court infuriated the labor leader. Every lawyer the union consulted, he stated, advised that no law favors the union. "The best we could possibly do would be to start litigation that would keep us in the courts for years. It would still be there when the Jacksonville agreement expired, long after it expired." Unless prompt federal action saved the union, operator repudiation of contracts would "spread like a rotten spot in an apple until the whole Jacksonville agreement is consumed."[37] Yet Lewis was helpless, for he had suffered a total loss of mastery. Deserted by his allies among Republican officeholders and his former admirers among coal operators, he could not retard the UMW losses in soft coal.

*   *   *

With what little strength he and his union retained, Lewis fought to the bitter end in anthracite. Relying on complete loyalty among the hard-coal miners, Lewis vowed to hold them out indefinitely, and he warned the operators that "they cannot break this strike." At the end of November an informer told Hoover: "The men may cuss their leaders . . . and the women become sorer than they are now, but there is nothing to indicate revolt or break." From late November until a settlement was achieved in mid-February, Lewis held fast to secure a compromise agreement suggested by Governor Gifford Pinchot that included a five-year contract based on existing wages, voluntary arbitration that might raise but not lower wages, and a voluntary checkoff. The operators, for their part, continued to insist on binding arbitration of all questions in dispute. To those who feared that Lewis might defer to the employers' insistence on arbitration, he assured: "I am quite sure that our position will remain the same as heretofore."[38]

Drained by four and a half months of industrial warfare, anthracite operators and miners declared a truce in mid-February. Exercising his singular flair for the dramatic, Lewis signed a new contract with the anthracite operators on his forty-sixth birthday, February 12, 1926. In a flower-filled room at the Bellevue-Stratford Hotel that included a huge birthday basket of roses sent by W. W. Inglis, chairman of the Anthracite Operators' Negotiating Committee, Lewis showed reporters a birthday gift, a copy of Carl Sandburg's *Life of Lincoln*, inscribed: "The Lincoln of Labor." Sighing with relief at the achievement of a strike settlement, he remarked: "Some birthday!" To a Tamaqua, Pennsylvania, miner who had telegrammed his union president as follows: "I desire to get married the day the strike is settled. Please advise," Lewis replied by wire: "Get married today."[39] Actually, except for promising anthracite miners five years of fixed wages, the 1926 agreement offered little else.[40] Yet this minimal achievement in collective bargaining was the one bright element in an otherwise gloomy scene for the UMW and John L. Lewis.

Even this one bright spot soon darkened. Markets lost by anthracite coal during the long strike were never recaptured. Between 1926 and 1930 anthracite production declined from 90 million tons annually to 68 million, a loss of almost 25%. By February 1929 an article in the *Nation* correctly noted: "anthracite . . . is a critically sick industry. A pall of gloom hangs over the sections of Pennsylvania which are dependent on the mining of coal."[41]

In the year 1926 Lewis faced only bleak prospects. A Bureau of Mines survey, based on conditions in the soft coal industry as of December 31, 1925, showed that 65.3% of all soft coal produced came from nonunion mines and 61.3% of all miners worked without a union contract.[42] Only his personal philosophy "that events run in cycles and that circumstances repeat themselves" sustained Lewis in these times that tried a union leader's soul.[43] He simply survived as best he could as the UMW entered its time of troubles and waited for the economic cycle to revive coal mining and rejuvenate the miners' union.

*   *   *

Unexpectedly, the year 1926 brought Lewis a temporary respite from his troubles. Events outside the nation—factors over which the UMW president exercised no influence—brought prosperity to bituminous coal and employment to miners. British coal miners walked out of the pits in 1926, starting the much-feared national general strike by the "Triple Alliance" of miners, transport workers, and dockers. The closure of British mines increased the overseas demand for American coal, inflated bituminous prices, and, for a short time at least, aborted the employer offensive against the UMW.

But the outcome of the British strike presaged disaster for the UMW. The once-powerful British miners' union, which had suffered setback after setback since the end of World War I, collapsed completely in the 1926 conflict. Opposed by the full repressive force of the national government, the British miners and their labor allies caved in. Government subsidies to the coal industry that hitherto had buttressed British miners' wages were eliminated; mine operators instituted the first of a series of across-the-board wage cuts; employment tumbled; and union membership shrank. In a depressed British national economy, the coal industry and its miners were among the most depressed of all sectors. Across the ocean in the United States—a prosperous, booming society in the years 1926-1928—coal mining, too, experienced depression, and its workers knew starvation.

If 1926 was not as bad a year for the UMW as 1924 and 1925 had been, it still saw many formerly unionized operators terminate their relationship with the UMW. Moreover, the Jacksonville agreement itself expired on March 31, 1927, and unless union and operators signed a new agreement for the industry, economic chaos impended.

With the future in doubt, union representatives and operators assembled in Miami on February 15, 1927, as required by the Jacksonville agreement, to negotiate a new contract. For one full week the negotiators hammered away at each other. On the opening day, despite intense heat that wilted many a collar, John L. Lewis, reported a newspaper correspondent, "a picturesque orator with his heavy mane of reddish hair and thundering voice—a massive figure of a miner—spoke for more than a hour." Lewis could have orated for ten hours, and it would have made no difference, as operators and union delegates engaged in a dialogue of the deaf. The union negotiating team had been instructed by the 1927 UMW convention to secure the best possible contract based on *no reduction in wages*. Employers, however, refused to bargain about any other issues until the union acceded to a downward revision of the Jacksonville wage scale and accepted the principle that wages should be automatically adjusted to changing prices for coal. Operators refused to discuss Lewis's suggestion that employers and union collaborate to obtain from the ICC freight rates more favorable to union mines; to coordinate sales policies in order to maintain prices at a profitable level; to obtain federal legislation liberating the industry from antitrust laws; and to share the expense of employing legal counsel, rate experts, and engineers to execute the above program and stabilize the soft-coal industry. Neither party to the conference being willing to compromise the issue of wages, the Miami meeting adjourned sine die on February 22, and the operators, the union, and federal officials planned for a nationwide soft-coal strike set for April 1, 1927.[44]

The 1927 strike, caused because the UMW had no alternative to its enunciated policy of "no backward step" on wages, ruined the miners' union everywhere outside of Illinois and Iowa.* Already extinguished in West Virginia, Kentucky, Virginia, Maryland, Alabama, and most of central Pennsylvania, the union struggled to hold on in western Pennsylvania and Ohio. In western Pennsylvania, where operators had initiated the violations of the Jacksonville agreement, coal companies evicted striking miners from their company homes, cut off credit at the company stores, used private armed guards and state police to turn mine towns into fortresses, and imported strikebreakers by the thousands—including many black miners from Tennessee and Alabama, whose arrival intensified local bitterness. A United States senator who in 1928 investigated the labor situation in the coal mines of Pennsylvania, West Virginia, and Ohio observed: "had I not seen it myself, I would not have believed that in the United States there were large areas where civil government was supplanted by a system that can only be compared with ancient feudalism."[45]

His union army a tattered remnant by the fall of 1927, Lewis sought external assistance. He had no choice, for the UMW had lost its economic muscle as the 1927 statistics of soft-coal production revealed. Despite the strike, the Labor Department reported that "the coal now in sight and to be produced this year will equal the total production for 1925 and surpass the total production of 1921, 1922, 1924."[46] At Lewis's urging, A. F. of L. President William Green convened a special convention in Pittsburgh to consider the coal strike and assist the UMW. Attended by over 300 A. F. of L. representatives—including the federation's most influential leaders—and addressed by Gifford Pinchot, Philip Murray, and John L. Lewis, the conference resulted in a resolution to call upon all international unions to send money, materials, and organizers to assist the strikers; to instruct the A. F. of L. executive council to confer with President Coolidge about the "intolerable situation" in Pennsylvania; and to appoint a committee to remonstrate with the governor of Pennsylvania about the role of the state police in breaking the strike. At a time when mine operators violated civil liberties wholesale, the A. F. of L. delegates beseeched coal miners to observe the law "and to pay no heed to power assumed by those who are unauthorized under the law to limit, circumscribe, or repress, their rights as citizens."[47]

Just as please to coal miners to obey the law exposed the American labor movement's flaccidity in the face of repression, so, too, did the request of labor

---

*One-year agreements were reached in these two states on the basis of current wages because operators there faced the least nonunion competition.

leaders that the Coolidge administration mediate the coal strike reveal obsequious-ness. On November 17, Green, fellow executive council members, and Lewis called on Coolidge, who shunted them off to his least influential cabinet member, Labor Secretary James J. Davis. A second conference with the president on November 21 proved equally fruitless. Coolidge advised the labor leaders that the coal operators had no interest in a government-sponsored union-management conference and that they simply could not meet the union's wage demands. Once again, he sent his visitors off to the Labor Department.[48]

Lewis now found himself in a completely new situation. In the past, especially during the coal strikes of 1919 and 1922 and the negotiations preceding the Jacksonville agreement, it had been federal officials and, to a lesser extent, mine operators who urged public mediation or arbitration. Then, an affluent, large, and stable UMW played the reluctant guest at government-sponsored bargaining sessions. Now, however, Lewis, representing a dying organization, acted the ardent suitor, wooing federal officials with every wile at his command. Rejected by Coolidge and neglected by Hoover, Lewis relied on Labor Secretary Davis to serve as matchmaker for a new relationship between an ardent union and a frigid operators' group. Davis played the role that Lewis cast him in, a role declined by Coolidge and Hoover because they knew that the operators preferred an irreparable divorce from the UMW.

On December 9, 1927, Davis telegrammed all the coal operators and UMW officials in central and western Pennsylvania, northern West Virginia, and Ohio asking them to attend a conference at his office on December 13. Speaking for his union, Lewis accepted the invitation with alacrity. But the largest mine operators either sent no response or rejected Secretary Davis's invitation. A second and third telegram from Davis to the operators elicited no better response.[49]

The replies that Davis received from the operators disclosed the sad state to which the UMW had fallen and John L. Lewis's complete loss of influence. A former warm admirer of Lewis and longtime union operator, F. E. Taplin, observed of his company's situation since the strike began on April 1: "We are not short of miners today. We are mining more coal than we can sell in open market competition. After we have fought and bled to put ourselves in a position to meet our competitors, what would be our idea in meeting now and giving up the ground that we fought for?"[50] J. D. A. Morrow, president of the Pittsburgh Coal Company and a leading antiunion advocate, informed Davis: "You are attempting to draw this company into a conference with the officials of the miners union. We have definitely and permanently severed all relations with that organization."[51] Another operator, F. E. Herriman, formerly a close associate of Lewis's and a key man in the 1922 and 1924 union-management agreements, now refused to partici-pate in any conference attended by representatives of the United Mine Workers. "So far as we are concerned," he wrote Davis on December 13, "that organiza-tion is entirely out of the picture. It is my sincere belief that freedom from union domination is the best assurance of future stability and peace for the industry and for the public.'' Moreover, added Herriman, Lewis and his fellow officers ''now represent nothing in Central Pennsylvania . . . whatever influence they have left should be devoted to releasing the few members they have . . . so they may find work. . . . We will not discharge our present employees to make room for those who deserted us.''[52]

The December 13 conference proved farcical. A full UMW delegation, including Lewis, Murray, and Kennedy, assembled in Davis's office. Only eleven operators (compared to fifteen union men), mostly from smaller companies, attended. Three days of separate meetings among federal officials, union men, and operators, as well as joint sessions, led nowhere.[53]

After his conference adjourned on December 15, Davis learned further from operators as to why they declined to bargain with the UMW. If Lewis knows any other way to unionize Pennsylvania and Ohio other than through the wage cut proposed by operators at the Miami conference, wrote F. E. Taplin, ''I would like to have him tell me how it can be done.'' There is simply no way, he concluded, that union wages can exceed nonunion rates by 50% when nonunion mines provide the nation with all the coal it needs.[54] ''There was a time,'' wrote another operator, ''when the Mine Workers Union was handled by constructive men, willing to give and take, and meet conditions as they existed. Today we feel that the union is handled by a bunch of men, the most of whom are not American citizens and is not handled for the best interests of the employer or the employees.''[55] Finally, a close personal friend of Davis's among the larger operators linked to the steel industry informed the secretary that his proposal for a conference had come too late, ''as there are now too many non-Union men employed in Union fields to make *any conference on wages with Lewis and his crowd practical*, as no employer is going to take back Union miners and displace non-Union workers.'' Davis's friend saw no cure for soft coal ''except through the working of economic laws. . . . Governmental interference at any time, *in my opinion, would be hurtful.*''[56]

By 1928 the UMW was involved in a headlong race to oblivion. The cost of supporting strikers in Pennsylvania and Ohio proved debilitating, and A. F. of L. assistance scarcely compensated for the drain on the union treasury. The millions spent on strike relief, moreover, seemed wasted, as more and more Pennsylvania and Ohio mines closed down or operated nonunion. By spring 1928 the UMW scarcely existed anywhere in the Appalachian fields; Pennsylvania and Ohio had gone the way of West Virginia, Kentucky, and Alabama. From a high of over 500,000 bituminous members in 1921-1922, the UMW membership had fallen to perhaps 80,000 by mid-1928, two-thirds of whom were in only one district: Illinois. And even in District 12, its last soft-coal stronghold, the UMW was in retreat. Not only did Lewis surrender completely the union's policy of refusing to negotiate separate district agreements in the Central Competitive Field, he also relinquished his edict of ''No backward step.'' Those districts, such as District 12, that still had agreements to renegotiate on April 1, 1928, were advised to accept the best terms offered. ''Under the circumstances confronting us,'' Lewis informed

Jett Lauck on July 25, 1928, "we had no alternative than to amend our policy."[57] By then, however, Lewis had little to save, for his organization as an effective trade union was dead everywhere except Illinois.

Having outlasted all his union rivals by 1928, Lewis was bereft of external influence. One hope remained—the election of Herbert Hoover as president, and to that objective Lewis committed himself in the 1928 election campaign. The best public speaker among labor Republicans, if not the party's most successful labor leader, Lewis appeared on a national radio network on the evening of October 17, under the auspices of the Republican National Committee, to deliver a major address for Herbert Hoover. In his speech, Lewis linked Hoover to the economic program expounded in *The Miner's Fight*. In his five years as Secretary of Commerce Hoover had, Lewis informed his listeners, established a "new economic order," in which higher wages, greater consumer power, and a rising standard of living created a domestic market that insured prosperity. "Industry and trade," Lewis asserted, "must be released from the restrictions of the anti-trust laws so that the maximum economies in production and distribution may be made possible." Now government must enable employers to introduce coordinated industrial planning and work toward the elimination of unemployment, "a necessary condition to the permanent prosperity of modern industry and of the country as a whole." To continue the "economic revolution" begun in 1923 and insure the elimination of poverty itself, American voters must, intoned Lewis, elect Herbert Hoover as the next president of the United States. Republicans were so pleased with Lewis's radio address that they published it in pamphlet form under the title, "Hoover's Tonic Safest for Industry," and distributed it widely among workers.[58]

Hoover's margin of victory over Alfred Smith in the November election proved so enormous that Lewis's contribution was at best marginal. Yet the UMW president expected substantial compensation for his endorsement of Hoover. As president, Hoover could, reasoned Lewis, urge Congress to pass legislation that would stabilize the soft-coal industry, foster the industrial cooperation that operators refused to provide themselves, and mandate a place in the system for organized labor. That prospect, however, offered only a long-term solution to Lewis's predicament, not a pleasing prospect for the UMW leader.

Lewis, ever the opportunist, saw a quicker way to turn failure into success. As soon as the presidential election was over, Lewis eagerly campaigned for appointment as secretary of labor. Working through Dan G. Smith, chairman of the Republican party National Labor Committee, Lewis contacted congressmen, senators, bankers, and businessmen on his own behalf.[59] By mid-January Hoover was deluged with telegrams and letters recommending that Lewis be appointed secretary of labor. Among the more prominent backers of the UMW president were W. Averell Harriman and E. N. Foss, former governor of Massachusetts.[60]

When Lewis heard no news by the end of January 1929, he instructed Jett Lauck to seek a private interview with Hoover concerning the cabinet position.[61]

Lewis's campaign had been in vain, for he had completely misread Hoover. Thinking himself the labor leader closest to the economic, political, and social ideas of the new Republican president, Lewis expected the appointment, the more so since he thought that he had had a long, close, and mutually profitable political relationship with Hoover. Hoover, however, had other ideas about John L. Lewis, as the president-elect revealed to an industrialist friend troubled by rumors that Lewis might be appointed secretary of labor. "You need have no fears in the direction you mention," Hoover assured his friend.[62] Thus Lewis was destined to remain as president of a decaying trade union and could scarcely turn for relief to a United States president who refused to consider him as a candidate for secretary of labor. The opportunism that had rewarded Lewis so well between 1911 and 1924 now failed him.

The plight of the UMW and the American coal miner in 1928 presaged the fate of the nation under Herbert Hoover. As affluent Americans celebrated the victory of "the Great Engineer," drank bathtub gin, danced the Charleston, drove fast cars, and speculated in the stock market, coal miners vainly sought work, burdened local relief agencies, and, sometimes, starved. The more ambitious among them fled the coalfields for the Pittsburgh steel mills, Akron rubber plants, and Detroit auto factories. As the universe of the American coal miner collapsed, his union and its leader watched impotently. No one conceived, in the late winter of 1929, that in less than three years, 12 to 15 million other American workers would share the plight of the coal miner and that Lewis would have considerable company as an impotent labor leader. For John L. Lewis, his union, and the coal miners, the Great Depression, when it arrived from 1930 to 1933, provided a quantitative rather than a qualitative change in circumstances. Economic, social, and political problems that had affected only the coal industry from 1922 to 1929 paralyzed the entire economy. Proposals Lewis originally broached to ameliorate the ills of soft-coal mining were subsequently expanded to apply to the entire national economy; they became an integral part of the New Deal and the "Roosevelt revolution," which followed the aborted "Hoover revolution."

The economic circumstances that shattered Lewis's union, turned his corporate allies into enemies, and reduced his political influence had no apparent influence on his private or family life. Lewis continued to live well, maintain three homes in Springfield, drive a large Cadillac, and support an extended family on the payroll of the union and the Indianapolis bank he headed. At the 1927 UMW convention delegates voted to increase his annual salary by 50%, from $8,000 to $12,000.

Myrta, too, suffered no diminution in what had become her accustomed standard of living. Lewis's wife and children traveled with him during the summer, though they ordinarily returned to Springfield for the school year, where Kathryn and John Jr. attended the local public schools. Kathryn as a teen-ager developed the physical traits that made her life so burdensome. Enormously overweight, Kathryn bore little attraction for the opposite sex, felt uncomfortable among teen-age female companions, and lived increasingly in a world bounded by family and father's career. John Jr., aside from occasional newspaper photos showing him at play on the beach at Atlantic City, remained the family's invisible member, seldom mentioned by his father, and, unlike his older sister, totally shielded from his father's trade union universe.

Lewis acted very much a man of the American 1920s. Not only the president of a prosperous bank, he was also, according to a business newsletter of February 1925, "one of the wisest small traders that ever takes a flier in the stock market. His success . . . shows that he knows economics far better than do nine out of ten coal operators. And, he is making more money for himself today than are ninety-five out of a hundred operators."[63] That an increasingly more frustrating relationship with coal operators had not soured Lewis on his association with industrialists is evidenced in the warm and friendly correspondence he engaged in between 1920 and 1927 with Tom Moses, who rose from the coal pits to high executive office in the United States Steel Corporation. When Moses became president, in 1927, of the H. C. Frick Coal Company and its subsidiaries, one of the most dedicated antiunion firms in the coal industry, Lewis wrote to him: "It is a long road you have travelled and no one knows its length or understands its difficulties better than I."[64]

Had Lewis desired merely a substantial income, a prosperous family, and influential associates, he might have been pleased with his status in 1929. Had he desired the sort of influence and wealth Tom Moses achieved, it probably could have been Lewis's for the asking in the corporate world. But he wanted political power and public esteem. In 1929, however, dreams of glory seemed beyond Lewis's reach, and the future promised only bleaker prospects.

Ann Louisa (Watkins) Lewis,
c. 1895–1900

Thomas H. Lewis,
c. 1895–1900

Thomas A. Lewis,
c. 1900–1905

Howard and Hattie Lewis,
c. 1908–1910

(Below left)
George Lewis,
c. 1910–1915
John's favorite brother

(Below right)
Sarah Edith Lewis Collins

"Jesse James in disguise";
written by Lewis on back of
photograph in 1917.
What can it mean?
*(State Historical Society of
Wisconsin)*

(Below left)
Howard Lewis,
c. 1918

(Below right)
A. Dennie Lewis,
c. 1918

(Left)
Hattie at her nursing school
graduation, 1922

(Right)
Lewis with his son, John L., Jr.,
on the boardwalk in Atlantic City,
1935

(Below)
Lewis' home in Springfield, Illinois,
c. 1937

CHAPTER 8
The Nadir, 1929-1932

From 1925 through 1929 American coal miners and their union suffered. While most Americans enjoyed prosperity during the late summer and early fall of 1929, three coal miners competed for every available job; those fortunate enough to find work seldom labored more than a couple of days a week; and their wages declined precipitously, in some places falling from the customary $7.50 union minimum to under $2.00 a day. Unemployed or partially employed, miners supported ragged wives and hungry children.

Their union scarcely presented a more pleasing prospect. Reduced to fewer than 80,000 members, the UMW no longer held a national contract with the operators, and it lacked effective district organizations, except in Indiana and Illinois. Even Illinois District 12, which in September 1928 had negotiated a four-year contract, acceded to a reduction in daily wages from $7.50 to $6.10. Elsewhere no union stood between coal miners and operators, who sought to survive a depressed market by cutting wages, intensifying labor, and turning a profit at company stores.

But life worsened for coal miners after November 1929 as economic depression paralyzed the entire nation. With rising unemployment and a shrinking consumer market, railroad traffic diminished, steel mills cut production, and utility companies transmitted less power. In a marketplace already glutted with soft coal, national depression spelled disaster for mine operators and their employees. Coal prices collapsed, as did miners' wages; more mines closed, additional miners joined the unemployment rolls, and others worked fewer days.

By 1932 average hourly earnings for soft-coal miners had fallen to fifty cents, and in the following year almost one-third of the nation's mines paid their workers less than $2.50 a day. In the absence of the union and its checkweighman, mine managers in effect reduced wages by crediting miners with less tonnage than they produced. Miners who rebelled at company exploitation heard the footsteps of the "barefootman," whom folklorist George Korson heard about. "There's a barefoot, hungry man outside waiting for your job," miners told Korson.[1]

Barefootmen and -women abounded in the coalfields. Social workers, welfare officials, and concerned citizens found the same scene everywhere: hunger, mental depression, stark poverty. Irving Bernstein describes a common miner's diet as " 'miner's strawberries' (beans—for variety, white beans one day and red the next); 'bulldog gravy' (flour, water, and a little grease); a 'water sandwich' for the miner's lunch pail (stale bread soaked in lard and water)." Rural families, to be sure, enjoyed fresh garden vegetables in season, but like most mining families they lacked meat, milk, and fruit.

Weakened by meager diets, miners and their families suffered from a variety of respiratory and intestinal diseases. Illness exacted a heavy toll in isolated Appalachian mine towns that had no doctors or hospitals. In some "communities" where companies provided medical services, miners so distrusted company doctors and company clinics that folklore conceived of the doctor and the hospital as institutions to visit only when death was near.

The plight of the union paralleled the fate of the coal miner. By 1932 little remained of what had once been the proudest trade union in the United States. Unionism had been erased as a functioning institution from the coalfields of West Virginia, Virginia, Maryland, Kentucky, Tennessee, and Alabama. Pennsylvania, which once included over 100,000 members in its two primary soft-coal districts, counted less than 1,500. Ohio's hitherto prosperous District 6 had lost nearly its entire dues-paying membership. The outlying districts of Iowa, Missouri, Kansas, Oklahoma, Montana, Wyoming, New Mexico, and Washington counted their members by the 100s. And the gem of the union, Illinois District 12, as we will see, had been shattered by corruption, purges, provisionalism, insurgency, open rebellion, and dual unionism.[2]

How the union paid its international officers and met its other financial obligations seems miraculous. The total union payroll, to be sure, declined by over $200,000 between 1920 and 1930, with the greatest decrease coming after 1924. In 1929 and 1930 the union practically ceased financial aid to striking and unemployed miners, such expenditures falling from over $3 million in 1928 to just over $17,000 a year later. Between $50,000 and $60,000 was saved simply by not calling the regular convention scheduled for 1929 and postponing indefinitely all future conventions.[3]

Yet Lewis cut expenditures shrewdly. Few of the cuts diminished the union president's authority or patronage. Reductions in manpower, materials, and miscellaneous expenses occurred proportionately more at the district than the international level. Economy, in this instance, perpetuated and enlarged the power of the union president. So, too, did the spread of provisionalism among the decaying union districts, as Lewis appointees on the international payroll replaced elected district officers. Districts without dues-paying members, in West Virginia, Kentucky, Tennessee, and Alabama, among other states, existed only by virtue of funds and officials dispatched to them by Lewis; Lewis's appointees also served as convention delegates and always voted with the administration. Yet Lewis's economic and administrative adjustments to depression kept the UMW barely alive and provided a cadre of officials who subsequently acted decisively when the New Deal sparked the rejuvenation of unionism among coal miners.[4]

Although the international union administration survived from 1929 through 1933, the UMW could do little to protect the American coal miner. Lewis's loss of mastery and the collapse of his union induced fresh challenges to his power from opportunistic union careerists, old UMW left-wingers who romanticized the union's pre-Lewis past, and militant Communists. Ironically, these challengers, rather than checking Lewis's influence in the union, in the end enhanced the UMW president's power. Opponents who sought to restore trade union democracy instead hastened the establishment of a more perfect union autocracy.

The most significant challenge to Lewis's authority came from Illinois District 12, the last bastion of union strength for coal miners and the one district over which the UMW president lacked complete control. For a brief time in the summer of 1928, some members of District 12 considered running John H. Walker against Lewis for the UMW presidency. But the Walker candidacy collapsed when Lewis, the unilateral interpreter of his union's constitution, again ruled Walker ineligible to run for office.* And Walker himself deemed it unwise to risk his position as president of the Illinois State Federation of Labor for the dubious prospect of unseating Lewis.[5]

Despite Walker's caution, the anti-Lewis elements in Illinois fought on. District 12 officials demanded autonomy in their relations with international officers and, as the spokesmen for more than two-thirds of the UMW's dues-paying membership, represented a real threat to Lewis's power. In addition to Walker, Frank Farrington and Adolph Germer retained considerable influence in District 12, and such other critics of Lewis as John Brophy, Powers Hapgood, and Alex Howat also intrigued in Illinois. As the UMW lost members, collective bargaining contracts, and revenue, critics blamed Lewis. "For downright blundering, mad, unreasoning, stupid, destructive, and disloyal leadership," Farrington asserted in a privately published pamphlet, "Lewis' action has never been equalled by any leader in the organized labor movement of America."[6]

Lewis struck back at his critics in Illinois. Using his own allies in District 12, international funds, and influence in state politics, he sought to restrain Illinois district officials. His younger brother, A. Dennie Lewis, who served as director of the Illinois Department of Mines and Minerals, rewarded his elder brother's supporters with state patronage (for example, appointments as mine inspectors).[7] But patronage proved too slow and cumbersome a device through which to assert hegemony over District 12; Lewis sought a more swift and certain means to his end. Corruption and financial chicanery among officials of one of the Illinois

*See Ch. 3, pp. 64-65.

subdistricts—No. 9, in Franklin County, the most productive coal county in the state and the union's largest subdistrict—gave Lewis his opportunity. On June 14, 1929, ostensibly acting at the request of Franklin County miners, Lewis suspended Subdistrict 9's officers, appointed his own men in their place, and established a provisional administration under the direct supervision of the international office.[8]

Not only did Lewis act first against his enemies in Illinois; their reaction also served his purposes. District 12 officials, rather than disciplining the Subdistrict 9 leaders charged with corruption, supported them against Lewis. District 12 President Harry Fishwick encouraged the suspended local officers to fight Lewis in court, where they secured an injunction against the UMW president's suspension of the subdistrict. Early in September 1929, however, Lewis summoned two of the suspended subdistrict officers to his union's Indianapolis headquarters, brought them before an in camera session of the executive board, and obtained from them a confession linking District 12 officials directly to the alleged corruption in Franklin County. With this confession in hand, Lewis set out to purge Fishwick and other elected District 12 officials. Charging them with fomenting dissension, rebellion, and dual unionism, Lewis, on October 10, 1929, suspended the charter of District 12, removed its officials, and replaced them with a provisional administration responsible solely to John L. Lewis.[9] Thus commenced a two-year union civil war in the state of Illinois that precipitated an unholy alliance among Lewis's critics and rivals.

District 12's elected leaders promptly fought back. They went to court to enjoin Lewis from establishing a provisional district, and they recruited prominent allies. John Brophy, inactive in union affairs since his defeat in the 1926 UMW election and his subsequent banishment, returned to the struggle. In a letter to Oscar Ameringer, the left-wing editor of the *Illinois Miner* and a vitriolic critic of Lewis, Brophy observed:

> To me it is evident that John Lewis is out to wreck the Illinois district. Exposure of the character of the man and his treacherous work . . . is necessary. . . . To defeat Lewis is of primary importance. Everything else is secondary. Until Lewis is disposed of there cannot be any rebuilding of the Miners' movement. . . . Resistance to one who has perverted the democratic principles of the union and almost destroyed it with his senseless policies is obedience to the miners' best interests.[10]

By November 1929, according to William Mitch, coal miners in his own state of Indiana were in a fever heat of turmoil, and the popular thing was to denounce union leaders.[11] The turmoil in the miners' union was intensified by an Illinois state court decision that in January 1930 ruled in favor of District 12 and prohibited Lewis from establishing a provisional government and removing elected officers without adhering to the UMW's constitutional rules concerning the filing of formal charges and hearings.[12]

These initial setbacks to Lewis instilled new courage among his enemies. By the end of January 1930, Frank Farrington, who had been driven from the UMW in disgrace in 1926, dreamed of leading a new miners' union. "Though I do not like to be identified with a dual miners' union," he wrote to a prospective ally, "I see no other hope for the Mine Workers of the Country, but to start another union. If the Mine Workers of the southwest were willing to accept my leadership in the formation of a new organization, I would be disposed to accept the proposition. I think I could get a large majority if not all, the Illinois Miners with me in a movement of that kind. . . . I can see no other way out, can you?" asked Farrington.[13] But he had strong competition for influence among coal miners in the Southwest from Alex Howat, who had rejoined the UMW in October 1928 by pledging to obey loyally the laws of the UMW and the authority of its president. With insurgency again rising in the UMW, Howat, in 1930, allowed his ambition to transcend his pledge of loyalty, and he seemed as eager as Farrington to lead a dual miners' union.[14]

If Farrington and Howat were prepared to leap into dualism, such other enemies of Lewis as Walker, Brophy, Germer, and Ameringer preferred to seek control of the existing United Mine Workers. At a secret meeting in Chicago attended by all the above-named individuals as well as the deposed District 12 executive board, their attorneys, and Sidney Hillman—president of the Amalgamated Clothing Workers of America, a trade union that itself had originated as a result of an internal organizational schism—the UMW insurgents plotted their strategy. The strategy they chose paralleled the action taken by Sidney Hillman's union fifteen years earlier. Instead of deciding to found a new miners' union, they accused Lewis of violating the UMW constitution and leading an illegitimate organization. "The definite understanding was," Germer later recalled, "that we would contend for the name of the organization in order to protect the contract in Illinois, and other districts." The insurgents based their claims on the sort of legal-constitutional sorcery that ordinarily delighted Lewis. Asserting that because Lewis had not held an international union convention in 1929 as mandated by the constitution, the UMWA lacked an international constitution and officers empowered to call conventions or administer union rules. Lewis's challengers thus called their own convention to reestablish the "true" United Mine Workers of America.[15]

At their Chicago conclave, the insurgents wisely chose a slate of prospective officers. Farrington, notorious for his personal ambition and greed, found no place on the ticket; indeed, Brophy and Germer especially argued that he not be allowed to attend the insurgent convention. Howat, exceedingly popular among coal miners and nonunion left-wingers, was slated for the vice-presidency, a position carrying prestige but not power. For the two primary administrative posts, president and secretary-treasurer, the insurgents selected men of principle and rectitutde: John H. Walker and John Brophy. Walker could be charged with neither personal ambition nor selfish motives, for he had to relinquish his secure and prestigious office as president of the Illinois Federation of Labor in order to serve the insurgent coal miners.[16]

The UMW insurgents' strategy seemed ingenious. Rather than commit the sin of dual unionism, which would bring down on them the wrath of organized labor, they claimed to be rescuing the real United Mine Workers from the usurper John L. Lewis and his corrupt machine. They chose three candidates for international office, two of whom, Walker and Brophy, appeared selfless; and before establishing their own UMWA at a convention scheduled to meet in Springfield, Illinois, on March 10, 1930, the insurgents offered a compromise to John L. Lewis. They suggested that Lewis join with them in convening a special convention attended only by delegates representing active locals, whose credentials would be screened by a committee appointed by the A. F. of L. executive council; that William B. Wilson and William Green serve as the convention's presiding officers; that a firm of certified accountants audit the books of the international union and District 12; and that officers responsible for any irregularities found were to resign. If Lewis accepted those conditions, the insurgents promised to postpone their convention scheduled for March 10 and seek instead a harmonious solution to the union's internal difficulties.[17]

Lewis, to be sure, planned no compromise with his opponents. Instead, he looked forward to routing them. No sooner did insurgents issue their call for a convention to meet in Springfield on March 10 than Lewis called his own UMW convention for Indianapolis on the same day. He could scarcely wait to battle enemies who asserted that "John L. Lewis killed more than the United Mine Workers of America. He killed more than the leaders of our union. He killed its very soul."[18]

On March 10, 1930, occurred one of the strangest moments in American trade union history. Two groups of delegates meeting in separate conventions in the respective capital cities of Indiana and Illinois each asserted the right to represent the legal, legitimate United Mine Workers of America. One convention, that called by John L. Lewis in Indianapolis, proceeded in clockwork fashion and completed its business faultlessly. The other convention, asembling insurgents in Springfield, degenerated into chaos and created more problems than solutions.

The Indianapolis convention saw Lewis in absolute control of his troops. And why not? As Lewis soon afterward informed Jett Lauck: "It was an excellent convention. Our enemies were all gathered in one boat at Springfield, which in many respects is not a bad situation."[19] Lewis's defenders in Indianapolis devoted the first five days of their convention to endorsing the UMW president's actions in Illinois. Delegate after delegate from District 12 charged the deposed Illinois officials with corruption, excoriated the insurgents as traitors, and threw mud at anyone who dared criticize John L. Lewis. They listened attentively as Lewis characterized the Illinois insurgents as "a little band of malcontents . . . a rag-tag and bobtail element who . . . are muttering in their biers" and linked them to Frank Farrington and communism. And delegates applauded vigorously when Lewis advised them that only one question lay at the heart of the Illinois controversy. "No man in our union," he proclaimed, "can be greater than the law of this union. It is axiomatic that he must, like all others, abide by the laws, and after all, when you get down to the real heart of the question that is what it amounts to today." Because John L. Lewis was "the Law" in the UMW, delegates agreed overwhelmingly with their president that the District 12 officials had been legally and constitutionally wrong to disobey Lewis's rulings. By endorsing Lewis's revocation of District 12's charter, the delegates in Indianapolis established one man's fiat as the undisputed law in the UMW.[20]

William Green arrived in Indianapolis on March 17 to offer additional support to Lewis. The A. F. of L. president pledged that "the United Mine Workers of America—*this* United Mine Workers of America here—is the only organization recognized by the American Federation of Labor." To thunderous applause, he assured the delegates that Lewis's organization "is the only United Mine Workers of America that will be recognized in the future by the American Federation of Labor."[21]

After excoriating their absent enemies for five days, the Lewis delegates devoted the remaining five days of their convention to transforming the UMW into a constitutional autocracy. Lewis easily withstood feeble challenges to his right to appoint organizers and field officers. Arguing as usual that the issue was one of efficiency and sound business administration and directing his appeal at ethnic and nonwhite constituents, Lewis asked, "Where could you logically expect in this organization as presently constituted, to be able to elect a colored field worker, or a Lithuanian, or a Slovak, or an Italian, or a Polish individual? It is impossible. It is impracticable."[22] More important, the delegates authorized the president to interpret the UMW constitution and to exercise unrestrained executive power between sessions of the IEB. They also expanded the president's prerogative to expel union members for fomenting dualism; to revoke the charters of districts, subdistricts, and local unions; and to create provisional governments in their places.[23]

Buoyed by the delegates' eagerness to enhance his authority, Lewis closed the convention with an unusually powerful, brief oration. Despite the adversity and misfortune that had befallen the UMW, Lewis assured the delegates that their union remained "a tremendous moral and economic force in the affairs of the coal industry and . . . the nation." The labor leader, who for the previous three years had been rebuffed by coal operators and scorned by public officials, proudly proclaimed to the miners that he had

> pleaded their case from the pulpit and the public platform, in joint conference with the associated operators of the country, before the bar of state legislatures, in the councils of the President's cabinet, and in the public press of this nation—not in the quavering

tones of a feeble mendicant asking alms, but in the thundering voice of the captain of a mighty host, demanding the rights to which free men were entitled.

Then, in an ironic peroration, Lewis confessed his personal impotency to the men who had just granted him autocratic power. "As an individual," he observed, "my opinion and my voice is of no more consequence in our world of affairs or in the coal industry . . . than the voice or the opinions of any passerby upon the street. It is only when I am able to translate your dreams and aspirations into words which others may understand that my tongue possesses any strength or my hand has any force."[24]

If unity prevailed in Indianapolis, disunity wracked the insurgents in Springfield. Even before their convention opened on March 10, their careful plans went awry. Hoping to confront the delegates with a slate headed by John Walker, the insurgent leaders met opposition from Howat, Ameringer, and a group of New York socialists and Brookwood Labor College radicals who favored the Kansan. Howat threatened to withdraw from the anti-Lewis movement if he was not chosen president, and his radical sympathizers pledged to withhold financial and moral endorsement if the new organization failed to choose militant leaders. Rather than experience a split, the two most active Illinois insurgents, John Walker and Adolph Germer, built a new slate. Walker withdrew in favor of Howat, a concession intended to elicit support from miners in the Southwest, rank-and-filers everywhere, and eastern socialists; Germer agreed to accept the vice-presidency; and Walker replaced John Brophy as secretary-treasurer-designate.[25]

But preconvention compromises failed to instill harmony among the insurgents. Their hunger whetted by Walker's withdrawal in favor of Howat, the radicals sought to substitute Powers Hapgood for Germer, a demand that intensified dissension. Worse the Springfield delegates engaged in a fractious floor struggle over the seating of Frank Farrington. After two days of debate, the majority supported Farrington, a decision that angered Walker, Germer, and especially Brophy, who noted: "I can't see that tying themselves up to Farrington would be any better than being tied to Lewis." Indeed, Brophy promptly decided "not to cooperate with a movement that gives Farrington a clean bill of health and that opens wide the door of its inner councils to him." By seating Farrington, the Springfield delegates, in Brophy's estimation, "taint[ed] the new movement in a fundamental way, just as John L. Lewis has befouled the miners' movement. . . . I see no more hope from a group dominated by Farrington than one dominated by Lewis."[26] During their convention, the insurgent leaders lost all control over their followers, who not only seated Farrington, but stripped union leaders of substantial power—especially appointive authority—and provided them with salaries less than half those the Lewis union paid.[27]

*   *   *

A union civil war followed immediately upon the adjournment of the two miners' conventions. Lewis entered the internecine struggle as the constitutionally autocratic leader of an organization that was in complete control of anthracite coal, firmly in command of all the bituminous fields except Illinois, and endorsed by the A. F. of L. The insurgents and their Reorganized United Mine Workers of America (RUMWA) began the battle with no substantial strength outside of Illinois; almost all the 456 delegates in Springfield had come from Illinois locals. Furthermore, they were crippled by internal divisions that worsened over time, and they possessed a structure that separated rather than united organizational power. The Great Depression insured that no labor organization could enhance its power or better its members' material conditions; under the circumstances, the best that a strong, united trade union could do was to survive. The RUMWA's leaders could neither end the depression, restore prosperity to the soft-coal industry, put miners back to work, nor negotiate better contracts than Lewis. Much as they criticized Lewis and blamed him for the collapse of the UMW, the insurgents lacked an alternative program.

Yet for six months and perhaps longer, the insurgents posed a threat to Lewis. The RUMWA started with a significantly larger paper membership in Illinois than the Lewis UMWA—at least 65% (perhaps 85%) of the state's miners to Lewis's remainder. But both organizations had fewer dues-paying than total members. Germer claimed 75,000 members for the RUMWA in Illinois, of whom 26,000 paid dues; and Lewis's District 12 claimed 16,000 dues-paying members.*[28] Because Illinois had numbered over two-thirds of the UMWA's total membership before the split and held the only contract with operators, the insurgents' numerical dominance in District 12 provided them with considerable strength. From the first, they aimed to solidify power in Illinois and then use District 12 as a club with which to smash the Lewis organization.

The greatest advantage Lewis exercised in the civil war flowed from splits among his rivals. Although Farrington scarcely figured in the RUMWA, Lewis and his spokesmen persistently associated the insurgents with Farrington and, by implication, with class collaboration and corruption. Furthermore, Alex Howat unconsciously served Lewis better than he led the RUMWA. Eager to play the role of radical labor leader, Howat, much to the dismay of Germer and Walker, sought advice from such non-Communist leftists as A. J. Muste and Tom Tippett.[29] The more Howat associated with alleged Communists and eastern urban "intellectuals," the more Lewis red-baited the insurgents, accusing them of seeking to "bolshevize" the mine workers and of subjecting workers to the influence of effete New York left-wing bohemians.

---

*According to John Walker's reliable financial records, the RUMWA never average more than 24,000-plus dues-paying members, and by the end of 1930 the number had dropped to 14,000-plus.

His flirtation with the political left proved the least of Howat's deficiencies as an insurgent union leader. Much worse was his administrative bungling and his thirst for hard whiskey. While Germer and Walker labored to hold Illinois and gain allies elsewhere in the coalfields, Howat spent most of his time away from the decisive arena of struggle and in local booze joints or in Kansas, among his idolators.[30] Germer was later to compose the following poem in Howat's honor:[31]

> A whiskey breath from Kansas came
> And said ''I am a man of fame;
> It's President I want to be
> I'll pledge to set the miners free.''
>
> And President was this man made
> To put John Lewis in the shade.
> The fight began a year ago
> With whiskey breath as the main show.
>
> The year has passed and whiskey breath
> Has almost drank himself to death.
> Is there a booze joint may I ask
> Where he has not yet had his flask?
>
> Is there a brand he has not sipped
> A bootleg joint where he's not slipped?
> In Springfield, Tovey, and in Troy,
> Our Alexander is the boy.
>
> This is our Alex, great and strong
> The whiskey breath who came along
> And told us that he is the man
> To put John Lewis on his can.

Howat, in turn, accused Walker of serving the coal operators and Germer of being too conservative. Germer employed ''spies'' against Howat, intercepted the latter's confidential correspondence, and even schemed to keep the RUMWA president out of Illinois. Lewis encouraged the divisions among his rivals by also obtaining confidential information about Howat, which he turned over to Germer and Walker.[32]

Lewis, moreover, benefited from Communist activity among coal miners. While Howat courted Communist support, the National Miners Union, the party's trade union, published leaflets accusing the insurgents of class collaboration, of being linked through Farrington to the Peabody Coal Company, and of racism.[33] Committed in theory to serving the coal miners neglected by the UMW, Lewis's opponents denounced each other.

Lewis cunningly assisted his enemies as they cannibalized each other. He threw all his resources into the struggle in Illinois. The union *Journal* slandered the insurgents; union funds flowed to Lewis supporters in Illinois; Phil Murray and Van Bittner traveled through the coalfields carrying Lewis's message; William Green declared the insurgents dual unionists, had John Walker purged from the Illinois State Federation of Labor, and closed the state labor movement to RUMWA locals;[34] Lewis's brothers, George and Dennie, used their political influence in the state to strengthen loyalists and punish rebels;[35] and Lewis's allies used force and violence against the insurgents. Wherever Germer traveled in Illinois, Lewis supporters heckled him, interrupted his meetings, and, in one instance in Royalton on April 18, started a gun battle that wounded six miners—two seriously. When Germer and other insurgents were not attacked by Lewis loyalists, they were deported from mining communities by local mayors and sheriffs who served the Lewis machine.[36]

The violence spilled over from Illinois to Indiana, where, on the last day of July 1930, several carloads of Lewis supporters kidnapped Indiana insurgent Joseph Claypool, placed a rope around his neck, threatened his life, and then tarred and feathered him. At the same time, the kidnappers ran down Claypool's wife with a car, breaking her ankle. Two weeks before the kidnapping, John Walker had written Claypool about the violence: "Our members now understand them [Lewis crowd] for what they were and were now going to defend themselves—not to let them get away with it."[37]

Treated as traitors to the labor movement by William Green, beaten in the streets by pro-Lewis goons, and harassed by pro-Lewis public officials, the insurgents received moral support from Mother Jones. Just after celebrating her hundredth birthday early in September, the "Miner's Angel" donated $1,000 to John Walker and the RUMWA. "I only hope that I may live long enough to see John L. Lewis licked," commented the redoubtable Mother Jones.[38]

The decisive struggle between Lewis and the insurgents materialized not in the streets with fists and guns but in Illinois courtrooms with writs and injunctions. Insurgents had won the first legal battle back in October 1929, when an Illinois judge enjoined Lewis from suspending the charter of District 12 and deposing its elected officers. For more than a year afterward the legal battle seesawed back and forth as Lewis sued to deny the insurgents the right to use the name UMWA for their organization (thus RUMWA) and his opponents secured writs citing Lewis et al. for violating the original October 1929 injunction.[39]

The climactic legal decision occurred in the Dixon, Illinois, courtroom of Judge Harry Edwards in February and March 1931. Judge Edwards, in a temporary decree of February 13 that he made final on March 6, suggested a compromise solution to the intraunion controversy. It was one that, in effect, handed Lewis a victory. To Lewis's dissatisfaction, Edwards ruled that the UMW president had illegally established a provisional administration in District 12 in October 1929;

that the officers elected by the Illinois miners in December 1930, including John Walker as District 12 president, were entitled to hold office; and that miners had paid their dues to the RUMWA in good faith and could not be reassessed by Lewis's UMWA. To the frustration of the insurgents, however, Edwards decided that the Indianapolis UMWA was the legal miners' organization; that Lewis, Murray, and Kennedy remained the legitimate international officers; and that District 12 must accept as binding the constitution, rules, and regulations of the Lewis UMWA. In return for offering the Illinois miners a measure of district autonomy, Judge Edwards asked them to dissolve the RUMWA.[40]

Lewis seemed well satisfied with the results of the year-long legal imbroglio. The insurgents found little to celebrate in Edwards' decree. In fact, even before the judge delivered his final decision, Howat had threatened in court and outside not to obey it if Edwards favored Lewis.[41] Walker and Germer later asserted that Howat had prejudiced their case before Edwards by impugning the RUMWA's good faith. In a sense, then, Walker and Germer had prepared in advance to quit the struggle in the event of an adverse ruling. Within days of Judge Edwards' final edict, Walker and Germer disbanded the RUMWA, turned over to Lewis the complete financial and organizational records of District 12, and abided by the law. For them the larger struggle was over, and all that remained was a secondary effort to preserve District 12 from absolute domination by Lewis.[42]

Many left-wingers and also rank-and-filers were left aghast by Walker's and Germer's hasty and complete surrender. They wondered why, as Norman Thomas put it in a letter to Germer, "a fight such as you waged must be dropped at one unfavorable or partly favorable decision?"[43]

To be sure, Germer and Walker refused to admit that they had been defeated by Lewis, and they warned that unless the UMW president behaved honorably in the future, they reserved the right to appeal Judge Edwards' decree. Yet they never intended to prolong the legal struggle, because, among other reasons, it cost money—a resource the RUMWA lacked. In truth, Walker and Germer accepted the legal ruling because it saved them from publicly confessing their own failure.

After a year of bitter and sometimes violent internecine conflict in Illinois, the insurgents claimed 26,000 members (a substantial loss from their initial asserted following of 75,000 miners) to Lewis's 16,000—an actual increase for Provisional District 12. In Kansas, all of whose members Howat promised to deliver to the RUMWA, the insurgents counted 65 dues-paying members, and in the neighboring states of Oklahoma and Missouri there were fewer than 200. In West Virginia, where the insurgents spent over $20,000 and subsidized a protracted strike, they ended up with fewer than 300 dues-paying members; and in Ohio an expenditure of $10,000 recruited 22 members. Among Pennsylvania miners, the insurgents lacked any following. The whole financial burden of the RUMWA, Germer confessed, fell on the Illinois miners, who, particularly after Judge Edwards' decision granted the Lewis organization legal control of the contract between District 12 and the coal operators, could no longer carry the burden. The only contracts held in March 1931 by coal miners, Germer added, belonged legally to Lewis, not to the RUMWA, and miners laboring under those contracts could do so only as long as they held membership in the UMWA. "It is not that the Ohio, West Virginia, and Southwestern miners did not want to pay dues," lamented Germer, "the poor devils just did not have the money." To strip the few miners who still had jobs and money of their contracts, argued Germer and Walker, would have been unconscionable.[44]

Good and substantial cause partly explained Germer's and Walker's surrender. But other less honorable and unspoken reasons underlay their decision. When they failed to succeed immediately and became dependent on external financial, material, and moral support, Germer, Walker, and their closest allies equivocated. Fearful that Communists were gaining inordinate influence with Howat, who relied heavily on the noncommunist A. J. Muste and Tom Tippett for advice, Walker and Germer, both old-guard socialists who since 1919 were more anti-Communist than anti-capitalist, decided that compromise with Lewis was necessary. And as their base of support among coal miners withered, they had to choose among a slow death, coalition with Muste (independent of the Communists but to the left of the socialists), or compromise with Lewis. In the event, much as they despised Lewis, Walker and Germer considered Muste, whom they falsely linked to communism, a greater evil.

Communists among the coal miners offered Germer and Walker ample cause for suspicion. From the start of the conflict in Illinois and more so after the founding of the RUMWA in March 1930, Communists proved as inept politically as the insurgents. Instead of initially supporting the Illinois rebels against Lewis, whom they considered the nation's most obsequious labor lieutenant for capitalism, the Communists, following "third period"* party policy, pleaded with coal miners to reject the RUMWA as well as the UMWA. Communist propaganda never distinguished among Lewis, Farrington, Brophy, Germer, Walker, and Howat; nor did it portray the RUMWA as any less pro-capitalist than the Lewis UMWA. Throughout the union civil war in Illinois, Lewis's avowed enemies proved to be his best friends, however inadvertent their support. The political and personal scruples that divided Communists from socialists and Musteites from Germerites and that made coalition among them impossible never fazed Lewis. In 1931, as he had done before and would do again subsequently, Lewis used Communists, socialists, and anti-Communists indiscriminately.

Thus the first round of the Illinois coal miners' struggle ended in March 1931, when a legal ruling, financial problems, and anticommunism drove Germer and Walker into Lewis's arms. With the collapse of the RUMWA, the anti-Lewis

---

*The declaration in 1929 by Stalin and the Soviet Communist party that capitalism was entering its final crisis, workers had become radicalized, and that Communists must engage in total class war—against "social fascists" (Social Democrats and trade unionists) as well as capitalists.

movement in Illinois was left in the possession of Howat and Muste who, during the week of March 17-22, 1931, met secretly in Saint Louis to establish a new, dual miners' union.[45] On April 15, this faction held a public convention in Saint Lous (the Rank and File Coal Miners International Convention) that was subsidized entirely by Muste and his eastern sympathizers and that pledged to continue endlessly the struggle against Lewis for an honest, democratic miners' union.[46]

Lewis simply ignored the new Howat-Muste organization, which lacked support among coal miners, and allowed Walker to combat it. Lewis now occupied an enviable position in the internecine conflicts that still wracked District 12. Although Lewis remained committed to ending District 12's autonomy, Illinois district President John Walker not only had to preserve his independence from Lewis; he also had to thwart Musteite and Communist threats.

At an international executive board meeting on June 12, 1931, Lewis gloated that he had emerged from the Illinois conflict with his union hegemony secure. Admitting that the coal industry had been demoralized by depression and that the union had been destroyed as an economic force in the major bituminous fields, he asked board members to take pride in a new long-term anthracite contract that guaranteed existing wage rates and to look forward with optimism to the day when the cycle of history swung from depression to prosperity. He also reminded board members of the trauma their union had just endured. "The enemy from within," he lectured, "is always more destructive than the enemy who knockes at our gates from without." Thankfully, the UMWA had preserved itself against treason, it had "lived through its winter of discontent . . . [and] emerged as a solvent, functioning business institution."[47]

Lewis's optimism initially seemed premature. In July 1931, Illinois miners at the Orient mines in West Frankfort began a wildcat strike. When Lewis went there on July 26 to urge the miners to return to work, they greeted their president with catcalls, boos, and hisses, and they stopped him from speaking.[48] Then in the spring of 1932, when District 12's contract came up for renegotiation, insurgency reappeared in Illinois. Since the current contract had been signed in 1928, miners' wages had fallen continuously in the nonunion fields, causing Illinois operators, by 1932, to suffer a severe competitive disadvantage. To maintain the $6.10 daily wage rate in the state implied economic suicide for the operators and unemployment for the miners. But Illinois miners (50,000 of them) preferred to strike on April 1 rather than accept a wage cut. Unable financially to sustain such a strike, District 12 officials, in early July, accepted a $5.00 wage, still the highest in any of the coalfields. But on July 11 the Illinois miners voted overwhelmingly to reject the new contract. Additional conferences between union officials and operators resulted in a renegotiated contract that provided a six-hour day—a concession that in effect raised hourly wages based on the $5.00 daily rate and promised to spread employment among more miners. Lewis assisted District 12 leaders in renegotiating the contract, and on August 2, 1932, in an official notice to Illinois miners, he advised them to ratify the contract. Unless they did so, Lewis warned, their wage rate would not be $5.00 but would decline to the abysmally low level "now being paid the distressed mine workers in Kentucky, West Virginia, and Ohio. Lest he who would destroy, consider the price of such destruction."[49]

The election on the revised contract shceduled for August 8 boded no good. Communists, Musteites, Howatites, and plain malcontents urged Illinois miners to reject a wage cut. In some locals, according to John Walker, rebellious leaders allowed only negative ballots to be cast. Early results presaged another rejection, but the referendum suddenly took a strange turn. On the morning of August 10, a Lewis lieutenant, one Fox Hughes, took the ballots from the official union auditors, who subsequently reported that they had been robbed. Claiming that a state of emergency existed in District 12 owing to the theft of the ballots, Lewis declared the revised agreement ratified. This incident gave birth to the following bit of doggerel:

> John L. Lewis blew the whistle;
> John H. Walker rang the bell;
> Fox Hughes stole the ballots,
> and the miners wages went to hell.[50]

The Illinois election, Irving Bernstein's assertions to the contrary notwithstanding, was not a case in which John L. Lewis autocratically usurped the authority of district officials. Bernstein errs when he asserts that Walker had ceded authority in District 12 to Lewis after the original contract had been rejected and that Walker was not a party to the revised agreement. Walker, in fact, signed the revised contract, urged Illinois miners to ratify it, and never criticized Lewis's August 10 action. Five years later, in 1937, Walker recalled, in a letter to William Green, that although he found it personally obnoxious to include Lewis as a party to and guarantor of a District 12 contract, "I signed that contract . . . to save what little there was left of the market for the Illinois miners in Illinois and to give them a chance to get back a portion of their share of their natural markets." In 1937 he also informed Robert McCormick, publisher of the Chicago *Tribune*, "I would have made that agreement whether the ballots had been stolen or not, and regardless of what the International union did or did not do."[51]

Many rank-and-file Illinois miners, however, did not share their district president's sentiments. Lewis's declaration of a state of emergency and his arbitrary ratification of the Illinois contract stimulated a new wave of rebellion in District 12. In several coal mining communities, especially in Macoupin County and the surrounding East Saint Louis-Belleville area (once the Germer insurgent stronghold), Illinois miners declared their independence from the Lewis UMWA and formed a dual miners' union: the Progressive Mine Workers of America. If the progressive miners did not pose as great a threat to Lewis's authority as the Howat-Germer-Walker insurgency, they demonstrated far greater staying power.

The durability of the progressive miners seems incredible when one considers the amalgam of factions it united in Illinois. Sparked originally by men linked to Communists and Musteites, the Progressives came to include Ku Klux Klanners, pure opportunists, pie-card artists, and the corrupt associates of Frank Farrington. Such dedicated anti-Lewisites as Germer and Walker rejected it. "The plain fact of the matter is," Germer advised a Socialist party associate, "that some of the leaders of the progressives were formerly Lewis henchmen of the worst type, and like the leopard, they have not changed their spots."[52]

What most depressed Germer undoubtedly was not the threat that the Progressives posed to the UMWA but their gratuitous destruction of District 12 and its autonomy. The Progressive rebellion shattered John Walker's influence among Illinois miners. Committed to enforcing the 1932 contract, Walker fought the Progressives and, in the process, bankrupted District 12. With his members slipping away to the dual union and his treasury empty, Walker, in February 1933, turned to Lewis for salvation, asking the UMW president to assume control of District 12 and to establish a provisional administration. From one of his most dedicated enemies, Lewis thus obtained what he most desired: absolute dominion within the UMWA, as the last powerful autonomous district became an administration satrapy.[53]

Early in 1933, then, Lewis had become an absolute ruler, the master of an empty empire. Autonomy for District 12 disappeared only after Illinois lost the bulk of its UMW membership. A skeleton institution in the nation's other coalfields since 1927, the UMWA, on the eve of the New Deal, had lost its flesh in District 12. First weakened by the collapse of the soft-coal industry, brought to a terminal stage by the Great Depression, and reduced to impotency by the 1930-1931 Illinois miner civil war, the UMWA seemed an anachronism.

Not that coal miners accepted their misery in silence or apathy. The years 1930, 1931, and especially 1932 saw mass violent strikes scar the coalfields of Kentucky, West Virginia, western Pennsylvania, and Ohio. But Communists and independents, not Lewis men, either instigated or assumed control of these walkouts— conflicts that represented a final challenge to the UMW before its revival during the Roosevelt years.

Despite hard times, massive unemployment, and poverty—perhaps because of them—American coal miners behaved as few other workers did in the early stages of the Great Depression. They struck. On the surface, the number of coal strikes in 1931 and 1932 barely increased, but the number of strikes proved a false indicator of the depth of discontent in the coalfields. Better measures of discontent were the total number of miners on strike and man-days lost as a result of labor disputes. In 1931 a total of 113,808 coal miners walked off the job, compared to the previous year's 46,877. The 113,808 striking miners remained idle for almost 2.2 million man-days (compared to 1930's 999,937 man-days), or 32% of the time lost to strikes in all American industries combined. The following year, 1932, the number of miners on strike slipped to 83,211, but the number of man-days lost rose to over 6 million, or 58% of the time lost to all American industries.[54]

The UMWA and John L. Lewis had few links to the renewed militancy among coal miners. In 1931 and 1932, Lewis was too involved in his battle with the Illinois insurgents and in Washington politics to devote attention to industrial strife in the coalfields. Leadership of the 1931-1932 mass coal strikes slipped into other, more radical hands, and the leaders of the coal strikes posed a final threat to Lewis's dominion in the miners' union.

One of the major 1931 strikes flowed directly from Lewis's conflict with District 12 and the creation of the RUMWA. Among the founders of the RUMWA was C. Frank Keeney, a former district president (No. 17) in northern West Virginia and a former socialist. Keeney, in the summer of 1931, called his West Virginia miners out on strike. Unfortunately for him, however, the reality of industrial conflict had not much changed in West Virginia since the 1919-1923 period, when employers had vanquished the union. Local law officers in 1931 still served the coal companies; the governor assisted the operators; and employers evicted striking miners from company houses and replaced them with strike-breakers protected by armed guards. The tread of the "barefootman" was heard everywhere in northern West Virginia. Keeney's radical northern sympathizers lacked the funds to support 20,000 striking miners for an extended period, and, as financial support dwindled, the defeated and depressed West Virginia miners drifted back to work, left the state, or subsisted on minimal relief allotments.[55] Keeney's defeat left West Virginia coal unionism, or what little remained of it, in the grip of John L. Lewis's provisional District 17.

American Communists represented a second challenge to Lewis's influence among coal miners and proved as eager as Keeney to lead strikes. At the end of the 1920's Communist trade union policy, both in Soviet Russia and the United States, shifted toward combating rather than "boring from within" existing labor movements. After the defeat of Brophy and Lewis's repression of the "Save the Union Movement" in 1927-1928, Communist trade unionists gave up all hope of capturing the UMWA. Instead, at a conference in Pittsburgh in September 1928, they formed a separate dual organization, the National Miners' Union, with John J. Watt, an old Illinois radical, as president, William Boyce, a black miner, as vice-president, and Pat Toohey, an old Lewis foe from Pennsylvania, as secretary-treasurer. The organization of the National Miners' Union presaged a new stage in Communist trade union policy, coinciding with the so-called third period and the Trade Union Unity League (TUUL); it was a time for all-out war against existing trade unions, social democrats, and liberals ("social Fascists" in Stalinist terminology).[56]

The Great Depression, the collapse of the RUMWA, and the revival of militancy among coal miners offered Communists an opportunity. Officials of the National Miners' Union, in 1931, led strikes in western Pennsylvania, eastern

Kentucky, and Ohio. They organized mass marches by unemployed miners, their wives, and children; challenged local and state law enforcement officials; and, for over a year, kept the three coalfields in a state of turmoil. By late summer of 1931, the Communists had won a larger following among the region's coal miners than Lewis.

In all three regions, and especially Harlan County, Kentucky, bloodshed and death marked the National Miners' Union strikes. In Pennsylvania alone 3 miners were killed during the struggle; 55 were hospitalized; and over 2,000 were gassed, injured, or wounded. In Harlan County, where the most publicized and notorious of the Communist strikes occurred, coal miners and party officials found prominent sympathizers. Such eminent left-wing writers as Theodore Dreiser, Sherwood Anderson, and John Dos Passos visited the region and compiled a book, *Harlan Miners Speak*, that vividly portrayed industiral feudalism in eastner Kentucky. Neither newspaper publicity, the Dreiser delegation, visits by civil libertarians, nor a United States Senate investigation ended repression as practiced by Harlan County's coal operators. Employers, who treated the UMWA with impunity, hardly would deal with a Communist union. By the end of 1932, the Communists had as little as Frank Keeney to show for their strikes. Depression defeated Communists just as it frustrated UMWA insurgents and John L. Lewis.[57]

On almost every front from 1930 through 1932—economic, political, and personal—Lewis suffered defeat or frustration. Ever since 1921 the UMW president had cooperated with Herbert Hoover, flattered the Republican statesman, and supported him politically in order to win federal assistance for the miners' union. But Hoover had refused to save the Jacksonville agreement. After his election as president, he rejected Lewis as a candidate for secretary of labor, and declined to support UMWA-sponsored federal coal legislation. Despite such rebuffs from Hoover, Lewis affirmed his political alliance with the Republicans.

Other events exposed Lewis's loss of political influence and acumen. In 1926 the UMW president had campaigned for Gifford Pinchot as governor of Pennsylvania; Pinchot lost the Republican primary. Four years later, in 1930, Pinchot again sought the governorship; this time, however, Lewis fought his candidacy, and Pinchot won first the primary and then the general election. Lewis's repudiation of Pinchot in 1930 was linked to the labor leader's larger political ambitions. The anti-Pinchot Republican primary ticket included as its senatorial nominee James J. Davis, the secretary of labor; a Davis victory in the November general election would necessitate the appointment of a new secretary of labor, a position still desired by Lewis. Conferences between Lewis and Hoover in late August 1930 led to renewed rumors concerning the UMW president's candidacy for the cabinet position; and in October 1930, the Associated Press reported that Lewis and William Doak were Hoover's two primary prospects to replace Davis. Jett Lauck, as he had done in 1928-1929, offered to assist Lewis's candidacy, which

Lewis assured his economic adviser was then being investigated by William Green. "Green has been looking into the matter," Lewis wrote on November 11, "and the situation is still rather hazy."[58] When the situation clarified, Lewis was once again left frustrated. Hoover appointed Doak (a railroad brotherhood man) as secretary, leaving his "friend" Lewis's career and ambitions tied to a moribund miners' union.

Rejected by his political allies, repudiated by the voters of Pennsylvania, and beset by enemies inside the UMW throughout 1930 and 1931, Lewis suffered yet another family tragedy. In March 1931 his younger brother, George W., the sibling closest to John, passed away unexpectedly. For more than ten years George had served his older brother loyally as the UMW's legislative and political agent (Springfield and Washington lobbyist, in other words). According to close associates of Lewis, George's death caused the UMW president to cry openly and honestly and thereafter to dwell on health and death.*[59]

Lewis's fixation on death is understandable, considering that at three crucial moments in his trade union career close family members died: in October 1917, his firstborn child, Mary Margaret; in September 1919, his father, Thomas; and now in 1931, his brother George. And before John L. Lewis died in 1969, four other close family members—his mother, his wife, his daughter Kathryn, and his brother Dennie—preceded him to the grave.

In the spring of 1931 Lewis sublimated his depression over family loss and his fixation about death to union business. As his union slid deeper into the pit of disaster and miners rebelled at their economic predicament in a series of mass walkouts, Lewis once more turned to Washington and to Herbert Hoover for salvation. In June he appealed to Hoover, beseeching the president to bring the operators and miners together in a national conference to save the bituminous industry from total disaster. Only coercive federal action, could save the industry, warned Lewis.[60]

Several operators now shared Lewis's belief that the decline of the miners' union had harmed rather than benefited northern bituminous coal, and they also urged federal action. "It must be admitted," F. E. Taplin, president of the North American Coal Corporation, wrote to the presdient, "that the situation is even worse than when we dealt with the union. . . . Personally, I would much prefer to deal with the United Mine Workers than with these ruthless, price-cutting, wage-cutting operators who are a detriment to the industry." "Boiled down to plain English," observed Taplin, the would rather deal "with a good union under a fixed wage scale . . . than compete with . . . wage-cutting operators, which latter policy fills the mines with Communists." Unless a well-managed national

*As a reward and in the spirit of an extended family, Lewis made George's wife, Hannah, the secretary at District 12 headquarters in Springfield.

union instituted a fixed living wage scale in all competitive fields—a policy operators would never institute themselves—disaster impended, for Communists threatened industries other than coal. But Taplin, like Lewis, realized that the UMW lacked the strength to organize all the coalfields, and the mine operator, like the union leader, looked to Hoover for a solution. "Please think this over carefully," he asked the president, "and let me know what comments you have to make of a constructive nature that will benefit the industry."[61]

Hoover, however, proved as uneager as Harding and Coolidge before him to involve presidential prestige in the insoluble economic dilemma of bituminous coal. The president instead suggested that the union and the coal operators take their problems to the secretaries of labor and commerce, William Doak and Thomas Lamont, respectively.[62]

In July 1931 Lewis did precisely that. Leading a delegation of UMW officials on the thirteenth to meet with Secretary Doak, he urged a government-sponsored coal conference, and warned that the coal situation was so desperate that only federal action could salvage it.[63] The next day Lewis's delegation met formally with Doak and Lamont to press the case for federal intervention. Lewis demanded that the federal government invite operators to join the UMW in a national conference to establish a joint wage contract—the only means to stabilize the industry. Lamont and Doak rejected the proposal, the commerce secretary insisting that "we simply cannot call a lot of men together without having a program." Lewis, however, unabashedly offered the government a program: Sanction the principle of collective bargaining and the right of miners to assemble and organize freely.

As Lewis pressed for a conference, government recalcitrance grew. "We never intended to call a conference," asserted Doak. "The President wanted us to find out if there could be a conference." When Lewis reminded the secretaries that on numerous occasions in the past, federal officials had demanded the right to intervene in coal crises, Doak replied that no crisis existed in 1931. To Lewis's response that coal faced the worst crisis in its history, as thousands of miners and their families went hungry and naked, Lamont observed: "I do not see that that can be corrected until this abnormal condition of the country can be corrected." The commerce secretary also noted that people everywhere were in distress "due to the world situation which we cannot control." "A start ought to be made somewhere," observed Phil Murray, "and where ought we to go if not to our own Government to ask assistance in the situation." As the conference ended late that afternoon, Doak and Lamont refused to commit the government to the conference idea, yet Lewis seemed optimistic when interviewed by reporters.[64]

A week later Doak and Lamont invited 160 coal operators to attend a national coal conference. Their invitation, however, disappointed Lewis, for it was not a direct request from President Hoover. Doak and Lamont received the response that they had expected and also wanted: 38 operators agreed to attend the conference, 21 questioned its value but consented to appear, and the remaining 101 either declined to attend or failed to reply. The operators who declined to attend represented a rated tonnage of 2 million tons daily, compared to only 450,000 tons for those willing to meet with the union. Doak and Lamont now had reason to postpone a national coal conference, and Lewis realized that another union demand had been rebuffed by Hoover. The UMW president intended to resort to Congress and seek legislative redress for the coal miners and their union.[65]

Lewis and the coal miners were not alone in the summer of 1931 in learning that Hoover and the Republicans preferred to combat the depression with a policy of masterly inactivity. As Jett Lauck wrote to Lewis at the end of August, "all classes—labor, employers, white collar, congressmen, bankers . . . want a leader, if he has a sound and constructive policy." Lauck suggested that Lewis be that leader, that the UMW president "take the field for the reival and stabilization of the soft coal industry" by demanding that Hoover call a special session of Congress to pass the union's coal stabilization bill and adopt an emergency plan to control production and stabilize prices in all industries, under government boards composed of employers, organized labor, and the public. Aware, to be sure, that Hoover was unlikely to adopt such a policy, Lauck proposed an intensive political and public relations campaign, for "I am sure that *now* affords an opportunity which will never occur again for generations. You could take the leadership of the whole constructive movement—all classes of organized labor . . . farmers, bankers, business men, and industrial leaders . . . a movement of real industrial statesmanship and accomplishment which you would start and lead to success."

Here in embryo was the program of Franklin Roosevelt's first "hundred days"—but with Lewis cast in the role of the statesman who would offer the nation industrial planning, labor-management cooperation, stimulation of the domestic economy (which consumed 92% of America's output), and a cure for depression. "You are a Shakespearean scholar," Lauck flattered his putative national savior, "and you know that 'There is a tide in the affairs of men which taken at ebb leads on to victory,' or words to that effect."[66] Lewis, indeed, claimed to be a student of Shakespeare, and he certainly believed in the tides of history; but he was also cautious, cunning, and opportunistic. "The suggestions have a distinct appeal," he informed Lauck, "but we would undoubtedly encounter substantial obstacles in the way of attainment of the desired objectives." The leader of a moribund trade union was not comparable to the rising patrician star of the Democratic party, and 1931 was not 1933. Lewis knew it and hence notified his economic consultant that "it is debatable that I could undertake, with propriety, to act as a spokesman for industries other than coal."[67]

Lauck, however, persisted in pushing his plans and dreams on Lewis. On September 4 the economist advised the union leader that such industrialists as Owen D. Young, of General Electric, favored national price and production controls and that many other businessmen shared Young's dismay with the negative attitude of President Hoover. Such industrialists, moreover, endorsed the UMW's coal stabilization plan and desired its extension to other industries. Lauck pleaded with Lewis to inaugurate the fight for national economic planning promptly, because "the present situation offers an opportunity to put through a stabilization measure and to rehabilitate the industry and the union which will not occur again for another generation at least."[68]

Although Lewis apparently disregarded his adviser's most ambitious ideas, some of Lauck's concepts had begun to germinate in the union leader's mind. In a Labor Day speech delivered in Des Moines, Iowa, on September 7, Lewis warned that unless the nation's political leaders took immediate action to combat depression, the United States faced radical changes. "Those in high places who rest serene in the thought that cycles must have their fling," he continued, "will soon have to go into action or face action which might bring radical changes in our recognized system of commercial enterprise." Regardless of the "less government in business ballyhoo," he asserted, "the people will undertake the performance on their own responsibility by exercising their voting strength in devising and enlarging the regulatory powers of their federal and state governments." Because statesmen and businessmen had failed to provide high wages and stable employment, the forces that sustained mass production, the people would have to organize themselves to insure the revitalization of domestic purchasing power through economic planning.[69]

A month later, in October 1931, Lewis consented to Lauck's proposal to have the UMW president appear as a featured witness at a congressional hearing scheduled by Senator Robert LaFollette to consider national economic planning and stabilization. "It is the occasion," noted Lauck, "I think, we have been waiting for." Throughout the remainder of October and all of November, as the LaFollette hearings were postponed, Lauck and Lewis discussed the details and substance of the latter's public statement. They also planned to publicize their policies and the incipient movement for national economic planning with the assistance of Louis Stark, the *New York Times* labor reporter and the man they selected as an outlet for well-timed news leaks.[70]

More important to Lewis, however, than leadership of a national political movement—an attractive proposal but a dubious one in 1931—was congressional legislation to stabilize the coal industry. From December 1931 through March 1932 Lewis lobbied intensively for passage of his union's bill. Lauck and Ellis Searles managed the arm twisting in WAshington; UMW district officials lobbied congressmen from coal mining states; and Lewis courted coal operators. Lauck and Searles won Labor Secretary Doak's endorsement of the UMW bill and the support of congressmen. And Lewis, by late February, thought he had gained the approval of several large coal operators for passage of the Davis-Kelly Bill, as the union's proposed law was known. "I find a good deal of sentiment for the bill in a private way," Lewis informed Lauck, "and some [operators] said they were exercising their private influence, but they are hardly in a position as yet to come out in the open. I am hopeful that some of the seeds I planted may produce results later."[71]

Whether Lewis, in fact, had influenced the operators or he had instead misunderstood their position on federal legislation is an open question. By 1932 most bituminous operators desired some sort of federal legislation to liberate coal from the antitrust laws and to sanction price-fixing and joint marketing arrangements. The UMW's bill provided that much, but it also mandated that coal operators respect their workers' right to organize and bargain collectively with them in good faith. In the event, then, most coal companies opposed the Davis-Kelly Bill, President Hoover never endorsed it, and it died in congressional committee.

Despite the history of his relationship with Herbert Hoover, the failure of the Jacksonville agreement, the Great Depression, federal inactivity during the economic crisis, and the president's refusal to endorse emergency legislation for coal, Lewis rather remarkably endorsed Hoover's reelection in 1932.[72] Why Lewis made this political choice seems inexplicable. It was certainly not a reward for favors Hoover had done for Lewis or the UMW. It did not flow from Lewis's rock-ribbed Republicanism, which was more a fabrication of his critics and biographers than a reflection of his actual political beliefs. And it could not have been a reflex of Lewis's essential conservatism, for by November 1932 the UMW president, at the prodding of Lauck and with full awareness of the proportions of the nation's economic crisis, began to flirt with radicalism. Most likely, Lewis in his typical opportunistic fashion was playing both sides of the political fence. For in the late spring or early summer of 1932 Lewis had privately informed a Roosevelt emissary that most labor leaders, himself included, "will support the democratic nominee unless Mr. Hoover withdraws. . . ." He also promised to work behind the scenes for Roosevelt's election.[73]

Lewis by 1932 had rejected absolutely what Jett Lauck referred to as Hoover's "old rugged individualism." By the fall of 1932 Lewis had been stirred by Lauck's dreams and by the possibilities of more radical solutions to the nation's crisis. After three years of somnolence in the face of depression, the American people seemed to be stirring from their lethargy. The violent, mass miners' strikes of 1931-1932 were only one manifestation of a new political consciousness simmering among the nation's exploited and oppressed. The emergence of the Farm Holiday Association in 1932—an organization of rebellious midwestern farmers angry at the government's inability to protect agriculture from collapse and under strong left-wing influence—revitalized the potentialities of a farmer-labor alliance, and Lauck suggested to Lewis that a lobbying coalition between the miners' union and the Farmers' Holiday Association be consummated. Although Lewis rejected Lauck's more ambitious political schemes, the labor leader, long a believer in the cyclical theory of history, perceived that in 1932 a new cycle was about to begin—that now was the time to ride a rising political tide to victory.[74]

The election of 1932 over, Lewis forsook Hoover and Hooverism. Now he, Lauck, and the UMW lobbyists in Washington looked to the new president and the Democratic leadership in Congress for action.[75] That a new chapter was about to begin in Lewis's personal history became evident at the November 1932 A. F. of L. convention. After acting the role of conventional, conservative labor leader for almost a full decade after his defeat by Gompers at the 1921 A. F. of L. convention, Lewis reverted to the style of his early union career. At the 1932 convention he criticized the labor barons who dominated the federation and who offered unemployed workers the principle of voluntarism instead of bread. Compulsory government-financed unemployment insurance must come, Lewis asserted, for "it is inevitable that the die-hards among those opposed to the principle will have to modify their position [opposition to all government welfare programs] or be defeated." He also battled unsuccessfully to enlarge the A. F. of L. executive council from eight to twenty-five members so that more affiliates would be represented, especially those linked to the mass-production industries, which lacked an effective voice in the federation.[76]

Well before Franklin Roosevelt entered office in March 1933, Lewis expressed the social and economic philosophy indelibly associated with the later New Deal. Ever since the mid-1920s he had been demanding that the federal government intervene more directly in private enterprise by stabilizing the soft-coal industry under public control, promoting the interests of the UMW, and stimulating a high-wage, mass-consumption economy. The time had come, Lewis informed the Senate Finance Committee in February 1933, to free industry from the grip of the investment bankers, to control prices and production in the national interest, to stimulate mass purchasing power among those who labored for wages and salaries, and to offer wage and salary earners direct participation in the management of industry.[77] Just as the violent miners' strikes of 1931-1932 were precursors of the labor upheaval of the Roosevelt years, Lewis's speeches and public statements in late 1932 and early 1933 presaged the New Deal reforms and the 1935-1936 industrial union rebellion against the A. F. of L.

III.

Years of Glory,
1933-1940

CHAPTER 9

Rebirth of a Union, 1933-1934

March 4, 1933, the day of Franklin Delano Roosevelt's inauguration as thirty-second president of the United States, dawned gray and wet in Washington, D.C. Nature reflected the mood of a nation whose banks had closed the previous day and in which 13 to 15 million men and women were jobless. American capitalism, whether of nineteenth-century vintage or Herbert Hoover's "cooperative" model, seemed dormant; the future of democracy itself appeared problematic. Some citizens toyed with the idea of ceding autocratic authority to the nation's chief executive. "Even the iron hand of a national dictator," lamented the Republican governor of Kansas, Alfred M. Landon, "is in preference to a paralytic stroke."

Sensing the mood of the nation, Franklin Roosevelt promised swift action. "We must act, and act quickly." Warning Americans that it might become necessary for their elected leader to assume powers ordinarily exercised only in wartime, the new president also played Dr. Pangloss, assuring his listeners that they had nothing to fear but fear itself. Roosevelt implored citizens to cast away their anxieties and to join with him in a program of action.[1]

One American knew precisely what he wanted from the new president and the sort of federal action required to meet the crisis. By 1933 John L. Lewis had had a decade's experience coping with economic crisis in the bituminous coal industry. Before the Great Depression, Lewis had already concluded that only federal intervention could revitalize an ailing soft-coal industry. For Lewis, the depression simply revealed further intrinsic deficiencies in the private corporate system and the necessity for government national economic planning. The labor leader and his advisers thus refashioned plans devised originally to nationalize the coal industry into a proposal to reform the entire national economy—a program in which the federal government compelled industry to function collectively, eliminated destructive competition, insured stable employment, inflated wage rates (and hence consumer demand), and granted organized labor full participation. What the United States needed, asserted John L. Lewis, was a "New Deal."

Lewis's testimony before the Senate Finance Committee, on February 17,

1933, presaged the essence of Franklin Roosevelt's March 4 inaugural address and the substance of the New Deal. The time for equivocation and halfhearted measures had passed, Lewis warned the senators; let businessmen and conservative politicians heed the lessons of history. "The Bourbons of France, like some of the modern Bourbons in our own country, indulged themselves in idle chatter and continued to believe in their own security, notwithstanding the suffering and degradation of the masses. They paid for their errors and their inaction with their heads." Let us stop uttering pious platitudes about the need to balance the budget, advised the labor leader. "The balancing of the budget will not in itself place a teaspoonful of milk in a hungry baby's stomach or remove the rags from its mother's back." Instead, let us act as if the nation were threatened by a foreign enemy, as if we faced an emergency comparable to 1917-1918. Legalize collective bargaining, allow workers to organize unions in the basic industries, replace corporate autocracy with industrial democracy, and organized labor, promised Lewis, would police industry "against communism, or any other false and destructive philosophy, more efficiently than can the government itself." Lewis demanded the creation of a board of emergency control composed of representatives from industry, labor, agriculture, and finance, which would have plenary emergency power to reduce the hours of labor, guarantee the right of collective bargaining, stabilize prices, and implement national economic planning. Some may criticize this proposal as the beginning of a dictatorship, conceded Lewis, but "it is the form of procedure resorted to . . . during the crisis of World War, when the enemy was three thousand miles from our shore. Today the enemy is within the boundaries of the nation, and is stalking through every community and every home, and, obviously, this proposal is the most democratic form of internal regulation that can be devised to deal with our economic and industrial collapse."[2]

Lewis wasted little time in discovering whether Franklin Roosevelt agreed with the UMW president's prescription for economic recovery. On Monday, March 27, John L. Lewis, Phil Murray, Tom Kennedy, Van Bittner, and Ellis Searles met with President Roosevelt and Secretaries of Labor and Interior Frances Perkins and Harold Ickes, respectively, to discuss federal stabilization of the coal industry. Although Lewis refused to comment to reporters after the meeting and the president issued a noncommittal public statement, behind the scenes presidential advisers busily laid the foundation for a reorganization of the economy along the lines suggested by Lewis in February.

Among the more influential of the administration economic advisers was the UMW's own consultant, W. Jett Lauck. President Roosevelt's "brain-trusters," especially Rex Tugwell and Raymond Moley, came from the same academic and institutional milieu as Lauck; their intellectual predispositions were identical, their values were similar, and their proposals for national economic planning were simply the UMW's coal industry plan writ large. Lauck thus exerted influence during the planning sessions that formulated the National Industrial Recovery Act (NIRA) and particularly the incorporation in it of Section 7a, the clause that guaranteed workers the right to "organize unions of their own choosing" and to bargain collectively with their employers.

As ultimately presented to Congress for action, the NIRA exempted industry from prosecution under the antitrust statutes if enterprises eliminated competition by stabilizing prices and allocating markets. In return for exemption from antitrust legislation, businessmen had to adopt presidentially sanctioned codes that established minimum wages and maximum hours, eliminated child labor, and recognized the right of workers to organize unions and bargain collectively.[3]

Roosevelt's recommendation that Congress enact the NIRA ignited a legislative and public struggle reminiscent of the conflict over federal coal legislation from 1928 to 1932 among UMW officials, mine operators, and politicians. Just as the mine owners earlier had sought relief from antitrust laws and the right to stabilize prices and allocate markets among themselves but balked at accepting trade unionism as the price for cartelization, most American industrialists in May and June 1933 favored the passage of NIRA—but without its labor clause, Section 7a. In the press, on the radio, and before congressional committees, industrialists and labor leaders clashed concerning how to save the economy. Free us from antiquated antitrust regulations, let us handle labor unencumbered by costly union practices, said industrialists, and we will restore employment, productivity, and prosperity. Guarantee workers the right to organize and compel employers to bargain in good faith with trade unions, asserted labor leaders, and the labor movement will secure the high wages and steady employment that industrialists had failed to deliver.

On June 1, Robert Lamont, representing the American Iron and Steel Institute, and John L. Lewis clashed in testimony before the Senate Finance Committee. Opposing Section 7a of the NIRA, Lamont asserted that iron- and steelworkers were content with their employment status, preferred to remain outside trade unions, and endorsed the industry's "open-shop" policy, which offered work to all applicants regardless of union membership. If congressional action compelled employers to deal with trade unions, he warned, labor agitators would cause turmoil among satisfied employees and disrupt economic recovery. Lewis proved equally adamant in defense of Section 7a. "A man who can say that labor relations in the last ten years in America were happy," the UMW president sneered, "is an optimist that dwells in a realm to which I can not ascend." The steel industry's open-shop policy, implied Lewis, was pure hypocrisy, for employment was available only to those workers who rejected the union; industry's private police guaranteed that union members had brief job tenure. To Lamont's prophesy that passage of Section 7a would disrupt economic recovery, Lewis countered: "American labor . . . in the very essence of things . . . stand[s] between the rapacity of the robber barons of industry of America and the lustful rage of the communists, who would lay waste to our traditions and our institutions with fire and sword." To those congressmen fearful of the implications of the New Deal's innovations, the labor leader offered his characteristic rhetoric. "Let there be no 'moaning at the bar'," Lewis intoned, "when we put out to sea on this great adventure."[4]

Two weeks later on June 16, when Congress by overwhelming majorities, passed the National Industrial Recovery Act, Section 7a remained intact, providing what Lewis proclaimed as the greatest single advance for human rights in the United States since Abraham Lincoln's Emancipation Proclamation. For organized labor, Section 7a substantiated Harold Ickes' description of the impact of Franklin Roosevelt's first hundred days in office. "It's more than a New Deal," said the Interior Secretary. "It's a new world. People feel free again. They can breathe naturally. It's like quitting a morgue for the open woods."[5] And none felt freer nor breathed more easily than American coal miners.

That Lewis desired the incorporation of Section 7a into the Recovery Act is indisputable; that he lobbied unstintingly for its passage is without question; but that he envisaged Section 7a, in the words of Saul Alinsky, as the means "to fertilize the egg of the CIO" and organize all the nation's mass-production workers is legend. In March and April of 1933 Lewis, as Alinsky wrote, may have met frequently with A. F. of L. President William Green to discuss organized labor's response toward the emerging New Deal. They may even have met covertly one early spring evening in a "dark alley" near the St. Regis Hotel in midtown Manhattan to consider the New Deal's implications for labor. But it is unlikely that Lewis returned to his hotel room from that nocturnal meeting knowing, as Alinsky dramatized,

> that industrial unionization of steel, autos, and the basic industries would never come out of the AF of L. Section 7a or a thousand sections would never inspire the AF of L or Bill Green to this inevitable task. It was then and there that I knew it was up to me. The die of the CIO was cast in those early morning hours in that dark areaway on 55th Street. I went to bed, and the next day I began to plan the CIO.[6]

In the spring of 1933 different thoughts and objectives were uppermost in the mind of John L. Lewis. Organization of the nation's mass-production workers, the timidity of the A. F. of L.'s leadership, and the necessity for a new national labor federation may have been ideas germinating in the deepest recesses of Lewis's imagination. But Lewis, in the spring of 1933, remained too much the realist and opportunist to plan an unprecedented organizing campaign in the mass-production industries and a potential rift in the labor movement when the great mass of the nation's coal miners remained unorganized and his own union was barely solvent. Before Section 7a could become the Magna Carta for all unorganized industrial workers, Lewis first had to attend to his own union's immediate needs. Just as Lewis, in 1931, had rejected Jett Lauck's recommendation that he serve as the leader of a radical national reform movement, Lewis in 1933 could scarcely lead the nation's unorganized industrial workers when he had yet to conquer antiunion coal operators or liberate the miners from "industrial autocracy." Lewis had no desire to play the false prophet or premature savior.[7]

While labor leaders and employers fought in Washington to obtain an industrial recovery program satisfactory to their respective interests, rank-and-file workers, coal miners included, seemed quiescent. Few symptoms of the discontent that had swept through the coalfields in 1931 and 1932 lingered; American workers again appeared as lethargic as they had been early on during the Great Depression. From one Appalachian coalfield a UMW member reported in February 1933 that "as far as West Kentucky is concerned there is no sign of organization. Now . . . you could not organize a *baseball team*." A week later, an Illinois District 12 miner observed: "Things are in a bad way. . . . The future is not bright."[8]

Yet by June coal miners seemed liberated—their lethargy transformed into militancy, their indifference to the UMW replaced by fierce union loyalty. On June 23, precisely one week after the passage of NIRA and Section 7a, Van Bittner reported from West Virginia that the UMW's current organizing campaign was like a dream, too good to be true. "We expect to be practically through with every mine in the state and have every miner under the jurisdiction of our union by the first of next week." Northern West Virginia had been completely reorganized, and the southern counties of Logan and McDowell, where the UMW had never functioned, were fast being conquered. Referring to southern West Virginia, Bittner exulted: "That field is completely organized and unbounded enthusiasm prevails among the miners and their people." What happened in West Virginia repeated itself in other coalfields. Begun on June 1, the UMW's organizing campaign was practically completed by July 1—August 1 in some of the more recalcitrant antiunion districts. Neither coal-company-instituted wage increases nor the establishment of company unions retarded the UMW advance.[9]

John L. Lewis's role in the revitalization of the UMW and the reunionization of the coalfields was central yet tangential. It was salient to the extent that his political influence led to the enactment of Section 7a and that afterwards he gambled his union's slender financial resources on an intensive organizing campaign. It was tangential in the sense that coal miners seemed to organize themselves in June and July 1933, even in the absence of UMW funds and organizers. Such organizers as Van Bittner did not have to plead with miners to join the union; all they needed to do was sign up recruits as fast as they appeared, which was rapidly, indeed.[10] In fact, the spirit of the New Deal, the accomplishments of Roosevelt's first 100 days, and a sense that substantial social and economic changes impended were more important than any speech or action by John L. Lewis in motivating coal miners to rebel against their employers and the conditions of their existence.

Equally important, the initial New Deal reforms and President Roosevelt's benevolent attitude toward labor left coal operators spiritually paralyzed. With minor exceptions, few coal companies openly resisted their workers' unionization, not because they now favored trade unions, but because the policies of the

Roosevelt administration confused them. As one astute observer of the UMW campaign later noted, the operators and their local law enforcement allies "stood by with one eye on Washington, wondering what it was all about and not sure of themselves when the organizers kept reassuring the men that the federal government was behind them and their right to organize." The UMW did its job so quickly, added the observer, "that organizations were established before the mine owners woke up."[11] Some mine owners, moreover, perceived the New Deal reforms and the unionization of the miners as an opportunity to resurrect a declining industry. Northern operators, unable to compete with lower-cost southern mines, favored the UMW as an instrument to equalize wage rates, and they saw the New Deal's economic recovery program as a means to control prices, allocate markets, and rationalize an otherwise anarchic industry.

Organization of the miners was only a first step in Lewis's campaign to restore UMW influence, improve working conditions, and, ultimately, build a powerful national labor movement. Once the mass of miners enrolled in the UMW, he sought to negotiate contracts with coal operators. Here Lewis encountered serious obstacles. Caught unawares by the UMW's lightning organizing campaign and the miners' alacrity to join the union, nonunion operators now regrouped to resist further UMW advances. Traditional open-shop operators in the South and the captive mines* everywhere refused to bargain with the UMW, discharged union militants, and attempted to crush the UMW before Roosevelt approved the NIRA code of fair competition for the bituminous coal industry, which would penalize employers who refused to bargain collectively in good faith.[12] One prominent West Virginia operator suggested in late July that "now is the time to clean out those that have indicated they would be leaders when the 'show-down' comes." There is no room in the jails for coal operators anyway, he added, and he doubted that the local judge "would turn a bootlegger loose to make room for us."[13] To the north, the same large Pennsylvania operators who a decade earlier had repudiated the Jacksonville agreement resorted to customary tactics in fighting the union. They discharged union leaders, recruited strikebreakers, set black against white miners, exercised repressive local police power, and created company unions. Particularly in southwestern Pennsylvania, the captive coal companies refused to recognize the UMW or bargain with labor. To recognize trade unionism in the mines, they feared, would set a precedent that might open the iron and steel industry to organized labor.[14]

In July and August 1933, however, coal miners were in no mood to tolerate employer resistance. Throughout the summer militant miners, acting on their own, walked out of the pits in wildcat strikes aimed at achieving union recognition. Rank-and-file impatience with the tedious process of negotiating a code for the coal industry under Section 7b of the NIRA led Lewis to develop a seemingly

---

*Mines owned by the major steel companies that produced coke for the steel mills and not coal for open-market sales.

contradictory but effective bargaining strategy. On the one hand the UMW president, eager to remain on good terms with the Roosevelt administration and to mollify operators, kept a tight lid on action in the coalfields. Lewis repeatedly urged miners to sit tight, remain at work, and allow their leaders "to bring home the bacon." On the other hand Lewis knew that if the coal miners in fact sat tight and worked diligently, operators would be less likely to bargain seriously with the UMW or to offer the union the terms it desired. Negotiations then under way in Washington to establish NIRA codes for the steel and auto industries revealed to Lewis (as if he did not already recognize) labor's inability to extract concessions from employers whose workers were neither effectively organized nor able to paralyze production. Lewis thus acted the moderate in his relations with the Roosevelt administration and the coal operators while a militant union rank and file threatened rebellion from below.

Early in August UMW representatives, coal operators, and federal officials began hearings on a code of fair competition for the bituminous coal industry. Two factors, aside from the militancy of coal miners, strengthened Lewis's position in the negotiations. No labor leader seemed to command more respect in the nation's capital, as evidenced by his appointment on August 5 by President Roosevelt to serve as a member of the Labor Advisory Board under the NIRA. Next to Leo Wolman, observed the *New Republic*, Lewis was the most important member of the advisory board.[15] Lewis also established a close personal relationship with the director of the National Recovery Administration (NRA)—the agency created to administer the NIRA—General Hugh S. Johnson. Johnson, like Lewis, was a self-made man habituated to bombastic rhetoric, stock phrases, and mixed metaphors; like the UMW president, the NRA director scowled in public, stared fiercely at all enemies, and threatened to sock recalcitrant employers right on the nose. Like Lewis's, Johnson's public persona turned into charm and gentlemanly graces when he met privately with individuals of equal or superior status. For years after their initial meeting in the summer of 1933, Lewis and Johnson exchanged New Year's, birthday, and good health greetings, sometimes consoling each other in times of personal and family illness. "In my opinion," Johnson privately informed Lewis on December 30, 1933, "you are one of the greatest influences on the President's New Deal—Toleration understanding—Statesmanship. You have no intelligent opponents on the part of employers. They regard you as a partner and so do I—but as for me—mainly . . . a friend."[16] The friendship between Lewis and Johnson was particularly crucial during the negotiations to write a coal code, for Johnson chose to intervene directly, often, and sometimes, inopportunely in the bargaining between coal operators and union officials.

The start of the bituminous industry hearings found employers and union far apart. Lewis's demands were numerous, fundamental, and costly. He sought an agreement that would cover the southern Appalachian fields as well as the old

Central Competitive Field; a uniform national minimum daily wage of $5 . . . (many southern mines were then paying as little as $1.50); the six-hour day, six-day week; the right to checkoff union dues and for miners to select their own checkweighman; the prohibition of noncash wage payments and compulsory company houses and stores; the elimination of child labor; and the creation of equitable grievance procedures. Divided about whether or not to deal with the UMW, the coal operators united in their insistence, as stated by their chief negotiator, Charles O'Neill, that they could not pay higher wages. Operators, said O'Neill on August 9, the first day of hearings in Washington, would gladly unite to set prices and allocate markets but absolutely rejected any legal requirement that employers must deal with labor. The next day, Lewis, speaking for his union, warned that the future welfare of the United States, if not the whole Western world, depended on the results of the code hearings. The NIRA, he stressed, "offers . . . not only a way out, but the only way out." Characterizing O'Neill's remarks of the previous day, Lewis pungently summarized employers' emerging attitude toward the New Deal recovery program. "More and more," observed the labor leader, "the framing of codes is a matter of bickering and barter, of surrendering just as little as possible and grasping just as much as possible." Industrialists, he concluded, seem "to be suffering from the delusion that we are on our way back to the conditions which prevailed in the summer of 1929."17

As industry and union representatives quarreled about the terms of a code for the soft-coal industry in sultry Washington offices, coal miners and mine managers fought a real industrial war in western Pennsylvania and other coalfields. In Pennsylvania, where strikes proved most common and often violent, Lewis had little direct influence. The miners, especially those who walked out of the captive pits, followed the leadership of such union insurgents as Martin Ryan, an old-line radical and Communist, and acted without orders from the UMW hierarchy. Indeed, most of the Pennsylvania strikers looked more to Franklin D. Roosevelt than John L. Lewis for salvation. Assurances from Roosevelt that if the men returned to work, coal operators would deal with the union and adopt an industrial code caused the strikers in mid-August temporarily to end their walkout.18

But when negotiations between employers and UMW officials brought no resolution to the dispute over code terms and General Johnson complicated matters by suggesting he might "clarify" the meaning of Section 7a—a public statement that led southern nonunion operators to believe the general would sanction the open shop and company unions—miners took matters into their own hands. Louis Stark, the *New York Times* labor reporter and a customary Lewis conduit for news leaks, wired Roosevelt on August 23 that "hell" was about to break loose in the coalfields. "Every day sees another walkout," he noted. "Today a bunch of miners in Bell County, adjoining Harlan County . . . went out. Part of Alabama was out yesterday . . . more trouble in the Pittsburgh coal mines." Lewis pleaded with his organizers, Stark reported, "to sit on the lid and get the men to be patient,'' but every day that passes without a code increases the danger of violence.[19]

The message in Stark's telegram suggests that Lewis, or a Lewis lieutenant, was the reporter's primary source of information. Stark's warning that ''seething discontent in the [coal] fields may break out worse than ever. From coal it will spread to steel and autos'' had to vex the president. Yet Roosevelt also must have been pleased by Lewis's attitude, as characterized by Stark. ''Lewis is holding tight. He knows that if the conflagration starts it may be disastrous for everybody.'' The key to peace, advised Stark, echoing Lewis's analysis of the coal situation, ''is an agreement between the union and the southern operators.''[20]

Other influential presidential informants buttressed Lewis's strategic campaign to win presidential sanction for the UMW. On September 5, Pennsylvania Governor Gifford Pinchot informed Roosevelt ''that if we have a prolonged general soft coal strike, bang goes Recovery.'' He also assured the president that coal miners trusted Roosevelt as the worker's friend, indeed worshipped him, and believed fervently that ''you are working to get them recognition of the United Mine Workers of America.''[21]

Lewis's strategy had its intended effect on Roosevelt, motivating the president to intervene directly in the code negotiations. On the evening of September 6, a day after he received Governor Pinchot's warning, Roosevelt invited UMW officials and leading coal operators to a private conference at the White House. Greeting his guests, the President joshed:

> Come along and sit ye down, let's make it a family party. I thought that when Cuba blew up yesterday it was about the only thing I was to have trouble with, so its up to you to clear this thing up. Remember Cuba only affects 3 million folk, but coal affects 25 million and we've got to straighten this situation out quick. We can't let things go on. . . . If you want my help, I'll fix em! Will some one tell me what this difficulty is about language? Now don't all speak at once, make yourselves at home and have a cigar.

The operators' representatives spoke immediately, asserting that they had already eliminated an open-shop clause from the proposed coal code, would never accede to the closed shop, and were morally compelled to protect the liberty of nonunion miners. To which Lewis asked: Where are the nonunion miners?

As the operators described a code more notable for its complexities than for its concessions to labor, Roosevelt observed: ''The contract you suggest and your contract are drafted in an English that 9/10ths of the miners can't understand—they simply won't read it.'' Reading aloud the clause operators suggested be inserted to protect nonunion miners, the president remarked that he didn't know what it meant, ''and if I, as a lawyer, can't figure it out—well that language is obscure.'' Roosevelt then asked that he personally be allowed to draft a supplementary statement encompassing the operators' aims that would say in plain words ''that a man shall have the right to work without being a member of a union." Weasel words, observed Roosevelt, "always add difficulties and finally land us in an endless mess."

Although the operators balked at the president's suggestion, Lewis, the only voice that spoke for the UMW, promised that the "United Mine Workers will accept your good offices, Mr. President." For the remainder of the conference Lewis and Roosevelt harmonized their positions, the president urging the operators to compromise and the labor leader offering revisions in the UMW's original demands. "You get that contract written up tomorrow," urged the president as he bid his guests goodnight, "and if you've anything else on your minds, just let me know."[22]

But a week after the White House conference, the UMW and the coal operators were no closer to agreement. On September 12 Pennsylvania miners, once more acting more militantly than their leaders, voted to strike the next day unless a satisfactory code was written. And once again Governor Pinchot urged President Roosevelt to act, for "one more outrage . . . might easily plunge the whole area into tumult and riot."[23] With the threat of a coal strike in Pennsylvania—one likely to spread throughout the bituminous fields—a real possibility, Roosevelt pressured UMW officials and operators to remain in daily bargaining sessions, weekends included.

On September 21 Lewis's strategy brought the UMW handsome dividends. Using rank-and-file rebelliousness to pressure both operators and the United States president, Lewis won for his union the first code written under the NIRA that awarded organized labor substantial concessions and a role in its implementation. The auto and steel codes, written earlier and already approved by the president, vested management with undiluted authority in labor relations, including hiring and firing, and—aside from the wages and standards mandated by law—offered minimal concessions to trade unionism. But the bituminous coal code, as approved by President Roosevelt on September 21, granted the UMW what it had fruitlessly struggled for since its foundation in 1890: a contract that covered all the major soft-coal producing districts: Pennsylvania, Ohio, West Virginia, Virginia, eastern Kentucky, and Tennessee—with supplemental agreements that covered Indiana and Illinois. Although Lewis failed to win uniform wage rates, the remaining differentials, though substantial in some instances, had been narrowed. No miner would henceforth earn less than the $3.40 a day awarded the lowest paid deep South coal digger nor more than the $5.63 granted the small number of miners in the Northwest where prevailing wage rates were high and the cost of living equally high. Miners in the hitherto low-wage districts of West Virginia, east Kentucky, Virginia, Maryland, and Tennessee, who had seen wages fall as low as $1.50 a day during the depression, were now guaranteed a $4.20 minimum, only forty cents a day less than Pennsylvania and Ohio miners and sixty cents less than Illinois miners, once the highest paid union members.[24]

Other benefits flowed to American coal miners as a result of the bituminous coal code. Statutory law now guaranteed them the eight-hour day, five-day week; the right to choose their own checkweighmen; and the abolition of wage payment in scrip and of the requirement to trade in company stores and dwell in company houses. The code outlawed child labor (defined as under age seventeen) and granted miners a grievance procedure culminating in arbitration. Although the UMW failed to win the union shop, it did gain the right to compel employers to check off union dues from the payroll. In a comment as apt as it was witty, belle-lettrist Howard Brubaker observed in the *New Yorker*: "the defeated mine-owners agreed to all things that deputy sheriffs usually shoot people for demanding." More revealing, a northern mine operator immediately wired Lewis: "I want to congratulate you on getting a code . . . which puts the United Mine Workers in every bituminous mine in the country which I am sure will do more to stabilize the . . . coal industry than anything which has been done in its history."[25]

The political relationship between John L. Lewis and Franklin D. Roosevelt that secured coal miners rights that had eluded them for almost half a century was caught in songs composed by black and white southern miners. In Trafford, Alabama, Uncle George Jones sang:

> In nineteen hundred an' thirty-three,
>   when Mr. Roosevelt took his seat,
> He said to President John L. Lewis,
>   "In union we must be."

> Hooray! Hooray!
>   Fer de union we must stan',
> It's de only organization
>   Protects de laborin' man.
> Boys, it makes de women happy,
>   Our chillun clap deir hands,
> To see de beefsteak an' de good po'k chops,
>   Steamin' in dose frying pans.

> When de President and John L. Lewis
>   Had signed deir decree,
> Dey called fer Mitch an' Raney—
> Dalrymple made de three:
> "Go down in Alabama,
>   Organize ev'ry laborin' man,
> Spread de news all over de lan':
>   We got de union back again!"

And in McDowell County, West Virginia, they sang:

> Some people don't know who to thank,
>   For this "State of McDowell" that's so free;
> Give part of the praise to John Lewis,
>   and the rest of it to Franklin D.[26]

However much truth the miners' songs revealed, they failed to give sufficient credit to the role of rank-and-filers. Without coal miners' loyalty to trade unionism and their willingness to walk out of the pits repeatedly, neither John L. Lewis nor Franklin D. Roosevelt could have compelled operators to acquiesce in the September 21 agreement. It was the militant behavior of coal miners, not the tough language and sharp bargaining of John L. Lewis, that threatened Roosevelt's plans for industrial recovery. However astute Lewis may have been during his negotiations with operators, his achievements would have been minimal had miners not occasionally "blown the lid." Lewis, moreover, knew this. His bargaining achievements, he realized, flowed not from his own tactical and strategic brilliance but instead derived from the power exercised by masses of angry workers. Alone, Lewis was impotent as a labor leader; backed by hundreds of thousands of loyal followers ready to struggle for their rights, he wielded real influence. "We [labor leaders] would be just as other people, as the man on the street, if it were not for the fact that back of us is the great force of the workers for whom we can speak in relation to their hopes and aspirations, and the attention we get, the favorable attention . . . comes as a result of the fact that *back of us is organization*"[27] (italics added).

The September 21 agreement placed the United Mine Workers in the strongest position in its history. The miners' union had finally won a contract that guaranteed it recognition and stability in the hitherto nonunion southern Appalachian fields. But one exception—and a glaring one—remained to the UMW's triumphant conquest of the coalfields. The captive mines, those owned and operated by the steel industry, refused to recognize the miners' union or bargain with it.

Although the captive mines produced only about 8% of the nation's soft coal and did not market their output commercially, their existence as bastions of the open shop threatened the security of the miners' union. Lewis remembered well how after World War I, when the UMW had achieved its peak membership, those Pennsylvania operators most closely associated with the open-shop iron and steel industry had fought the UMW and precipitated the breakdown of the Jacksonville agreement. Lewis never doubted his union's ability to dominate smaller operators and independent coal companies, but he feared the economic power symbolized by an alliance among Wall Street investment bankers, major railroads, and mass-production industries (the Morgan-Rockefeller-Mellon-Dupont nexus—the economic royalists repeatedly condemned by the presidents of the miners' union and of the United States). If the UMW tolerated the open shop in the captive mines, commercial operators might demand similar arrangements. Moreover, the possibility always existed that the steel companies and their Wall Street allies might, in the future, lead a campaign, reminiscent of the antilabor crusades of the 1920s, to eliminate the UMW from the coal industry.

Steelmen, on the contrary, believed that recognition of the coal miners' union would set a bad example for labor relations in the iron and steel industries. Since the first decade of the twentieth century, when United States Steel defeated the Amalgamated Association of Iron and Steel Workers and made the entire industry open shop, the steel industry had successfully defeated all attempts at unionization. Through a combination of fringe benefits for their workers, astute public relations, and plain repression, the steel companies entered the New Deal years an open-shop bastion. They were not prepared to allow the labor enemy to breach any part of their defenses by conceding recognition to the UMW, however separate the mining of coal may have been from the production of steel. And just as United States Steel, since its organization in 1901, had set the industry's labor policies, the H. C. Frick Company, U. S. Steel's subsidiary in the coal industry and the nation's largest coke producer, led the captive mines' struggle against the UMW.

The central role of U. S. Steel and the H. C. Frick Company in the captive mine dispute of 1933 featured two notable ironies. Frick's president, Thomas Moses, was the son of an Iowa coal miner and had been a miner in Illinois District 12, a former UMW member, and a warm personal friend of John L. Lewis's. The chief executive officer of U. S. Steel was Myron C. Taylor, who in 1937 made history when, as a result of secret negotiations with John L. Lewis, he signed a contract with the Steel Workers Organizing Committee that opened the steel industry to penetration by the CIO. Unlike Moses, Taylor was born to his role as an "economic royalist." He was the son of a wealthy manufacturer, the descendant of prominent colonial forbears, and the beneficiary of an upper-class education. By age twenty-one, he had established a Wall Street law practice, and by middle age, on the eve of the Great Depression, he claimed a personal fortune estimated at $20 million. The possessor of a town house on Manhattan's Upper East Side, a country home on the estate-dotted north shore of Long Island, and a Medici villa in the hills above Florence, he lived more like a patrician gentleman than an active industrialist. His life-style was more comparable to that of Franklin D. Roosevelt than that of such anti-New Deal steelmasters as Eugene Grace and Tom Girdler. Taylor and Roosevelt, in fact, admired each other, corresponded with each other as statesmen (though one represented a public state and the other a private government), and, during the tense days before and during World War II, worked jointly to guide the nation toward an interventionist and internationalist foreign policy.[28] In the autumn of 1933 these four men—Lewis, Roosevelt, Moses, and Taylor—whose lives and careers were so intertwined, found themselves engaged in an industrial dispute that threatened the New Deal's plans for economic recovery.

Lewis pursued precisely the same strategy to organize the captive mines as he had applied against the commercial coal operators. A whirlwind organizing campaign succeeded in enrolling most of the captive miners in the union before employers realized what had happened. Lewis again relied on a militant rank and file to threaten the president's plans for economic recovery. And he alternately "kept the lid" on his miners' behavior and allowed them to explode rebelliously until the resultant pressures forced Roosevelt to wrench from reluctant employers a limited victory for the UMW and the first substantial breach in steel's hitherto impregnable antiunion wall.

As the commercial mines fell before the UMW onslaught in September 1933, the captive mines beat a strategic retreat. On September 21, the owners of the captive mines agreed to comply with the terms of the Bituminous Coal Code and to maintain as favorable hours, wages, and working conditions as those prevailing under the agreements between commercial coal operators and the UMW. On September 29 President Roosevelt approved the agreement, and on October 1 the captive mines implemented the new working conditions.

Conceding to their workers and the president on the question of wages and working conditions, the captive mine operators refused to relinquish arbitrary control of their labor force. A policy statement issued by United States Steel on September 27 covering labor relations for its coal mining subsidiaries specified "that if request is made to sign a Union scale or an Agreement with the Union, statement can be made that same cannot be done."[29]

The Frick Company's refusal to bargain with the UMW precipitated another crisis in the coal industry. Although Hugh Johnson believed that on October 1 he had succeeded in arranging an understanding between Tom Moses and Phil Murray, the UMW's chief negotiator for the captive mines, the general could not have been more mistaken.[30] A telegram from Pennsylvania Governor Gifford Pinchot to President Roosevelt, also sent on October 1, more realistically described the situation among the state's coal miners. Reporting that the meeting Johnson had arranged between Moses and Murray was a complete failure, Pinchot advised that "unless you [Roosevelt] can force Taylor to recognize union at least seventy five percent of entire Pennsylvania bituminous field will be out tomorrow and the rest by Wednesday or earlier. Rank and File miners complaining they are being kidded. Era of good feeling is over. Looting of food stores has begun. . . . It seems a shame," lamented the governor, "that pigheaded obstinacy of handful of men should force this calamity upon us and endanger your whole recovery program."[31]

Precisely as Lewis had expected, the militancy of Pennsylvania's miners and the threat that they posed to the New Deal's recovery program induced Roosevelt to intervene forcefully in the captive mines dispute and, more important, to assist the UMW. On October 4 the president wrote to Myron Taylor, informing the steel executive that the clause in the September 21 captive mines' agreement concerning "working conditions" encompassed the dues checkoff and collective bargaining. "I beg you to remember," Roosevelt informed the industrialist, "that the old doctrine of 'pigs is pigs' applies. Coal mining is coal mining. . . . Therefore, as a matter of public policy, I must hold that the conditions of work in the captive coal mines must conform to the conditions of work in the average run of commercial coal mines." To guarantee that the captive mine owners negotiated an agreement with the UMW, Roosevelt invited Myron Taylor and the operators to a conference at the White House on the morning of October 7.[32]

Although Taylor assured the president that the steelmasters were equally desirous of solving the dispute, the industrialists' position, as stated in a letter of October 6, suggested the contrary. Insisting that the captive mines were in an entirely separate category from the commercial coal properties and that the NIRA mandated neither union recognition nor collective bargaining, the operators asserted that their agreement of September 21 covering wages and working conditions satisfied all legal and moral obligations. "The Steel Industry as a whole stands firmly where it has always stood, for the 'open shop' . . . and we believe this policy complies with Section 7a of the National Industrial Recovery Act." Refusing to concede on the issue of union recognition, the captive mine owners argued that their employees were satisfied with conditions and remained away from work solely because of union-instigated violence. Not for one moment would they consider abandoning their employees' rights to contractual freedom by imposing the checkoff and a closed or union shop on them, the industrialists informed the president. We "are unwilling to do by indirection what [we] cannot do directly."33

During the October 7 White House conference and in a subsequent letter to the operators on October 9, President Roosevelt persisted in defining the phrase "working conditions" to encompass negotiations with the union and the dues checkoff. Buffeted by the president on one side and rebellious miners on the other, the operators offered a small concession: They agreed to check off dues for any miner who voluntarily requested it. Yet they refused to negotiate with union representatives and engaged in what Phil Murray characterized as "sparring on . . . irrelevant technicalities." When Murray offered to bargain only for those miners he represented and promised that the UMW had no desire "to control the operation of your mines," Moses replied that the Frick Company "will only make contracts of employment with our employees"; that is, the company would deal only with individuals, not labor organizations. Letters from Myron Taylor and W. A. Irvin, president of U. S. Steel, exemplified company recalcitrance. The two industrialists assured Roosevelt that only "violence and intimidation" prevent their miners, who "have no real grievance," from laboring. And Irvin stressed that the company would never be a party to inducing its employees to become union members, advising the president that the open shop is "an essential principle of personal liberty under our Constitution and laws."34

Wisely remaining in the background during the dispute, Lewis allowed Murray to represent the union and Roosevelt to manipulate the operators. In this instance the president did not disappoint Lewis. Roosevelt appreciated Lewis's and Murray's moderation—their appeals to the miners for restraint. Irked at the obstinacy of the captive mine owners, Roosevelt, on October 18, berated them. He told them that their collective bargaining policy was hypocritical and that he was at a loss to understand how their insistence on negotiating with individual employees was "consistent with your agreement [to] enter into negotiations at once, in good faith, with representatives of their workers." The president reiterated his principle that "pigs is pigs" and demanded that the operators accept his interpretation of the obligations that all captive mine owners had assumed in their agreement with the president on September 21, 1933.[35]

For two more weeks the dispute dragged on, as the recalcitrant steel executives weighed their options. Unable to sway the president or to resume full production at their strike-plagued mines, the operators, on October 30, finally accepted a presidential compromise. The UMW promised to call off its strike on November 6, and the companies pledged to implement the terms of the Appalachian agreement and to accept the principle of the checkoff. The thorny issue of union recognition was left in abeyance. The UMW and the operators agreed to abide by the results of representation elections, to be conducted by the National Labor Board, in which miners would select collective bargaining representatives with whom employers would negotiate a contract. In the event that no settlement was achieved through collective bargaining, the NLB would resolve the issues in dispute.[36]

In late November the NLB conducted representation elections at the captive mines. Except at the Frick properties, the UMW won substantial majorities among the miners, who voted for slates consisting of Lewis, Murray, Kennedy, and the respective district officials. Out of thirty such elections, the UMW won twenty, tied one, and lost nine—the defeats almost all coming in Fayette County, Pennsylvania, the stronghold of the Frick Company, where wages were highest, company unions firmest, and repression most common. Afterward, however, the steel companies failed to execute collective bargaining agreements with the UMW, which resorted to the National Labor Board for relief.[37]

Hearings conducted by the NLB in January 1934 revealed the steel companies' steadfast recalcitrance on the issue of union recognition and the UMW's inability to conquer the captive mines even with presidential support. The companies' attorney, Nathan Miller, former governor of New York, asserted during the hearings that the NIRA did not require employers to bargain with unions. The phrase that employees "shall have the right to bargain collectively through representatives of their own choosing," suggested Miller, meant that workers negotiated as individuals and not through a union. "How can an association negotiate?" he asked. "Individuals have to negotiate."[38] Thus when an agreement was finally reached, in mid-January 1934, the captive mines signed it with the individuals elected by the miners—Lewis, Murray, and Kennedy—not with the UMW as an organization, and the NLB declined to rule whether such an agreement constituted legal union recognition.[39]

The first clash between Lewis and the nation's leading industrialists had ended with the most crucial issues unresolved. Compelled to hold representation elections, to check off union dues, and even to bargain with union representatives, the steel operators nevertheless refused to concede the principle of union recognition. Having succumbed temporarily to political and economic pressures, they intended in the long run not to allow unions to dilute company authority. Guided by the Frick Company, operators hardly bargained in good faith, schemed to replace independent labor organizations with company unions, and discharged their most militant union employees.[40]

If Lewis had breached steel's hitherto impregnable antiunion walls, his union's penetration scarcely shattered the fortress of the open shop. Indeed, in late 1933 and early 1934, Lewis watched workers in steel, autos, and other mass-production industries suffer successive union defeats. And as President Roosevelt and his advisers repeatedly favored employers over trade unionists, Lewis became convinced that the Morgan-Rockefeller-Mellon-Dupont financial elite had lost none of its economic and political influence. Like the French ruling family, America's economic "Bourbons," thought Lewis, had failed to learn the lessons of history. Himself a student of popular history, an admirer of Napoleon, and a firm believer in historical cycles, Lewis was prepared to teach America's ruling class its lessons and to play labor's Napoleon to Wall Street's Bourbons.

In the autumn of 1933 Lewis expressed publicly his desire to build a more powerful labor movement. At the October 1933 A. F. of L. convention, he again demanded that the organization's executive council be expanded from eight to twenty-five members in order to represent better the full spectrum of the labor movement and allow a voice to mass-production workers. His proposal defeated by a delegate roll call vote of 14,133 to 6,410, Lewis clashed verbally—and almost physically—with Dan Tobin, president of the teamsters' union and the most outspoken critic of industrial, or mass-production, unionism. As reported by Louis Stark in the *Times*, only William Green's diplomatic intervention averted fisticuffs between Lewis and Tobin. To Tobin's allegations that Lewis's recommendation to enlarge the executive council betrayed the A. F. of L.'s traditions and the authority of President Green, Lewis shouted: "I hurl those statements back in your teeth, Dan Tobin."[41]

Lewis reaffirmed his commitment to the mass-production workers at the January 1934 UMW convention. UMWA delegates, meeting in a mood of jubilation, listened as their officers recommended that the A. F. of L. relinquish the claims of craft unions in the mass-production industries and allow industrial unions to emerge in the interest of a more comprehensive form of labor organization. The inability of mass-production workers to benefit from the NIRA and the failure of the craft unions to aid them necessitated new policies for the American labor movement. "Without question," advised Lewis, Murray, and Kennedy, "the problem of organizing the workers in . . . automobile, steel, rubber, lumber, electric and other industries is of paramount importance to American labor. There is imperative necessity by the American Federation of Labor of a sound and practical policy that will meet the requirements of modern industrial conditions."[42]

But before Lewis could transform the structure of the American labor movement, he had loose ends to tie up in his own industry. As 1933 passed into 1934 and

Roosevelt's New Deal entered its eleventh month of experimentation and innovation, the UMW had yet to conquer such obdurate antiunion regions as Harlan County, Kentucky; equalize wages between north and south; or gain miners the material improvements that their revived power justified. For years, as one knowledgeable observer reported, coal miners had endured "starvation wages," persecution by mine owners, and prosecution by the law while they dreamed of the day when they would resurrect their union and win decent wages and conditions. "From now on," miners told him in early 1934, "we get things," for Lewis's much vaunted cycle of history had swung in the miners' favor, causing them to seek a standard of living far in excess of their past expectations or achievements. "How long they will wait for better conditions, how long it will take them to rebel when better conditions and wages are not forthcoming," the observer concluded, "it is impossible to say. But . . . the United Mine Workers must be able to deliver, or they will be pushed aside."[43]

Lewis heard his miners' angry voices, and he meant to deliver what the rank and file demanded. When negotiations commenced, in Washington, on the last day of February 1934, between the UMW and the Appalachian coal operators, Lewis expressed his union's extensive demands, relating them to the aims of the New Deal as well as to the material needs of America's coal miners. The time has come, proclaimed Lewis, to end the baseless and inequitable wage differentials between districts and to establish uniform wage levels. Trust the New Deal, the NRA, and its coal code, he assured operators, and prices for coal will be set high enough to cover increased wages and still produce a profit. Reminding the operators of their financial plight before June 1933 and the passage of the NIRA, Lewis argued that coal's economic recovery necessitated cooperation with the UMW, President Roosevelt, and the New Deal. Miners' wages not only must be equalized, but they must be increased substantially, he warned, for the New Deal's effort to revive the national economy depended on high wage levels and expanded consumer purchasing power. Raise wages, lower hours (the UMW reiterated its call for a six-hour day, five-day week), widen employment opportunities, Lewis demanded, and American consumers will then save industrialists from their own past mistakes.[44]

Northern operators proved willing collaborators with Lewis and the UMW. The coal code had saved them from financial ruin, and Lewis's demand for wage equalization promised them further competitive benefits. But southern operators, partly stripped of substantial competitive advantages and price dominance in the marketplace, refused to make further concessions. Southern West Virginia operators early on left the Appalachian Joint Conference, and Alabama mine owners never attended. And those southern interests remaining in the conference fought hardest against the UMW's demands. Not till the early morning of March 31—described by the UMW *Journal* as "the last minute on the last day before the expiration of the old contract between operators and miners"—did the operators make substantial concessions to the UMW. Rather than risk a nationwide coal strike on the following day and the likelihood of federal (presidential) intervention on behalf of the miners, southern operators joined with their northern colleagues in accepting a new Appalachian joint agreement with the UMW to run from April 1, 1934, to March 31, 1935.[45]

The 1934 agreement granted the UMW a substantial victory. Miners won the seven-hour day, five-day week and a narrowing of wage differentials, as $5.00 became the basic daily minimum wage in all the large northern districts and $4.60 the minimum throughout the South. The union also won complete recognition, the full dues checkoff (meaning, in effect, the establishment of the union shop, insuring that all workers in union mines would have to join the union), and the right to discipline militant union members and wildcat strikers. So complete was Lewis's victory that even a majority of the Harlan County operators signed the new agreement, and in a separate arrangement, southern West Virginia mine owners accepted terms. Only Alabama's operators refused to respect the 1934 Appalachian agreement.[46]

What Lewis failed to win through union power, he obtained through federal intervention. Almost as soon as he had negotiated the 1934 agreement, Lewis requested Hugh Johnson to make its terms part of an amendment to the September 1933 bituminous coal code, a process that would apply the revised wages and working conditions to all soft-coal producers. Johnson needed no convincing from Lewis, and the general immediately announced hearings scheduled for Washington on April 11 to amend the bituminous coal code to encompass the seven-hour day, five-day week and a rise in minimum daily wages in southern Appalachian mines from $3.40 to $4.60. Not unexpectedly, the Alabama operators, speaking through their attorney, Forney Johnston, rejected the amendments and vowed to obtain a legal injunction against implementing them. Johnston's antiunion adamance, phrased in antiquated nineteenth-century southern rhetoric, occasioned a notable Lewis response. To applause from the hitherto bored code-hearing audience, Lewis accused Johnston of bombast and hyperbole for implying that Alabama's operators were capable of declaring war on the United States. "If they think they are, and care to resort to that method to maintain their arrogant position," barked Lewis, "the United Mine Workers of America is ready . . . to furnish the President . . . with 20 army divisions to help make the Alabama operators comply with the law of the United States." Turning once again to an appreciative audience, he ridiculed his legal adversary: "I assume Mr. Johnston . . . was somewhat inebriated by the exuberance of his own verbosity."[47]

Prior to the rhetorical exchange between Lewis and Johnston, the UMW president had presented the hearing a dispassionate economic analysis of the case for uniform wage rates. Marshaling his evidence carefully, presenting detailed statistics on comparative living costs and wage levels, and defending the right of southern workers to a decent existence, Lewis shattered the operators' case of a lower southern cost of living, especially for black miners, who composed half or more of their labor force. Black coal miners lived more poorly than their white brothers and tolerated a lower standard of living, Lewis proved, not because their needs and standards were more primitive, but because they had no choice. Racism not only depressed black wage levels but compelled black miners to pay more than whites for identical housing.[48] Operators had no answer to Lewis's statistical presentation, and, as the UMW president expected and Johnson promised, the bituminous coal code was amended as Lewis recommended.[49]

The UMW was now secure, for at least a year, if not longer, in the nation's commercial soft-coal mines. Government-sanctioned and union-approved wage rates and working conditions covered miners from northeastern Pennsylvania to Alabama, from eastern Ohio to Washington State. In the vast majority of coal mines covering more than 90% of working soft-coal miners, Lewis had won contracts that provided union recognition, the checkoff, and the union shop.

Simultaneous with his triumphs in the coalfields, Lewis extended peace feelers to his former left-wing critics. In October 1933 Lewis recommended that William Green appoint Adolph Germer, long-time District 12 insurgent, old-guard socialist, and advocate of industrial unionism, as a voluntary organizer for the A. F. of L.[50] The same month Lewis, at the urging of Phil Murray, met with John Brophy in Washington and restored his former foe to good standing in the UMW. That a new phase was about to begin in the career of John L. Lewis was revealed in the labor leader's comment to Brophy during their reconciliation. "I suppose," observed Lewis, "our differences in the past were largely ones of timing."[51]

Not only did Lewis reconcile himself to former union enemies; he assigned John Brophy to a delicate "diplomatic" mission. With the signing of the first Appalachian agreement in September 1933 and the concessions wrenched subsequently from the captive mines, the UMW seemed more secure than ever in the soft-coal fields—with one exception: District 12 in Illinois, where the Progressive Mine Workers of America continued to challenge UMW authority. Eager to discover the actual strength of the PMA, to learn if the Illinois rebels might, in fact, endure as an independent union, and to probe the prospects for peace between the progressives and the UMW, Lewis dispatched Brophy to Illinois. The UMW president assumed that Brophy, an outspoken critic of Lewis and known publicly as still a union renegade, would have no difficulty making contact with the progressives and obtaining confidential information. Lewis was right.[52]

Brophy's confidential report on conditions in Illinois pleased Lewis. Although Brophy observed that past hatreds remained too intense and fresh to induce progressives to consider reconciliation, he noted that the UMW's recent successes under the NRA had shaken the progressives' self-confidence. The rebels, reported Brophy, "are getting a sense of isolation." His report also indicated that the PMA's influence had declined and that its members had begun to realize that their organization was "only a pocketed sectional union in Illinois . . . closed out of any promise of becoming a national union." Consequently, the progressives' morale had disintegrated, and in the war of attrition being waged in District 12, the PMA was "on the losing side." One old-time miner and PMA member even told Brophy: "In about a year everybody in Illinois will be back in the United Mine Workers." Such information led Brophy to conclude that "disintegration of the P. M. A. is . . . inevitable."[53]

Although Lewis may have appreciated Brophy's report, the UMW president rejected his agent's advice. Brophy recommended that peace be made with the dispirited progressives and that they be restored to membership in the UMW without penalty.[54] Certain now that the PMA posed no threat to the UMW, Lewis preferred to compel his Illinois opponents to disintegrate slowly or return to the UMW only by individual petition. A most forgiving battler when it suited his purposes, Lewis could also be an unrelenting vengeful foe.

One aspect of the Brophy report provides an interesting sidelight on Lewis's character and beliefs. Trying to explain the PMA's survival despite UMW triumphs, Brophy suggested that the progressives' organization of a woman's auxiliary "has enlisted a sustaining fervor and emotional support to the cause of the P. M. A. that has undoubtedly prevented serious breaks."[55] For years rank-and-file UMW miners had proposed the establishment of a woman's auxiliary—a demand usually expressed in resolutions introduced at union conventions. The January 1934 UMW convention proved no exception; delegates introduced a resolution calling for the creation of a woman's auxiliary. Despite Brophy's observations on the success the Illinois progressives had achieved with women, Lewis, in 1934, cherished values more suitable to a nineteenth-century Victorian gentleman than to a 1930s class warrior. Opposing the resolution, Lewis commented that he was happy that among American coal miners, at least, men did the fighting while women remained at home. "If there is anything that has caused me great concern in some of our industrial conflicts," he stressed, "it has been the tendency of certain men to shove their women out on picket lines while they remained at home and did the cooking."[56] Lewis expected coal miners to replicate their leader's family life, an existence in which the wife exemplified "the cult of true womanhood," isolated herself from her husband's career, and raised the children.

The year-long struggle to build labor influence with Franklin D. Roosevelt and to reorganize the coalfields under the NRA had taken its toll physically on John L. Lewis and also Phil Murray. Lewis's apparent physical vigor and vitality cloaked a constitution vulnerable to collapse. His resistance to respiratory infections weakened by his early years in the mines and later years in ceaseless travel, Lewis was immobilized by the common cold. Colds not infrequently confined Lewis to his bed for a week or longer. Apparently fatigued by the feverish and protracted negotiations that resulted in the last-minute agreement with mine operators on March 31, 1934, Lewis became ill and left Washington to recuperate. As was his style, Lewis vacationed in the haunts of the "idle rich," in this instance the Fort Sumter Hotel, in Charleston, South Carolina. Writing to Phil Murray from the hotel on May 6, Lewis joked: "Am still a little below par, but improving. Am up and around and eating with enthusiasm. Meals on the American plan. One tries to eat his way right down through the menu." Rejuvenated by his retreat from union affairs, Lewis offered Murray advice. "Am sorry, indeed, that you are ill—Hope you are much improved. Trust you will take plenty of time to get well. Stay away from the downtown office. . . . Things seem to go just as well when we are both taking time out. Let us therefore, says I, take more time out."[57]

Lewis soon had another opportunity to "take more time out." No sooner had he returned to Washington than Secretary of Labor Frances Perkins appointed him as one of the American labor delegates to the upcoming International Labor Organization meeting in Geneva, Switzerland.[58] Traveling with Myrta, Lewis holidayed in style. Myrta and John celebrated their twenty-seventh wedding anniversary at sea on June 5 aboard the S. S. *President Roosevelt*, where the captain entertained them at dinner. In Paris the Lewises were flooded with dinner invitations from wealthy American expatriates, businessmen, and diplomats, as well as foreign officials. Lewis even appeared as the featured guest at a reception held by the American Chamber of Commerce in Paris. Throughout his month-long European trip, Lewis spent more time with diplomats, foreign dignitaries, wealthy exiles, and socialites than with the labor leaders he met in Geneva. Myrta used the occasion to collect expensive additions to her gallery of antiques. Picture postcards that the Lewises mailed to their family and friends suggest that Myrta and John made the most of their journey and followed an itinerary available only to affluent tourists.[59]

Refreshed by his southern spring holiday and European summer tour, Lewis returned to the United States in midsummer 1934 ready to open a new chapter in his own career and in the history of American trade unionism. The labor lamb who had laid down with corporate wolves from 1924 to 1932 was about to become the union lion who roared at industrialists and congressmen. The man who, in 1933, seemed "merely a labor boss of the most conventional kind," "a big-bellied, oldtime labor leader . . . an autocrat, per capita counter, egotist, power seeker" was about to become the idol of labor radicals, social reformers, and militant workers.[60] The labor leader characterized by A. J. Muste in October 1934 as an "essentially reactionary" and obsequious follower of the Roosevelt administration would soon win a reputation as a radical and eventually become the labor movement's bluntest critic of Franklin D. Roosevelt.[61]

CHAPTER 10
The Challenge, July 1934-
October 1935

While John L. Lewis vacationed in South Carolina and toured the European continent in May, June, and July 1934, American workers rebelled.[1] In Toledo, Ohio; Minneapolis, Minnesota; and San Francisco, California, strikers, police, and troops waged a bloody class war. In their morning newspapers Americans saw photographs that depicted Ohio National Guardsmen with fixed bayonets clearing Toledo's streets of strikers. They read stories describing the violent confrontation between teamsters and police in Minneapolis's main square, during which sixty-seven persons were wounded—two fatally. And they read anxiously of events in San Francisco, where the deaths of two strikers and the presence of state militia armed with machine guns and armored vehicles ignited a citywide general strike that, much to the dismay of the Bay Area *bourgeoisie*, left the city at the mercy of a central labor union administration.[2]

More significant than the violence associated with the three conflicts was the reality that all erupted independently of the American Federation of Labor. In Toledo strikers walked out under the leadership of A. J. Muste and his Workers' Party, a schismatic Trotskyite organization. In Minneapolis Roy Grant and Miles Dunne, ex-Wobblies and Communists turned Trotskyists, together with Farrell Dobbs, a brilliant labor strategist and also a Trotskyist, led the local teamsters' strike, commanding members of a trade union whose international president, Dan Tobin, exemplified conservative Democratic politics, antipathy toward industrial unionism (Tobin called mass-production workers "the rubbish at labor's door"), and anticommunism. And in San Francisco, Harry Bridges, an Australian immigrant, self-educated leftist, and associate of Communists, guided that city's waterfront workers in a rebellion that not only liberated them from an exploitative work situation but also freed longshoremen from the authority of the corrupt and unimaginative president of the A. F. of L.'s International Longshoremen's Association, Joseph P. Ryan. Not only did strikers in the three cities act without A. F. of L. authorization and sometimes against the federation's wishes; in Minneapolis and San Francisco they won more complete victories for trade unionism than "legitimate" A. F. of L. unions had achieved in 1933 and 1934.

Signs of labor unrest flared among workers in other organizations associated with the A. F. of L. Auto workers flooded federal labor unions in late 1933 and early 1934 or joined several independent labor organizations especially active in the Detroit area. Eager to improve working conditions, gain job security, and build an industrial union encompassing all employees in the industry, auto workers, in March 1934, threatened a nationwide strike. Only presidential intervention averted the walkout. Roosevelt inveigled A. F. of L. officials and representatives of the auto workers into accepting an agreement on March 25, 1934, that established an Automobile Labor Board to govern labor relations in the industry. But the new board proved more susceptible to employer than to union influences, because automobile manufacturers were intransigent, wealthy, and influential, whereas the auto workers were divided, poor, and represented by A. F. of L. organizers whose resistance collapsed before employer obduracy and federal pressure.[3]

Similar stories repeated themselves in the steel, rubber, aluminum, and other mass-production industries. Acting under the impetus of Section 7a and President Roosevelt's sheltering embrace, mass-production workers by the thousands enrolled in newly chartered federal labor unions or flooded old lodges of such established unions as the Amalgamated Association of Iron, Steel, and Tin Workers. Wanting action and immediate gains, the new union members demanded solidarity—industrial unions that encompassed all workers in a single industry regardless of skill, job classification, or earnings, not craft unions that parceled them out among Heinz's 57 varieties of labor organizations. But in steel and rubber, as in autos, A. F. of L. leaders refused to charter unrestricted industrial unions,* advised against militant action, feared the power of employers, and deferred to President Roosevelt's desire for industrial peace.[4] By the summer of 1934 the initial gains organized labor had made in the mass-production industries had been completely dissipated by equivocal union leadership. When Robert and Helen Lynd completed their sociological reinvestigation of Muncie, Indiana, in mid-1935, they found scarcely a sign of trade unionism or unrest among the local workers at General Motors, who only a few months earlier had joined federal labor unions in the great wave of union fervor that had inundated even traditionally open-shop Muncie.[5]

Even where A. F. of L. affiliates acted vigorously in 1934, the results proved disappointing. In June, the United Textile Workers of America inaugurated a

*Instead the A. F. of L. chartered federal unions directly under federation control and without autonomy, which served as stopgap institutions intended to exist only until their members could be assigned to the craft union that claimed exclusive jurisdiction over their type of work—machinists to the Machinists' Union; in-plant drivers and out-of-plant haulers to the Teamsters' Union; maintenance men to such building trades unions as the carpenters, plumbers, electricians, etc. The mass of unskilled and semiskilled laborers were to be left in a form of trade union purgatory or to be tolerated as second-class citizens of the dominant craft unions.

general strike in the textile industry that spread from Maine to Alabama and involved between 300,000 and 400,000 workers. Employer resistance, marked by the introduction of thousands of professional strikebreakers; extensive violence; and the use of police, sheriffs, and state militia crushed the textile workers' union and its strike. And not a finger was lifted in Washington among members of the Roosevelt administration to ease the textile workers' plight. For millions of American workers, Roosevelt's New Deal was turning into a raw, old deal.[6]

Two years' experience with the NIRA and Section 7a taught even the A. F. of L.'s old guard the reasons for organized labor's ineffectiveness during the early New Deal. "Only where labor was well organized," wrote John Frey, the custodian of the A. F. of L.'s craft union tradition and its voluntaristic political policy, "was there anything like adequate enforcement. . . . Labor did have a voice in N. R. A.," he informed an English trade union friend in September, 1935, "but business had a greater voice and much more control of the situation."[7] No truer words could have been written, for the inability of workers to organize, especially in the mass-production industries, guaranteed an impotent national labor movement—one that employers could disregard and Washington officials treat cavalierly.

Beyond coal and the needle trades, organized labor had won little of positive value during the New Deal's first two years. Slightly more than 3 million workers, or about 12% of the nonagricultural labor force, belonged to trade unions in 1934—a smaller proportion than in 1922. By midsummer 1934 labor's upheaval had produced more company unions than independent unions and more aborted strikes or industrial defeats than victories. John Frey appeared right: Employers were better organized, more class conscious, more determined to prevent union growth, and, consequently, more influential in Washington.

Unless something happened, and quickly, to alter the prevailing distribution of power, organized labor's advances under the New Deal would be few and far between. Yet labor leaders seemed to face an insoluble dilemma. Without mass organization, labor lacked effective political influence; without the guardianship of a benevolent government, unions could not defeat recalcitrant employers. During the New Deal years, more so than ever before in United States history, the federal government acted as society's arbiter; it determined the outcome of conflicts between private disputants. While publicly defending its actions as promoting justice and equality, in reality it customarily shifted its influence to favor the better organized and, hence, stronger party to the conflict. Simply put, until organized labor achieved mass membership, its political influence would remain minimal; yet lacking influence in Washington, the labor movement appeared unable to advance.

Doubtless, even while he recuperated from illness in Charleston and enjoyed a tourist's Europe, John L. Lewis pondered labor's dilemma. His own experience with the coal strikes and code negotiations of 1933-1934 had convinced him that federal officials would henceforth exert a decisive influence in labor relations and that only a militant, organized group of workers could compel public officials to assist unions against management. Lewis realized that labor's economic and political futures were inextricably linked and that union leaders had to lobby intensively for support among Washington politicians and then use legislative or executive sanction to organize workers who would vote for their "benefactors." Politicians, like businessmen and union leaders, Lewis sensed, operated in a utilitarian universe; how much you invested depended on your estimation of the potential payoff. No businessman put his money in an enterprise unless he expected a substantial return on his capital; no labor leader expended union funds on organizing workers unless he hoped to gain enough new members to strengthen his union and add to its income; and no politician endorsed controversial legislation unless it promised to win him votes. Such utilitarian values prompted Lewis to cast aside all ideology, all respect for hoary labor traditions. Where William Green, John Frey, and Matthew Woll (once Samuel Gompers' heir apparent) viewed the issues of the 1930s through the lens of the past, Lewis counted votes, estimated power, and seized opportunities.

If A. F. of L. leaders allowed the ghost of Gompers and respect for labor traditions to determine their policies during the 1930s, they were insuring their own impotence. New times called for new methods, and Lewis, the perfect union politician, was also the complete chameleon, always ready to change colors to suit a new milieu. A man who previously had transformed himself from a Wilson Democrat to a Coolidge Republican, a union militant to a "labor statesman," a bankrupt grain dealer to a successful banker, could easily, once historical cycles changed, play the multiple public roles of ardent New Dealer, A. F. of L. rebel, "united fronter," and class warrior. Life was a contest to Lewis in which success went not to the best sportsman or the man who followed rules but to the man who made his own rules and played the game according to present needs, not past rituals. As he explained to William Green in June 1936: "I am not concerned with history . . . I am concerned with the problems of today and tomorrow."[8] While other labor leaders of his generation and origins turned to the past to guide them in the present, Lewis never allowed what had been to limit what might yet be, and he turned to a younger generation—the restless, rebellious, and even "red"—to point him toward the future.

Lewis returned home from Europe in the summer of 1934 with one aim in mind: to organize the nation's mass-production workers and build a labor movement of 25 million to 35 million members. The political implications of such an achievement needed no exegesis; nor did one have to be a prophet to perceive that such an accomplishment would establish Lewis as the nation's most influential labor leader.

From June 1933 through July 1934, the A. F. of L.'s leaders had squandered an opportunity, letting power slip through their grasp as their hesitancy, fear of militancy, and respect for outdated jurisdictional boundaries caused them to dismay or betray millions of mass-production workers. In the summer of 1934, however, labor's future remained open; latent power still existed in the factories, streets, and neighborhoods of working-class America. And Lewis proposed to offer his fellow barons of trade unionism another chance to build a powerful mass working-class movement in the United States.

Because Lewis eventually succeeded in organizing mass-production workers, most Lewis biographers and historians of the American labor movement during the New Deal suggest that the UMW president pursued a consistent, calculated strategy, one that necessarily split the American labor movement. The birth of the CIO as an independent national labor center originated, according to such versions of history, as the product of John L. Lewis's fertile imagination. Saul Alinsky has been most responsible for propagating the concept that from June 1933 on Lewis plotted the creation of the CIO. Citing numerous interviews with Lewis and quoting them verbatim, Alinsky describes a strategy that proceeded inexorably to the formation of an innovative labor center for industrial unionism.[9]

Yet Lewis's entire character and personality belie the notion that he plotted two years in advance to split the American labor movement. Much to the dismay of such advisers as Jett Lauck, Lewis rejected long-range factors; despite the public image he cultivated as a student of history and literature, Lewis's reading seldom transcended the newspapers and news magazines. He had no deep feel for history (he may indeed have shared Henry Ford's belief that "history is bunk") and naively believed that strong men, if they seized the main chance, could transcend tradition and environment.[10] He wrote few of his own speeches and articles, limiting his contributions to the addition of the purple passage, mixed metaphor, or singularly effective malapropism.[11] His social and economic ideas were few, simple, and timeworn; with minor variations he tailored them to fit all times and circumstances.

His genius for timing consisted of the abilities to know precisely when to counterattack an opponent and to perceive when his enemies were most vulnerable. The story of Lewis's crusade to organize mass-production workers into industrial unions and convert the A. F. of L. executive council to the cause is a tale of thrusts and counterthrusts, of quick advances and rapid retreats, of rhetorical triumphs and substantive defeats. In this saga of parry and thrust, Lewis's decision to create the CIO flowed as much from the actions of his critics in the A. F. of L. as from the logic of a preconceived plan.

By late summer of 1934 the New Deal seemed at a dead end. With full recovery from depression no nearer than it had been during the Hoover days, left-wingers and right-wingers freely criticized the Roosevelt administration. Trade unionists, especially, accused Roosevelt of subservience to big business and denigrated NRA as the "national run-around."

But if Roosevelt had fooled the nation, so, too, had the majority of American labor leaders. The attitudes and practices of the A. F. of L. hierarchy made American industrialists by comparison seem innovative, adventurous, and almost radical. More concerned with defending than expanding their existing fiefdoms, most craft union leaders raised barriers to the organization of the less skilled, mass-production workers. Such union presidents as Arthur Wharton of the machinists, Bill Hutcheson of the carpenters, G. M. Bugniazet of the plumbers, and Dan Tobin of the teamsters had learned from history that the less skilled were "unorganizable." On the one hand, the craft unionists believed that the unskilled were "unorganizable," and hence that any funds expended on organizing efforts would be wasted. On the other hand, if unexpectedly the mass-production workers were in fact organized, their presence inside the A. F. of L. would threaten the hegemony exercised by the craft unionists. Rather than squander money or risk a diminution of their own power, the craft unionists preferred to cite union traditions and jurisdictional claims as reasons not to build mass industrial unions. Simply put, they lacked the will to organize masses of workers and used American labor's sanctification of craft unionism to cloak their inaction.

John L. Lewis, by contrast, was a gambler. Successful organization of the mass-production workers in no way threatened his union power. Indeed he might well ride organization of the masses to increased power inside the labor movement. The potential expense of organizing millions of workers also did not trouble Lewis. In the summer of 1933 he had gambled the remainder of the UMW's treasury in an organizing campaign among coal miners—and won. In late 1934 he was willing to take the same risk in a bid to unionize much larger numbers of workers. Lewis, who could cite jurisdictional claims with the most legalistic of craft unionists, implored that labor leaders submerge their particular union's jurisdictions to the greater necessity of organizing workers. Organization first, jurisdiction later, became Lewis's battle cry. In a Labor Day 1934 statement, Lewis asserted that the A. F. of L. *must* authorize a policy of industrial unionism for employees in the mass-production industries.[12]

If Lewis played the radical and militant inside the labor movement, he acted the reformer and moderate outside. Nowhere was this aspect of Lewis's character better revealed than in a speech he delivered on October 10, 1934, before the Commonwealth Club, the association of the San Francisco Bay Area's financial, industrial, and social elite. Delivering to his prestigious audience ideas formulated by Jett Lauck (who referred to the speech as "simply made up of our old lines of thought in a rearranged form"), Lewis defended the New Deal and (its) NRA as the "Middle Way," an American democratic response to depression preferable to Fascist or Communist dictatorship.[13] He forcefully reminded his listeners of what had recently happened in Germany (Hitler) and Italy (Mussolini) and what might occur in the United States if "those reactionary industrial groups who have 'eyes but see not' and 'ears but hear not' " thwart sound public policy and the labor movement. Placing the responsibility first for depression and then for violations of Section 7a squarely on a Wall Street financial elite (the Morgan-Dupont-Rockefeller triumvirate central to the Lauck-Lewis demonology), Lewis warned that their indefensible tactics would inevitably cause "an industrial revolt . . . attended by the menace of Communism or Fascism. . . . If I may speak as a prophet," he told his audience,

> I . . . say that full organization on the part of free labor, with the free right to enter into collective agreements with employers, is bound to come sooner or later, if the economic system, as we now know it, is to endure. . . . Labor cannot, and will not, and should not ever be content until its partnership becomes a real one and not merely one in theory. To oppose such a movement is, to paraphrase an old saying, not only a crime against labor—it is a social blunder which may lead to the toppling over of our whole economic edifice.

Lewis mixed old concepts drawn from *The Miner's Fight for American Standards* (1925) with his analysis of the current totalitarian threat. Take organized labor into an equal partnership, make industrial democracy as common as political democracy, Lewis promised, and trade unions would join with employers in promoting industrial efficiency and social planning and in replacing cutthroat nineteenth-century capitalism with cooperative twentieth-century capitalism. Finally, after making a ritualistic reference to the beneficence of natural economic laws (again recalling the conventions of *The Miner's Fight*), Lewis offered San Francisco's elite his real message. "Our whole economic system," he suggested, "is man made . . . and will have to be judged by its fruits in human welfare and happiness." The world today, Lewis continued, "is seething with new ideas and new desires [that] . . . are better than the old . . . hold[ing] up a better organized economic system, in which there will be no unemployment of those who wish to work, a more equitable distribution of income, and far more intelligent use of the earth's natural resources." But, he warned, "ideals do not realize themselves" and must instead "be worked out by human beings with many frailties."[14]

While Lewis invited the Bay Area's elite to support the New Deal in seeking a "middle way" for the United States, he told the A. F. of L.'s resolutions committee and its 1934 convention delegates that there was only one way to organize the nation's mass-production workers, and it was not the "middle way" preferred by craft unionists. Mass-production workers could not be parceled out by trade to competing craft unions, nor could the less skilled among them be offered an inferior status.

Powerful as was Lewis's voice in the Resolutions Committee and on the convention floor, it spoke for and to an A. F. of L. minority. The majority, weighted with the votes of Wharton, Hutcheson, and Tobin (the machinists, carpenters, and teamsters unions, respectively) and the parliamentary leadership of John Frey and Matthew Woll—lawyers and legalists more than labor leaders or organizers—preferred craft to industrial unions and determined to guard the jurisdictional claims of the former. The more militant among the craft unionists were even willing to repudiate the advocates of industrial unionism—Lewis included. But Woll and Charles P. Howard of the Printers engineered a compromise acceptable to Lewis through the Resolutions Committee. It won unanimous approval on the convention floor. It recognized the principle that the mass-production industries must be organized on "a different basis" and that charters, implicitly industrial in character, be issued to unions in the automotive, cement, aluminum, and other mass-production industries as deemed necessary by the executive council. The executive council, moreover, was charged with inaugurating promptly an organizing campaign in the iron and steel industry. Having moved that far in satisfying Lewis and the industrial unionists, the A. F. of L. majority recommended that "the jurisdictional claims of existing unions be protected by authorizing the executive council, for a provisional period, [to] direct the policies, administer the business, and designate the administrative and financial officers of . . . newly organized unions."[15]

The 1934 A. F. of L. convention had thus recommended a "middle way" in the dispute between craft and industrial unionists. Lewis accepted this singular compromise, of which Howard Brubaker wrote in the *New Yorker*: "The A. F. of L. has adopted the industrial form of organization without abandoning the craft-union plan. If it can be horizontal and vertical at the same time, prizefighters would be pleased to know the details."[16] Why, then, did Lewis defer to labor's "middle way" advocates?

Brubaker's sarcasm notwithstanding, the convention seemed a triumph for Lewis. He thought so, as also did his adviser and friend Jett Lauck, who, in responding to Lewis's messages from the West Coast, observed: "You certainly brought about an epoch-marking change in the A. F. of L. and have given everybody new hope about unionization and a strong, aggressive labor movement."[17] So, too, did Louis Stark, who reported in a feature article in the *New York Times* on Sunday, October 21, that the A. F. of L. convention had signified a victory for Lewis, the industrial unionists, and new-blood elements. Not only had the convention endorsed the principle of industrial unionism, however equivocably; it had also expanded the executive council from eight to fifteen members, elected Lewis to one of the new seats, and welcomed the Amalgamated Clothing Workers of America and its president, Sidney Hillman, an outspoken advocate of industrial unionism, into the A. F. of L.[18]

Although the convention left the issue of industrial unionism and the campaign to organize mass-production workers to the discretion of the executive council, on which Lewis represented a minority (among the other newly elected council members were Hutcheson and Tobin, the most bitter opponents of industrial unionism), the UMW president obviously expected to influence the council's decisions. Lewis's ego surpassed that of any other council member, and his intellect, wit, and command of the English language far exceeded that of his fellow labor barons. Accustomed to absolute dominance in the inner councils of the miners' union, Lewis hoped to replicate his power on the A. F. of L. executive council, where his arrogance, self-assurance, rhetorical prowess, and adamance would overwhelm less verbal and more epicene colleagues. One might also assume that Lewis expected sympathy and support from the A. F. of L. president, William Green, who had served in Lewis's shadow within the UMW and been elevated to his position in the federation through Lewis's influence.

Convinced that he would dominate the executive council, Lewis, in late 1934, had no intentions of splitting the labor movement or forming his own industrial union federation. Quite the contrary, as he revealed in a letter to Adolph Germer. Germer had written to Lewis asking the latter to endorse Germer as an organizer for the A. F. of L. Lewis's response revealed his persistent intolerance for union insurgents. "You know, I am sure," Lewis informed Germer, "that I believe in adherence to the fundamentals effecting the laws and wage policies of the United Mine Workers of America, as well as the American Federation of Labor; that I expect those who become paid advocates . . . of the American Federation of Labor to become defenders and champions of the policies and practices of these organizations." Lewis then offered to endorse Germer if the latter followed "a policy consistent to supporting the trade union movement, rather than continuing to occupy the position of a critic."[19]

Lewis's advice to Germer proved singularly ironical, as the UMW president, from January through August 1935, occupied a position on the A. F. of L. executive council as a persistent critic of the trade union movement. The first meeting Lewis attended as a member of the A. F. of L. executive council from January 29 to February 14, 1935, brought into sharp focus the clash between craft unionists and industrial unionists. The related questions of issuing an industrial union charter to the auto workers and organizing the steelworkers occupied much of the council's time and occasioned the most heated discussion, in which Lewis participated prominently.

Whereas the council's majority—especially Wharton, Hutcheson, and Bugniazet—appeared most concerned with guarding the jurisdictional claims of the craft unions, Lewis addressed the realities of economic and political power. The failure of the A. F. of L. to organize the auto workers and its alacrity at accepting presidential awards for the industry that subverted trade unionism, warned Lewis, "is an exhibition of public weakness that reflects itself in the White House and makes it possible for the Recovery Administration and the White House to make decisions with impunity or without fear of any successful challenge from the American Federation of Labor. Our weakness is fundamental." We are weak, he added, because the public believes, and rightly, that we have no organization among auto workers. Our enemies, as well as our potential allies in Washington, measure labor's strength, analyze its possibility as an adversary. "Our weakness to get anything is the absence of effective competent organization." Remember, advised Lewis: "It is axiomatic . . . that you can get just about what you are ready to take."[20]

Pursuing the same line of argument, Lewis asserted that the time had come to *take* the auto workers, to use the energy and talent of the young men in the industry, and to "give them an international union and money enough to carry on a campaign." It must be done, he proceeded, for "we are all on trial. . . . There is a distinct anti-Federation sentiment abroad. The White House is tainted with that anti-Federation sentiment. So many stories have been given to the White House about our weakness that they have become contemptuous." We must throw money and men into the auto industry and postpone jurisdictional disputes until the men are actually organized. Lewis formulated a seven-point program for organization of the auto workers that, in effect, temporarily placed the auto union under executive council guardianship and hence conformed to the 1934 convention resolution on industrial unionism. Lewis pleaded with the craft unionists to subordinate their jurisdictional claims "for the greater consideration of safeguarding American labor in mass production industries and regenerating and again restoring to normal the lowered prestige of the American Federation of Labor before the American people." He concluded his appeal with typical Lewisian rhetoric, as notable for its sound as its sense. "We have too long been straining at a gnat and swallowing the camel."[21]

Preferring to swallow Lewis's metaphorical camel and ignoring his impassioned plea that "contention over the fruits of victory [jurisdictional claims] be deferred until we have some of the fruits in our possession," the council's craft union majority defeated Lewis's motion to postpone the settlement of jurisdictional claims in the auto industry until after the workers were organized by a margin of twelve to two (only David Dubinsky of the ladies' garment workers voted with Lewis).[22]

Lewis was also frustrated in his effort to institute industrial unionism in the iron and steel industry. Again Lewis addressed the realities of power, reminding his colleagues that the A. F. of L. was threatened by its own ineffectiveness and that the Amalgamated Association of Iron, Steel, and Tin Workers, the old craft union that claimed absolute jurisdiction in the steel industry, had been bypassed by history and relegated to the dustheap. The past, the present, and common sense all teach, advised Lewis, that the steel industry can only be organized by placing the workers in one union. "If you believe otherwise you may as well save your efforts, your trouble and your money." Lewis appealed to the craft unionists' reflexive anticommunism, warning them that if they deserted the militant young industrial union insurgents in the Amalgamated Association, who, he alleged wrongly, were untrained and unexperienced in the labor movement but non-Communist, the A. F. of L. would make Communists out of them. Let the A. F. of L. charter a new industrial union for steel, suggested Lewis; allow the Amalgamated to sit on the sidelines and perhaps later merge; but act, and act now. "I do not know about the cost," admitted Lewis. "I only know it should be done whether we win or lose."[23]

But the executive council again preferred equivocation to decisiveness and, instead of granting an industrial union charter to a new organization in steel, it authorized Lewis, Tobin, and Wharton as a three-man committee to negotiate with the officers of the Amalgamated Association—Michael "Grandmother" Tighe and Louis "Shorty" Leonard—concerning Lewis's proposal for industrial unionism. Naturally, Tighe and Leonard refused to relinquish their union's jurisdiction in the steel industry (they could be as legalistic as any other craft unionists) or to allow a special A. F. of L. committee to organize steel for them. Rebuffed by the AA, the executive council refused to act in steel.[24]

A twice-defeated Lewis persisted in claiming that labor's "fundamental obligation is to organize people." Either we are going to try to organize autos and steel, as well as other mass-production industries, he implored, "or the world is going to believe we are not going to try, or perhaps we do not want to." The Amalgamated Association may be "just as unchangeable as the laws of the Medes or Persians," declaimed Lewis, but the A. F. of L. had time and reason to change, and on its decision "impinges [sic] the destiny of the labor movement."[25]

On matters vital to the security of the mine workers' union, however, Lewis could be as selfish and illogical as his craft union adversaries. He argued, for example, that unless the Federation organized the steelworkers, the steel industry would attack labor organizations on the industry's fringes, such as the UMW. An industrial union in steel would necessarily protect the UMW's foothold in the captive mines. And the same man who castigated Wharton, Tobin, and Hutcheson for placing jurisdiction above organization rushed to defend the jurisdictional claims of the International Union of Mine, Mill, and Smelter Workers and, by implication, the UMW. Long an ineffective union, the IUMMSW had for more than two decades been unable to exert its theoretical jurisdiction among workers in the nonferrous metals industry. Particularly in Butte, Montana, local metal trade unions had organized workers in mills and smelters, and a new agreement negotiated between the metal trades and the Anaconda Copper Company in 1934 had sanctioned the arrangement. The craft union leaders defended their own organization of workers, theoretically within the jurisdiction of the IUMMSW, precisely as Lewis pleaded for industrial unionism in autos and steel. Because the IUMMSW had failed to unionize Butte's skilled mill workers, they would have remained unorganized unless the metal trades unions recruited them. Organization, asserted the metals trades spokesmen, must in this case transcend jurisdiction. In response, Lewis could only cite the history of the IUMMSW's affiliation with the A. F. of L. in 1911, consummated only after Gompers, at the insistence of the UMW, awarded the IUMMSW complete jurisdiction over all workers in and around the mines, mills, and smelters. In this case, to infringe on the jurisdiction of an ineffective union threatened the UMW's comparable claim to all workers in and around the coal mines, and Lewis unabashedly, if hypocritically, defended trade union tradition, legitimacy, and jurisdiction.[26]

Prior to the next A. F. of L. executive council meeting, scheduled for the first week of May 1935, Lewis decided to force the issues of industrial unionism and organization of mass-production workers to a resolution. Hints began to emanate from UMW headquarters that Lewis needed the assistance of the young, the rebellious, and the "red" to organize the nation's workers. On April 23, Germer, again on the UMW payroll, learned that a bitter feud was on between Lewis and William Green, no doubt because the A. F. of L. president had failed to endorse Lewis's demand for unionization of the auto, steel, and other mass-production industries.[27] Even as the executive council met, from April 30 to May 7, Louis Stark reported in the *New York Times* of May 3 that the formation of a bloc of unions into a separate national labor federation led by the UMWA appeared an eventual possibility because, according to the miners, the executive council had repudiated the San Francisco convention's resolution on industrial unionism.[28] Earlier in April, Lewis welcomed union insurgents from the steel industry to meet with him in his office at UMW headquarters. The same local leaders expelled from the AA for their alleged Communist connections were embraced by the president of the mine workers.[29]

Lewis's tactics upset the A. F. of L.'s old guard. On March 21, John Frey, craft unionism's most pedantic defender, worried that William Green had joined the "industrial unionists." Certain, however, of support for his position by fellow craft unionists on the executive council, Frey prophesied a showdown between industrial and craft unionists at the 1935 convention. "There must be a show down," he informed an English acquaintance, "for it is becoming intolerable to have some International Unions determined that other International Unions must change their form of organization against their desire."[30]

Frey's prophesy concerning the 1935 A. F. of L. convention proved accurate; but his fears about Green's loyalty were unwarranted. When the executive council reconvened on April 30, again to consider the issue of industrial unionism and organization of the mass-production workers, Green offered Lewis neither solace nor support.

Focusing his case for industrial unionism this time on the rubber industry, Lewis insisted that its workers demanded solidarity—a union structure that encompassed all employees of the industry regardless of job classification or skill. Let craft unions serve their members and even flourish, Lewis said, but do not allow theories about union structure to obstruct the organization of mass-production workers never before unionized and employed in industries traditionally resistant to craft unionism. Six months had passed since the San Francisco convention, he warned, and there has been no administration of that policy and no execution of the promissory note that the Federation held out to the millions of workers in mass production industry . . . and neither do I understand that there is any immediate desire to carry out that policy. . . . It appears that the American Federation of Labor is not going to liquidate [a typical Lewisian malapropism] the policy outlined by the San Francisco convention.[31]

To Lewis's consternation but not surprise, the overwhelming majority of executive council members (fourteen to two) evinced more concern about jurisdictional rights than about organizing the unorganized. Not even the prospect of imminent passage of the Wagner Labor Relations Act, the most prounion legislative act ever to emerge from Congress, motivated the A. F. of L. old guard to heed Lewis's advice.[32]

Not long after the executive council adjourned on May 7, rumors again circulated in print predicting a split in the labor movement. "It has grown increasingly clear," commented an editorial writer in the *Nation* of May 22, "that secession of industrial unions from the A. F. of L. may be inevitable if the young industrial unions are to grow. Leadership will naturally fall to John L. Lewis of the United Mine Workers and Sidney Hillman of the needle trades."[33] Earlier in the month, when Louis Stark had published information leaked by Lewis or his associates in the pages of the *New York Times*, the purpose had obviously been to pressure the executive council majority into granting industrial union charters to auto, steel, and rubber workers. That bluff having failed, the *Nation*'s story suggested quite plainly that Lewis finally had decided to act independently concerning industrial unionism unless the old guard in the A. F. of L. changed its collective mind between May 1935 and the convention in October.

Lewis's actions threatened a rift in the trade union establishment. He attended neither the August 1935 nor the October 1935 session of the executive council. Not one to accept minority status equably, the lord of the UMW refused to play vassal in the councils of the A. F. of L. In July he dispatched John Brophy to represent the UMW at a conference in Boston convened by federal unions in the gas and by-product coke industries. Lewis, Brophy assured the Boston delegates, would waive his union's jurisdiction over the coke workers, cooperate with them, and not obstruct their efforts if they built a permanent organization. Moreover, if the delegates adopted an inclusive structure for their union, he promised to help them achieve success. All William Green offered workers at the same conference was a biblical injunction. "He who keepeth his head," advised the A. F. of L. president, "is stronger than he that taketh a City. Remember gentlemen keep your head and respect jurisdictional rights."[34] In July Lewis also embraced the American Left more firmly. Writing to his wife on July 24, Powers Hapgood observed: "It's surprising how many radicals think I ought to see Lewis, saying it's much less of a compromise to make peace with him and stay in the labor movement than it is to get a government job and cease to be active in the class struggle.'' To reject a reconciliation with his old enemy Lewis, Hapgood concluded, would be tantamount to letting the left wing down.[35] Early in September Lewis asked Adolph Germer to attend the Atlantic City A. F. of L. convention in order to assist in countering criticism of the UMW and jurisdictional attacks on it by Dan Tobin and other craft union officials.[36]

Lewis also occupied himself in the spring and summer of 1935 lobbying Congress and cementing political alliances that would prove essential to his campaign to organize mass-production workers. First Lewis had to protect the UMW from economic competition and antiunion operators. He did this by joining with northern coal operators in pressuring Congress to enact legislation that would transform the soft-coal industry into a federally regulated utility. Winning the support of coal-state congressmen (a significant voting bloc), northern big-city Democrats, and the Roosevelt administration, Lewis and his operator allies obtained passage of the Guffey-Snyder Bill. The act, which established a little NRA for bituminous coal, guaranteed miners the right to organize and bargain collectively, mandated minimum wages and maximum hours, and created a federal commission to fix prices and allocate production (and thus markets). After a decade of struggle, Lewis and Lauck had won their most cherished objective.

May and June 1935, however, brought Lewis frustration as well as triumph. A series of Supreme Court decisions in May paralyzed the New Deal. On May 27 the Court, in a unanimous decision, declared the National Industrial Recovery Act unconstitutional—a ruling that threatened labor's rights under Section 7a and presidential employment codes setting minimum wages and maximum hours; it also presaged a similar legal fate for the Guffey-Snyder Act.

But in June Congress passed the Wagner Act, granting organized labor far greater protection than it had been ceded under Section 7a. Signed by President Roosevelt in early July, the new labor law effectively outlawed company unions, declared illegal the most widely used employer antiunion weapons, placed no restraints on trade unions, and created a National Labor Relations Board to administer the new law. Never before had the federal government, or for that matter any American political jurisdiction, offered the union organizer and the worker eager to join a union such substantial protection against employers. The Wagner Act indeed provided organized labor with Lewis's oft-cited once-in-a-lifetime opportunity to unionize the nation's mass-production workers.[37]

By early September Lewis acted as one of the nation's most ardent Roosevelt admirers. Speaking to a Labor Day rally in Fairmont, West Virginia, on September 2, the largest outdoor meeting ever held in the area and attended by 40,000 coal miners and their families, Lewis demanded the reelection of Franklin D. Roosevelt. In the same city where ten years earlier on Labor Day he had been served with a fistful of antilabor injunctions, Lewis now told an enthusiastic audience that "the era of privilege and predatory individuals is over." He called on American workers to join Roosevelt in a struggle against the Liberty League and the reactionary elite that for too long had dominated the United States.[38]

Its 1935 convention in Atlantic City was like no other in the A. F. of L.'s fifty-year existence. The brisk October sea breezes and salt air scarcely cooled the passions about organizing the unorganized that Lewis had inflamed during the year that had passed since the San Francisco convention; nor did they chill the ardor of the young and rebellious who came to New Jersey's resort determined to participate in the building of a mass labor movement. "This year you could feel the challenge," later recalled Len DeCaux, a left-wing labor journalist. "On the boardwalk, in lobbies, in lower-priced restaurants, you could hear them laugh and kid—making jokes about the Old Guard. A treasonous mood."[39]

The hotel chosen as convention headquarters personified the character of the A. F. of L. old guard. In its rococo design and garish elegance, the Chelsea Hotel reeked of late nineteenth-century Victorian respectability—an antiquarian relic in depression America. Lewis consciously and calculatingly set himself and his union apart from the ambience of the Chelsea; he established UMW convention headquarters in the more modest President Hotel, where he held court and advised the militant young delegates from the steel, auto, and rubber industries. Welcomed by a labor leader with power, the youngsters, in Len DeCaux's words, "came away glowing." As Powers Hapgood had discovered in July, a new Lewis was in the making, one who seemed not to care whether his associates in the labor movement were left or right, red or pink.[40]

But Lewis was too experienced a labor politician to believe that he could stampede the convention delegates. The fate of his efforts to promote industrial unionism during executive council sessions presaged the results of the convention. The craft unionists who opposed Lewis on the council (usually by twelve to two) controlled the votes of their convention delegates as tightly as Lewis dominated his UMW group. What support Lewis had, aside from the needle trades unions and several old A. F. of L. affiliates with industrial union traditions, came largely from state federations and city centrals, which each cast only a single vote, and from federal labor unions, whose voting rights bore no relation to actual membership. Even if the vast majority of organized workers favored Lewis's bid to organize the unorganized—and later evidence would suggest they did—they had no means to express their sentiments in Atlantic City. Hutcheson spoke for the carpenters, Wharton for the machinists, and Tobin for the teamsters, and their voices would strike the same chords at the convention that they had hit at every session of the executive council. What, then, was Lewis's strategy? What motivated his desire to associate himself with younger insurgent delegates in a losing cause?

The first question is easier to answer. As he had done so often in the past, Lewis determined to make his adversaries suffer, to embarrass them before their own constituents. Waiting until the last minute, he introduced two resolutions directly on the convention floor aimed at Matthew Woll and John Frey, the ideological spokesmen for the old guard. One resolution declared that any official of the A. F. of L. who held office in the National Civic Federation—an association of corporation executives, trade unionists, and public citizens, once reformist in character but by 1935 increasingly antiradical and even antilabor—could not serve both organizations simultaneously. Thus Matthew Woll faced a dilemma: He could fight Lewis's resolution, defend his own association with the NCF, and rationalize "class collaboration" at a time of heightened class feeling; or he could admit that his association with the NCF had been mistaken (as John Mitchell had done two decades earlier when faced with the same choice by UMW socialists), resign his position, and endorse Lewis's resolution. Committed to opposing industrial unionism in the mass-production industries, Woll could not also defend "class collaboration." He could bear one cross, not two, and hence, he resigned from the NCF. The second Lewis resolution declared that the *American Federationist* (the A. F. of L.'s monthly journal) should not publish advertisements by antiunion corporations. This, too, was directed against Woll, who was an insurance agent as well as labor official, and who solicited ads (as did Frey for the *Molders' Journal*) from corporations with persistent records of union busting. Again, Woll, Frey, and the old guard offered no resistance to the resolution.[41]

Yet those resolutions—guaranteed to carry and introduced merely to embarrass Lewis's loudest critics—were only diversions to the main battle: organizing the unorganized. On this issue, defeat loomed for Lewis. Why, then, did this most egotistical of labor leaders risk repudiation? Several likely answers come to mind. First, the possibility of long-term gains for Lewis far outweighed the short-run risks. If he read reality correctly and gauged political power accurately, the moment was propitious for organizing mass-production workers. Even if defeated on the convention floor, Lewis would leave Atlantic City as the heroic advocate of industrial unionism, the brave spokesman for the aspirations of millions of unorganized workers. Second, defeat in October 1935, did not foreclose an ultimate victory. If Lewis was right, most rank-and-file trade unionists sympathized with his policy, as did millions of unorganized mass-production workers. He not only sought to organize the unorganized; Lewis also called on craft union members to rebel against an unresponsive and unrepresentative leadership. Third, a mystical quality underlay Lewis's decision to fight for industrial unionism in 1935, a quality captured in Heber Blankenhorn's later remembrance which cannot be verified of a chance meeting on the boardwalk with Lewis the night before the convention's climactic debate on industrial unionism.

> Late that evening [October 15, recalled Blankenhorn] I went for a walk on the Boardwalk . . . when a sudden shower came up and I took refuge under a tin shelter over some benches. Before long a big man with his coat collar turned up and his hat

brim pulled down, sat down at the other end of the bench. . . . When he struck a match . . . I said, "Hello, John."

Lewis waved the match in my direction . . . and said, "Hello, Blank," without cordiality. . . . I mentioned his industrial union resolution at the 1934 convention . . . and asked if he had been thinking about organizing the new units in the basic industries on an industrial union basis.

Lewis' big hand fell on my forearm with an iron grip. He said, "I have been thinking of nothing else for a year. Day and night. Night and day. Last night I could not sleep. I sat in my bathrobe, at the window, facing east, looking over the sea, where I could see nothing but dark night, not even the ocean or the sky. Mrs. Lewis called, asking why I did not go to bed, what was I waiting up for? I said, 'I am waiting for the sun to rise!' After a little while the first ray appeared and I could see the line of sky and sea, and gradually the rays slowly spread and dawn was breaking. Then with startling speed, the sun's rim glinted and I said, 'Behold, at last the sun arises, the day is here, day has come.' And I went to bed and slept soundly."

I was awed by this mystic. When he took his big hand off my forearm it was numb. We sat there silently, while he tried again to light his cigar. The rain stopped, and Lewis stood up. He said, "I shall go back to my hotel now and tonight I shall sleep for the day is here and I am ready."[42]

The climactic day indeed arrived on October 16, as delegates to the 1935 A. F. of L. convention debated from 2:30 P.M. to 11:45 P.M. a report by a minority of the Resolutions Committee that the A. F. of L. issue industrial union charters to workers in the mass-production industries. The minority report, introduced by Charles P. Howard—an official of one of the most tradition-bound craft unions in the federation, the International Typographical Union—stressed the failure historically of the A. F. of L. to organize workers in the basic industries along jurisdictional lines outmoded by technological change. Of almost 40 million wage workers, said Howard, the A. F. of L. at most represented 3.5 million, a record that should not cause labor leaders to rejoice. No one, including the most militant of industrial unionists, added Howard, desired to strip craft unions of their members. The real issue, he implied, was not craft versus industrial unionism; it was whether or not the A. F. of L. would authorize a large-scale organizing campaign among the mass-production workers on the only foundation that promised success: industrial unionism.[43]

After Matthew Woll delivered a lengthy rebuttal to the minority's position— studded with misread history lessons, arid legalisms, and an exegesis of the A. F. of L. constitution worthy of a Medieval divine—Lewis arose and made the debate's most dramatic speech.

a year ago at San Francisco [he declaimed] I was a year younger and naturally I had more faith in the Executive Council. I was beguiled into believing that an enlarged

Executive Council would honestly interpret and administer this policy—the policy we talked about for six days in committee, the policy of issuing charters for industrial unions in the mass production industries. But surely Delegate Woll would not hold it against me that I was so trusting at that time. I know better now. At San Francisco they seduced me with fair words. Now, of course, having learned that I was seduced, I am enraged and I am ready to rend my seducers limb from limb.

The labor movement, Lewis proclaimed, "is organized upon a principle that the strong shall help the weak." Calling upon the strong craft unions to assist their weaker brothers in the mass-production industries, Lewis repeated the rhetorical devices he had used twenty-four years earlier (1911) in his pseudonymous pamphlet attack on Duncan MacDonald and the leaders of Illinois UMW District 12. Lewis now asked A. F. of L. delegates to "heed this cry from Macedonia that comes from the hearts of men." If you reject the minority report, he warned the delegates, "despair will prevail where hope now exists [and] . . . High wassail will prevail at the banquet tables of the mighty."[44]

The debate raged on for several more hours, ever more heated, ever more ad hominem and scurrilous in character, but it changed few votes. In the event all the large international craft unions, the dominant sector of the federation, voted against the minority report. The UMW; the brewery workers; the mine, mill, and smelter workers; the needles trades unions; and the state federations, city centrals, and federal labor unions voted in favor of the report. However much more representative of rank-and-file sympathies the latter bloc may have been, its voting strength represented only 38% of convention delegate ballots. Thus by a margin of 18,024 to 10,933, the minority report went down to defeat, rapidly followed by the adoption by voice vote of the majority report.[45]

On the succeeding three days the advocates of industrial unionism suffered further setbacks, all by virtually the same voting margin. Indeed, not satisfied with voting victories, the triumphant old guard even sought to silence the industrial unionists through parliamentary rulings. When a delegate from the rubber workers raised the question of jurisdiction for his union, Hutcheson, of the carpenters, interjected a point of order. It was a moment Lewis had waited for, an event he would have manufactured if necessary. "This thing of raising points of order all the time on minor delegates," Lewis challenged the burly, oversized carpenters' leader, "is rather small potatoes." More heated words passed between the two labor barons, with Hutcheson finally calling Lewis a "bastard." At that, Lewis jumped to his feet. Quick as a cat, he leaped over a row of chairs toward Hutcheson, jabbed out his right fist, and sent the carpenters' president sprawling against a table. Moments later the fight was over, as a blood-streaked Hutcheson left the convention floor guided by friends. "Lewis," wrote the labor journalist Edward Levinson, "casually adjusted his tie and collar, relit his cigar, and sauntered slowly through the crowded aisles to the rostrum."[46]

Cool calculation, not passion; purposeful tactics, not anger, explained Lewis's resort to physical force. Hutcheson, unlike Tobin, was neither an old enemy nor personally obnoxious to Lewis. Instead, they were old Indianapolis poker cronies, a relationship that would be resumed in the 1940s. Lewis's blow to Hutcheson's jaw was intended to symbolize publicly the UMW president's irrevocable rupture with labor's old guard. It also dramatized, as no number of words or convention resolutions would, the split between Lewis and his critics. No one could now doubt that Lewis was serious about his plans to organize the unorganized. Lewis's punch resonated through the working class. One of Hutcheson's own constituents, a Kansas City union carpenter, wired Lewis: "Congratulations, sock him again."[47]

CHAPTER 11

Founding the CIO,
October 1935-October 1936

Lewis quickly took the offensive against the A. F. of L. old guard. On the morning of Sunday, October 20, the day after the 1935 convention adjourned, Lewis met with Phil Murray, Tom Kennedy, John Brophy, Sidney Hillman (men's clothing workers), David Dubinsky (women's garment workers), Charles Howard (printers), Thomas McMahon (textile workers), and Max Zaritsky (cap makers) for breakfast at the President Hotel. Lewis told his eight companions, who also had endorsed industrial unionism during the convention, that only they could answer the pleas of the unorganized, that they must not let their defeat obstruct efforts to unionize mass-production workers. But the breakfast ended with the advocates of industrial unionism as far from achievement of their primary objective as they had been when the A. F. of L. convention opened the previous week.[1]

Less than three weeks later, on November 9, 1935, Lewis invited his Atlantic City breakfast associates as well as Thomas Brown (mine, mill, and smelter workers) and Harvey Fremming (oil workers) to a meeting at UMW headquarters. There the eleven labor leaders created the Committee for Industrial Organization as an organized bloc inside the A. F. of L. dedicated to unionizing mass-production workers along industrial lines, a policy the federation majority had just rejected. Beyond appointing Lewis as chairman, Howard as secretary, and Brophy as director, and obtaining $5,000 pledges from the UMW, ACWA, and ILGWU, the labor leaders at the November 9 conference made no plans, adopted no policies, and simply reiterated their commitment to promote the organization of mass-production workers inside the A. F. of L. They also invited other trade unionists sympathetic to industrial unionism to join the CIO.[2]

Ten days later, on November 18, John Brophy opened the CIO's first office, in the Rust Building, at Fifteenth and K Streets in Washington, across the street from UMW headquarters. Aided by two secretaries—Katherine Pollack and Bernice Welsh—Brophy planned, in the words of a "Proposed Outline of Activities for the CIO" prepared by Pollack, "to foster recognition and acceptance of collective bargaining in [mass production] industries; to council and advise unorganized and newly organized groups of workers; to bring them under the banner and in affiliation with the American Federation of Labor." Brophy and his assistants prepared pamphlets explaining the history and principles of industrial unionism, circulated them among workers and union groups, and intended to publish a regular newsletter (the *CIO News*).[3] Shortly afterward, with Lewis's consent, Brophy hired Len DeCaux—a talented journalist of British origins, a Communist, and a persistent former critic of Lewis—as editor of the newsletter and CIO publicist.[4] DeCaux's appointment was yet another indication of the transformation in Lewis's values and his apparent willingness to collaborate with leftists.

In late 1935 the CIO amounted to scarcely more than Brophy and his two secretaries, Len DeCaux, a cubbyhole for an office, and Lewis's dreams. Only the prospect of generous material and financial support from the UMW, which meant Lewis, made the CIO a force within the labor movement.

Indeed, in a real sense the CIO, at birth, was Lewis. Brophy, who administered the early CIO, was an extension of the UMW president, a man who served at Lewis's pleasure and was paid by the mine workers' union. Lewis's fellow committee members David Dubinsky and Max Zaritsky lacked national influence and seemed as eager to maintain the respectability that the A. F. of L. conferred on them as to please Lewis. Fremming, Brown, and McMahon represented weak unions, negligible political influence, and no power in the A. F. of L. Howard, perhaps the most principled and unselfish of all the CIO founders, spoke only for himself, not his union, which never affiliated with CIO. Only Sidney Hillman approached Lewis in stature and influence. Much admired by labor journalists, academic labor specialists, and social reformers, Hillman, however, led a union— the Amalgamated Clothing Workers—that operated in a peripheral industry and represented a narrow strata of the American working class: largely Jewish and Italian immigrants. Among the CIO's founders, then, only Lewis had in the past bargained as an equal with the men who ran the A. F. of L., and only Lewis led a union situated at the heart of the American industrial economy.

With the founding of the CIO, the struggle to organize the unorganized turned into a personal conflict between William Green and John L. Lewis—a clash with dark, unconscious Freudian undertones. In the past, whether as a UMW official or as president of the A. F. of L., Green had customarily deferred to Lewis's more arrogant and commanding personality. Now, suddenly, in November 1935, Green sought to establish his personal prowess, to prove to the more "manly" members of his executive council—especially Tobin, Hutcheson, and Wharton—that he was their equal and that he would discipline Lewis as a rebellious child. In Green's mind, the creation of CIO challenged his personal authority—a challenge he accepted.

In late November before the CIO had done anything that could be construed as a violation of A. F. of L. policies, Green sent a letter to each member of the committee warning him to desist from his current course of action. Apparently, if newspaper reports were accurate, Green made a special point of having the letter hand-delivered to Lewis so that the CIO chairman received it late on the evening of the twenty-second or early on the morning of the twenty-third, before any other CIO member had had a chance to read it.[5] Green filled his missive with dire warnings and exaggerated allegations, even accusing the CIO's founders of "dual" unionism. From your actions, he prophesied, "bitterness and strife would inevitably follow." In a particularly pointed warning, Green stressed that the minority inside the A. F. of L. must abide by the decisions of the majority and not interfere with or even oppose the policies of the majority.[6]

Lewis responded immediately. Although he acted without first consulting his CIO associates, an act some scholars consider imperious if not arrogant, he had good reason.[7] Green's letter may have been sent separately to all members of the CIO, but its message was aimed at Lewis and framed in terms descriptive of the UMW's internal practices. Green, moreover, had made a point of having the letter specially delivered to Lewis. Lewis's reaction was equally dramatic. "Effective this date (November 23)," he wrote to Green and for release in the newspapers, "I resign as vice president of the American Federation of Labor." Those fourteen words captured the headlines in the Sunday newspapers, producing more publicity for the CIO than any event since its founding on November 9. As Lewis subsequently informed first Hillman and then other CIO members, his resignation from a "worthless post" where his future membership "would avail nothing" had electrified the nation and stimulated interest in the CIO.[8]

Lewis intended to make the most of the publicity attendant on his resignation. On Monday, November 25, he held a well-attended press conference in his office during which he expounded freely on the necessity for industrial unionism as a means to organize the mass-production workers. And on Thursday, November 28, he delivered a radio address on the CBS network, written by Jett Lauck and titled "The Future of Organized Labor," that explained to an audience of millions why economic evolution and technological innovation dictated the establishment of industrial unionism in the mass-production industries. Seeking to assuage the anxieties of nonworking-class listeners and also to appeal to white-collar workers, Lewis linked American antiunionism to fascism in Italy and Nazism in Germany and asserted that only the emergence of effective industrial unions would guarantee "real recovery and reform" from depression. Industrial unionism, he proclaimed, "offers the only way to emancipation from industrial autocracy—to economic and political freedom to those who work by hand and brain."[9]

Lewis's response to Green's letter won the CIO "four days of continuous publicity," newspaper coverage that Hillman and others found exceedingly favorable to their point of view. It also reinforced Lewis's conviction that he had acted wisely—that, in the words he used when justifying his actions at a meeting of the CIO executive board on December 9, "Fine price, I sold out for—my worthless job.'' Admitting that his resignation and subsequent actions might have seemed impetuous, Lewis noted that ''it was a methodical attempt to dramatize what the committee is trying to do,'' and it did evoke ''a healthy response back in the field.''[10]

Green's letter of November 23, however, required an official response from the CIO. More concerned about publicity than questions of union legitimacy, Lewis preferred that members of the CIO planning board respond individually and that subsequently the committee print a pamphlet containing Green's original letter and the CIO replies.[11] Contrary to Irving Bernstein's version of events, Charles Howard wrote no authorized CIO rejoinder to Green; nor did Lewis desire such a step in November 1935.[12] In fact, Harvey Fremming, of the oil workers, replied first to Green, and his letter captured the essence of the dispute. ''Whether industrial unionism is right or wrong is not the issue,'' wrote Fremming. ''The whole question is one of *tactics, not of principle*'' (our italics). Additional responses from Thomas McMahon, David Dubinsky, John Sherwood (mine, mill, and smelter workers), and Sidney Hillman emphasized that the founders of the CIO intended to strengthen, not weaken, the A. F. of L. ''We all feel,'' wrote Hillman on December 12, ''that the activities of this Committee will help the American Federation of Labor in extending organization to the unorganized mass production industries.''[13]

But the most dramatic response, as might be expected, came from Lewis. As usual, he acted without consulting his CIO colleagues—informing them of what he intended to do only a day earlier—and with care to obtain maximum publicity.[14] Precisely two weeks to the day after he had resigned from the executive council, Lewis, on Saturday, December 7, released to the press a letter addressed to William Green that would dominate the next morning's newspapers. ''Your official burdens are great,'' Lewis commiserated with Green.

> I would not increase them. I do not covet your office. . . . It is bruited about . . . that your private sympathies . . . lie with the group espousing the industrial type of organization, while your official actions and public utterances will be in support of their adversaries. Such a policy is vulnerable to criticism and will hardly suffice to protect you against attacks that may ensue from advocates of the craft philosophy. . . . Why not return to your father's house? You will be welcome. If you care to dissociate yourself from your present position, the Committee for Industrial Organization will be happy to make you its Chairman in my stead. The honorarium will be equal to that you now receive. The position will be as permanent as the one you now occupy. You would have the satisfaction of supporting a cause in which you believe inherently and of contributing your fine abilities to the achievement of an enlarged opportunity for the nation's workers.[15]

Lewis's offer to Green was a typical calculated gamble, one that he was certain would cost the CIO nothing. He addressed himself directly to Green's weakness of character. Lewis presented the A. F. of L. president a choice: Green could occupy his present position and serve as a supine agent for the most powerful craft unionists, with whose philosophy he did not sympathize, or he could serve Lewis in a cause in which he believed. In a memorandum of December 6 to CIO members explaining the reasoning behind his offer, Lewis conceded that Green "may not accept" but added that "it makes no material difference whether or not he does." Two days after he had released his letter of December 7 and received Green's rejection, Lewis observed, at the December 9 meeting of the CIO executive board: "If Green had accepted my invitation, it would have revolutionized the American labor movement."[16]

By early December 1935 Lewis had formulated a strategy to organize the mass-production workers, and his letter to Green formed part of a larger plan. Reports from his fieldworkers, especially Adolph Germer from Cleveland, Toledo, Akron, and Detroit, and other agents in rubber and steel, indicated to Lewis that considerable union sympathy remained alive among mass-production workers but that employees in autos, rubber, and steel associated the A. F. of L. with craft exclusiveness and labor failure. Such workers rejected organizing ventures promoted by the A. F. of L. To gain their loyalty, Lewis learned, CIO organizers would have to differentiate themselves from A. F. of L. agents.[17] Thus Lewis consciously declared war on the craft unionists, derided the possibility of neutrality in the conflict, and compelled Green to choose sides. If Green had accepted Lewis's proposal, scarcely a likely prospect, the craft unionists in the A. F. of L. would have lost an influential ally. If Green, instead, allied with the craft unionists, as Lewis, who had "spies" inside the A. F. of L. expected, the issue between the advocates of craft unionism and industrial unionism would be more sharply drawn. As CIO organizers proselytized for industrial unionism in the mass-production industries and enrolled members, the A. F. of L. would either tacitly recognize the success of Lewis's committee and impotently watch the formation of a new power bloc inside the federation, or Green and his associates would reject Lewis's union army. In no event, however, would Lewis secede voluntarily from the A. F. of L.; instead, he preferred to make his craft union enemies their own executioners. Tobin, Hutcheson, Wharton, et al., would be forced to accept minority status inside the A. F. of L. or maintain their hegemony only by expelling the CIO and compelling Lewis to form his own independent national labor center, which, if it successfully organized the mass-production workers, would far outnumber the A. F. of L. in members. In either case, Lewis would become the dominant power in the national labor movement, a leader whose massive union army would guarantee him unprecedented economic and political influence.

The December 9 CIO executive board meeting adopted policies in accord with Lewis's grand strategy. The board agreed unanimously to organize along industrial union lines in autos and rubber, a campaign to be initiated by Lewis speeches in Akron and Cleveland. It sanctioned Lewis's observation that "We ought to show results. . . . If we don't do anything, we lose our prestige. Now everyone is talking about us—even politicians, bankers, the Pennsylvania Railroad, and one of the Wall Street magazines.'' Expect reprisals from the craft unions, warned Lewis, for ''we are likely to be made the object of an attack by the A. F. of L.,'' but give them no cause for conflict. Which is precisely what the CIO resolved to do, delaying action in the steel industry until the A. F. of L. executive council acted first and refusing to accept donations from individuals and organizations outside the A. F. of L. In an official press release issued the next day, the CIO cited its determination to organize auto and rubber workers and ''to encourage them in building strong unions, *within the A. F. of L.*''[18] (our italics).

In the days and weeks that followed the December 9 CIO executive board session, Lewis's agents were busy among the auto and rubber workers. Even the more conservative and reactionary of trade unionists in the Detroit area, according to one report, responded to the CIO with ''progressive sentiment'' and ''warm friendliness.'' Although CIO representatives encouraged organization among auto and rubber workers without regard to craft union jurisdictional claims, they also advised against precipitous action or divisive steps prior to the A. F. of L. executive council session scheduled for January 15, 1936.[19]

In strategy formulated by Lewis and implemented by John Brophy at Washington headquarters, Adolph Germer among auto workers, and Powers Hapgood among rubber workers, the CIO acted to incorporate the auto workers' and rubber workers' unions within the A. F. of L. as industrial organizations, sought an accommodation with the craft unionists—not an internecine conflict—yet prepared for the worst. By January 6, 1936, Lewis had decided that unless the A. F. of L. recognized the claims of the industrial unionists, industrial unionism would have to be implemented outside the federation. And he bluntly warned Green of the likely result if the executive council again repudiated industrial unionism. ''Opportunity to organize may knock more than once at labor's door,'' John Brophy wrote to Green on January 10, delivering Lewis's message. ''But seldom has it knocked with such insistence . . . and never perhaps has disregard of its call been fraught with such peril not only for labor but for our country as a whole.'' Brophy advised Green that rejection of industrial unionism in the mass-production industries by the council would result in serious consequences and would deal a deadly wound to labor unity ''that will be all the harder as coming from the hands of labor leaders.''[20]

Lewis's warning had no discernible impact on the craft unionists who dominated the A. F. of L. and manipulated Green. As these men gathered in Miami on January 15 for the first executive council session of 1936, their minds were far removed from organizing the unorganized. The night before the meetings began, one question dominated discussion among the A. F. of L.'s ''Council of Patriarchs'': During what hours should they remain in session. ''Those who desired to remain up until the 'wee sma hours', to engage in their favorite pastime [poker],'' reported an informant of Sidney Hillman's, ''favored afternoon sessions . . . as usual. Those who desire to visit Tropical Park and Hialeah, where the 'bangtails' perform for the suckers, wanted the hours fixed at 9 A.M. to 1 P.M. The latter element prevailed . . . and then some difficulty was experienced in finding a member who would agree to meet the President [Green] when he arrived and tell him how the matter had been arranged.'' On the issue of industrial unionism, however, no differences of opinion divided the "Council of Patriarchs": They refused to consider any compromise with the CIO.[21]

Lewis was too busy with the real business of the labor movement to worry about his foes on the executive council, whom he ridiculed publicly as sybaritic birds of passage "who follow the Council in its seasonal peregrinations from the Jersey beaches in the summer to the golden sands of Florida in the winter."[22] While Hutcheson, Tobin, and Wharton bet on the ponies, Lewis traveled to Akron and Cleveland, Ohio, to deliver speeches to auto and rubber workers. On the afternoon and evening of January 19, despite one of the worst winter blizzards in Ohio history, thousands of workers packed meeting halls in Cleveland and Akron; indeed, in both cities the halls were too small to contain the crowds, and thousands stood in the streets outside in driving snow and numbing temperatures to listen to Lewis over a loudspeaker system. The speech, written, as was customary, by Jett Lauck, stressed the traditional theme of industrial democracy versus industrial autocracy, of the need for mass-production workers to organize economically and politically to save the nation from fascism or communism, and of the role of the labor movement in liberating the United States from thralldom to a reactionary financial élite. Lewis also sounded one new, clear note: the CIO's commitment to rescue mass-production workers from the antiquarian union practices of the A. F. of L. and its craft union majority.[23]

As Ruth McKenney wrote in her historical novel about the organization of Akron's rubber workers, Lewis's speech made a profound impression. "His audience went out of that chilly hall to make John L. the most talked of man in town. A hero to his listeners, he was next morning a hero to every second man in the rubber shops." His impact was similar in Cleveland, and it spread from there to auto workers in Toledo, Detroit, Milwaukee, and Kansas City. Every CIO fieldworker and industrial union organizer began to demand a Lewis personal appearance. Workers responded enthusiastically to Lewis's oratorical style—his purple passages and hyperbolic flourishes notwithstanding—for, as McKenney noted, workers "liked hearing their dreams, their problems, their suffering cloaked in Biblical phrases [the stock quotations that Lewis carefully inserted into Lauck's learned addresses]. They felt proud that a workers' leader could use so many educated words with such obvious fluency, and they were pleased and a little flattered by hearing their own fate discussed in such rolling periods and such dramatic phrases." Lewis's sonorous voice transformed clichés into battle cries, malapropisms into epic prose, solecisms into revelations. He did not enlighten his audiences; he hypnotized them. When he sneered at the advocates of partnership between labor and capital, and observed that "labor and capital may be partners in theory, but . . . are enemies in fact," Lewis caught the gut feelings of auto and rubber workers, who left the hall determined to battle their employers. Whatever the A. F. of L. decided in Miami, Lewis assured his listeners, they could count on him, the UMW, and the CIO; there would be no repeat of the betrayal that mass-production workers had experienced in 1933-1934.[24]

Miami's winter sun may have warmed the bodies of A. F. of L. leaders, but it failed to soothe their temperaments. When Charles Howard appeared before the council to defend the CIO, his inquisitors, led by Green, castigated the industrial unionists for instigating dualism, divisiveness, and bitterness within the labor movement. "If you could be convinced that activities of the Committee would lead to . . . discord, hate and injury to the American Federation of Labor," Green asked Howard, would you be willing to continue it? "No," replied Howard, "I would lay down my life to prevent that."[25] His reply failed to assuage anti-CIO council members, who proceeded, with Green's blessing, to ram through a resolution that accused the CIO of dual unionism, ordered the CIO to dissolve forthwith, commanded CIO members to abide by the majority decisions of the 1935 convention, and appointed a committee of three (George Harrison, G. M. Bugniazet, and Joseph N. Weber) to confer with CIO representatives and hand them the executive council's ultimatum. In rapid order thereafter, the council rejected industrial union charters for auto, rubber, aluminum, and radio workers.[26]

The executive council's action stunned many trade unionists. Matthew Smith, a skilled tool and die maker in the auto industry and a leader in the Detroit Mechanics Educational Society of America (MESA), reacting to the order to dissolve the CIO, told Germer: "Never, Never! Haven't these fellows any sense? Don't they know what is going on among the rank and file of labor? Our people refuse to be parceled out like fish on the market. We want unity. . . . They want to force us into a guerilla warfare, and much to our regret, it looks like that is what it is going to be." Germer personally advised Brophy that although most auto unionists preferred to avoid a break with the A. F. of L., "rather than allow their organizations to be dismembered by the Executive Council, they are willing to pool their fate with the CIO, should the break come."[27]

Lewis, however, took the news from Miami in stride. Green, who had asserted his manhood vigorously in Miami by leading the assault against the CIO, would soon be humbled in his "father's house," the UMW.[28] Lewis eagerly awaited the UMW's 1936 convention, scheduled to open in Washington on January 28, where he would set the stage for a dramatic confrontation between himself and Green, the CIO as labor's wave of the future and the A. F. of L. as heir to an ebbing nineteenth-century union tide. In the ensuing contest of wills and personalities, Lewis had no doubt as to who would emerge triumphant.

The 1936 UMW convention opened in a triumphant mood. "We are meeting," the miners' president informed over 1,800 delegates, "at a time when our industry is more completely organized than ever before, when collective bargaining is more universally accepted in the coal industry than at any time in the lives of any of us, when the membership of our Union is greater than ever before, when the financial resources of our Union are greater than every before, and when the potential strength of our organization . . . transcends the imagination of the organized labor movement.'' Whenever he addressed the delegates, which was frequently, Lewis, in the words of a *Nation* editorial, ''drew forth roaring cheers, rising votes, and hostile boos as he desired.'' ''John certainly has a hold over that crowd,'' Sidney Hillman, a convention guest, later reflected.[29]

One issue more than any other stirred emotions and stimulated debate at the miners' convention: the A. F. of L. executive council's demand that the CIO dissolve. Referring to that order, Lewis observed that the executive council ''seems to have buried its head in the golden sands of Florida and is issuing pronunciamentos that cause the worker to despair.'' Phil Murray threatened that ''the sooner we get the hell away from them [the A. F. of L.] the better it will be for us.'' And in his most powerful speech, midway through the convention, Lewis declared that ''all the members of the Executive Council of the American Federation of Labor will be wearing asbestos suits in hell before the committee [CIO] is dissolved. . . . I don't work [for the American Federation of Labor]. . . . I work for the United Mine Workers of America . . . and . . . I do not . . . intend . . . to see a policy ratified and followed that is designed to disrupt, emasculate, and destroy the union that I have the honor to represent.'' The nation needs a labor movement, Lewis stressed, that represents the millions of unorganized workers whose exploited condition makes them a drain upon the well-being of every American citizen whether a hand or brain worker. Lewis promised to devote all his strength to the organization of the unorganized. ''As ye may help these other workers out of the fullness of your own strength,'' he declaimed, ''ye also stand to aid and help yourselves. If that be your policy I want you to say so to the world now, and when the time comes I will say to the American Federation of Labor . . . just what I think you want me to say to them under the circumstances.'' At the conclusion of Lewis's speech, the delegates, by a unanimous rising vote, empowered their officers to withhold per capita dues payments from the A. F. of L. ''The feeling of the crowd toward the A. F. of L.,'' Hillman noted, ''is very bitter.''[30]

That bitterness was exemplified on the convention's last day, when William Green returned to his ''father's house'' to plead with the delegates to remain loyal to the family of American labor. In his plea to the miners to respect labor unity, Green resorted to the same domestic metaphor that Lewis had used when he invited the A. F. of L. president back into his ''father's house.'' ''A child and some associate children of the organized labor family of the nation are in open rebellion against the action of a convention,'' warned Green. ''I plead with you to show loyalty and devotion to your father, your parent, the great organization that chartered you and that has fathered you and protected you. Remain at home, for the American Federation of Labor will remain supreme.''[31]

Green's emotional one-and-a-half-hour speech failed to save the parents of the American labor movement against a rebellion by their metaphorical children in the miners' union. Miners instead saw their decision more in terms of a divorce between freely consenting adults whose longtime union had been strained by the emergence of irreconcilable differences.

When Lewis asked all the delegates who had changed their minds as a result of Green's speech to rise, he observed two delegates. Lewis then asked those delegates who believed that the CIO should be dissolved to rise. "The Chair," recorded the official convention proceedings, "sees one delegate arise." And when Lewis requested that all those who believed that the convention's policies should be executed by the UMW president rise, the delegates rose *en masse* and applauded. "President Green," responded Lewis, "you have received the answer of the United Mine Workers to your ultimatum."[32]

Lewis, reported Heywood Broun, "knocked out William Green in precisely three minutes." Broun also observed that when Lewis asks a dissident delegate to stand up, "it is rather more a challenge than an invitation." And Jett Lauck recorded in his diary for February 3, 1936: "Very dramatic scene. Green ruthlessly obliterated."[33]

The advocates of industrial unionism were exhilarated by the UMW convention. "I have never been as proud of my membership in the miners' union as I was during the convention," wrote John Brophy. "True, it wasn't absolute perfection, but as compared with any other group in the country today it was a beacon of light for the workers and those who value the democratic political structure." The miners' convention, observed the *Nation*, "was a rich and lively manifestation of mass strength pushing toward genuine power in national affairs." And Heywood Broun concluded that within two years John L. Lewis would be in command of the labor movement because of his drive, courage, and "extraordinary grasp of popular psychology."[34]

Not all Lewis's allies, however, were pleased by his behavior at the UMW convention. David Dubinsky, Max Zaritsky, and other Social Democrats among the New York garment workers seemed troubled by Lewis's threat to desert the A. F. of L. To them, Lewis had not displayed good judgment and diplomacy, because by "striking a belligerent note [he] will tend to drive friends away who want to preserve the unity of the trade union movement."[35] Even Charles Howard and Sidney Hillman were vexed by the militancy displayed at the convention. Howard tried to convince himself that Lewis had no serious thought of withdrawing from the federation because "to withdraw would play into the hands of those who have been crying 'dual unionism'." Howard preferred that the CIO advocates remain inside the A. F. of L. and win a majority. Hillman agreed completely with Howard "that the way to fight the industrial question is on the inside and that sooner or later we are bound to get on top."[36]

Lewis, however, kept his ultimate aims a closely guarded secret. He did nothing publicly or overtly to indicate any intention of splitting the labor movement. His

CIO director, John Brophy, asserted that fears about a split in the labor movement were much exaggerated, especially by those who opposed a mass labor movement and whose negativeness caused them to accuse the CIO of disruption. "It is true," he suggested, "that our work jars the inactive and to them that seems like dualism and a split." Brophy, like Howard and Hillman, expected time to give the CIO a majority inside the A. F. of L. In his position as director of the CIO, Brophy witnessed the workers' widespread and sustained response to committee literature and organizers. "After long years of apathy and apparent stagnation," he noted, "the stir within the ranks of labor is welcome and the upsurge of interest is the promise of a stronger labor movement."[37]

Events after the 1936 UMW convention proved the truth of Charles Howard's contention and Lewis's private prediction that some members of the A. F. of L. executive council "would rather retain control of the organization with a small membership than to lose control through doubling or tripling the present membership."[38] For while the CIO sought to organize workers under the auspices of the A. F. of L., Green treated the CIO as a schismatic organization. On February 5 the A. F. of L. president directed his staff not to recognize any requests or communications from John Brophy. Two days later, Green wrote to Lewis and other members of the CIO executive board informing them of the executive council's January 15th ruling that the CIO must dissolve and asking Lewis and his representatives to confer with the A. F. of L.'s three-man committee to discuss preservation of labor unity.[39]

Lewis and his associates promptly accepted Green's invitation to a conference. (Lewis indeed offered to meet the A. F. of L. committee on any of three days during the week of February 19.) But A. F. of L. leaders evinced little desire to compromise the issues in dispute with the CIO, as evidenced by George Harrison's decision to attend an overseas labor conference precisely when Lewis agreed to confer with the Harrison committee.*[40]

Unable to confer with the A. F. of L. committee, the CIO held its own executive board session at UMW headquarters on February 19. Board members decided to respond bluntly to the A. F. of L.'s order to disband. On February 21, in a letter signed by Lewis and his associates and addressed to Green, the CIO spokesmen emphasized that they "were trying to remove the roots of dualism by making it possible for the millions of mass-production workers now outside the A. F. of L. to enter on the only basis they will accept—industrial unions." Denying vigorously that they intended to usurp the federation's functions, CIO leaders implied that they were forced to conclude "that many of those who are trying to brand us falsely as dualists are themselves none too eager to see the unions in the mass-production

*The committee, consisting of Harrison, G. M. Bugniazet, and Joseph N. Weber, all of whom were marginal figures on the executive council, lacking power and influence, illustrated the A. F. of L.'s arrogant attitude toward the CIO.

industries grow in influence.'' Once more offering to meet with the Harrison committee, Lewis warned that any attempt by the executive council to interfere with the CIO's organizing activities "would be completely undemocratic and contrary to the policies of the labor movement."[41]

Not until mid-May 1936 did the Harrison committee confer with CIO representatives. By then, however, prospects for accommodation between the advocates of industrial unionism and the A. F. of L. old guard had evaporated. Nevertheless, the A. F. of L. and CIO committees met for about two hours on May 19, with John L. Lewis and George Harrison dominating the discussion. Almost immediately, Harrison revealed to Lewis the A. F. of L.'s recalcitrance, stating that the executive council would consider a "solution" to the industrial union impasse only after the CIO dissolved. As Lewis replied to Harrison: "You shoot victim before you confer. Can't AFL confer?'' Harrison, moreover, refused to identify industries in which the A. F. of L. might establish industrial unions and instead asserted that his purpose was "to urge CIO members to go along with Council views." Aware that Harrison not only refused to negotiate but lacked the authority to do so, Lewis bluntly informed the A. F. of L. committee: "I am not going to advocate dissolution. Proceed with your judgment of execution. . . . We're part of the AFL and like to remain. We hold AFL responsible because of eternal policy of doing nothing. You can talk about convention mandate but you have no policy except frittering away time and shutting the door to those clamoring. No longer believe in your promises. I have mandate."[42]

Lewis knew that while Harrison talked, the A. F. of L. executive council, then concluding its quarterly session, had decided overwhelmingly to submit another ultimatum to CIO members. Before it adjourned on May 20, the executive council authorized Green to summon all international unions affiliated with the CIO to appear before the council beginning on July 9 (one union in the morning and a second in the afternoon) to answer charges that the CIO was a dual organization in violation of the A. F. of L. constitution and its rules. But first the Harrison committee sent a letter to CIO affiliates on May 20, again demanding that the CIO dissolve forthwith. "We are confident," Harrison's committee wrote, "that such action is necessary if the unity of the labor movement is to be preserved and the solidarity and prestige of the American Federation of Labor maintained."[43]

As expected, CIO members refused to comply with the Harrison committee's ultimatum. Those who responded formally, such as David Dubinsky and Charles Howard, denied emphatically that the CIO was dual in character or that its activities threatened the A. F. of L. Howard quite rightly observed that the CIO, not the A. F. of L., was acting on the primary principle of the labor movement that "the interests of the workers transcends every other consideration—even jurisdictional claims which have never existed in reality. Any legal and ethical policy that will promote organization is justified. Any policy that interferes with and prevents organization cannot be justified and will not prevail."[44] Lewis refused even to reply to Harrison and instead instructed Thomas Kennedy to write directly to

William Green. Our international executive board directed me by unanimous vote, Kennedy informed Green on May 29, to

> question the right and authority, or the propriety, of the Executive Council . . . to make such demands upon . . . the Committee for Industrial Organization; or upon any International organization to cease constructive work . . . in bringing about effective organization . . . in the mass production industries . . . I am instructed to say further to you . . . that the United Mine Workers of America emphatically refuses to accede to either the call or the request of the American Federation of Labor to discontinue its constructive and logical course of action.''[45]

Throughout the protracted war of words, letters, and ultimatums between the A. F. of L. and CIO, Lewis attended to his main objective: organization of the unorganized. As Brophy informed field organizer Adolph Germer early in June 1936: "The line of development continues very much as originally laid down in the early stages of formation of the C.I.O. The prestige of the C.I.O. continues to grow." That "line of development" meant that Germer labored round the clock in Detroit, Toledo, Cleveland, and other auto production centers to spread industrial unionism among auto workers and to encourage hitherto independent unions in the industry to merge into a large, all-inclusive international union.[46] And it brought Powers Hapgood and other CIO organizers to Akron, Ohio, to act as midwives at the birth of industrial unionism among rubber workers. Hapgood and other organizers, nearly all on the UMW payroll, assisted local Akron labor leaders in transforming spontaneous worker militancy into organized power, in using the aggressiveness of a small minority of rubber workers to spread unionism among the great mass. CIO funds and Hapgood's astute leadership helped Goodyear workers win a strike in late March 1936—a victory that increased union membership in the Goodyear plants from the small handful that had initiated the walkout to over 5,000 by March 29.

Lewis used his political influence to assist the Goodyear strikers. When the company threatened to break the strike with scabs and armed guards after the workers rejected a settlement offer, Lewis told federal mediators that he would make a national network radio speech in which he would accuse Goodyear officials of outright repression and that the likely aftermath would be a general strike in Akron and a consumer boycott of Goodyear products and Chrysler cars that used Goodyear tires. Lewis's threats brought action. Federal mediator Ed McGrady contacted Chrysler and Goodyear executives, whom he warned what might happen unless strikers were offered better terms. As a result, Goodyear resumed negotiations with its workers, which brought an improved settlement accepted by the strikers.[47]

From late 1935 through the first half of 1936, Lewis personally devoted his energy to organizing steelworkers. Before the rupture between the CIO and A. F. of L. became irrevocable, Lewis pursued a variety of tactics aimed at pressuring Green to initiate an aggressive organizing campaign along industrial union lines among steelworkers. Because Mike Tighe, the ancient and ailing president of the Amalgamated Association of Iron, Steel and Tin Workers, the A. F. of L. affiliate with jurisdiction in the industry, showed little interest in organizing the mass of semiskilled steelworkers, Lewis dispatched his own agents among the rank and file. In late November 1935, Pat Fagan, director of UMW District 5, conferred with John Chorey, a militant rank-and-file leader among Pittsburgh area steelworkers, about the prospects for unionizing the industry. During the conference Fagan drafted a letter that was sent to Lewis, under Chorey's signature, on November 30. Referring to Lewis's role at the 1935 A. F. of L. convention and his subsequent radio address espousing industrial unionism, the letter asked Lewis to confer with Pittsburgh area steelworkers about launching an intensive organizing campaign in the Monongahela River Valley. "We feel confident," Chorey wrote in Fagan's words, "that an organizing drive, immediately begun and carried on under the leadership of the United Mine Workers and other unions in your committee [CIO], can soon bring these thousands into the Amalgamated Association of Iron, Steel, and Tin Workers, thus strengthening the American Federation of Labor against its enemies."[48] By the end of 1935, then, Lewis had decided to unionize steel, yet he still preferred to function under A. F. of L. auspices and within the jurisdictional authority of the Amalgamated Association.

During the first five months of 1936 Lewis repeatedly urged an intensive organizing drive among steelworkers and then equivocated. Jett Lauck and Nathan Fine, the latter a free-lance union adviser and scholar, both submitted elaborate plans to Lewis for unionizing the steel industry, which he rejected.[49] Yet suddenly and without prior warning, Lewis acted. On February 21 he sent a letter to Green that bore his signature as well as Howard's and that suggested the inauguration of an organizing effort in the steel industry. The time was ripe, Lewis wrote, but to be successful the campaign must avoid the pitfalls that in the past had undermined organization of the steel industry. Lewis offered the services of trained organizers and $500,000 of a suggested $1,500,000 organizing fund. He demanded that organization must be along industrial lines and "that all steel workers organized will be granted the permanent right to remain united in one industrial union." Finally, Lewis declared that a responsible, energetic person (meaning an organizer outside the AA) who understood the industry must direct the campaign. Time being of the essence, Lewis promised to confer with Green at the earliest convenient opportunity, for "we are sincerely anxious for immediate action to organize the steel industry."[50]

As usual, the A. F. of L. equivocated. On March 2, Green agreed to discuss Lewis's plans but would not promise $1 million or to charter an unrestricted industrial union for steelworkers.[51] In fact, the dominant members on the A. F. of L. executive council had already decided that any "skilled" workers organized in the steel industry must be parceled out among the craft unions. Green, moreover, never conferred with Lewis, nor did the A. F. of L. president offer Amalgamated Association officials an acceptable organizing plan. Meantime, however, many locals inside the AA urged that their union undertake an organizing drive in cooperation with the CIO.[52]

By mid-April Lewis could wait no longer. On April 15, he wrote to Mike Tighe directly, repeating the offer he had originally made to the A. F. of L. in his letter of February 22. Lewis assured Tighe that the rights of the Amalgamated would be honored and that the CIO, unlike the A. F. of L., would respect the steel union's right to an unrestricted industrial union charter. He then presented the following terms to the AA "regardless of the stand taken by other organizations": (1) assurance that all steelworkers would remain united in one industrial union and be protected against future division among craft unions; (2) the establishment of a joint committee on which the AA would be represented as well as the CIO and other unions willing to contribute to a joint campaign. The committee would select a "responsible and energetic person" to direct the organizing drive. Lewis again promised to provide $500,000, and he asked that Tighe bring this proposal before the delegates to the AA convention scheduled for April 28. Finally, Lewis insisted that if the AA accepted his proposal, the steel industry organizing committee would have to have a free hand in regard to incorporating independent and company unions into the AA and keeping initiation fees and dues sufficiently low to attract masses of workers.[53]

Tighe proved as leery of Lewis's plans as Green. The AA president feared opposing the A. F. of L. and aligning himself with the CIO against Green's wishes. He was even more fearful of Lewis's proposal to create an organizing committee separate from the AA under an outside director. "Under no circumstances, while I am President," Tighe told fellow executive board members, "will I surrender to any other organization the right to direct the affairs of our organization."[54]

Events, however, soon forced Tighe into Lewis's grasp. Delegate sentiment at the AA convention clearly favored an aggressive organizing campaign along industrial union lines, a type of campaign the A. F. of L. proved unwilling to sponsor. Heber Blankenhorn, an adviser to rank-and-file militants in the steel industry, informed Lewis, on May 6, from Canonsburg, the convention city, that "my guess is you can have steel right now if you want it."[55] Two days later, May 8, Lewis wired the AA convention disparaging the A. F. of L.'s proposal to organize steel through a committee of craft unions that would later parcel out union members among a variety of crafts. The A. F. of L. offer, he wrote,

> is a rehash of the ancient and futile resolutions . . . which have resulted in the frittering away of years. . . . The policy . . . would immediately fill your industry with a horde of organizers attached to craft unions, fiercely competing with each other for the new members . . . and for the few dollars which might be taken in. . . . It would set aside your claim to industry jurisdiction. The policy . . . would preserve . . . leader-

ship . . . in the hands of men who have through the years demonstrated their utter incapacity to establish stable organization and modern collective bargaining in the mass production industries. . . . The policy . . . is inadequate, futile, and conceived in a mood of humiliated desperation.

Lewis concluded by reaffirming his original offer of funds, organizers, and the creation of a special organizing committee.[56]

Still fearful of losing his authority and influence in the steel industry to Lewis, Tighe desperately negotiated with Green to arrange an A. F. of L. alternative. But Green refused to promise unlimited jurisdiction to the steelworkers; nor did he seem eager to organize steelworkers. Consequently, on May 30, Louis Leonard, secretary of the AA, wired Lewis to arrange a meeting between AA and CIO representatives.[57]

On June 3, 1936, Leonard and his associates conferred with Lewis at UMW headquarters. Lewis minced no words in explaining what he desired. He promised immediate action, large sums of money, industrial unionism, and no red tape provided that the AA accepted CIO leadership. An executive committee appointed by Lewis would be established in Pittsburgh, where it would direct the organizing drive. The committee would rely on the AA's technical knowledge of the steel industry, but the CIO would dominate the organizing drive. In a small concession, Lewis promised to appoint to the steel organizing committee any two men the AA chose, but, in return, the AA had to join the CIO, which, as Lewis observed, "I'm so goddamned proud of." Refusing to consider Leonard's reservations to his proposal, Lewis said bluntly, "Don't tell me that." He gave the AA committee twenty-four hours to make up its mind. "If you don't want it," warned Lewis, "we want to find out as soon as we can. We're tired—want action. I think we're going to help steelworkers with or without you. If you spurn it, we'll announce to country and you can do your own explaining. If accept, you stand to have great power, encomiums, etc."[58] As Leonard subsequently reported to his own union's executive board: "Lewis . . . made it very plain that the Committee for Industrial Organization had practically decided to begin a campaign of organization . . . whether they had the cooperation of the Amalgamated Association or not."[59]

Presented with Lewis's ultimatum, the AA officials made their choice on June 4. As Lewis expected, they accepted his terms and signed a written agreement to affiliate with the CIO and serve as part of the Steel Workers Organizing Committee (SWOC), consisting of persons appointed by Lewis. In every essential respect the June 4 agreement bound the AA to the terms Lewis had enunciated at the previous day's meeting. All executive power rested with the SWOC, and all significant decisions would be made by SWOC and the CIO. Lewis had scored an absolute victory. Compelled to choose between the A. F. of L. and the CIO, the AA, a charter member of the Federation, elected to ally with Lewis. Lewis not only secured a new affiliate for the CIO—one whose charter conferred legitimacy on the CIO's organizing drive in steel; his triumph publicly ridiculed Green and the

A. F. of L. old guard. The AA, moreover, had surrendered all vestiges of its authority to Lewis, who selected his longtime right-hand man, Phil Murray, as chairman of SWOC; staffed the committee with fieldworkers from the UMW; and funded it from the mine workers' treasury.[60] If the SWOC organized the steel industry, Lewis would add control of the labor force in a second vital industry to his labor empire in coal.

Lewis's seizure of the Amalgamated Association infuriated Green. A day after the leaders of the AA accepted Lewis's plan to organize the steel industry, the A. F. of L. president blasted the CIO publicly and derided its plan to unionize steelworkers. Green's angry outburst occasioned a notable Lewis riposte, once again ridiculing the A. F. of L. leader's manhood. "I overlook the inane ineptitude of your statement published today," Lewis wrote Dear Bill on June 6. "Perchance you were agitated and distraught. . . . It is inconceivable that you intend doing what your statement implies, i.e. to sit with the women, under an awning on the hilltop, while the steel workers in the valley struggle in the dust and agony of industrial warfare." Reminding Green of his honor and obligations to the UMW, Lewis observed that members of the A. F. of L. executive council intended to suspend the ten unions associated with CIO. "I cannot yet believe," wrote Lewis, "that you would be a party to such a Brutus blow." If Green joined the anti-CIO majority, Lewis warned,

> you [Green] would destroy yourself. . . . It is known to you that your shipmates on the Executive Council are even now planning to slit your political throat and scuttle your official ship. They are caviling among themselves over the naming of your successor when the perfidious act of separation is accomplished. Why not forego such company and return home to the union that suckled you, rather than court obloquy by dwelling among its adversaries and lending them your strength? An honored seat at the Council table awaits you, if you elect to return.[61]

The same day Green replied to Lewis in a letter in which he stressed his own personal honor, integrity, and organizational loyalty. "I am the President of the American Federation of Labor," wrote Green.

> I took a solemn obligation to uphold its laws, to be governed by its decisions and to be loyal to its principles and policies. . . . Nothing can be offered as a justification for the sacrifice of honor and a solemn obligation. The mandate of the American Federation of Labor Convention becomes law to me. There will be no resort to subterfuge or expediency in order to evade the discharge of this solemn obligation.[62]

Compelled to choose between subservience to Lewis in a cause in which he believed or alliance with a majority of his executive council, whose policies he rejected, Green elected the latter course, for while Lewis challenged his manhood, the craft union leaders extolled Green's dignity and courage.[63]

Again Lewis acted with alacrity in publicizing his disagreement with Green and his commitment to action in steel. Ridiculing the A. F. of L.'s failure to organize a single worker in the steel industry as contrasted to its intention of expelling CIO unions, Lewis acidly rebuked Green. "Your lament is that I will not join you in a policy of anxious inertia. . . . Candidly, I am temperamentally incapable of sitting with you in sackcloth and ashes, endlessly intoning, '*O tempora! O Mores*'." Let us discuss personal honor no more, concluded Lewis. "For myself, I prefer to err on the side of America's underprivileged and exploited millions, if erring it be."[64]

The bitter public exchange between Lewis and Green worsened the rupture between the A. F. of L. and the CIO and intensified the executive council majority's desire to punish the insurgents. As Lewis had suggested in his letters to Green, the executive council planned to suspend from federation membership all affiliates of the CIO at its July session. So much did the Tobins, Hutchesons, and Whartons despise Lewis, so bitterly did Green resent Lewis's insults, that the A. F. of L. leaders, men customarily enamored of tradition and legitimacy, intended to violate their organization's constitution and precedents in order to expel from membership unions representing over one-third of the federation's total membership.

The federations's attorney, Charlton Ogburn, had advised Green that the council could suspend autonomous unions after they had been presented with a bill of particulars, provided a formal hearing, and found guilty as charged.[65] Ogburn acted the typical lawyer; knowing what his clients wanted, he rationalized a legal justification for their action. Yet he also personally abhorred the CIO leaders as potential subversives. "It has been frequently said," Ogburn wrote to Green in June 1938, "that Hillman, Russian-born, has the aspiration of becoming the Lenin of America."[66]

Lewis and his CIO associates refused to believe that the executive council would suspend them—at least not in July 1936. Lewis informed members of the CIO executive board, on July 2, that Green seemed confused: "Saw Green on a train—the more I talked with him, the woozier." Lewis thus advised his associates to ignore the A. F. of L. threats and edicts. "Doubt if we can spare time to go one after another like boys—and be lectured—Unless Ex Ccl completely insane, will not suspend at this meeting. . . . I think members of organized labor will straighten [them] out. Am tired of conversation and letters," concluded Lewis. Hillman agreed that CIO members should disregard the A. F. of L. executive council. "Let them go ahead and discuss—we work." Aware as always of reality and public relations, Lewis concluded that it was "inconceivable that AFL Ex Ccl could split labor" and that if the CIO leaders ignored the council's fulminations, it would "make them [A. F. of L. leaders] ridiculous."[67]

With CIO officials absent and David Dubinsky, the lone member of the executive council sympathetic to the CIO, away on other business, Green and the craft unionists, at their July meeting, followed Ogburn's script. John Frey presented a bill of particulars against the CIO affiliates that accused them of "dual unionism," infringements on established jurisdictions, violations of the A. F. of L. constitution, and even communism. The council adopted Frey's specifications, and on July 16, Green sent a letter to all CIO leaders that presented them with Frey's charges and ordered them to appear at an A. F. of L. hearing on the afternoon of August 3.[68]

Within a week Lewis called a meeting of the CIO executive board to discuss an official response to Green's order and Frey's charges. In his comments to CIO associates, Lewis remarked that he had tried to compromise the dispute through private conferences with Green, who preferred accommodation to conflict. Under pressure from the carpenters, however, who threatened to leave the A. F. of L., and other arrogant craft unions, Green had violated the confidence of his private negotiations with Lewis and thus killed the prospects for a peaceful accommodation. A. F. of L. leaders, Lewis reported, lacked the will to negotiate or compromise on the issue of industrial unionism, and their executive council members planned to arrogate to themselves "powers not in the constitution." Lewis consequently advised that for CIO members to appear before the executive council on August 3 "would weaken the position of the associated organizations, prolong the agony, and add to newspaper notoriety, which detracts attention from the organizing campaign." Moreover, he believed that pressure from their constituents might yet restrain executive council members from taking precipitous action.[69] As Lewis well knew, most major-city central labor organizations and state federations of labor as well as scores of locals, including many in the most tradition-encrusted craft unions, had petitioned or wired the executive council advising against the expulsion of CIO unions.[70]

Organized labor's rank and file, by an overwhelming majority, sympathized with the CIO, and Lewis cultivated that sentiment through press releases suggesting that the CIO organized workers while the A. F. of L. divided the labor movement. Counting on support from the rank and file and favorable press coverage, the CIO leaders, at their July 21 meeting, drafted a joint reply to Green's letter of July 16.

In their reply, the CIO officials pointedly criticized the unconstitutional and undemocratic nature of the council's action. They also derided the "heads of certain craft unions" who feared the inclusion of industrial workers in the A. F. of L. "as a jeopardy to their own dead-hand control of the Federation. Satisfied now, as they have been for years, they regard the labor movement in America as having culminated. They are mistaken; it has just begun, and if it cannot continue within the Federation it will be because of the desperate course of the Council itself." The fundamental issue in dispute, argued the CIO, was neither "dual unionism," labor traditions, legalisms, nor craft versus industrial unionism; it was primarily one of organizing the unorganized in the mass-production industries. Labor leaders must remember that they

> have an obligation that ought to outweigh their personal ambitions, and may even call for some sacrifice of real or fancied advantages enjoyed by crafts they represent. That obligation is to organize the unorganized for the common benefit of all who toil, whether craftsmen or unskilled. . . . In the fair and just solution of those problems rests the welfare of all our working millions and the heritage they shall leave their children. The Committee for Industrial Organization will carry on.[71]

In the ten months that had passed since its formation in November 1935, the CIO had with the exception of SWOC's creation been careful to respect A. F. of L. rules and traditions. Most CIO leaders proclaimed their devotion to the Federation and their desire to remain within it. Even John L. Lewis, whom historians and biographers subsequently have charged with "plotting" from the first to establish a rival labor federation, from November 1935 to August 1936 denied having any desire to split the A. F. of L. Indeed, evidence suggests that he negotiated secretly with Green to avert a split in the labor movement, if the A. F. of L. would sanction industrial unionism. To be sure, Lewis was an ambitious man eager to become the dominant figure in the American labor movement. But he aimed first to achieve dominance inside the A. F. of L. as the result of an expansion in trade union membership among mass-production workers. In other words, Lewis would have much preferred to act as the leader of a united labor movement than serve as the chief of one faction in a divided movement. By August 1936, however, the A. F. of L. executive council compelled CIO leaders to choose between organizing the unorganized or remaining inside the federation. "It appears," Sidney Hillman wrote to Charles Howard on July 22, "that the Council would rather break up the organization than lose its face. The feeling at the last CIO meeting was very strongly against submitting to the Council's arrogance."[72]

Arrogance was the proper word to characterize the executive council's attitude toward the CIO. As scheduled, the council met in Washington on August 3 to consider Frey's allegations against the CIO. No witnesses appeared to rebut Frey; nor did any council member challenge his evidence. One incident during the hearing best revealed the character of labor's old guard. The August 3 session had been preceded by a flood of petitions and wires from local unions, city centrals, and state federations pleading with the executive council not to suspend the CIO. Referring to the unprecedented volume of appeals demanding accommodation with the industrial unionists, Matthew Woll said: "That is no part of the trial and should not be part of the record." To which Vice-President Knight added: "We might be intimidated by them."

As expected, the executive council sustained all Frey's charges against the CIO and instructed Green to transmit its finding to all CIO members, who were given until September 5, 1936, to abandon the CIO or stand suspended from the A. F. of L.[73]

Four days after Green informed CIO members of the executive council's ruling, Lewis called a meeting of the CIO executive board—a session during which Lewis, as usual, dominated discussion. Lewis evinced more concern with the impact of the CIO's response on the media, the "man-in-the-street," and workers' morale than with the legalities or ethics of the A. F. of L.'s decision. More fatalistic than legalistic, more concerned with economic reality than trade union tradition, Lewis now relished the impending split in the labor movement and planned to obtain the most from it. He rejected as futile any legal action against the executive council or an appeal against the ruling. "The only thing that could change the position of the craft leaders would be counter expressions from their members, though what effect these will have is uncertain. It would seem best," concluded Lewis, "to reaffirm our previous attitude."[74]

Responding to their leader's advice, members of the CIO executive board unanimously reaffirmed their position as stated in the letter of July 21, declined to undertake legal action against the council, and agreed to boycott the November 1936 Federation convention in Tampa. The executive council having split the labor movement, the CIO leaders shared Lewis's belief that they should all ignore their suspension and pursue forcefully union organizing and political activity.[75]

Having split the labor movement, the A. F. of L. old guard now decided to divide the CIO. Max Zaritsky and David Dubinsky unwittingly served as the agents of the A. F. of L. strategy. Zaritsky's organization, the Cloth Hat and Cap Makers' Union, had recently been restored to membership in the federation as a result of its merger with the United Hatters.* Zaritsky was not inclined to lead his organization once again into the wilderness by relinquishing its link to the A. F. of L.[76]

Dubinsky had his own insecurities. An immigrant and ex-socialist, still hand-icapped outside his own union by heavily accented English speech, he was rapidly shedding a radical past for a role as a super-American, the nation's most assiduous pursuer of trade union Communists. In 1936 Dubinsky was the only representative of the "new immigrants" on the A. F. of L. executive council—a position he had been elected to only two years previously—and he, too, enjoyed the respectability conferred by membership among the trade union elite. It is likely that he also harbored jealousy and resentment of Sidney Hillman, another labor leader of East European immigrant extraction but one who was better known nationally and exercised greater political influence. Inside the A. F. of L. Dubinsky surpassed Hillman; within the CIO Dubinsky moved in Hillman's shadow.[77]

---

*From 1918 to 1934, the cap makers had been expelled from the A. F. of L. for practicing dual unionism and violating the jurisdiction of the hatters' union.

Other factors also motivated Zaritsky and Dubinsky to seek an accommodation between the advocates of the CIO and the leaders of the A. F. of L. Both men were associated with the *New Leader* and its old-line socialist staff, a group of political intellectuals who feared that an independent CIO would become a center of strength for left-wing socialists sympathetic to a coalition with the Communist party.[78] To preserve their links with the A. F. of L. and to avert what they deemed potential Communist penetration of the labor movement, Zaritsky and Dubinsky, in October 1936, conducted, independently of Lewis, peace negotiations with the A. F. of L.'s Harrison committee.

The Zaritsky-Dubinsky peace offensive began early in October at the convention of the United Hatters, Cloth Hat and Cap Makers' Union. Zaritsky introduced a resolution endorsed by his union's delegates that requested the A. F. of L. to lift the suspensions against the CIO affiliates and to resume negotiations between the Federation's three-man committee and a similar group from the CIO. Subsequently, both Zaritsky and Dubinsky contacted Green and also the Harrison subcommittee.[79]

Green promptly aggravated the emerging divisions within the CIO by offering the industrial unionists the shadow, not the substance, of a compromise. The Harrison subcommittee consented to resume negotiations with the CIO, although the executive council refused to lift the suspension of the CIO unions prior to the Tampa A. F. of L. convention.[80]

Despite the insubstantial nature of Green's peace proposal, Zaritsky and Dubinsky pleaded with Lewis to compromise. First they urged Lewis to reschedule for an earlier date the CIO executive board meeting set for Pittsburgh on November 9 and 10 in order to allow more time for a compromise to be arranged before the A. F. of L. Tampa convention began on November 16. "The door for negotiations has been . . . opened wide," Zaritsky informed Lewis. "I hope that every effort will be made to keep it open and unobstructed."[81] Zaritsky and Dubinsky also took a tactic out of Lewis's own book; together with Matthew Woll they leaked information about the pending peace agreement to *New York Times* reporter Joseph Shaplen, whose newspaper dispatches heralded the likelihood of a compromise between the A. F. of L. and CIO and hinted that only John L. Lewis stood as an obstacle to reuniting the divided labor movement.[82]

Lewis, however, understood the character of the A. F. of L. leaders far better than Zaritsky or Dubinsky; after all, he had been one of them for two decades. He knew that the new Harrison subcommittee lacked the authority to negotiate a compromise because its members (Matthew Woll and Felix H. Knight in addition to Harrison) could not speak for an executive council majority; in fact, Hutcheson, Wharton, and Tobin dominated the council in 1936, and they evinced no desire to accommodate Lewis and the industrial unionists. Lewis also felt it to be ethically, legally, and pragmatically improper for the CIO to resume negotiations before the A. F. of L. lifted its unconstitutional suspensions.[83] As Charles Howard informed Zaritsky on October 24, the suspended unions would be at a distinct disadvantage in peace negotiations. How, he asked, can suspended unions negotiate equally in such a situation? The CIO, according to Lewis and Howard, had been asked to make all the concessions without receiving any commitments from the A. F. of L. The Harrison subcommittee, for example, refused to identify those unions that would be granted unrestricted charters in the mass-production industries; nor would the executive council identify them. If the CIO affiliates resumed paying their per capita dues to the A. F. of L., which they had discontinued at the time of their suspension on September 5, the executive council refused to guarantee them representation and voting rights at the Tampa convention. In fact, both Lewis and Howard prophesied that if CIO affiliates paid their back dues (a considerable sum of money) and sought admission at Tampa, a simple delegate majority would deny their appeal. And then, Howard notified Zaritsky, "a precedent will . . . have been established that constitutes a menace to every National and International Union. Disqualifying the opposition is the most effective method of maintaining autocratic control."[84]

Later, after the Tampa convention, George Harrison admitted to George L. Berry, president of the printing pressmen's union, that the executive council had refused to cede his subcommittee authority to negotiate a settlement with the CIO. Lewis, to be sure, knew this from the first. "Mr. Harrison," Lewis informed Berry on December 21, "has no authority and doubtless cannot secure any."[85]

Ever the realist, Lewis had more important things on his mind in October 1936 than fruitless negotiations with an impotent committee from the A. F. of L. He was then deeply involved in Franklin D. Roosevelt's campaign for reelection and in SWOC's organizing drive among steelworkers. Protracted negotiations with the Harrison subcommittee, believed Lewis, would only distract attention from the CIO's more significant political and economic offensive. His involvement in electoral politics, not a desire to render compromise with the A. F. of L. impossible, as Dubinsky suspected, explained Lewis's decision to convene a CIO executive board meeting after the presidential election and on the eve of the Tampa convention. Lewis consented, however, at Dubinsky's request, to convene the executive board two days earlier: November 7 and 8 instead of November 9 and 10.[86]

The November 1936 session of the CIO executive board sealed the split in the American labor movement. Zaritsky and Dubinsky came to Pittsburgh eager to urge a compromise with the A. F. of L., but their voices found no echo among CIO associates. Lewis, Hillman, and Murray exemplified the prevailing sentiment. "The question of peace is secondary to organizing the unorganized," remarked Lewis. "This is the premise on which the fight was made in the convention, and on which the C.I.O. was formed. Why," he asked, "continue on a course of action that means only embarrassment to the C.I.O.?" Mass-production workers, he observed, "have lost confidence in the A. F. of L. Affiliation with it means nothing to them." Hillman echoed Lewis. "Can we afford to do anything that may make it impossible to take advantage of what may be the last opportunity to organize," he asked? "We know that the C.I.O. is an absolutely necessary instrumentality. I am for peace," Hillman continued, "but I do not believe that the Executive Council have the intention of allowing any peace that will make organization possible." Peace conferences, thought Hillman, had already demoralized CIO people. Clearly committed by now to go their own way independently of the A. F. of L., the CIO majority ritualistically pledged its loyalty to a united labor movement. "Not a single member of this Committee wants a split," remarked Phil Murray. "The C.I.O.," he stressed, "was formed in desperation because there was no room for expansion under prevailing policies."[87]

Despite their pessimism about the prospects for accommodation with the A. F. of L., CIO executive board members made one last effort at peace negotiations. At Lewis's suggestion, they voted unanimously to sanction their leader to engage in direct peace negotiations with William Green. The peace proposal was merely intended to assuage Zaritsky and Dubinsky, for Lewis openly told the executive board: "I am conscious that a conference with Green will lead nowhere. I suggested so that some of you will be satisfied."[88] Lewis, moreover, practically declared the rift in the labor movement permanent. From the beginning, he informed his associates, he knew that the A. F. of L. would never organize steel, auto, or rubber workers. "When we met on the Sunday morning after the Atlantic City convention, I knew what we were doing, what obligations we were putting on our organizations." Some of you, Lewis continued, may not have thought the question out clearly, but we in the UMW have our minds made up. "We have thrown the cream of our staff into the fight [organizing steel]. We knew we had crossed the Rubicon." Think about it, he advised, take time (but not too much) for I want you to join me in this "great enterprise for the weal or woe of the nation." We in the UMW will go it alone, if need be, but prefer your assistance. "My patience," Lewis observed, "is a bit worn by this [AFL] cowardly undermining of a great movement." Be proud of this organization, he concluded, for "people everywhere are looking to us for leadership, and it is time to give it to them."[89]

The executive board also made decisions that rendered an accommodation with the A. F. of L. impossible. Two new industrial unions—the United Electrical Workers and the Marine and Ship Building Workers—involved in jurisdictional disputes with A. F. of L. affiliates were admitted to membership in the CIO. And Heywood Broun, of the Newspaper Guild, suggested that if Green did not accept the CIO's peace terms without reservation by November 15, the next day the CIO would establish a permanent new labor federation.[90] Lewis gleefully observed that not only had the executive council suspended the CIO unions unconstitutionally; the Tampa convention, he gloated, lacked the constitutional power to reelect Green as president. With the suspension of the UMW, Green had lost his membership in the Federation, his right to serve as a convention delegate, and hence his eligibility for office.[91]

The proposed Lewis-Green negotiations never occurred. On November 8 Green agreed to meet with Lewis but advised the CIO executive board that the suspension of CIO unions would not be lifted and that peace negotiations would better be conducted with the Harrison subcommittee. Lewis wired back the same day declaring that discussions with Green would now be futile. "When the American Federation of Labor decides to reverse and rectify its outrageous act of suspension and is ready to concede the right of complete industrial organizations to live and grow in the unorganized industries," Lewis told Green, "it will be time to discuss and arrange the details of a reestablished relationship."[92]

Lewis, however, did not, in Irving Bernstein's piquant words, shoot down Zaritsky's "angel of peace." Nor was his primary aim "to seal the split in the labor movement immediately."[93] The only "angels" that floated over the American labor movement in 1936 existed in the imaginations of Zaritsky and Dubinsky. Neither Green nor any of the influential members on the A. F. of L. executive council desired to compromise with the CIO. To be sure they offered to readmit CIO affiliates to the federation—but only on terms that had caused the original split. Executive council overtures to Zaritsky and Dubinsky aimed to split the CIO. Green chose the two immigrant union leaders as the A. F. of L.'s instruments to divide the CIO internally and cause its collapse. Lewis could have floated in the stratosphere with Zaritsky's "angels," but that would have placed him, in the phrase with which he ridiculed Green, above "the steelworkers in the valley [who] struggle in the dust and agony of industrial warfare."

Ambition, even egomania, may have fired Lewis's refusal to negotiate on Green's terms in November 1936. But had he negotiated in good faith and had he accepted the peace agreement offered, Lewis would have surrendered only personal power, if that. The true losers would have been the mass-production workers in steel, autos, rubber, and elsewhere, struggling desperately to build stable, independent trade unions. As Lewis knew and stressed repeatedly, an accommodation between the A. F. of L. and CIO could only come at the expense of the mass-production workers.

Even if Lewis's actions in the autumn of 1936 were motivated solely by personal ambition, a debatable proposition at best, they nevertheless served the real interests of the nation's mass-production workers. Lewis's decision to discontinue negotiations with the A. F. of L. and to concentrate the CIO's energies on organizing the unorganized created the modern mass American labor movement. From 1937 through 1940 Lewis and the CIO would transform the American labor movement from an association of select craft unions on the fringes of the economy with limited political influence into a significant power situated in the economy's core with potent influence in the national Democratic political coalition. This, then, was clearly a case where Lewis's personal interests coincided with the welfare of the American working class.

Only at the deepest, perhaps most unconscious, level of human behavior did Lewis, in November 1936, act irrationally and arrogantly. The split between the CIO and A. F. of L., as we have seen, flowed from substantive issues on which Lewis argued the stronger case. The clash between Lewis and Green derived from more personal and psychological roots. Ever since the emergence of the rift inside the A. F. of L., Lewis had cast aspersions on Green's manhood, no small insult to an ex-coal miner who shared the exaggerated sense of manliness associated with that occupation. Indeed, ever since Lewis vaulted into the UMW presidency in 1919, Green had had to suffer cruel remarks and cavalier treatment from the UMW president. Thus Green's intransigence about the CIO perhaps derived more from a need to assert his manhood and equality with Lewis than from the substantive issues in dispute.

Lewis, in turn, intended to diminish further Green's self-esteem. Acting vindictively, Lewis, on November 11, 1936, had his union bring formal charges against Green. Walter Smethurst, clerk to the international executive board, informed Green that the board, on November 18, two days after the A. F. of L. convention began in Tampa, would consider allegations that Green had conspired illegally to suspend the UMW from the A. F. of L.; failed to conform to the established policies of the UMW; associated and fraternized with avowed enemies of the UMW; and distorted and misrepresented the aims of the UMW.[94]

Green, of course, refused to appear before the international executive board and denied all the charges out of hand. The IEB hearing went ahead as planned and, in the event, found Green guilty on all charges. "Life in the mines is naked and elemental," Smethurst informed Green on November 18 in words likely written by Lewis. "Relationships are not cushioned with sophistry. This Union yields to none the right to appraise the act of a servant or the perfidy of a member. William Green wears the insignia of this Union. Let him abide by the decision of its Convention." Lewis, in effect, ordered Green to cease and desist from criticizing the CIO—that is, to resign as president of the A. F. of L. or lose his membership in the UMW.[95] In the abstract, that may have seemed an easy, painless decision for Green. But in reality, Green's emotional ties to the mine workers, as a charter member and longtime official, were deep and binding. In compelling Green to snap those emotional bonds, Lewis achieved precisely the psychological blow he desired.

Contrary to Irving Bernstein's assertion that the UMW's punishment of Green was an instance in which Lewis "in his passion . . . had overreached himself," Lewis's vindictiveness toward Green made scarcely any public impact. Nor had the mouse (Green) bitten the lion (Lewis).[96] Political and economic developments had a national impact from November 1936 to March 1937, and those events heightened Lewis's stature as they diminished Green's. By mid-1937, Lewis had become both the nation's most admired and most feared labor leader.

CHAPTER 12

CIO! CIO! CIO!
Labor on the March,
June 1936-June 1937

Although the CIO functioned as an independent national labor center by mid-1936, Lewis temporarily subordinated its trade union function to its political role. The politics of the New Deal, as David Brophy has observed, was not only central to the rift within the A. F. of L.; it was the most salient factor in Lewis's thoughts and activities during the year 1936.[1] For he had concluded that the future of the CIO depended on a sympathetic federal government. Without federal allies, Lewis realized, organized labor could not conquer the mass-production industries. His estimation of economic and political reality impelled Lewis to forge a political marriage of convenience with Franklin D. Roosevelt. Yet the Lewis-Democratic party coalition was, from the first, based on common necessity, not shared values. As the *Nation* magazine wisely observed about Lewis's political plans: "When the labor movement has become under his generalship a genuine force, he may be expected to turn it to [independent] political ends."[2]

Politics was indeed so central to Lewis's plans in 1936 that during the summer he neglected the CIO's campaign to unionize steelworkers and convinced Philip Murray, who headed SWOC and directed the actual organizing drive, that the effort to unionize steelworkers must be linked to the political situation.[3] In the spring and summer of 1936, this meant that Lewis concentrated on securing the reelection of Franklin D. Roosevelt.

Organized labor in the United States, as exemplified by the A. F. of L., traditionally participated in national politics in a nonpartisan manner. Although since Woodrow Wilson's initial election in 1912 the A. F. of L. had implicitly formed a part of the Democratic party coalition, the Federation lacked its own independent political arm. Those labor leaders sympathetic to the Democratic party, the large majority, served on its national committee's labor divison. Other

248

labor leaders more sympathetic to Republicanism served a similar function, as Lewis had done for Coolidge and Hoover from 1924 to 1932.

In 1936 Lewis transformed labor's political traditions. Together with George L. Berry, of the printing pressmen's union, and Sidney Hillman, Lewis, in April 1936, formed Labor's Non-Partisan League as organized labor's own political instrument, dedicated to the election of Roosevelt but independent of the Democratic party. Both Lewis and Hillman, for example, declined invitations to serve as members of the Labor Finance Division of the Democratic National Committee. Although the Non-Partisan League ostensibly united A. F. of L. and CIO spokesmen—craft unionists and industrial unionists—its finances and manpower came largely from the CIO and mostly from the United Mine Workers. Berry, the league's director, may have been a craft unionist and an A. F. of L. member, but Lewis and Hillman represented the organization's political brains, and appointees from the mine workers and the men's clothing workers dominated the leadership of the league at the state and local levels.[4]

Lewis supported Roosevelt's reelection through an independent labor agency rather than as an integral part of the Democratic party for substantial reasons. In 1936 Lewis lacked a principled commitment to Roosevelt, one that transcended the labor leader's immediate political goals. Lewis's loyalty to Roosevelt hinged on the president's ability to satisfy the needs of the labor movement as defined by Lewis. Indeed, less than a month after the founding of the Non-Partisan League, Lewis and his adviser Jett Lauck discussed the possibility of forming a labor party after November 1936.[5] But Lewis, ever the realist as distinguished from the more idealistic Lauck, desperately needed Roosevelt's assistance in 1936. Not until the CIO had organized the great mass of industrial workers—a development dependent, in Lewis's estimation, on a benevolent federal administration—could labor exert its political influence independently.

President Roosevelt, for his part, relied on organized labor's political assistance in 1936. In the spring and summer the president could scarcely imagine the landslide victory that would be his in November. Instead, he feared a close election, one that might leave him without a clear mandate for further reform. Roosevelt thus sought a commitment from organized labor to deliver the vote, and to achieve that goal he looked more to the CIO and "its" Non-Partisan League than to the A. F. of L. and Dan Tobin, head of the Democratic party's labor committee. At a White House conference with Lewis and Berry on May 11, the president waxed enthusiastic about the work of the league.[6]

The political relationship between Lewis and Roosevelt, however, faced a crisis in mid-June 1936. The single piece of congressional legislation most dear to Lewis, the Guffey-Snyder Bituminous Coal Act, had been defeated in the Senate partly as a result of the opposition of the Senate Majority Leader, Joseph Robinson, of Arkansas. But the crisis, ironically, reinforced the Roosevelt-Lewis alliance. The Guffey act failed on Saturday night June 20. On Monday morning,

June 22, Roosevelt invited Lewis to the White House for a conference that lasted an hour and a half. More important than the conference's length was its substance. The president promised Lewis that he would protect the United Mine Workers in every way possible until Congress reconvened in January and enacted new coal legislation. Roosevelt also pledged to cooperate in the unionization of the steel industry. Finally, the president read to Lewis sections of the Democratic party platform then being drafted that contained strong prolabor clauses and recommendations for an amendment to strip the Supreme Court of the power to declare reform legislation unconstitutional. Lewis emerged from the conference to inform the press that he was entirely in accord with Roosevelt's proposed party platform, legislative recommendations, and labor program.[7]

Even then, however, Lewis refused to link his political fortunes totally to Roosevelt and the Democratic party. Only a week after his conference with the president, Lewis attended a meeting at the office of Wisconsin Senator Robert LaFollette, Jr. The conferees on this occasion (June 29) discussed the creation of an effective farmer-labor political coalition, one that would campaign for Roosevelt in 1936 but lay the basis in the future for an independent farmer-labor party.[8] Alternatives to Roosevelt, the New Deal, and the Democratic party always remained a salient element in Lewis's political thought and strategy.

Yet in the summer of 1936 Lewis lacked political options. The immediate future of the CIO and the steel campaign hinged on Roosevelt's reelection. Consequently, Lewis inaugurated the drive to unionize steel with a national radio address that reiterated the message of Roosevelt's acceptance speech at the 1936 Democratic convention in Chicago. During the week prior to his speech, delivered over NBC on Monday evening, July 6, Lewis and Lauck, who wrote the speech, discussed how to relate its theme to the New Deal. They decided that Lewis should link the steel industry's repressive labor policies to the "economic dictatorship" Roosevelt had castigated in Chicago and to identify J. P. Morgan and Company as the banking house at the heart of an American empire of "economic royalists."[9]

The actual radio address distilled in pure form Lewisian oratory and self-esteem. "I salute the hosts of labor who listen," Lewis began. "My voice tonight will be the voice of millions of men and women unemployed in America's industries, heretofore unorganized, economically exploited and inarticulate." Lewis then ripped into the Morgan financial dictatorship that selfishly sought to recreate the degenerate system of finance capitalism that had caused the Great Depression. A struggle impended, Lewis warned, in which the primary question will be "whether the working population of this country shall have a voice in determining their destiny or whether they shall serve as indentured servants for a financial and economic dictatorship which would shamelessly exploit our natural resources and debase the soul . . . and . . . pride of a free people. On such an issue there can be no compromise." Freedom can only be won, Lewis told steelworkers, and also textile, lumber, rubber, and auto workers, by breaking the shackles that bound them to industrial servitude, joining an industrial union, and voting for Roosevelt.[10]

Three days after the speech, Roosevelt invited Lewis to the White House. Lewis, who feared that the president had extended the invitation in order to compel a compromise between the CIO and A. F. of L., found instead that Roosevelt only desired assurance of labor's political solidarity. Lewis took the occasion of his July 9 visit to stress the link between national politics and the steel organizing campaign. The steel operators, whose hostility to labor was unsurpassed in American industry and who supported the Republican party, commented Lewis, motivated workers to unite for the reelection of Roosevelt.[11]

In late July, as the presidential campaign intensified, Lewis's own role became magnified. At a meeting of the Montana Banker's Association, on July 25, a Chicago newspaper editor charged that Lewis had endorsed Roosevelt in 1936 in return for the president's pledge to favor Lewis as the Democratic party nominee in 1940.[12] The next day, Lewis himself discussed with Lauck how to influence Roosevelt to take a more decided leftward approach in his campaign speeches in order to court additional votes from "Labor and Masses."[13] The Republican party, moreover, intended to use the Lewis-Roosevelt political friendship to transform A. F. of L. leaders into Republicans.[14]

Lewis, his open links to Roosevelt and the Democratic party notwithstanding, continued to stress labor's political independence. Never did he publicly repudiate the alternative of forming a labor party in 1940 with Lewis as its candidate. But such ambitions, if they existed, were kept private. Publicly, Lewis simply denied his prophetic abilities. "We cannot forecast the future," he told Louis Stark. "There may be new alignments in the next few years. It may be well to be prepared with a strong labor movement so that we can shift our weight around."[15]

Lewis reiterated labor's political independence at the first convention of the state chairmen of Labor's Non-Partisan League in Washington on August 10. The convention, to be sure, defined its sole objective for 1936 as the reelection of Roosevelt. In the meeting's major speech, Lewis stressed the absolute necessity for labor to preserve its own autonomous political organization.[16]

In September Lewis devoted most of his time to politics. On Monday, September 7, he delivered a Labor Day address over the CBS network that again vilified the nation's "corporate dictatorship." And in keeping with an old theme, he called on workers to organize as "the best guarantee . . . and best insurance against the spread of alien and subversive doctrines."[17] Four days later, September 11, he arrived in Chicago to attend a conference of "progressives" who organized the National Progressive Conference with Senator LaFollette as chairman. Attended by more than 100 delegates, including 18 congressmen and governors and 27 labor leaders, the conference endorsed Roosevelt, but not the Democratic party, and promised an inevitable future realignment of party politics.[18] A week later, on September 17, Lewis traveled to Pottsville, Pennsylvania, in the heart of the anthracite district, to deliver his first major campaign address. Speaking to an audience of over 30,000 gathered at the local fairgrounds, Lewis, as usual, castigated J. P. Morgan and the financial dictatorship that the New York banker personified—a dictatorship whose stranglehold on the nation could only be broken by the reelection of Roosevelt. But Lewis also introduced a theme that foreshadowed his subsequent political break with Roosevelt. Not only did Lewis charge the finance capitalists with causing the Great Depression and exploiting labor; he suggested that J. P. Morgan was responsible for United States' entry into World War I and that the interests of investment bankers and munitions makers threatened to involve the United States in another bloody world war. "I am convinced," he announced, "that the freedom of our country from war—the assurance that it will not be drawn into another world war—are dependent upon the reelection of President Roosevelt."[19]

If September was a hectic political month for Lewis, October proved busier. Early in the month, Lewis promised Roosevelt: "Command me any time I can be of service."[20] As the days passed the political alliance between Roosevelt and Lewis gathered momentum. Lewis campaigned for the Democrats in Ohio, Kentucky, and Indiana coal mining centers, as well as the nation's two most populous industrial states: New York and Pennsylvania.[21] On October 27 Lewis addressed his largest audience of the campaign. At a meeting sponsored by the ALP in Madison Square Garden, Lewis spoke to an estimated 20,000 packed inside the sports arena and over 8,000 crowded into the street outside, where they listened to the speech over amplifiers. The audience responded ecstatically to Lewis's customary theme: Labor must organize politically as well as economically to free workers from the clutches of an unscrupulous economic dictatorship. And it roared with laughter when Lewis described Landon as "just as empty, as inane, as innocuous as a watermelon that had been boiled in a washtub."[22] Two days later Lewis closed his campaign schedule with a joint appearance with Roosevelt in Wilkes-Barre, Pennsylvania.

Lewis provided Roosevelt with more than oratorical assistance. The UMW spent almost $600,000 to reelect the president—an unprecedented expenditure of labor funds. Of that amount $148,378 went to Labor's Non-Partisan League; $206,250 went directly to the Democratic Committee; and $94,250 was spent on Non-Partisan League political broadcasts in September and October.[23] For that investment Lewis expected a substantial return.

Roosevelt, to be sure, won a landslide victory, losing only Maine and Vermont and carrying by huge majorities industrial precincts heretofore customarily Republican. The extent of Roosevelt's victory, particularly the size of his margin in the steel towns of Pennsylvania's Monongahela Valley, exulted Lewis. At the CIO executive board meeting held just after election day, Lewis challenged: "We . . . must capitalize on the election. The CIO was out fighting for Roosevelt, and every steel town showed a smashing victory for him. . . . We wanted a President who would hold the light for us while we went out and organized.''[24] The political lesson, as read by Lewis, was clear: The CIO must initiate an aggressive organizing drive and look to Roosevelt for assistance. Lewis also reminded the president publicly that working-class voters had produced his landslide—an electoral triumph that portended a political realignment four years hence into liberal (labor) and conservative national parties.[25]

Some commentators saw Lewis as a greater victor than Roosevelt in the 1936 election. The *New York Times*, for example, wondered editorially whether Lewis's unconcealed political ambitions would lead him to organize a labor party with the intention of gaining absolute control of the government in 1940. ''With a man of his temper, his record, and his ambition,'' the *Times* noted, ''it will be difficult to deal amicably.''[26]

Lewis, to be sure, pressed his political influence with the president. He suggested soon after the election that the federal government guarantee economic freedom and democracy to all wage and salary workers and introduce extensive national economic planning. On November 20, his union's international executive board, in a public statement, demanded that Congress exercise its popular mandate to limit the power of the Supreme Court to restrain reform and curb economic planning. And Lewis, together with Berry and Hillman, urged Roosevelt to heed their advice before making decisions affecting the office of secretary of labor or other matters concerning the labor movement.[27]

Events, however, soon tested the Roosevelt-Lewis alliance. On December 30, 1936, workers at two General Motors Fisher Body plants in Flint, Michigan, occupied the factories, stopped the assembly line, and sparked the great General Motors sit-down strike of 1937. The subsequent conflict between the United Auto Workers-CIO and the largest industrial corporation in the world ineluctably involved Roosevelt and Lewis and tested the strength of labor's alliance with the Democratic party.

Lewis immediately demanded that Roosevelt deliver on his campaign pledges to labor. On New Year's Eve, 1937, Lewis addressed a nationwide radio audience over the NBC network. The speech, prompted by the previous day's sit-down strike in Flint, saw Lewis, as customary, assert his right to speak for the nation's toiling masses. But the heart of the speech stressed the significance of the 1936 presidential election. ''The people of our nation,'' said Lewis, ''have just participated in a national referendum. By an overwhelming majority they voted for industrial democracy, and reelected its champion, Franklin Delano Roosevelt.'' Now, he suggested, it was time for the agents of the federal government to enter the plants of General Motors and gut them of the deadly weapons that federal investigators had discovered there in order that workers might exercise their rights as free men. ''Labor,'' proclaimed its leader, ''demands a new deal in America's great industries. . . . Labor demands legislative enactments making realistic the principles of industrial democracy.'' Lewis's peroration challenged President Roosevelt. ''The time has passed in America,'' asserted Lewis, ''when the workers can be either clubbed, gassed, or shot down with impunity. . . . *Labor will . . . expect the protection of the Federal Government in the pursuit of its lawful objectives"*[28] (our italics).

The General Motors strike thus promised to determine the future direction of the CIO, to establish the sagacity of Lewis's politics, and to test the strength of his relationship with Roosevelt. It would also make 1937 a decisive year for United States labor history.

The year 1937 was without parallel in the history of the American labor movement. In 1937, as in 1919, militant union organizers and angry workers carried industrial warfare to the core of the nation's economy: steel and autos. In 1937, as in 1919 and also 1934, industrial violence rocked the nation as workers and their adversaries fought pitched battles in the streets of such cities as Flint, Michigan; Youngstown, Ohio; Johnstown, Pennsylvania; and Chicago, Illinois.

But 1937 differed from previous turbulent years in United States working-class history. The conflict, violence, and even deaths that punctuated events brought workers impressive and lasting gains. Before winter moderated to spring, CIO organizers had unionized workers in the two most powerful, oligopolistic, and antiunion basic industries: autos and steel. By mid-March 1937, CIO affiliates had wrested union contracts from the General Motors Corporation, the world's largest and wealthiest industrial firm, and United States Steel, for more than three decades a bastion of the open shop.

As a consequence of such major victories and subsequent lesser triumphs, organized labor gained more than 3 million members in 1937, a membership increase of nearly 100%. By December, the labor movement claimed almost 23% of the nation's nonagricultural workers among its members, the greatest proportion as yet unionized in American history. More significantly, the vast majority of newly organized workers belonged to CIO affiliates that, by the end of 1937, boasted a larger membership than the A. F. of L.

Just as 1937 was an unparalleled year for American workers, it was unequaled in the life and career of John L. Lewis. The triumphs that blessed the labor movement inflated Lewis's own power and prestige. Newspaper headlines and editorials, magazine feature stories, leftist and liberal journalists, and prominent politicians credited Lewis—not the workers who struck, suffered, and sometimes died—for labor's victories in autos and steel. Established labor unions and newly born ones implored Lewis to address their conventions; magazine and newspaper publishers beseeched him for articles on the future of American society; newspaper reporters clustered around mine workers' headquarters in Washington waiting for leaks from the UMW president's office or for Lewis's frequent and dramatic press conferences; millions of citizens gathered around their radios on the evenings Lewis spoke over national networks to listen to his mellifluous voice as it blended malapropisms and biblical invocations; and governors, congressmen, and the president himself sought Lewis's political support. Once again Lewis achieved the status of "Labor Statesman," but this time, unlike the years 1922-1924, he represented not solely mine workers, but instead claimed to speak for the entire American working class.

Lewis set the scene well for his 1937 triumphs. Committed to organizing mass-production workers in the nation's steel and auto industries, he knew that success or failure would hinge on the outcome of industrial battles in the crucial states of Pennsylvania, Ohio, Michigan, Indiana, and Illinois; he also realized that support from President Roosevelt, whatever its precise form, would be essential. That was why he had poured so much of his own energy and his union's money into the 1936 election and why the results exulted him. Not only had Roosevelt won an unprecedented national landslide; prolabor Democratic governors had been swept into office in Michigan, Ohio, Indiana, and Pennsylvania, where the new lieutenant governor was not only a Democrat but also the secretary-treasurer of the UMW: Tom Kennedy. More remarkable, in scores of mill towns across the industrial heartland, working-class voters, hitherto loyal to Republicanism and deferential to their employers, rebelled, electing Democrats and union members to local offices.

In 1937 the economy also favored the CIO. New Deal reforms, especially the pump priming that preceded the 1936 election, brought results. For the first time since the depression's onset, manufacturers optimistically expanded production and recalled workers. By spring 1937 gross national production approached predepression levels, the auto industry forecast record profits, and steel companies relit long-banked blast furnaces.

When a militant minority of rebellious auto workers occupied Fisher Body Plant No. 1 in Flint, Michigan, on December 30, 1936, they selected a propitious moment to act. Although the Flint strikers acted without direct authorization from John L. Lewis (Lewis in fact planned to attack steel before autos), the CIO leader had no choice in the circumstances but to place realities before preferences and endorse the struggle against General Motors. By unexpectedly stopping the assembly line and sitting down inside the plant instead of picketing outside, as was customary in labor disputes, a militant minority of auto workers catalyzed prounion sentiment among the vast majority of apathetic workers in Flint and forced the hand of General Motors. On the evening of the initial Flint sit-down, as we saw in the previous chapter, Lewis spoke on a national radio network to assure the auto workers of CIO support and to demand that Democratic officeholders, especially President Roosevelt, pay their debts to organized labor and working-class voters.

The scene had been set, the struggle joined. Auto workers, through their militancy, courage, and solidarity, and Lewis, through bluff, bluster, shrewd bargaining, and political manipulation, assured the triumph of mass-production unionism.[29]

* * *

The General Motors sit-down strike of 1936-1937 pitted the infant United Auto Workers-CIO against the nation's wealthiest industrial corporation and brought John L. Lewis into direct confrontation with the financial oligarchy that he repeatedly had criticized. Financed by Wall Street investment bankers and linked directly to the Duponts, who owned the largest single bloc of its stock, General Motors had more than tripled its net sales between 1933 and 1936. By 1936 its net profits had risen thirty fold, to well over $200 million, and it had converted its financial losses of 1932 into a pretax profit of about $163 million in 1936, a rate of return of 37.9% on invested capital. The company had sixty-nine plants in thirty-five cities, fourteen states, and two foreign countries (Germany and England), with total assets in excess of $1.5 billion. It also produced buses, trucks, and home appliances. In short, General Motors was an immensely powerful international (multinational) corporation.[30]

More than enormous capital resources and rising profits contributed to General Motors' ability to thwart organized labor. Between January 1, 1934, and July 1, 1936, the company spent about $1 million on private detectives who spied on union activists and ferreted out dissident workers. (General Motors was the largest corporate client of the Pinkerton Detective Agency.) In the words of the LaFollette Committee on Civil Liberties, General Motors "stands as a monument to the most colossal super-system of spies yet devised in any American corporation."[31]

Throughout the protracted struggle centered in Flint, the disparity in power between General Motors and the UAW-CIO clouded the prospects for a labor victory. Past organizing failures among auto workers—especially during 1934—and President Roosevelt's greater solicitude toward manufacturers than trade unionists in settling the 1934 dispute had led John L. Lewis's agents in Michigan auto centers, especially Adolph Germer, to counsel caution in November and December 1936. Sensing that strike sentiment was gaining momentum among UAW leaders and rank-and-file militants, Germer warned Lewis, on November 30, that the time was not propitious for action. If the union had the strength to pull the men out of the key plants in Flint, Cleveland, and Detroit, Germer advised, then a strike might succeed. But with only about 1,500 of the 42,000 Flint General Motors workers in the union, he asked, how could the UAW paralyze production? Before a strike could even be considered, Germer concluded, the union must first submit a list of demands to General Motors.[32]

Lewis acted on Germer's advice. Meeting in Washington on December 18 with John Brophy and UAW leaders Homer Martin (president), Ed Hall (vice-president), and Wyndham Mortimer (director of the Flint campaign and a left-wing Communist militant), Lewis formulated the CIO's strategy for an impending confrontation with General Motors. Lewis's approach called for the UAW to communicate formally with the president and executive vice-president of General Motors enumerating the auto workers' primary grievances and suggesting a joint conference to negotiate all questions in dispute between the union and the company. Lewis, to be sure, expected General Motors to reject the UAW's suggestion.

"The whole policy," Brophy informed Germer the next day, "is to move towards a climax in January in the event that General Motors refuses to confer and negotiate on a broad scale."[33]

Lewis was particularly anxious that no walkout occur before January 1, 1937, when Democratic governors would come to power in Michigan and Ohio. After January 1, if a strike occurred in the auto industry, as Lewis anticipated, strikers would more likely win political support not only from President Roosevelt but also from Governor Davey of Ohio and, more particularly, Governor Murphy of Michigan. Two other federal agencies also promised to assist Lewis in a struggle against General Motors: the National Labor Relations Board and the LaFollette Committee on Civil Liberties. Heber Blankenhorn, a sometime associate and critic of Lewis, coordinated efforts to involve the NLRB and the Senate Civil Liberties Committee in the General Motors strike.[34] Clearly, then, Lewis saw the role of the state as vital to CIO success in the auto industry.

Lewis understood politicians and the factors that motivated them to intervene in industrial conflicts on behalf of labor. He never expected politicians to reward labor simply for past favors; however much CIO assistance had benefited Roosevelt and Murphy in 1936, what was done had been done. Politicians, Lewis assumed, were moved far more by fear of prospective retribution than gratitude for retrospective favors. Past experience had taught Lewis as much; he never forgot the lessons taught by Woodrow Wilson during the 1919 coal strike and Herbert Hoover from 1924 through 1932. Lewis, moreover, believed that politicians reacted to power, not sentiment, and that workers could advance their cause only through the exercise of power, violently if necessary, not through appeals for sympathy as oppressed Americans. When Gardner "Pat" Jackson, the socially prominent son of a Colorado banker, New Deal liberal, and advocate of the southern tenant farmers, proposed, during a dinner at the Cosmos Club in Washington, the germ of the idea that ultimately took substance as the Senate (LaFollette) Committee to Investigate Civil Liberties, Lewis patronized Jackson as a naive, immature lad unaware of power realities and congressional behavior. "Not until there was blood flowing in the streets of our cities," Lewis declared, "would we ever be able to get an investigation . . . of the denial of civil liberties through the application of force in our country."[35]

Power and force, then, proved central to Lewis's strategy in the General Motors conflict. That was why Germer's advice fed Lewis's natural caution, leading him to counsel UAW leaders to avoid acting as the aggressors and to delay a strike. And that was why when the sit-down came to Flint ahead of schedule and without Lewis's authorization, he nevertheless supported the strikers wholeheartedly. For by their surprising and decisive action, the Flint militants had established an unescapable reality: their *power* to paralyze two essential General Motors plants and, apparently, to win the support of a substantial majority of the hitherto nonunion workers. During the forty-four days between the workers' seizure of the Fisher Body No. 1 and 2 plants on December 30, 1936, and their victorious march out on February 11, 1937, Lewis, despite entreaties from Labor Secretary Perkins, Governor Murphy, and President Roosevelt, never ordered the strikers to surrender the power they wielded through the seizure and occupation of company property by withdrawing from the plants before victory was theirs.

Had Lewis himself planned the Flint organizing campaign, he could not have devised a more ingenius strategy. But events in Flint flowed not from the actions of top CIO officials but from the labors of such UAW stalwarts as Wyndham Mortimer, Roy Reuther, and Robert Travis and such local leaders as Bud Simons. The sit-down tactic enabled the union to magnify its own limited power and to compound General Motors' problems. By timing the factory occupation to occur when shifts changed, union strategists immediately doubled the number of activists (militants) available to stop the assembly line. And by actually stopping the line and successfully occupying the plant, the militant minority forcefully impressed the apathetic majority with the power of the union and attracted thousands of new recruits to the cause. By occupying company property on the inside instead of picketing it on the outside, strikers escaped the worst vicissitudes of a midwinter walkout. Indeed, owing to fear that pipes might burst or sit-downers might wreck the plants if heat was turned off, General Motors operated its heating system. Finally, instead of strikebreakers marching into a picketed factory under armed guard in order to restart idle machinery, strikers themselves remained inside to ensure that the machinery stayed idle.

Other advantages blessed workers as a result of the sit-down strategy. Forced to exist together around the clock and away from the influence of family and other external forces, the strikers developed a sense of solidarity. With the factory silent as the assembly line lay still, strikers talked to each other conversationally, became more sociable with one another, and developed a "consciousness of kind." Perhaps recalling his own experience during World War I, one sit-downer observed: "It was like we were soldiers holding the fort. It was like war. The guys with me became my buddies."[36]

Strikers evinced their new solidarity in a variety of ways. They formed committees that voluntarily and cooperatively administered the daily needs of the sit-downers. Different groups supervised sanitation, feeding, fire drills, recreation, and, in the event of the worst, preparations for defense. Group sings were especially popular, and the strikers opened and closed every meeting with a verse from their favorite song:

> Solidarity forever
> Solidarity forever
> Solidarity forever
> For the Union makes us strong.

So impressive was the community and solidarity that the sit-downers had forged that journalist Paul Gallico wrote: "They had made a palace out of what had been their prison."[37]

Labor solidarity extended beyond the occupied factories' gates. Auto workers from other cities came to Flint to assist their union brothers whenever events took a turn for the worse. And outsiders, both UAW members and sympathizers, provided the steady flow of food and messages that maintained the strikers' health and morale. Wives and children, too, played a crucial role. An unhappy wife or a forlorn child could do more to weaken the spirit of a sit-downer than company intransigence. Thus those strikers' wives and daughters most committed to the struggle organized an emergency brigade to enlist the energies of Flint's females. And it worked. "I found a common understanding and unselfishness I'd never known in my life," observed a striker's wife. "I'm living for the first time with a definite goal. . . . Just being a woman isn't enough any more. I want to be a human being with the right to think for myself." Another female activist believed that the strike had produced a new type of woman. "Women," she wrote, "who only yesterday were horrified at unionism, who felt inferior to the task of organizing, speaking, leading, have, as if overnight, become the spearhead in the battle for humanism."[38]

The solidarity established by the strikers on the inside and their families and supporters on the outside provided Lewis with the power that enabled him to play the role of negotiator-extraordinary. Personally, Lewis had little to do with day-to-day events in Flint or elsewhere on the broad national General Motors strike front. Even Germer and Brophy, his two primary CIO aides in the conflict, generally deferred to the wishes of such UAW leaders as Mortimer and Travis. At the most Lewis and his lieutenants restrained UAW president Homer Martin. Martin, a former intercollegiate hop, skip, and jump champion and an ordained minister (thus sometimes known as the "leaping Parson"), was, according to Germer, an inept negotiator. A bombastic platform orator, Martin was a liability for the strikers, and Lewis arranged for Martin to be occupied elsewhere during the final critical strike negotiations. Uninvolved in the more conventional activities of the strike, Lewis concentrated on eliciting federal and state support for the sit-downers and forcing General Motors to the bargaining table.[39] Put another way, during the General Motors strike, the sit-downers personified labor power, power that Lewis could exert to win for unionism an unprecedented triumph in mass-production industry.

General Motors had no intention of negotiating seriously with the union or conceding to the strikers. Instead, the corporation's top executives, especially Alfred P. Sloan, fully expected to smash the strike. And they had good reason for their optimism. Flint was a company town: Its public officials, civic organizations, and newspapers served General Motors. Substantial numbers of local workers declared loyalty to the company, not the union, and some among them belonged to the Black Legion, a Fascist-style organization that opposed unions, the foreign-born, and nonwhites. The law, too, seemed to favor the company. If the sit-downers were not revolutionaries, they had nevertheless seized company property—a seizure in violation of statutory and common law. General Motors thus had reason to anticipate that the judiciary would order the strikers to return company property to its rightful owners and that public authorities would enforce such an injunction. And once the sit-downers had been evicted from the plants, the strike would collapse.[40]

On January 2, 1937, the General Motors Corporation obtained from the Genesee County Circuit Court a "temporary restraining injunction" ordering the union to cease and desist from obstructing entrance to and exit from the plants, to halt mass picketing, and to order the sit-downers to evacuate the factories. The next evening at a union strategy meeting, Adolph Germer, the CIO's adviser in Flint, suggested that the judge who issued the injunction, one Edward D. Black, an elderly local resident, probably owned General Motors stock. Lee Pressman, whom John L. Lewis had appointed as CIO's legal adviser, immediately contacted friends in New York, who informed him that Judge Black indeed owned more than $200,000 in General Motors stock. The brilliant, handsome, and cocky young Pressman, who less than a year earlier had severed his formal relationship with the Communist party, though he still remained radical in sympathy, promptly released to the press news of Black's material interest in the General Motors Corporation and demanded that the temporary injunction be lifted. An embarrassed Black let his order lapse, and an equally embarrassed General Motors turned to another judge for relief. The CIO had rescued the auto workers from the strike's first crisis.[41]

During the first weeks of January, then, the real battle was fought by auto workers in Flint, the strike's nerve center, and in GM plants elsewhere in the nation. What negotiations occurred during that time—and they did take place among Martin and Mortimer for the UAW, Germer and Brophy for the CIO, several General Motors officials, Governor Murphy, and federal mediators—were partially a charade. If General Motors edged closer to the union's demands, it still resolutely refused to countenance the UAW's central demand: exclusive representation. The company's primary objective remained first to compel the sit-downers to evacuate the plants and only then to bargain with the union. If the strike leaders debated evacuation, they still desired to gain exclusive representation for the union before marching the sit-downers out. In short, the company and the union as yet had nothing to compromise.

Even force failed to break the resistance of the stubborn sit-down strikers. On January 11, 1937, the Flint police, perhaps in collusion with General Motors, attacked the strikers at their weakest point, Fisher Body Plant No. 2, a factory occupied by at most 100 strikers whose spirits had been sagging. About noon on

January 11, the company suddenly turned off the heat inside Fisher No. 2. Early that same evening, company guards turned away union men about to deliver dinner to their brothers on the inside. As cold and hunger inflamed tensions, the sit-downers, with the consent of UAW leader Victor Reuther, acted. A group walked down to the main plant gate, demanded the key from the guards, and, on being refused, broke the lock and established contact with supporters on the outside. The captain of the guards immediately phoned the Flint police, asserting that he and his men had been captured by the strikers; and then the guards fled to the ladies' room where they took sanctuary until the following morning.

Sometime after 9:00 P.M. the Flint police arrived on the scene armed with tear gas and masks. About fifteen officers approached the plant, ordered the strikers to open the gates, and, receiving no response, fired tear gas canisters into the factory. Inside, the strikers, listening to commands from Victor Reuther outside in a union sound car, retaliated. Using fire hoses, steel auto door hinges, bottles, stones, and other handy weapons, the sit-downers drove the police back.

As the tide of battle ebbed and flowed, the police regrouped and again attacked the plant with tear gas. Once again the sit-downers and the pickets outside fought back with hoses, cans, hinges, ice balls, and every available implement. Pelted by the strikers' missiles and with the wind whipping the tear gas back into their own faces, the police retreated. Suddenly the police halted, turned, drew their pistols and riot guns, and fired directly at their pursuers.

When the shooting stopped, fourteen strikers and sympathizers as well as two spectators lay wounded—thirteen by gunshot. Eleven law officers also had been injured; a deputy sheriff had been wounded by a stray police bullet; a policeman had been the victim of his own agency's gas; and the others had been cut by the strikers' flying weapons. The "Battle of the Running Bulls" ended "with the strikers and their allies in command of the battlefield."[42]

The next morning, when a Detroit reporter examined the plant, he found the floor inside flooded with water and the plant windows pocked with bullet holes. Car bodies had been formed into barricades, and the strikers stood guard with iron bars, door hinges, and night sticks seized from company guards. Across the street, among the even more resolute strikers in Fisher No. 1, an observer sensed "a determination that in this desperate struggle between capital and labor they should not lose nor retreat till every man was dead or unable to fight anymore."

The "Battle of the Running Bulls" ushered the strike into a new phase, one that demanded a more active role by John L. Lewis. As was usually the case in labor disputes, the eruption of violence presaged the intervention of the state. After the events in Flint on January 11, Michigan Governor Frank Murphy had to act decisively, for his earlier efforts at mediation had ended in warfare, not peace. As soon as he learned of the violence in Flint, Murphy ordered elements of the Michigan National Guard to duty in the embattled city. Perhaps that was precisely what General Motors wanted. The appearance of troops during a strike customarily spelled disaster for strikers. Military men dispersed pickets, scattered congregations of strikers, spread fear among them, and returned property to its rightful owners. But this was not to happen in January 1937.

Governor Frank Murphy entered the Flint dispute with a deserved reputation as a friend to labor, a reputation that he meant to maintain. According to his biographer, Sidney Fine, Murphy "had great compassion for the weak, the afflicted, the down-trodden, the flotsam and jetsam of humankind." He had also been unique among public officials during the 1920s in his concern for civil liberties and for the welfare of working people. As a local criminal court judge and later depression-era mayor of Detroit, Murphy allied politically with organized labor and strived mightily to serve the "down-trodden." In the Philippines, serving as President Roosevelt's governor-general for the American colony, he evinced a similar concern for the cause of labor. And when he returned to the United States in 1936 to campaign for the governorship of Michigan, he linked his political future to the rise of organized labor. Without the manpower and money organized labor supplied his 1936 campaign, Murphy might indeed have lost, as he ran far behind Roosevelt in Michigan. After winning the election, he informed William Green, "I am certain that you will find that my administration . . . will mark a new day for labor in Michigan."[43]

After the arrival of the state troops in Flint on January 12, peace returned to the troubled city. Although Murphy believed that the sit-down strike created an illegal trespass on private property, he never intended to use force to evict the strikers. If he desired to restore the occupied plants to General Motors, the governor nevertheless preferred the strikers to leave voluntarily. Thus Murphy used his considerable influence to compel UAW representatives and corporation officials to negotiate.

Beginning on January 15, General Motors met face-to-face with union officials in the governor's presence. For almost fifteen hours the negotiators argued their respective positions. Corporation spokesmen demanded that the strikers evacuate the plants; that accomplished, the company promised to bargain freely with the UAW concerning its demands of January 4.* Speaking for the union, Brophy, Mortimer, and Martin (who were in phone contact with Lewis) insisted that the strikers would evacuate the plants only if General Motors agreed to bargain exclusively with the UAW and made no attempt to open the struck plants during the subsequent negotiations. Finally, in an agreement in which the corporation surrendered more than it liked and the union accepted less than it wanted, Murphy arranged for a temporary truce in the sit-down strike.

Under the terms of the agreement, the unions agreed to evacuate all the occupied plants and the company promised not to resume production or to move dies and other machinery from Flint to other domestic plants and to bargain exclusively

*Eight demands presented by Homer Martin to William Knudsen, of which the most important was recognition of the UAW as exclusive bargaining agent for the auto workers.

with the UAW over its January 4 demands. Murphy acted as the guarantor of the truce, which was to last for a period of fifteen days from the start of the evacuation in Flint on January 17. What would happen if no final settlement was reached during the fifteen-day truce was left unmentioned.[44] Events, however, immediately shattered the truce.

General Motors, not the union, broke the truce. Whatever his real intention, William Knudsen, the chief operating executive of the company and the man least hostile to trade unionism among General Motors executives, gave the sit-downers cause to delay evacuation. Knudsen, acting either for himself or at the direction of his company superiors, invited George E. Boysen, leader of the Flint Alliance, a General Motors-sponsored organization of loyal employees, to join the negotiations as spokesman for the majority of nonunion workers. William Lawrence, a reporter then covering the Flint strike for United Press, leaked word to the union of Knudsen's invitation (in a telegram to Boysen of January 17) to the Flint Alliance. Union representatives immediately informed Governor Murphy that General Motors had violated its promise to bargain exclusively with the UAW and that the sit-downers would now remain inside the occupied plants.[45]

Frank Murphy's truce having collapsed, the federal government, through Secretary of Labor Frances Perkins, intervened. On January 19, Perkins met all day and into the early evening with Murphy and John L. Lewis. The Michigan governor remained committed to evacuation by the sit-downers and offered to surround the Flint plants with militia, keeping them idle while negotiations ensued. But Lewis refused to recommend evacuation before the strikers won substantial concessions from General Motors. "Lewis's position," Perkins reported to President Roosevelt, "remains absolutely unchanged."[46]

Unable to crack Lewis, Perkins pursued Alfred Sloan, president of General Motors. For four hours the secretary of labor pleaded over the telephone with the corporation executive to bargain with the union. Finally, Sloan consented to go to Washington to confer with Perkins and also Frank Murphy—but not John L. Lewis. Not only did Sloan refuse to meet with the CIO leader; he insisted that his visit to the capital be kept in absolute secrecy; he wanted no sign that General Motors could be influenced by public officials to bargain with organized labor. Despite Secretary Perkins' best efforts to cloak Sloan's visit, reporters uncovered the General Motors executive's presence in Washington, publicized it, and thus ruptured the new round of strike negotiations.[47]

Federal intervention in the conflict offered Lewis the opportunity to apply his singular skills. As Sloan refused to meet with him and Perkins assiduously cultivated a peaceful settlement, Lewis delivered a direct message to President Roosevelt. During a news conference at UMW headquarters on the afternoon of January 21, the CIO leader told a crowded room full of reporters,

We have advised the administration that for six months the economic royalists represented by General Motors contributed their money and used their energy to drive this administration out of power. The administration asked labor for help to repel this attack, and labor gave its help. The same economic royalists now have their fangs in labor. The workers of this country expect this administration to help the workers in *every legal way*, and to support the auto workers in the General Motors plants (our italics).[48]

Press commentators promptly asserted that Lewis had lost his political acumen. How could a labor leader have the temerity to make such demands of the nation's chief executive, especially one who had been so friendly to organized labor? Lewis must be mad, they suggested, to rupture the CIO's alliance with Roosevelt and the Democrats, a political coalition that delivered substantial rewards to organized labor. And when President Roosevelt, at a press conference on January 22, implicitly criticized Lewis for his remarks of the previous day, pundits were satisfied that their analysis of Lewis's political gaffe had been proved correct.[49]

In reality, however, Lewis had lost none of his political acumen between the fall of 1936 and mid-January 1937. His public statement of January 21 simply reiterated the central message of his radio address of December 30, delivered the night Flint workers had occupied the factories. Moreover, he had merely asked the Roosevelt administration to assist the auto workers "in every legal way," meaning the enforcement of the Wagner Act and federal pressure on employers to bargain collectively with labor. And he had not asked the president to make new commitments; during a series of private conferences between Lewis and Roosevelt in the summer of 1936, the chief executive had promised precisely that.[50] If Roosevelt had needed organized labor's, especially the CIO's, support during the election of 1936, he had no less need for it in January 1937, when he was proposing new welfare legislation to Congress as well as planning to restructure the Supreme Court. That Lewis intended no break with Roosevelt was made obvious in the labor leader's public response to the president's alleged rebuke. "Of course," Lewis observed, "I do not believe the President intended to rebuke the working people of America who are his friends and who are only attempting to obtain the rights guaranteed them by Congress."[51]

Why, then, did Lewis engage in public controversy with Roosevelt? He apparently did so for two reasons. First, he perhaps intended to let Sloan and other General Motors executives know that in January 1937 they could not expect federal authorities to assist them in thwarting organized labor, as had happened in 1934, when workers were poorly organized and politically impotent. Sloan apparently received this message, for immediately after Lewis's January 21 press conference, the General Motors executive informed Perkins that he was terminating all negotiations and departing Washington.[52] Second, Lewis addressed the strikers, reminding them that the CIO, unlike the A. F. of L., would not surrender their vital interests in negotiations with the federal administration. As long as they held firm in their occupation of Flint's auto plants, the sit-downers could rely on Lewis.

In a telegram to the Flint strikers on January 22, Lewis clarified his strategy. He pledged the sit-downers undiluted support from the CIO and its fifteen affiliated international unions. Criticizing General Motors as the spearhead of the nation's industrial and financial elite's crusade to crush independent unionism, Lewis pledged the Flint workers "complete and unanimous support in the conduct of the strike and in the attainment of a negotiated peace that will definitely establish the principles of collective bargaining in the automotive industry." Ridiculing Sloan, Knudsen, Donaldson Brown, and John T. Smith (the latter two, lawyers and GM strike negotiators), men whose combined income exceeded $1 million annually, for fleeing a collective bargaining conference with labor, Lewis applauded the courage of the Flint strikers.

> You men who are now in Fisher Plants Number one and Number two are undoubtedly carrying through one of the most heroic battles that has ever been undertaken by strikers in an industrial dispute. The attention of the entire American public is focussed upon you. Every working man . . . and representative of labor in this country owes a debt of gratitude to each of you and I trust that this knowledge will cheer you through the long weary hours of waiting for the honorable settlement which in the nature of things must inevitably come.

And for Sloan and his refusal to negotiate, Lewis offered a choice comment: "perhaps," the labor leader declared, "he feels his intellectual inferiority to me."[53]

Despite Sloan's departure from Washington and Lewis's sarcasm, Perkins continued her efforts to bring the disputants together. In the event, however, her efforts collapsed. Evacuation of the General Motors plants in Flint remained the central issue. Sloan resolutely refused to bargain with the union until the plants were evacuated, a condition neither Perkins nor Governor Murphy could meet. Not that federal and state officials failed to try. On January 26, Murphy offered to keep the plants closed with troops for two weeks if the sit-downers evacuated, and two weeks longer if negotiations failed to produce a settlement during the initial fortnight. But Lewis rejected the governor's proposal. In a phone conversation with Adolph Germer, Lewis said bluntly that he had turned down Murphy's evacuation proposal and didn't think it so hot. He also warned Germer that the administration would keep working on the proposal and that labor leaders in Michigan should not raise publicly the issue of evacuation.[54]

Lewis's political influence and his refusal to consider evacuation prior to a settlement produced positive results for the strikers. Unable to settle the strike, federal officials fell silent about the intransigence of their friends in the labor movement but criticized publicly their enemies among the "economic royalists." At a press conference on January 26, President Roosevelt rebuked Sloan for ending negotiations in much sharper language than he had directed at Lewis, and Perkins the same day criticized Sloan more emotionally and acidly.[55]

*　　*　　*

As the first month of the new year ended, the General Motors strike seemed as far from settlement as ever. A month of fruitless negotiations, unsuccessful state and federal intervention, and continued occupation of the Fisher Body plants had rubbed nerves in Flint raw.[56]

In the tense, volatile atmosphere that was Flint, Michigan, on January 31, 1937, General Motors acted to worsen matters. Unable to win state or federal assistance in its attempt to remove the sit-downers, the company again resorted to the courts for relief. General Motors petitioned Circuit Judge Paul V. Gadola to issue an injunction ordering the sit-downers to vacate company property. The judge scheduled a formal hearing for February 1.

Before Gadola could act, the leaders of the Flint strike engineered a remarkable tactical coup. In one unexpected but devastating step, the auto workers intensified the economic pressure against General Motors. Of the many General Motors factories in Flint, none was more vital to the company's economic empire than Chevrolet No. 4, where the bulk of the top-selling car's engines were produced. Throughout the strike, however, the Chevrolet plant had remained open and in production. It became the logical target for strike strategists. On the afternoon of February 1, fighting erupted in front of the gates at Chevrolet No. 9, and rumors spread that its militant workers were about to sit down. Immediately, company guards and city police raced toward No. 9, as did elements of the National Guard. As masses of union men, strike sympathizers, and curious spectators gathered around No. 9 to await the impending battle between law officers and auto workers, another group of union members entered the gates of Chevrolet No. 4, walked inside the plant, and gave the signal to begin a sit-down. After a brief battle with supervisory personnel and anti-union workers, during which the nonunion majority fled, the UAW's militant minority occupied the most vital General Motors plant in the city.[57] As the day ended, the corporation found itself in an extremely parlous predicament.

At the moment that the auto workers occupied Chevrolet No. 4, Judge Gadola heard arguments in the injunction case. The next day, February 2, after a temporary delay, Gadola delivered his decision. The judge satisfied all General Motors' desires. He ordered the strikers in Fisher Plants Nos. 1 and 2 to depart by 3:00 P.M., February 3; forbade picketing and other union activities around the plants; and threatened to fine the UAW $15 million if its members failed to heed the injunction.[58]

The conflict was once again in Governor Murphy's hands. Only he possessed power adequate to enforce the injunction if the strikers refused to obey Gadola's order. Only he had the resources to avert the civil war that impended in Flint as city and company officials organized a volunteer force to implement the court order and union men prepared to resist.

But Murphy still declined to use state power to break the strike. When advocates of law and order insisted that the governor enforce Judge Gadola's order, Murphy allegedly said: "I'm not going down in history as 'Bloody Murphy!' If I sent those soldiers right in on the men there'd be no telling how many would be killed. It would be inconsistent with everything I have ever stood for in my whole political life." Instead, the governor sought to reopen negotiations between the company and the union and to bring Lewis to Detroit.

President Roosevelt endorsed Murphy's strategy, and for good reason. As long as negotiations occurred in Detroit, not Washington, and Murphy, not Roosevelt, was the central public figure involved, the president could separate himself from a sensitive, explosive political situation. If Murphy, however, could manage to settle the conflict amicably with behind-the-scenes presidential assistance, political credit would flow to all New Deal Democrats.[59]

Lewis reentered the General Motors strike in typical melodramatic fashion. Leaving Washington's Union Station on the morning of February 3 for the overland train trip to Detroit, the union leader told reporters, "Let there be no moaning at the bar when I put out to sea."[60]

If Lewis's departing statement at the train station seemed pompous, his role in the final negotiations was dramatic. He arrived in Detroit late on February 3 and immediately entered conferences with General Motors representatives and Murphy that lasted until February 11. As pressure built up on the governor to enforce Gadola's injunction, Murphy labored to bring the union and management closer together. Understanding Murphy perhaps better than the governor did himself, Lewis refused to relinquish the union's primary demand: exclusive representation. Nor would he consider evacuation by the sit-downers until General Motors agreed to negotiate exclusively with the UAW.[61] Lewis realized that Murphy wanted the sit-downers out, but he knew that Murphy would not use force to evict the strikers.

Initial bargaining between Lewis and General Motors representatives on February 4 and 5 slightly narrowed the differences between the union and the company. Lewis demanded exclusive bargaining rights only for workers in plants still on strike—some twenty in all. General Motors offered to bargain with the union for those workers it represented, promised not to discriminate against union members, pledged not to undermine the union, and stated that it would not sign a better contract with any other labor organization. The company, however, still refused to concede exclusive representation to the UAW, which remained Lewis's primary aim.[62]

With the strike differences narrowing, President Roosevelt again intervened. Acting on the advice of Secretary of Labor Perkins, Roosevelt spoke by phone to Lewis, Knudsen, and Donaldson Brown. He asked Lewis either to postpone exclusive representation for four months or to accept it for only two months; he requested Knudsen and Brown to implement the terms that General Motors had already offered the union, especially the pledge not to make more favorable agreements with other organizations during the life of the contract with the UAW or to encourage the emergence of any other union, and, most important, to "agree to give any guarantees required by the Government for the faithful performance of no discrimination, interference, restraint, or coercion.''[63]

But neither Lewis nor General Motors would defer to the president's wishes. Lewis would not relinquish possession of the occupied factories unless he could be more certain of winning union security. The company had little inclination to grant exclusive representation as long as the law validated its claim to possession of the occupied plants and the A. F. of L. endorsed the corporation's position on collective bargaining. Indeed, A. F. of L. officials publicly appealed to Roosevelt, Murphy, and General Motors to reject implementation of an exclusive bargaining agreement with the UAW and instead to protect the rights of A. F. of L. craft unionists in the auto industry.[64]

Throughout the tortuous and tense negotiations, Lewis acted typically. As always, he believed that power, not principle; might, not right, prevailed. In this case, the sit-down strikers personified raw power. As Lewis told Heber Blankenhorn only two weeks after the strike had been settled, in what is perhaps the most accurate and detailed version of the CIO leader's role in the negotiations: ''We held those key dies in Flint and we were not going to let go of them. They crippled General Motors.'' (General Motors car production had fallen from a rate of 50,000 for the month of December to only 125 for the first week in February.) Moreover, added Lewis, ''Those were splendid boys in those plants. Nothing would have gotten them out except troops. They were all set to lick any army of vigilantes and police that Flint could muster. They were set to lick anybody except cannons and bayonets.''[65]

General Motors, in fact, could achieve its aims only with the assistance of Governor Murphy, who had the power to break the strike. Lewis understood this. He had gone to Detroit, Lewis informed Blankenhorn, primarily to deal with the governor, whose attitude was the key to union success. ''I had studied up Murphy and again and again had to deal with his wobbling over the Flint sit-down.'' Lewis played on the governor's intense political ambitions. ''I had an impression,'' the labor leader told Michigan's governor,

> that Frank Murphy was a man of ambition. You left an $18,000 job in the Philippines, where you were living like a potentate with cars and country places in the mountains to enter a precarious race here. President Roosevelt swept this state by nearly 200,000, you carried it by 40,000 because labor supported you. Labor put you here. . . . If you break this strike that washes us up and washes you up. General Motors fought you in the election and when we are gone you are gone. If you stand firm you will aggrandize your political position enormously and there will be talk of Governor Murphy in 1940.

Here, Blankenhorn recalled, ''Lewis picked up a cartoon contrasting a large and growing Governor Murphy, pro-C.I.O., with a dark and diminishing Governor Hoffman of New Jersey, anti-C.I.O., and said he was going to send that cartoon to Murphy.''[66]

Ever the realist, Lewis adroitly parried all Murphy's threats to enforce the law. When Murphy repeatedly led the labor leader outside the conference room and begged him to withdraw the sit-downers voluntarily or face forcible evacuation, Lewis, Blankenhorn reported, abruptly told the governor,

> I am not going to withdraw those sit-downers under any circumstances except a settlement. What are you going to do? You can get them out in just one way, by bayonets. You have the bayonets. Which kind do you prefer to use—the broad double blade or the four-sided French style? I believe the square style makes a bigger hole and you can turn it around inside a man. Which kind of bayonets, Governor Murphy, are you going to turn around inside our boys?

Murphy responded, as Lewis, to be sure, anticipated, that he would do no such thing. "Then," the labor leader retorted, "why bellyache to me about my getting those boys out to save you?"[67]

Lewis vexed the three General Motors negotiators—Knudsen, Brown, and Smith—with a combination of bluster, bluff, and sarcasm. "Whenever it was necessary for me to break up their argument," Lewis told Blankenhorn, "I went for them with Pinkertons." During the critical February negotiations, the press reported that a Pinkerton employed by General Motors had been found in Alexandria prowling near the Lewis home. The day that the story broke Lewis interrupted a particularly strong corporate line of argument and queried:

> What's the basis for your statement? Some lousy Pinkerton? I want to know who of you sent a Pinkerton bastard to spy on me and my home in Alexandria. I look on my home as my castle and I guard my privacy jealously. Who sent that Pinkerton, was it you, Brown? [Donaldson Brown was visibly taken aback and said he had no idea who sent Pinkertons.] Was it you, Smith? [The usually arrogant Smith insisted on his own innocence.] Well how is this General Motors run anyway? What about the third one, you Knudsen?

"Well, I guess it must be my department," Knudsen replied. By the time Lewis finished, General Motors' negotiators had completely lost track of their line of argument.[68]

The strikers' occupation of the three General Motors' plants in Flint remained throughout the protracted negotiations, as it had been during the entire conflict, the key to union success. None of Lewis's rhetoric or sarcasm carried as much weight in the balance of the bargaining as the sit-downers' determination to risk their own lives. As long as the sit-downers remained inside, General Motors could not produce cars and suffered substantial financial losses, even the possibility of losing a permanent share of the market to its competitors. One way or another, the corporation had to regain possession of its plants. Neither the Flint police nor judicial orders, however, seemed sufficient to remove the strikers. Only the state and federal governments had the power in February 1937, to break the strike by enforcing the law—that is, Judge Gadola's injunction of February 2.

But Lewis knew that neither President Roosevelt nor Governor Murphy would break a strike in February 1937, especially if bloodshed resulted. No matter how often Murphy raised his obligation to enforce the law in the public interest, Lewis realized that the governor would never order the State Guard to attack the strikers. The labor leader was also aware that Roosevelt, whose principal desire was a peaceful settlement in which the union won recognition, put no pressure on Murphy to restore General Motors to its occupied property. Publicly and privately, however, the governor and the labor leader acted out a strange charade, one in which Murphy threatened to uphold the law and Lewis challenged the governor to spill human blood.

As documented in Sidney Fine's definitive history of the sit-down strike, on February 9 Murphy did, indeed, prepare an order to enforce the injunction; but the governor never intended to issue it. It was drawn entirely to protect the governor against prospective political criticism for being a captive of organized labor unable to enforce the law, and it was not revealed publicly until January 1939, when a United States Senate committee was considering Murphy's nomination as attorney general. Perhaps the governor also prepared the order in hope of bluffing Lewis into a voluntary evacuation of the occupied plants. And Lewis, as recorded in Heber Blankenhorn's report on the General Motors negotiations, responded to Murphy's threat to enforce the law, with the following riposte: "Your grandfather was executed for resisting real law, law passed by the Lords Spiritual and Temporal and assented to by the Commons and sealed with the King's imprimatur. My compliments to your ancestors and I hope they will be able to look down and be proud of their Governor Frank B. Murphy, who was willing to resist not law but a General Motors' suborned injunction."[69]

Lewis's refusal to retreat and his alacrity at calling Murphy's insubstantial bluff showed his sagacity as a bargainer for labor's rights. When Lewis became ill, on the eve of the settlement and took to bed, the governor and the corporation executives came to the labor leader's room to seal an agreement. On point after point General Motors conceded to Lewis's demands, causing the militant Robert Travis to advise his boss, "We've got 'em by the 'balls,' squeeze a little." General Motors insisted that strikers convicted of acts of violence not be rehired; Lewis asserted that the corporation must rehire *all* strikers and union members without discrimination; the labor leader prevailed. The company offered the union a three-month period during which it would not bargain with any union other than the UAW unless it received permission from Governor Murphy to do so; Lewis demanded a six-month exclusive bargaining arrangement; he received it. And so it went. Finally, on February 11 after General Motors retreated on one point after another, a gratified Murphy could carry a completed agreement to Lewis's bedside. "We have left a place for you to sign at the top," the governor informed the labor leader. Lewis insisted on signing at the bottom, as befit the man without whose consent there would have been no settlement.[70]

*   *   *

If the strikers had not won a total victory, they had nevertheless wrenched a good deal from the world's largest industrial corporation—one that for two decades had resolutely repelled every trade union advance. General Motors formally recognized the UAW as the collective bargaining agent for employees who belonged to the union. It promised not to interfere with the workers' right to join the union or to discriminate on the basis of union membership. The company also pledged to start bargaining with the UAW on February 16 concerning the union's January 4 demands. For its part, the union agreed to evacuate the occupied plants and not to interfere with production pending negotiation of a final agreement. Most important, William Knudsen, in a letter to Governor Murphy, promised that the company would not inspire activities among other worker groups that might weaken the UAW; and for six months after auto production resumed, Knudsen pledged that General Motors would not deal with any other union or representative of its employees in the twenty plants covered by the agreement without Murphy's permission.

Lewis's own evaluation of the strike settlement a month later at a meeting of the CIO executive board was to the point. "GM strike," Lewis exulted, "CIO faced a united financial front—GM settlement broke it."[71]

Rank-and-file auto workers felt the same way. The day the strike settlement was announced a committee of eight Ford workers came to visit Lewis in his hotel room. One of the eight, the son of a UMW member, leaned over the sickbed with his hand on his heart and said to Lewis, in broken English, "Mr. Lewis, my heart is glad today. The hearts of 100,000 are glad for the union. Now we got the sons of bitches."[72] Flint workers felt even more elated, one stating that recognition "was the most wonderful thing that we could think of that could possibly happen to people." And a hitherto antiunion man added, "We now . . . are treated as human beings, and not as part of the machinery. . . . It proves clearly that united we stand, divided or alone we fall."[73]

The UAW victory over General Motors legitimized the CIO as a national trade union center competitive with the A. F. of L. and magnified Lewis's role and influence as a labor leader. In the aftermath of Flint, the auto workers' union surged ahead to build a mass membership. Claiming 88,000 members in February 1937, within a month the UAW practically doubled its membership to 166,000; nearly another 100,000 joined in April, and by mid-October the union claimed 400,000 dues-paying members.[74]

The example set by Flint's workers proved contagious. The year 1937 experienced 477 sit-down strikes affecting 400,000 workers. Twenty-five sit-down strikes occurred in January, 47 in February, and 170 in March. "Sitting down," proclaimed *Time* magazine hyperbolically, "has replaced baseball as a national pastime."[75]

Sitting down also played a role in the UAW-CIO's victory against a second of the "Big Three" auto manufacturers: the Chrysler Corporation. Having defeated General Motors, proved its potency in battle, and built up its membership, the UAW determined to win a better agreement from Chrysler, whose executives were quite ready to cede the union precisely what General Motors had granted. This time, however, the union demanded exclusive representation for all company employees, and when the company refused, UAW militants sat down on March 8. By then political conservatives and the press had stimulated a powerful, apparently popular repudiation of the sit-down technique. In March 1937 the governor of Michigan and the president of the United States perceived greater political gain in enforcing the law than in "appeasing" strikers. Murphy prepared to use force to evict the Chrysler strikers, and Lewis, ever the realist, quickly worked out a peaceful accommodation with the governor and company negotiators. After a typical round of bargaining, in which Lewis threatened one Chrysler executive with physical force and exposed another to ridicule, he accepted a strike settlement identical in every respect with the earlier General Motors agreement.[76]

But sit-downs, rank-and-file militancy, illegal trespass, violence, and dramatic confrontations played no part in what was perhaps the single most significant result of the Flint strike: the CIO's achievement of a collective bargaining agreement with the United States Steel Corporation, the traditional bastion of the antiunion open shop. To this development we must now direct our attention.

However decisive the auto workers' victory over General Motors, many contemporary commentators and several scholars subsequently interpreted the Flint strike as a fortuitous or accidental incident in the CIO's basic strategy to organize mass-production workers. To them, activity among the auto workers appeared mainly as a diversionary or flanking tactic to the main battle that Lewis intended to wage in steel. After all, had not the irreparable rupture between A. F. of L. and CIO been precipitated by Lewis's seizure of the Amalgamated Association in the summer of 1936? Did not Lewis's selection of Philip Murray as director of SWOC, the small army of UMW officials dispatched to organize steelworkers, and the huge sums of money CIO (the UMW, in fact) provided SWOC betoken the primacy of the steel campaign? Was it not more than a coincidence that Lewis chose to proclaim publicly, in a national radio network speech in July 1936, that the CIO organizing effort would begin in steel? Finally, had not much of the political bargaining between Lewis and Roosevelt in the summer of 1936 focused on administration support for the CIO drive among steelworkers?[77]

Other facts lend credence to the belief that Lewis, in 1936 and early 1937, planned to attack steel. Rumors abounded that Lewis had never forgotten the defeats he had suffered as an A. F. of L. organizer (1911-1917) in the Pittsburgh area and that he thirsted for revenge against the city's dominant industry: steel. Substantial evidence revealed also that he considered organization of the steel industry vital to the long-term security of the UMW in the coalfields and the best means to conquer the captive coal mines. The steel industry, moreover, more so than any other sector of the economy, symbolized the Wall Street financial oligarchy's dominance in the United States—a reality Lewis had persistently criticized. Finally, Lewis's economic adviser, W. Jett Lauck, repeatedly urged a frontal assault against the steel industry's resistance to trade unionism.[78]

Yet to examine steel the CIO drive in steel before the conflict in autos, and accord primacy to the CIO's settlement with U. S. Steel over the agreement with General Motors (as Irving Bernstein and Walter Galenson do) is to mystify history and distort the reality of the CIO's rise to power.[79] History is the study of persistence and change *over time*, and chronology is its essence. How, then, can an agreement reached on March 2, 1937, be interpreted as more significant than one ratified on February 11, 1937—indeed be characterized by one labor economist as "the most important single document in the history of the American labor movement"?[80] Ironically, and almost unconsciously, Bernstein and Galenson lend credence to what might be labeled a *Fortune* magazine and "New Left" version of labor history. In that interpretation, Myron C. Taylor bulks larger than John L. Lewis and corporate manipulation (*cooptation* is the "New Left's," if not *Fortune*'s preferred word) of labor leaders appears more significant than working-class struggle.[81] An element of truth underlies such an interpretation, but to stress a small truth is to obscure the larger reality that never eluded John L. Lewis or, for that matter, Myron Taylor.

Just as dramatic stories of the confrontation between Lewis and Murphy during the Flint strike make better reading than sober analyses of the economic and political realities of the dispute, so, too, do the secret negotiations between the CIO chief and the U. S. Steel executive appear more intriguing than the counter-play of the same economic and political forces that brought labor victory in autos. Let us examine briefly the story of the Taylor-Lewis negotiations and then place it in its proper historical context.

On Saturday, January 9, 1937, Lewis was having lunch in the dining room of the Mayflower Hotel with his good friend Senator Joseph F. Guffey, when Mr. and Mrs. Myron C. Taylor entered. On the way to their own table, the Taylors passed Lewis's table, whereupon the business executive bowed. After seating his wife, Taylor returned to Lewis's table, where the three men chatted for about a minute. According to *Fortune*, so dramatic was this event that waiters and other diners lost all interest in lunch—an interest that diminished even more several minutes later when Lewis, having completed his own meal, walked over to the Taylor's table, where he conversed animatedly for almost half an hour.[82]

The following day, Sunday, January 10, a day Lewis ordinarily devoted to his family, found the CIO leader in Myron Taylor's Mayflower Hotel suite. For the next several days the two men continued to meet secretly in this conspicuous Washington hotel.[83] Events in Michigan, however, interrupted the negotiations when Lewis traveled to Detroit to bargain for the auto workers in the General

Motors dispute. Not until February 17, when Lewis arrived in New York to participate in collective bargaining between the UMW and the coal operators, did he resume negotiations with Taylor. Then, for the next two weeks, Lewis and Taylor again met secretly, this time in the executive's gracious Upper East Side town house. There the two men put the finishing touches to what became the final agreement between U. S. Steel and SWOC. On Sunday, March 1, Lewis assembled Lee Pressman, Sidney Hillman, and Philip Murray in his suite at the Essex House. He told his associates in the labor movement that he had just returned from Myron Taylor's house; that he had secured an agreement with the steel corporation, the terms of which he quickly rattled off; and that if Murray and Pressman went down to Pittsburgh on Monday morning and met Benjamin Fairless (president of U. S. Steel) in his office, Fairless would sign an agreement with SWOC. A stunned Murray, the director of the steel organizing campaign, had been presented with a fait accompli, the securing of a labor agreement in which he had played no role. As Lee Pressman later reflected on this moment in history, "That's his [Lewis's] function, to meet the Myron Taylors and knock down the doors of the might[y] citadels of the U.S.A., and then say, 'Now, go down to Pittsburgh and get your contract'.''[84]

The contract that Murray and Fairless signed, on March 2, 1937, for SWOC and U. S. Steel offered less than the February 11 UAW-GM contract. The steel corporation agreed to recognize SWOC and to bargain with it solely for the workers it represented; U. S. Steel, like GM, refused to relinquish the principle of the open shop. The corporation also accepted rudimentary grievance and seniority procedures; granted its workers an across-the-board wage increase; and conceded the basic eight-hour day, five-day week with time and a half for overtime.

But why had U. S. Steel conceded prior to a strike? Why would a corporation that alone produced almost as much steel in 1934 as Germany; that controlled 38.4% of all American capacity, with assets of over $2 billion; and that possessed its own iron and coal mines, ships, railroads, basic steel and fabricating plants, as well as marketing agencies surrender to trade unionism without a struggle? *Fortune* magazine provided one answer: the far-sighted leadership and vision of Myron C. Taylor. Lee Pressman offered another: the character of John L. Lewis. Let us examine them.

In the summer of 1936, according to *Fortune*, Myron Taylor left the United States for his customary vacation in Italy's Florentine hills in a particularly philosophical mood. The emergence of the CIO had convinced Taylor that "a great change had come over the face of U. S. industry. The blood and brimstone labor philosophy of his predecessor, Judge Elbert H. Gary, was out of tune with the times. So was . . . the idea of the big steel 'family, for instance, and good will toward the worker, and social welfare. Labor was in arms'." A summer's reflection led the executive to formulate what *Fortune* characterized as "the Myron Taylor formula for industrial peace." Simply stated, U. S. Steel's new labor policy would be as follows:

The company recognizes the right of its employees to bargain collectively through representatives freely chosen by them without dictation, coercion or intimidation in any form or from any source. It will negotiate and contract with the representatives of any group of its employees so chosen and with any organization as the representative of its members, subject to the recognition of the principle that the right to work is not dependent on membership or non-membership in any organization and subject to the right of every employee freely to bargain in such manner and through such representatives, if any, as he chooses.[85]

Fortune, then, and many scholars, subsequently, viewed the Taylor formula of industrial relations as a substantial shift in company policy, an innovation that made possible the peaceful agreement between SWOC and U. S. Steel. A close reading of the above statement and supporting evidence suggests, however, that Taylor never altered company labor policy in principle. U. S. Steel, even in the days of Judge Elbert H. Gary, had never denied its workers the theoretical right to join unions, provided the rights of nonunion workers received equal consideration and protection. Company executives believed, in Gary's era, as Taylor tried to convince himself from 1935 through 1941, that most workers preferred *not* to join unions. And Taylor, quite contrary to *Fortune*'s assertion, still preferred "the idea of the big steel family." In a private memorandum of September 11, 1935, to President Roosevelt, Taylor expressed his deepest personal feelings on labor policy. Referring to the emergence of company unions in the steel industry after the passage of Section 7a and the Wagner Act, Taylor asserted that his company's employees "have shown a decided preference in managing their own affairs and the tendency, therefore, has been toward the formation of company unions." To be sure, he added, the American labor movement has never been as strong as elsewhere, because "the average American worker considers that he has an opportunity to qualify himself for and eventually be promoted to an executive position." The overwhelming percentage of our employees, he asserted, lack class consciousness and "do not want to become members of outside labor organizations, to which workingmen who become members are required to pay dues and assessments." Taylor never deviated from the principles he enunciated to the president in September 1935. But in 1937 the events in Flint forced him to dilute his principles when faced with the reality of labor power. Yet, in 1941, he risked Roosevelt's displeasure and brought on the notorious captive mines' strike to defend the rights of a handful of nonunion miners.[86]

Taylor and U. S. Steel shifted labor policy between July 1936 and March 2, 1937, not because a summer's reflection transformed Taylor's beliefs, but because workers and their labor movement had refashioned American economic and political reality. The results of the 1936 elections displeased steel executives. Not only had Roosevelt been returned to office by a landslide, but in states and local communities that the companies had long dominated, their candidates fell before labor's. In a new political milieu, many more steelworkers signed up with SWOC, and scores of company unions declared their independence. For the first time since

1919, a national strike in the steel industry seemed a real possibility, and if it came, executives could not rely on the power of the state to smash it.

Taylor and his steel associates thus watched events in the auto industry carefully. They saw what a militant minority achieved in Flint. More important, they noticed, with trepidation, that neither President Roosevelt nor Governor Murphy had enforced the "law" against the sit-downers. Labor's victory in Flint presaged a bitter conflict in steel, one that might cause untold damage to property and life. Rather than risk such a conflict and sacrifice the profits his company was now making* as a consequence of the New-Deal-stimulated economic recovery, Taylor chose to beat a strategic retreat in labor policy. He voluntarily agreed to recognize SWOC and committed U. S. Steel to collective bargaining with the labor organization, yet he steadfastly refused to surrender the open-shop principle or to believe that most workers voluntarily preferred to join unions.

Clearly, the success of the auto workers in Flint was the single most important reason that the CIO triumphed over U. S. Steel without struggle. Lewis freely admitted as much on March 9, 1937, when he told fellow CIO executive board members, "a GM strike—sweeping effect on steel. CIO faced united financial front—GM settlement broke it."[87]

What remains to be explained is why Lewis settled for less in the U. S. Steel agreement than he had wrested from General Motors. The steel company, like the auto company, consented to bargain with the CIO union (SWOC) for the workers it represented; but it refused to rule out negotiations with other labor groups for any time period, and it reiterated its commitment to the open-shop principle. Frankly, only one explanation seems plausible: Lewis believed that he was bargaining from a weaker position in steel. But why?

To this last question no easy answer emerges. Comparing the situation in steel to that in autos, *Fortune* asked, in the spring of 1937, if the sit-down strike could "tie up the auto industry, which had been hastily organized, what would prevent it from tying up steel, where the CIO was firmly and forethoughtedly entrenched?"[88] Lewis, to be sure, had devoted greater attention, manpower, and money to the campaign in steel. Yet the strengths of the CIO's position in steel paradoxically produced significant weaknesses. So completely was SWOC administered from the top down, so firm was its oligarchic leadership, that officials could not be sure how the rank and file would act in a crisis. The steel union lacked the Mortimers, Travises, Simons, Johnsons, and Reuthers—militant cadres who could force the hands of both corporation executives and labor leaders. And in steel as in autos only a minority—and a small minority at that—of workers belonged to the union on the eve of victory.[89] Steel also differed from the auto industry in structure. Not dependent on assembly line methods of manufacture, though continuous flow characterized some aspects of steelmaking, the steel industry was not as vulnerable

---

*At the time, U. S. Steel was also negotiating with a representative of the British government on a large armaments contract—one that could not be fulfilled in the event of a strike.

to economic damage inflicted by worker occupation of a single strategic plant. Furthermore, the CIO's strategists in steel were convinced that the Iron and Steel Institute (the industry's major trade association) had established an agreement among its members that in the event of a strike against one company, profits on orders then filled by other companies would be shared with the struck company.[90] Finally, the state, at least as personified by Democratic officeholders, had strengthened labor's position during the auto strike. Could state and federal officials be relied on again to disregard judicial injunctions or blink at labor violence in the event of a steel strike? Lewis wasn't sure. In the event, then, rather than risk a protracted industrywide general strike, possible repudiation by public officials, and an irremediable defeat for labor, Lewis chose to accept Taylor's terms.

Lewis, moreover, realized the importance of symbols and images, that what people believed to be true was often more significant than what in fact happened. When Myron Taylor, representing U. S. Steel, accorded recognition to organized labor in March 1937, newspaper columnists, public officials, scholars, and many labor leaders did not examine the terms of the settlement microscopically. They were awestruck by news that the fortress of the open shop, the company that for four decades had used every weapon in its arsenal to combat trade unionism, had surrendered without a struggle to the CIO. The U. S. Steel-SWOC agreement coming just three weeks after the General Motors-UAW settlement proved the potency of the CIO. If the outcome of the auto strike had certified the legitimacy of the CIO, the U. S. Steel contract apparently made Lewis's organization the dominant national labor center. What the A. F. of L. had failed to accomplish in half a century the CIO had achieved in three weeks. Having conquered autos and steel, the CIO's future, in March 1937, seemed unlimited.

The CIO signified a new epoch in the history of American labor. Lewis certainly thought so. Addressing fellow CIO leaders at the March 9, 1937, executive board meeting, he observed: "As years go by, this period will be marked as epoch in life of labor organizations—and economic, social, political history of America. Gigantic implications."[91]

The CIO meant to capitalize on those implications. Its director, John Brophy, told the same March 9 meeting that although it was impossible to draw blueprints in such a rapidly changing situation, the organization must centralize its operation in order to lessen the danger of unmanageable local situations. Brophy urged that the board appoint additional national representatives, authorize the formation of central bodies (counterparts to the A. F. of L.'s city centrals and state federations) where the situation warranted, and move the CIO into more commodious office facilities in Washington. Less than two weeks later, Charles Howard advised Brophy that the CIO should consider seriously the affiliation of a large number of new unions, including such substantial A. F. of L. affiliates as the meat cutters (butcher workmen), bakery and confectionary workers, government employees, hotel and restaurant workers, and retail clerks. Howard proposed a strategy that avoided conflict with the most stable and powerful A. F. of L. affiliates yet allowed the CIO to charter local unions in certain cases where jurisdiction remained disputed.[92]

Acting on the advice of Brophy and Howard, the CIO embarked on an aggressive organizing campaign that competed directly with the A. F. of L. for members. William Green soon complained to his executive council that "the country seems to be filled with CIO organizers. Every town and every city, small and great, seems to be filled with organizers employed, appointed and assigned to work for and by the CIO."[93]

By the end of August 1937 the CIO laid claim to 3,419,600 members (more than the A. F. of L. claimed at that time) organized in 32 national unions and 510 local industrial unions directly affiliated to the CIO. Among the national unions were some of the giants of the American labor movement: the mine workers with 600,000 members; the UAW, with 375,000; SWOC, with 500,000 (463,000 actually held union cards, but 510,000 were employed by companies under SWOC contract); the Textile Workers' Organizing Committee (TWOC), with 400,000; the Amalgamated Clothing Workers, with 200,000; and the ladies' garment workers, with 250,000.[94]

In October CIO prepared to celebrate its successes. And it could find no more suitable location for a festival than Atlantic City, where in November 1935, John L. Lewis had thrown the first punch in American labor's civil war. In mid-October the new hosts of labor gathered along the worn boardwalk and in the rococo hotels of Jersey's resort city for their first national conference. They came from the steel towns of the Monongahela Valley, Akron's rubber factories, Detroit's auto plants, the West Coast waterfront, New York's subways, and the rain forests of the Pacific Northwest. The delegates included gnarled old class warriors from the coalfields and young militants from the mass-production industries, pure and simple unionists and flaming Reds. Practically every shade of labor and radical opinion found a spokesman in Atlantic City, and the old joined the more numerous young in toasting the labor movement's bright future. "I attended the Atlantic City conference," Adolph Germer wrote a friend, "and I assure you it was an educational treat. There was as much difference between that meeting and the A. F. of L. conventions I have attended as there is between night and day."[95]

But the man whose imagination, drive, and daring had breathed life into the CIO could not fully share in the celebration. As now seemed to happen more frequently when the sun shone less strongly and the temperature fell, John L. Lewis took to his bed, a victim of the flu. The man who exuded such exuberance publicly and enormous vitality in his formal speeches suddenly seemed inordinately susceptible to physical ailments. Yet remember that Lewis was now fifty-seven years old, his life had taken its toll, and he had paid a price for labor in the coal mines and years of ceaseless train and auto trips broken only by strange hotels and best-forgotten restaurants.[96]

There can be no doubt that Lewis created the CIO. From June 1936, when it began its real existence, to September 1937, the month preceding its first national conference, the CIO was *not* a self-sustaining organization. In the fifteen months from June 1936 to September 1937, the CIO spent $1,745,968 and earned only $308,388 (despite a membership in excess of 3 million by the end of the period), leaving a deficit of $1,437,580. Of the total funds the CIO received to support its operations, the UMW alone provided $1,245,000 (SWOC received $960,000 from the mine workers); without Lewis's generosity, then, there would have been no CIO.[97]

In 1937, Lewis's gamble, his decision to use UMW funds to build a new labor movement, seemed a wise investment. "In a little over a year," Benjamin Stolberg wrote in the *Nation* of February 20, 1937, "the C.I.O. has changed significantly the relation of social forces in American industry. It is changing both the structure and orientation of American labor. . . . It is gradually killing off the A. F. of L. in all but the most craft-ridden industries. It is profoundly affecting our two major political parties. It is transforming the relationship of government to industry." Lewis's extraordinarily shrewd leadership, Stolberg concluded, had made the CIO "the most progressive and vital force in American life today."[98] In 1937, then, to the public and to millions of workers, Lewis was the CIO, and the CIO was Lewis.

CHAPTER 13
The Man Behind the Mask: Lewis in Legend and Reality

The year 1937 was undoubtedly the zenith of John L. Lewis's career. The year began with *Nation* magazine placing the labor leader on its 1936 honor roll "for continuing to give strength and backbone to the American labor movement." A short time before, Amelia Earhart, the woman pilot and popular culture hero, had written Lewis to endorse his position in the controversy with the A. F. of L. "I hope," she wrote, "that CIO will maintain the advantage of breadth and simplicity, for therein lies an extraordinary opportunity for progress." Heywood Broun—the columnist, social commentator, and quondam radical—compared John L. Lewis to Joe Louis, the Negro heavyweight champion (the "brown bomber") and idol of the black masses. Arguing that Lewis the labor leader had done more for black people by organizing the mass-production workers than Louis the fighter had done by annihilating white boxers, Broun quipped, "I think that Lewis is the greatest heavyweight of our day."[1]

Wherever Lewis went in 1937, masses of people seemed to share Broun's opinion. Invited to address an anti-Nazi rally in New York's Madison Square Garden sponsored by the American Jewish Committee and the Jewish Labor Committee, Lewis found himself wildly, ecstatically cheered minute after minute by a crowd estimated at 20,000. In May 1937, when Lewis addressed the convention of the International Ladies' Garment Workers, delegates rose to their feet for several minutes and cheered in unison: CIO! CIO! CIO! And in August, at the United Auto Workers convention, in Milwaukee, delegates preceded Lewis's featured speech with twelve minutes of wild applause, punctuated the address itself with more applause, and followed it with five minutes of raucous snake dancing through the aisles.[2] This scene was repeated as Lewis became the labor movement's most sought after public speaker, a man who commanded the rapt attention of hundreds of convention delegates and millions of radio listeners.

Public esteem and mass popularity seemed to alter Lewis's character and mode of behavior as a labor leader. Some of Lewis's closest associates sensed the change. John Brophy, for one, later reflected "there's no question in my mind that Lewis's aims in those early years of the C.I.O. were definitely tied to the good of the general labor movement, and the workers as a whole. . . . I think that he too was stirred by the drama. I think he was moved by the sense of opportunity and fulfillment that lay in the situation."[3] Gardner Jackson, who went to work for the CIO late in 1936 and came to know Lewis personally as well as officially, believed that the CIO transported Lewis out of his narrow trade union power role and into leadership of a mass popular uprising. Lewis would show Jackson letters from dentists, shopkeepers, teachers, and small-town professionals saying, "This will bring a new day to our country if you expand this movement [CIO] to embrace all of us." At the time, remembers Jackson, even Lewis seemed overwhelmed by the CIO's size and the popular response it evoked.[4] The masses of workers and small people who appealed to Lewis for leadership in 1937 fired the labor leader's imagination, recalls Lee Pressman, the CIO's chief counsel and one of Lewis's most trusted advisers in the early CIO period. Lewis, Pressman suggests, dis- covered a new life career in 1937, one in which the labor leader would embark on a long march that would carry the common people to the pinnacle of national power.[5]

How did Lewis's personality and character in 1937 compare to what it had been in the past? What were his essential beliefs and goals? What manner of man was he? And how did he relate to others in official and personal capacities? How did his private life and values contrast to his public persona and behavior? Was Lewis a Churchillean enigma wrapped in a riddle cloaked in mystery? Or was there a consistency and logic to his public career and private existence?

From the summer of 1936 through the summer of 1937 many Americans and also foreigners asked themselves the same questions. Newspapers and magazines hastened to provide their readers with answers. Who was this powerful public figure about whom Ben Stolberg wrote in a three-part sketch in the *Nation*: "it seems to me that in the second half of this decade the most significant leader in American society will be John Lewis—unless we get fascism." Newspapers featured articles exploring Lewis's origins, life, and career. Stolberg dissected the labor leader's tactics and beliefs in the *Nation*; Louis Adamic, an astute observer of American mores, probed Lewis in *Forum*; and in the *Atlantic Monthly*, a French journalist examined the United States labor leader from a European perspective.[6]

From these prose portraits and scores of similar brief biographies, there emerged an image of John L. Lewis as labor leader and public figure—one that he cultivated assiduously. For those journalists eager, whether knowingly or un- knowingly, to gloss Lewis's image, the labor leader appeared, in the words of Heywood Broun, the most visible sight in the nation's capital next to the Washing- ton Monument.[7] For C. L. Sulzberger, who, as a young reporter for United Press, made his journalistic reputation by publishing the first popular biography of

Lewis in 1938 (*Sit-Down with John L. Lewis*), Lewis seemed always to have a spare moment, time to prepare a written statement of his beliefs and goals. For Louis Stark of the *New York Times*, a CIO sympathizer, there were always timely and significant news leaks. For Louis Adamic and other free-lancers preparing sketches for mass circulation weeklies and monthlies, there was time for a gracious luncheon in Lewis's favorite dining place, the Carlton Hotel. And for the mass of working journalists, there were the dramatic press conferences that Lewis staged as successfully as his chief competitor for news space, President Roosevelt.

First and foremost, Lewis cultivated an image of size, strength, and anger. "Big" is one of the first words that tumble into the description of John L. Lewis, reported Adamic. "He weighs in the vicinity of 230 pounds . . . but has little excess flesh anywhere about him. . . . Lewis," added Adamic, though in his late fifties, "seems to have just reached his prime. His great body is a marvelously fit and efficient organism, all its parts, working, clicking, integrated . . . he does not know from experience what illness is. . . . Lewis' head is the most impressive affair I have ever seen on top of a man's neck. . . . Alongside it, the average male head is something faint and inane." The whole impressive face dominated by aggressive features could register every important human emotion, according to Adamic, "but seems most effective in wrath, scorn, contempt and bulldog tenacity. . . . The face holds just a hint of incongruity. Above the nose is the face of a philosopher, a brooder; below, that of a fighter, a man of action. The two are not fused or integrated. The fighter dominates the brooder."[8]

Lewis refused to alter that image when friends suggested that he cultivate public favor. Asked by Gardner Jackson not always to frown publicly, Lewis rejected the suggestion outright. "Why, Gardner," he responded, "my stock in trade is being the ogre. That's how I make my way." To Frances Perkins, the labor leader observed: "Madame Secretary, that scowl is worth a million dollars." And to a business acquaintance who suggested that the labor leader hire public relations men to improve his image, Lewis replied that if he were going to fight for the coal miners, he was simply going to have to be disliked and disrespected by the majority of American people.[9]

One story, undoubtedly apocryphal but repeatedly printed in sketches of Lewis, illustrated his physical prowess. It was said in one variation that in Lewis's days as a young coal miner, a man-killing mule named "Spanish Pete" cornered Lewis in a mine corridor and attacked him. Lewis immediately lashed out with his right fist, stunned the mule, grabbed a piece of timber, and drove it deep into the enraged animal's brain. Realizing that the mule's death might cost him his job, the young miner filled the gaping head wound with clay and reported that "Spanish Pete" had died of heart failure.[10]

Nothing was allowed to obscure Lewis's image of size and strength. Cyrus Ching recalls meeting Lewis for lunch at the Carlton in 1940 or 1941 and then being rebuffed by the labor leader for at least a year afterward. Unable to fathom

Lewis's coolness to him, Ching was eventually told by one of the labor leader's associates, "When you had those photographs taken at the Carlton Hotel [reporters had photographed the men before the luncheon], you towered over him, and John resents anyone towering over him. You should have been sitting."[11]

Alongside the image of size and strength went the notion of Lewis as the center of all attention. When the UMW finally moved into its luxurious new Washington headquarters in the former University Club building, no visitor could escape Lewis's eyes. Every passageway, corridor, wall, and office bore a photograph of Lewis, usually full-face. Marquis Childs, the newspaper columnist, described a visit to Lewis's office in this way. "You go to see him and he receives you almost like—I once went to Mussolini's office in the Palazzo Venezia and he gave somewhat the same impression. A great office and you waded through the rug a couple of miles and got over to the great man."[12]

Wherever he went Lewis tried to foster that image. There is the story of Lewis pausing in front of his home in Alexandria, bending over, and tying his shoelace as a bus full of tourists passed by. All the tourists craned their necks to get a clear view of the sight outside. Lewis was to say, "Even the posterior of a great man is of interest."[13]

Len DeCaux tells an equally revealing story of Lewis's grip on public attention. After the victory over GM at Flint, Lewis arrived for a rally at a large local stadium. As the crowd surged around the labor leader, he headed away from the platform and in another direction. DeCaux, together with hundreds of others, decided to remain close to Lewis, who forged slowly ahead. As the procession halted, DeCaux pushed ahead to see where Lewis had disappeared. Finally, at the head of the large crowd stationed at a respectful distance from the labor leader, DeCaux witnessed a strange sight. "They were watching solemnly," DeCaux wrote, "while the great man relieved himself at a urinal. No one cracked a smile or a jest. Least of all Lewis. He zipped up his pants and washed his hands. Then he headed into the ranks of his admirers."[14]

Such public behavior by the labor leader led the newspaper reporter Kenneth Crawford to quip: "Lewis had come to believe that his own birthday should be celebrated instead of Christmas." "To ask Lewis to exercise magnanimity, to ask him to be humble," wrote John Chamberlain, "is just about as futile as trying to get gold from pyrites or blood from a turnip."[15]

The final element in the public image that Lewis cultivated was the picture of himself as the prototypical coal miner. "Think of me as a coal miner," he told Saul Alinsky, who spread the word in his life of Lewis, "and you won't make any mistakes." Trying to capture the essence of Lewis's personality, John Chamberlain concluded: "The man is still a miner in his psychology, still a 'man from the picks'."[16]

Did Lewis's private behavior among those he preferred to be with fit his public image? Scarcely! For one thing, Lewis was not an accessible person. Marquis Childs, for example, described Lewis as "a pretty aloof figure. . . . He lives in a kind of Olympian way. I don't know any newspaperman, except maybe one or two, who ever got very close to him."[17] Ed Levinson, another newspaperman more familiar with Lewis because he went to work for the UAW in 1937, asserted that Lewis understood the psychology of making himself inaccessible, "thus making himself more effective for public assemblages and gatherings."[18] John Brophy and Lee Pressman, who, as close associates and advisers in the CIO, knew Lewis well, agreed. "Friends?" John Brophy responded to an interviewer's question. "I don't think he [Lewis] had any real friends. I think he lives—I was going to say in lonely grandeur, using grandeur facetiously. I think he likes to appear in the grand manner. . . . Grandeur for him is a material and formalized thing." Pressman remembers Lewis as close personally to only one associate in the labor movement, his right-hand man, Phil Murray. Only Murray could call Lewis "Jack" (other close associates might refer to him as "John"). Every morning during the SWOC campaign, Pressman recalled, Lewis and Murray chatted with each other by phone between Pittsburgh and Washington. And whenever Murray visited Washington, he and Lewis met for lunch.[19] And Jett Lauck, who saw more of Lewis than anyone else associated with the UMW and CIO and who handled the family's real estate and tax transactions, often found himself rebuffed when he was most eager to have a word with his "friend" and employer.[20]

Rather than being a perfect physical specimen of prodigious strength and undiluted health, Lewis was especially susceptible to respiratory ailments—and at the most inopportune moments. During the final days of the 1925 anthracite coal strike negotiations, Lewis lay ill in a Philadelphia hotel bed, as he did during the climactic moments of the General Motors negotiations in Detroit. And flu restricted Lewis's personal appearances at the October 1937 CIO national conference in Atlantic City. Flu was the least of Lewis's health problems. In 1941, he suffered a severe heart attack that kept him in a Washington hospital on the critical list. He had future heart problems and perhaps past ones, which he labored to keep out of the press and secret.[21]

The ogre's image that he presented to the public, the abruptness with which he treated associates in the labor movement, and his unrestrained egotism quickly dissolved when Lewis was among the corporation executives, high government officials, diplomats, military men, and socialites whose company he seemed to prefer. Cyrus Ching remembered Lewis in private meetings as a "shy, bashful man, the soul of courtesy." Rather than acting flamboyantly in private conversation, Lewis, according to Ching, spoke softly, with a dry, keen sense of humor; he was "a brilliant conversationalist," a wonderful man to sit down and talk with. James M. Landis, too, recalled the Sunday afternoon tea parties at the Lewis's Alexandria home, where prominent public officials came, and good talk flowed, as Lewis acted the perfect gentleman. It is quite remarkable, indeed, how often the image of Lewis as gentleman, frequently as "Southern gentleman," crops up in the remembrances of socially prominent individuals who knew him.[22]

The portrait of Lewis as prototypical coal miner also suffers from a glimpse at private reality. Contrary to the stories spread in most biographies and sketches of Lewis, John did not descend from a long line of Welsh coal miners. Moreover, no one can be certain how much time John Lewis himself actually spent in the mines, a vocation he had fled successfully and permanently by 1909. The further Lewis removed himself from the mines by career, income, and life-style, the less he resembled the typical miner in behavior, character, and values. Unlike the ordinary coal miners, among whom comradery and brotherhood were two of the strongest values, Lewis, according to Brophy, "had the arrogance of the boss, the superior." Brophy illustrated this with one particularly graphic story. Joe Kovner, a young attorney employed by the CIO, was asked by Lewis one day to get a couple of cigars down in the hotel lobby. Kovner returned to Lewis with a couple of good cigars and the change from the money Lewis had provided for the purchase. Whereupon Lewis turned to the young man and said, "You keep the change."[23]

Pressman describes how Murray, not Lewis, maintained the UMW hierarchy's contact with common coal miners. On weekends, Murray and his wife would travel to a small town outside of Pittsburgh, where he had once worked in the mines, and sit on the front porch and chat with the local miners. Comparing Murray to Lewis, Pressman observed that "Murray never did enjoy sitting and talking with the so-called great. He always felt much better going back to the homely people, and getting the feeling of knowing what was going on in the mines, with the guys back home. It wasn't just a show with him. He actually felt refreshed when he did that."[24]

The discrepancy between Lewis's public image and private behavior led Pressman to conclude that "he's just one of those strange creatures that God throws up every now and then." Marquis Childs reached almost the same conclusion: "This is a very curious man, this man Lewis."[25]

Perhaps Lewis's role as trade union official and his leadership of the United Mine Workers and the CIO can illuminate his character and personality. In his 1938 history of the CIO, Edward Levinson presents a Lewis who appears every bit the counterpart of the stereotypical corporate executive whose work never ends and who must exert total control of his enterprise. "Hours after the sun has set and marked the end of a working-day for the rest of Washington," wrote Levinson, "the lights burn in Lewis' oak-paneled office at the United Mine Workers office. During the crises of the General Motors strike, of the U.S. Steel negotiations . . . he kept telephone wires open nightly, determined that no important detail should escape his attention."[26]

Precisely what Lewis did during those long days and evenings in the office, aside from speaking on the phone, remains uncertain. One can search the extant files of the UMW and the CIO in vain for any policy statements, administrative reports, or detailed proposals of union objectives bearing Lewis's signature.

Reports and policy statements proliferated—but they were the products of John Brophy, Jett Lauck, Lee Pressman, Ralph Hetzel (a young academic economist Lewis hired as a CIO consultant), and scores of other little-known or undistinguished individuals who labored for Lewis. David Dubinsky remembers how surprised he was whenever he visited Lewis at the latter's Washington office to find the leader of the largest single international trade union and the dominant labor federation of the late 1930s sitting behind an immense desk absolutely devoid of the smallest scrap of paper. How, wondered Dubinsky, did Lewis administer his affairs without a clutter of correspondence, memorandums, and reports?[27] A good question.

Although reporters might compare Lewis to a corporation executive and the labor leader himself preferred the appellation *executive* to that of *union official*, Lewis operated more in the style of big-city political boss than modern business executive. He dealt in power, not policy; patronage, not principles. Many of the deals he negotiated and methods he used were best left unrecorded. The telephone was preferable to the letter (or written memorandum); the private face-to-face conversation was preferred to the impersonal communication. And after he was convinced that the FBI at the behest of President Roosevelt, was tapping his phones and eavesdropping on office and hotel room conversations, Lewis preferred to do business over lunch or dinner in crowded restaurants.[28] To unveil Lewis's methods as a trade union administrator is as difficult as to penetrate the secrecies of Tammany Hall in the days of Boss Charles F. Murphy; perhaps it is impossible.

There are hints, however, of Lewis's mode of union operation. As in the universe of the political boss, in Lewis's labor world loyalty to the organization (the extended shadow of its leader) was the element essential to success. Nearly any error, sin, or crime could be forgiven except disloyalty. As Tammany Democrats scarcely blinked at coalitions of convenience with organization Republicans, Lewis easily countenanced alliances with Communists, anti-Communists, Democrats, Republicans, trustbusters, and business tycoons—provided the union benefited. Also, like the political boss, Lewis used the trade union as an institution to reward family members, whose loyalty to the chief could never be doubted, with lucrative positions. Finally, Lewis approached the development of young trade union leaders much as the boss chose his political heirs. Asked by John Brophy one day in 1938 how he would educate workers for union leadership, Lewis replied, "whenever I see a bright young fellow I pick him out and place him on the payroll of the union." "This," observed Brophy, "was his conception of how leadership was developed."[29]

Brutality and perhaps physical force played a part in Lewis's administration of union affairs. If no evidence that would hold in court and no written records that would convince a trained historian tie Lewis to crimes of violence, still the testimony of those who knew him best suggests a penchant for direct force. Trying to describe Lewis's behavior toward those who had allegedly betrayed him,

Brophy could only find one word: brutality. When Lewis feels betrayed, Brophy said, "he strikes with all the venom of which he is capable." Gardner Jackson sensed the same streak of violence in Lewis's character. When Jackson returned to Washington from Denver, where he had been sent by Lewis in 1937 to attend a convention called to unite the Southern Tenant Farmers Union and the CIO's United Association of Cannery and Packing Workers, he complained to his boss about the tactics of Donald Henderson, the leader of the cannery workers. "There is only one way to handle that, Gardner." Lewis responded. "You ought to have chosen your opportunity, found Don Henderson alone, and slugged him until he never forgot it. That was the only recourse you had." Subsequent relations with Lewis and his associates convinced Jackson that Lewis "has actually relied a considerable number of times on the use of direct violence in achieving his end." Asked by an interviewer if Lewis had a capacity for ruthlessness, Lee Pressman replied: "Oh, completely so. He was the kind of guy would commit murder."[30]

In one way, and an important one, Lewis differed from the political boss. If he preferred to exert power behind the scenes and perhaps use violence to achieve his ends, Lewis nevertheless desired to be esteemed publicly as a man of influence. Not satisfied with the knowledge that he exerted power, his inordinate pride commanded him to seek public manifestations of his potency. Thus none who saw or read a Lewis letter could mistake the fact that here was a puissant individual. The signature proved it—carefully practiced large, flowing letters that flooded the page and shrank every other word or phrase in the document. President Roosevelt, especially, experienced Lewis's thirst for power. To compete with the president of the United States, whose stationery bore the simple imprint at the top of the page, "Office of the President," and the presidential seal, Lewis would reply by letter on unofficial UMW stationery that also featured at the top the imprint, "Office of the President"; and just below it and barely visible to the human eye was the union seal.

The combination of secrecy, brutality, and egotism that characterized Lewis's behavior as union leader led some to compare him not to Roosevelt but instead to Mussolini, an equally effective poseur. Brophy, for example, settled on Mussolini as most comparable to Lewis. Both men, observed Brophy, acted the showman, strutted about, and exuded arrogance. Brophy, however, had to admit that in one essential respect Lewis differed from the Italian dictator. "Lewis," Brophy observed, "would never let himself get into the situation where he was knocked off, and hung up by the heels. He'd compromise with power before that end."[31] But none of those who compared Lewis's personality traits to the Italian dictator ever suggested that the American labor leader shared fascist beliefs.

A strange creature, a most peculiar man, this man Lewis, who could simultaneously impress different acquaintances as either a brutal individual or as the soul of southern courtesy.

*   *   *

If Lewis's public behavior serves more to cloak his character than reveal it, perhaps the values he espoused during the late 1930s offer glimpses into his personality. Here, too, however, the student of Lewis meets insuperable problems. Almost all Lewis's major addresses and publications were written by Jett Lauck. Only rarely during sessions of the CIO and UMW executive boards or the mine workers' conventions did Lewis voice thoughts that expressed his values rather than tactics. If one relies on Lewis's statements before congressional committees, on the air, and on the speaker's platform (the same could be said of newspaper, magazine, and opinion journal contributions) to fathom the labor leader's beliefs, one may, in fact, be learning more about the ideology of Jett Lauck, Lee Pressman, Ralph Hetzel, or even K. C. Adams.

At times Lewis sounded radical, at other times conservative, and sometimes downright reactionary. Before union groups he sounded the tocsin of militancy; the more militant the union he addressed, the more radical Lewis seemed. Before congressional committees and audiences of prominent individuals, he extolled organized labor as the primary bulwark against communism and the defender of Americanism. To businessmen he promised to behave as one practical entrepreneur to another.

No single issue caused Lewis more problems in the late 1930s than his association with Communists. Two of his closest and most trusted advisers in the CIO were one-time party members or sympathizers: Len DeCaux and Lee Pressman. Some of the most prominent new generation of labor leaders who emerged within the CIO—Joe Curran, of the merchant seamen; "Red Mike" Quill, of the transit workers; Harry Bridges, of the West Coast longshoremen; James Matles and Julius Emspak, of the electrical workers; and Wyndham Mortimer, of the auto workers, to name just a few—were linked either to communism generally or the party specifically. To such staunch A. F. of L. types as John Frey and Matthew Woll, to southern Democratic and Republican congressmen, to most of the nation's press, and to many antiunion businessmen, the CIO, in its halcyon days, seemed bolshevism's American vanguard, and John L. Lewis seemed the head of a subversive Trojan Horse.[32] Yet this was the same labor leader who had routed all varieties of "Reds" from the UMW during the 1920s and exceeded any other trade unionist in his red-baiting. He was the same man to whom Walter Chrysler allegedly said, "Mr. Lewis, I do not worry about dealing with you, but it is the Communists in these unions that worry me a great deal."[33]

What, indeed, was Lewis's relationship to Communism in the late 1930s? Without doubt, he had no sympathy with or even understanding of communism's principles and objectives. Determined by late 1936 to build a new national labor center, one that would surpass the A. F. of L., he needed all the help he could find. And he found no more dedicated and selfless union organizers than the young Communists who rallied to the CIO cause. Here were men and women who risked bodily injury and even death; who worked anywhere, anytime; and who asked little material recompense to organize the unorganized. For a labor movement such as the CIO, lacking its own sound financial base, unpaid or poorly paid organizers were a great boon. And as Lewis allegedly remarked to David Dubinsky: "Who gets the bird, the hunter or the dog?"[34]

Asked to analyze Lewis's relationship to communism, Lee Pressman responded this way. Lewis never contemplated for a moment that Communists or socialists or any other group—Catholics included—could try to develop independent influence or strength in the CIO. Never could Lewis, Pressman asserted, have developed Phil Murray's subsequent fear about Communist party influence in the CIO. "To contemplate him [Lewis] being aware of somebody else's power or influence over the organization that he had given birth to—that's something you just couldn't contemplate. I mean, it would be like talking to him about the atmosphere on Mars."[35]

Yet many trade union Communists considered Lewis their advocate in the internecine struggles between Left and Right that roiled many new CIO unions, especially the UAW. So well did Lewis disguise his own goals that John Frey castigated Lewis publicly for abetting Communist penetration in the United States, trade union Communists looked to him as their protector, and influential businessmen such as Walter Chrysler valued him as a bulwark against bolshevism.

Appearing to be all things to all people, did Lewis have any consistent or central values? Was there a solid, unshakable core to the man, or was he simply an ideological chameleon who discarded principles as easily as the lizard changed colors?

Despite his own adamant refusal to be drawn out during interviews and discussions on matters of philosophy, a consistent core of beliefs motivated Lewis's public behavior.[36] He believed that cycles governed history, that the present invariably repeated the past, that bad times inevitably followed boom times, and, hence, that men must seize the main chance during prosperity and act defensively during adversity. But his belief in cyclical history was more intuitive than intellectual, more acted out in practice than expressed in words or theory.[37]

The same might be said of his relationship to religion. Raised by a Mormon mother and a nonbelieving or nonpracticing father, Lewis, as an adult, evinced no interest whatsoever in formal religion. To the best knowledge of his closest associates in the labor movement, he attended no church, never referred to religion openly, and, if he subscribed to Christianity at all, he did so as part of a broader civic religion subsumed under the rubric *Americanism*. Like politics, he treated religious controversies opportunistically. When Gardner Jackson went to work for the CIO, the patrician reformer was an active supporter of the Spanish Loyalists in their struggle against Franco and the rebels. Lewis immediately asked Jackson to abandon all links to the Spanish Republicans because so many of the second-line CIO leaders, as well as the rank and file, were Catholic and possibly sympathetic to Franco.[38]

The rubric *Americanism* characterized Lewis's fondest beliefs. It was a word he had used frequently in *The Miner's Fight for American Standards* and continued to use repeatedly during the 1930s. To Lewis, Americanism had many connotations: It meant a society in which prosperity and well-being were widely diffused. And prosperity, in turn, was founded on technological innovations and high wages. Technological innovation—that is, the introduction of new and superior methods of production—increased per capita industrial productivity and, hence, provided the source of wage increases. Unless wages rose in direct proportion to increases in productivity, consumers would be unable to purchase the products of American industry, and depression would follow as logically as day passes into night. Experience, moreover, had taught Lewis that employers refused to raise wages voluntarily. Selfish (as Lewis thought most people in fact were) businessmen preferred to pocket the entire value of increased labor productivity. Only the power of organization, the trade union, enabled workers to reap the material rewards of technological innovation, to win for themselves the higher wages that kept the American economy prosperous. When Louis Adamic asked Lewis if he did not sometimes worry about excessive labor power, the CIO leader replied, "Recently a businessman of my acquaintance asked me a similar question. . . . I answered him, 'No one can guarantee the future; but I am certain that if labor does develop great power it cannot possibly make a worse mess of things than did big business in the last two decades, to go back no further in our history'." Linked to his belief in the necessity of trade union power to maintain economic prosperity, was Lewis's distrust of a conspiratorial financial elite that he associated with Wall Street and the House of Morgan. Two sources contributed to his antipathy to eastern bankers and monopoly capitalists. One was the geographical and cultural environment of the first three decades of his life—Iowa, Illinois, and the Mountain West, a region in which hostility to Wall Street flourished along with corn, wheat, pork, beef, coal, and precious metals. The other was the advice of his friend and longtime economic consultant Jett Lauck, an intellectual critic of the House of Morgan and unregulated oligopolistic enterprises.[39]

Paradoxically, Lewis's distrust of Wall Street and finance capitalism scarcely influenced his more general attitude toward businessmen and capitalism as a system. Some of his best friends were businessmen, and capitalism was for Lewis the source of the American success story. As Brophy later recalled, Lewis never sought a fundamental change in the national economy; instead, he appeared perfectly satisfied to work with the business community. More specifically, Brophy suggested, "I think Lewis accepts the basic relationships set up by the business community. I think he accepts completely their dominance."[40]

Businessmen saw the same characteristics in Lewis. Alfred Staehle, publisher of *Coal Age*, the industry trade journal, from 1942 to 1955, perceived no difference whatever between Lewis's and the operator's position on mechanization in the mines; they simply quarreled about the proper division of the proceeds of technological improvement. Staehle, moreover, had never met anybody "with a more penetrating and precise knowledge of what makes industry work, what produces profits than that possessed by John Lewis."[41]

Why not? Hadn't Lewis been a successful bank president in Indianapolis during the 1920s and kept his bank liquid even during the Great Depression? Had he not been a business associate of one of the nation's great capitalists and bankers, Jacob Harriman? And would he not in the future once again control a bank, this time a larger one in the nation's capital—the National Bank of Washington—and make it an integral part of the post-World War II mine workers' union empire? And finally, was he not the man who, in the 1950s, formed a financial alliance with another business tycoon, Cyrus Eaton, aimed at centralizing control of coal mines, power companies, and coal-carrying railroads? To businessmen even more than to fellow labor leaders, Lewis personified integrity. "I could trust John L. Lewis," said Cyrus Ching, "and if he ever gave his word on anything, you could rest assured that's the way it was going to be. John L. Lewis is a man of very high integrity."[42]

At a time when Lewis appeared to the public most radical and dangerous to the established order, the year 1937, Louis Adamic grasped, as few others have, the labor leader's essence: possessive individualism. Lewis, thought Adamic, believed that every individual desired to improve himself, that selfishness—the intensive human desire for material possessions, social mobility, and status—was the root of human progress as well as misery. "Though an exceptional man," Adamic wrote in 1937,

> Lewis is also a deeply ordinary one . . . he has a chauffeur in whipcords to drive him about in the twelve-cylinder automobile his union bought for him; which is what every ordinary American would like to have . . . there ride in that shiny car . . . vicariously—the four hundred thousand United Mine Workers of America, most of them ordinary men . . . full of the instinct and impulse to improve themselves, to get on, to acquire the material symbols of well-being, power, and progress that are the chief contemporary elements of the American "Dream." That fine machine and the snappy cap on the chauffeur's head are ordinary symbols, generally craved in America, though rarely attained, and which, incidentally are apt to be an important source of Lewis's power in this country.[43]

Occasionally Lewis himself openly revealed his possessive individualism and status striving before union audiences. The same man who excoriated the financial and corporate dictators of Wall Street told delegates at the 1938 UMW convention that their union "stands for the proposition that the heads of families shall have a sufficient income to educate [their children who] . . . go forth when given that opportunity. . . . They become scientists, great clergymen in the church, great lawyers, great statesmen. . . . Many of our former members are successful in great business enterprises." No dream or visions of contented craftsmen or self-respecting laborers—not even a great labor leader in the bargain. In 1938, after almost ten years of depression—in fact in year one of the new Roosevelt depression—Lewis still beguiled coal miners with the gospel of individual success. Two years later, at his union's 1940 convention, Lewis stated his belief in possessive individualism more bluntly. "You know," he said, "after all there are two great material tasks in life that affect the individual and affect great bodies of men. The first is to achieve or acquire something of value or something that is desirable, and then the second task is to prevent some scoundrel from taking it away from you."[44]

One may well wonder, given Lewis's belief in individualism, the gospel of success, and status striving, why he was content to act in the role of labor leader? A good question. Could he not have followed in the footsteps of Tom Moses, who rose from an Illinois coal mine to one of the highest executive positions in United States Steel? Or Tom Lewis, John Mitchell, and John White, his predecessors in the UMW presidency, all of whom became executives for employers' associations? A position in big business might have offered Lewis greater material remuneration than a union presidency (though his UMW salary and perquisites were not to be sneered at) and certainly conferred heightened status. But union leadership offered Lewis one compensation business could not provide: overt power and the public esteem that flowed from it. Not to the manor born, nor himself the creator of a business empire, Lewis could never be a Morgan, Harriman, Ford, Rockefeller, or Carnegie. Like other labor leaders who deserted the union for corporate careers, Lewis would likely have disappeared from public view had he chosen to be lured by the salary and status of an executive position. Lewis's colossal ego, however, required more; it demanded attention, esteem, and, most of all, social, economic, and political power.

In the labor movement, Lewis could have his cake and eat it. The UMW provided him a substantial salary, unlimited expenses, and assorted fringe benefits; it also enabled him to become a financier through the National Bank of Washington and through the Union's subsequent role as trustee for its members' pension and welfare funds; and it brought him into contact and business relationships with such latter-day lordly entrepreneurs as Cyrus Eaton. As a labor leader—moreover, one who commanded a large and militant union situated in a strategic industry—he could command public attention whenever he chose, exert economic and political power, and directly challenge presidents of the United States.

There he was, this strange creature, this most peculiar man, this man Lewis. No matter how deeply his public behavior is probed, Lewis remains an enigma wrapped in a riddle cloaked in mystery. Perhaps only the creative insight of a novelist can delineate the man's character. The British novelist Richard Hughes' comments may also apply to John L. Lewis. Those who criticize Lewis for indecision, opportunism, and lack of scruples fail, in Hughes' words, "to grasp that *what* you do often matters so very much less than *when*." Hughes' description of the perfect politician also fits Lewis's role as labor leader. "The 'Idealist Statesman's' essential gift is a righteous right hand blissfully unaware what his crooked subliminal left is up to. In short, political life is as full of unconscious meanings and motivations as poetry."[45]

*   *   *

Lewis's private life appears still more unfathomable. He guarded his and his family's privacy zealously. Journalists and associates in the labor movement (he had no friends among trade unionists) were scarcely if ever invited to the Lewis home either in Springfield, Illinois, where the family lived from 1917 to 1933, or Washington, D.C., where they rented an apartment at the Wardman Park Hotel in 1933-1934, or in Alexandria, Virginia, where they first rented a notable old American colonial home and later purchased one of the Washington suburb's more famous colonial domiciles. Lewis also seldom referred to his family life, past or present, in conversations and interviews with inquisitive reporters or prospective biographers, which is why. so many of the sketches and biographies of the labor leader contain inaccurate personal data or, more often, neglect Lewis's private life.

Still, from scraps of information that appear in the unlikeliest places, observations by prominent individuals who knew Lewis, and inference, certain conclusions may be drawn about the character of the Lewis family and its pater familias. Victorian respectability characterized the Lewis family. Nary a hint of social deviancy touched any member of the Lewis clan, an extended family that included sons, daughters, brothers, sisters, nephews, nieces, and in-laws. Husbands and wives remained outwardly loyal and faithful to each other; children were obedient to their parents; and all family members were temperate in their private behavior. Neither John L.; Myrta; the daughter, Kathryn; nor the son, John Jr., drank. At the Lewis's Sunday afternoon parties for Washington influentials, presided over by Myrta and Kathryn, tea, not liquor, was the beverage served. Welsh temperance and Iowa Presbyterianism, if not formal church membership, exemplified the Lewis family's value system. Sunday, moreover, held a special place for Lewis, as a sort of secular sabbath, the one day of the week on which he abandoned union affairs and devoted himself to family matters.[46]

Family loyalty seemed Lewis's dominant belief. As Phil Murray once told John Brophy, "John, when any member of the family wants something and another person gets in the way, well, it's just simply too bad." Lewis's intense family loyalty protected and rewarded materially all members of the extended clan. His younger brothers served as union functionaries either on the UMW or CIO payrolls, and his sister Hattie ran the UMW's district headquarters in Springfield, Illinois, where she could live in one of the three homes Lewis owned in that city and care for her elderly mother. Floyd Bell, his brother-in-law, whom Lewis had earlier made treasurer of the United Labor Bank and Trust Company of Indianapolis, in 1936 became comptroller of the CIO. And daughter Kathryn served as her father's private secretary and later sought office as secretary-treasurer of the CIO—a desire, as we will see in a subsequent chapter, that caused conflict between Lewis and Sidney Hillman, among others.[47]

Blood, not ability, motivated Lewis's selection of relatives for important official positions in the labor movement. When Lewis decided that the CIO should compete directly with the A. F. of L. for membership among building trades workers and established the Construction Workers' Organizing Committee, he selected Dennie Lewis as director. A Chicago labor reporter succinctly characterized Dennie Lewis's talent. "I mean," said Edwin A. Lahey, "Denny's [sic] a meathead. . . . I can't imagine Denny [sic] doing anything more responsible than going for coffee. He's a likeable guy, a saloon fighter, a crap-shooter, living on his brother's eminence."[48] Kathryn may have been more intelligent and talented—Lee Pressman remembers her as exceedingly intelligent and acute, though without philosophical insight—but as a female in an overwhelmingly male trade union universe she suffered irremediable handicaps. Yet Lewis selected his daughter as secretary-treasurer of UMW District 50, the union's catchall subdivision for all noncoal miners and, after Lewis's departure from CIO in 1942, his own organizational competitor to the CIO and A. F. of L. Though District 50 recruited few women and the male trade unionists associated with it believed that women belonged in the home, Kathryn remained, as long as her father desired it, the district's secretary-treasurer.[49]

The outward manifestations of closeness among members of the Lewis family and the intense loyalty that characterized their behavior hid a variety of tensions and peculiarities. Just as John L. Lewis tended to shrink all those he came into contact with officially, and indeed desired to do so, he undoubtedly had the same impact on family members. Myrta Lewis seemed to disappear physically and affectively in the presence of her husband. The Gardner Jacksons, who, during the 1930s, frequently invited John, Myrta, and Kathryn to dinner and developed a relationship with the Lewis family, found Myrta so retiring in her relationship to her husband that she scarcely spoke. Other individuals who dined with the Lewis's recall Myrta as a dim figure who seemed to vanish into obscure corners of the home. Small, sensitive, reserved, unexpressive, without John L.'s command of the English language—those were the words and phrases that Gardner Jackson used to describe Mrs. Lewis. At a loss otherwise to comprehend the relationship between the diminutive, diffident, and demure wife and the imposing, expressive, and flamboyant husband, the Jacksons inferred that Myrta was the most thoughtful member of the family and the influence that motivated John L. Lewis to read literature.[50] But even about that, one must wonder. Every sketch and biography of Lewis stresses Myrta's role as cultural tutor to her husband. Yet Lee Pressman, who worked closely with Lewis for five years and tried to talk with his boss about intellectual and philosophical matters, concluded that John L. Lewis had no interest in books, literature, history, or culture. Lewis's reading, according to Pressman, ended with the newspapers and news magazines.[51]

However that may be, other factors undoubtedly strained the relationship between Myrta and John. Myrta Lewis had extravagant social pretensions, a desire to be accorded status as an upper-class Virginian who traced her lineage back to the colonial era. But her husband's role as a public figure threatened Myrta's status striving. Virginia's colonial dames detested the plebeian, loathed public controversy, and feared the New Deal and the labor movement as subversive to their concept of the United States. John L. Lewis's image in the 1930s as radical labor leader, ardent New Dealer, and tribune for American plebeians caused the grand dames of Alexandria to remove the Lewis home from their annual tour of notable colonial residences—likely a blow to Myrta's self-esteem, as she had devoted considerable time, energy, and money to decorating it in exquisite and costly style.[52]

The relationship between parents and children was fraught with unconscious conflicts and personal tragedy. Kathryn, the eldest child after the death of her sister, Mary Margaret, worshipped her father, who, in turn, showered affection and attention on her. No acquaintance of the Lewis's ever remarked about the mother-daughter relationship or thought to compare Kathryn to Myrta. A bright, precocious girl, Kathryn excelled in the public primary and secondary schools of Springfield, Illinois. Upon her graduation from high school, she entered Bryn Mawr College in suburban Philadelphia, a labor leader's child in a universe of women to the American ruling class born. Unhappiness marked her college days, a time when her weight problem—she weighed upwards of 300 pounds—caused grave psychological problems. Another time she isolated herself for two years in a little cottage in Croton-on-Hudson, New York, and practiced Yoga. And finally, she fell under the spell of a mystic and guru named Nicholas Roerich, whose paintings decorated Kathryn's bedroom walls.[53]

John L. Lewis tried hard to compensate Kathryn for her physical handicap. He made her his secretary, later offered her an official position in the labor movement, pressured the Roosevelt administration to appoint Kathryn as one of the U. S. delegates to a Pan-American labor conference in Lima, Peru, and took her wherever he went. Father also protected daughter from photographers, whose lenses threatened to embarrass the obese young woman already so traumatized by her weight.[54]

Kathryn was the complete subject of her father—"Daddy's girl"—and she in turn sought to shield her protector from any criticism or snub. Kathryn, in fact, came to hate Franklin D. Roosevelt because the president did not obediently bend to her father's will; and, in her own way, Kathryn played a part in the political rupture in 1940 between John L. Lewis and Franklin D. Roosevelt. Intense and loyal as was the surface relationship between daughter and father, Kathryn was in a continuous state of rebellion against her dependency, as revealed by her adventures with psychoanalysis, Yoga, and Roerich.[55]

Father and son developed an entirely different, almost impersonal, relationship. For most of the 1930s, John L. Jr. seemed to be the missing member of the family. When the Lewis's dined out as a family, the son was absent. When the Lewis's entertained others at home, John Jr. was not to be seen. To be sure, he was away from home during most of the decade as a student at a private secondary boarding school and at Princeton University; still, friends and acquaintances of the Lewis family came to believe that Myrta wanted her son completely shielded from the influence and controversy that surrounded his father. Rather small physically—unlike his sister—shy, and retiring, John Jr. turned his life into a flight from his father's reputation, a desire inculcated in him by his mother. The son evinced no interest in his father's career or the labor movement. John Jr., like his maternal grandfather, chose a career in medicine upon graduation from Princeton in 1941. He matriculated at the Johns Hopkins Medical School and eventually specialized in psychiatry. Closeness to his mother compensated John Jr. for distance from his father. When John L. Lewis and Kathryn occupied themselves during the summer of 1936 on trade union business, Myrta and John Jr. traveled together in Europe. If later in life, at various stages of his own career, John Jr. remained dependent on his father for financial assistance, he remained personally and emotionally distant from his father's world. Indeed, after John L. Lewis's death in 1969, John L. Lewis Jr., the only surviving heir, actually sought to destroy all remaining traces of his father's career.[56] One can only wonder at what John Jr.'s life reveals about Myrta Lewis's deepest feelings toward the man to whom she was married for thirty-five years.

Social climbing occupied as significant a place in the Lewis's family life as outward respectability. Permanent residence in Alexandria afforded Myrta and John the chance to climb that they had lacked in Springfield. A part of their social ascent derived directly from John L. Lewis's role as labor leader. Regular invitations to White House dinners, receptions, and presidential inaugurations were the respect the nation's leading politician paid to the dominant figure in the labor movement. The same might be said of invitations to address the National Press Club and to appear as a featured guest at the annual Gridiron Club Dinner—the most prestigious event sponsored by newspaper publishers.

Much of the social climbing, however, was carefully and consciously planned. Kathryn was not sent to a snobbish women's college by chance; nor was John Jr. enrolled at Virginia's Woodbury Forest Academy* and Princeton University by accident. The Lewises, moreover, did not first rent and then purchase seventeenth- and eighteenth-century homes in Alexandria because of an abstract love for the architecture of the era. An original colonial-style home provided the ideal setting in which Myrta Lewis could display the expensive antiques that for more than ten years she had been purchasing in American and European shops. The choice of social acquaintances and dinner companions, a choice that excluded all trade unionists, was also not fortuitous. Thinking about his own relationship with

---

*G. William Donhuff, in his book *Who Rules America*, groups Woodbury Forest with the preparatory schools to which the American ruling class sends its sons.

Lewis—the fact that the Lewis family dined not with the Murrays, the Brophys, or the Hillmans, but with him and his wife—Gardner Jackson wondered about "John L.'s preoccupation with status, his environmental desires, his reach for lavish surroundings in his own personal life. . . . In retrospect, I think that very possibly John regarded me as in a strata of relationships that was different from his, and to which he aspired actually."[57] Lewis made clear to Jett Lauck his eagerness to gain entry among the elite of the nation's capital. For weeks and months, precisely at the moment he was forming the CIO, Lewis pestered Lauck with requests that the economic consultant use his influence to have the labor leader accepted as a member of the Cosmos Club, Washington's most prestigious private men's social institution.[58] And that was why the guest list to the Lewis home, whether for dinner or Sunday afternoon tea parties, featured senators, cabinet members, diplomats, Supreme Court justices, military leaders, and men and women of inherited wealth.

The Washington elite reciprocated. Lewis became the first labor leader invited regularly to dine at the Cosmos Club. Drew Pearson invited the trade unionist to attend his regular stag dinners, a meeting place for many influential Washingtonians. Kingman Brewster invited Lewis to spend a weekend at the former's Catoctin Lodge in Thurmont, Maryland. And Evelyn McLean Walsh, the dowager queen of Washington society, showered dinner and cocktail party invitations on the Lewises.[59]

By 1937 the social activities of the Lewis family made the newspapers. In a story that appeared on the society page of the New York *Telegram* in July 1937, Helen Worden reported that, "The phrase 'Rich as John L. Lewis' was born in the antique shops of Alexandria, Va., during the past year." According to Worden, Mrs. Lewis—who refused to shop on Sunday because, as she told a local antique dealer, "I'm an old-fashioned Presbyterian. I don't like to do anything on the Sabbath that can be done on a week-day"—claimed to be descended from old Virginia aristocracy. Everyone among Alexandria's best society, to which the Lewises belonged, according to the society columnist, spoke well of Myrta, a small, quiet, gray-haired woman of conservative inclinations. "It isn't as if the Lewises were strangers," remarked Mrs. R. R. Sayers, the wife of a local doctor and occupant of the Robert E. Lee house. "In coming to Alexandria they are really coming home. You know, her people, were Virginians. He's very well connected in Wales." Myrta had certainly arrived socially, one Washington society reporter even speculating in October 1937 that Mrs. Lewis might entertain the Duke and Duchess of Windsor in "her resplendent antique-filled home."[60]

The Lewis family lived as sumptuously as the wealthy individuals whose behavior they emulated. Mrs. Lewis shopped at the Shoreham Market, the capital's most exclusive butcher and grocery store. Helen Worden, the society columnist, asserted that Mrs. Lewis never questioned price. Bills and receipts for the antiques, furniture, tapestries, rugs, and paintings that Mrs. Lewis purchased on two continents proved as much. When Myrta attended church on Sunday mornings, as she did regularly, her husband's chauffeur-valet, James Lewis,* drove her to the Washington church she preferred. Not only did John L. Lewis, Sr., possess a twelve-cylinder Lincoln limousine upholstered in plush velvet and leather and fitted with the most expensive accessories (all paid for by the UMW); John Jr. had his own late-model sedan, garaged together with his father's vehicle at a monthly cost of forty dollars.[61]

No luxury was spared the Lewis family in the 1930s. Besides employing a chauffeur-valet, the Lewises hired a Negro cook-maid and a second maid. In 1937, it was estimated that the chauffeur earned $40 weekly; the cook-maid, $30 weekly; and the second maid, $80 monthly—for a total annual wage bill of approximately $4,600, or 37% of Lewis's annual UMW salary of $12,500 until it was doubled to $25,000 in 1938. (Even then, servant expenses consumed 18% of annual salary.)[62]

Lewis himself enjoyed the good life, not only the limousine and snappy chauffeur in whipcords that so impressed Louis Adamic, but also fine clothes, good cigars, superb food, and costly vacations. Lewis had his well-tailored suits, vests, and trousers custom-made by a clothier, A. J. Treat and Son, he had come to know when the UMW had its headquarters in Indianapolis. Silk shirts, ties, and even underwear he ordered, again custom-made, from A. Sulka and Company on Fifth Avenue in New York. As always, wherever he traveled, Lewis stayed in the best hotels and occupied their finest suites. He lunched regularly in the Carlton Hotel's plush dining room, and on days when he remained late at the office, he also dined there. Lewis regularly stopped at the florist shop next door to UMW headquarters to buy flowers for the women who served as union secretaries or the society hostesses who constantly entertained the Lewis family. The Gulf Coast of Florida and a group of islands just off the Tampa-Saint Petersburg peninsula became his favorite vacation haunt. There, first in a rented cottage and later one he purchased himself on Pine Island, Lewis took the sun, relaxed, and enjoyed his favorite sport: deep-sea fishing on a charter boat. For a time, he even considered buying his own small offshore island; and fragmentary evidence hints that in September 1942, Lewis considered taking an option on a piece of Florida property valued at $95,000.[63]

The labor leader, in the case of John L. Lewis, could indeed live the good life. His was a true American success story, striking proof that in the United States ambition combined with talent brought material rewards, individual success was more than myth, and possessive individualism had proved itself a valid system of belief.

Much as Lewis's life-style may have impressed coal miners and inflated their self-images, as Adamic suggested, it was nevertheless an existence that Lewis

---

*No relation to Lewis, and the loyal black servant that was absolutely de rigueur among the fashionable Virginia suburban set.

could scarcely defend before his union rank and file. When delegates at the 1936 coal miners' convention rebelled at a recommendation that they double their officers' salaries (in Lewis's case from $12,500 to $25,000), Lewis beat a hasty retreat, reporting to delegates on the convention's final day that he and his fellow officers would not accept salary increases. In what can only be termed the most vulgar rationalization, Lewis asserted that union officials sought office only to serve mankind, not to enrich themselves; "their hand," he swore, "is always giving, giving, what they have to give." Aside from the clothes that they wear and the food they eat, Lewis assured the delegates, the UMW's executive officers "are just as poor in this world's goods as any delegate to this convention." No man, asserted the UMW president, "holds a lesser quantity of this world's goods than the executive officers of your International organization."[64]

When Lewis returned home to Alexandria after the convention and sat down in his living room filled with Myrta's antiques, one may wonder how Lewis squared his private life with his public role as the captain of a mighty host of plebeians.

CHAPTER 14

Denouement,
June 1937-December 1939

For much of 1937 and 1938 John L. Lewis symbolized the emergence of organized labor as a significant force in economics, politics, and society. To most Americans and many Europeans the accomplishments of the CIO and Lewis seemed indistinguishable. It was Lewis, not auto and steel workers, who had stormed the ramparts of monopoly capitalism and battered into defeat General Motors, Chrysler, and United States Steel. It was Lewis, alone among labor leaders, who publicly criticized trade unionism's protector and the common man's idol: Franklin D. Roosevelt. It was Lewis who, in numerous network radio talks and even more frequent public speeches, asserted his prerogative to articulate the aspirations of 40 million American workers—hand and brain, blue- and white-collar—hitherto mute in national affairs. And it was Lewis, according to two early biographers, who dreamed of becoming the United States' first labor president. "He would like to be President of the United States," wrote Cecil Carnes in 1936, and "the prospect of leading perhaps 30,000,000 voters does not frighten him." Two years later, in 1938, C. L. Sulzberger glowingly portrayed the mine workers' chieftain as a prospective presidential candidate, a man Sidney Hillman imagined placing in the White House.[1]

Yet the same historical moment that brought Lewis acclaim and power also produced a series of setbacks to the man and his movement—reverses that revealed inherent flaws in the character and principles of John L. Lewis. By the end of 1938 Lewis's claim to articulate the aspirations of *all* the nation's workers had been vitiated by events scarcely visible to a public badly served by its news purveyors but quite noticeable to major party politicians and fellow labor leaders. Less than two years after its unprecedented triumphs over General Motors and United States Steel, CIO had lost momentum, members, and direction. Simultaneously, the A. F. of L. and its affiliates recovered from the initial shock of schism, regrouped, and surged ahead of CIO in membership, income, and political influence. Lewis, too, like the organization that he personified, lost momentum and floundered about in a search for new directions, a fruitless endeavor in which he never recaptured the esteem, labor power, and political influence that had been his from the summer of 1936 through the summer of 1937.

The single most substantial obstacle to John L. Lewis's claim to act as the unrivaled leader of the American labor movement was the split between the A. F. of L. and CIO. As long as the A. F. of L. survived, Lewis necessarily shared influence with his Federation counterpart, William Green. Not only did the persistence of the rift in the labor movement diminish Lewis's claim to power; it also limited organized labor's political influence, as politicians could and did play one faction off against the other. In theory, then, for Lewis to achieve maximum power required a united labor movement. Indeed, if Lewis actually had presidential ambitions, a most unlikely prospect as we will see below, a united labor movement would have been essential. Even if Lewis desired only labor, and not presidential, power, trade union unity remained the sine qua non for its achievement.

For almost five years, from 1937 through 1941, presidential emissaries, several A. F. of L. officials, and some CIO leaders maneuvered to reunite the labor movement. All their efforts, however, failed, and as their dreams dissolved, the quondam peacemakers most often blamed John L. Lewis. Lewis's role in the negotiations between CIO and A. F. of L. from 1937 through 1941 is well worth examining for what it reveals about Lewis's personality, the character of the American labor movement, and the nature of national politics.

In analyzing Lewis's behavior during the unity negotiations, certain factors must be borne in mind. First, Lewis had everything to gain and little to lose from an agreement that recognized the principle of industrial unionism for mass-production workers. Second, one must distinguish carefully between those in the A. F. of L. who served as peacemakers and those who wielded organizational power. One must also differentiate between the positions of the Federation's publicists and its power barons. If that is done, the A. F. of L. may well appear the more intransigent party in the negotiations, and Lewis's obduracy seems more understandable. Third, one must separate President Roosevelt's public pleas for labor unity from his essential political motives. A united labor movement might, in theory, strengthen working-class support for the New Deal, but Roosevelt could, in fact, exercise power more comfortably by playing one labor faction off against the other—a political reality noted by David Dubinsky, perhaps trade unionism's most ardent peacemaker.[2]

While the CIO and Lewis sought to avert needless conflict with the craft unions in the A. F. of L., the same could not be said for the Federation. At the February 1937 session of the A. F. of L. executive council, just after the UAW had defeated

General Motors, its members voted to issue A. F. of L. charters to workers in the suspended CIO trade unions and to cede discretionary authority to Federation officers carrying the battle against the industrial unionists.[3]

Perhaps to avoid the labor civil war threatened by the A. F. of L. executive council's action in February 1937, Lewis met secretly with William Green on April 16 and 18 in Washington to arrange, according to Jett Lauck's diary, a formula to reunite A. F. of L. and CIO. If Lauck's diary entry is correct, and there is no reason to doubt its accuracy, Bill Hutcheson of the carpenters' union, perhaps the most stubborn and influential of the Federation's barons, had thrown down an ultimatum to Lewis. Lauck failed to specify the ultimatum's substance, but one may properly guess at its contents. And a good guess would be that Hutcheson warned that unless Lewis returned the suspended unions to the A. F. of L. on the latter's terms, the Federation would declare open war on the CIO and its affiliates.[4]

Only a day after the second Green-Lewis conference on April 19, 1937, members of the executive council authorized Green to organize workers in textiles (a month earlier the CIO had established a Textile Workers' Organizing Committee, TWOC*), other mass-production industries, and most surprisingly, to issue a charter to the Progressive Mine Workers of America, the UMW's Illinois rival.[5] The A. F. of L., which less than a year earlier had suspended twelve affiliates for fostering dual unionism, now eagerly chartered its own dual unions, one of which was certain to enrage John L. Lewis.

Despite the enmity between Green and Lewis, bitterness that was personal as well as ideological and institutional, external factors impelled the CIO to launch new peace feelers in the fall of 1937. Having lost the momentum it achieved during the Flint sit-down strike and the subsequent settlement with United States Steel, the CIO could not afford to fight enemies inside the labor movement. Shorn of his political influence with Roosevelt, Lewis desired to confront the president with a united labor movement. Finally, prominent individuals inside the CIO, including David Dubinsky, Max Zaritsky, Charles P. Howard, and, perhaps, Sidney Hillman, found themselves uncomfortable tenants in labor's divided house. To keep such vital associates content Lewis initiated peace negotiations with the A. F. of L., however unpromising the actual prospects for achieving labor unity.

Not surprisingly, then, in the second week of October 1937, as the A. F. of L. convened in Denver and CIO delegates conferred in Atlantic City, unity negotiations resumed. On October 12 Harvey Fremming wired A. F. of L. Secretary Frank Morrison suggesting that each union federation select a committee of 100 to meet jointly in order to discuss labor unity. Fremming's wire also stipulated that the A. F. of L. must accept the principle of industrial unionism in the mass-production industries, maritime trades, public utilities, service, and basic fabricating industries.[6]

Both the size of the proposed conference and the CIO's insistence on prior

*See p. 315.

commitments disturbed A. F. of L. leaders, as Lewis undoubtedly assumed would happen. Although the CIO proposals that the negotiating committee consist of 200 members and that the A. F. of L. concede the primary issue in dispute prior to meeting seemed absurd, it nevertheless reflected Lewis's perception of power realities in the labor movement. Lewis knew such A. F. of L. leaders as Dan Tobin, Bill Hutcheson, Arthur Wharton, and G. M. Bugniazet too well to believe that they would ever voluntarily offer concessions to CIO or sanction unrestricted industrial unionism. Only if those men and their associates served as a minority of a larger A. F. of L. delegation more representative of the rank and file's desire for unity would Lewis and the CIO have a chance to enter a reunited labor movement without sacrificing principle. Frankly, Lewis expected little from negotiations; yet he wanted to ensure that Green and the A. F. of L. bore the responsibility for sabotaging labor unity.[7]

Thus, after a series of snide and sarcastic telegrams among Fremming, Morrison, and Murray between October 13 and 17, the CIO and A. F. of L. agreed to meet jointly at the Willard Hotel in Washington on October 25. The Federation chose to send its three-man peace committee as originally appointed by the executive council in the summer of 1936, and the CIO selected a ten-man negotiating committee that included such prominent industrial unionists as Hillman, Murray, Dubinsky, Howard, Joseph Curran and Mike Quill but excluded John L. Lewis, a most significant omission.[8]

Why the CIO and A. F. of L. delegations elected to confer on October 25 when their leaders saw no room for compromise and less prospect for unity seems inexplicable. On October 18, only a day after the two groups agreed to meet, Lewis confided to Jett Lauck during a phone conversation that no hope then existed for peace with the A. F. of L. and that independence would better assure the CIO's size and prestige.[11] The A. F. of L. hierarchy harbored as little enthusiasm about the conference's prospects. Even had Green and the three-man A. F. of L. committee been eager to compromise, the most powerful craft union leaders in the Federation—Hutcheson, of the carpenters; Tobin, of the teamsters; Wharton, of the machinists; and even William D. Mahon, of the transit workers—stressed that the Federation's negotiating committee lacked the authority to arrange a settlement with the CIO delegation and that only the full executive council could make peace. Hutcheson even threatened to withdraw the carpenters from the A. F. of L. if the CIO were invited back on terms he deemed unacceptable. Green, of course, assured his testy labor barons that their interests would not be sacrificed.[9]

Despite the dim prospects for peace, the negotiations opened as scheduled. Discussion during the first day, October 25, degenerated into a series of pointless, protracted, and heated arguments about procedures. Suddenly, the next day, Philip Murray presented a breathtaking proposal for unity. It called for the A. F. of L. to ''declare as one of its basic policies that the organization of the workers in the mass production, marine, public utilities, service and basic fabricating industries be effectuated only on an industrial basis.'' Murray also demanded that the

Federation create a department known as the Committee for Industrial Organization to which all national, international, and local industrial unions now affiliated with the CIO would be admitted. The new department would be entirely autonomous, operate under its own constitution, designate its own officers, and exercise "complete and sole jurisdiction" over the organization of workers in industries and their members. Finally, Murray proposed that the CIO and A. F. of L. call a joint national convention to be attended by all their current affiliates to sanction the CIO proposal and arrange for its implementation.[10]

Murray's comprehensive proposal left the A. F. of L. negotiators speechless. Its audacity, the suggestion that the Federation simply violate the principles that had precipitated the original schism, apparently stunned them. In a statement issued to the press on October 26, the A. F. of L. declined to discuss the substance of the CIO offer, which it characterized as too broad and vague for comment.[11]

But the A. F. of L. could not cavalierly reject Murray's proposal, for that would serve Lewis's objectives and fix responsibility for the collapse of negotiations on the Federation's committee. So, on the morning of October 27, the A. F. of L. presented its counterproposal, an offer equally unacceptable to the CIO committee. The Federation committee proposed that the nine international unions originally chartered by the A. F. of L. reaffiliate, leaving the disposition of the other twenty-three unions associated with the CIO to be settled on the basis of the organizing policies adopted by the 1934 and 1935 conventions. As Phil Murray promptly observed, the Federation proposal reaffirmed the policies that had caused the initial split in the labor movement, rejected the principle of unrestricted industrial unionism for the mass-production industries, and suggested that the A. F. of L. remained determined to stifle organization of the unorganized.[12]

Despite the width of the chasm that separated the two labor centers, peacemakers sought to build bridges. Neither party wanted to appear responsible for breaking off negotiations, and each sought to blame the other for failure. Lewis and his principal advisers, Lee Pressman, Len DeCaux, and Jett Lauck, maneuvered to portray the A. F. of L. as unyielding and regressive, and its leader, Green, as ridiculous. Lauck, for example, advised Lewis to hold fast to the CIO's original unity proposal, and he assured his boss that the CIO leader would appear to the nonlabor public and to workers as a reasonable man who wanted unity "but was thwarted by a group of self-seeking, short-sighted A. F. of L. job holders." Stand fast, Pressman, DeCaux, and Lauck assured Lewis, for you are "sitting pretty," and the A. F. of L. will consequently "be forced to make concessions to industrial unionism."[13]

Lewis's advisers proved correct. The A. F. of L. did indeed make concessions to industrial unionism. During a series of further peace conferences from November 4 through November 10, the A. F. of L. committee made two crucial concessions: (1) to recognize industrial unionism in certain industries then being organized by the CIO and (2) to convene a special A. F. of L. convention in the event of a peace agreement.

Having achieved that much, Lewis sought more. As the Labor Department mediator John Steelman reported to Frances Perkins, Lewis stated confidentially that the CIO would absolutely reject any agreement that did not amend the constitution of the A. F. of L. to deny its executive council the right to suspend unions or interfere with jurisdictions between conventions. Lewis, Steelman reported, also wanted more specific commitments concerning the scope of industrial unionism—a promise, one might assume, that charters for auto and steel workers, for example, would not exclude machinists and building tradesmen employed in the two industries.[14]

After a delay of almost three weeks, the peace conference resumed on November 29 and met intermittently and without success until mid-December. Numerous historians, in trying to explain the failure of the negotiators to achieve labor unity, either suggest that answers are impossible owing to the absence of conference records or more commonly blame Lewis and his megalomania for the impasse. A typewritten copy from penciled notes of the discussion between the A. F. of L. and CIO committees on November 29 found in the John Brophy Papers provides some of the missing answers and absolves Lewis of sole responsibility for the collapse of negotiations.

According to Brophy's notes, two men dominated the negotiations: Murray for the CIO and George Harrison for the A. F. of L. The discussions between Murray and Harrison revealed that on November 29, 1937, after more than a month of negotiations, the A. F. of L. still declined to specify which industries organized by unions not originally in the Federation were susceptible to industrial unionism or to put such an agreement in writing. In response to a question by Murray, Harrison refused to offer a commitment regarding industrial unionism until all matters in dispute were first settled. Indeed, Harrison agreed only to the readmission of the nine unions originally suspended.[15] Harrison, in fact, suggested that the auto workers, rubber workers, and steelworkers could not be readmitted to the A. F. of L. until the jurisdictional claims of carpenters, machinists, and teamsters were satisfied. Disband the CIO, Harrison told Murray, and the remaining differences can be solved. Define the rights and extent of industrial unions, challenged Murray, and then we can consider the CIO's place inside the Federation. "Do you agree to abandon the CIO?" responded Harrison. Let's have a written understanding, demanded Murray. Whereupon Harrison agreed that twelve unions could return to the A. F. of L., changing his mind to include autos, steel, and rubber, yet still refusing to put such an understanding in writing or to waive the rights of machinists, carpenters, and teamsters in those three industries. As Murray exasperatedly reminded the A. F. of L. negotiator, after a month of discussion, the committees had made no progress.[16]

Further discussions continued the first week in December in Murray's absence between the two committees, and the labor leaders in attendance allegedly produced a satisfactory peace settlement. No incontrovertible evidence, however, exists to indicate that the Harrison committee went beyond its offer of November

29, terms scarcely acceptable to the CIO. Only the self-serving statements of the Harrison committee in reports and documents to the full A. F. of L. executive council and the comments of such needle trades unionists as David Dubinsky and Max Zaritsky, whose desire for labor unity blinded them to power realities, offer supporting evidence. According to that evidence, which takes several forms and has received numerous embellishments, Murray himself eventually accepted the peace accord but refused to commit the CIO until he spoke to his principals, meaning John L. Lewis. Then, just as unity seemed to bless the labor movement, the megalomaniacal Lewis sabotaged the peace agreement. In Dubinsky's own dramatic version, as told during an interview in September 1972, Murray took the proposed unity agreement to his chief's hotel room. Picking up the piece of paper with the peace terms on it, Lewis glanced quickly at its contents, sauntered toward the window, tore the paper into little pieces, and tossed the shreds to the street below. There, said Lewis, you have my answer.[17]

What really happened? The answer, to be sure, is scarcely as dramatic as Dubinsky's version of events. Throughout the protracted peace negotiations, the A. F. of L. committee refused to put in writing the precise rights or extent of industrial unionism, and it never retreated from its demand that the CIO disband prior to a final peace settlement. These were terms that most CIO unions could not accept, especially the twenty-three affiliates that had not originally been A. F. of L. members. This was made clear at a CIO policy conference held at UMW headquarters on December 21, 1937, attended by all thirty-two affiliates. Lewis informed the assembled delegates that peace negotiations had reached an impasse, that the A. F. of L. refused to negotiate except on its own terms, and that he would recommend termination of negotiations until such date as the Federation became more reasonable. After a prolonged and open discussion, during which delegates from the clothing trades unions offered several alternative peace formulas, the conference unanimously sanctioned Lewis's policy and adopted his motion to terminate peace negotiations.[18]

A few blind advocates of labor unity within the CIO, such as Dubinsky, might also misconstrue Lewis's behavior and leak items to the press suggesting that the CIO leader had rendered labor peace impossible. But most CIO members, especially those closest to Lewis, shared Adolph Germer's belief that "I am . . . firmly of the opinion that the controlling men on the A. F. of L. Executive Council do not want to see the mass production workers organize and that they do not want peace between the C.I.O. and the A. F. of L." How, asked Germer in May 1938, could CIO make peace with a labor organization (A. F. of L.) that chartered the Progressive Mine Workers of America as a direct assault on the UMW, criticized CIO steelworkers during the 1937 Little Steel Strike, charged the CIO with fostering communism, and allied with the Chamber of Commerce in an attempt to amend the Wagner Labor Relations Act?[19]

*   *   *

The year 1938, then, was a year for war, not peace, in the labor movement. As Germer had suggested, the A. F. of L. attacked the CIO directly on a broad front. State and city centrals, under executive council orders, purged all CIO affiliates and sympathizers. A. F. of L. unions recruited new members as aggressively as the CIO, disregarded hallowed craft and jurisdictional lines, and competed in the same industries as CIO affiliates. Federation officials, most notably John Frey, appeared regularly before congressional committees, especially the Dies committee (House Committee on Un-American Activities) to allege Communist influence in CIO and to seek amendments to the Wagner Act that would restrict mass-production unionism. The A. F. of L., moreover, tended to oppose candidates for public office endorsed by the CIO—a policy that undercut the New Deal and the liberal left wing of the Democratic party.

Lewis readily accepted the A. F. of L.'s challenge. By the fall of 1938 the CIO could no longer continue in an anomalous institutional position. Its nine original affiliates and three later ones having been expelled from the A. F. of L. and its twenty other international unions never having been a part of the Federation, the CIO could no longer claim to exist as a legitimate A. F. of L. committee that had been unconstitutionally ejected. By November 1938, the CIO functioned as an autonomous, independent, effective national labor center in all but name. It was time to end the charade, call a constitutional convention, and announce to the nation the formation of a permanent new trade union federation.

Lewis thus instructed all CIO affiliates to select delegates to attend a constitutional convention in Pittsburgh on November 15. Because such a convention would doom labor unity, David Dubinsky, refused to allow his union, the ILGWU, to attend the Pittsburgh convention. Dubinsky's action, not unexpected by Lewis, prompted the CIO leader to issue a statement so strained in its literary allusions and marked by mixed metaphors that it would have embarrassed any other public figure. "Mr. Dubinsky, whom I highly esteem," remarked Lewis, "is apparently giving an imitation of Eliza crossing the ice. Like Lot's wife he is looking backward. He must decide for himself whether he is fish, fowl, or good red herring."[20]

In Dubinsky's absence, newspaper reports to the contrary notwithstanding (and Dubinsky and his then adviser, ex-Communist Jay Lovestone, may have been the source of those stories), harmony and enthusiasm prevailed among the CIO delegates present in Pittsburgh. Press reports, especially by Louis Stark in the *New York Times*, that hinted at dissatisfaction and incipient rebellion by so-called Communist delegates mistook a fundamental difference between how "old" and "new" unionists operated their unions for ideological conflict. Hillman, Murray, and Lewis, who dominated the Pittsburgh convention, were accustomed to administering their own unions—the UMW and the ACWA—with an iron hand; conventions were run under the tightest discipline, and union officials customarily presented delegates with faits accomplis. Only rarely did delegate votes or actions determine or alter union policy. Hillman, Murray, and Lewis, undoubtedly without giving the matter a second thought, intended to run the CIO convention as they would their own unions. Asked to vote on constitutional clauses that they had scarcely seen, delegates representing the newer unions—many of whom were indeed red and rebellious, where convention procedures were looser and debate freer—balked. Such minor convention splits—and they were minor—appeared in the press greatly magnified as a "red revolt." In fact, the alleged "red" delegates, led by Harry Bridges, Joe Curran, and Mike Quill, met privately with Lewis to pledge their loyalty and publicly tumbled over themselves to prove the CIO's solidarity. "What struck me most forcibly at Pittsburgh," reported Robert Bendiner in the *Nation,* "was not a trend toward factionalism but rather the advance notice served by John L. Lewis . . . that no such tendency would be tolerated—and the complete humility with which the left-wing . . . accepted the rap on the knuckles. . . . Not division but excessive unanimity was the order of the day." Bruce Bliven earlier reported similarly in the *New Republic*. The CIO delegates, wrote Bliven, "applaud and whistle and cheer like freshmen at a Big Game rally. . . . When the nomination of John L. Lewis for president. . . came . . . the Grotto's wall could barely contain the thunder. And who could blame them?"[21]

As expected, delegates unanimously elected Lewis as CIO's first president (still, it might be noted, an unsalaried position) and Philip Murray and Sidney Hillman as vice-presidents. CIO's "big three" had been confirmed in their respective leadership roles. The only surprise, if it could be called that, saw young James Carey, of the United Electrical Workers, elected as secretary-treasurer—the one salaried executive position. Many stories, most without foundation, spread concerning Carey's election, and John Brophy, the man passed over for the slot, may be the source of those tales. In his Columbia oral history interview and in the autobiography extracted from it, Brophy alleged that Lewis intended to make his daughter Kathryn CIO secretary but was discouraged by objections from Murray and Hillman.[22] Lewis certainly felt no embarrassment in practicing nepotism. But logic suggests that he was unlikely to have considered Kathryn a candidate for office in the CIO. First, throughout his association with the CIO, Lewis conducted all his official business from an office at UMW headquarters and devoted more attention to the affairs of the mine workers than to those of the CIO. Hence, Kathryn could serve him better as a UMW official, as the president's personal secretary. Second, Lewis might reasonably expect, given his own cultural values, that a convention of predominantly male delegates would rebel at electing a woman to high union office, even their esteemed leader's daughter and hand-picked choice. Third, too many individuals from the UMW and Lewis's own personal circle already held influential positions in the CIO. More diversity was needed.

Carey's selection was natural and logical. He represented the "new unionists," coming from the second largest union outside the original CIO nine. He was young, personable, a good man to meet the press and circulate on the Washington cocktail party circuit, but not hardworking or capable enough to threaten Lewis. For some reason, moreover, Kathryn liked him, and Lewis was always susceptible to his daughter's influence. Finally, among the leading "new unionists," Carey was the one clearly not linked to the Left or communism. Much as Lewis may have collaborated with Communists from 1936 through June 22, 1941, and much as he may have been their labor idol, he remained a rigid anti-Communist, a man unlikely to allow a Communist to hold high elected office in the CIO or UMW.

The creation of the CIO as an independent national labor center with its own constitution, bylaws, and *elected* officers should have logically ended for a time talk and action aimed at labor unity, as Dubinsky believed it would. Yet the CIO convention, paradoxically, served to reinvigorate unity moves. Why?

Peace negotiations resumed between the CIO and A. F. of L. in March 1939. They had begun informally in December 1938 through the initiative of Secretary of Labor Frances Perkins, whose agent, Father Francis J. Haas, contacted Hillman, Murray, and George Harrison (chairman of the Federation's peace committee). Fragmentary evidence suggests that as early as July 1938, Lewis and Roosevelt had discussed labor unity. Although the Perkins-Father Haas effort failed, the president persisted in raising the issue of labor unity with Lewis. When A. F. of L.-CIO negotiations finally resumed, as they did early in March 1939, they revived largely in response to President Roosevelt's public demand for labor peace, a request labor leaders could not refuse.[23]

Roosevelt's role in the negotiations raises more questions than it answers. On the surface, as disclosed by materials in the Roosevelt Library and by the president's overt behavior, he ardently desired labor unity and acted to achieve it. From December 1938 through February 1939, he met privately with both Lewis and Green to urge the two labor leaders, described by the president's aides as "prima donnas," to unite the labor movement. Roosevelt also arranged with his closest aides and cabinet members—Perkins, Harry Hopkins, and Frank Murphy—a well-coordinated campaign to compel negotiations between A. F. of L. and CIO. The president personally asked Green and Lewis, in letters sent on February 23, to resume unity negotiations not only to aid American workers, but also to serve the national interest.[24]

Many explanations have been offered to explain the president's desire to promote unity between A. F. of L. and CIO. Most boil down to Roosevelt's political needs. Labor's civil war weakened the New Deal, as the A. F. of L., after 1936, fought the president's labor and social welfare legislation and aided the emerging conservative congressional coalition of northern Republicans and southern Democrats. As foreign affairs threatened to involve the nation in war, national unity became Roosevelt's imperative concern. Finally, if, as many suspected, the president had chosen to break with tradition and seek a third term in office, the support of a united labor movement would be essential. All these considerations make Roosevelt's behavior logical, and, if true, they serve to convict John L. Lewis of sabotaging prospects for trade union unity.[25]

However much Roosevelt desired labor unity, he may not have been displeased when negotiations collapsed. A united labor movement theoretically may have offered Roosevelt political benefits; it also involved potential dangers. Just as a united labor movement could pressure Congress and produce Democratic voters on Election Day, it could also undermine presidential policies that it opposed. Bernstein and others have suggested that a reunited labor movement, by diluting the authority of John L. Lewis, would have rendered him less able to threaten the president's domestic and foreign policies. But what of the other possibility? What if Lewis emerged as the dominant figure in a reunited labor movement and if he allied with Bill Hutcheson, labor's leading Republican and an arch-isolationist in foreign affairs? Such a prospect could only frighten Roosevelt, and it was as likely to occur as any other result of a peace agreement between the A. F. of L. and CIO.

The evidence suggests inferentially that the CIO approached negotiations more seriously than the A. F. of L. Although Green responded to the president's letter of February 23 first, the three-man committee he chose to represent the A. F. of L. in the proposed negotiations boded ill for success. Green selected Matthew Woll, Harry Bates, and Dan Tobin, who soon withdrew to be replaced by Tom Rickert. The A. F. of L. could not have chosen a more inept, less imposing trio. After Tobin's departure none represented a major union; Woll was more a lawyer and insurance agent than a labor leader; Bates was scarcely known outside his own union, the bricklayers; and Rickert was an aged functionary best known for splitting his own union in 1914 and engaging in numerous corrupt practices. Such a committee could not negotiate seriously, nor could it have been granted much authority by the executive council. The CIO's negotiators were a different matter. Lewis informed the president, on February 28, that he, Sidney Hillman, and Phil Murray would be pleased to serve as negotiators for the industrial unionists. They certainly had full power to act for their organization.[26]

Formal negotiations between the A. F. of L. and CIO committees began in the White House on March 7, with President Roosevelt in attendance. Three days before the first session, Lewis, during lunch with Brophy, Tom Kennedy, and Lee Pressman, discussed the peace proposal that he would unveil at the president's conference. Lewis's peace plan, undoubtedly the product of memorandums and conversations among Pressman, Len DeCaux, and Jett Lauck, promptly disrupted peace negotiations. Lewis called on representatives of the A. F. of L., CIO, and the four railroad brotherhoods to convene not later than June 1, 1939, in the Daughters of the American Revolution Hall in Washington to form the American Congress of Labor. This entirely new national federation would elect its own officers for one-year terms, excluding Lewis and Green. Green and A. F. of L.

Secretary Frank Morrison, Lewis recommended, should be pensioned at their current salaries, an action befitting their status as supernumeraries in a militant labor movement. The ACL's executive board would consist of an equal number of representatives from the Federation and the CIO, with proportional representation from the railroad unions, from whose ranks would come the Congress's president. During the first year after the formation of the new organization, Labor Department agents would assist affiliated unions in settling all jurisdictional questions. Finally, Lewis proposed that President Roosevelt serve as presiding officer during the founding convention.[27]

Not only did the A. F. of L. promptly reject Lewis's peace proposal and Roosevelt refuse to endorse such an outrageous plan; Sidney Hillman also opposed it.[28] Yet negotiations proceeded the following day in Washington, recessed for only a day, and resumed in New York City on March 10. During the next three weeks the negotiators continued to meet, sometimes in New York (where Lewis and Murray were involved in coal negotiations) and other times in Washington; but they made absolutely no progress. Finally, on April 5, by mutual agreement between Woll and Lewis, all meetings were indefinitely postponed, never to be resumed. Lewis announced the termination of negotiations to reporters, whose stories portrayed an angry, militant Lewis glad to be done with peacemaking. Matthew Woll's confidential memorandum to Green and the Federation executive council revealed a different Lewis, a labor leader who had terminated negotiations because bargaining between the miner's union and the coal operators had reached a crisis that would occupy all Lewis's time for the foreseeable future. As Woll informed Labor Secretary Perkins, his final conversation with Lewis had been entirely friendly. "Lewis did not manifest or evidence any militancy . . . he did not indicate either in the words used or his manner of approach that he intended our conferences should be postponed for all time. To the contrary . . . he . . . left the distinct impression with me that he would undertake to resume negotiations."[29]

Woll's impressions notwithstanding, negotiations were indeed dead, not to be resumed, and for the same reasons that had doomed the 1937 peace proposals. As Lewis reported in a confidential memorandum sent to members of the CIO executive board on March 25, the A. F. of L. still demanded that CIO unions make most concessions. To a question from Lewis concerning whether or not CIO unions as now constituted would be invited to return to the Federation, the A. F. of L.'s answer was evasive. In theory, the federation spokesmen pledged to respect the structure of CIO unions; but in practice, they demanded that the UMW confer with the Progressive Miners, surrender members organized in UMW District 50 to A. F. of L. federal unions with jurisdiction in related fields, and that all CIO unions transfer members recruited by expansion to the A. F. of L. unions that may have legitimate jurisdictional claims to them. Finally, the A. F. of L. insisted that no settlement could be arranged until a mutually approved firm of certified public accountants examined and audited the books of the A. F. of L. and CIO in order to determine true paid-up membership as a basis for allocating real jurisdictions and voting rights at a joint convention. Such a procedure posed a threat to the CIO, which followed the UMW practice of exonerating unemployed union members from dues payment, a policy that produced a paper membership far in excess of the paid-up membership as calculated by A. F. of L. unions. In short, the A. F. of L. asked the CIO to respect *all* Federation affiliates' jurisdictional claims and to reenter the federation as a numerical minority, a peace proposal that was as unacceptable to Lewis in March 1939 as it had been in December 1937.[30]

At the urging of his Secretary of Labor, President Roosevelt dutifully went through the motions of trying to beat life into a dead horse. During the summer of 1939 he spoke to Lewis on the phone and discussed labor unity in private White House conferences. As far as can be determined nothing substantial resulted from their talks. When the president, in a letter to the 1939 CIO convention, again pleaded for labor unity, Lewis replied on October 15 that "Our Committee does not possess any information which would lead to the belief that conferences, if resumed at this time, would be fruitful."[31]

Indeed, by that time, despite press reports to the contrary, conflict between A. F. of L. and CIO had intensified.[32] On July 31, 1939, Lewis announced the creation of the Construction Workers Organizing Committee (CWOC), led by his younger brother Dennie and intended to carry labor's civil war directly to the most influential bloc of unions in the Federation: the building trades. Early in January 1940 Dennie Lewis informed Jett Lauck that the CWOC would bring peace to the labor movement by breaking the building trades power in the Federation.[33]

Peace within the labor movement now depended on a clear victory either for the CIO or the A. F. of L. or on the disappearance from the scene of William Green or John L. Lewis. The latter being an unlikely alternative, both labor federations fought for ascendancy among workers—before the NLRB, in Congress, and with President Roosevelt. In the course of this struggle, a frustrated Lewis watched his adversaries grow more numerous and influential as his own relationship with President Roosevelt soured.

The first sign that the CIO had lost its momentum came in the spring and summer of 1937, when SWOC waged a bloody, protracted, and unsuccessful strike against the so-called Little Steel companies, small only in the sense that they operated independently of the industry's giant, United States Steel. The Little Steel Strike also precipitated a rift between Lewis and his labor lieutenant Murray, further strained the relationship between Lewis and Roosevelt, revealed the CIO's political weaknesses, and suggested that mass-production unionism was less than invincible.

SWOC's unexpected and easy triumph over U. S. Steel made its officers and organizers eager to unionize the remainder of the industry's major concerns, known collectively as Little Steel.* It also may have upset Phil Murray emotionally. Finally the commander of his own labor organization, SWOC, Murray had been thrust into the background during negotiations with U. S. Steel by John L. Lewis. Who can say what went on in Murray's mind, reminisced Lee Pressman, when "the Myron Taylors didn't come to Phil Murray, but they went to John Lewis. . . . It's the kind of thing a man doesn't talk about, to any intimate."[34] Saul Alinsky and David McDonald, SWOC's secretary in 1937, like Pressman, alleged that Murray's emotional needs and insecurities compelled him to authorize a strike against Little Steel in order to prove his manhood. According to Mac-Donald's recollections, as told to an interviewer in 1967, "Lewis thought the strike stupid. . . . He said, 'I think you guys are crazy, Dave'." And Alinsky asserted that Lewis stated specifically, "this was the first time in Murray's life that he acted without requesting my advice. I told him what I thought, and he has never forgotten that."[35]

Here we have a version of the CIO's first major setback that implies that a jealous lieutenant impetuously entered battle against the better judgment of his commanding officer. Historical reality, however, is more complex. Murray's decision flowed as much from pressure on him by SWOC organizers and subalterns as from any emotional desire to prove his manhood. "Our own people in the field," recalled Lee Pressman, SWOC's legal adviser, "told us that we have to keep marching forward, and go into Little Steel. We had Big Steel, now we had to have Little Steel. If we didn't we'd lose the momentum." At a conference of SWOC officials, nearly everyone present, especially the local leaders from the mills, favored a strike; as Pressman remembers, the local leadership concluded, "Let's have a strike."[36] Never at this prestrike stage of affairs did Lewis, according to the evidence, counsel Murray against a walkout. And never during the course of the battle did Lewis ever lend less than his total support to the strikers. Perhaps, when it was over and SWOC had lost, Lewis might have remarked to Murray, as Pressman thinks possible, "Phil, I don't know whether you should have done that. I don't know why you didn't check with me."[37]

Pushed by his rank and file and scarcely dissuaded by Lewis, Murray authorized a strike against Republic Steel and Youngstown Sheet and Tube to begin on May 26, 1937. "He sent the men out to prepare for it," recalled Pressman. "And he walked into it. And we took a terrific drubbing on that Little Steel Strike—a terrific drubbing."[38]

The steel companies, led by Republic's Tom Girdler, as resolute and intransigent an antiunion entrepreneur as existed in the nation, fought SWOC with a full arsenal of antilabor weapons. Company spies honeycombed SWOC locals; firms hired strikebreakers and stocked their plants with weapons and tear gas; local police and country sherrifs broke picket lines and terrorized strikers; clergymen,

*Republic, Bethlehem, Youngstown Sheet and Tube, Jones and Laughlin, Inland, and Wheeling were the primary Little Steel companies.

local professionals, and newspaper publishers red-baited SWOC and CIO merci-
lessly; and a core of loyal antiunion workers led "back-to-work" movements
conceived by the struck companies.[39]

Strikers waged the struggle with equal intensity. In the streets of Youngstown
and Massillon, Ohio; Bethlehem and Johnstown, Pennsylvania; and Gary, Indiana, they fought strikebreakers, police, and deputies. However freely blood
flowed in the streets of steel towns, the single most violent and notorious incident
of the strike occurred on one occasion when strikers had had no intention of
resorting to force.

On Memorial Day, 1937, Republic Steel strikers and their wives, children,
friends, and sympathizers—between 1,500 and 2,000 people—gathered in a
holiday mood on a broad vacant lot near the company's South Chicago mill to
protest police interference with legal picketing. As the crowd later marched
peacefully toward the mill gate, an altercation erupted with the Chicago city police
on duty there. Suddenly the front ranks of the police fired guns and tear gas
point-blank into the crowd, and its members fled hastily across the field. "The
police advanced," writes Irving Bernstein, "continuing to fire their guns and
beating the fallen, now lying in tangled masses, with billies and hatchet handles."
When the shooting stopped, ten marchers lay dead—seven wounded by bullets in
the back and three in the side; thirty others had been wounded by gunshot; and an
almost equal number had been the victims of lacerations and contusions.
"Wounded prisoners of war," later observed the LaFollette Committee, "might
have expected and received greater solicitude."[40]

This, then, should have been the occasion for Lewis to use the CIO's vaunted
political influence to obtain relief for the Little Steel strikers. The governors of
Pennsylvania, Ohio, Illinois, and Indiana had all been elected with CIO support,
and Roosevelt was reputed to be labor's president. Lewis, in fact, urged the
governors in whose states the strike was centered and also Roosevelt to assist the
strikers by using state power to thwart corporate terror. But to no avail. The
governors of Indiana and Ohio dispatched militia to strife-torn industrial cities—
only, however, to disperse pickets, protect property, and guard strikebreakers.
And in Pennsylvania, where the lieutenant governor was the UMW's own Tom
Kennedy, the state implemented a neutral policy that in practice aided the steel
companies to break the strike.

President Roosevelt's role in the conflict exposed graphically the limitations of
Lewis's and the CIO's political influence. On June 21, Lewis, referring to twelve
steelworkers dead and ten more "gaping for their lives in hospital beds" as a result
of Little Steel's terroristic policies, demanded of the president, "Labor will await
the position of the authorities on whether our people will be protected or butchered."[41] A week later, at his regular press conference, on June 29, Roosevelt
observed about the Little Steel Strike that "the majority of the people are saying
just one thing, 'A plague on both your houses'." Newspaper headlines the
following day stressed that the president had cast a plague equally on Little Steel

and CIO—Tom Girdler and John L. Lewis. When reporters read Roosevelt's statement to the CIO leader at his own subsequent press conference, one journalist noted afterward that Lewis "said nothing, but his heels drummed against the desk's lower panels with a violence that just missed reducing them to splinters."[42]

Roosevelt acted as he did for good political reasons. His advisers warned against his becoming involved in a dangerous situation from which he had little to gain. The new unionization movement in the mass-production industries, reported one presidential adviser, "is a complicated situation, and full of all kinds of dynamite, political as well as social." Advising Roosevelt that the Little Steel Strike was then (July 2) coming to a natural end, the adviser counseled the president against offering public encouragement to Lewis. "Nothing the President could now say would make any difference. If he chided the employers, he would once again be charged with playing Lewis's game. Time is needed for things to cool off. . . . I think Lewis will be willing to compromise. There is a strong reaction against the C.I.O., and Lewis will need time to reorganize his forces."[43] Such advice apparently persuaded the president, who gave no encouragement to Lewis or SWOC. By summer 1937, presidential support for the CIO and mass-production unionism carried as many, if not more, political liabilities as benefits. Ever the politician, Roosevelt maneuvered to avoid the labor-capital quagmire, in the process diluting the CIO's political influence and straining the relationship between charismatic labor leader and popular president.

The CIO defeat in Little Steel was merely one example of its loss of momentum during the summer of 1937. A similar tale repeated itself in the textile industry. On March 9, 1937, the CIO had established the Textile Workers' Organizing Committee (TWOC), which in every essential feature replicated the creation of SWOC. The new organizing committee simply swallowed whole the long-dormant United Textile Workers' Union. Two CIO officials, Sidney Hillman and Tom Kennedy, acted as TWOC's leaders, and the Amalgamated Clothing Workers and other CIO affiliates provided the bulk of the committee's finances and organizers. After winning several contracts rather easily from northern textile mills, TWOC's organizing drive fizzled in the South—the center of cotton textile production. Unable to organize more than 5% of the region's mill workers, TWOC, by the late autumn of 1937, as the economy again declined, acceded to wage reductions and experienced a loss of membership in northern mills. And in November 1937, the organization's commander, Sidney Hillman, collapsed physically, the victim of a severe case of pneumonia from which he did not recover fully until April 1938. In Hillman's absence, TWOC suffered further setbacks, none more unsettling than the emergence of a competing textile union in the A. F. of L.—the United Textile Workers—which by 1939 successfully seized contracts and members from TWOC.[44]

Other Lewis-CIO organizing gambits endured similar fates. On June 21, 1937, Lewis announced the creation of a new union—the United Federal Workers—to organize an estimated 800,000 federal employees. Opposed by federal officials, including most New Dealers, who doubted that public employees had the right to unionize or to strike, the new organization made little headway.[45]

An even more ambitious Lewis scheme to organize more than 3 million workers laboring on WPA and other federal emergency employment projects suffered a ruder administration rebuff. Lewis presented his idea directly to New Dealers Harry Hopkins and Aubrey Williams, saying bluntly, "It's the least that the Administration can do for the C.I.O." Not only did Lewis's proposal shock Hopkins and Williams; they simply refused to consider the notion that the government should actively recruit members for CIO.[46]

All across the labor organizing front, by the end of 1937, Lewis surveyed an uninviting terrain for CIO. In the Pacific Northwest, Bill Hutcheson's carpenters and Dave Beck's teamsters united to thwart the organizing forays of the CIO International Woodworkers of America. Up and down the entire Pacific coast conflict between Harry Bridges and Harry Lundeberg wrecked the Lewis-CIO vision of a united industrial union of all maritime workers.[47]

Before 1937 ended worse news awaited the CIO. In August, just as the industrial union drive faltered, the American economy cracked. During the next four months all the economic gains made since 1935 evaporated. Industrial productivity plummeted, stock prices fell precipitously (the Dow-Jones average dropped from 190 in August to 115 in October), and between Labor Day and the end of the year 2 million workers lost their jobs. By early 1938 starvation again threatened millions of Americans. "In Chicago," writes the historian William Leuchtenberg, "children salvaged food from garbage cans; in Cleveland, families scrambled for spoiled produce dumped in the streets. . . . during the first six days of 1938, sixty-five thousand Clevelanders on the relief rolls went without food or clothing orders. One reliefer committed suicide. . . . In seventeen southern states . . . people were starving. . . . In New York City, Mrs. Sarah Goodman, the sixty-year-old mother of a WPA worker, died of malnutrition and anemia."[48]

If Roosevelt and his New Dealers had assumed credit for the economic improvement between March 1933 and July 1937, they could not escape responsibility for what soon became identified as the "Roosevelt depression." Believing the national economy healthier than it actually was early in 1937, Roosevelt had reduced federal expenditures and maintained revenues, hence seeking one of his fondest ambitions: balancing the federal budget. He could not have calculated more incorrectly. As the federal money pump dried up, the economy reverted to depression levels of consumption, production, and employment. The economic collapse that occurred between August and October 1937 struck more rapidly and deeper than even the Great Depression of 1929-1933.

Lewis and the CIO paid an enormous price for Roosevelt's economic miscalculations. The CIO's membership strength was concentrated in those industries most sensitive to the economic cycle. Steel, autos, rubber, electrical goods, and other mass-production workers experienced a second wave of mass unemployment, economic hardship that made it impossible for many CIO members to pay union dues and for other workers to consider joining a labor organization. The coal and garment industries, too, experienced unemployment; but, at least in their case, stable, financially secure trade unions functioned. The impact of the depression on the CIO makes all estimates of the organization's membership for the years 1938-1939 totally unreliable. How many of the members claimed by the CIO in steel, autos, and rubber actually paid dues in 1938 and 1939 may never be known. Suffice it to say that most A. F. of L. leaders were convinced that by the end of 1938 their organization far surpassed CIO in paid-up membership.[49]

Lewis's own behavior reinforces the conclusion that the "Roosevelt depression" cost the CIO dearly. He responded to the altered economic circumstances much as he had reacted to hard times in the past. Retrenchment became the order of the day in the CIO. Lewis instructed Brophy to prune headquarters and field-workers; CIO organizing drives lost organizers and received less financial assistance from the UMW; Lewis strove to make the promptest and least demanding agreements with employers; and his primary goal became to conserve union resources during depression and to hold on tightly to what the CIO already had and then wait for better conditions. As customary, Lewis once again trusted his fortunes to the cycles of history.[50]

Critics and enemies of the CIO lost no time in gloating over the misfortunes of their adversary. "The C.I.O.," reported John Frey in April 1938, "is slipping definitely as industrial movement." Not only did Frey find the CIO losing its organizing momentum; he considered its once potent political influence gone.[51]

The downturn in the CIO's fortunes left Lewis temporarily rudderless. Aside from retrenchment and conservation of resources, Lewis, in 1938, appeared unsure of his economic and political strategy. His uncertainty, moreover, was compounded by personal, political, and ideological disputes that threatened to demoralize industrial unionism and the CIO. Economic prosperity and union success had stimulated organizational solidarity; depression and failure induced recrimination and factionalism.

Factionalism practically paralyzed the United Automobile Workers and entangled Lewis in a sordid trade union power struggle. Only six months after the great General Motors victory and a month after the UAW national convention celebrating that victory, the UAW seemed a shambles. "You can see from this fragmentary report that our [UAW] affairs are in one hell of a shape," Wyndham Mortimer informed John Brophy on September 29, 1937, "and now when the International is in a period of decline instead of being on the upgrade it is particularly difficult." Three days later, Mortimer, now complaining about UAW president Homer

Martin's reliance on Jay Lovestone, the ex-Communist and current associate of David Dubinsky, wrote: "Some sanity must be injected into this whole affair very soon or the CIO will be compelled to step in and take charge as they [Martin and Lovestone] are out to either rule or ruin the organization."[52] Brophy, no friend to the left-wing Mortimer, agreed with the latter's diagnosis of the UAW's ailment. "Homer's troubles," Brophy advised a friend, "are largely the result of being advised by people completely outside the trade union movement [Lovestoneites] . . . who, for their own selfish purposes, play upon his fears."[53]

Lewis, too, worried about developments in the UAW. In November 1937 he instructed Jett Lauck to investigate the Detroit situation and to submit recommendations for action. Lauck, more sympathetic than Lewis to Lovestone, suggested that the CIO leader should personally persuade Homer Martin to adopt policies that would eliminate the persistence of unsanctioned wildcat strikes in the auto industry, introduce improved grievance machinery, and rationalize union administration. "My ideal," Lauck informed Lewis, "is not for you to impose upon or suggest these to Homer unless you wish. I can make them to him, and urge them upon him, and he would undoubtedly ask you to advise him which you could then do." Further to allay Lewis's anxieties, especially concerning the reports that he received from Mortimer and Brophy, Lauck reported that the UAW radicals were a small minority who could easily be rendered impotent by an effective union administration.[54]

Initially, Lewis apparently acted on Lauck's advice. From late 1937 through June 1938, he separated himself from UAW factionalism and took no overt action to control affairs among auto workers. But conditions in the UAW continued to deteriorate. Auto manufacturers raged at the union's inability to prevent wildcat strikes and threatened not to renew contracts. Dues-paying membership declined, and the UAW's officials spent more time quarreling among themselves than recruiting members. The factional politics of the UAW proved too much even for Lewis. Martin had fallen completely under the influence of Lovestone, who in his new anti-Stalinist incarnation remained as conspiratorial as he had been in his halcyon Bolshevik days. Indeed, Lovestone convinced Martin that every challenge to the latter's authority in the UAW emanated from Stalinists. Lovestone's definition of *Stalinist* encompassed every variety of trade unionist from such Communist party stalwarts as Mortimer and Robert Travis to the socialist Reuther brothers and the apolitical Richard Frankensteen and George Addes. At Lovestone's urging, Martin removed alleged Stalinists from appointive union office, replaced them with Lovestoneites, and even sought to purge his critics from the UAW executive board. A comic opera red scare spread throughout the UAW. The maladroitness of Martin and Lovestone ultimately produced the impossible: an alliance among socialists, Communists, and pure and simple trade unionists that looked to Lewis and the CIO for relief.[55]

In June 1938 Lewis complained to Germer about Lovestoneite influence in the

UAW, and by August the CIO leader seemed to be cooperating with UAW Communists preparatory to making the union a ward of the CIO. In early September Lewis dispatched Hillman and Murray to Detroit, where they delivered an ultimatum to Martin. Lewis's lieutenants ordered Martin to reappoint forthwith the members that he had purged from the union's executive board, eliminate Lovestoneite influence in the UAW, and rely on advice from the CIO.[56]

Lewis's intervention in UAW affairs through the Hillman-Murray mission neither ended factionalism nor restored union stability. Martin and Lovestone accused Lewis of serving Communist objectives. Martinites and anti-Martinites continued to fight each other throughout 1938, and the battle raged with great intensity until January 25, 1939, when a frustrated Homer Martin officially resigned from the CIO executive board, accusing his UAW opponents and Lewis's lieutenants of operating a dual auto workers' union. Martin's letter of resignation bore the imprint of Jay Lovestone. Practically every paragraph hinted at Stalinist manipulation of the CIO; it noted the Dubinsky-Lewis quarrel; and it reeked of conspiratorial notions. Soon afterward, Martin marched "his UAW" into the A. F. of L., and in April 1939 dual unionism entered the auto industry as it already plagued other industries in which the CIO and A. F. of L. competed for members.[57]

Lewis, however, seemed satisfied with the outcome of the UAW's factional struggle. "The opposition, with crystallized resistance, made the victory all the greater," Lewis wrote to Germer on May 16, 1939. "I feel sure the settlement will be of value to our entire movement."[58]

Despite Lewis's optimism, the UAW, at the end of 1939, was weaker in many respects than at any time since its March 1937 victory at Flint. And the same might be said of the CIO. The personal and political quarrels that produced factionalism and red-baiting among auto workers repeated themselves in the CIO during 1938 and 1939. There, too, depression dissolved harmony and euphoria, replacing them with cacophony and anxiety.

The solidarity that characterized the first constitutional convention of the CIO at Pittsburgh in November 1938 cloaked quite real differences, political and personal, that divided the organization's hierarchs. Dubinsky and Zaritsky, to be sure, left the CIO even before the 1938 Pittsburgh convention. But the relationship among Lewis, Murray, and Hillman appeared cordial and secure. Lewis's attitude toward Hillman was expressed privately in a note occasioned by Hillman's illness and forced retirement from union business in November 1937. "It has been lonely without you," Lewis assuaged his ill associate. "I am glad you are better and are going south. . . . In all important matters I have tried to consider what you would think. . . . Our affairs are in sound condition. No worries for you. 'Go south young man.' You know my wishes and hopes go with you."[59] And at Pittsburgh in

November 1938 Lewis and Hillman considered each other's thoughts on all important matters.

Beneath the surface, however, real differences divided Lewisites and Hillmanites. By late 1938, Lewis, Hillman, and their respective followers perceived political and economic realities quite differently. The Hillman wing of the CIO, and also Phil Murray, linked their political fortunes to Roosevelt and acted deferentially toward the president. Lewis and his loyalists preferred to exercise some independence from the Democratic party and expected the president to respect labor, not patronize it. On foreign policy, Hillmanites shared Roosevelt's internationalist-interventionist sympathies and had few reservations concerning an activist United States foreign policy overseas, especially in Europe. Lewis, on the contrary, persistently opposed active United States intervention in European affairs and recurrently warned the nation against drifting into war. Differences regarding domestic and foreign policies were complicated by the anomalous role of Communists within the CIO. Members of the organization's far-left wing, whether actually party members or simply "fellow-travelers," preferred Lewis's domestic policies to Hillman's but supported the latter's foreign policies—that is, until the signing of the Nazi-Soviet Non-Aggression Pact in August 1939. Hillman and his associates, moreover, grew increasingly sensitive about Communist influence in the CIO while Lewis refused to consider Communists a threat to his power.[60]

The opponents of the CIO in labor, business, and politics tried to aggravate factionalism among the industrial unionists. Led by John Frey, the A. F. of L. assiduously red-baited the CIO. Appearing as a star witness before the Dies committee (House Committee on Un-American Activities), Frey accused several CIO affiliates of operating as Stalinist front organizations and charged that between forty and fifty CIO leaders belonged to the Communist party.[61] In leaflets, public speeches, and leaks to newspaper reporters, other A. F. of L. officials made similar accusations. Journalists sympathetic to the CIO, in 1938 and increasingly in 1939 became critical. Louis Stark, of the *New York Times*, who from 1935 through 1937 served as a conduit for Lewis's proindustrial union propaganda, beginning with the 1938 CIO convention, began to print stories about the role of Communists in the CIO. Benjamin Stolberg, the free-lance journalist, whose essays in the *Nation* and other magazines in 1936-1937 found no encomium too flattering to describe the CIO, in 1938 published *The Story of CIO*, a critical analysis of the organization. Stolberg's book, widely publicized by the A. F. of L., conservative politicians, and business associations, told the story of a great idea turned sour, of a decent labor organization subverted by Stalinist agents.[62]

The rising chorus of red-baiting had its intended effect on the CIO. As the organization's 1939 convention approached, divisions between Lewisites and Hillmanites widened. Hillman had been drawn ever deeper into the web of Roosevelt-New Deal politics while Lewis increasingly asserted his independence from the president. Conflicts over foreign policy also intensified as the situation in Europe worsened. Hillman, like Roosevelt, supported Britain and France against Hitler's Germany, was stunned by the Nazi-Soviet Pact, and believed America's security directly linked to overseas events. Lewis, although no advocate of Hitler and no ally to the Communists, thought that America's security depended primarily on avoiding entanglement in Europe's misfortune. The warm relationship between Lewis and the left wing troubled Hillmanites, one of whom warned Adolph Germer on September 12, 1939, that unless Lewis changed his tactics and restricted Communist influence in the CIO, the ACWA, like the ILGWU a year earlier, might be forced to secede from the organization.[63]

CIO factionalism, as well as his relationship to trade union Communists, obviously troubled Lewis. Certainly he was the last man to feel comfortable in a role as the labor movement's spokesman for the far Left. Equally vexing was the fact that a majority of the CIO ardently supported Franklin Roosevelt and desired the president to run for a third term. These factors as well as the CIO's loss of momentum caused Lewis to consider resignation as CIO president. Shortly before the 1939 convention opened in San Francisco, Lewis on October 8, prepared a statement for release to the press and also to the CIO's executive board. Referring to President Roosevelt's plea that labor leaders cast aside self-interest in this time of national crisis, Lewis responded, ''I readily conform to his wishes. My personal pride and self-interest is of pitiful inconsequence as compared to the requirements of national interest. I will not be a candidate for reelection and at the close of the convention will retire as President of the Congress of Industrial Organizations.''[64] The statement, of course, was never released; nor did Lewis resign as CIO president.

In 1939 and subsequently, various explanations have been offered to account for Lewis's threatened resignation. Most analysts refuse to believe that Lewis was serious; they prefer to think that his threat was tactical (he made the threat at the preconvention executive board meeting and also discussed it at length with Murray) and intended to compel delegates to sanction Lewis's domestic and foreign policy positions.[65]

Yet it can be argued with equal effect that Lewis meant what he said. He knew that Hillman and his followers and, perhaps, Phil Murray and other UMW delegates simply would not endorse Lewis's politics. To compel the delegates to vote for an antiinterventionist foreign policy and to reject Roosevelt meant, on the one hand, to split CIO irrevocably; that Lewis had no intention of doing. To achieve completely his aims meant, on the other hand, to appear publicly to some as a captive of the Communists; that, too, Lewis would not consider.

The resolutions adopted by the 1939 convention also belie the notion that Lewis's resignation was a tactical ploy. First, delegates voted to endorse Roosevelt's proposal to amend neutrality legislation in order to lift the embargo against the shipment of materials to belligerents, meaning Britain and France. Lewis personally endorsed the revision of the neutrality laws, doing so in response to a direct plea from the president, a plea drafted by none other than Sidney

Hillman.[66] Second, although the convention declined to endorse Roosevelt for a third term, it did *not* directly oppose his reelection, Lewis's preferred policy. Third, Lewis's original report to the convention, a document that criticized Roosevelt's domestic and foreign policies, was never read to the delegates.[67] Fourth, Lewis reserved his harshest criticism at executive board sessions and in private meetings for Communists, not Hillmanites. Adolph Germer, for example, noted in his diary on October 14 that at a meeting of CIO executive board members and regional directors, John L. Lewis "took a healthy fling at the communists." Lewis, indeed, warned that no known Communist was to be employed in any capacity; and to prove that he intended to limit Communist influence in the CIO, he restricted Harry Bridges' role as West Coast regional director to California, placing two nonleft-wingers in charge of Oregon and Washington. He also replaced John Brophy—who was then, a left-wing sympathizer—as national director of the CIO with Allan Haywood, a UMW loyalist.[68]

Other factors also suggest that Lewis's threat to resign was more than tactical. By late 1939 the presidency of the CIO brought Lewis as many headaches as compensations. Receiving no monetary compensation for his administrative labors, Lewis devoted considerable effort to steering the CIO safely through the rough waters of political factionalism. At public and private meetings during the 1939 convention, Lewis had to warn CIO affiliates to pay full per capita dues on claimed membership or suffer the consequences. Lewis did not even deign to offer the convention delegates a written report on the organization's finances or organizational status, so anarchic were the CIO's administrative operations. And as we saw in a previous chapter, the CIO was not financially self-supporting.[69] Such considerations may well have led Lewis to ponder resignation—an act, moreover, that would not have left him bereft of influence in the CIO. He could have selected Phil Murray as his heir apparent with minimal opposition (he indeed discussed that prospect with Murray prior to the convention), and ex-UMW officials still dominated the leadership positions in numerous CIO affiliates. The roster of delegates to the 1939 convention bore further witness to the influence Lewis exerted. He attended the convention as a delegate from a Maryland city industrial council; daughter Kathryn represented the UMW; Lee Pressman appeared as a representative from the Utility Workers Organizing Committee and served as secretary of the Resolutions Committee; and Ralph Hetzel, Len DeCaux, and other CIO central office bureaucrats received credentials from local industrial unions. "The impression is," reported an A. F. of L. observer at San Francisco, "that the CIO remains in the main a sort of large holding company, in which the miners hold the controlling shares."[70] Lewis's resignation from the presidency would not have altered the distribution of shares in the CIO.

What needs to be analyzed, then, is why Lewis chose not to resign at the 1939 convention. The threat may have led Hillman, as some contemporary observers believe, to cancel an open attack on Lewis's leadership and preserve instead the

CIO's facade of solidarity. But it brought Lewis no further gains. As late as November 1, two weeks after the convention adjourned, Jett Lauck considered Lewis's talk of resignation sincere.[71] Why, then, did Lewis change his mind? No ready answers come to mind. Indeed, only one possibility suggests itself. By the fall of 1939 Lewis may have realized that an open break with Franklin Roosevelt was inevitable and that when the rupture came, as it must, Lewis would need every ally he could possibly attract. With that thought in mind, October 1939 was no time to resign as president of the CIO.

Much of the nation's political history between 1936 and 1940 and the most salient features of its labor history oscillated around the shifting relationship between John L. Lewis and Franklin D. Roosevelt. Saul Alinsky wrote that "The break between them ruptured an incipient new American revolution. . . . The break between them broke the militant surge of the labor movement and broke much of the New Deal. Historians will describe it as the great American tragedy of the labor movement."[72]

Alinsky, however, is at a loss to explain why two leaders who, in his version of history, shared a commitment to political reform and economic egalitarianism split. Unwilling to comprehend the rupture as the result of Lewis's and Roosevelt's respective roles as spokesmen for objectively opposed political tendencies, Alinsky interpreted the quarrel in terms of personality, abnormal psychology, and hatred. "Roosevelt's hatred for Lewis festered," wrote Alinsky, "and became as deep as Lewis's hatred for Roosevelt." Alinsky cites several stories to establish his case. Lewis, it is alleged, reminisced, during an interview in 1948, that "it was during the winter of 1937, when we were gripped in the fatal conflict with the Corporation of General Motors, that I discovered the depths of deceit, the rank dishonesty, and the doublecrossing character of Franklin D. Roosevelt." Roosevelt, in turn, supposedly told the journalist Max Lerner, "You know, Max, this is really a great country. The framework of democracy is so strong and so elastic that it can get along and absorb both a Huey Long and a John L. Lewis." Upon hearing this story from Alinsky, Lewis quipped, "The statement is incomplete. It should also include 'and a Franklin Delano Roosevelt'."[73]

Irving Bernstein, in his magisterial history of labor during the New Deal, endorses Alinsky's interpretation. Dismissing policy differences as the cause of conflict between Lewis and Roosevelt, Bernstein suggests that "more fundamental was the clash of personalities and of roles. The styles of the two men were completely different. Lewis was dour, angry, direct, and demanding. Roosevelt was cheerful, chatty, effusively vague, a master of indirection." In this irrational clash for individual power between the chief executive of the CIO and the chief executive of the American nation, the American presidency naturally carried all the advantages. "The fire in Lewis's belly," asserts Bernstein, "made it impossible for him to accept this fact.'' Thus Bernstein, like Alinsky, infers that Lewis ''entertained the ambition'' of succeeding Roosevelt in the presidency in 1940 and that when Roosevelt chose to run for a third term, the labor leader vainly sought the vice-presidential nomination. Thwarted in his political ambitions, Lewis turned bitter, and a relationship with Roosevelt ''that had earlier been merely strained . . . degenerated into hatred.''[74]

Such history makes good reading and drama. But it also mystifies the past. Both Lewis and Roosevelt were too experienced and adept at politics to allow personal idiosyncracies or irrational hatred to thwart the achievement of their goals. Lewis, to be sure, often seemed dour, angry, and demanding; yet when it suited his purposes he could be sweet, charming, and amenable to compromise, just as Roosevelt, in private, could be harsh, sullen, and recalcitrant. Lewis, moreover, certainly knew that the president of the CIO could not share power equally with the president of the United States. True, in 1936 and early 1937, when Lewis appeared most popular and influential, talk abounded about Lewis as the labor movement's first presidential candidate. But by late 1937 and 1938, when conflict between Lewis and Roosevelt gathered momentum, the labor leader had lost much of his popularity and influence. A Gallup Poll released in October 1938 that asked its sample, ''Which labor leader do you like better: Green or Lewis?'' reported that 78% preferred Green and 22% favored Lewis, an 11% loss for Lewis since the previous July. The pollsters added that a substantial majority of Americans in the middle and upper classes feared Lewis, scarcely a good omen for a prospective presidential candidate.[75] Those closest to Lewis during the 1930s—Jett Lauck, Lee Pressman, and Len DeCaux (none of Lewis's biographers, their claims to the contrary notwithstanding, spent much time in his presence)—saw little overt evidence of the labor leader's ambition to be president. As Pressman commented, Lewis was far too realistic to get the presidential bug the moment his name appeared in a newspaper column as a prospective candidate.[76]

If neither personality differences nor the contest for individual power nor Lewis's desire to succeed Roosevelt as president explain the clash between the two men, what, then, does? Social and class factors do. However much Roosevelt conceived of himself as an idealistic social reformer dedicated to the interests of the American people, in practice he acted largely as the defender of the existing order. His aim was to preserve the existing structure of society, not to transform it; to save a social and economic system that offered more to capitalists than to workers. By the mid-1930s only two approaches promised to preserve the economic system that had caused the Great Depression: repression through an American variant of fascism or extensive social reform. Roosevelt exemplified those members of the American ruling class who preferred reform to repression and believed that the discontented could be assuaged more easily with carrots than sticks. As with David Lloyd George during Great Britain's pre-World War I Edwardian crisis, Franklin Delano Roosevelt, in the American political crisis of the 1930s, found revolutionary class rhetoric indispensable. For it frightened the powerful into concessions and won working-class voters for the Democratic party. Just as Lloyd George intensified the earlier British crisis in order to ease its solution, Roosevelt did the same in New Deal America.[77]

Lewis, however much he preferred to think of himself as an executive rather than a labor leader, however little he associated with the working class personally, functioned as the leader of a militant working-class movement. Where Roosevelt sought to contain working-class militancy through reform, militant workers pressured Lewis to demand more than the president or the ruling class were willing to concede. As is now well known, none of the New Deal reforms cured the American economy fully or ended mass unemployment, and the more evident became Roosevelt's failures, the more heatedly labor militants demanded a fundamental reordering of the American economy and society—demands that Lewis, as leader of the CIO, came to express more forcefully than any other trade unionist. "No matter how much Roosevelt did for the workers," writes Len DeCaux, "Lewis demanded more. He showed no gratitude, nor did he bid his followers be grateful—just put on the squeeze all the harder." DeCaux captures a part of the Roosevelt-Lewis relationship in these words: "Roosevelt may not have thought of himself as the liberally inclined head of a capitalist government; nor Lewis of himself as a momentary leader of an insurgent working class. But that is how they behaved to each other in the early years of CIO."[78]

Lewis, unlike the British labor leaders of Lloyd George's generation who found in the Labour party an alternative to the prime minister's "New Liberalism," had no substitute for Roosevelt's New Deal. The lack of a political alternative, whatever its cause, frustrated Lewis politically from 1937 through 1940. In the United States the president mastered the labor leader.

Despite the material forces that made inevitable a break between Lewis and Roosevelt, for most of the years 1936-1939 they required each other's support and strived to remain political allies. Louis Adamic, in a notation in his diary made on October 4, 1936, described the Roosevelt-Lewis alliance from that date to June 1937. "For the time being," wrote Adamic, "they are using one another. Roosevelt is holding the fences for Lewis, who is momentarily helping him to be reelected so that he can hold the fences. . . . Lewis will not be surprised if after the election Roosevelt's passion for labor cools all of a sudden."[79]

Adamic proved prescient in his analysis of Lewis's evaluation of the president. During the General Motors sit-down strike and during the early stages of the organizing campaign in steel, Roosevelt acted precisely as Lewis desired, and expected. Without administration sanction the CIO could scarcely have conquered either General Motors or United States Steel. To that extent Roosevelt paid his political debt to Lewis. And Lewis, contrary to Alinsky's assertions, never complained privately about the president's behind-the-scenes role in the Flint sit-down strike.[80]

In the late winter of 1937 and into the spring, Roosevelt still needed and sought Lewis's political friendship. As the president struggled unsuccessfully to reform the Supreme Court by increasing the number of sitting justices, Lewis and the CIO provided Roosevelt with one of his few unswerving sources of support. On May 14, 1937, Lewis spoke on the CBS radio network and offered a ringing endorsement of the President's plan to reform the Supreme Court. "Why then should we set up over ourselves a tyrannical and oligarchic tribunal, which arrogates to itself even the power of defying the wishes of the people of the United States?" he asked his audience. "The time for reckoning is at hand. I believe that the overwhelming majority of Americans are in favor of the President's Court plan. . . . The future of labor in America," he concluded, "is intimately connected with the future of the President's proposal to reform the Supreme Court."[81]

The fight over the Supreme Court, the rise of the CIO, and Roosevelt's daring proposals for reform produced, in Congress and elsewhere, an anti-New Deal conservative coalition that united northern Republicans, southern Democrats, antilabor businessmen, and A. F. of L. hierarchs. Roosevelt required CIO assistance against these political enemies. And Lewis gave it unstintingly, appearing before a congressional committee in May 1937 to plead for passage of the administration's minimum wage-maximum hour bill and regularly using CIO funds, publications, and lobbyists to urge the implementation of Roosevelt's public works, housing, and Social Security programs.[82]

Yet ill feelings between Roosevelt and Lewis festered beneath the surface of an apparently cordial political alliance. Lewis, for example, as early as March 1937 voiced dissatisfaction with the administration's mine safety program, although he kept his complaints private in order not to undermine Roosevelt. The labor leader also felt disappointed that the president paid scant attention to Lewis's recommendations for federal appointments. Whether in the case of the Supreme Court, the Labor Department, or the Social Security Administration, Roosevelt rejected Lewis's nominees. "I hear John Lewis is miffed," the President remarked to Frances Perkins in August 1937, "because you have not answered his letters, especially the one about filling the vacancy of Assistant Secretary of Labor."[83]

As late as June 23, 1937, however, the *New York Times* reported in a front-page story that John L. Lewis had initiated a movement in Pennsylvania to make Roosevelt the Democratic presidential nominee in 1940.[84]

Thus many journalists and observers were stunned when only a week later the rift between Roosevelt and Lewis surfaced as a consequence of the president's refusal during the Little Steel Strike to support the steelworkers. When Roosevelt, on June 29, declared a plague on both houses—labor and capital—Lewis quipped, "Which house: Hearst or Dupont?" A week later, at a presidential press conference on July 6, and at another two days later, reporters queried Roosevelt about his relationship with Lewis. "Will you comment on reports that you and Mr. John Lewis are going to break off friendly relations?" asked reporters on July 6. "I don't think that a report like that needs comment," replied the president. Asked again two days later about stories alleging a break between the administration and Lewis, Roosevelt commented, "that is the same old story, press reports," which he would neither deny nor confirm. Such interchanges led Irving Bernstein to conclude pungently that "a brief and not very beautiful relationship had come to an end."[85]

During the midsummer months of 1937, however, journalists and politicians were confused about what was happening to the Roosevelt-Lewis political alliance. For both men played an opportunistic, sometimes duplicitous, political game. At various times in July and August, Lewis threatened to build a new third party that would unite the nation's majority of dispossessed workers and farmers. At other times, he denied that he planned to found a third party and asserted that he expected both Republicans and Democrats to offer organized labor its just demands. Lewis did, however, tighten his personal control over the Labor Non-Partisan League, force George Berry to resign as league director, and focus his political efforts in the most populous coal mining states, especially Pennsylvania, Ohio, and Illinois. Throughout July and August Lewis persistently criticized the Democratic party for allowing a clique of conservatives on the House Rules Committee to thwart reform legislation. Such criticism prompted conservative Democrats to charge, on August 23, that a Lewis-Roosevelt alliance planned to seize total control of the Democratic party by 1940. Lewis still asserted publicly that labor had most to gain by working with Roosevelt and would only consider a third party in 1940 if the Democrats failed to implement their own reform program. As August drew to a close, Lewis, interviewed in Chicago on August 27 on his way home from the UAW convention, again raised the prospect of a third party in 1940. Millions of Americans, he asserted, now desired a third party, and if the two old parties failed to act decisively to reorder national priorities, farmers and workers would know what to do.[86]

Precisely one week later, on September 3, Lewis amazed millions of American workers. Speaking over the CBS network to an audience estimated at 20 to 30 million, Lewis delivered what the press described the next day as a bitter, angry, graceless personal attack on President Roosevelt. Listeners and reporters remembered best the labor leader's rhetorical flourishes—purple passages in which Lewis accused Roosevelt of stabbing his trade union friends in the back. Referring specifically to the events of the Little Steel Strike, Lewis grieved, "Labor, like Israel, has many sorrows. Its women weep for their fallen, and they lament for the future of the children of the race. It ill behooves one who has supped at labor's table and who has been sheltered in labor's house to curse with equal fervor and fine impartiality both labor and its adversaries when they become locked in deadly embrace."[87]

Such hyperbole led many reporters and listeners to miss Lewis's real message to the president, which was clear, direct, simple, and unexceptional. The CIO leader calmly explained that the labor movement was the true ally of the New Deal and the last defender of the American system. "Workers," he declared, "have kept faith in American institutions," and their unions have unreservedly recognized the "institution of private property and the right to investment profit." Workers, Lewis answered those who charged labor with promoting communism, "free in their industrial life, conscious partners in production, secure in their homes and enjoying a decent standard of living, will prove the finest bulwark against the intrusion of alien doctrines of government." To the president, Lewis promised the prospect of a farmer-labor alliance that would defend the achievements and aims of the New Deal against those who fought it. Roosevelt, Lewis implied, could demonstrate his commitment to the New Deal by assisting the mass-production workers and their agrarian allies, whose votes alone could save reform from congressional and corporate Tories.[88] Lewis tried to push the president to the left while he simultaneously restrained left wingers inside the CIO.

The president apparently understood the political message implicit in the speech, for the next day at his press conference Roosevelt refused to satisfy reporters eager for a story blasting the CIO leader. Asked his reaction to Lewis's radio address, Roosevelt said, "There wasn't any."[89]

John Brophy proved as sage as the president. When Sidney Hillman chided Brophy and Lee Pressman for their failure to restrain the "Big Boy" from criticizing Roosevelt publicly, Brophy remarked, "I didn't think it was serious as the newspapers made it out. At this stage Lewis and the President needed each other and it would work out all right."[90]

Ironically, as Turner Catledge suggested in a story in the *New York Times*, Lewis's September 3 speech benefited Roosevelt politically. Because of popular reaction against the sit-down strikes and the labor turbulence associated with the CIO's rise, Lewis, Catledge implied, had become "a great political inconvenience, if not a downright liability, to the President." The future of the Roosevelt-Lewis relationship, concluded the reporter, would hinge on whether the president stood to gain or lose politically by a break with Lewis.[91]

It soon became apparent that the Lewis-Roosevelt quarrel was more a late summer squall than a winter storm. On September 14, the two men met at the White House for a pleasant forty-minute chat, which reporters observed reestablished the "entente cordiale" between the CIO and the Roosevelt administration.[92] As the 1937 elections approached, Lewis needed Roosevelt, and the president required CIO assistance, motivating them to patch up their alliance and cooperate during the campaign. As the year ended, some presidential advisers, Rex Tugwell among them, counseled Roosevelt to be more gracious to Lewis. Hold Lewis's hand once every three weeks regularly, Tugwell recommended. "Life for all of us will be so much easier if you will!"[93]

Throughout 1938 Roosevelt apparently stroked Lewis often enough to maintain their political relationship in good order. CIO and Non-Partisan League lobbyists proved the most ardent and effective pressure group for administration reform legislation. Rebuffed by Roosevelt in his attempt to elect Tom Kennedy governor of Pennsylvania, Lewis nevertheless promised to support Roosevelt's aborted efforts to purge anti-New Deal Democrats during the 1938 primaries, providing the president with money, campaigners, and publicity among trade unionists—especially in such mining states as Kentucky (where the UMW supported New Dealer Alben Barkley against Albert "Happy" Chandler), Alabama, Maryland, and Tennessee.[94] On the eve of the CIO's first constitutional convention in Pittsburgh and only a week after the 1938 election, Lewis informed Louis Stark and other reporters that although conservative Democrats such as Governor Martin Davey of Ohio and Mayor Frank Hague of Jersey City must be defeated, the great majority of American people overwhelmingly supported Roosevelt. The Republican party, he charged, "for years past has done nothing but betray the interests of the common people. . . . it offers no program . . . except their . . . reiterated wail that the clock of time be turned back to yesterday." Only Roosevelt, Lewis asserted, offered the nation a constructive program for reform.[95]

In 1939 Lewis continued to defend what remained of the New Deal's domestic reform program against its critics. The nation had no greater advocate of public employment programs, public housing projects, and Social Security improvements than John L. Lewis. When the A. F. of L. and numerous employer groups sought to amend the Wagner Act and other basic New Deal labor legislation, Lewis testified before congressional committees with his customary rhetorical brilliance. In 1939, when Vice-President John Nance Garner exerted his influence among congressional conservatives to thwart his own administration's wages and hours law, Lewis ridiculed the Texas politician publicly as a "labor-baiting, whiskey-drinking, evil old man." The bill passed as Roosevelt and the CIO desired, and Garner never recovered politically from the impact of Lewis's ridicule.[96]

Yet the apparent political reconciliation engineered by Lewis and Roosevelt in the autumn of 1937 failed to eliminate fundamental sources of conflict between the two men. Throughout 1938 and 1939 the president continued to disregard Lewis's nominees for federal office. Roosevelt would neither appoint Michael Mussmanno, a political ally of the coal miners in western Pennsylvania, to a vacancy on the circuit court of appeals, nor would he accept Josephine Roche, a close personal friend of Lewis's, as head of the new Federal Security Agency. Rather than offer Lewis what he requested, Roosevelt acted on the advice of Frances Perkins that he chat with the labor leader by phone in order to "sweeten his [Lewis's] disposition a bit."[97]

But it was hard to sweeten Lewis's disposition when he had substantial policy disagreements with the administration. Most of Lewis's dissatisfaction with Roosevelt in 1938 and 1939 flowed from two sources separate in their origins but related in their impact. The onset of the "Roosevelt depression" in the fall of 1937 and the ensuing loss of momentum by the CIO left Lewis frustrated and confused. Roosevelt simultaneously lost not only his claim to have restored the nation's economy; his political influence slipped, as congressional conservatives defeated the president's court reform plan, diluted New Deal legislation, and triumphed generally in the 1938 primary and general elections. Thwarted in Congress and baffled by the new depression, Roosevelt became more interested in foreign than domestic affairs. And as the president sought to expand congressional and popular support for his foreign policy, especially among political conservatives and business groups, he perceived fewer political benefits in Lewis's recommendation that a farmer-labor coalition become the core of the Democratic party. Rather than ally with Lewis in a militant domestic reform crusade, Roosevelt sought to undercut his labor rival in several ways. The president assiduously cultivated the friendship of such Lewis associates as Sidney Hillman and Philip Murray, consciously seeking to separate them from the "Big Boy." His new appointees to the National Labor Relations Board proved more sympathetic to the A. F. of L.'s jurisdictional claims than their predecessors. And by late 1939 the president ceased scolding "economic royalists" and "Congressional Tories."

As early as December 1937 Lewis began to rail against the New Deal's economic failures. On December 12, Jett Lauck finished writing a long speech for Lewis's delivery at a SWOC meeting that indicted federal economic policies since 1933 for aiding business, not labor.[98] In the spring of 1938 Lewis demanded that the federal government find jobs, on the public payroll if necessary, for 13 million unemployed workers; that it spend billions, not millions, on public housing; and that it cure the Roosevelt depression by guaranteeing that one-third of the nation no longer remained ill-fed, ill-clothed, and ill-housed. Throughout the remainder of the year and all of 1939, Lewis refused to soften his demands for increased federal expenditures—jobs for public workers, billions for subsidized housing, and a Social Security system sufficiently generous to allow the elderly to retire in dignity and comfort. To achieve his goals, the labor leader persistently threatened to build a left-wing, farmer-labor alliance that would incorporate student radicals and racial minorities either in an independent third party or as the dominant element in the Democratic party.[99]

Yet the most bitter and the deepest source of the rift between Lewis and Roosevelt derived not from economic problems and domestic politics; rather, it originated in a fundamental disagreement about the nation's foreign policy. The seeds of conflict flowered in Lewis's and Roosevelt's quite different conceptions of the United States' place and role in the world arena. The labor leader exemplified a tradition that dated back to Grover Cleveland, William Jennings Bryan, William Borah, George Norris, the LaFollettes, and Herbert Hoover—a tradition that perceived the American world role as largely symbolic. The United States would serve the world best by domestic example, not foreign adventure. Roosevelt exemplified the world view of William Henry Seward, John Hay, his own cousin Theodore, and Woodrow Wilson—a perspective that promoted a vigorous, sometimes adventurous, foreign policy. What Lewis expected from Roosevelt in foreign policy the president could not deliver. "I am convinced," Lewis proclaimed in a 1936 campaign speech, "that the freedom of our country from war—the assurance that it will not be drawn into another world war which now impends abroad—also depends upon the re-election of President Roosevelt."[100] No prediction could have been more incorrect.

As Roosevelt, in 1938 and 1939, increasingly devoted himself to the situation overseas, he and Lewis ineluctably split apart politically. At an anti-Nazi rally in Madison Square Garden in March 1937, Lewis warned an emotional audience of Jewish-American trade unionists that "Europe is on the brink of disaster and it must be our care that she does not drag us into the abyss after her." From this position he never deviated, insisting consistently that the United States' security lay in domestic economic reform, not overseas entanglements. Lewis even refused publicly and privately to lobby in favor of the president's preparedness (rearmament) program—a program that promised to reduce unemployment considerably.[101]

Marginal disputes over foreign policy also separated labor leader and president. Proud of his reputation as "Good Neighbor" to Latin American nations, Roosevelt was disturbed by Lewis's own Pan-American diplomacy. At a time when the United States was involved in delicate negotiations with the Cardenas government in Mexico over the property claims of foreign oil companies, Lewis conducted his own discussions with the Mexican President. In Mexico City, in September 1938, at a conference to discuss the founding of a new left-wing Latin American labor federation to replace the A. F. of L.'s defunct Pan-American Federation of Labor, Lewis attended a mass meeting of the International Congress against War and Fascism. Appearing before 50,000 Mexican workers gathered in a bullring decked with red flags, Lewis warned the audience that fascism also threatened the United States. Two days previously Lewis had conferred privately with President Cardenas, who asked the labor leader to deliver diplomatic messages directly to the American president.[102]

If Lewis's adventures in Mexico City upset Roosevelt, as they undoubtedly did, the president was even more perturbed by Lewis's oil diplomacy. Working closely with William Rhodes Davis—a Texas entrepreneur, oil wildcatter, and sometime Democratic party financial backer—Lewis used his own Mexican contacts to enable the Texan to purchase oil from the recently nationalized properties for sale to Hitler's Germany.

Precisely what motivated Lewis to engage in this enterprise to this day remains obscure. Davis's motives, to be sure, are lucid: profit, made by buying oil cheaply from Mexico and selling it dearly to Germany. Cardenas's reasons for supplying oil to Nazi Germany are also obvious: It provided an opportunity to break the blockade imposed on the shipment and sale of nationalized Mexican oil by the dominant Anglo-American petroleum companies. But what did Lewis seek? It is unlikely that the labor leader was involved, unwittingly or not, as Ladislas Farrago implied in his *The Game of Foxes*, in Nazi espionage schemes.* Only one explanation seems likely for Lewis's behavior. By enabling Mexico to evade the oil blockade, he hoped to earn the friendship of Cardenas and the left-wing Mexican Federation of Labor (CTM), link CIO to Latin American labor, and establish his own influence as an anti-imperialist** throughout the Western Hemisphere.[103]

Events in Europe, however, remained at the heart of the Lewis-Roosevelt conflict. In his traditional Labor Day radio address in 1939, shortly before the outbreak of World War II, Lewis warned interventionist American politicians about the irrationality of their policies. "War has always been the device of the politically despairing and intellectually sterile statesmen," Lewis observed in referring to Democratic leaders unable to cope with the domestic economy.

> It provides employment in the gun factories and begets enormous profits for those already rich. It kills off the vigorous males who, if permitted to live, might question the financial and political exploitation of the race. Above all, war perpetuates in imperishable letters on the scroll of fame and history, the names of its political creators and managers.
>
> Labor in America wants no war nor any part of war. Labor wants the right to work and live—not the privilege of dying by gunshot or poison gas to sustain the mental errors of current statesmen.
>
> During the last fortnight our country has been subjected to an overdose of war propaganda. Patently an attempt is being made to create the illusion that when war breaks in Europe, the United States in some mysterious fashion will forthwith be involved. Such a concept is of course a monumental deception and amounts to a betrayal of national interest.[104]

Lewis had good reason for his anxiety about possible United States involvement in European conflict. He knew that contingency plans were being prepared in Washington for possible American involvement and that an emergency war production proposal was then under consideration. Equally disturbing, Lewis had been informed by his friends and sources inside the Roosevelt administration that the president had been selecting prominent businessmen as the principal administrators of the war production planning program. Once again, as had happened during World War I, a thought never far from Lewis's mind, labor, it seemed, would be treated as less than an equal partner during a national crisis. Much as Lewis opposed United States intervention in the European war, he nevertheless intended to insure that labor won its *full and equal* share of all appointed positions on war planning agencies. Every hint that Roosevelt seemed more eager to involve corporation executives than trade unionists in emergency planning further angered the CIO leader.[105]

---

*See p. 345.
**Lewis associated imperialism primarily with British policy and Wall Street financiers (the Morgans and Rockefellers especially) not necessarily with American foreign policy.

As war threatened to envelop first Europe and then the United States, Lewis's old friend, Tom Moses, the United States Steel executive, pleaded with him to intercede with the president on behalf of peace. "The issue of peace or war," Moses informed Lewis in a phone conversation on September 30, 1939, "is solely in the hands of the President of the United States." War, Moses prophesied, would open all Europe to Communist penetration. Roosevelt's power is so great that he can have war or peace as he chooses. "Germany wants peace now. Our influence should be exercised in that direction." Asserting that regardless of the outcome of European hostilities, the United States faces economic debacle, Moses concluded, "Common sense requires that peace should be made within the next few weeks."[106]

Moses's desperate phone call had been occasioned by Roosevelt's request for modification of American neutrality legislation and the lifting of the embargo against the shipment of war materials to belligerents. The corporation executive was certain that such a policy change would inevitably entangle the United States in war, and he was equally certain that Lewis shared his belief. Yet as we have already seen, Lewis, at the October 1939 CIO convention in San Francisco, endorsed Roosevelt's request for revision of the neutrality laws, telling delegates that "the President's program . . . should be supported by the Congress and by the people, and caviling should cease."

Why Lewis supported Roosevelt, other than his alleged compromise with Hillman to maintain CIO unity, remains puzzling. The only clue is an entry in Jett Lauck's diary for September 15, 1939, in which the economic consultant observes, after an hour-and-a-half conversation with Lewis on the embargo question, that the labor leader perceived revision of the neutrality laws as a means to reduce unemployment and to obtain for labor equal representation with industry on all war production boards.

That Lewis's position on the embargo entailed no change in his attitude toward foreign affairs or in his growing disenchantment with Roosevelt was immediately made evident in words and action. During the same convention speech in which he endorsed Roosevelt's neutrality legislation, Lewis reaffirmed his conviction "that our nation is not called upon to participate in any manner on one side or the other of a European conflict. Safety and security for Americans," he added, "lie in non-participation in this conflict and the addressing of ourselves to the major problem now confronting us in our internal economy and domestic establishment." Two weeks after the convention, Lewis scotched a proposal by western Democratic governors and so-called political progressives to involve the CIO's Non-Partisan League in a conference to plan a third-term nomination for Roosevelt.[107]

The year 1940 promised to bring a unique presidential election to Americans. Lewis certainly thought so. In his Labor Day 1939 speech, the CIO leader prophesied: "In the march of years 1940 will be one of the crossroads of destiny for the people of the United States. . . . Let those who will seek the votes of the workers of America be prepared to guarantee jobs for all Americans and freedom from foreign wars."[108] Roosevelt, in accepting his party's 1936 nomination for the presidency, referred to America's "rendezvous with destiny." Four years later, during another presidential election, John L. Lewis would seek his own "rendezvous with destiny."

John L Lewis
Act g Pres.
United Mine Workers of America.

(Top left)
An Official portrait as a minor union official, 1917
(State Historical Society of Wisconsin)

(Top right)
Acting President of the UMWA, 1919–1920
(State Historical Society of Wisconsin)

(Below left)
Dressed for a presidential reception
(State Historical Society of Wisconsin)

Addressing the mine workers in West
Virginia, c. 1923–1935
(State Historical Society of Wisconsin)

Mr. and Mrs. Lewis with daugther Kathryn
after a visit to the White House, 1923
*(State Historical Society of Wisconsin,
Miller Photo, Photograms, New York)*

A trophy from his favorite sport:
deep-sea fishing
(*State Historical Society of
Wisconsin*)

In the garden of his Alexandria,
Virginia home
(*State Historical Society of
Wisconsin*)

With Kathryn's bulldog, Socrates,
1936
(*State Historical Society of
Wisconsin*)

As a debonair Washingtonian, 1941
(State Historical Society of Wisconsin)

Raymond Lewis, UMW Vice President, c. 1950

Probably at Jackson Hole, Wyoming, 1944
(State Historical Society of Wisconsin)

CHAPTER 15
Naked to Thine Enemies:
The Politics of 1940

The year 1940 proved a fateful year for Western civilization, the American political system, Franklin D. Roosevelt, and John L. Lewis. Seldom had an American presidential election occurred at a more crucial historical moment, and never had a labor leader sought so decisively to tip the political balance in the favor of one candidate. The outbreak of European war in September 1939 and the fall of Poland had been followed by a period of military inaction sometimes referred to as the ''phony war.'' But in late winter and early spring of 1940, Nazi armies invaded Denmark, Norway, Holland, Belgium, and France with devastating results. By the time the Republican party convention met in Philadelphia in mid-June, France had fallen, the remnants of Britain's European army had fled the Continent at Dunkirk, and only the English Channel and Winston Churchill's eloquence stood between Hitler's Germany and total domination of Western Europe. When the Democrats convened in July, Great Britain, alone in Europe, bore the brunt of aerial bombing by Goering's Luftwaffe; it was a nation apparently doomed to invasion and defeat.

The year 1940 scarcely seemed a good year for tradition. It was a year in which the adversaries of Western liberal capitalism—from Berlin and Rome to Moscow and Tokyo—were in the ascendancy. Thus, not surprisingly, both major American political parties shattered precedent. First the Republicans selected a dark-horse candidate for president, a man who only a few years previously had been a registered Democrat and whose experience was administrative and managerial, not political. The nomination of Wendell Willkie shocked old-line Republicans, causing the crusty Indiana politico James Watson to quip: ''I don't mind the church converting a whore, but I don't like her to lead the choir on the first night!'' A month later the Democrats broke an older tradition by nominating Franklin Roosevelt for a third term, making him the first chief executive in United States history to seek more than two terms in the White House.

John L. Lewis observed these events with great interest. The same factors that had led Republicans and Democrats to fracture tradition prompted Lewis to intervene dramatically in the politics of 1940. If Willkie, and especially Roosevelt, saw the fate of Western civilization tied to the outcome of the American presidential election, Lewis believed that the future of the United States hinged on the election results and that freedom and democracy depended on American insulation from Europe's debacle. A victory for Roosevelt, Lewis felt, would do more than shatter the two-term presidential tradition; it would also inevitably drag the United States into a European conflict, create the preconditions for the establishment of an "imperial presidency," transform the United States into an imperialist power, subvert the nation's democratic liberties, and enable a corporate-financial elite to control economic policy. To avert such dire results, Lewis, in October 1940, staked his leadership of the CIO and his personal prestige on the result of the election. He implored America's workers to choose between Lewis and Roosevelt, a demand that has led many historians of labor and biographers of Lewis to question the UMW leader's sense and sanity. Lewis's action, rather than being senseless or insane, derived from a consistent set of beliefs concerning domestic politics and foreign affairs.

The most sensational and often repeated story that purports to explain Lewis's behavior in 1940 was published initially in Frances Perkins's *The Roosevelt I Knew*. According to that tale, allegedly told to Perkins and Dan Tobin by President Roosevelt personally, Lewis came to the White House one evening in January 1940. "Lewis was in a most amiable mood," the president told Tobin and Perkins,

> and he talked about the third term too, Dan, just the way you have, only much smoother. . . . When I told him what I told you, that the people wouldn't like a third term and that it would be very hard going politically, what do you think he said, Dan? He said, "Mr. President, I have thought of all of that and I have a suggestion to make for you to consider. If the vice-presidential candidate on your ticket should happen to be John L. Lewis, those objections would disappear. A strong labor man would insure full support, not only of all the labor people but of all the liberals who worry about such things as third terms."

Asked by Tobin and Perkins how he responded, Roosevelt replied, "Why, he didn't press, he didn't press me. He just asked me to think it over and give it consideration."[1]

Rejected as a vice-presidential candidate, Lewis, the Perkins story continues, engaged in the politics of vengeance. Even Saul Alinsky, to whom Lewis refused to confirm or deny the Perkins story, asserted that the former secretary of labor might be correct, that Lewis indeed harbored presidential ambitions, and that the vice-presidential nomination in 1940 might then have seemed the smoothest avenue to the White House. Printed first by Perkins, this account of the Roosevelt-Lewis political negotiations in 1940 has been repeated numerous times since, with few of its tellers ever seeking to establish its veracity.[2]

New evidence and logical analysis, however, cast grave doubt on the truth of Perkins's story and her role as its source. For one thing the Lewis-Roosevelt conference she cited allegedly occurred shortly before the 1940 UMW convention. Yet the only recorded meeting between the two men in that period took place at the White House on January 10, when Lewis visited with his son John Jr., in whose presence a delicate and tense political discussion was unlikely.[3] For another, Edwin A. Lahey, a labor reporter for the Chicago *Daily News*, has asserted that he leaked the original story of Lewis's vice-presidential ambition based on a tip from Lee Pressman and that Perkins picked up the story later.[4] In his own oral history interview, Pressman has further compounded the mystery of the story and conflated Perkins's version of it. According to Pressman, Roosevelt first reported the essence of his conversation with Lewis to Phil Murray from whom Pressman heard it, not Perkins and Dan Tobin. Moreover, in Pressman's version, Lewis specifically warned the president: "Mr. President, I think if you run for a third term, you may be defeated, unless you have a representative of labor on the ticket, and unless that representative is myself." To which Roosevelt supposedly replied, "That's very interesting, John, but which place on the ticket are you reserving for me?"[5]

Yet in the same oral history interview, Pressman refers to the story as possibly apocryphal and suggests logical reasons why the conversation differed from Perkins's version. No doubt Lewis and Roosevelt, in 1940, discussed the political situation and organized labor's role in the forthcoming presidential election, perhaps on January 19 at an unrecorded White House conference. No doubt Lewis informed Roosevelt that labor deserved greater influence in national affairs and warned the president that he needed labor's political support. But for Lewis to have asked Roosevelt to select the labor leader as his vice-presidential running mate was unlikely, asserts Pressman. "Lewis is not the kind to put himself so completely at the mercy of another man, who would have the power and be in the position to say 'No.' That's why for Lewis to have made that specific request that he is alleged to have made would have been entirely out of character."[6]

The entire history of the Lewis-Roosevelt relationship between 1936 and 1940, as described in the previous chapter, also casts suspicion on Perkins's story. By January 1940 whatever ardor Lewis had once had for Roosevelt as president had cooled. Recall that shortly after the 1939 San Francisco CIO convention Lewis had quashed an effort by western political "progressives" to initiate a Roosevelt third-term boom and simultaneously promoted the presidential aspirations of Montana Senator Burton K. Wheeler. Recall also that by January 1940 the differences in foreign policy between Lewis and Roosevelt were so great that only a marked switch in United States policy could have reconciled the two men. Consider that the personal snubs and insults that had flared between Lewis and Roosevelt from 1937 through 1939 would multiply in 1940, and it seems even more unlikely that the labor leader could have supported a third term for Roosevelt or that he aspired to be the president's running mate.

Whatever the actual substance of the Lewis-Roosevelt conversations in January 1940, the labor leader faced grave political problems that demanded solutions. Having eliminated Roosevelt as a presidential candidate, what alternative did Lewis have? Were any Democratic candidates, other than Wheeler—a dark, dark horse—more favorably disposed to organized labor? Would the Democrats, regardless of their candidate, dare to offer the second spot on the ticket to a labor leader, especially one from the CIO, or adopt a blatantly prolabor platform? If the Democrats offered no satisfaction, could Lewis reasonably expect a better bargain from the Republicans, whose leading prospects seemed to be such anti-CIO spokesmen as Robert A. Taft? Rebuffed by Democrats and Republicans, would Lewis consider the creation of a third party, an alliance of farmers and workers that would also attract the then antiwar American Communists? What real alternatives did Lewis have in 1940, and when would he indicate his choice among them? The first hint of Lewis's new politics, and it was more than a hint, came at the 1940 Golden Anniversary convention of the United Mine Workers.

To the 2,000-plus convention delegates who had gathered in a festive mood to toast their union's fiftieth anniversary, Lewis, as the opening speaker at the second meeting's session, on Wednesday, January 24, recommended that the delegates endorse no presidential candidate in 1940—a rebuke to many in the audience who had swamped the Resolutions Committee with Roosevelt reelection endorsements. Lewis minced no words in criticizing the president's desire for a third term. If Roosevelt unwisely and egotistically sought another term in office and the Democratic party acceded to his ambition, Lewis warned that "with the conditions now confronting the nation and the dissatisfaction now permeating the minds of the people, his candidacy would result in ignominious defeat."[7]

Lewis addressed his speech as much to Democratic politicos as to miners' delegates. For organization Democrats, Lewis provided a lesson in practical politics. The Democratic party, he taught, was a minority organization in twentieth-century America. Limited by their southern sectional prejudices and commitment to the fallacious policy of free trade, Democrats achieved power only "under abnormal circumstances when [they] receive the support of the national independent vote. . . . Psychologically and politically," he thundered, "organized labor created the atmosphere of success that returned the Democratic party to power with an ample margin of safety." Yet today, three years after that great victory (1936), organized labor lacked any substantial points of contact with the administration in power. No labor leader occupied the office of secretary of labor; nor did representatives of trade unionism hold any policy-making positions in federal agencies; nor did the president consult labor's spokesmen in handling unemployment, national economic planning, and foreign affairs. Such ingratitude by the Roosevelt administration to organized labor could have but one result: Democratic defeat in 1940. The key states of Illinois, Indiana, Ohio, Pennsylvania, New Jersey, and New York were already leaning toward the Republicans, Lewis cautioned, and Frank Murphy's defeat in Michigan in 1938 combined with Roosevelt's failure to purge Democratic reactionaries during that same year's primaries revealed lucidly Democratic weaknesses and a Republican resurgence. The Republicans could be prevented from winning in 1940, Lewis lectured, "only by an accord between the Democratic party and organized labor."[8]

Lewis's break with Roosevelt and open challenge to the Democrats startled many observers. TRB, in the *New Republic*, commented that some thought on Wednesday morning ". . . Mr. Lewis got out of the wrong side of the bed, put on his socks inside out, cut himself while shaving, [and] squirted grapefruit juice in his eyes." And an even more confused Arthur Krock concluded on January 25 in his daily *New York Times* political commentary that Lewis was now the left-wing leader of an antithird-term movement who spoke as a conservative critic of the New Deal in the language of a nineteenth-century classical liberal.[9]

It was little wonder that Lewis confounded friends, sympathizers, critics, and observers. Sharing the same foreign policy perspective in 1940 as Communists and hinting at the possibility of a farmer-labor alliance, Lewis could appear the herald of a new left-wing movement. Yet criticizing the federal government for not doing enough to combat unemployment, on the one hand, and lambasting it for interfering too freely in voluntary collective bargaining on the other, Lewis seemed sometimes a leftist advocate of national economic planning and other times a voice from the Republican 1920s.

A day after his initial attack on Roosevelt, Lewis proved that his dissatisfaction was with the president personally and politically, not with the Democratic party. He introduced Senator Burton K. Wheeler as a featured convention speaker, thus offering the Montana Democrat an opportunity to launch his bid for the presidency before a sympathetic audience. Lewis's preference for Wheeler was neither accidental nor gratuitous. In January 1940 the two men shared many beliefs concerning foreign affairs and domestic policies. Both Lewis and Wheeler remembered World War I with regret. To them it had been a time when a reform president, Woodrow Wilson, had misled the nation into an unnecessary foreign war and then allowed reactionary businessmen and politicians to repress labor and persecute radicals in the guise of national security.[10] In 1940 Franklin D. Roosevelt seemed likely to repeat Wilson's mistakes of 1917-1918, to involve the United States in someone else's quarrel, and to terminate the New Deal and domestic reform, as Wilson earlier had gutted the New Freedom. Roosevelt, argued Wheeler and Lewis, must be stopped. Unfortunately for Lewis, the Montana Senator failed to stir the audience of union delegates and lost credibility as a Democratic presidential nominee.

Wheeler's failure to excite the coal miners did not deter Lewis from further attacks on Roosevelt. Repeatedly during the remaining week of the convention the UMW president reiterated the themes of his opening speech. He gloried in the role that Mike Quill, left-wing president of the transit workers' union, thrust on him. "We look to him [Lewis]," Quill informed the convention delegates, "as a tower of strength, as the man with the one loud voice who can see to it that the American people will never be dragged into the blood bath of Europe, that we will stay home in America and defend our American institutions, our American flag, that we will stay home in America to fight the war against unemployment, and to send men and women back to work in the mines, the shops, the farms, and the factories."[11]

Picking up on Quill's theme, Lewis indicted Roosevelt for failing to end unemployment and called on the president to confess, "I am not equal to my job." He dismissed Secretary of Labor Perkins with contempt. "She is a nice lady," Lewis conceded. "I like her a lot. I think she would make an excellent house-keeper, but I do not think she knows as much about economics or the problems affecting this country as a Hottentot does about the moral law." And he warned Roosevelt and the businessmen who now seemed in charge of national economic policy that labor intended to be consulted by those who in past years ruled. Something had better be done to combat unemployment and to allow workers to participate in the making of domestic policy, Lewis warned bankers, industrialists, and politicians. What must be done, the labor leader stressed, absolutely did not include involvement in war.

> Let no politician or statesman believe or dream that he is going to solve the unemployment question . . . by dragging America into war with foreign countries. . . . The answer to the questions that concern our nation is not, may I advise the politicians of this country, the formula of taking our young men and making cannon fodder out of them and covering the rest of the nation with grief and lamentations. . . . That day is gone if my voice and my strength can make any contribution to prevent it.

Finally, in his closing address to the convention on February 1, Lewis served notice on the nation's leaders "that labor in the United States wants no war or any part of war, and that it will hold to strict accountability any statesmen who depart from that declared policy."[12]

Those who tried to assess Lewis's politics in 1940 paid little attention to his strictures on foreign affairs. During a press conference at his Cincinnati hotel headquarters, Lewis, according to a report by Louis Stark in the *New York Times*, remained silent about foreign policy, devoting more than an hour to criticizing the Democratic party for failing, during its seven years in power, to solve the nation's major domestic problems. Lewis simultaneously indicted the Republican party as being explicitly hostile to labor compared to the Democrats, who at least sympathized with trade unionism. Yet to reporters who asked him what alternative existed to Roosevelt, Lewis had no response.[13] TRB, in *New Republic*, also perceived Lewis's tactic at the convention as an attempt to influence domestic policy and to obtain more bargaining influence with the Democratic and Republican parties as their 1940 conventions approached. "Whether or not Mr. Lewis is right in breaking so spectacularly with Mr. Roosevelt," concluded TRB, "I submit that he cannot be called whimsical, petulant or frivolous."[14]

TRB was indeed correct. Lewis's position in 1940 flowed from two decades' reflection concerning World War I's impact on the labor movement and domestic reform. With every day and week that passed after the outbreak of European war in September 1939, Lewis saw Roosevelt repeat what the labor leader considered to be Woodrow Wilson's mistakes. With "Dr. Win-the-War" about to replace "Dr. New Deal" in the White House and corporation executives becoming more prominent than labor leaders and academic types in the administration, organized labor's future looked dim. Lewis worried, and quite rightly, as antilabor corporations that refused to heed the Wagner Act's mandate to bargain with unions of their workers' own choosing received lucrative defense contracts. With a stroke of the pen, a simple executive order, Roosevelt could, Lewis asserted, compel such companies as Ford Motor and Bethlehem Steel to bargain with labor or lose their defense contracts. And when the president, despite numerous letters and entreaties from Lewis, refused to do so, was Lewis not correct in asking, "Is the law just for the weak and lowly, or is the law to be enforced against the powerful and the strong?"[15]

Domestic affairs as well as a desire to influence the 1940 party conventions undoubtedly explain part of Lewis's behavior in January 1940. But one should not underestimate his passionate beliefs concerning foreign affairs and his commitment to American neutrality. The most ardent advocates of the Allied cause (that is, the defense of Great Britain), such as Gardner Jackson, literally believed that Lewis's megalomania drove him to play any side of the fence internationally that he thought was going to win. "There is just no question in my mind on that," Jackson told an interviewer years later.[16]

But Lewis, numerous allegations to the contrary notwithstanding, was neither a Nazi nor a Soviet sympathizer in 1940 and had no desire to leap to the Nazi-Soviet side of the fence. The charges that Lewis either was sympathetic to the Nazis, or perhaps was duped by William Rhodes Davis (the oil entrepreneur associated with Lewis's Mexican diplomacy and also with financing part of the labor leader's anti-Roosevelt campaign in 1940) into advancing German plans, recently have been revived in Ladislas Farrago, *The Game of Foxes* (New York, 1971), and in Hugh Ross, "John L. Lewis and the Election of 1940," *Labor History* (Spring, 1976, pp. 160-190). Their allegations fall under the weakness of their evidence. First, for direct evidence of Lewis's attitude, both authors cite accounts of William Rhodes Davis's conversations with Goering. Among the assumptions Farrago and Ross make is that Davis accurately reported Lewis's position to the Nazis. Yet we have found no evidence which would substantiate Davis's assertions that Lewis looked favorably upon German diplomatic moves and much—presented throughout the book—that would contradict it. Even Farrago and Ross recognize that

Davis was prone to inflate the extent of his influence with others to both leaders of the Third Reich and President Roosevelt. Secondly, both Farrago and Ross stress Lewis's apparent willingness in 1939 to try to arrange a meeting at which Davis could present Roosevelt with a Nazi-approved plan for restoring peace to Europe. Such action, if true, simply emphasizes Lewis's strong desire for peace, and represents the behavior of a responsible citizen trying to facilitate the transmission of important information to an American president.*

Moreover, Lewis honestly believed, as did his old political associate Herbert Hoover and the Republican presidential aspirant Robert A. Taft, and his corporation executive friend Tom Moses, that the European struggle did *not* directly threaten the United States security and that the Atlantic and Pacific oceans provided the nation with unbreachable defenses. To go to war unnecessarily, thought Lewis, Taft, Moses, and Hoover, would transform the United States into a garrison society, expand dangerously the power of the presidency, make America an imperialist nation, and turn its citizens into servants, not masters, of the state.

By February 1940 little common ground remained available for Lewis and Roosevelt to occupy. Yet those most intrigued by Lewis's politics, including Roosevelt's closest advisers, still had great difficulty fathoming the labor leader's position. His anti-interventionism combined with criticism of the Democratic party as too conservative led some to consider Lewis as a Communist ally. Reports from the United States Embassy in Mexico hinted that Lewis and his union acted as a conduit for Soviet funds provided to the Mexican labor movement, money intended to promote Latin American independence from United States foreign policy and to keep the Latin nations out of the European war. Such reports apparently convinced Roosevelt that Lewis again had engaged in personal diplomacy with President Cardenas of Mexico, a pro-Soviet diplomacy that the president believed threatened national security. J. David Stern, publisher of the Philadelphia *Record*, whom Roosevelt assigned in 1940 to keep Lewis in line politically, later recalled that one night in his Mayflower Hotel suite, he concluded a seven-hour discussion with Lewis with the comment, "John, you talk like a Commie."[17]

Lewis, however, had a consistent record as a red-baiter and enthusiast of American values, the themes he had sounded in his one and only book, *The Miner's Fight for American Standards*. Those who remembered Lewis's policies as president of the UMW during the 1920s and his politics during that decade wondered if he might not again opt for Republicanism. Most Republicans, especially the party's apparent front-runner for the nomination, Taft, and its elder statesman, Hoover, shared Lewis's foreign policy sentiments, and Republicans

*See p. 183.

scarcely exceeded in bitterness Lewis's indictment of Roosevelt and the New Deal.

For most of the late winter, spring, and summer of 1940, however, Lewis seemed entirely liberated from his Republican, conservative political past. He repeatedly appeared on public platforms as the angriest man on the American Left, the most outspoken and effective critic of the New Deal's domestic failures. Confining his public appearances largely to trade union, youth, Negro, and radical meetings, he uttered words and sentiments that stirred receptive, often ecstatic, audiences. Isolationists, youthful radicals, staunch Communists, militant trade unionists, and gentle pacifists saw Lewis as a man whose policies could end unemployment while keeping the United States at peace, and many among them ached to enlist with the labor leader in a popular left-wing, third-party movement that would sound twentieth-century American populism's "first hurrah."

Initially, Lewis gratified his left-wing admirers. Only ten days after the miners' convention adjourned, Lewis again challenged the president. On the weekend of February 9-11, 1940, radical youth affiliated with the American Youth Congress rallied in Washington to demand jobs and peace. Invited to hear the president on the White House lawn, the young people gathered there early on the afternoon of Saturday, February 10. Their youthful enthusiasm scarcely dampened by the steady cold rain that fell, they eagerly awaited Roosevelt's words. But the president did more than the inclement weather to chill youth's ardor; he sternly told them that unemployment could not be cured overnight and that they were too immature to adopt resolutions on foreign affairs.[18]

Thus lectured by their president, the young people marched on to the Labor Department auditorium for an afternoon of formal speechmaking, the featured talker none other than John L. Lewis. With the president's wife, Eleanor, long a sympathizer of the Youth Congress, seated on the stage, Lewis promptly ridiculed the president. Referring to Roosevelt's response to the youth's demand for jobs that under certain forms of government young people would not have had the opportunity of standing on the lawn, in the rain, to ask for jobs, Lewis retorted, "Some answer! How many years, how many years can you stand to be without a job? . . . How many years must you wonder and hope that you will have an opportunity here in your native land to live the normal life of the normal citizen?" Concerning the president's advice to immature youth to keep their hands off diplomacy, Lewis countered, "After all, who has a greater right to protest against war or any part of war, or the diplomatic intrigues of war, or the subtle policies preceding war, than the young men who in the event of war will become cannon fodder?" And he assured his auditors that "Americans as I understand them will hold to strict accountability any politician or any statesman who undertakes to involve this country in a war in Europe or a war in the Pacific." Instead of using the FBI and other secret agents to ferret out putative "Fifth Columnists," the Justice Department, asserted Lewis, should use its power to abolish the poll tax and ensure southern blacks the right to vote. The time had come, Lewis proclaimed, for the common people and the youth of America to unite. "As chairman of the Labor's Non-Partisan League I issue an invitation to the American Youth Congress to become affiliated or come to a working arrangement with Labor's Non-Partisan League of America."[19]

Ovation after ovation punctuated Lewis's speech, writes the biographer of Eleanor Roosevelt. And when Lewis finally finished, comments Joseph Lash, "bedlam ensued." The American Left had found its leader; John L. Lewis would lead young people, black people, farmers, and workers to the promised land of jobs and peace.[20]

Lewis waited almost two months before expressing himself again publicly on political questions. Again he chose his audience wisely. On April 1, 1940, the coal miners' annual national holiday, Lewis addressed an enthusiastic gathering of 20,000 coal miners, their families, and their friends at an open-air meeting in Monongah, West Virginia. The UMW *Journal* later published Lewis's speech under the apt headline, "President Lewis Gives the Politicians a Warning."[21]

In his talk to the West Virginia miners Lewis repeated the themes he had first raised at the 1940 UMW convention and reiterated to the American Youth Congress. Again he stressed the Roosevelt administration's failure, despite seven years in office, to reduce unemployment substantially and the Democrats' increasingly "imperialistic" foreign policy. Insisting that he expected nothing from the Republican party "because it is obvious that he who pays the fiddler calls the tune" and that Americans will not allow their nation "to drift, drift, merely to drift, while politicians, hope, hope, merely hope," Lewis suggested the creation of a great new people's coalition to consist of the CIO, the old-age pension movements, the national Negro organizations, youth groups, and liberal farmers' organizations. And he informed his audience that in the weeks and months to come he planned to deliver major addresses at the conventions of the National Negro Congress, the NAACP, and the Townshend Old-Age Association.[22]

Lewis also delivered his usual strictures against United States intervention in foreign wars. Politicians will not be allowed to solve domestic economic problems by having the nation participate in a European war, he asserted, stressing that America's youth, "are not again going to be butchered in a European country, or upon a foreign shore."[23]

Five days later, on April 7, speaking to 10,000 auto workers in Flint, Lewis predicted that "any statesman, politician or public figure who puts his hopes on expecting that the American people are going to send their sons to be butchered in another foreign war, is going to show himself as nothing more or less than a fool."[24] Throughout the spring, summer, and autumn, Lewis's remained the labor movement's loudest and most consistent voice for peace.

Roosevelt, despite refusing to comment publicly or even off the record about Lewis's political threats, worried.[25] And the president schemed to undercut

Lewis's influence in the labor movement. As relations between the president and the labor leader cooled, Roosevelt cultivated his association with Phil Murray and Sidney Hillman, men much more susceptible than Lewis to White House influence and more deferential in the presence of power. On May 28, 1940, with France on the verge of military collapse, the president announced the appointment of a National Defense Advisory Council (NDAC), with Sidney Hillman as labor's representative on the council. At a press conference the same day, Roosevelt explained his choice of Hillman in these words: "for heaven's sake do not attribute it to me because somebody will call me names—he [Hillman] is just half way between John Lewis and Green."[26]

Ostensibly, then, Hillman's appointment seemed logical, a compromise between the divided factions of the American labor movement. In fact, Hillman was no compromise choice, for the ACWA president was as unacceptable, if not more so, to the A. F. of L. than to Lewis. Roosevelt selected him for two reasons: (1) Hillman would neither challenge nor deviate from the president's domestic and foreign policies and (2) Hillman's appointment was sure to enrage Lewis, create dissension in the CIO, and, hence, insure that the industrial union federation would not present a united front against Roosevelt's reelection chances. Hillman's appointment, in short, was Roosevelt's response to Lewis's political challenge.

The president calculated correctly. Lewis was, indeed, enraged by the Hillman appointment; not, however, simply because of Roosevelt's choice, but primarily because of its manner. The president neither approached the CIO leader prior to making his selection, nor did Hillman speak to Lewis before accepting appointment. Clearly, Roosevelt intended to subvert Lewis's authority as president of the CIO, and Hillman had cooperated in that plan. As Lee Pressman later expressed Lewis's feelings, the manner of the appointment "made Hillman a Government representative in the ranks of labor, rather than a representative of the ranks of labor in the field of Government."[27]

Lewis quickly demonstrated that he expected Hillman to serve organized labor ineffectively. Only a day after the establishment of the NDAC, Lewis released to the press a copy of a letter to Senator Thomas Walsh demanding that Congress protect labor standards during the war crisis. And he continued to insist that the administration deny defense contracts to firms in violation of the Wagner Act, a policy that could be implemented by simple executive order.[28]

In June, at a session of the CIO executive board called to discuss the national defense emergency, Lewis again assailed the administration's failure to involve organized labor fully and equally in defense planning. After his customary astringent comments about those politicians who sought to involve the United States in Europe's imperialistic quarrels, Lewis dismissed outright the notion that Hillman represented labor. "Labor," asserted Lewis, "wants a seat at the council table, labor wants to maintain its dignity. . . . It wants to cooperate and not be driven to the work bench or the factory by violent action, repressive legislation, nor the rantings of men who are merely interested in the entire proposition from the standpoint of enhancing their political prestige [a barb hurled at Hillman]. Labor as represented in the CIO wants a partnership in this enterprise."[29]

As Lewis expected, Hillman proved more committed to defending the administration's labor policies than to pushing the CIO's demands. To Lewis's demand that Roosevelt issue an executive order that required recipients of defense contracts to bargain collectively with organized labor, Hillman pleaded the exigencies of practical politics and the overriding importance of national security. Supplying Britain with war materials to defend itself against the Nazi onslaught, argued Hillman, was more important for the moment than pleading the CIO's case, however justified—an argument that Lewis would not buy.[30]

Hillman would not even accede to direct requests from Lewis. In late July, Lewis wrote to Hillman concerning the latter's refusal to appoint James J. Matles, left-wing, allegedly Communist leader of the United Electrical Workers, to a role in the defense planning establishment. I hope, wrote Lewis, that charges concerning Matles's political nonconformity will not influence policy. The UE, added Lewis, "has a record of which I am officially and personally proud. I may be counted upon to defend its integrity and its policies at all times . . . I do hope," he concluded, "that you will undertake to review this situation from the viewpoint of according a fair treatment to this great organization." Early in August, Hillman dismissed Lewis's request curtly: "I find it . . . impossible to accept the notion that non-inclusion of an individual on the committee is tantamount to unfairness to an organization of which he is a member."[31]

Another door in Washington had shut in Lewis's face. His influence at the White House minimal, Lewis now discovered that labor leaders close to him (or to his policies) stood little chance of serving in defense planning agencies.

All during the time that Lewis parried and thrusted with Hillman concerning organized labor's role in defense planning, the CIO leader's political plans solidified. By the time the Republicans convened in Philadelphia in mid-June 1940, Lewis knew what he wanted and what he must do. Speaking to the national convention of the NAACP on June 18, the eve of the Republican convention, Lewis delivered a typical speech. He referred, as was by then quite customary, to the CIO's commitment to win for American Negroes their full civil and political rights and criticized those statesmen who had no solution to domestic problems other than involvement in a European war, a policy "repugnant to every healthy-minded American." Toward the close of his speech, Lewis however, delivered an analysis of the Great Depression that presaged a new politics. As if drafted by Herbert Hoover, Lewis's analysis of the depression asserted that it had been caused by European economic problems originating in World War I, that the United States and every other democratic nation had been rising from the economic trough in the spring of 1932, and that the United States alone in the

Western world slid backward economically after the election of Franklin D. Roosevelt, whose policies made depression and unemployment "a chronic fact in American life." Not content to make his point, Lewis drove Hoover's lesson home. As a matter of simple justice, contended Lewis, Hoover had nothing whatever to do with the depression. "It was laid at his doorstep when he came to the White House. It is only the self-seeking politicians that blame Mr. Hoover. The policies he pursued . . . had a powerful effect in the start at recovery in 1932."[32]

The next day Lewis appeared personally before the Republican party Resolutions Committee to denounce Roosevelt's policies, especially the president's compulsory universal military service bill, characterized as "a fantastic suggestion from a mind in full intellectual retreat." Speaking before the committee for a full two hours, Lewis demanded no alterations in the Wagner Act, no favoritism to the A. F. of L., the abolition of hunger and unemployment, and full civil rights for blacks and other American minorities. In response to a question from Alf Landon, he threatened to lead a third-party movement unless Republicans met labor's demands.[33]

More interesting than Lewis's speech to the NAACP or his personal appearance before a convention committee was his behind-the-scenes activity. In conjunction with Herbert Hoover, the labor leader plotted to promote a convention boom for the former president. According to Lee Pressman, Lewis believed that Hoover had a chance to stampede the Republican delegates. And Lewis enlisted Pressman as a messenger boy in the plot to promote Hoover's candidacy.[34] More remarkable still, Lewis prepared a statement that the labor leader hoped would sway the Republican delegates. So amazing is the statement that it deserves to be quoted at some length.[35]

"Labor has been observing with great anxiety the action of the Republican convention," Lewis intended to say. "This is a time of crisis when national interest transcends in our thought every other consideration. We have a nation to save. We have a system of life to save which will provide employment for our people."

> I believe that the working people of the United States need and want the leadership of Herbert Hoover. His sense of service, his idealism, his great common sense, his knowledge of economics and his administrative abilities, his knowledge of world affairs and foreign trade have created for him the universal respect of the American people and his humanitarian aspirations have won their complete affection.
>
> I realize that some will protest what I say, but I was a member of the Republic Pary [sic] and supported it continuously for 30 years [simply not a true history of Lewis's political past]. I worked against it in 1936. I have endeavored to work with the New Deal in the interests of labor. Despite its high promises and its many admirable acts, the New Deal is heading the country toward disaster. Under these circumstances, I can no longer withhold this statement which my conscious [sic] compels me to make.
>
> This country above all needs industrial peace.
>
> I . . . and many of my colleagues and friends among labor are prepared to extend the

hand of labor to the employers of America to bring an end to conflict and confusion. We can extend that hand through Herbert Hoover alone, the man in whose probity and vision we have complete confidence.

It is said by politicians that Mr. Hoover can not be elected. He is the only Republican whom I and my colleagues can support. He can be elected because the workers of America con [sic] provide the ropes. And there will be associated with us the plane [sic] people on the farms and in the homes. If you will nominate him, we will elect him.

In the event, however, Hoover laid as big an egg among Republicans as Burton Wheeler had among Democrats. No mass Hoover sentiment emerged among convention delegates, and Lewis never had the opportunity to read his prepared statement. Still, one must wonder what inexplicable reasons prompted Lewis to consider Hoover a potential presidential candidate in 1940 or to believe that any substantial proportion of the American working class would vote for a man whose name was inextricably linked to depression.

That Lewis, by June 1940, detested Roosevelt was common knowledge; that he considered the New Deal a domestic failure was equally true; that the CIO's influence in Washington had declined since 1936 none denied. But why Hoover as an alternative to Roosevelt? During the early depression years, 1930-1932, Hoover had done little for labor in general and less for Lewis and the coal miners. Lewis knew that in the past Hoover had rejected him as a candidate for secretary of labor and also refused to endorse the UMW's proposals for national coal legislation. Why Hoover in 1940? Only one answer comes to mind. Lewis, in 1940, considered foreign policy more crucial than domestic affairs. Much as he wanted to end unemployment and cure the nation's economic ills, he refused to do so by recourse to war. Lewis sincerely believed that however much United States involvement in Europe's conflict might do to solve unemployment temporarily, it would come only at the greatest long-range expense to American society. War, Lewis prophesied persistently, would create a puissant presidency and an imperial nation; if unemployment and economic collapse did not follow eventual peace, it would be only because the United States remained a garrison state whose armed forces stalked the globe in the name of citizens who had surrendered their customary rights and freedoms. To Lewis, Roosevelt's compulsory conscription bill seemed an omen of the future, a future in which the federal government would command without restraint the services of its citizens. Hoover shared Lewis's fears of a puissant presidency, harbored no imperial dreams, and believed that national security lay in noninvolvement in foreign wars. In foreign affairs, Hoover, then, was the perfect candidate—perhaps the only major party choice likely to share Lewis's conception of the United States' proper role in world affairs.

What the Republicans offered Lewis, however, was worse than he expected. Not only did the Resolutions Committee recommend a platform antipathetic to organized labor's demands; the delegates nominated Wendell Willkie, whose foreign policy barely differed from Roosevelt's and who was to become famous as an advocate of an interventionist American policy under the rubric "One World."

A month later the Democratic convention met, renominated Roosevelt, and left Lewis in a quandary. Both major parties had chosen candidates unacceptable to the labor leader. What choice did he now have but to form a third party, a political organization dedicated to noninvolvement in foreign affairs and radical reform at home, a party dependent on Communist and other left-wing supporters?

Speaking to the Townshend Movement national convention on July 2, Lewis disparaged the Republicans, prophesied defeat for the president if he ran again, and hinted at the need for a new people's party. Later that same month, on July 30, Lewis addressed the auto workers' union's national convention. After receiving a raucous thirty-five-minute ovation from the excited delegates, Lewis tore into Roosevelt. "Build up . . . a gigantic military instrumentality . . . and quarter it upon the people under a Roosevelt or under any other President, call it a defensive mechanism," he warned, "but sooner or later will come a Chief Executive, . . . a man on horseback, who will believe this instrumentality is not a defensive instrument but an offensive instrumentality that will carry out his imperialistic dreams and conceptions." Some day, Lewis suggested, the American people will lose their confidence in the two old parties and form their own. To delegates who perhaps expected Lewis to beseech them to join him in building that new party, he advised anticlimactically that a third party was for the future to develop—advice that Louis Stark reported in the next day's *New York Times* sounded a death knell for the advocates of a third party in 1940.[36]

Having found the choices of the Republican and Democratic conventions unacceptable, having declined to lead a third party, what political choice was left for Lewis? As Lewis pondered the future, friends of Roosevelt, advocates of Willkie, and labor leaders maneuvered to influence the CIO president's politics. Everyone seemed to believe, especially Lewis himself, that his choice of candidate in 1940 would be crucial, perhaps decisive, to the outcome of the presidential race.

As Lewis weighed his political options and perplexed his associates in the labor movement by engaging in a singular blend of pressure politics, bluff, and suspense, personal and substantive factors made inevitable his choice of presidential candidate. The influential CIO leaders—including Phil Murray, Van Bittner, and John Brophy of the UMW—who in July and August endorsed the reelection of Roosevelt, neither vexed Lewis nor embittered the CIO leader by a show of disloyalty.[37] R. J. Thomas of the UAW may have called for Roosevelt's reelection, but when Lewis appeared at the UAW convention, the delegates treated him as labor's unchallenged leader. Moreover, by the late summer of 1940, few of those closest to Lewis criticized his politics. The left-wing and Communist unions and their leaders in the CIO applauded Lewis's criticism of the president, especially in foreign affairs, where the party line demanded American neutrality. The two men on the CIO central office staff closest to Lewis—Len DeCaux and Lee Pressman—opposed Roosevelt's domestic and foreign policies. Jett Lauck, Lewis's economic consultant and friend for more than two decades, persistently declared the New Deal a failure and urged Lewis to lead a radical reform crusade. And K. C. Adams, the Republican, isolationist, and peddler of anti-semitic canards, returned to the UMW, at Lewis's invitation, as editor of the union *Journal*.[38] No close associates urged Lewis to reconsider his criticism of the president or to alter his position on foreign affairs.

This became clearer as Lewis continued to speak out publicly on politics, war, and peace. Appearing before the convention of the left-wing International Union of Mine, Mill, and Smelter Workers, in Denver, in mid-August, Lewis castigated those labor leaders who had endorsed Roosevelt for selling labor's influence too cheaply. "Labor can endorse a politician for some high office today and tomorrow he will come out and kick labor in the face by advocating conscription. Just like that," observed Lewis, referring sarcastically to Roosevelt. He also reminded the delegates that the president sought war because, among other things, "war writes with imperishable letters on the scroll of history the name of the statesman who first conceived the war; who, second, led his people into the war; and, third, who either won or lost the war." And when Roosevelt had his war, Lewis warned, American liberties would disappear as "the United States . . . first becomes a militaristic nation, and second, becomes an imperialistic nation, to carry out the dreams of conquest of some would-be dictator."[39]

Two weeks later, in his annual Labor Day radio address, Lewis issued further political warnings. "Labor Day in 1940," he observed, "finds labor and the things in which labor believes more in jeopardy than at any time during the history of the modern labor movement." War hysteria had been manufactured and merchandised wholesale in order to turn the nation's attention away from the New Deal's domestic failures, and peacetime conscription as urged by the president, asserted Lewis, "would be the beginning of the end of our democratic way of life." Before it is too late to save the lives of our youth and cure unemployment, all Americans must, Lewis pleaded, "become articulate and . . . demand consideration of American problems, if America as we know it is to be preserved."[40]

Roosevelt's advocates inside and outside the labor movement also believed that the 1940 election would determine the nation's future and that the result would preserve our liberties or threaten them. But where Lewis perceived dangers in foreign intervention and neglect of domestic ills, the president's supporters believed, to the contrary, that Hitler's Germany posed the real threat to national security and American freedom and that, for the moment, foreign policy considerations transcended domestic problems. Such individuals desperately tried to patch up the Lewis-Roosevelt relationship and effect a political reconciliation between the two men. Unfortunately for their plans, Roosevelt advocates lacked direct influence with Lewis, who, as the election approached, withdrew even more tightly into the confines of his family.

The closer the election drew, the fewer friends and associates Lewis saw, at least among those unlikely to support a Republican candidate. Lee Pressman, for five years a Lewis confidant, suddenly found himself isolated from his chief. Jett Lauck, for whom Lewis had always made time available in the past, was unable to see Lewis personally at any time during the month of October 1940.[41]

Such treatment of Pressman and Lauck makes questionable Saul Alinsky's story of last-minute efforts to reconcile Lewis and Roosevelt. According to Alinsky, he and Roman Catholic Bishop Bernard J. Sheil, of Chicago, with Roosevelt's permission, approached Lewis, urging the labor leader to meet privately with the president in order to patch up their differences. The Sheil-Alinsky maneuver, according to the story, resulted in a White House conference on October 17 between Lewis and Roosevelt.[42] This conference, as we will see below, indeed occurred, but probably not as a consequence of Sheil's and Alinsky's intercession in presidential politics. Lewis, who in October 1940 refused even to talk with Jett Lauck because the economist saw no alternative to the Democrats, would scarcely treat Saul Alinsky with more respect or openness. Lewis, who insisted consistently throughout his career that trade unionism and religion could not be mixed, would hardly engage in political maneuvers in the company of a Roman Catholic bishop.

If the above fails to cast doubt on Alinsky's story of last-minute presidential politics, his references to Kathryn Lewis's role in the 1940 election complete the case. Alinsky wrote that Kathryn cooperated in the Sheil-Alinsky ploy and that she urged a reconciliation between Lewis and Roosevelt. Yet Lauck, Pressman, and Len DeCaux, all of whom were closer to Lewis than Alinsky (Lauck indeed was a family friend), agreed that Kathryn was an unalloyed Roosevelt-hater and also a member of the America First Committee and the last person to seek a rapprochement between her father and the president.[43]

Whatever the truth or provenance of the Alinsky story, Roosevelt had excellent reasons to seek a political reconciliation with Lewis. In mid-October Roosevelt's prospects for reelection seemed dicey; the two-term tradition presented one obstacle; foreign policy and the threat of war made the votes of many ethnic blocs, especially the Irish, questionable; and the persistence of mass unemployment eight years after Roosevelt's initial election threatened to cost the Democrats votes. When Louis Stark reported in the *New York Times* on October 16 that Lewis was leaning toward Willkie and would endorse the Republican candidate unless Roosevelt quickly assuaged the labor leader's grievances, the president and his advisers took notice. More so because they probably shared Lewis's reading of the forthcoming election, as noted by Stark, that support for Republicans and Democrats was closely balanced, that a small vote margin in several key industrial and agricultural states would decide the outcome, and that a few thousand CIO votes might swing New York State.[44]

Not unexpectedly, then, the day after the Stark story appeared, Roosevelt invited Lewis to the White House. This is the conference Alinsky asserts that he and Bishop Sheil arranged. But Stark was probably more accurate about the

October 17 White House meeting when he reported, on October 18, that it had been arranged by a close confidant of the president in response to the *Times'* story of October 16.[45] No one can be sure precisely what happened during the conference. Neither participant commented to reporters afterward and both referred to their discussion as secret.[46]

One can only imagine what transpired in the White House on October 17. Undoubtedly the president turned all his redoubtable personal charm on the labor leader. Roosevelt perhaps promised Lewis that the federal government would require industries with defense contracts to obey the Wagner Act, that the A. F. of L. would not be favored over the CIO, and that labor would have as large an influence as business in shaping defense policies. The president probably said little, if anything, about foreign policy, and if he did so, it would not have been to Lewis's liking. Lewis, it is clear, went to the White House determined not to be charmed by Roosevelt—in fact, determined to reject a reconciliation. Instead of discussing substantive political issues, Lewis immediately accused the president of ordering the FBI to eavesdrop on him and subject him to total surveillance. He demanded that Roosevelt end all such infringements on his personal privacy and civil liberties.[47]

Lewis had thus placed the president in a position in which he could not mollify the labor leader. If Roosevelt now ordered the FBI to cease and desist from eavesdropping on Lewis, the president would have admitted publicly that he had originally issued such orders. If Roosevelt denied having issued such orders, Lewis would have further proof of the president's duplicity. Nothing Roosevelt might do or say could satisfy Lewis; by the evening of October 17 their political rift was complete.

That Lewis actually accused the president of tapping his phones and invading his privacy there can be no doubt. On October 30 the New York *Herald-Tribune* reported that such a confrontation had occurred and that Lewis cited three men in the Justice Department as the source of his information. Characteristically, however, a day later, for official purposes and in response to the *Herald-Tribune* story, J. Edgar Hoover issued a formal denial of the charges. "The fact of the matter is," wrote Hoover, "that this Bureau never has and is not now making any investigation of John L. Lewis."[48]

Saul Alinsky also repeats the FBI story—with the customary dramatics and inaccuracies. Alinsky contended that Frank Murphy, then attorney general, informed Lewis of the FBI surveillance ordered by the president, an assertion rejected by Murphy's biographer, Sidney Fine, who has discovered no evidence to suggest that Murphy knew of any bureau surveillance of Lewis or leaked such information to the labor leader.[49]

Did Roosevelt order the FBI to place Lewis under surveillance, or did J. Edgar Hoover do so without authorization? Those questions perhaps will never be answered satisfactorily until Hoover's personal files become open to public examination.* Why Lewis charged the president with ordering his surveillance can be answered. First, Lewis remembered that during the post-World War I labor crisis in 1919, then-attorney general A. Mitchell Palmer had had the phones of Lewis and Gompers tapped and all UMW officials placed under surveillance. Second, for more than a year, Lewis, in a series of public speeches, had alleged that the Roosevelt administration used the foreign policy crisis to build up a domestic secret police force that spied on the private lives of alleged "fifth columnists." Third, and finally, a Lewis associate later informed the authors of this biography that the CIO president literally observed FBI agents trailing him wherever he went. For these reasons, Lewis had cause to believe that Roosevelt ordered wiretapping and personal surveillance.[50] But the wiretapping charge was scarcely a necessary or sufficient cause for the political rift between Lewis and Roosevelt. It simply offered Lewis an excuse to feign anger and outrage, stalk out of the president's bedroom, and break off all further discussions aimed at rapprochement. As we will shortly see, Lewis had made a firm decision about the presidential election three weeks prior to the October 17 conference.

On October 22 the press reported that Lewis would speak to the nation on Friday night, October 25, at 9:00 P.M. on all three national radio networks. By then, most knowledgeable political observers, including Roosevelt, knew that Lewis would endorse Willkie, though the president, at his press conference of October 22, denied any advance knowledge of what Lewis would say. And Lewis, to insure obtaining the largest possible audience subject to his influence, telegrammed UMW districts requesting them to inform all local unions immediately of the scheduled October 25 radio address and the "fact that political issues of the campaign will be discussed."[51]

In the week before his October 25 speech, Lewis retreated into almost total isolation, soliciting ideas from none of his close associates or advisers and, according to Lee Pressman, even writing his own speech. Leaders in the CIO, the Republican party, and the Democratic party expected no surprises in Lewis's speech. The estimated 25 to 30 million Americans who listened to Lewis on the evening of October 25 over 322 local stations on the three networks, however, had no idea what the labor leader would say. They listened expectantly.

Almost before his radio audience settled down, Lewis disclaimed any intention of speaking for labor or of controlling the vote of any man or woman. Instead, he promised to speak only for himself. Lewis then repeated the essence of every public political speech he had made since the January 1940 UMW convention. Roosevelt's motivation and objective, he stressed, was *war*. "The President has

*The U. S. Senate Investigation of internal security in the fall of 1975 insisted that Hoover and the FBI did engage in domestic surveillance of civilians as authorized by President Roosevelt. *New York Times*, December 4, 1975, p. 1; December 7, 1975, IV, p. 1.

said that he hates war and will work for peace, but his acts do not match his words." He, Lewis charged, created an unprecedentedly powerful presidency— one rendered even more unprecedented by "the spectacle of a President who is disinclined to surrender that power, in keeping with traditions of the Republic. . . . Personal craving for power, the overweening abnormal and selfish craving for increased power, is a thing to alarm and dismay. . . . America needs no super-man," thundered Lewis. "It denies the philosophy that runs to deification of the state. America wants no royal family." The United States, Lewis quipped nastily, has had enough of the "economic and political experiments of an amateur, ill-equipped practitioner in the realm of political science."

Having castigated the president's domestic and foreign policies, as he had done the entire year, Lewis, more than halfway into his speech, finally struck its most dramatic, new note. Whom do I recommend, he asked? Why, of course, he answered, Wendell Willkie! Then, as if in unconscious parady of Harold L. Ickes's dismissal of the utilities tycoon Willkie as "the barefoot boy from Wall Street," Lewis portrayed the Republican candidate as follows: "He is not an aristocrat. He has the common touch. He was born in the briar and not to the purple. He has worked with his hands, and has known the pangs of hunger." To reject Willkie and elect Roosevelt, Lewis warned, "would be a national evil of the first magnitude."

Roosevelt, Lewis concluded, could win only with labor's support, and he implored CIO members not to give it. If CIO members spurned his advice, if they voted for Roosevelt, Lewis pledged to resign as CIO president. Then came what should have been the speech's peroration. "Through the years of struggle, you have been content that I should be in the forefront of your battles. I am still the same man. Sustain me now, or repudiate me." But instead of closing his address on that dramatic challenge to his union constituents, Lewis restated the issue that really separated him from Roosevelt. "You," he asked the youths among his audience, "who may be about to die in a foreign war, created at the whim of an international meddler, should you salute your Caesar?" And to their mothers, he pleaded in his best Victorian tone, "May I hope that on election day [you] . . . with the sacred ballot, lead the revolt against the candidate who plays at a game that may make cannon fodder of your sons."[52]

After the speech, an obviously satisfied Lewis remained at UMW headquarters for several hours posing for newsreel cameramen, taking phone calls, and opening telegrams.[53] Among the wires was one from Herbert Hoover, assuring Lewis "that speech will resound over years to come," and another from Harvey Fremming, of the oil and chemical workers' union, also congratulating Lewis for being at his "unequalled best." "I agree and support your conclusions pridefully," said Fremming. "If I can aid you in the crusade, please command me."[54]

The Republican presidential candidate, too, was among those who wired Lewis immediately complimenting the labor leader for making "the most eloquent address I ever heard.'' Interestingly, Willkie's telegram bore a Wilkes-Barre, Pennsylvania, postmark, indicating that Lewis's radio speech had been timed to coincide with a Republican campaign swing through that crucial state ending in the anthracite district.[55] And several days later, on October 28, the 1936 Republican candidate, Alf Landon, added his flattery. In endorsing Willkie, Landon complimented Lewis, ''you had more courage, and were sticking your neck further out, than the stuffed shirt business man who is supporting Willkie . . . making the issue with the people who should be loyal to you a direct one between you and Roosevelt was a master stroke.''[56]

Lewis's family and his closest associates in the labor movement rallied round their leader or kept silent, as did Phil Murray, a Roosevelt advocate. On October 28, CIO publicity director Len DeCaux announced that 90% of the post-speech telegrams, many from trade union rank-and-filers, favored Lewis's endorsement of Willkie. DeCaux assured newsmen that Lewis thought that his radio speech had elected Willkie and that he would probably not have to speak on the air again. Illinois, Indiana, Ohio, Pennsylvania, and New York, DeCaux alleged, were safely in the Republican column; New Jersey remained doubtful; and one more Lewis effort would win Kentucky and Tennessee for the Republican candidate.[57]

Those expected to rally around Lewis but who failed to do so immediately became targets for pressure. The left-wing and Communist union leaders Lewis had welcomed into the CIO and sheltered received phone call after call from Dennie Lewis demanding that they endorse Willkie. The Harry Bridgeses, Joe Currans, and Ben Golds applauded Lewis's repudiation of Roosevelt; but, as left-wingers, they could scarcely countenance promoting the candidacy of a Republican ''barefoot boy from Wall Street.'' Consequently they strained to avoid Lewis after October 25, and in the words of Lee Pressman, ''were running so fast you couldn't see their coat-tails from then on.'' Mike Quill, unfortunately, failed to run fast enough, and when asked by Lewis personally to support Willkie, the militant Communist leader of the New York City transit workers deferentially said, ''Willkie is my man for President.'' Thereafter Dennie deluged Quill's office with Willkie literature, which the union's staff incinerated as soon as it arrived.[58]

In the ten days that remained between Lewis's initial endorsement of Willkie and the election, the labor leader drew the line ever sharper between himself and Roosevelt, reiterating that workers must choose between the two. On Sunday, November 3, Lewis released to the press a statement he had composed in laborious longhand on official UMW presidential stationery. ''Labor will decide the election,'' he wrote. It ''will determine whether it is capable of following its own developed leadership or whether it will accept the leadership of an erratic war mongering politician. The issues are joined. Labor can sustain or cut down its own leader. I have confidence in the result. Wendell Willkie will be elected.'' And a day later, on election eve, Lewis spoke briefly on radio to warn voters that

Roosevelt's reelection meant war and that only Willkie and the Republicans could preserve peace.[59]

Lewis's endorsement of Willkie caused consternation inside the CIO and among the entire American political Left. Resentment against Lewis's new politics had been mounting ever since the 1940 UMW convention, and it reached a climax after the October 25 speech. Many city and state industrial union councils repudiated Lewis's endorsement of Willkie, though they generally expressed their confidence in the CIO president as a labor leader. Hillman and the Amalgamated Clothing Workers directly challenged Lewis's politics. Over the radio and also at an American labor party rally at New York's Madison Square Garden on October 31, Jacob S. Potofsky, vice-president of the ACW, asserted that "neither John L. Lewis nor any other man can dictate labor's vote. . . . The Amalgamated Clothing Workers along with the overwhelming majority of the workers in the C.I.O. and A. F. of L. *think* for themselves. . . . They will vote to continue the New Deal; they will vote for President Roosevelt. Labor will not scrap its newly won rights because of one man's personal grudge."[60] On October 27, Gardner Jackson, one of the few CIO officials Lewis had associated with socially, submitted his resignation as legislative representative of Labor's Non-Partisan League in an open letter to Lewis published in most metropolitan newspapers that took sharp exception to the CIO president's endorsement of Willkie.[61]

More vexing to Lewis was the emergence of dissent and division within the UMW. Even before his October 25 speech, Lewis's criticism of Roosevelt had led more UMW locals to submit nominations of Phil Murray for the union presidency than Lewis (500 to 200). After Lewis's Willkie speech, observed Powers Hapgood, "The miners are all disturbed about Lewis's speech." Hapgood noted that most coal miners probably shared Van Bittner's observation that, "I am 100% for John L. Lewis as head of the CIO and also 100% for the reelection of Roosevelt."[62] Senator James Murray reported to Roosevelt from Montana that, "All workers and their unions in Montana have repudiated Lewis. His action is a boomerang." To which the president responded, "That is grand news." And another presidential informant noted that he had never seen the coal miners worked up to such a pitch of excitement. Except for officials appointed directly by Lewis, all the miners and their locals had rallied behind the president. In the Ohio coalfields, the informant observed, were many dummies of Lewis hanged in effigy with cards proclaiming, "Judas, Traitor, Dictator."[63]

Roosevelt's papers, in fact, contain three file boxes crammed with letters and telegrams supporting the president and repudiating Lewis, many from UMW locals, coal miners, and hundreds of CIO affiliates. Scores of notes from nonunion correspondents linked Lewis to communism and Stalinism. And most of those who wrote to the president shared the sentiments expressed by one J. Q. Ferguson: "The following to John L. Lewis: Tremendous, stupendous, colossal! not since Judas Iscariot has God created such a traitor. Maybe Barnum was right."[64]

When the votes were counted, they convicted Lewis of a glaring political miscalculation. Not only did Roosevelt win reelection by a substantial, if reduced (5 million votes, down from 11 million in 1936) margin; the president's support remained firmest among working-class voters, especially those in regions of union strength, including coal miners. Lewis's troops had deserted him en masse.

Yet the day following the election Lewis seemed not the least depressed. Refusing to be drawn into a discussion of the election campaign during a press conference, he nevertheless impressed reporters as cheerful and good-natured. Lewis, moreover, seemed as willing to abide by his pledge to resign the CIO presidency as to accept the election results.[65]

In an ironic footnote to the election, it turned out that Lewis himself did not cast a ballot. Although then living in Alexandria, Virginia, he had retained his legal, and hence voting, residence in Springfield, Illinois. "I consider it unfortunate," Lewis informed the chief clerk in Springfield when applying for an absentee ballot in December 1943, "that circumstances prevented my voting at the time of the last presidential election."[66]

At this point, one might well ask, what really prompted Lewis to endorse Willkie? Why did he stake his future as CIO president on Roosevelt's defeat? Why, moreover, did he risk splitting the UMW as well as the CIO in what many considered a vain political gamble? How does one analyze or explain Lewis's political behavior in the year 1940?

Len DeCaux, who was at the radio studio with Lewis the night of his election-eve endorsement of Willkie, asserts that during a long chat later that evening, Lewis assumed that Roosevelt would win. Why, then, did he back Willkie? DeCaux's only answer is that Lewis resented the divisions Roosevelt had created inside the CIO and that if the president was reelected, Lewis then had an excuse to retire as CIO president. If, unexpectedly, Willkie won, Lewis would have the right to stay on as president of the CIO and demand absolute loyalty from his followers.[67]

Saul Alinsky provides more evidence for DeCaux's answer. Lewis allegedly told his biographer, "I carefully examined that election [1940], and there never was a momentary doubt in my mind but that Mr. Roosevelt was going to be re-elected. That was the very reason I deliberately publicly committed myself and my organization to the camp of Wendell Willkie. You see, I wanted to, I had to get out of the presidency of the CIO if I were to be effective in uniting the divided forces of labor." And TRB, in the *New Republic* of November 4, 1940 (even before the returns had come in), observed that Lewis's primary motivation was "to preserve the labor movement as a separate, independent entity under its own leaders. If Mr. Willkie were President, there would be no confusion about whether he or John L. Lewis spoke for organized labor. There would be no difficulty in rallying labor against Mr. Willkie."[68]

In October and November 1940, Roosevelt intimates suggested that personal peeves and ambitions explained Lewis's behavior. The president had refused to heed Lewis's advice in making federal appointments, declined to issue executive orders demanded by the labor leader, and rejected entreaties to lend federal funds to Josephine Roche's bankrupt coal company—a concern heavily indebted to the UMW. Other rumors from the White House alleged that Lewis was especially piqued by Sidney Hillman's role as presidential labor adviser; and Senator Robert Wagner asserted publicly that Lewis's great desire was to become secretary of labor, a position Willkie had promised the labor leader.[69]

Lewis and his associates naturally characterized such rumors as fantastic. Lewis personally ridiculed Senator Wagner's assertion, claiming falsely that "in the past, I have been offered the portfolio of Labor and I have declined it. If, in the future, it should again be tendered me, I would decline it."[70]

The essence of the White House rumors can be dismissed easily. First, Lewis never allowed personal pique to influence, let alone control, crucial political decisions. Second, with the exception of the 1932 election, in which he played a distinctly secondary and largely invisible role, Lewis never consciously backed a sure loser. His whole career in the labor movement had reflected virtuosic opportunism—the ability to change policies, positions, and parties hastily as attitudes inside and outside the labor movement shifted. In the past he had evolved from a Wilsonian reformer to a 1920s-style Republican to an ardent New Dealer. Whatever the times demanded, or Lewis thought they did, he tried to supply. That, however, does not mean that Lewis rejected risk-taking. Far from it. He was, as the history of the CIO proved, a consummate gambler, a man able to bluff industrialists and politicians as well as poker cronies. Need it be said, however, that no good gambler bets all his chips on a sure loser? A long shot, to be sure, offers greater prospective rewards to its backer than an odds-on favorite, and Willkie, the underdog in 1940, carried precisely the right odds, provided Lewis could deliver his candidate some slight edge in the race.

Anyone who followed Lewis's public speeches from January through October 1940 could see that substantive issues divided the labor leader from Roosevelt. Personal pique may have embittered the relationship, but mass unemployment, the failure of the New Deal to ameliorate the nation's economic problems, and the threat of overseas war remained the root causes of the break. Lewis, by 1940, believed that labor had received all it would from the New Deal, that continued support of Roosevelt would only vitiate labor's political influence and, worse yet, lead the nation into war.

Willkie as president, on the contrary, promised labor clear advantages. As early as April 1939 Lewis and Willkie, during a dinner discussion at a party given by liberal Democratic lawyer Morris Ernst for what he referred to as his "favorite Tories," agreed on a program for reducing unemployment substantially.[71] More significantly, during the 1940 election Lewis and Willkie had a secret meeting on September 28, at which the Republican candidate assured the CIO leader that organized labor would be recognized as a real factor in national affairs and its leaders would receive key positions in the administration if the Republicans won.[72] Although Willkie's interventionist foreign policy displeased Lewis, Republicans, as a party, thought Lewis, were less likely to involve the nation in war; and their protectionist economic policies, compared to the Democrats' free trade propensities, promised greater job security for American workers.

Willkie's promises and Republican foreign policy would have meant nothing to Lewis in the absence of victory. But the labor leader had been reading the election returns since 1938, and was certain, as he stated publicly at the 1940 UMW convention, that a Republican trend was in the making. Knowing that Democrats depended on the labor vote in 1940 as never before, certain that the election would be close, and egotistical enough to believe that he could influence the votes of a substantial number of CIO members, Lewis endorsed Willkie. Alinsky is right, when he writes that Lewis used his threat to resign as CIO president as a trump card. "He took the whip and laid down the ultimatum. 'It's either Roosevelt or me. Take your choice. You cannot have both'."[73] In the event that Willkie won, the Republican candidate would know whom to thank for his success. What better, more calculated gamble could a poker player take?

No one close to Lewis challenged his gamble. His family encouraged the break with Roosevelt. Daughter Kathryn and brother Dennie played the politics of pique. They worshipped respectively their father-older brother and interpreted every presidential rejection of Lewis as a personal insult, none more so than the appointment of Sidney Hillman rather than John L. Lewis as wartime presidential adviser. Moreover, some acquaintances of the Lewis family suggested that Myrta was the rock-ribbed family Republican and political conservative—a wife pleased by her husband's return to the true faith in 1940.

In the event, Lewis had no alternative to Willkie. Roosevelt was out of the question. Much as the American Communists and pacifist Left approved Lewis's attacks on the president, Lewis still despised Communists and only by accident shared their foreign policy in 1940. Lewis remained too much the opportunist, too much the personification of vulgar pragmatism and business values, to lead a third-party political crusade.[74] During the same union convention in August 1940 at which Lewis lashed out at Roosevelt and threatened the creation of a third party, he informed delegates that trade unions today must compete with big business on the basis of efficient, practical business administration of union affairs. "It takes money to operate a modern business enterprise," he advised, "and it takes money to operate a modern, successful labor organization. After all, we get in value about what we pay for."[75] A third party would cost too much and obviously offer too little in return. Committed fundamentally to the central values of a business civilization and to the myth of the indestructability of the two-party system, Lewis had nowhere to turn in 1940 but to Willkie.

His turn to Willkie, however, cost Lewis and the American labor movement dearly. Democrats and Roosevelt-worshippers in the labor movement called Lewis's political bluff, and, in this event, they held the better cards. Roosevelt's triumph, despite the wishes of CIO draft-Lewis advocates and the fears of CIO anti-Lewis leaders, sealed Lewis's resignation as CIO president and precipitated his eventual departure from the organization. A labor movement already split between A. F. of L. and CIO would soon be divided in three, as Lewis and the mine workers chose in 1942 to function independently. Having backed the rejected candidate in 1940 and stepped down subsequently as president of the CIO, Lewis would never again exercise the influence inside and outside the labor movement that he had wielded from 1936 through 1940.

Well before Lewis endorsed Willkie and threatened to resign as CIO president if Roosevelt were reelected, many CIO members looked forward to the November 1940 convention with foreboding. Beyond the long-standing dispute between Hillman and Lewis and the internal schism in the United Auto Workers, trouble between Murray and Lewis had developed by early October. On October 9, Powers Hapgood informed his wife, Mary, that although "Phil Murray will never oppose John L. publicly, they have severe differences owing mainly to Lewis's refusal to consult anyone before he makes an important move and he insults people with whom he disagrees." Later that month, a day after Lewis's radio speech for Willkie, Hapgood grew more worried about the upcoming CIO convention. "The [Lewis-Hillman] fight is now bitter," he wrote Mary. "If FDR is elected, there will be no split as Lewis will retire and Murray will probably be president. If Willkie wins Lewis will make life so embarrassing for the A.C.W. and other unions that they will probably secede."[76]

But even after Roosevelt won, Hapgood and other critics of Lewis feared what Lewis might say or do at the convention. "There is a strong sentiment growing," Harvey Fremming, of the oil workers, reported to Adolph Germer from the West Coast on November 9, "in an effort to draft President Lewis to succeed himself." Two days later, Hapgood, after a long conference with several officials of the Amalgamated Clothing Workers, informed his wife that Lewis might accept a draft movement being organized by Joe Curran, Harry Bridges, Mike Quill, and representatives of other Communist party-controlled unions. If Lewis acceded to a draft or Murray declined to accept CIO leadership, Hapgood concluded, "there is going to be a split. . . . There will be an awful fight unless the convention is fair and that depends on Lewis and Murray." Indeed, Hillman's lieutenants were so worried about Lewis's tactics, including the prospect of his using anti-Semitism against his critics, that the Amalgamated planned to send all the "Gentiles" it could find as delegates to the CIO convention.[77]

The last session of the CIO executive board shortly before the convention offered critics of Lewis further cause for anxiety. At this meeting, Lewis clashed explicitly with representatives of the clothing workers, and he accused Hillman, in the latter's role as labor representative on the NDAC, of relinquishing trade unionism's legitimate rights. Why, asked Lewis, did Hillman tolerate the awarding of defense contracts to nonunion firms? Why did Hillman refuse to demand that President Roosevelt issue an enforceable executive order requiring the recipients of federal contracts to bargain with organized labor? Such questions led Hillman's associates to believe that Lewis would not relinquish the CIO presidency gracefully.[78]

In Atlantic City, on the boardwalk, in the Chelsea Hotel, at the site where Lewis had slugged Hutcheson in October 1935, with 2,600 CIO delegates in an expectant mood, the stage seemed set, on November 18, 1940, for another dramatic John L. Lewis performance. Crucial convention committees, especially the Resolutions Committee, with Tom Kennedy as chairman and Lee Pressman as secretary, were firmly in the hands of Lewis loyalists. A large majority of the delegates, excluding only those from the ACW and a few of their allies, could not conceive of a CIO without Lewis. Whatever their president wanted, they would grant. Let Lewis order; the delegates would implement. Moreover, as president, Lewis would deliver the convention's first major address. What would he say? Would he tender his resignation or encourage a draft?

As Lewis made his way to the lectern to speak, delegates erupted in an enthusiastic demonstration. According to the biographer of Sidney Hillman, Matthew Josephson, who presents the ACW's version of what happened on the convention's opening day, suddenly many of the delegates arose wearing huge "We Want Lewis" buttons. Placards with the same motto sprang up everywhere. "There were visible," writes Josephson, "all those little signs and warnings of what political scientists . . . characterize as a 'stampede'." For forty-three minutes, faithful mine workers, Communists, and other delegates exhibited their draft-Lewis placards. They "paraded, yelled, sang, wept, and embraced each other," Josephson continues. "For a long time the chanting and roaring went on—'*Lewis is our leader! Lewis is our leader!*'—while he smiled and waved and drank in the intoxicating sight. Only the Amalgamated delegates and their allies sat impassively, and if they could be suppressed or driven out," concluded Josephson, "the road would be open to the Lewis steam roller. As the convention proceeded it became apparent that this was Lewis's intention."[79]

Josephson is perfectly right in his description of the pro-Lewis demonstration and the consternation that it caused among Amalgamated delegates. Even the UMW *Journal* described the delegates' reaction to Lewis's appearance in similar language. "It was a display of loyalty," the union *Journal* observed, "that could not be misunderstood, and it must have warmed the cockles of his [Lewis's] heart."[80] But Josephson was wrong about Lewis's motivation. Much as it may have warmed his heart, the CIO leader played no part in organizing the demonstration or initiating the draft-Lewis movement; nor did any of his lieutenants.[81] Subsequently, Lewis indeed clashed with Hillmanites, insulted them, and even humiliated them rhetorically; but his opening address must be taken at face value, and, as such, it was a valedictory—some even said an example of a man reading his own eulogy.

The opening address was vintage Lewis. For it, Lewis drew freely from his well-thumbed book of aphorisms, stock phrases, purple passages, and platitudes. Borrowing from poets, philosophers, and politicians, the banal as well as the brilliant, Lewis echoed familiar themes and uncharacteristically, made several heart-felt private confessions. From his opening paraphrase of the Gettysburgh Address ("Three score months ago a new union was formed; conceived in liberty and the spirit of progress and forever dedicated to the proposition that the workers in our modern industries should be organized into industrial unions. Today we are engaged in a great struggle to determine whether a union so conceived and so dedicated can endure") to his closing lines, Lewis played his audience for all it was worth. He intended to depart the CIO's stage in a display of emotion, tears, and histrionics.[82]

Lewis also left no doubt, for anyone who listened carefully to his words, that he planned to resign. He informed the delegates that their worst enemy was internal dissension and a lack of confidence in labor's leaders. Divide among yourselves, he observed, and at night there is the sound of revelry and rejoicing in the camp of the adversary. The meaning of his words should have been obvious. After his endorsement of Willkie and pledge to resign if Roosevelt was reelected, Lewis obviously could not remain as president of CIO without causing dissension. To his most ardent supporters at the convention, the left-wing and Communist delegates, he uttered the most discomforting words. "I yield to no man the right to challenge my Americanism nor the Americanism of the organizations which at this moment I represent." For those in the press who misrepresented Communist influence in the CIO, Lewis remarked, "they lie in their beard and they lie in their bowels. My remark goes for Old Lady Green down in New Orleans, too, and old as she is, she really should know better."[83]

After advising the delegates to avoid dissension and abjure "un-American" philosophies, Lewis stated explicitly that, "I won't be with you long. In just a day or two I will be out of this office which at the moment I occupy." Do not trouble yourself or grow heartsick over my departure, he begged, giving the delegates his own philosophy of existence. "That is the way of life. Some are able to carry through and some fall, but there is nothing to worry about. We should not dwell in the past [the most hallowed of Lewis's beliefs]. Yesterday is gone and tomorrow is another day. I am concerned with tomorrow and I care nothing what happened yesterday." And then, with tears streaking his cheeks and his voice quavering, Lewis observed, "Some great statesman once said that the heights are cold. I think that is true. The poet said, 'Who ascends to the mountain's top finds the loftiest peaks encased in mists and snow.' I think that is true." That being the way of man and life, "we can't stop to weep and wear sackcloth because something that happened yesterday did not meet with our approval or that we did not have a dream come true. Tomorrow is the day that always faces the men and women." To any delegates who still thought that Lewis desired to continue as president, he reiterated, "You know when you first hired me I was something of a man, and when I leave you in a day or two I will still in my own mind be something of a man." And after reminding delegates that they must choose a new president, Lewis thanked them for receiving him so warmly, recalling the words of the Jesuit Gratian three centuries ago, "He shortly turns from the well who drinks his fill and the squeezed orange falls from the golden salver to the dung." In an extremely revealing final remark, particularly so coming after several references to his strength and manhood, Lewis reflected, "I only wish sometimes that men had half the strength and half the fortitude and half the courage and half the wisdom of the ladies."[84]

Thus did Lewis bid farewell as president of the CIO. Never before had he confessed publicly the personal loneliness that had been his life as labor leader. Having lived, in his own words, "among men and sometimes in far places," Lewis lacked intimate friends and the stable family relationships he most cherished. His sacrifice freely made, Lewis, in November 1940, fell to the ground like Gratian's squeezed orange—the departed leader of an army whose troops no longer rallied undivided behind their general.

Despite Lewis's explicit pledge to resign on his own, friends and critics of the CIO leader refused to believe he would voluntarily relinquish the presidency. Communist and left-wing delegates still hoped that Lewis might be drafted, and the Hillman-ACW coalition feared that Lewis might change his mind. Instead of taking Lewis at his word and letting him depart gracefully and quietly, the ACW delegation assaulted the CIO president. They submitted a resolution criticizing the *CIO News* (still fearful of attacking the "big boy" openly, they chose Len DeCaux as surrogate) for printing no news on the Roosevelt campaign, and, losing that battle, charged Lewis directly with disrupting A. F. of L.-CIO unity negotiations. The ACW delegation, joined by Phil Murray, also demanded the passage of a resolution repudiating communism. When left-wing delegates appeared at Lewis's hotel room well after midnight to complain about the anti-Communist resolution in the works, Lewis responded, "What can you expect when the old man leaves, everybody will set their dogs howling at his heels. What can I do?" he asked. "What can a man do, a general who is being harried from the scene of battle? Whipped as his cohorts."[85]

The ACW assault prompted Lewis to one last rhetorical flourish. Angered especially by the charge that he had sabotaged negotiations with the A. F. of L., Lewis rose to defend himself. Promising to spare the delegates a speech, Lewis delivered one of the longest and most frequently cited addresses of his career. To those who demanded further discussions with the A. F. of L. in order to explore its position on unity, Lewis characterized the Federation's negotiators disdainfully.

> I have been an explorer in the American Federation of Labor. Explore the mind of Bill Green? Why, Bill and I had offices next door to each other for ten years. . . . I have done a lot of exploring in Bill's mind, and I give you my word there is nothing there.
>
> Explore Matthew Woll's mind? I did. It is the mind of an insurance agent who used his position . . . to promote his insurance business.
>
> Explore Tom Ricket's mind? I did, and here is what was in his mind. . . . I said he

was getting $20,000 a year graft . . . and I had a paper in my pocket to prove it. He knew . . . that as true. And I thought then I had explored his mind enough.

Well, after all I think there is a limit to which the membership of my organization should permit me to waste my time and their money.

Lewis next laid into the leaders of the needles trades unions, raising the suspicion that he planned to stir the anti-Semitism latent among many convention delegates. Dubinsky, remarked Lewis, had sworn by bell, book, and candle to remain loyal to the CIO. And where is he today?

He has crept back in the American Federation of Labor. . . . He is crying out now, and his voice laments like that of Rachel in the Wilderness, against the racketeers and the panderers and the crooks in that organization.

And Zaritsky. . . . He said, "Me too." And now above all the clamor comes the piercing wail and the laments of the Amalgamated Clothing Workers. And they say, "Peace, it is wonderful." And there is no peace.

Then, staring at the Amalgamated delegates, Lewis sneered, "Dubinsky took the easy way. Zaritsky too the easy way. If there is anybody else in the CIO who wants to take the easy way, let them go on."[86] At this juncture, according to Matthew Josephson, "a great roar of applause came from the crowd, which burst into a renewed 'draft parade. . . . The whole convention seemed on the verge of riot and bloodshed'."

Other observers at the convention, including most reporters who were then hostile to Lewis, saw it differently. Lewis, indeed, had many advocates among the delegates; but they scarcely seemed on the verge of riot and bloodshed, nor was Lewis eager to encourage such behavior. But the anti-Lewis element, especially that part associated with the Amalgamated, probably saw events as Josephson describes them. Ridiculed and frightened by Lewis, they hastened to phone Hillman, then in Washington on official defense business, asking him to come to Atlantic City in order to assume command of the anti-Lewis forces.[87]

On November 20, the convention's third day, Hillman arrived at the Chelsea well before the session's opening benediction in order to avoid a later entry which might engender an angry reaction from the Lewis claque. Advised by his lieutenants that Lewis intended a draft, Hillman acted to prevent that likelihood, a possibility that existed more in the fevered imagination of ACW delegates than in reality. Hillman spoke softly and unemotionally. If Lewis could steal from Shakespeare, so, too, could Hillman, though less dramatically. Playing the role of Mark Antony at great Caesar's funeral, Hillman heaped praise on the departing CIO president. His harshest words were reserved for the convention's most inviting target, the Communist delegates, already tongue-lashed by Lewis and the object of Phil Murray's wrath. Pledging that his own union would never desert the CIO, Hillman regretted that in the future John L. Lewis would not lead the organization. "I know that there is nothing else that he can do and will do and will agree to do but what he believes to be the best for the organized labor movement.

. . . It is my considered judgment that when John L. Lewis steps down there must be a demand for Phil Murray.'' Those words, according to Hillman's effusive biographer, coldly, logically buried the draft-Lewis movement.[88]

If Hillman believed that his premature nomination of Murray for the CIO presidency killed the impending Lewis draft, he was deceiving himself. For Murray was already Lewis's hand-picked candidate as successor. All that stood between Murray and the CIO presidency in November 1940 was not the prospect of a Lewis draft but Murray's own fear about following in his master's footsteps. Although the press fussed about Murray's insistence that the CIO unanimously condemn communism before he would consider the presidency, that factor was the least of his worries. Lewis, in his opening address, had condemned communism, Nazism, and other alien philosophies in words practically identical with a resolution later passed unanimously by the delegates, including the Communists among them. Murray knew Lewis too well to consider alleged Communist influence in the CIO as a reason to decline the presidency. What he feared was that Lewis expected him to act in a subservient capacity to the UMW president. Prior to accepting the presidency, Murray, according to Lee Pressman, ''went through the pangs of hell, because he knew that Lewis was putting him there . . . expecting him to act as an agent for Lewis, and that Lewis would have the hold over him as vice-president of the United Mine Workers. And Murray was . . . trying to ask himself . . . was he going to be a man in his own right, or not?''[89]

But even Murray lacked alternatives. A successful Lewis draft would have rescued Murray from his dilemma; Lewis's lieutenant knew, however, that under no circumstances would his chief remain as CIO president. And Murray also realized that he was the only candidate acceptable to Lewis, the UMW delegates, the Hillman crowd, and, to a lesser degree, the Communists. Crudely put, the choice for the CIO on November 20, 1940, was Murray or chaos. A left-wing successor to Lewis would have driven the Amalgamated and its allies out of the CIO; a right-wing nominee would have prompted Lewis, the miners, and a large majority of the delegates to rebel. Thus Murray allowed Lewis to weaken his resistance and to place his name in nomination on November 22, as a man ''splendidly equipped with every natural and inherent talent, a gentleman . . . a scholar . . . a natural leader, an administrator, a family man, and a God-fearing man.''[90]

Elected president of the CIO unanimously, Murray rose to deliver a peculiar acceptance speech, an address in which he sought to dispel the self-doubt that had plagued him from the moment Lewis annointed him as successor. ''I think I am a man,'' Murray remarked, recalling his chief's opening day allusion to his own manhood. ''I think I have convictions, I think I have a soul and a heart and a mind. . . . With the exception, of course, of my soul, they all belong to me, every one of them.''[91] With this assurance to the CIO delegates that he would act for himself and no longer play the role of Lewis's loyal, unquestioning servant, Murray took the crown offered him by the CIO's departing champion.

For Lewis the 1940 CIO convention closed the most brilliant chapter in a long, varied, and tumultuous career as a labor leader. All that remained was leadership of the organization that he had built into the nation's largest and most powerful trade union. Rejected by the nation's voters and voluntarily cast out from the CIO presidency, Lewis, in Lee Pressman's classical allusion to the Greek mythical figure Antaeus, who lost all his strength if lifted from the ground, returned to solid ground, the source of his strength, the United Mine Workers. "When Lewis uttered the words 'United Mine Workers of America'," recalled Pressman, "you had a feeling there that that was something much more important than when he said 'United States of America'."[92] Or as Len DeCaux wrote in 1970, "John L. Lewis and the miners alone together—John L. Lewis/UMW—that for him may have been a closer identification of man with many than was John L. Lewis/CIO."[93]

CHAPTER 16

A Man and His Union:
John L. Lewis, the UMW, and
the Coal Industry, 1935-1940

For four decades the headquarters of the United Mine Workers had been in Indianapolis, a city close to the major bituminous coalfields, the home of several other large national trade unions, and a railroad center. The UMW's location in Indianapolis reflected the dominance of the Central Competitive Field in the soft-coal industry and, despite some exceptions, the private, voluntary character of collective bargaining in the coal industry. Convenient to the union's largest districts (Illinois and Pennsylvania) and to the largest operators' home offices (Pittsburgh, Cleveland, and Chicago), Indianapolis had served the UMW well. It had also been handy for John L. Lewis, who kept his family residence in Springfield, Illinois, only a three-hour train ride away on a regularly scheduled Baltimore and Ohio passenger route.

With the coming of the New Deal, however, Indianapolis lost its locational advantages. Changes in the structure of the coal industry during the 1920s also rendered the Indiana capital less desirable for the UMW. The rise of the southern Appalachian coal producers weakened the hegemony of the Central Competitive Field, and bargains struck in Pittsburgh, Cleveland, and Chicago no longer guaranteed stability in the nation's coal mines. More significantly, after the passage of the National Industrial Recovery Act in June 1933, decisions reached in Washington became as important to the future of coal mining as contracts between the miners' union and the operators. The locus of economic power in the coal industry had shifted for both union representatives and operators' associations from the coalfields to the nation's capital and from Capitol Hill to the White House and presidential appointees in the National Recovery Administration and the Departments of Labor and Commerce.

John L. Lewis grasped the significance of this change for his union. In 1934 he transferred UMW headquarters to Washington, first in rented space in the Tower

Building, an undistinguished office block close to the White House and federal agency offices, and two years later to the University Club, at 15th and K Streets, N.W., which the UMW purchased for a half million dollars, remodeled, and refurnished in a style fitting a labor baron.[1] Perhaps this was Lewis's way of showing that America in the 1930s had been turned upside down, that those born to wealth and power now had to share it with those who had thrust themselves up from the bottom.

From his new union headquarters in the nation's capital, John L. Lewis pressured the Roosevelt administration about coal mining legislation, urged federal officials to enforce the basic coal industry codes of fair competition, and appeared regularly before congressional committees to testify in support of legislation. Lewis now entertained cabinet officers, ambassadors, congressmen, Labor Department bureaucrats, and the cream of Washington society. Wheeling and dealing among the American power elite, Lewis, by 1940, fashioned his labor organization into the largest, most secure, and most powerful single trade union in the nation.

Lewis built the mine workers into the nation's strongest union despite a protracted depression in soft and hard coal. The economic factors that had undermined the UMW during the prosperous 1920s continued to beset coal mining in the depressed 1930s. During no year in the decade 1930-1939 did bituminous coal production ever equal levels reached during the 1920s. Anthracite coal, too, steadily declined in output.[2]

Coal miners suffered as the industry in which they were employed declined. Although coal miners, by the late 1930s, earned higher hourly wages than other blue-collar workers, including all-male workers in the manufacturing sector (one of the highest paid sectors), irregularity of employment reduced their weekly earnings. Among workers employed in manufacturing industries, only females in 1939 had substantially lower average weekly earnings than coal miners; even unskilled male workers earned almost as much as coal miners: $22.82 a week compared to $22.99.[3]

The economic plight of the mining industry plus the strength and stability of the UMW combined to bring five years of relative labor peace to the coal industry. Between 1934 and 1940, according to a special labor department report on strike activity in the coal industry, an average of only 16% of all labor idleness caused by strikes nationally occurred in the coal industry, as compared to 61% from 1927 through 1932 and 42% from 1942 through 1944. Twice, in 1935 and again in 1939, national strikes closed down the bituminous mines; but in each case the dispute was more bargaining ritual than class war.[4]

Labor stability, however, only relieved one of the coal industry's chronic ailments. Too many small operators still produced on the fringes of the soft-coal industry and, whenever spot prices rose, reentered the marketplace and intensified competition. Substantial differentials in wages, the largest factor in the cost of mining coal, still existed between districts and even within districts, further compounding the competitive difficulties of mine owners, especially the higher-wage-paying northern operators. Despite the code of fair competition adopted by the bituminous coal industry in September 1933 and amended the following year, many operators continued to cut prices and also wages.

By mid-December 1934 Lewis bemoaned the NRA's coal section's inability to compel observance of the code of fair competition. In a letter of December 17 to Wayne Ellis, coal administrator, Lewis alleged that in many areas the minimum price structure of the bituminous coal industry had practically collapsed. Demanding immediate action by the NRA, Lewis warned that failure to act decisively would compel the UMW on "its own initiative to take such steps as may be deemed necessary to protect the interests of its membership."[5]

In January 1935, at a public hearing to consider amendments to the bituminous coal code, Lewis continued to urge stricter enforcement of its provisions. He reminded coal operators and NRA officials at the hearing that the UMW no longer intended to tolerate the NRA's neglect "to enforce the provisions of the code upon those who flagrantly or otherwise evade its provisions," a failure that threatened to involve the coal industry in "a species of gorilla [sic] economic warfare," in which the union becomes responsible for maintaining the wage and price structure through incessant industrial conflict. Rather than endure an annual ritual of enforcing contracts and fair competition by strikes, Lewis preferred, he alleged, to shut down the entire coal industry until its economic structure could be thoroughly rationalized either by federal edict or labor-management cooperation.[6]

Lewis's threats and the desires of most northern operators to limit competition caused Wayne Ellis, the NRA's coal administrator, to amend the code by making any attempt by operators to market coal at a price below the minimum level fixed by the administrator a violation of the code. Theoretically, now, at least, the code had teeth, and its administrator had the authority to punish transgressors.[7]

Lewis and the northern operators nevertheless preferred special federal legislation to regulate the soft-coal industry rather than rules of competition set under the NRA. Their desire for such special legislation intensified in May 1935, when a unanimous Supreme Court decision declared the price-fixing provisions of the NIRA unconstitutional. From February through October 1935 the UMW and the northern operators lobbied Congress and the White House to obtain passage of the Guffey Coal Stabilization Bill, which would mandate the creation of a federal administrative agency to set minimum sale prices for soft coal, allocate markets equitably among different producers, eliminate wage differentials that caused unfair competition, and rationalize the entire structure of the industry. As the UMW officers told union delegates at the 1936 convention, "The fundamental objective of the United Mine Workers . . . lies . . . in a system of proper Federal regulation, which will encompass a synchronized system of price fixing and allocation of tonnages on a basis equitably fair to mine workers and operators alike.''[8]

While Congress debated the Guffey bill, Lewis and the mine operators bargained about a new union-management contract. Uncertainties about the future of federal coal legislation, however, caused the collective bargaining to break down repeatedly between February and October 1935. Unwilling to risk a strike when unemployment remained high, Lewis gladly acceded to requests from the Roosevelt administration that the UMW extend its 1934 bituminous agreement until a new contract could be negotiated. Yet he used the strike threat as a weapon with which to pressure Roosevelt into supporting the miners' bargaining position. If only the president would compel the operators to sign a new contract, Lewis advised Roosevelt, no walkout would occur.[9]

But coal operators were too divided among themselves to come to terms with the union. Northern operators sought the abolition of southern wage differentials; southerners demanded the retention of such differentials; and operators everywhere worried that existing inter- and intra union wage differentials offered some producers "unfair" competitive advantages.

From March to September, as the operators refused to discuss the union's demands or even to offer an alternative, Lewis, at President Roosevelt's behest, agreed to several extensions of the 1934 agreement. Each extension assumed congressional passage of the Guffey bill, an event that never occurred. In the absence of new legislation, Lewis, during bargaining sessions that resumed on September 5, cut his union's demands to minor revisions in the wage terms of the 1934 contract.

The operators, however, remained intransigent and sat silently as the miners' representatives did all the talking. Even after the entrance of federal mediators on September 12 and Roosevelt's personal intervention later that same day (in response to a strike threat by Lewis), the operators pointedly refused to make concessions and broke up the conference.

Lewis remained calm. His minimal terms for a new contract rejected on September 13, he readily accepted another ten-day extension in the old contract. Finally, when further bargaining brought no concessions from operators, Lewis, on September 23, called the miners out. What collective bargaining had failed to achieve in eight months, economic power won in a single day. On September 24 the operators made their first offer to the UMW, and on the evening of September 29, union negotiators reached agreement with the operators. On October 1 the miners resumed work, and stability of a sort returned to the soft-coal industry.[10]

The 1935 bituminous coal agreement extended the terms of the 1934 contract, retained the basic North-South wage differential and other customary district differentials, and granted a marginal upward revision in wages. By October 4 the captive coal mines also signed new contracts incorporating the wage increases into their basic 1933 agreement with the union.

The 1935 negotiations revealed graphically what had become the standard pattern in coal industry-union bargaining as practiced by Lewis. The strike functioned more as a threat than a reality, more as a weapon to inveigle presidential intervention than as a club to beat employers. Rather than risk precipitous or protracted strikes, conflicts that threatened to harm an industry in parlous economic condition and weaken the finances of a union recently recovered from the ravages of the 1920s, Lewis preferred temporary contract extensions and short, though massive, strikes that illustrated the UMW's potential power. The Roosevelt administration's commitment to economic growth, its aversion to industrial conflicts that threatened recovery, and its relative sympathy for organized labor made Lewis's tactics effective. In the event, Roosevelt usually put more pressure on operators than union negotiators. Sooner or later, then (unfortunately, ordinarily later rather than sooner), operators would offer more generous contract terms to Lewis.

In 1937 collective bargaining, without even the hint of a union strike threat, produced a two-year renewal (until March 31, 1939) of the basic 1935 bituminous coal union agreement. Again operators consented to a modest advance in day and tonnage rates, although the 1937 agreement sanctioned traditional regional wage differentials. Under its terms $6.00 became the basic minimum daily wage in coalfields north of the Ohio River and $5.60 the rate in fields south of the Ohio.

By 1937 the miners' union and coal operators also seemed to have achieved their legislative goals. Congress, in 1935, had enacted the original Guffey-Snyder Coal Stabilization Bill—but only after collective bargaining in the industry had collapsed and a short strike had occurred in late September. The Guffey-Snyder act, which mandated collective bargaining in coal, fixed minimum wages and maximum hours, legitimated price-fixing and allocation of markets, and created a federal agency to enforce its provisions, was declared unconstitutional by the Supreme Court less than a year later, largely because of its wage and hours provisions. Eventually, after a legislative struggle of more than a year during which several amended Guffey coal stabilization bills went down to defeat in the Senate, Congress, in 1937, passed the Guffey-Vinson bill, an act that retained all the economic stabilization provisions (primarily price-fixing and market allocation under federal administration) of the 1935 bill but eliminated the wage and hour clauses. This bill survived review by Roosevelt's reconstructed Supreme Court and provided the federal rationalization of the soft-coal industry that Lewis for more than a decade had sought fruitlessly.[11]

The relative peace between union and operators and the enactment of basic federal coal legislation in the late thirties tempted Lewis to focus on new concerns. If his union had stability and the miners a satisfactory union contract, the existence of the coal miner remained less than satisfactory. For one thing, technological innovations continuously transformed working conditions in the industry, eliminating jobs and altering the character of many more. Not only did new machinery make the work of many miners redundant and transform others from craftsmen practicing an ancient skill to machine tenders; it frequently increased the physical risks, already great, of mining. State and federal mine safety legislation originally passed to protect miners against the risks of their occupation often lacked provisions to regulate the dangers associated with the introduction of new mining technologies. By the time safety legislation caught up with past changes in the character of mining, innovation had transformed working conditions once again. In the race between the enforcement of mine safety and technological change in the coal industry, technology triumphed every time. Throughout the 1930s, as the UMW *Journal* persistently stressed, American coal miners suffered more injuries than their brothers in Western Europe; fatalities per 1,000 miners in the United States were double the rate of most European nations and three times the rate in the Netherlands.[12]

The unemployment, injuries, and deaths that technological innovation caused coal miners led Lewis, by the late 1930s, to become increasingly interested in union welfare systems. Although he lobbied incessantly and loudly for generous federal Social Security programs for unemployed, injured, and retired workers, Lewis also sought to cushion federal programs with a private, voluntary union system less subject to political trends and manipulations. At the 1938 UMW convention and every two years thereafter, one or more union officers would propose the establishment of a coal industry welfare plan for injured and retired miners. In 1938 Secretary-Treasurer Tom Kennedy recommended that a small tax on the coal produced in this country (the method used to pay the administrative costs of the Guffey-Vinson act) would generate adequate funds to finance a union program for the health and welfare of its members.[13] Eight years later the plan first proposed by Kennedy would come to fruition as a result of a bargain struck between John L. Lewis and the federal government.

Lewis sought a direct method to regulate the impact of technological innovation on American coal miners. And he found such an instrument in the 1937 agreement between the union and the soft-coal operators. The 1937 contract provided for a mechanized mining commission to consist of an equal number of union and operator representatives that would meet regularly, investigate conditions in the industry, and seek to moderate mechanization's negative impact on miners. Lewis also toyed with the notion of federally financed work-retraining programs for miners made redundant by technological innovation.[14]

During the 1930s Lewis first began to badger the president and Interior Department officials about the nonenforcement of mine safety legislation and the need for more stringent federal laws to compensate for weak controls in those states whose legislatures were subject to the influence of coal operators. Although he received scant satisfaction from federal officials, most of whom still considered safety legislation largely a state function, Lewis persisted in his complaints and recommendations, building up a record he could cite when rank-and-filers or union insurgents complained about the UMW's failure to insure mine safety.[15]

Lewis took great pride in what he had accomplished for his union and also for the soft-coal industry. No better testament existed to Lewis's success than the words written by a prominent northern coal operator. Writing in response to a request asking him about labor relations in the coal industry, William Taylor, executive vice-president of The Valley Camp Coal Company, observed on November 23, 1938, that

> it would be impossible for better and finer labor relations to exist anywhere than exists between our companies and that organization [UMW]. . . . John L. Lewis . . . [has] a record of taking care of . . . contractual obligations, in our opinion unsurpassed by anyone in any line of business endeavor. . . . They have done a lot to stabilize the bituminous coal industry and have endeavored to have it operate on a profitable basis, in fact though one dislikes to admit it their efforts along that line have in the main . . . been a bit more efficacious . . . than the endeavors of coal operators themselves. We thoroughly enjoy our relations with this union—and . . . we hope the time will never come when we ever again are in the position of having to operate our coal mines on a non-union nor [sic] open shop basis.[16]

Harmonious relations between the UMW and the mine operators failed, however, to restore economic prosperity to the soft-coal industry. During the two-year life of the 1937 agreement, the period of the "Roosevelt Depression," bituminous production stagnated; coal companies operated at a loss; machinery continued to displace miners. Thus, as the moment approached in 1939 to negotiate a new contract between the UMW and the Appalachian Operators' Association, the time seemed less than propitious for Lewis to advance the claims of his membership.[17]

Collective bargaining in the soft-coal industry, which opened on March 14, 1939 (precisely two weeks prior to the formal expiration of the 1937 agreement), manifested Lewis's character as union negotiator. As usual, during collective bargaining sessions between the UMW and the coal operators, Lewis, though accompanied by an international policy committee that numbered over 150 members and a smaller negotiating group that included all the union district presidents, thoroughly dominated his bargaining team. Indeed, Lewis's voice was the only one that counted. A. H. Raskin, then a young *New York Times* reporter covering his first soft-coal crisis, later recalled that at one crucial moment during the 1939 negotiations, Lewis declined to react to a presidential initiative until after he had received instructions from the full UMW International Policy Committee. Eager to see union democracy in action, Raskin planned to watch how the UMW representatives instructed their leader. When the doors to the Policy Committee's meeting room in the Biltmore Hotel inadvertently opened, the young *Times* reporter saw a strange sight. Instead of busily discussing President Roosevelt's proposed settlement terms, the committee members sat at tables concentrating intently on poker, gin rummy, and pinochle games. The card playing continued until Lewis entered the room to instruct the union delegates on how to vote, after which the Policy Committee endorsed unanimously the negotiating position of its president.[18] Absolutely in command of his union team, Lewis could act at the bargaining table without fear of repudiation.

From the first, Lewis sought no costly new benefits for coal miners. He focused primarily on achieving union security. He thought that operators might concede one of two union demands that cost no money: abolition of the penalty clause—a contract provision that fined miners and the union for strikes allegedly in violation of the contract,* or institution of a closed shop. Throughout eight weeks of collective bargaining, from March 14 to May 14, and a combination strike-lockout that lasted a month, Lewis struggled solely to achieve one of his two nonmonetary objectives.[19]

Lewis also pursued what had become by 1939 his customary strategy for achieving union goals. Once again he sought to obtain federal endorsement for the miners' claims. Only when moderation failed to produce tangible results did Lewis play labor's angry man, promising a full-scale nationwide strike that, he hastened to advise Labor Secretary Frances Perkins and President Roosevelt, threatened the economy with severe damage. Lewis offered the operators a blend of promises and threats.

The Appalachian Joint Conference opened in New York on March 14 with both sides far apart. Asking for a six-hour day (and thirty-hour week) and an advance in wages, the UMW negotiating team responded caustically to the operators' suggestion that the 1937 agreement be extended two more years with a fifty-cent reduction in the daily wage rate. Phil Murray replied to the employers' proposal in words redolent of his boss "I know operators cannot eat losses," quipped the UMW vice-president, "nor can mine workers live on wind." The next day Lewis softened the union's position, asking the operators to join with him in pledging that there would be no closure of the mines on April 1 if a new contract had not yet been negotiated. Yet for the next two weeks the operators would neither discuss the union's proposals nor join with Lewis in pledging to keep the mines open on April 1.[20]

Thwarted by the operators, Lewis turned to the federal government, asking federal mediator James Dewey to enter the negotiations. Joining the bargaining at the last minute, March 31, Dewey found the situation a complete mess. One operator informed him that "we can reach a settlement without governmental

*Abolition of the penalty clause would enable the union to call strikes if and when the employment of nonmembers or members of another union (the Progressive Miners) threatened union security. In effect, then, the closed shop would be achieved through economic power, not contractual arrangements.

intervention. . . . We always have and we always will." The federal mediator characterized the operators as "bitter, nasty, and antagonistic," even eager to risk a strike. Lewis, on the contrary, acted respectfully toward Dewey and pleaded for federal intervention.[21]

Lacking an agreement on April 1, the Appalachian mines fell silent. April 1 was a miners' holiday and April 2 was a Sunday, another nonworking day; but on April 3, all the union miners in the region laid down their tools, following the UMW custom of "No contract; No work." Yet Lewis preferred to consider the shutdown a lockout, because he had offered to recommend that union members remain at work in the absence of a new agreement if operators pledged to bargain seriously.[22]

Despite the silence in the Appalachian coalfields, industry and union negotiators continued to talk in New York. During the lockout-strike's first week, the conferees made no progress. Although Lewis dropped all but one of the union's original twenty-eight demands—abolition of the penalty clause—the operators remained intransigent.

According to Dewey, who apparently had become an advocate of Lewis's beliefs and shared the labor leader's perceptions, the coal operators saw themselves as surrogates for large industry fighting to save American capitalism from the closed shop and union tyranny. The great steel companies, railroads, and utilities, Dewey reported to his superiors in Washington, had interfered in the negotiations and pressured the coal operators to reject Lewis's proposal.[23]

Throughout the month of April, despite pleas from federal mediators Dewey, John Steelman, Secretary Perkins, and President Roosevelt, the coal operators refused to grant either the closed shop or the abolition of the penalty clause. Indeed, the operators made clear to Dewey and Steelman that the coal industry spoke for "big business" all over the nation in its commitment to the open shop in basic industry. On April 11 Lewis called a press conference to denounce the interference of outside influences* in the negotiations and the obduracy of the operators. "Deep silence prevails," he observed, "as the negotiators gaze at each other's pallid faces." Unless the operators compromised, Lewis warned, he would have no choice but to shut down the outlying districts and also call out the anthracite miners when their contract expired on April 30. "If the bituminous operators . . . will be satisfied with nothing less than war in the industry, the United Mine Workers will be able to accommodate them and will be able to protect themselves."[24]

The first week in May brought no resolution to the dispute, and the situation deteriorated when Lewis called out the miners in the outlying districts on May 4 and 5, thereby denying the nation all supplies of coal. On May 7, Lewis made public a letter addressed to Steelman which placed total responsibility for the impasse on the operators and criticized the federal role in the dispute. The UMW,

*Railroads, steel companies, and investment bankers.

he sneered, never sought a closed shop; it granted employers the right to hire whomever they pleased, provided new employees, as a condition of work, joined the union within a stated period of time; all miners wanted, he jibed, was the "union shop," a status legitimated by New Deal legislation. Moreover, Lewis added, he would gladly waive even the union shop if employers eliminated the penalty clause from future agreements. The union had certainly acted on the president's advice of the previous day to "give and take." Of the twenty-eight union proposals made to the conference, Lewis noted, "the operators have taken 27. . . . Is it unfair to suggest that the Mine Workers propose to take the 28th point?" The Roosevelt administration's failure to sustain the mine workers, he declared, "caused many coal operators to believe that they had carte blanche from the Government to disembowel the Mine Workers' Union if they could. In consequence, your Department [Labor] must accept responsibility for its own administrative blunder."25

Lewis's May 7 letter had the intended effect. The next day the joint Appalachian conferees met in special session, joined by Dewey, Steelman, and Secretary Perkins. Perkins pleaded with the operators to grant the union shop and presented, without modification, the union's case for it. Her plea was unanswered by the mine owners, who preferred an invitation to meet with President Roosevelt in the White House the next day, May 9, in an attempt to resolve the dispute. The president proved noncommittal. Perhaps to the surprise of the participants, he repeated worn platitudes. Warning of the national damage that would result from a protracted strike, Roosevelt asked the conferees to return to New York and, with assistance from Steelman, reach an agreement within twenty-four hours.26

The president's injunction had little effect. On May 10, Perkins informed Roosevelt that the operators and miners were further apart than ever—indeed were so angry with each other that federal mediators thought it best to keep them in separate rooms. "John Lewis is mad, rough and angry and everybody is mad," reported the secretary. "There is no more of that peaceful talk that the President heard yesterday. John Lewis is very ugly today—very ugly," lamented Perkins, "and we don't know how to handle him. One of those moods are on him. I really believe it would be a wise thing," she suggested, "for the President to call John Lewis at the Hotel Biltmore . . . and pacify him—give him a little flattery. It will go a long way with John."27

Secretary Perkins obviously did not know her man or his personality quirks. Lewis's anger was feigned, not real—a tactic he had found useful in the past during collective bargaining and would use persistently in the future. The labor leader wanted material support from the president, not sweet words. Throughout the coal controversy, Roosevelt had sweet-talked Lewis without explicitly endorsing the miners' claim to union security. This presidential approach only angered Lewis. Now, on May 11, as the coal conflict reached its climax, Lewis demanded federal support, a commitment from the president or his lieutenants sanctioning the union shop for coal miners.

Precisely what Roosevelt did in response to Perkins's suggestion and Lewis's demands remains unknown. Certain inferences, however, may be drawn. On May 13 Lewis informed Jett Lauck that he was delighted with the president's endorsement of the bituminous miners' position, a fact that had restored cordial relations between the labor leader and the White House. On May 11, Lewis had ordered the miners in the outlying districts back to work under a contract that included the union shop. And the next day, May 12, the northern Appalachian operators consented to a new contract with the UMW that extended the 1937 agreement to March 31, 1941, and granted coal miners a union shop. The southern operators left the conference and declared their intention of fighting to preserve the open shop. But with the immediate coal crisis past, the Roosevelt administration intensified its pressures on recalcitrant operators. Within days of the May 12 agreement between the UMW and the northern operators, the southern Appalachian mine owners acceded to Lewis's demand for the union shop. And on May 19, a contract signed between the UMW and the captive mines of U. S. Steel in Harlan County, Kentucky, set the pattern for the captive mine industry. That agreement simply extended the terms of the existing contract without including a union shop provision, because it never included a penalty clause. Pleased with his work, federal mediator Steelman reported to Perkins on May 19 that everything looked better now, especially for the UMW.[28]

If Steelman smiled, the UMW *Journal* gloated. In its May 15 issue, under the headline "United Mine Workers Win First Union Shop Contract," the *Journal* bragged about the greatest victory ever achieved by the UMW—a union-shop contract for the entire bituminous coal industry. "The new agreement," UMW members read, "makes it impossible for any rival organization to obtain a foothold in the bituminous mining industry . . . and makes certain the future integrity, security, and permanence of the United Mine Workers of America."[29]

Lewis had finally conquered the commercial mines, placing his union in an ideal position to reap the material rewards that would flow its way in 1940 and 1941 as the nation armed for war. Only the captive mines, 95% of whose employees belonged to the UMW, still refused to concede the union-shop principle, primarily because of its implication for the steel industry. So complete did Lewis's triumph of May 1939 seem that—despite the fact that he gained for miners neither an additional penny in wages, a minute more off from work, greater autonomy on the job, nor increased safety—editorialists and columnists interpreted the settlement as a personal victory for Lewis, "strengthening his position in labor ranks to a point approaching dictatorship."[30]

The character of the mine workers' union in the late 1930s lent credence to press portraits of John L. Lewis as a labor dictator. *Autocratic, imperious, bureaucratic*, and *machinelike* seemed terms most expressive of the nature of the UMW. By 1940 the internecine union struggles of the predepression years and the recurrent challenges to union leadership by insurgent rank-and-filers seemed only a distant memory—a memory, indeed, best forgotten. Served in the UMW hierarchy by close family members, loyal lieutenants, and sycophantic followers, Lewis ran a frictionless machine.

The men who had challenged Lewis's domination of the UMW from 1919 to 1932 had either disappeared from the scene or allied with their former foe. Frank Farrington, Alex Howat, John Walker, and Duncan MacDonald no longer disrupted union conventions nor disturbed Lewis. They could vent their hatred for Lewis only through correspondence among themselves and with William Green and antilabor congressmen. John Brophy, Adolph Germer, and Powers Hapgood now served Lewis loyally, primarily in the CIO and secondarily in the United Mine Workers.

Lewis, in 1940, commanded an army of union troops many of whom were unfamiliar with their organization's past history. Although a lack of concrete evidence makes it impossible to quantify what proportion of UMW membership was new to the union in the late 1930s, reasonable guesses can be made. The regions in which the post-1933 UMW grew most rapidly included southern Appalachia and southwestern Pennsylvania—districts traditionally resistant to trade unionism. Most West Virginia, Virginia, Kentucky, Tennessee, Alabama, and Pennsylvania miners who joined the UMW in the 1930s had not hitherto been union members. Even in the Central Competitive Field and the once well-organized northern outlying districts, the UMW membership had fallen so low by 1933 that the members recruited during the New Deal years, especially the younger ones, probably had joined the union for the first time. Union members such as these sang the praises of John L. Lewis for building up the union, although they were ignorant of his role, however inadvertent, in debilitating the UMW during the prosperous 1920s.

With the old union insurgents absent or tamed and the new members and their convention delegates ecstatic about Lewis, the UMW conventions in 1936, 1938, and 1940 proceeded placidly. Delegates no longer roared insults at each other, raced round the aisles, or stormed the platform. Lewis handpicked the chairmen of the major convention committees, who diligently served the interests of the international officers. Barring one exception that proved the rule, debate never flared among delegates on the convention floor. Two events at the 1938 convention proved that Lewis chaired the biennial union meetings as frictionlessly as he ran his administration. When a solitary delegate rose to oppose an amendment to the UMW constitution barring membership and office to Wobblies, Ku Klux Klanners, and Communists, among others, Lewis silenced him without protest by simply stating: "This is not open for debate because the section has been adopted. I merely recognize the delegate so he could get rid of that speech." A little earlier at the same session, the Resolutions Committee introduced a motion insisting that the UMW's international officers accept retroactively the 100% salary increase granted them in 1936, a raise then refused by Lewis, Murray, and Kennedy. In

1938 only two delegates demurred from the recommendation, and the union's triumvirate this time eagerly doubled its salary.[31]

The one issue that ignited debate at the 1936, 1938, and 1940 conventions—the question of district autonomy, that is, the right of the UMW's separate districts to elect their own officers—exposed both Lewis's dictatorial power in the UMW and his singular interpretation of union democracy. Ever since the UMW began to decline in the mid-1920s, Lewis had seized provisional control of many once independent, semiautonomous union districts. In 1936 most union districts, instead of possessing the right to elect their own officers, were governed by officials chosen by Lewis and responsible directly to the UMW president, not the district membership. By the late 1930s, however, as the union's size and strength grew, some districts began to demand the right to elect their own officers. Yet to each demand from below for district autonomy, the UMW's officers responded identically. "We believe," the officers reported to the conventions of 1936, 1938, and 1940, "that the International Executive Board should continue to exercise its good judgment . . . and to act at such time with respect to autonomy in any particular district as in their judgment will best meet the needs of the situation." In short, Lewis, not the membership, would decide whether and when to restore to UMW districts the right to elect their own officers.[32]

Lewis and his fellow officers also spelled out precisely what factors in their judgment would "best meet the needs of the situation." Democracy, for one thing, the officers declared not pertinent to autonomy. "Some people," they implied, "confuse democracy with license." But not the UMW's officers, all of whom defined democracy as that which best "protects and advances the . . . interests of the membership." In their view, the primary responsibility of international officers was not to extend the voting rights of union members but rather to ensure that the UMW faithfully observed the terms of its contractual obligations. "The primary interest of the International Union," they stressed, "is establishing an absolute recognition of the principle of collective bargaining." Such faithful observance of contracts, not "so-called 'autonomous right'," guaranteed absolute freedom to union members.[33]

Lewis proved blunter in castigating the advocates of autonomy. "Do you want an efficient organization or do you want merely a political instrumentality?" he asked delegates. "That is all that is involved in this matter—business administration, effective internal policies, and no denial of the fundamental principles of democracy . . . learn to walk before you run and learn to wait while you train some of these young men . . . to be the successor of Van Bittner and President Mark and the men from these other districts." Remember, warned Lewis, "we do not want the [political] ambitions of a few of our young men to jeopardize the well being of the hundreds of thousands of other members of our Union." And Lewis invariably reminded delegates that in the past autonomy had often elected district officials who absconded with union funds, squandered such funds foolishly, and in other ways weakened and bankrupted the organization. We are not discussing a fundamental principle, Lewis suggested, but rather a question of "business expediency," that is, "whether you prefer to sacrifice the efficiency of your organization in some respect for a little more academic freedom in the selection of some local representatives in a number of districts." For Lewis, the answer was clear, and the advice that he gave delegates never varied: business before democracy, efficiency above "academic freedom."[34]

Remarkably, during the autonomy debates, most advocates of union democracy unfailingly complimented Lewis for his administration of union affairs and swore fealty to him as president. Even more striking were the words of the delegates who rose to defend their president's interpretation of union democracy. One defender of Lewis at the 1936 convention mixed the Bible and boxing. Scolding the advocates of district autonomy for griping about their leaders, this delegate declared that Lewis "has sacrificed his time, and energy and ability—Moses did. And when that thing came down to a close there was but two or three children that got into the Promised Land—they all died in the wilderness—just like you are going to do if you don't let John Lewis alone." Accept your defeat, he concluded, and "do just like Max Baer did when Joe Louis whipped him—take it."[35]

Yet in 1936 the advocates of autonomy were sufficiently numerous to demand a roll call vote on which they won the support of 602 (37%) delegates compared to 1,014 (63%) who supported their officers. How many of the 602 defenders of autonomy would have voted for union democracy had the choice been clearly between the legitimation of district autonomy and Lewis's continuance in office remains questionable. What is noteworthy is that such a large majority of the delegates in 1936 voted against the democratic principle and in favor of presidential prerogatives.[36]

Two years later, at the 1938 convention, the terms and language of the autonomy debate remained the same. Only the strength of the union "democrats" diminished. Philip Murray again lectured delegates on the difference between democracy and license, assuring them that the UMW was the nation's most perfect democratic organization. And Lewis warned delegates that Reds and mine owners used the autonomy issue, a matter that affected no vital principle, to stir up dissension in the UMW. UMW members, he intoned, had the right to elect their leader, the union president, the man alone responsible for the actions and conditions of the provisional districts. "That," Lewis declared, "is democracy." In conclusion, he beseeched all union members "to demonstrate to the world at large that the integrity, cohesion and solidarity of our Union rises supreme over any minor consideration that can be raised or over any question of who holds office in any district."[37]

Many rank-and-filers had no qualms about participating in John L. Lewis's guided democracy. Delegates from provisional Alabama District 20 resolved publicly, "We know we are not able to lead and are satisfied to follow our very able leaders. We know we are not in any way ready for autonomy."[40] The autonomy advocates of 1938 could not even obtain a roll call vote, having to be satisfied simply with recording their own votes for democracy. Only 80 delegates, moreover, compared to the previous convention's 602, recorded themselves in favor of autonomy.[38]

Two years later, at the 1940 convention, delegates and officers repeated without variation the autonomy debate. Lewis advised delegates that there was nothing to debate as the UMW had a policy on autonomy, one that treated the issue for what it was, a "business proposition." After all, he lectured, the UMW could not allow members to elect inadequate officers. "A child can only be given so much responsibility," Lewis philosophized, "and if we sometimes elect men to office who are either inexperienced or . . . not sufficiently honest to be true to their membership, someone has to pay the fiddler," that someone invariably being the international and members from other districts. When members were mature enough to elect competent officers, the executive board would, Lewis assured delegates, restore autonomy, as had happened in 1940 with Districts 2 and 6. Again no roll call vote occurred on the question, and fewer than eighty delegates declared themselves opposed on the record to "guided democracy."[39]

Such placid, even harmonious, miners' conventions disappointed labor journalists. By 1940 reporters assigned to the UMW convention struggled to dramatize the banal and, as a consequence, manufactured imaginary insurgencies. Two incidents in 1940 that journalists cited to prove rank-and-file dissatisfaction with Lewis instead revealed the UMW president's invincibility. First was the issue of President Roosevelt's third term bid. By January 1940 Lewis, as seen above, opposed Roosevelt's reelection, although the vast majority of coal miners idolized the president and expressed their affection in scores of resolutions submitted to the convention by union locals endorsing a third term. Daily newspapers reported rank-and-file pro-Roosevelt resolutions as a revolt against Lewis. Much as convention delegates may have admired Roosevelt, however, they made no substantial protest when Lewis ridiculed the president, nor did they demur when Lewis buried all the third term resolutions in committee and demanded instead that the UMW endorse no candidate in 1940. Whatever discontent flared among the UMW rank and file as a result of the Lewis-Roosevelt rupture produced at best a silent revolt, one that in no way threatened Lewis's hegemony in the miners' union.

Second, near the close of the convention's third day, as Lewis delivered a national radio network speech in commemoration of the union's golden anniversary, a red flag with the hammer and sickle of the USSR rose behind the rostrum. Obviously intending to embarrass Lewis, who characterized the appearance of the Soviet flag as "a cowardly, reprehensible, and dastardly trick," the perpetrators of the incident were never discovered.[40] Communists and labor leftists certainly had no reason to embarrass Lewis in January 1940, as he was then their firmest ally in the labor movement and an outspoken critic of Roosevelt's interventionist foreign policies. Insurgent UMW members would more likely have criticized Lewis for his class collaborationist tendencies than for his leftist sympathies. Whatever the source of the red flag incident, and it was more likely the product of right-wing nuts than trade union rebels, in no way did it lessen Lewis's domination of the convention or his union.*

In fact, the morning after the flag incident, Lewis cajoled delegates into a display of solidarity. Reacting directly to press reports suggesting rank-and-file discontent with his leadership, Lewis observed sarcastically that in 1940, for the first time in the history of the UMW, not a single grievance had been filed against its officers. Where, he asked, "are the complaints against the dictator of the United Mine Workers of America? Where is the man in the United Mine Workers of America whom John L. Lewis has injured?" Beseeching delegates to vote on a resolution of confidence in their leaders, Lewis snarled, "Every once in a while I get a good laugh at our enemies." After the vote, he proclaimed that 2,400 delegates had unanimously "affirmed that peace and tranquillity and confidence dwell in the ranks of the United Mine Workers."[41] Not satisfied with a unanimous vote of confidence, Lewis turned to reporters at the press table and remarked: "I commend that report to the attention of the Chicago Tribune, the New York Herald-Tribune, the Scripps-Howard newspapers, and various other publications in the country . . . who have been utterly convinced that the ruthless and terrible John Lewis was totally inconsiderate of the rights of members of his organization. Think it over gentlemen!"[42]

Words Lewis first trumpeted before a miners' convention in 1930, when the UMW was torn by internecine conflict, bore real meaning ten years later. To a desperate band of men gathered in Indianapolis in March 1930, striving solely to preserve their union's integrity during a labor civil war, Lewis proudly proclaimed that he "pleaded their case from the pulpit and the public platform, in joint conference with the associated operators . . . before the bar of state legislatures, in the councils of the President's cabinet, and in the public press of this nation— not in the quavering tones of a feeble mendicant asking alms, but in the thundering voice of the captain of a mighty host." Those words were indeed a fitting description of Lewis's labors for coal miners and their union during the New Deal years. They would prove even more descriptive during World War II when Lewis astutely and courageously led his own domestic army, acting as the captain of a mighty host of American coal miners.

---

*John Owens and George DeNucci alleged, during the course of interviews, that the American Legion planned the incident.

IV.
From Resistance
to Resignation,
1941-1969

CHAPTER 17

A Man Alone, 1941-1942

John L. Lewis's dramatic retirement as CIO president symbolized his break with the New Deal phenomenon of which he had been an integral part. From the UMW organizing drive of 1933 to the presidential election of 1940, Lewis had enjoyed the role of charismatic leader of the masses. Now, in the 1940s, he found himself isolated as the lone defiant labor defender of free enterprise and voluntary collective bargaining against government encroachment.

At the close of the 1940 CIO convention, Lewis still possessed considerable influence and numerous allies. His close associate for over a quarter of a century, Phil Murray, had ascended to the CIO presidency. The Lewis forces, moreover, had dominated the convention and defeated attempts by the Hillmanites to link the organization to Roosevelt's administration. Lewis's outspoken support of a noninterventionist foreign policy led Communist-oriented unionists, Midwestern Populists, and conservative, probusiness America Firsters all to seek him as an ally.

Yet these were weak alliances. Over the next two years the bonds of friendship between Lewis and Murray proved unable to withstand the tensions of political and personal differences. And joining Murray in his forced departure from the UMW would be some of the organization's most able field generals: Van Bittner, Pat Fagan, William Mitch, and others. The Nazi invasion of Russia would terminate the Communists' comradeship with Lewis, and Pearl Harbor would silence the remaining antiwar coalition. Lewis's economic policies, moreover, would alienate many in the business community and general public who had not already condemned him for his isolationist views. The desertion of quondam friends and supporters was followed by the death of his wife, Myrta. By the fall of 1942, Lewis and his union faced a world of enemies—alone.

In the months immediately following the 1940 CIO convention, Lewis retreated from public view. He sincerely hoped that his withdrawal from the limelight would enable Phil Murray to establish his own leadership of the CIO. A low profile might also help dissipate dissension inside the UMW that stemmed from Lewis's personal opposition to Roosevelt. In the union elections held in December 1940, approximately 20,000 miners directly expressed their disapproval of Lewis by refusing to endorse his uncontested reelection while casting ballots for Murray and Kennedy, both of whom also ran unopposed.[1]

In either late January or early February 1941, Lewis's voluntary withdrawal from public view became mandatory, when he suffered a heart attack. Now sixty-one and faced with the first serious threat to his health, he hid his condition from the press and his own union membership. Aside from his immediate family, he allowed only Phil Murray and Lee Pressman to see him incapacitated, and as soon as the doctor permitted, he escaped to Florida to convalesce. It was not until the convening of the Appalachian Joint Wage Conference in New York City on March 11 that Lewis made his first major public appearance since laying down the mantle of the CIO.[2]

Lewis believed the 1941 bituminous coal negotiations to be critical. Naturally, a major bargaining success would assure him the continued support of the miners; and the revived prosperity of the coal industry, generated by war abroad and mobilization at home, created an environment in which such advances could be won. Equally important, Lewis feared that the United States would soon enter the global conflict, and he wanted to achieve maximum gains for his organization before the government imposed stringent wartime economic controls. In large measure Lewis's behavior in the spring of 1941, as throughout the mobilization and war period, stemmed from his remembrance of the negative impact World War I had had on his union's members. Viewing the coal miners in 1917-1919 as the "innocent victims of an ill-advised wartime economy," he vowed that they would not suffer again.[3]

On the opening day of the Appalachian Joint Wage Conference, Lewis presented the union's demands to the assembled operators: (1) the continuation of the 7-hour day, 5-day week; (2) a pay increase of one dollar per day for daymen and comparable advances for other workers; (3) a minimum of 200 guaranteed working days each year; (4) a 2-week vacation with pay; (5) a strengthening of seniority rules; (6) the right to participate in selecting physicians and supervising medical facilities financed through deductions from miners' pay; (7) the right to appoint safety committees to inspect mines; (8) the right to call mourning periods in honor of those who died in the pits; and, finally (9) the elimination of inequitable differentials within and between districts.[4]

At the next session of the wage conference, operator spokesman Charles O'Neill ritualistically rejected the miners' demands. Lewis then proposed that mining operations continue without interruption in the event that an accord could not be reached by April 1, when the existing contract terminated; he further stipulated that any increases in wages embodied in the new agreement be retroactive to that date. As Lewis no doubt anticipated, the operators promptly rejected his offer. They were not about to negotiate seriously until certain of the future of the Guffey coal act—in particular, that aspect of the law which permitted price adjustments for increases in labor costs. Although the act would expire in late April, Congress had not yet made provision for its renewal. At this point a strike would aid the operators by creating further pressures on Congress to act.

Lewis understood the operators' predicament and tolerated their procrastination at the bargaining table. He absented himself from the wage conference until March 25. When he finally reappeared, eager reporters queried him on the progress of the negotiations. "That's what I'm hoping to find out," he cryptically remarked.[5]

Serious negotiations resumed with Lewis's return. In exchange for the union yielding on its proposal for a guarantee of 200 working days a year, the operators granted a dollar-a-day increase to daymen and commensurate raises to other classes of workers—contingent, of course, on congressional renewal of the Guffey act, which passed the added wage cost on to the consumer.

With one issue settled, Lewis reintroduced the union demand for removal of wage differentials. Southern operators had long enjoyed a lower wage bill than their northern competitors. The South justified this advantage on the basis of the region's lower cost of living; the union and northern operators in the past begrudgingly accepted it in order to keep the Appalachian Conference united.

Lewis now felt that reenactment of the Guffey act would remove any justification for regional wage differentials, and he viewed the defense mobilization drive as a propitious moment for the UMW to act. He also feared that if war came and the government froze prevailing wage differentials, competitive advantages would work to shift coal production to the southern fields, where hostility to the union remained greatest. Northern operators endorsed Lewis's proposal. Lewis insisted on ending the forty-cent gap in wages for daymen—a fraction of the Southern mine work force. Southern operators realized, nonetheless, that Lewis was attacking the principle of wage differentials. If they yielded on rates for daymen now, the union would come back in future negotiations and attack the remaining differentials. Thus, southerners emphatically answered: Never!

When the old contract expired on March 31, President Roosevelt issued his customary plea for the mines to remain in operation and sent Dr. John R. Steelman, director of the Department of Labor's Conciliation Service, to New York to sit in on the negotiations. April 1 being Miners' Day, a traditional UMW holiday, the mines would have closed anyway. On April 2 the miners continued to stay away from the pits, honoring the union's policy of "No contract, No work." According to government estimates, the nation then possessed a thirty-day supply of soft coal.[6]

Northern operators and the union united in a de facto alliance to compel the South to abandon the wage differential. Seventy percent of the nation's coal operators and the UMW agreed to abolish the wage differential, they asserted.

Only the southerners refused to accept this provision and sign an agreement.[7]

The southerners refused to yield and, on April 11, abruptly withdrew from the Appalachian Conference, formed a new group, moved to Washington, and appealed to Roosevelt and Perkins to certify "the case of the south" to the National Defense Mediation Board (NDMB). To create the image of moderation, they invited the union to confer with them in Washington. Lewis promptly rebuffed their gesture, criticizing it as unreasonable, since negotiations were still proceeding in New York with both the northern operators and representatives of the anthracite industry.[8]

The president's signing of the renewed Guffey act on April 12 removed one impediment to a settlement. With the coal stabilization program assured for another two years, the mine workers and northern operators arrived at a tentative agreement on April 16. Despite a personal request from the Secretary of Labor, however, both parties refused formally to sign the contract and reopen the northern pits. The northern operators and the union intended to keep the heat on the southern operators by blaming them for the continued curtailment of coal production.[9]

Apparently, both Roosevelt and Perkins viewed the South's efforts to send the dispute to the NDMB as an attempt to escape the consequences of free collective bargaining. Yet the southern operators succeeded in whipping up support for their position in Congress, where several antistrike bills were introduced. On the evening of April 12, in a last-minute move to avoid certification of the dispute to the NDMB, President Roosevelt issued a two-part appeal to the nation's miners and operators:

1. The miners and operators already in agreement resume coal production under the terms of that agreement.
2. The operators and miners who have not yet reached an agreement enter into wage negotiations and at the same time reopen the mines, the agreement ultimately reached to be made retroactive to the date of resuming work.[10]

The next morning representatives of the southern operators hurried to the White House, where they talked to presidential secretary Major General E. M. Watson. After the meeting a spokesman for the group informed the press that they were returning to New York to meet with the union "at the request of President Roosevelt." At 9:00 that night the Appalachian Southern Coal Operators Wage Conference commenced bargaining with a delegation from the UMW. Negotiations resumed the following day as Lewis shuttled back and forth between the southern meeting in the Hotel Commodore and the northern conference in the Biltmore Hotel.[11]

Then, at 7:00 that night, word reached the southerners that the UMW and northern operators had accepted the president's plan. In doing so, Lewis and the northern operators skillfully blended Roosevelt's two-part proposal into one:

Northern mines would open on the basis of the unsigned contract *with* the resumption of mining in the southern fields and the continuation of negotiations along the lines outlined by Roosevelt. The responsibility for accepting the president's plan now rested solely on the southerners. Realizing they had been outflanked, southern operators walked out of the conference without saying a word. Later that night conciliation chief Steelman informed newsmen that the southerners had not answered Roosevelt's plea. "By leaving the negotiations and by failing to comply with the President's request to open the mines," he observed, "they have taken upon themselves a grave responsibility."[12]

The next morning, April 24, Secretary of Labor Perkins certified the dispute to the NDMB. The board appointed a panel to hear the case headed by William H. Davis, a New York patent attorney and NDMB vice-chairman. The panel, after taking testimony, recognized that it could not devise a settlement of the wage differential issue satisfactory to all parties; and so on April 27 it simply recommended that the southern operators follow the lead of the union and northern operators and accept the president's April 21 proposal.[13]

No longer able to evade Roosevelt's proposal, the southern operators agreed to the plan on April 28. During the next two days the union negotiated temporary agreements with the northern and southern operators reopening the Appalachian fields. With coal production renewed, the UMW consented to a request by the southern group for a recess in talks until May 12.[14]

The southerners, lacking substantial support from the northern coal operators, Congress, the Truman committee, or the Roosevelt administration, faced certain defeat. "The world and every school boy knew," Lewis later gloated, "that when they returned to work under the President's proposal they had lost the battle."[15]

Throughout May and June bargaining between the union and the Southern operators brought no results. The NDMB, taking up the case a second time, recommended that the Southern operators eliminate the differential for day men and on June 9, they agreed to do so.

But Lewis sought more for his men. He demanded that the Southerners sign a contract identical to the one the UMW had negotiated with Northern operators on June 19 that the NDMB did not fully endorse. One of the clauses the NDMB disliked granted the union the right to call workers out of the pits for "memorial periods." Another provision, the Protective Wage Clause, authorized the UMW to "call and maintain strikes throughout the entire Appalachian Area when necessary to preserve and maintain the integrity and competitive parity of this Agreement." In correspondence with William Davis, President Roosevelt observed "that the Protective Wage Clause, giving Mr. Lewis the right to interpret the clause all alone, and call a strike on that interpretation, is contrary to the spirit of any agreement. It is like giving the sole right to one party to a written contract to determine, with or without pretext or good reason, that the contract had not been lived up to and thereupon tear it up without review or redress by the other party."[16]

Lewis fully appreciated the potential of the clause. Yet his insistence on securing points beyond the recommendations of the mediation board in part stemmed from anger over the southerners' refusal to yield in early May and, more importantly, from a desire to implant firmly in coal operators' minds the fact that he would not tolerate any attempt to use the NDMB to dilute union demands.

The southern operators, naturally, resisted the additional clauses, but after some compromises and more threats by Lewis, twelve of the thirteen southern associations at the conference consented to a contract almost identical to the one the North had signed. Harlan County, the lone holdout in 1939, still objected to the imposition of the union shop. Lewis refused to sign with the other operators until Harlan County joined the fold. Following more negotiations and the intervention of William Davis, a settlement was finally concluded on July 5.[17]

The 1941 bituminous contract constituted a significant victory for Lewis and the union. The UMW had compelled the South to accept a contract almost identical to that of the North. Lewis, despite marginal concessions, attained the union's primary objectives of a dollar a day or its equivalent in pay increases, elimination of the forty-cent differential, vacations with pay, and the union shop throughout the field. The Protective Wage Clause and the memorial period provision, moreover, granted Lewis additional weapons with which to impose his influence on the industry.

Aside from the union's advances, the prolonged negotiations heralded a shift in Lewis's style. Always a resourceful negotiator, he now began to display a love of strategy for its own sake. No doubt the war news competing for headlines with UMW activities partly stimulated his fascination with the subtleties of maneuvers. Yet his increased concern also reflected the miners' lack of labor allies: The smaller the army, the more skillful must be the general. To the members of the northern wage conference, Lewis relived "the great coal drama of 1941" as a veteran would a war. Pleased with his own performance, he found the "strategy and generalship" of the southern leaders "deplorable from every standpoint."[18]

Lewis also found little to praise in the conduct of the government. The administration's intervention in the coal dispute, he charged, displayed a lack of coordination, direction, and even wisdom. Given the salience of the Guffey act, the president could have encouraged Congress to renew it before the existing contract expired. Moreover, twice during March, William S. Knudsen, director general of the Lewis-despised Office of Production Management, conferred with operators on ways to keep the mines open. Yet he failed to consult with Lewis on either occasion, and in presenting his plan to the operators, Knudsen ignored the union's concern with insuring retroactive pay. Similarly, the National Defense Mediation Board, in its initial recommendations, failed to solve the dispute, and Lewis easily subverted its subsequent award.[19]

Indeed, nothing the Roosevelt administration did by the spring of 1941 would satisfy Lewis. Although the president pressured the operators to meet the UMW's demands, Lewis was not grateful. Rather than thank Roosevelt for his behind-the-scenes intervention, Lewis preferred to humiliate the president publicly.

*　　*　　*

Nothing, including mobilization efforts, came between Lewis and his feud with the Roosevelt administration. Yet Lewis adroitly avoided assailing the president personally, focusing his criticism instead on Roosevelt's lieutenants, particularly Sidney Hillman. At a testimonial dinner for Phil Murray in April 1941, Lewis raged about Hillman's collaborationist policies. Again, at a CIO leadership conference in July, he castigated Hillman for endorsing Roosevelt's use of the army to break a strike at North American Aviation in Inglewood, California. The denunciation caused an indignant Jacob Potofsky, acting president of Hillman's Amalgamated Clothing Workers, to indict Lewis for "playing politics" in the national emergency and creating disunity within the CIO. Although many CIO delegates may have concurred in Potofsky's characterization, they nonetheless voted to uphold "the stand of President Philip Murray, UAW President R. J. Thomas and UMW President John L. Lewis in emphatically condemning the use of the armed forces to break strikes."[20]

The CIO delegates' endorsement of an anti-Hillman resolution testified more to Murray's efforts to promote unity than to Lewis's popularity. Throughout 1941, Lewis's influence in the labor movement deteriorated. As defense efforts intensified, numerous CIO officials turned deaf to Lewis's cry of labor independent and unregulated, and they joined Hillman in working with the administration. At the United Automobile Workers' convention in mid-August, for instance, the Hillmanites, led by Walter Reuther, trounced George Addes and other Lewis supporters in a contest for control of the union's executive board. Moving quickly to consolidate their victory, Reuther's forces persuaded the convention to pledge UAW support for Murray's reelection as CIO president, thereby eliminating Lewis from consideration.[21]

Hitler's invasion of Russia on June 22, 1941, further splintered the Lewis anti-Roosevelt coalition, as pro-Communists switched their foreign policy. Lewis remained silent on the international situation until early August, when he joined Herbert Hoover, Alfred Landon, Charles Dawes, and other conservatives in an appeal to Congress to halt Roosevelt's step-by-step projection of the country into the conflict. Immediately, Communists and fellow travelers allied with New Dealers to attack Lewis. Left-wingers such as Lee Pressman and Len DeCaux divorced themselves from the man they once esteemed. Albert Fitzgerald, the newly elected president of the CIO's United Electric, Radio and Machine Workers, fervently denounced Lewis, and delegates to the State, County and Municipal Workers convention acted as if the former CIO president had never existed.[22]

Respect for Lewis diminished throughout the labor movement. In a poll of the nation's leading labor editors, fifty-two participants supported the administration and its defense policies; only a lonesome triad endorsed Lewis's views. Another survey, conducted by *Fortune,* indicated that factory workers disapproved of Lewis's part in labor relations more than they did the roles of Bethlehem Steel,

General Motors, Henry Ford, or Roosevelt. Even in his citadel, the United Mine Workers of America, discontent with his policies emerged. Irritated over the increased union assessments by checkoff collection, anthracite miners staged a wildcat strike against the union's leadership in September and October.[23]

Lewis reacted to the loss of influence in his customary manner. First, he strengthened his own position by fortifying the mine workers' union. The assessment policy, which provoked the September anthracite rebellion, was part of a drive to strengthen the organization against economic adversity. He also reorganized catchall District 50, placing Ora Gasaway at its head and his daughter, Kathryn, as secretary-treasurer. Intending to breathe new life into his private labor movement, Lewis demoted or forced into premature retirement about thirty District 50 officers. Leaders in both the A. F. of L. and CIO took note of this refurbishing as a threat to their domains.

Lewis also lashed out at his antagonists with a zeal reminiscent of his attacks on Farrington, Howat, Brophy and other opponents in the 1920s. In testifying before the Truman committee he engaged in petty squabbling with Senator Tom Connally. On several occasions he seemed determined to humble Roosevelt. William Davis witnessed one such episode during the captive mine controversy in the fall of 1941, when he, Lewis, and Myron Taylor were meeting in a Washington hotel room with Taylor on the telephone trying to arrange a conference with the president. "We could hear FDR's voice. 'Come right over. Glad to see you, come right over'," recalled Davis. "Taylor looked at John L. Lewis and said 'All right?' John said, 'I will go to the White House if I'm invited to the White House.' And it was just in the tone of his voice—that's what he wanted. It was a victory to him to have gotten himself in a position where he was invited to the White House."[24]

Visions of conspiracies against himself and his union pervaded Lewis's speeches and writings. He depicted Sidney Hillman as the sinister force behind the scenes who convinced the administration to inject the NDMB into the bituminous dispute. During the subsequent captive mine controversy, he once again accused Hillman of responsibility for "the fantastic procedure" followed by the mediation board and of harboring an "attitude of vengeful and malignant opposition to the interest of the United Mine Workers of America."[25] Likewise, he charged John Brophy with leading "a poison squad in the headquarters of the C.I.O." "This group," he maintained, "systematically and quite maliciously have been disseminating misinformation and propaganda to favored newspaper correspondents, radio commentators and columnists, designed to besmirch the character and impair the standing" of the head of the UMW.[26]

Such behavior suggested to many, including Roosevelt, that Lewis no longer controlled his full mental facilities. Yet behind each of Lewis's accusations lay some factual basis. Hillman and Roosevelt did, indeed, actively interject themselves in the mediation board's handling of coal disputes. And someone at CIO headquarters was releasing malicious stories about Lewis to the press. Lewis, moreover, had learned early in his career that his paranoid style generated sympathy among both coal miners and ordinary citizens. To observers, then, Lewis appeared as an extremely complex individual with one foot rooted in reality and the other in fantasy. Lewis-watchers continually debated which foot was more firmly planted.

Accounts of the captive mine controversy in the fall of 1941 ascribe a host of sinister motives to Lewis. No longer able to attack him as a defender of Moscow, a few critics shifted to castigating him as an agent of Berlin. More frequently, commentators asserted that Lewis, unsympathetic to the defense program, opportunistically grasped any occasion to embarrass his rival, Roosevelt. A third hypothesis suggests that Lewis sought to reestablish his leadership of the labor movement by challenging the emergency mobilization program's restraints on unions.[27]

Such explanations reflected the conventional notion during the defense crisis and war period that anyone who acted in a manner seemingly detrimental to the nation's security must be either power hungry, traitorous, or mentally disturbed. Yet Lewis demanded the union shop in the captive mines neither as a megalomaniac, a paranoid hater of the president, nor even a saboteur of national defense. Rather, he behaved primarily as an aggressive labor leader who failed to anticipate fully the impact of his actions.

After settling with the northern and southern Appalachian operators in early July, the officers of the UMW began negotiating contracts with the nation's other coal producers. All of the outlying districts accepted the miners' demands except the steel companies' captive mines. Willing to grant most of the provisions in the. basic contract, the steel industry steadfastly rejected the union shop. In 1939 the union had acquiesced to steel's intransigence. But in the summer of 1941 Lewis feared that the nation would soon enter the war and that prevailing labor standards would be frozen for the duration of the conflict. Under such circumstances, he felt it imperative "to 'batten down the hatches' and see to it that when the mine workers union was frozen, it would be with a union shop prevailing every place a man dug coal."[28]

An industrywide union shop including the captive mines, moreover, represented a reasonable and natural growth of the UMW. By the fall of 1941, 99% of the workers in mines under contract were union members, including 95% of the coal diggers employed in the captive pits. Because 90% of the total annual bituminous production was mined under union-shop agreements, Lewis thought it only logical for the UMW to demand a similar status in the captive mines, where all but 5% of the eligible employees had joined the union. In more normal times, with the union free to unleash its full arsenal of weapons, it seems probable that the steel companies would ultimately have yielded to the demand for a union shop.

Indeed, hints exist that the steel executives recognized the logic of the UMW's position. Throughout the controversy industry spokesmen seemed aware that the union possessed both the rationale and the power to win its point. Yet they opposed the demand out of fear that if they granted the union shop in the collieries, they would be forced to do likewise in the steel mills and shipyards. Apparently, steel company executives preferred that the government impose the union shop on the captive mines. A federally mandated union shop in the "captive mines" would enable the industry to argue during negotiations with SWOC and other labor bodies that the union shop in the mines should be considered neither a precedent nor a change in the steel industry's basic policy. In a memorandum to Roosevelt marked "Personal and Confidential," Myron Taylor expressed his belief that the directors of U.S. Steel "would abandon the defense of the freedom of the workers to join or not to join a union only if you issued an executive order in the captive mine case, or if Congress enacted legislation which took from the shoulders of the Board the responsibility for that decision. In either of those instances, I am confident the corporation would promptly comply."[29]

Throughout the summer of 1941 the union and captive mine operators haggled over the union-shop issue. With the talks going nowhere, Lewis ordered a walkout of the 53,000 captive mine workers on Monday, September 15. Lewis's behavior suggests that he recognized that the operators wanted the government to act for them and that he initiated the strike knowing full well that it would immediately bring the National Defense Mediation Board into the controversy. Lewis held the miners out for a full week in order to impress the board with the union's determination. Finally, on September 17, with his point made, Lewis offered a plan, which the operators accepted, to reopen the mines for a month while the NDMB considered the dispute.[30]

For the next thirty days the miners worked, the steel industry profited, and the NDMB panel procrastinated. The union waited patiently, expecting the logic of the situation to compel the panel to recommend in its favor. Finally, on October 21, Lewis informed Davis that he wearied of delay and that the temporary agreement under which the mines operated would terminate at midnight October 25. Because October 26 fell on a Sunday, when the mines normally closed, the NDMB still had five days to render a decision.[31]

The pace of activity at the board promptly quickened. According to the UMW *Journal*, Sidney Hillman led "Chairman Davis up to the White House where the captive coal problem was tucked into the category of a political issue."[32] Roosevelt, Hillman, and Davis probably explored ways to settle the controversy without compelling the government to order workers to join the union, a policy the president detested. But on October 24 the NDMB subcommittee investigating the dispute released an opinion adroitly sidestepping the central question. "It became clear to the members of the Mediation Board," the report explained, "that there could be no meeting of minds in the conference before it with respect to the two conflicting rights asserted in the present dispute, because of the possible repercussions of any agreement here made on the steel and shipbuilding industries, in one or both of which most of the interests involved in this dispute are engaged.''[33]

Although unwilling to rule on the union shop issue, the members of the NDMB subcommittee proposed in their report two new ways of resolving the controversy. First, they suggested submitting the question to the full mediation board, with both parties pledging beforehand to accept the final verdict. Second, they recommended renewed collective bargaining and, if that failed to produce agreement, binding arbitration. In either event, mining operations were to continue.[34]

A memorandum presenting the president's views accompanied the panel's opinion. The memorandum expressed the president's hope that ''if the parties to the dispute adopt the second alternative procedure recommended by the Mediation Board'' that Myron Taylor of U.S. Steel and Lewis of the mine workers would assume the leading positions on a joint conference board. To make the second procedure more appealing to Lewis, Roosevelt magnified Myron Taylor's role. In previous dealings with Taylor, including the famous 1937 steel negotiations, Lewis had won great victories.[35]

Whatever hope Roosevelt harbored of achieving a private, voluntary solution to the crisis collapsed the following day, October 25, when he received a note from Taylor. The former chairman of the board of U.S. Steel informed the president of his disappointment at being nominated ''for a joint activity with Mr. John L. Lewis to settle a question which the Mediation Board seems not to be courageous enough to act upon themselves. It will be no surprise to you to know,'' he continued, ''that I immediately wired Mr. Davis that I was not available for service.'' Taylor outlined for the president the two factors that shaped his decision. First, as a result of his previous dealings with Lewis, his credibility with Little Steel had suffered, and he doubted that he could provide the industrial leadership needed in this crisis. Second, he asserted that the board of U.S. Steel would withhold the union shop until the government ordered it. Taylor, in effect, handed the crisis back to the president.

Taylor also informed Roosevelt that he had telephoned Lewis that morning and urged the miners' leader to extend the temporary agreement for two more weeks. He also indicated that if a two-week truce was arranged, he and Lewis could meet in Washington. ''This sort of conference, however, would not be a part of the Mediation Board activities but only a personal and private conference between Mr. Lewis and myself,'' Taylor stressed.[36]

Lewis responded to Roosevelt's October 24 memorandum after his 8:00 A.M. telephone conversation with Taylor and was aware, therefore, that the plan outlined in the memorandum would never materialize. He politely accepted the president's invitation to meet with Taylor but then fumed at being given the runaround by the government. The NDMB's approach to the captive mine dispute, he lamented, appeared ''casual and lackadaisical to the point of indifference. . . . The Board now emerges with a report devoid of conclusions as to merit, evasive as to the responsibilities of the Board, and dumps its own sorry mess into the already over-burdened lap of the Chief Executive.''

Then came the crucial point of the letter. "Under these circumstances," Lewis maintained, "I do not feel warranted in recommending an additional extension of the temporary agreement . . . in advance of an opportunity to negotiate with the qualified policy making executives of the corporations." Lewis, in effect, informed the president that it was unfair to demand that the miners continue work before the steel industry officially agreed to enter negotiations with the union.[37]

The dispute now entered a new crisis. The steel industry would not formally respond to the president's memorandum and the NDMB's report until at least Tuesday, October 28, when the directors of U.S. Steel were to meet. Lewis, however, had ordered the coal miners not to report to work after midnight, Saturday, October 25. For strategic and personal reasons, Lewis could not postpone the work stoppage without some concessions from the steel industry. To do so would relieve the pressure on the industry to seek a rapid settlement of the dispute and would be tantamount to abandoning the right to strike under the preparedness program. Roosevelt, however, insisted that the international situation demanded the uninterrupted operation of all defense industries. To him the union shop was far less vital than full military production. Yet unwilling to impose the union shop, Roosevelt preferred to force Lewis to cancel the strike in order to suppress a practice that other unions might later emulate.

On Sunday, October 26, Roosevelt sent Lewis a letter, which he also released to the press. Acknowledging Lewis's communique of the previous day but ignoring its substance, Roosevelt, "as President of the United States," asked Lewis and his associate officers "as loyal citizens, to come to the aid of your country" by keeping the captive mines in operation. "That is essential to the preservation of our freedoms, yours and mine."[38]

The notion that a miners' strike threatened the mobilization program served Roosevelt's purpose of turning public opinion against Lewis but did not conform to reality. The U.S. Steel Corporation's mines, Myron Taylor had informed the president, could be closed "for two or three weeks in the North and about five weeks in the South without affecting steel production." Likewise, the Bureau of Mines estimated that the steel companies possessed at least a thirty-day supply of coal.[39]

Lewis raged at Roosevelt's transformation of a labor-management dispute into a confrontation between the union and the government. "There is yet no question of patriotism or national security involved in this dispute," he challenged Roosevelt. "Defense output is not impaired, and will not be impaired for an indefinite period. This fight is only between a labor union and a ruthless corporation." In a clever move designed to remind an incited public that the controversy was essentially a labor dispute, that it involved one of the titans of Wall Street as well as himself, and that Roosevelt had displayed a lack of fair play, Lewis jibed: "If you would use the power of the State to restrain me, as an agent of labor, then, Sir, I submit that you should use the same power to restrain my adversary in this issue, who is an agent of capital. My adversary is a rich man named Morgan, who lives in New

York." If Morgan will permit Myron Taylor to implement the Appalachian agreement in the "captive mines," Lewis concluded, then the entire problem could be settled in ten minutes, and coal production could be quickly resumed.[40]

Lewis's snide letter provoked Roosevelt to issue, on October 27, yet another public appeal to the UMW leadership from "your Government, through me" urging the immediate resumption of work in the captive mines.[41] And in his Navy Day address broadcast later that night, in a clear reference to Lewis, he assailed "selfish leaders."[42] More privately to Thomas Lamont of U.S. Steel, Roosevelt expressed anger "at Lewis' unwarranted, untrue, and demagogic statement about Jack [Morgan]." When you see Morgan, he instructed Lamont, "tell him for me not to concern himself any more about Lewis' attack, for after many years of observation, I have come reluctantly to the conclusion that Lewis' is a psychopathic condition."[43]

The president's public pronouncements fed popular indignation against Lewis and the mine workers. As international developments entangled the nation in the global conflict, journals of liberal and conservative opinion alike accused Lewis of deliberately jeopardizing the country's security. Antistrike measures once again gained support in Congress, as conservative legislators charged the coal union leader with treason and urged the president to act decisively. "I have never seen such unanimity of opinon on any one subject as the strike situation and your impasse with Lewis," Sherman Minton informed Roosevelt. "The people support you with unprecedented agreement. . . . I read in the paper that you are trying to keep the controversy between you and Lewis from becoming an issue between you and him. Personally I think that's what you want. You don't want to make it a controversy between you and Labor. . . . It isn't Labor. It is Lewis. He is hated like no one else in America. Now is the time to clip his wings."[44]

Tuesday, October 28, dawned on 53,000 miners in six states remaining away from the captive collieries. In New York, directors of U.S. Steel learned that the firm's earnings for the first nine months of 1941 were almost one-third greater than they had been during the same period the previous year. They also decided to allow the federal government to resolve the captive mines dispute by asking the full mediation board to arbitrate the issue. Immediately following the directors' meeting, Myron Taylor journeyed to Washington, where he conferred with Roosevelt and William Davis.

The following morning Lewis and Taylor began bargaining. As a possible solution emerged, they summoned William Davis and informed him of their desire to have the full NDMB hear the case and issue a recommendation concerning the union shop. Neither party, however, would be bound by the board's decision. Lewis also demanded that the mines stay closed while the NDMB pondered the case; but the mediation board chairman refused to acquiesce. To break the impasse, Taylor led his fellow conferees to the White House, where, apparently after a personal plea by the president, Lewis agreed to order the miners back to work. In announcing the plan to newsmen, Lewis intentionally minimized

Roosevelt's role. "Once again," he pontificated, "Mr. Taylor and I have been able to render a service at a time when it is in the national interest and in a manner that has secured the gracious approval of the President."[45]

At 11:30 A.M., Thursday, October 30, Lewis summoned the captive miners back to work. At 2:30 that afternoon—in an act designed to reaffirm labor's right to strike—he informed the press of a new strike deadline of November 15. At the time most commentators viewed this last move as a symbolic gesture rather than a serious threat. They generally believed that the NDMB would simply follow the precedent set in a decision made in June granting the closed shop to the A. F. of L. metal trades in Bethlehem Steel's shipyards on the West Coast. With the outcome of the board's deliberations predictable, the captive mine controversy seemed settled.[46]

Then, on November 10, the unexpected happened. By a nine-to-two vote the NDMB rejected the union shop in the "captive mines." Only Philip Murray and Thomas Kennedy supported the union's case. All four employer representatives, all three public representatives, and both A. F. of L. alternatives voted in the negative. The unexplained absence of the two regular representatives from the A. F. of L. on a question of such critical importance to organized labor heightened some observers' suspicions that political intrigue lay behind the decision. The board's report, moreover, failed to clarify the vote.[47]

The day after the ruling, Lewis maintained an uncustomary silence while Murray and Kennedy captured headlines by resigning in protest from the NDMB. The board's opinion, they proclaimed, "discloses that regardless of the merits of any case, labor unions shall be denied the right of normal growth and legitimate aspiration, such as the union shop, and the traditional open-shop policy of the anti-labor employers shall prevail." Their departure from the board led to its collapse.[48]

Roosevelt, realizing that the mine workers would not accept the NDMB decision and that Lewis would now enforce the November 15 strike threat, summoned Benjamin Fairless, of U.S. Steel; Eugene Grace, of Bethlehem; and Frank Purnell, of Youngstown; along with the three top UMW leaders to the White House on Friday, November 14. At the conference, the president forcefully threatened antistrike legislation and implied his right to seize mines if the pits failed to stay open. He urged both parties to resume negotiations and, if they were unable to reach agreement, to appoint "an arbiter, or arbiters, or anyone else with any other name, and that in the meantime coal production continue." The union shop, he insisted, could only be achieved by voluntary collective bargaining and not through government decree. "I tell you frankly that the Government of the United States will not order, nor will Congress pass legislation ordering, a so-called closed shop." To do so "would be too much like the Hitler methods toward labor." Jawboning completed, Roosevelt requested the gathered parties to continue coal production as they negotiated. "And let me have some kind of a report on Monday next,'' he concluded, ''a report of agreement, or at the least a report that you are making progress.''[49]

On Monday, November 17, the president met disappointment. For the third time in as many months the captive coal miners refused to work. Fairless, Grace, and Purnell gave formal notice that negotiations had broken off. Lewis, moreover, raised the ominous specter of a complete shutdown of the bituminous industry should his union's demands go unmet.[50]

For the next few days, the president seemed stymied. He suggested that if the union would abandon the union-shop demand, he would personally encourage the remaining 5% of the captive miners who did not belong to the UMW to join the organization voluntarily. The implication that Roosevelt might do Lewis's job angered the labor leader.[51]

Some members of the administration, if not Roosevelt, also toyed with the idea of having the president order the miners back to work. To explore this option, the administration sounded out captive miners' views on November 8 and 9, prior to the NDMB decision and the ensuing crisis. Ninety-two percent of those surveyed wanted the union shop. A majority, however, indicated that they had not favored the October walkout, and the group divided nearly evenly when queried about their willingness to strike if the NDMB ruled against them. ''There is little doubt that the men would follow John Lewis if he called a strike,'' the report indicated. ''But there is also little doubt that the men would *prefer* to follow the President.''[52]

During the opening days of the strike, prospects that the miners would return to work if appealed to by the president still seemed good. According to early reports to the Federal Conciliation Service, the majority of captive miners supported the walkout more from a sense of union discipline than a belief in its justice. After a few days out picketing, informants advised the service, the coal diggers will be ready to go back to work.

But time worked against the administration. On November 20 news reached Washington of increased violence between pickets, law enforcement agencies, and some miners wishing to work. Confrontation polarized the situation and led the striking captive miners to close ranks. Simultaneously, thousands of coal diggers from the commercial collieries walked out to demonstrate solidarity with their union brothers. ''Whereas previously it had been reported that there was a strong movement among the miners back to work Tuesday and Wednesday,'' a conciliation service summary noted of West Virginia, ''the same source today reports that sentiment is rapidly changing to the opposite direction. It is said that this can be attributed partly to the bungling job of the state police on Wednesday.'' Additional reports of growing solidarity among mine workers the following day lessened the prospect that a presidential plea would induce miners to return to work.[53]

On November 19 Roosevelt again requested Lewis either to accept the status quo for the duration of the national emergency or to submit the union-shop issue to arbitration. Lewis promptly informed him that a final decision on the president's request would be made by the UMW Policy Committee, which was unable to meet for a few days. He then practically rejected Roosevelt's proposal. "Your recent statements on this question, as the Chief Executive of the nation," Lewis noted, "have been so prejudicial to the claim of the Mine Workers as to make uncertain that an umpire could be found whose decision would not reflect your interpretation of government policy, congressional attitude and public opinion."[54]

Whether intentional or not, Lewis's statement provided the key to ending the crisis, for it carried the implication that the mine workers would agree to arbitration if assured beforehand of a favorable decision. This was the route the union had thought it had traveled when it resubmitted the case to the NDMB. Its expectations then had been disappointed; now it demanded certainty.

As the UMW Policy Committee gathered at 10:00 A.M. on November 22 to respond formally to the president's request, Lewis received a telephone call from Secretary of Labor Perkins urging him to take no action until Roosevelt made a final appeal. With the committee waiting in the basement, Lewis left union headquarters, returned at 11:15 A.M., and then sat in his sixth-floor office until shortly after noon, when a messenger delivered the president's letter. In it, Roosevelt informed Lewis that the steel industry had agreed to arbitration, and therefore he was appointing Fairless for steel, Lewis for labor, and Dr. John R. Steelman for the public as a board to settle the dispute. Steelman's appointment guaranteed Lewis his victory, for it was well known that the conciliation service director favored the union's position. The Policy Committee, following Lewis's recommendation, eagerly agreed to the plan.[55]

The president's letter and newspaper stories suggested that the steel companies had accepted arbitration without knowledge of the board's full composition. Such ignorance may have served the industry's purpose, for it simply approved of a process and allowed the president to determine the outcome by appointing the board. This scheme met the steel industry's desire to have the union shop in the mines imposed through governmental action, if it had to be instituted at all. Finally, to satisfy Roosevelt's pledge that the government would not order the union shop, Steelman resigned from his post in the conciliation service, and the board's meetings were held in New York rather than Washington to disassociate it from the government.

After two weeks of discussions, the board issued its anticipated decree granting the union shop to the mine workers. Lewis and Steelman composed the majority; Fairless defended the steel industry's commitment to the open shop.[56] A controversy that involved only 53,000 workers in a nation of over 100-million, yet that had kept Congress, the presidency, and the general public in heated agitation, ended. After three months of dispute, three short strikes, and the collapse of the National Defense Mediation Board, Lewis once again appeared triumphant. But no one paid much attention. The board announced its decision on December 7; the Japanese had just attacked Pearl Harbor.

*   *   *

After the United States entered into the world conflict, Lewis pledged the UMW's full cooperation in defeating the nation's enemies. Partly out of patriotism and partly out of the realization that his motives were always suspect, he imposed upon his union a strictly formal and proper posture toward the war. From the beginning, the national organization and its affiliates fully subscribed to every loan drive. The pages of the UMW *Journal* and the speeches of the organization's leaders persistently urged the miners on to new production records. Throughout the war years, Lewis advocated policies that he, at least, felt did not seriously threaten the success of the GIs in battle. Yet despite such caution, the public image of Lewis as an enemy of the nation persisted. In part his outspoken criticism of the administration's conduct of the war on the home front reinforced this view, as did the UMW's strikes in 1943. Lewis's opponents in politics and labor, moreover, in order to discredit him, kept the memories of his prewar views alive.

Amidst the spirit of unity prevailing for the first few weeks after Pearl Harbor, Lewis appeared on the verge of regaining some of his lost prestige within the labor movement. When the president's conference of labor and management leaders convened on December 17 to consider means of settling disputes without interrupting production, Lewis arrived with a detailed plan of action. Although his program was not accepted, his foresight combined with his commanding presence allowed him to polish his tarnished reputation.[57]

On January 17, 1942, Lewis, as chairman of the CIO's standing peace negotiating committee, publicly called upon Philip Murray of the CIO and William Green of the A. F. of L. to resume unity talks. "It is obvious," he declared, "that if accouplement could be achieved, with unified and competent leadership, the result would be advantageous and in the public interest." The wartime crisis, the increasing pressures to curtail labor's rights, and the possible economic dislocations at the end of the conflict made it mandatory, in Lewis's opinion, for the two houses of labor to merge. "If labor is to be mobilized, transported here and there under terms and conditions set by employers and bureaucrats, with its forces divided," he pointed out, "there could be but one result—labor will be shortchanged in the process."[58]

Lewis's act elicited favorable responses from a number of prominent union officials and opinion makers. After consulting the A. F. of L. executive board, Green immediately accepted the peace overture. ILGWU President David Dubinsky expressed delight over the prospects of unity, as did Hillman's lieutenant Emil Rieve, who welcomed the proposal regardless of its source. To Eleanor Roosevelt the idea of unity was simply "grand." For a few brief days a labor merger seemed likely. Still to be heard from, however, were Murray, the president, and the *New York Times*.[59]

On Monday, January 19, the *Times* carried a front page story by A. H. Raskin describing secret negotiations between Lewis and Daniel Tobin of the A. F. of L.

teamsters. Together they reportedly had devised a scheme for merging the two organizations that called for Green's retirement, George Meany's promotion to the presidency of the new federation, and Murray's demotion to the position of secretary-treasurer. The A. F. of L. executive board, according to Raskin, had already informally accepted the plan. Press accounts the following day embellished Raskin's story by contending that Lewis, Norman Thomas, Senator Burton K. Wheeler, and other opponents of the president had concocted the plot at a cocktail party.[60]

Although the news releases created bitterness and jealousy inside the labor movement, the accuracy of the journalistic accounts cannot be substantiated. In fact, almost everyone who explored the story came up with a different version. Whereas Raskin argued that Lewis and Tobin were the principal characters, Anna Rosenberg, in checking it out for Roosevelt, concluded that the cabal consisted of Lewis, David Dubinsky, William Hutcheson, and Matthew Woll. Relying on different informants, Undersecretary of Agriculture Gardner Jackson reported to the president that "those definitely in the play were Matt Woll, Dan Tobin, and George Meany, along with John [L. Lewis] and Bill Hutchinson [sic]." George Meany, however, informed his biographer that only Hutcheson and Lewis plotted secretly. Finally, in a letter to Murray, Lewis contended that he had made "no commitments of any character to anyone that affect any phase of this problem."[61]

In all probability no secret maneuvers occurred at all. Rather, unity proposals constituted cocktail party chitchat and a subject of conversation among labor leaders, particularly those belonging to the A. F. of L. The mentioning of such firm supporters of the president as David Dubinsky and Daniel Tobin in accounts of behind-the-scenes dealings belie implications of a conservative plot against Roosevelt. Of major union figures, only Murray and Hillman seemed to have been left in the dark.

Lewis's failure to consult with Murray before making the merger proposal wounded the CIO president deeply. Absent from Washington when Lewis made the announcement, Murray learned of the proposal the next day from the newspapers. "No one has the right to trade me for a job," he bellowed to reporters when finally contacted for a statement. "My manhood requires a little reciprocity—and, by God, despite this feeble frame of mine, I will fight any living man to maintain my manhood."[62] In an official reply to Lewis, begun coldly with "Dear Sir and Brother," Murray curtly informed the miners' leader that all arrangements in behalf of unity "will necessarily have to be initiated through the office of the President of the Congress of Industrial Organizations."[63]

Lewis's reasons for not consulting Murray can only be surmized. In one sense, perhaps he was testing Murray's subordination: If the CIO president proved willing to have Lewis trade away his post, the UMW leader's prestige in the labor movement would be enhanced, while Murray would be forever doomed as Lewis's lackey. In Lewis's eyes, moreover, Murray's choice was not between Lewis and independence, but Lewis and Roosevelt.

To a large extent the unity proposal constituted an attempt by Lewis to end the CIO's subordination to the president. Seen from Lewis's perspective, a united labor movement would end the administration's strategy of divide and control, would strengthen the antiadministration forces by placing Lewis and Hutcheson in the same camp, and would weaken the influence of Murray and Hillman by compelling them to share power with individuals less deferential to Roosevelt. Evidently, Lewis calculated that a wave of favorable sentiment, both among the general public and within the labor movement, would compel Murray, and indeed Roosevelt, to go along with a merger despite their suspicions. Raskin's story in the *Times*, whatever its merits, clothed the affair with a sinister cloak that enabled Murray and the president to resist.

Roosevelt, realizing that a merger would weaken his influence over labor, moved quickly to thwart unity. Within a week of Lewis's proposal, he created the Labor Victory Committee, composed of three representatives each from the A. F. of L. and the CIO. According to the president, the committee would consult with him frequently on labor problems and would provide sufficient unity for the successful conduct of the war. Desiring to wield some influence with Lewis and also to have the three largest unions in the CIO represented, Roosevelt requested Murray to appoint the leader of the miners to the new committee. Enraged at Lewis's treatment of him, Murray refused. Disagreements between Lewis and Murray now erupted into full-scale war.[64]

With the advantage of hindsight, the bitter estrangement between Lewis and Murray can be traced to fundamental differences in philosophy as well as personality. Throughout his career, Lewis envisioned the labor movement as a force able to exert its will independently, beholden to no one. The attainment of that vision proved impossible during the lean years of the 1920s and 1930s. In the New Deal period Lewis freely accepted Roosevelt's aid, but he did so not as one receiving a gift, but as one being given his rightful due. When, after 1937, Roosevelt failed to meet Lewis's expectations, the latter felt ill-disposed to perpetuate the relationship for the sake of securing a few more crumbs. Murray, to the contrary, acted much more deferentially to a president whose policies had rejuvenated the UMW, and he had no wish to bite a benevolent hand.

For most of the 1930s, a dynamic labor movement and Murray's loyalty to Lewis served to mute the differences between the two men. Omens of Murray's divorce from Lewis, however, had appeared much earlier than the contentious unity movement of January 1942. Lewis's secret and dramatic negotiations with U.S. Steel in 1937 perturbed Murray and perhaps led him to launch the ill-fated drive on Little Steel without seeking Lewis's advice. Lewis's failure in 1940 to consult with him in advance of the Wendell Willkie endorsement further exasperated Murray, as did the assertions by reporters and convention delegates that Lewis would remain the power behind the throne after Murray's elevation to the CIO presidency.[65]

Actually, Lewis made a sincere effort in early 1941 to allow his associate to establish his own claim to leadership. Attempting to diminish his own presence, Lewis stayed away from CIO headquarters more than was his custom, and when union officials dropped into his office in the mine workers' building to chat about CIO business, he would drive them out and order them to consult Phil Murray.[66]

Temperament and fate combined, however, to prevent Lewis from sustaining this role for long. A few months after Murray's accession to the CIO presidency, for instance, the mine workers' leader accepted an invitation to attend a testimonial dinner for the new CIO chief. His absence, Lewis realized, would be interpreted as an affront to Murray. Yet when he arrived at the affair the delegates rose to their feet and cheered, and on the following morning the newspapers featured Lewis's remarks while giving only cursory treatment to the guest of honor.[67]

Murray also seemed temperamentally unable to adjust to his new station. Rather than operate out of the CIO headquarters, he did all his work from the miners' building. "It became almost like a Freudian symbol," observed Lee Pressman, "the act of leaving there to go over to the C.I.O. building." He became extremely sensitive, interpreting every act by Lewis as a rebuke. And what Lewis indiscretions Murray might inadvertently overlook were quickly pointed out by a band of followers eager to win the ear of the new president and dedicated to the demise of the old. When the CIO leader suffered a heart attack in the summer of 1941, his Pittsburgh partisans—David McDonald, Vin Sweeney, and others beholden to Murray for their place—went so far as to contend that Lewis consciously sought to drive Murray to his death so he could regain the presidency of the Congress of Industrial Organizations.[68]

According to some acquaintances, enmity between their kin further widened the rift between the two men. Shortly before the United States entered the war, Kathryn Lewis and Mercedes Daugherty, Murray's niece and ward, vacationed together. During their travels they engaged in a violent feud, and thereafter, David McDonald maintains, "they set out deliberately to poison the minds of Murray and Lewis against each other."[69] Apparently unaware of this occurrence, James Robb nevertheless felt that Kathryn "did more than anyone else to create the split. . . . She was so jealous of anyone who was close to him."[70]

The struggle between the Lewis and Hillman wings of the CIO over defense policy further complicated Murray's position. Murray was a man split in two, with old loyalties linking him to one camp and personal convictions pushing him into the other. Into the summer of 1941 he tried to equivocate between the two groups hoping to preserve some semblance of unity within the CIO. With news of the Nazi invasion of Russia and reports of German and Japanese attacks on American vessels, this precarious stalemate collapsed as more and more unionists entered the Hillman camp. Murray, reacting both to international developments and the changing political situation in the CIO, began to shift toward the emerging anti-Lewis majority.

In an effort to reach an accord, Lewis and Murray conversed in Atlantic City in mid-October 1941. Afterward each party to the talks related a different story of what had happened, though both men agreed that the meeting terminated their long relationship. To Lee Pressman, Murray painted a scene of Lewis pleading with him not to endorse Roosevelt's foreign policy. In response, a composed Murray asserted that he was going to follow the dictates of his conscience even if it meant that the two men would part.[71]

Lewis's version is presented in much more dramatic fashion by Saul Alinsky, who claimed to be at Atlantic City and in close contact with Lewis. Alinsky depicts Murray, still convalescing from his heart attack, as emotionally unstable. He refused to talk directly on the issues, speculated about his place in heaven, and broke into fits of tears. "Frankly," Lewis reportedly informed Alinsky, "I think he is a little bit out of his mind." Disclaiming concern over the foreign policy position to be taken by the forthcoming CIO convention, Lewis wanted to know what the CIO chief intended to do about the slander aimed at the UMW head. Lewis criticized Van Bittner and CIO Secretary-Treasurer James Carey in particular for their part in the defamation campaign, and he expressed his opposition to Carey's reelection. Emotionally upset, Murray nonetheless refused to concur. "He believes Bittner and Carey over me," the UMW leader thought in disbelief. Ending the conversations with Murray, Lewis reportedly remarked: "It was nice to have known you, Phil."[72]

Regardless of which account is nearer the truth, the fight between the two men did not degenerate into open hostilities until Lewis's ill-fated A. F. of L.-CIO unity proposal in January 1942. On November 11, 1941, Murray demonstrated his solidarity with the mine workers by resigning in protest from the NDMB. And although the CIO convention later that month reelected Carey and endorsed Roosevelt's foreign policy, it also approved Murray's motion of support for the striking captive miners. At the mid-December presidential labor-management conference, the CIO president still appeared to follow Lewis's lead. The aborted unity maneuver and Murray's decision not to appoint the miners' chief to the Victory Board ended the period of coexistence.

Administratively, Lewis had little choice but to expel Murray from the UMW and then to cut the miners' ties with the CIO. Otherwise an intolerable situation would have existed, in which UMW Vice-President Murray would be championing, as president of the CIO, policies that Lewis and the mine workers rejected. Such a situation would weaken the UMW internally as the rank and file took sides, and it would undercut the union's credibility with employers by exposing a divided organization.

The problem confronting Lewis was to devise a method to dispose of Murray that would least alienate the union's membership, long accustomed to supporting both men. The Atlantic City talks in October 1941 represented an unsuccessful attempt by Lewis to entice Murray's favor. The January 1942 merger proposal constituted a maneuver by Lewis to subvert Murray's influence indirectly. With its failure, Lewis proceeded to force a direct confrontation with his former colleague. His strategy would be to pit Murray's responsibilities as CIO chief against his obligations as a UMW officer.

First, Lewis engaged in a series of jurisdictional conflicts with other CIO affiliates, thereby skillfully cornering Murray into supporting either District 50's claims or those of other organizations. Next, Thomas Kennedy notified the CIO, on March 18, that the mine workers' union would not pay its monthly assessments but, rather, wished the sum deducted from the congress's $1,665,000 indebtedness to the UMW. When the CIO executive board refused to recognize the mine workers' claim, Murray again had to choose between the UMW and the larger federation that he headed. To side with neither, as he initially attempted to do, would enable Lewis to depict Murray as both indecisive and anti-UMW.[73]

Lewis's conduct provoked numerous CIO officials to denounce him. Seizing the opportunity, Lewis and his agents magnified this criticism to demonstrate to the miners the hostility of the CIO. The UMW *Journal* charged R. J. Thomas and Walter Reuther, in particular, of comparing the coal union leader to Robert Ley of the Nazi's labor front. Lewis personally twisted Murray's statement that he would not be Pearl Harbored into unity talks with the A. F. of L. into an accusation that the CIO head had called him a "Jap." Some attacks required no embellishment. On the evening of April 24, "Red Mike" Quill led about 200 of his transit workers in a raid on District 50 headquarters in New York. Primarily angered over invasions of his union's jurisdiction, "Red Mike" also charged Lewis with engaging in "a plot to build an isolationist labor movement and to thwart the nation's efforts at unity and victory."[74]

Lewis's lieutenants applied constant pressure on Murray to repudiate the assaults on the UMW and its leader. Murray tried to avoid a touchy situation by praising Lewis's patriotism and devotion to the labor movement without acknowledging that unfair charges had been made against his person. The UMW chief had no intention of settling for such gestures. In early April 1942 Ray Edmundson, Lewis's appointee as president of Illinois District 12, resigned as regional director of the CIO in protest against the attacks on the UMW. Recognizing their cue, mine workers officials across the country withdrew from the Congress of Industrial Organizations. Meanwhile, Lewis acted the victim of a slander campaign.[75]

In early May Murray ended his efforts at appeasement and initiated a Lewislike attack on Lewis. Speaking to coal miners and steelworkers in western Pennsylvania, the Scotsman rebuked his "traducers" in the UMW—"men who steal about in the silence of the night spreading poison and seeking to disorganize instead of organize." Charging Lewis and his henchmen with "back-stabbing" and "Tom Girdler" tactics, he declared that he would yield to "no dictator in or out of the labor movement."[76] Despite his new aggressiveness, however, Murray recognized that Lewis's hold on the mine workers' union was too firm to be broken, and on Friday, May 22, he accepted the salaried presidency of the United Steelworkers of America.

The following Monday, May 25, Murray ventured to the subterranean level of the coal diggers' headquarters, where, in a chamber filled with Lewis's mementos, the Policy Committee and executive council gathered to transact pending business. Throughout the day's session he waited nervously. When he finally spoke, he uttered not the pugnacious phrases of the past few weeks but mellow statements of praise and loyalty to the union's president. After he finished, the two men shook hands, Lewis giving few hints of an impending confrontation.

At the next day's executive council session, Lewis commenced his attack. In a dramatic performance, he flared out at Murray for failing to act against the UMW's detractors, criticized his response to the January unity proposal, and lambasted him for repudiating the CIO's outstanding financial debt to the UMW. Several times the CIO chief attempted to correct the "nasty record" being presented, but he was cowed by Lewis and the hostile delegates. When the miners' chief finally yielded to his "former friend," Murray, stunned by the brutality of men he had thought of as comrades, offered a meek rebuttal.

Murray's aggressiveness reemerged the following day, when the executive council began to consider formal charges against him. His spirits rejuvenated by a conference with Roosevelt the previous evening, Murray based his defense on his authority as president of the Congress of Industrial Organizations. Lewis retorted that Murray's first obligation must be to the United Mine Workers of America, and then he raised the issue of Murray's new salaried position with the Steelworkers. When Murray asserted that Lewis had also held other positions in the labor movement, the leader of the miners replied that he had never done so for pay and always "in behalf of our union." Lewis had found the issue that the rank-and-file members would accept as grounds for Murray's dismissal. The heated debate ended when Murray departed for another meeting with Roosevelt. With the victim closeted with the president, the executive board expressed Lewis's will by voting seventeen to one to declare the office of vice-president vacant.[77]

The lone ballot supporting Murray came from Martin Wagner, former leader of District 50, whom Lewis had promoted to an inconsequential post in order to put a more trusted supporter in a position of real power. Having registered his protest against Lewis, Wagner soon resigned and joined a number of other UMW officers who decided to risk their fortunes with Murray and the CIO. Among them were Allan Haywood, Van Bittner, Clint Golden, Pat Fagan, William Mitch, and David McDonald. Lewis attempted to persuade some of his old lieutenants not to leave, and he unsuccessfully tried to entice James Robb with the security of a post in a provisional district. Yet his efforts failed, and, as a consequence, the UMW lost some of its most talented leaders.

Rank-and-file discontent over Murray's expulsion proved less disastrous to the union's future. A number of locals throughout the coalfields, and particularly in the area around Murray's home district, sent resolutions of protest to the national headquarters. And when the CIO leader addressed a Slavic Day rally in Bellaire, Ohio, in June, some 200 miners and their families came to hear him. During the occasion a few local union presidents even posed for pictures with the deposed Murray. Yet while Murray criticized Lewis's actions, no one in the crowd jeered the UMW leader's name. Pete Phillippi, a UMW executive board member on the scene to evaluate the situation, reported that most of the miners present felt that Murray acted too piously and among themselves raised such questions as "Why didn't he use his influence to grant District Autonomy when he was Vice President if he [is] such a great liberal; [Why] does he want two jobs; . . . if he wants to win this war so bad why doesn't he get his Son to enlist.''[78] To quell discontent, Lewis elevated John O'Leary, a resident of Murray's district, to the vacant vice-presidency and sent the popular Colonel Percy Tetlow to West Virginia to assume Van Bittner's duties.

Throughout the summer Murray and his associates aimed a steady barrage of criticism at Lewis. Demonstrating a style he learned from over two decades of study with the master, Murray depicted himself as Christ, Lewis alternately as Peter or Judas, and the basement of UMW headquarters as the Garden of Gethsemane. Lewis devoted little time to replying, pausing only long enough to utter his characteristic blend of ridicule and pomposity. Life, he observed, "is too short for me to answer the yappings of every cur that follows at my heels. I hear the pack in my rear at times. I can turn my head and see the lap dogs and the kept dogs and the yellow dogs in pursuit. But I am serene in the knowledge that they won't come too close.''[79]

During the summer of 1942 Lewis delegated fighting the CIO to K. C. Adams, O'Leary, Edmundson, and other lieutenants, while he sought to cope with his wife's long illness. In February and again in March 1942, Myrta underwent major surgery for relief from a brain malignancy and spent most of the eight months before her death on September 9 in the hospital. She died at home in Alexandria, with her husband and daughter by her bedside, and she was buried in the Lewis family plot at Springfield.

Myrta's death saddened Lewis. For thirty-five years they had been man and wife. Some biographers and commentators, however, have tended to dramatize unduly the impact of her passing on Lewis. "Those who saw the anguish and deathly pallor of Lewis marked up 'finished' to Lewis's career,'' Alinsky wrote. "Those who saw Lewis and knew what Myrta Lewis had meant to him not only marked up 'finished' but underscored it.''[80]

Lewis's career was not "*finished*," to be sure, and it is doubtful that Alinsky or many others actually understood what Myrta had meant to him. The miners' leader worked hard at keeping his private life private. What public information he provided about his wife took the form of a Linconian myth with Myrta in the role of

Mary Todd, carrying culture and sophistication to the folksy coal miner who had been born on February 12. Although there are doubtless parallels in the wifely roles of Myrta and Mary Todd—such as applying pressure on their husbands to attain success and material possessions—for the most part, the myth lacks credence.

Whatever grief Lewis felt at Myrta's death hardly showed when he presided over the UMW's 1942 convention one month later. He hinted at his bereavement only once during the seven-day proceedings. In a report on the convention for the Russell Sage Foundation, Edward Wieck noted "that judging by close observation of his manner and demeanor at the convention, his recent personal tragedy, as far as his public life is concerned, has left him the same fighting Lewis. Somewhat mellowed, adopting a fatherly attitude to the mineworkers in the convention, but quite ready and able to lash out in biting, cutting attacks on opponents. He appeared to be in good health."[81]

The 1942 convention testified to Lewis's power over the miners. Since the last gathering in January 1940, he had led his union into situations that would have disrupted most organizations: a confrontation with a popular president; two coal strikes that antagonized both government and public opinion; outspoken and unpopular criticism of the nation's foreign policy; the expulsion of Philip Murray; and, finally, the separation of the union from the CIO. Yet despite such potential sources of discontent, open disagreement with Lewis's views was marginal and not militant. Lewis's machine, his agility as a union politico, and above all the fact that he "brought home the bacon" kept most miners in his camp and enabled him to sway the convention to his will.

Along with sanctioning the UMW's withdrawal from the CIO, the convention strengthened the union by granting even more authority to its president. The delegates increased monthly assessments, thus adding a projected $2,400,000 annually to the UMW treasury of $6,346,852. They also amended the constitution of the Gas, By-Product Coke, and Chemical Workers, District 50, to give it jurisdiction "in such other industries as may be designated and approved by the International Executive Board." Another amendment permitted supervisory personnel to join the union. Despite demands from some delegates for more autonomy, Lewis retained his power to establish provisional districts and received additional authority to grant dispensation relating to dues and assessments.

The convention also provided Lewis with a forum from which to issue policy statements on the war and government economic regulations. Defensive of the union's official position before Pearl Harbor, he insisted that since December 7 the organization had supported the war effort to the utmost. The record—in terms of miners joining the armed services, purchases of bonds and donations to relief agencies, services of UMW officials to government boards, and, above all, increased efforts to meet the nation's coal needs—"should commend this Union and its officers to the representatives of our government," he declared. "That record should entitle the United Mine Workers of America to be consulted with relation to the economic and industrial policies of this government necessary in pursuit of the war. That record . . . should cause the administrators of our government to lift that blacklist, figurative or real, which in the minds of many people has been imposed upon the United Mine Workers of America by officials in Washington.'' Lewis, in effect, challenged Roosevelt to readmit him to the circle of power. If the president refused, Lewis made clear, he would work to undermine what he perceived as unfair wartime regulations.[82]

CHAPTER 18
"Damn His Coal Black Soul": The Wartime Strikes, 1943

After the Japanese attack on Pearl Harbor, Lewis stilled his public opposition to Roosevelt's foreign policy and announced his support of the war effort. Soon afterwards he concurred with other labor leaders in a "No-Strike Pledge" to prevail for the duration of the struggle. He was disappointed at Roosevelt's choice of William H. Davis as chairman of the new National War Labor Board, but he consented to Thomas Kennedy's participation on the body. Throughout early 1942, the UMW *Journal* projected the all-sacrifices-necessary-to-win-the-war attitude then dominating national sentiment. The union backed the numerous war loan drives; it encouraged the miners on to record levels of production; and it heaped praise on the men in uniform. Personally, Lewis maintained a skeptical but essentially cooperative stance. In a time of national crisis, he told the union's Policy Committee, "every individual owes an obligation to temper his utterances to a point where the rights of the whole and the interests of the many are not set aside, intellectually or otherwise, by the arbitrary intellectual conclusions of an individual."[1] "Our nation is at war and coal production must not cease," he lectured wildcat strikers in July, 1942: "our every effort must be directed toward this end."[2]

By late 1942 the spirit of national solidarity had begun to fade. Various wartime controls, which the nation initially greeted with enthusiasm, now came under criticism. Along with other segments of society, miners felt aggrieved by unfair rationing standards, victimized by administrative chaos, and abused by preferential treatment for the rich and powerful. In the midst of the 1943 coal dispute, a leader of a UMW local traditionally hostile to Lewis explained to John Brophy why his rank and file now stood behind the miners' chief. "The bungling job that the O[ffice of] P[rice] A[dministration] has done has had a great share in this changed attitude of the miners," he opined:

> Gas rationing has also had some effect, and gas rationing is a crime in the coal fields with black market gas plentiful. It would require a book instead of a letter to explain all

415

the troubles the miners have had imposed upon them by blundering ration boards. And then there are the stories of how the Jews have cornered the market on vegetables and chickens and even potatoes. . . . And then the hogish attitude of the coal operators who accepted the increased selling price for coal to enable them to operate the six day week and then under any pretext refuse to operate the sixth day. . . . All this plus the 40 days of stalling by the operators in conference has had a very bad effect on appealing to the miners' *Patriotism*.[3]

Such sentiments among the rank and file enabled Lewis to speak more freely on wartime policies. Past events had made it practically inevitable that Lewis would become a leading critic of Roosevelt's domestic policies. His disdain for the President and his disavowal of the New Deal removed any political reason for remaining silent. The UMW's experience during World War I, moreover, had convinced him that domestic wartime policies inevitably operated to the detriment of workers and trade unions. He viewed World War I as an unfortunate "interregnum" in the development of the labor movement, and in a 1939 speech he predicted that in a future war prices and profits would soar while the government would restrain labor from adjusting wages to the rising cost of living.[4] Lewis's concern carried beyond the immediate impact of war on workers to the potential nature of post-war society. "My mind is oppressed," he told his lieutenants, "with the weight of responsibility that comes from considering what may be the position and the status of men and women of labor . . . as affecting the problems that will face them with the end of the war."[5]

Lewis recognized the need for some government regulation of the economy during the national emergency, but he wanted the government to limit its role to what was absolutely necessary. In particular, he desired minimal interference in labor-management relations. By and large he felt that the government should confine its activities to assuring fair play between contending parties and upholding basic labor standards. On all regulatory and policy boards—not just those dealing with labor matters—he wanted union spokesmen granted equal representation with delegates from capital. Reflecting his continued belief in the primacy of voluntary associations, Lewis also desired the formation of industry councils, composed equally of labor and management representatives, and charged with coordinating the policies of specific industries with the national defense effort.

The reality of wartime policy differed substantially from Lewis's concept. Conservative businessmen and bureaucrats came to dominate government councils while labor leaders enjoyed only limited participation in the affairs of state. "Indeed, there seems to be a blacklist against effective labor spokesmen," the UMW *Journal* complained, "and only those are admitted to the inner circle who can be trusted to nod acquiescence after decisions are made by others."[6] Nothing significant ever came of Lewis's industry council idea, although other labor leaders endorsed it. Nor was Lewis successful in having a code of principles formulated that would serve as a guide for the government's labor policies. Finally, the federal government substantially restricted collective bargaining as the National War Labor Board (NWLB) evolved from an agency to adjust differences between labor and management to an institution to check inflation through wage controls.

As the outline of government policy became clear, K. C. Adams, Lewis's spokesman as editor of the UMW *Journal*, unleashed a vehement attack on the administration and its supporters. Finding much to criticize in the confusion engulfing wartime Washington, Adams coined the term "burrocrat" to describe the "jitterbug Babitts who unloaded themselves in the various agencies and took over the affairs of government. . . . We have with us, and in power, more half-wits attempting to devise and blueprint our war-time conduct than have ever before periled the lives and future of any nation," Adams grumbled. He gleefully characterized Hillman, Green, and Murray as "weak-kneed" union officials who meekly sacrificed labor's independence "for a mess of political pottage or the crumbs doled out by any self-announced set of palace burrocrats."[7]

Such vituperation often obscured the UMW's basic criticism of Administration policy. For Lewis, the wartime measures threatened to reverse his life-long struggle to attain for labor an equal position with capital in the chambers of power. He saw Roosevelt's actions now as placing the American worker in a position of second class citizenship. If the Administration permitted labor a small role in shaping policy, it demanded an inordinately greater sacrifice from the men and women who toiled than it did from the owners of mines and mills. In Lewis's view the government implemented "a paradoxical policy that runs to the premise of rewarding and fattening industry and starving labor. . . ."[8]

Lewis was acutely aware of the extreme sacrifice made by some coal miners. The longer hours and increased mechanization imposed by the war-time demand for coal made mining—already one of the most dangerous jobs in America—even more dangerous. When Lewis came under attack during the 1943 dispute for jeopardizing the lives of the GI's on the battle front, he would paraphrase a Department of Interior report, however inaccurately, to the effect that until mid-1943 "the deaths and injuries in the mining industry since Pearl Harbor exceeded all casualties in the military forces of the United States since Pearl Harbor."[9] The statistics of miners dead and injured offered Lewis an ultimate justification for wartime strikes. He understood as neither Roosevelt, William Davis, nor most Americans did, that for miners the battle for production on the homefront produced its own body count. An awareness and sensitivity to such suffering constituted one of the factors that impelled Lewis to challenge the government in 1943. He did not think the dangers of mining could be substantially eliminated, but felt that his miners should be awarded adequate compensation for risking their lives.

The government policies most vexing to Lewis were those implemented to combat inflation. He believed that an increase in the cost of living was unavoidable during a military conflict. "Inflation to some degree is a concomitant of any war," he lectured Senator Harry Truman's watchdog committee. "War is a destroyer of economic and human values. It utilizes and destroys material of every character, virile manpower in the armies, while subsequent famine and pestilence decimate civilian population. All this creates scarcity and resultant higher values on remaining and available commodities and manpower."[10]

More to the point, Lewis believed that Washington's favorable treatment of defense industries actually intensified inflation. The government, he instructed the Truman Committee, "superinduces inflation by the excessive rewards to industry for producing essential war commodities. . . ."[11] Under the system of cost-plus contracting, in which the government guaranteed the cost of production plus a percentage profit, firms operating under defense contracts had little incentive to promote efficiency. Indeed, higher production costs meant higher profits. Furthermore, the Administration's wartime tax policies, accelerated depreciation allowances, and the general demand for greater production encouraged companies to rebuild their facilities and thus further contribute to the high cost of scarce materials.

Treating industry generously, the nation's policy makers, Lewis charged, were "saying to 50,000,000 workers in America gainfully employed and largely employed in war industries, 'We cannot do for you what we are doing for industry because that would cause inflation. You must not ask for a wage increase above and beyond a certain formula which we have arbitrarily computed; and as a patriotic duty you cannot expect your wages to keep pace with the rising cost of living.' " Behind such an argument, Lewis pointed out, "there is an implication that the individual worker is unpatriotic if he asks the same consideration as industry from his government."[12]

Of all government measures, the NWLB's "Little Steel Formula" most upset Lewis. He contended that Roosevelt had created the National War Labor Board in January, 1942 "to hand down in every wage controversy a decision based upon a *judicial determination of the issue,*" in exchange for labor's "No-Strike Pledge."[13] This bargain ended in July, 1942, he maintained, when the Board promulgated the "Little Steel Formula" and thereby transformed itself from a court of equity into an anti-inflation instrument. "The WLB violates the government agreement with labor each day that it operates," Lewis raged in February, 1943. "Under its arbitrary and miserably stupid formula, it chains labor to the wheels of industry without compensation for increased costs, while other agencies of government reward and fatten industry by charging its increased costs to the public purse."[14]

On July 16, 1942, the National War Labor Board first applied its "Little Steel Formula," which was intended to regulate the wage demands of all workers. In the Little Steel case, a fact-finding panel had informed the NWLB that the four steel companies involved in the dispute with the steel workers were able to afford a wage increase without raising prices. The Board felt that this fact alone was not a sufficient safeguard against inflation. It therefore calculated that since the cost of living rose approximately fifteen per cent between January 1, 1941, and May 1, 1942, workers were entitled to a composite fifteen per cent wage increase above their base rate on New Year's Day, 1941. The Board further contended that the President's anti-inflation program, announced on April 27, 1942, would restrain any significant increase in living costs and thus eliminate the need for future wage advances above the fifteen per cent ceiling, except in cases of unusual inequities. Although William Davis had originally proposed July 1, 1941 as the most suitable date for establishing the standard wage, the Board finally used New Year's Day as the base date so that the wage gains made by the major unions in the spring of 1941 could be charged against the fifteen per cent formula.[15]

John L. Lewis felt that the "Little Steel Formula" imposed a great injustice on the members of the UMW. Since the miners had won a sixteen per cent wage advance in the spring of 1941, they were automatically ineligible for any further increases under the "Little Steel Formula." The union had interpreted the sixteen per cent gain as an adjustment to cover the pace of inflation and other factors for the period from April 1, 1939 to April 1, 1941. In fact, then, the "Little Steel Formula" actually limited the coal diggers to slightly more than a sixteen per cent increase over their base rate in April, 1939 for the indefinite duration of the war, regardless of rises in the cost of living.[16]

According to Lewis, the War Labor Board "fouled its own nest" when it proclaimed its wage control policy. "When the mine workers' children cry for bread, they cannot be satisfied with a 'Little Steel Formula,'" he taunted. "When illness strikes the mine workers' families, they cannot be cured with an anti-inflation dissertation. The facts of life in the mining homes of America cannot be pushed aside by the flamboyant theories of an idealistic economic philosophy."[17] Cost-plus contracting for industry but the "Little Steel Formula" for labor epitomized for Lewis the government's "paradoxical policy." In testifying before Truman's Senate committee, the miners' leader warned that "Congress can't condone a policy in this country that fattens industry and starves labor, and then call upon labor patriotically to starve."[18]

The injustices of domestic wartime policy and the suffering of his miners influenced on Lewis during the hectic months of 1943. Yet other important but less articulated forces were also at work. By 1943 many workers demanded the elimination of the "No-Strike Pledge," and unauthorized wildcat strikes infested American industry. Lewis definitely hoped that his actions would thrust him once more to the forefront of the labor movement. This ambition was rooted as much in his psychological need for power as it was in his desire to take labor down a different path. The same factors underlay his gestures at humiliating Roosevelt, William Davis, and the National War Labor Board.

Many commentators at the time interpreted Lewis by assuming that he was a psychopathic personality and that his ideological arguments simply manifested his psychosis. For those who began with this belief, Lewis's deviant behavior in 1943 confirmed the theory. Yet, for those observers who recognized considerable merit in Lewis's criticism of wartime policy, his actions—while perhaps anti-social— were nonetheless rational. Not even Lewis understood his own motivation. "What makes me tick?'' he once asked himself. "Is it power I'm after, or am I a Saint Francis in disguise, or what?"[19]

As 1943 began, Lewis still remained uncertain on how to fulfill his threats against Washington's wartime policies. The nation's involvement in a conflict of unprecedented scale made it difficult for him to predict how the Administration would respond to various moves on his part. More importantly, Lewis recognized that his rank and file confronted conflicting pressures which made their loyalty uncertain. With many of their own friends and relatives in military service, they naturally desired to do everything necessary to protect the men at the battle front. At the same time, they felt that the government's domestic program called upon them to make unnecessary and unreasonable sacrifices.

In January, 1943, the anthracite miners helped Lewis arrive at his course of action. During the first week of the new year various locals initiated wildcat strikes, apparently to Lewis's surprise. Each day the walkout gained momentum until by January 9, almost half of the 40,000 hard coal miners remained away from work. While initially in opposition to an increase in union dues, the protest quickly shifted to an attack on the "Little Steel Formula," with the wildcatters demanding that Lewis immediately negotiate a two dollars a day pay boost from the operators.[20]

Lewis normally responded ferociously to such challenges to union discipline, but now he seemed intent on seeing how the situation would develop. Although he denounced the strikers for the public record, he proved less decisive in exercising his more effective powers for getting the miners back to work. Not until the morning of January 15—only hours before he testified before the National War Labor Board on the stoppage—did he send telegrams to the locals in the anthracite districts ordering their members to remain at work. Even at that, the telegram expressed more concern over the insurgent character of the committee formed to coordinate the wildcat than it did over the walkout.[21]

In the end, the strikers demonstrated their determination to correct their grievances by first ignoring a NWLB back-to-work directive, and then resisting an appeal from Roosevelt to resume production. The strike finally ended in late January after Lewis, having publicized his determination to win a pay increase for the miners, expelled from the union the leaders of the walkout.[22]

Lewis found the unauthorized strike highly instructive. For one thing, it revealed to him the government's lack of decisiveness when confronted with a challenge to its authority by labor. Although the full contours of any future government response remained problematic, drastic, punitive action seemed ruled out. Equally important, the strike illustrated the commitment of the rank and file to action. Neither patriotism nor Presidential pleas had deterred the wildcatters from their unpopular strike. Lewis, recognizing that the membership had decided the direction it would march, artfully maneuvered his way to the head of the parade.

He seized his January 15 appearance before the National War Labor Board as an opportunity to embrace the rebel's cause. In a masterful performance directed more at his membership than the Board, he relegated complaints over increased union dues to a secondary issue "when as a matter of fact the basic trouble in the anthracite industry has been low wages and part-time employment." He condemned the walkout—not in terms of a violation of the "No-Strike Pledge" —but as a breach of the union's contract with the operators. Lewis supported a wage increase for bituminous as well as anthracite miners, but he insisted that the proper way to attain the advance would be through the regular contract negotiations in the spring.[23]

Throughout the subsequent 1943 upheaval, Lewis would be doing his miners' bidding as well as executing his own assault on wartime regulations. The secret of the miners' support for Lewis during the unpopular wartime strikes rests simply in the fact that he was championing their cause. The figure of two dollars a day that Lewis initially demanded at the beginning of negotiations was set by the January wildcatters, not by the union's economists after scrutiny of cost-of-living indexes. Indeed, Lewis called upon W. Jett Lauck, K. C. Adams and Percy Tetlow to develop a statistical justification for this sum. Likewise, when Lewis, following the advice of Lauck, decided to achieve the wage advance through the subterfuge of portal-to-portal pay, he stumbled on to a genuine rank-and-file grievance. Throughout the coal controversy, tremors from his membership forced Lewis to act in particular ways.[24]

On March 10, Lewis led the UMW delegation into New York's Roosevelt Hotel for contract talks with the Northern Appalachian Wage Conference. He had forewarned them in public statements since February of the miners' insistence on a two dollar a day wage increase. Other major demands now outlined by Lewis included the elimination of occupational charges, an increase in vacation pay, and compensation for travel time within the mine. Traditionally, American coal miners had been paid only for the time they spent digging at the mine face. Lewis now proposed that they be paid from the time they passed through the mine portal into the dark underground, until they re-emerged through the portal at the end of their day's work.

Although portal-to-portal pay would become a central issue in the 1943 coal dispute, its inclusion among the original demands was apparently to provide the union negotiators with an item that they could trade away for a two-dollar wage increase. Lewis's correspondence in February and March with his chief economic advisor, W. Jett Lauck, reveals no deep interest in the issue. In 1940, moreover, the UMW had arrived at an understanding with the Appalachian operators and the Department of Labor that the travel time provisions of the 1938 Fair Labor Standards Act would not apply to the coal industry. All parties involved then assumed that travel time would have had to be calculated on an individual basis for each miner. The union naturally wanted to avoid the divisiveness this would foster among the rank and file. The union also feared that in establishing travel time in line with the Fair Labor Standards Act, which also provided for the forty-hour week, the mine workers would weaken their claim to a seven-hour day.[25]

Following the formal presentation of demands, Lewis orated for four hours. "The mine worker is at a great disadvantage working under the present wage structure of the industry," he contended. "His compensation is insufficient to enable him to maintain his living standards, and it contains no a protection against the vicissitudes of tomorrow." Food items in the stores where miners shopped, he insisted, had advanced an average of 124.6 percent since August, 1939. Lewis castigated the National War Labor Board for preventing workers' earnings from keeping pace with rising prices, and he warned the operators not to plan to "sit back and permit the mine workers to break their lances on the Little Steel formula." "The world knows that Mr. Davis inserted his long knife into the defenseless body of the United Mine Workers of America three times in 1941, and that he is waiting with ill-concealed impatience to insert that same long knife into the body of the mine workers in 1943. Well, he just isn't going to do it."[26]

Neither the northern nor southern operators believed Lewis would defy the government in time of war. Consequently Charles O'Neill, leader of the northern producers, refused to consider any wage increases and calmly evaded meaningful bargaining trusting that the NWLB would force the miners to change their demands. Edward Burke, representing the southerners, initially insisted that the coal diggers take a pay cut, and then proposed that all negotiations be suspended until the war ended. On March 15, after five days of sitting through aimless talks, Lewis emphatically informed the operators "that without a negotiated contract the miners will not trespass on your property on the first of April."[27]

Unlike Edward Burke, whose blind hatred of Lewis and unionism led him to underestimate his adversary, Charles O'Neill paid Lewis some heed. His interest in negotiating became further aroused when he learned that the U.S. Court of Appeals in Alabama had upheld portal-to-portal pay for iron ore miners. The court decisions thrust the travel time issue to the center of negotiations, causing O'Neill to explore with Lewis a thirty-day extension of the 1941 contract so that the talks could continue after April 1. The southern operators, alarmed at the weakening of the North, appealed to Roosevelt to turn the dispute over to the National War Labor Board.[28]

The President refused. Instead, on March 22 he sent identical telegrams to Lewis, O'Neill, and Burke requesting them to arrange a temporary settlement while negotiations continued. In a situation that required a decisive statement, Roosevelt proved equivocal. The operators took comfort in the President's assertion that any wage adjustment had to conform to the Stabilization Act of 1942 and Executive Order No. 9250. Lewis, however, interpreted Roosevelt's failure to send the dispute to the NWLB and his reference to the vague statute and executive order rather than the precise "Little Steel Formula" as indications that the 15 percent wage ceiling could be broken. Supporting this view was the telegram's closing paragraph which indicated the Administration's willingness to consider a price increase if the operators suffered "undue hardship" from a retroactive pay increase.[29]

The UMW, northern operators, and various outlying fields, consummated a thirty day contract extension by March 24. The southern operators proved more reluctant, and wavered for a week until, on March 29, Dr. John R. Steelman of the Conciliation Service arrived on the scene and prevailed upon the southerners to accept an extension. The nation was now guaranteed coal production until May 1.

In the ensuing negotiations, Steelman unsuccessfully sought a compromise that circumvented the "Little Steel Formula" by increasing the miners' total earnings without altering their basic wage rate. During these talks, Lewis began to view portal-to-portal pay as his ultimate weapon if the government interpreted a straight pay increase as a violation of the "Little Steel Formula." His economic advisor, W. Jett Lauck, sent him a series of notes in early April outlining both the long term and immediate benefits to the coal industry and the miners of portal-to-portal pay. The establishment of a seven-hour day on a portal-to-portal basis, Lauck predicted, would mean "a 'new heaven and a new earth' for mine workers." And the attractive thing about portal-to-portal pay at this particular time was that "it could be claimed effectively that the miners should at least, as human beings and American citizens, be accorded this request."[30]

Lewis concurred in Lauck's assessment and entered into a general give-and-take with O'Neill upon the issue.[31]

Then, on April 8, President Roosevelt issued a "hold-the-line" order, one provision of which directed the NWLB to allow no further wage increases other than those necessary to correct sub-standard conditions. The order also instructed the Director of Stabilization to approve all NWLB decisions, thus ending the Board's independence. Although Roosevelt may not have prepared and timed his order intentionally to undermine Lewis, he hardly could have been unmindful of its impact on coal negotiations. Only a fortnight earlier he had sent a telegram hinting at room for a wage increase. The contract having been extended as he requested, he now issued a definitive wage freeze order. Naturally, Lewis was peeved, for the operators interpreted the President's order as a vindication of their refusal to yield to union demands and stopped negotiating over portal-to-portal pay.[32]

Lewis now faced the three unpleasant options: surrender to the operators, send the case to the NWLB where the union's position would automatically be rejected as a violation of the "Little Steel Formula," or lead a direct confrontation against the government. In a vain hope of avoiding any of these courses, he made one last effort to salvage both collective bargaining and something he could claim as a union victory. The mine workers would drop the demand for two dollars a day, he promised, if the operators would guarantee six days of work a week. Lewis pointed out that the operators had already received a price hike to cover the additional cost for six days of operation and that part of the increase was designed to offset the higher wage bill. A guaranteed six day week, moreover, would only result in the miners earning the amount that the operators publicly contended the coal diggers were averaging under the old contract.[33]

Edward Burke and the southern operators promptly rejected the proposal. O'Neill spent three days considering the offer and then joined Burke in petitioning the President to send the coal dispute to the NWLB. With no compromise in sight and the contract extension running out, Secretary of Labor Perkins certified the dispute to the National War Labor Board on April 22.[34]

With the National War Labor Board's formal entrance into the coal dispute, tension gripped the nation. According to one survey, fifty-eight percent of the nation recognized some justice in the miners' demands. Yet this sympathy was far outweighed by the public's hostility toward Lewis, who was surely one of the most hated men in America. In one poll, eighty-seven percent of those canvassed viewed him unfavorably.[35] Most newspapers and journals reinforced this animosity by interpreting coal developments in light of Lewis's opposition to Roosevelt. Meanwhile, the operators, who consciously promoted a confrontation between Lewis and the government, went largely unscathed by editorial criticism.

Politicians and other popularity seekers quickly learned that attacks on Lewis won public approval. In late March, with the coal dispute at a critical stage, the Truman Senate Committee investigating of inflation, absenteeism, and other assorted subjects decided that Lewis's testimony was needed forthwith. In response to a letter from the committee's counsel, Lewis indicated his willingness to attend on the designated date unless prohibited by important developments in the coal negotiations. Some members of the committee saw an opportunity to insult publicly Lewis and, claiming that his assurance was unsatisfactory, subpoenaed his presence. At the hearing, Senators Ball, Brewster, and Connally engaged in a bearbaiting session that aroused Lewis's ire, and his contemptuous responses generated further editorials condemning him.[36]

Franklin Roosevelt could not, as President, act as overtly hostile to Lewis as members of the Senate. Yet his animosity toward the miners' chief was well known. Under the President's orders the Justice Department sought grounds to indict Lewis, including tax evasion, conspiracy with the Illinois operators in fighting the Progressive Miners, and violation of the Smith-Connally Act after its passage in July, 1943. He kept informed of Lewis's dealings with the antiadministration camp through a series of reports from personal associates and the F.B.I. At one point during the 1943 coal dispute Roosevelt hinted at the depths of his rancor when he joked of his willingness to resign if only Lewis would commit suicide.[37]

Lewis also loathed Roosevelt, but there were fundamental differences in the nature of the hostility they displayed toward each other. To a large extent,

Roosevelt's public personality was shaped by his political career. A master of the politics of compromise, he perceived himself as a broker seeking the just means. Viewing perfection as unattainable, he excelled in developing amiable, workable solutions to the immediate problems at hand. He displayed the political skill of giving something to everyone; and in exchange he expected everyone to behave. His commitment to a consensus society ill-prepared him to deal with those unwilling to play the game of compromise. Accustomed to persons who would arrive at a polite accord, he could not cope with a Lewis who preferred polarization. The wartime crisis further strengthened Roosevelt's desire for a harmonious, solidified nation. Believing that those who promoted division subverted the operations of civilized society, he reacted with an emotional vehemence held in check primarily by his appraisal of the American people's sense of fair play.

Lewis, on the contrary, was a master of the politics of confrontation. In over two decades of dealings with the coal barons, he had found this the most effective approach. It also served as the *modus operandi* within the union, as Lewis's struggles with Howat, Farrington, Brophy, and others attest. To a large degree it was Lewis's skill at the politics of confrontation that enabled him to establish the CIO and lead it to several victories.

Whereas Roosevelt, the broker in the politics of compromise, emphasized the complexity of problems as he sought to blend differences and diminish controversy, Lewis, as a combatant in confrontation politics, worked to polarize issues and differentiate policies so that the alternative became simplisticly self-evident. Lewis, moreover, tolerated opposition and rancor as part of conflict resolution. Animosity was a weapon he used; it was rational as well as emotional; he could turn it on or off almost at will. In preparation for the biennial negotiating sessions he could curse all operators, but once the contract was signed his vehemence died. For public consumption he could punch William L. Hutcheson or vilify Green, but it is doubtful that he hated them personally. Of all his public enemies he came closest to despising Roosevelt. Yet, because he accepted the legitimacy of confrontation, he always restrained his feelings. In 1943, he set two goals: 1) winning an advance for the miners; and 2) in the process tearing down the wartime economic regulation structure. Humiliating Roosevelt was less important.

From the start of the coal controversy, Lewis sought to achieve his ends by confrontation. Both the operators and the government, he believed, had absorbed the lesson of the 1941 captive mine dispute and would do everything necessary to avoid another crisis. Despite his March 15 strike threat and his March 26 statement before the Truman Committee that the "No-Strike Pledge" was "not necessarily binding," Lewis seems not to have planned a walkout. His strike threat to the Truman Committee came when he knew that a thirty-day truce would be negotiated; Lauck's correspondence with him in February, March, and April contained no hints of strike plans; and the UMW *Journal*, as late as April 15, predicted long negotiations and the possibility of several contract extensions, but no closing of the mines.

Lewis was, after all, posing as the champion of "free" collective bargaining against government wartime regulations, and apparently he felt he could win his objectives at the negotiating table. Prior to Roosevelt's hold-the-line order, he had moved the northern operators to an exploration of occupational charges and portal-to-portal pay. And Lewis believed that where the northern operators traveled, the southerners would begrudgingly follow. But, after the hold-the-line order, the operators reverted to their initial intransigence. Lewis had expected that the Roosevelt Administration would deal with him through the politics of compromise. Instead, Roosevelt, motivated in part by principles but also by passion, stepped out of character and engaged in the politics of confrontation. With the certification of the dispute to the NWLB, Roosevelt called Lewis's bluff.

In speech after speech since November, 1942, Lewis had made his objections to the War Labor Board clear.[38] On March 31, 1943, to emphasize his determination to have nothing to do with its deliberations, he had instructed Thomas Kennedy to resign as a member. Even if the Board had possessed the freedom to set aside the "Little Steel Formula" —a freedom it lost with Roosevelt's hold-the-line order— Lewis contended that the UMW could not receive a fair hearing from a group of men hostile to him. William Davis, the Board's chairman, still brooded over the humiliation he suffered at Lewis's hands during the 1941 captive mine dispute. Public member Wayne Morse held Lewis and his methods in complete disdain, while two CIO representatives, Van A. Bittner and John Brophy, resented their former chief. Other Board members and alternates, if less antagonistic toward Lewis, still had scant respect for him.

On April 22, Lewis learned that the coal dispute had been turned over to the NWLB. Immediately he dashed off a letter to Conciliation Director Steelman informing him that the union would consider the thirty-day contract extension terminated with any discontinuance of negotiations. Ignoring the strike implications in Lewis's message, the northern operators journeyed from New York to Washington to appear before the NWLB. Burke and the southerners also made the trek, although they left behind a contingent of negotiators to keep up the image of bargaining with the union so as to not prejudice their case with the NWLB.

On April 24, representatives of the Mine Workers boycotted the Board's preliminary hearings. Simultaneously, groups of miners across the nation failed to report to work, apparently on their own initiative. Ignoring these scattered walk-outs, the Board proceeded to outline the ground rules for the coal controversy with Chairman Davis announcing that any wage settlement must be resolved within the limits of the "Little Steel Formula." The Board also ordered uninterrupted production of coal and called upon the parties each to appoint a representative to a tripartite panel to hear the case. When Lewis ignored the Board's communique, Davis, determined not to be rattled, appointed David B. Robinson of the Brotherhood of Locomotive Firemen and Engineers as surrogate representative of the miners.[39]

As Lewis and the NWLB maneuvered for advantage, more miners refused to work. By April 26 sixteen thousand coal diggers from Pennsylvania, Kentucky, and Alabama had left the pits; three days later the number had grown to 75,000 and the area had expanded. On Wednesday, April 28, Davis followed traditional NWLB policy and suspended all hearings on the dispute until the miners resumed production. He then referred the matter to the President for appropriate action.[40]

On the following day Roosevelt sent Lewis and Kennedy a telegram which he also released to the press because it was really intended for the rank-and-file miner and the general public. Roosevelt appealed for an end to the strike, "not as President—not as Commander-in-Chief—but as the friend of the men who work in the coal mines." He condemned the stoppages as "not mere strikes against employers of this industry to enforce collective bargaining demands. They are strikes against the United States government itself." "The continuance and spread of these strikes," he warned, "would have the same effect on the course of the war as a crippling defeat in the field." Then the President issued an ultimatum: "if work at the mines is not resumed by ten o'clock Saturday morning [May 1], I shall use all the power vested in me as President and as Commander-in-Chief of the Army and Navy to protect the national interest and to prevent further interference with the successful prosecution of the war."[41]

The miners' first response to Roosevelt's telegram came that same day in Ohio where another 9,700 diggers walked off the job. A more formal reply was sent the following morning—the last day in April—by the UMW Policy Committee meeting in New York. Under Lewis's guidance the committee specified its objections to the NWLB and "its fixed mathematical measuring device." And again the committee stressed the miners' patriotism and productivity. But the committee ignored Roosevelt's warning.[42]

When Saturday, May 1, arrived millions of Americans waited nervously as the moment of reckoning drew near. A calmer atmosphere prevailed in miners' homes with some of the men folk still slumbering as the hour of ten approached. The thirty-day extension agreement had officially expired at midnight and without a contract a union miner would not work. Lewis had not ordered the stoppage, although the miners knew he approved. Nor did they stay home out of spite for Roosevelt, although they also knew he disapproved. Pride, self-respect, and loyalty to the union motivated these patriotic citizens to engage in a nationwide strike during wartime.

Roosevelt now had to execute his ultimatum. Lacking statutory authority, he could not imprison Lewis and his lieutenants. Inducting the miners into military service would be too time consuming and disruptive of production, and many of the miners were over draft age. If once drafted, the miners still refused to work, it would be self-defeating to lock them up for as Harold Ickes reminded the President, "a jailed miner produces no more coal than a striking miner."[43] Sending troops into the coal fields would not work either, for as a miners' saying went, 'bayonets can't mine coal.' In considering his options, Roosevelt believed that the public would not condone any extreme use of force or punishment against the men who actually dug the coal. Except for surrendering to Lewis, in the end the President had only one alternative. He could seize the mines and hope that Lewis would cooperate. Consequently, on May 1, Roosevelt directed Secretary of Interior Harold Ickes to take possession of the nation's bituminous mines and to manage them in the public interest until a threat of strike no longer prevailed.[44]

Although Roosevelt dramatized his move, Lewis had won a significant victory. The miners lost nothing through seizure; the operators lost formal control of their businesses. Lewis felt that before long the coal barons would squirm under government control as their fears about the eventual nationalization mounted. In the meantime Lewis could engage in his accomplished tactic of pitting one government official against another. Finally, the President's action allowed him to call off the strike in the name of patriotism and therefore avoid a prolonged shutdown that would have undoubtedly produced a vicious attack on the union.

The President having made his move, it was now Lewis's turn to respond. To compel the labor leader to act promptly, Roosevelt scheduled a radio address to the nation for Sunday, May 2, at 10 p.m. On Saturday Lewis contacted Secretary of Labor Francis Perkins who arranged a meeting for him with Secretary of Interior Ickes for Sunday afternoon. After journeying from New York to Washington, Lewis and three associates conferred for three hours with the new custodian of the mines and his staff. Lewis saw Ickes as a man with whom he could do business. The Secretary was not enamored of the "Little Steel Formula" and wanted to insure coal production for the duration of the war. New to the job, he asked Lewis to send the miners back to work for at least two weeks so he could have time to evaluate the situation. Lewis responded that such action would need the approval of the UMW Policy Committee in New York. With the meeting ended, Lewis made the return trip.[45]

The train bearing Lewis pulled into New York City at 9:10 p.m. Sunday night. He went straight to the Hotel Roosevelt where the Policy Committee was already in session and awaiting his arrival. Lewis briefed the committee on his talk with Ickes and then presented the Secretary's request for a two-week resumption of work. Although the resumption would abridge of the union's no contract-no work tradition, the Policy Committee concurred in the request. At 9:40 Lewis telephoned Ickes the good news. By 9:44 the President's advisors knew of the miners' decision to return to work for two weeks beginning on Tuesday, May 4.[46]

At 10:00 Roosevelt delivered his scheduled radio talk to the nation "and in particular to those of our citizens who are coal miners." It is hard to believe that the President had no knowledge of the Ickes-Lewis talks that afternoon, or that his staff had not drafted an alternate speech to be presented if the strike was settled before air time. Possibly overtaken by anger, Roosevelt delivered a hardline talk that ignored the Policy Committee's decision. In a stern but fatherly style he asked the miners to end the strike and resume coal production. His tone toward Lewis was unmistakably hostile. "The responsibility for the crisis we now face," he told an already exasperated nation, "rests squarely on the national officers of the United Mine Workers, and not on the Government of the United States."[47]

The President's vindictive speech after the walkout ended constitutes one of several perplexing events in the coal crisis. Supporters of Roosevelt attempted to excuse his action by contending that Lewis delayed announcing the resumption of work until the last minute in order to embarrass the President. Although Lewis was capable of such a vengeful deed, the fact remains that a decision from the Policy Committee could not have come more than fifteen minutes sooner and the White House should have been prepared.

Roosevelt remained in a tempest the following day. While the overwhelming majority of messages coming into the White House reflected the public's hostility toward Lewis, a flow of pro-Lewis correspondence also arrived. Asked if he wanted to see any more letters supporting Lewis, the President responded with an emphatic "No." That same day an aide posed a far more important question. Now that the government was operating the coal mines, would it be proper procedure to attempt to reach an agreement with the union? "No!" scribbled Roosevelt. Then, in error, he added: "U.S. cannot make an agreement with its employees."[48]

On Tuesday, May 4, the nation's bituminous miners returned to work. Technically they were now employees of the United States. Yet, although the American flag flew over the tipples, the old managerial personnel greeted the miners as they passed through the portals.

In Washington, Harold Ickes announced the President's decision that the government would not negotiate with the union. If the UMW wanted a contract, he stated, it would have to deal with the coal operators under the watchful eyes of the NWLB. Lewis, perhaps having been partly misled in Sunday's conference with Ickes, responded to the Secretary's pronouncement with exaggerated cries of double-cross and deceit. For the most part his outburst was for public consumption. Lewis viewed Ickes as one of the few reasonable men in Washington and sensed that pressures from the War Labor Board lay behind the Secretary's announcement.[49]

On May 6 the NWLB's fact finding panel opened public hearings on the coal case. As before, the UMW refused to send representatives causing the Board to appoint one of its own legal counselors as union spokesman. On May 14 the full Board ordered the miners and operators to resume collective bargaining under NWLB guidance. Coal production was to continue during negotiations and the parties were to report the results of the talks to the Board in ten days. Any agreement arrived at would be subject to the NWLB's approval and by implication had to conform to the "Little Steel Formula."[50]

Lewis would have nothing to do with the Board's May 14 directive, and in his opinion only Ickes as the government official in charge of the mines could order contract talks. As if to underline his responsiveness only to Ickes, he granted the Secretary's request that the two week back-to-work order scheduled to expire on May 18 be extended to June 1. The members of the NWLB were outraged at Lewis's affront with Chairman Davis accusing him of giving "aid and comfort to our enemies." To prevent Lewis from subverting their authority, they forbade any further negotiations involving Ickes, the operators, or anyone else until the union complied with its May 14 Interim Directive.[51]

Throughout May the public remained agitated over the coal situation. Newspapers, taking up a theme from Roosevelt's May 2 speech, published column after column on the GIs' irritation with Lewis. The words from an editorial in *Stars and Stripes* became a national chant: "Speaking for the American soldier, John L. Lewis, damn your coal-black soul!" At a CIO Executive Board meeting, Phil Murray, Allan Haywood, John Brophy, and Van Bittner all denounced Lewis as a self-seeking demagogue trying to get revenge against the President. On Capital Hill conservatives and liberals alike bitterly assailed the UMW leader.[52]

Lewis responded to the widespread hostility with a bold move designed to unsettle his foes. On May 17 he sent William Green a letter requesting reaffiliation with the American Federation of Labor. To make the idea more palatable to the business unionists in the Federation, he enclosed a check for $60,000 to cover the first year's dues. The UMW's application, sponsored by William Hutcheson and greeted as "wonderful" by Green, created the intended consternation among the White House 'Palace Guard,' CIO leaders, NWLB members, and others striving to isolate the miners' chief. Lewis knew full well that AFL action on his petition would not occur until the fall at the soonest. In the meantime, the idea would haunt those charged with resolving the coal crisis.[53]

For eight days a deadlock prevailed in the coal crisis as a result of the War Labor Board's May 14 ban on collective bargaining until Lewis recognized its authority. Finally, the Board on May 25 broke its own impasse by issuing a new Directive on the case. Aspects of the Directive sustained Lewis's charge of NWLB prejudice. Parts of the order had been written as early as March 3, before the NWLB had received jurisdiction, and depended on biased wage earnings and employment statistics. [54] On the basis of such data, the War Labor Board denied the UMW's demand for a two dollar a day direct wage increase. It did find in the union's favor on the issue of occupational charges and it also increased vacation pay. On the troublesome portal-to-portal pay question, the Board called for resumption of collective bargaining. Unlike the May 14 directive, the new order did not place the NWLB in the role of overseer of the talks, although the Board again instructed the parties to report back on their progress within two weeks.[55]

With only days left before the expiration of the third contract extension on June 1, Secretary Ickes frantically tried to prevent another walkout, even summoning Lewis and O'Neill to his office at 5:00 P.M., May 31, where he proposed a temporary compromise to the portal-to-portal question. Under his plan the mines would stay open with the miners receiving $1.50 a day in travel time pay while a commission studied the issue. Later a final figure would be negotiated on the basis of the commission's report.[56] Lewis accepted Ickes's proposal, subject to the approval of his Policy Committee. O'Neill simply agreed to meet with representatives of the miners and explore the plan. At 8:30 that night Lewis arrived at the Statler Hotel to negotiate with O'Neill. The latter refused to meet with him and insisted that their conference was not scheduled until 10:00 the next morning. Since mid-night brought an end to the latest contract extension, half a million miners refused to report to work the next day.[57]

The second bituminous coal strike caused the operators to reconsider temporarily their strategy of letting the government restrain the union. They now feared that they might become a casualty in the intensifying warfare among Lewis, Ickes, Roosevelt and the NWLB, and they began to think that Lewis might win. Thus, at 10:00 A.M., June 1, with the nation in a furor over another coal stoppage, the operators started negotiating seriously with Lewis. By adjournment that evening, individual mine owners had begun to break rank, and as the parties reconvened the following morning the Washington *Post* reported that only fifty cents separated the contending parties.[58]

Members of the National War Labor Board responded adversely to the prospect of an agreement. They viewed the stoppage as an "insurrection" and the continuation of negotiations during the strike as a negation of the Board's authority. If negotiations did not cease immediately, the board members feared that strikes would be legitimized. Equally important, they apprehended that the NWLB would be placed in an embarrassing position if its own guidelines compelled it to reject a negotiated contract. Lewis would then publicly assail the Board as the sole obstacle to a settlement. To avoid these prospects, the Board ordered all negotiations to cease until the miners returned to work, and again remanded the dispute to the President.[59]

On the afternoon of June 2, Secretary of Interior Ickes, Stabilization Director James F. Byrnes, and members of the War Labor Board gathered at the White House to discuss the coal crisis with the President. At the end of the conference Roosevelt issued a public statement as "President and Commander in Chief" instead of his May plea as a friend of the miners. In forceful language he ordered "the miners who are not now at work in the mines to return to their work on Monday, June 7, 1943." On the afternoon of June 4, Ickes repeated the government's demand that Lewis order the miners back to work.[60]

By Friday, June 4, Lewis was also eager for the miners to return to work. The strike had prodded the operators into serious negotiations. Yet the NWLB had suspended the talks just when a breakthrough seemed imminent. Lewis recognized that the only way to win was to discontinue the strike so negotiations could resume. Thus, the Policy Committee ended the strike but set June 20 as the termination date for this latest contract extension.[61]

For the next two weeks, Lewis labored at the conference table to divide the operators and then to negotiate a contract with at least part of the industry. He thought he had split Charles O'Neill and the Central Pennsylvania Coal Operators' Association from the larger Appalachian Joint Conference, yet this endeavor collapsed over the issue of retroactive pay to cover the four contract extensions. Lewis undertook to arrange another settlement with the Illinois operators, but U.S. Steel's captive mines in the state temporarily stymied this effort.[62]

While Lewis endeavored to break the operators' ranks, legislators on Capitol Hill strove to end his defiance of the government. After the outbreak of war in Europe, anti-labor Congressmen and Senators had sought to use the crisis as a justification for imposing restraints on unions. During both coal strikes of 1941 conservative solons had proposed antistrike legislation. Support for such a law waned in the climate of national unity that prevailed immediately following Pearl Harbor, yet each flurry of labor unrest produced renewed cries for Congressional action. Senator Thomas Connally had an antistrike bill prepared, and when the miners struck in May he capitalized on the public uproar to push it through the Senate and send it on to the House. Interest in the measure declined when the miners returned to work, but with the second strike on June 1 Representative Howard Smith brought the bill to the floor. By June 15 the Smith-Connally bill, more formally known as the War Labor Disputes Act, had cleared Congress and awaited Roosevelt's signature.

The bill contained several provisions designed to enable the government to deal with Lewis. To terminate Lewis's boycott of the NWLB, for instance, the bill gave the Board power to compel parties to appear before it. The Board also received authority to make a final, binding determination in any dispute. The President's power to seize production facilities threatened by strikes was confirmed and criminal penalties were established for anyone who would strike or otherwise disrupt property under government control. The provisions of the bill requiring an NLRB supervised strike vote and a cooling-off period also had application in the coal situation. In sum, if the President chose to sign the measure, the bill seemed to provide the government ample powers to cope with Lewis and the miners.

Roosevelt recognized, however, that the bill would punish his labor friends as well as his enemies. He also realized that Congress had passed the bill in a fit of passion and that many of its provisions would not fulfill their intent and could possibly cause even greater havoc. Advised by both Ickes and Davis to veto the measure, Roosevelt chose for the time being to hold it as an ax over Lewis's head as the next deadline in the coal crisis drew near.[63]

Members of the NWLB also hoped that the threat of the Smith-Connally bill would compel Lewis to capitulate. On June 18, two days before the next contract termination date, the Board issued another Directive Order. The new Order essentially rewrote the 1941 contract to include the Board's recent rulings. It increased the miners' vacation pay, transferred occupational charges to the operators, and raised the "substandard" pay of inside unclassified labor and slate pickers. The Board refused to guarantee the six day week, and in a move to weaken Lewis's power over the coal industry, it nullified the controversial Protective

Wage Clause. Finally, the Board made no provision for portal-to-portal pay, the union's right to take its claim to court though it upheld to seek a settlement of the issue through collective bargaining, with any final agreement subject to NWLB approval. In closing, the Board instructed both the UMW and the operators to accept these terms as the contract in force until March 31, 1945.[64]

Accusing the Board of attempting to "economically disembowel" the miners, Lewis characterized the Directive Order as an "infamous yellow-dog contract."[65] The rank and file agreed and on June 19, two days before the contract expired, they began to lay down their tools; 58,000 miners stopped work that day; a full 500,000 quit the next.

Officially the strike lasted only two days. On Sunday, June 20, when the operators refused to negotiate further, Lewis prepared a Policy Board statement for proclaiming that the UMW would not sanction a wartime strike and would urge miners to continue work under the direction of Ickes or anyone else chosen by the President.[66] In a meeting with Ickes and his staff on June 21, Lewis forthrightly expressed his desire to end the walkout. All present agreed, however, that the problem was not only "of returning the miners to work, but also of retaining enough morale so that maximum production would be assured." Ickes continually pointed out that he had no authority to deal with the wage controversy, while Lewis repeated the theme that something needed to be done "which would permit the miners to go back to work with good will." On that note the meeting adjourned until the next day while the participants developed ideas.[67]

By the following morning Lewis determined his new strategy. Unwilling to accept the NWLB's dictates, but with nowhere else to turn, he planned to sit tight with the mines under government control. He spent most of his second meeting with Ickes discussing the widening of the Secretary's management of the collieries.[68] After the conference, he summoned the Policy Committee and attained its approval of a back-to-work order. The members of the UMW, Lewis informed the press, would willingly dig coal "for the Government itself under the direction of the custodian of mines. The mine workers have no favor to grant the coal operators nor the members of the War Labor Board, who have dishonored their trust, but will make any sacrifice for the Government, the well-being of its citizens, the upholding of our flag, and for the triumph of our war effort." Lewis's effusive patriotism, however, had definable limits. As long as the government kept possession of the mines, he announced, the contract extension would last until October 31.[69]

Lewis's official call terminating the third soft coal strike defused Roosevelt's counter-attack. On June 23 the President issued a statement menacingly asserting: "It's a good thing that the miners are returning to their work." He still refused to acknowledge publicly the degree of rank-and-file militancy and concentrated his criticism on the UMW's leadership. Lewis's behavior, he informed newsmen, "has been intolerable—and has rightly stirred up the anger and disapproval of the overwhelming mass of the American people."[70]

The President renewed his attack on Lewis two days later in a message accompanying his veto of the Smith-Connally Bill. Although most of the message concentrated on his objections to the bill, he did indicate approval of those provisions which would strengthen his hand in dealing with the coal dispute, and he went on to request that the Selective Service Act be amended so that men up to age sixty-five could be inducted into the service. Lewis was sixty-three. The Congress, eager for an immediate weapon to wield against Lewis, overrode Roosevelt's veto and made the Smith-Connally bill law.[71]

Clusters of miners across the coal fields, incensed over the NWLB's June 18 Directive Order, Roosevelt's hostile comments, and Congress's passage of the Smith-Connally Act, continued to remain away from the mines despite the union's back-to-work order. One June 30, eight days after the Policy Committee called off the strike, Ickes reported that 130,000 men still remained away from work. Production at the pits did not reach normal levels until July 5. Although such rank-and-file militancy served Lewis's immediate purposes, the continuation of local strikes as well as the premature walkouts that had occurred on June 19 represented a breakdown of union discipline. With the possibility of his membership taking events out of his control, Lewis was perhaps glad that the next contract termination date was four months away. By then, he hoped, the dispute would be over.[72]

Throughout the 1943 coal dispute, Lewis publicly projected the image of a stern, inflexible individual, determined to achieve all or nothing. In reality, however, he had made substantial concessions by the end of June. When negotiations began in March, he had demanded four primary items: a two dollar a day wage increase, portal-to-portal pay, an increase in vacation pay, and payment of occupational charges by the operators. In its May 25 Directive, the NWLB granted the last two demands, but the first two, which the miners most desired, remained unsettled. Seeking compromise, Lewis first offered to yield on the two dollar increase and travel time pay in exchange for a guaranteed six-day work week, but the operators balked. In late May, Lewis merged the two dollar proposal and portal-to-portal pay into one demand: an increase of two dollars a day granted as travel time pay. Then, in his aborted early June negotiations with the Central Pennsylvania and Illinois operators, he conceded more ground by accepting a combination of portal-to-portal pay, vacation increases, and occupational charges that would average out to approximately two dollars a day. As the crisis worsened during the summer and fall, Lewis dropped public advocacy of the two dollar figure and the UMW *Journal* no longer heralded it as the miners' battle cry.

Lewis's tactics had also changed between March and June, 1943. He opened negotiations in March certain that he could secure a contract from the operators at the bargaining table and then force its acceptance by the NWLB. When the operators found sanctuary in the NWLB's temple, Lewis shifted tactics and created a confrontation between Ickes and the Board. Ever mindful of Lewis's strategy, Roosevelt blocked the labor leader's machinations by denying Ickes the right to negotiate a settlement.

By the end of June, Lewis conceded privately that any agreement he arranged with the operators would necessitate NWLB approval. Indeed, the expanded powers granted that body by the recently enacted Smith-Connally Act dictated that Lewis could no longer flout the Board. The Act also made his previous tactic of quick strikes too risky to continue. Now he hoped that the prospect of long term government control of the mines would motivate the operators to seek accord with the union.

Fortunately, Harold Ickes acted as a willing accomplice in Lewis's design. The Interior Secretary believed that only Lewis's voluntary concurrence in an agreement would assure full coal production for the remainder of the war. As if intentionally seeking to disturb the mine owners, Ickes appointed Carl Newton as Coal Mine Administrator. Newton was president of the coal-hauling Chesapeake and Ohio Railroad and an associate of Cyrus Eaton with whom Lewis was beginning to form one of his few close personal friendships. Soon after taking the post, Newton upset the operators by warning them in indirect but unmistakable terms that the longer they delayed negotiating an agreement with the UMW, the greater the pressures would be to nationalize the coal industry.[73]

Ickes also advanced Lewis's objectives through his interpretation of the Smith-Connally Act. Under the law plants or mines seized by the government had to be returned to their owners within sixty days of the resumption of normal production. Ickes realized that terminating government possession of the mines would likely generate a strike, and thus he sought to interpret the "normal production" provision narrowly. At first he asserted that the entire industry had to achieve pre-strike production levels before a single mine could be returned to private ownership. Roosevelt rejected this interpretation in mid-July, leading the Secretary to mandate stringent requirements which the owners had to fulfill before they could individually regain their property.[74]

The enactment of the War Labor Disputes Act emboldened both the operators and the National War Labor Board in their struggle with Lewis. The operators backed the NWLB in its efforts to compel the UMW to accept the June 18 Directive Order as the new contract for the industry. They also joined with the Board in petitioning Roosevelt to return the mines to their private owners. On July 13 the President announced that the mines would revert back to the operators within sixty days. A month later the cause of the operators and the Board received another assist when Roosevelt interpreted the punitive provisions of the Smith-Connally Act as authorizing the NWLB to sequester the dues of unions failing to comply with the Board's order. He also threatened to cancel the draft deferments of strikers.[75]

In a counter maneuver Lewis attacked his opponents' flank. Illinois had enjoyed a rejuvenation of its coal industry as a result of the booming wartime economy. In relations with the union, however, it was compelled to follow the decisions made by the Appalachian operators. Lewis sensed that the Illinois operators would gladly negotiate a contract favorable to the UMW in return for a more influential role in the coal industry. And the NWLB, when confronted with a labor agreement achieved through voluntary collective bargaining, would be under pressure to bend its "Little Steel Formula" and approve the contract rather than endure public odium as the sole impediment to a settlement. Once the Board submitted, the Illinois contract would become the model for the whole industry.

On July 21, the Illinois Coal Operators Association presented to the NWLB for its approval a contract negotiated with the UMW. The agreement would run until April 1, 1945, with the UMW pledging no strikes during that time. It incorporated all the awards previously granted by the NWLB, provided for a forty-hour work week, and contained a settlement of the portal-to-portal pay issue. Two days later Lewis courteously wrote Davis to ask for approval of the agreement and to indicate his willingness to appear before the Board personally to discuss the contract's provisions. Actually, the Board's new subpoena power granted by the Smith-Connally Act made Lewis's appearance mandatory.[76]

On August 3, with cameras clicking and reporters swarming around him for a statement, Lewis appeared before the men he had so recently vilified. The UMW chief wanted his new contract approved. For most of the hearing he sat by contemplatively, while an attorney presented the union's case. When he finally did speak, Lewis expressed none of the belligerency toward Davis and the others that he had formerly sounded. Now was the time to be ingratiating.

Neither the attorney's presentation nor Lewis's presence satisfied the Board. In issuing the majority opinion on August 25, Davis pointed out that although most of the contract complied with previous NWLB directives, the portal-to-portal arrangement failed to constitute "a genuine settlement of alleged claims arising under the Fair Labor Standards Act." Davis proceeded to warn the union that the Board would not approve a wage increase in the guise of travel time pay.[77]

In scattered mines in Ohio and Alabama miners reacted to the Board's decision by staging brief wildcat strikes. Most UMW members, however, waited for Lewis to act. Having few options open, Lewis resumed negotiating with the Illinois operators and emerged on September 23 with a new contract for the NWLB's consideration.

Lewis felt that the Board would uphold the new agreement. In line with NWLB criticism of the first contract, negotiators had changed the underground miners' work day from seven hours at the face to eight and one-half hours from portal-to-portal, thus putting the contract more in harmony with the provisions of the Fair Labor Standards Act. Lewis also utilized a 1936 Bureau of Labor Statistics report to justify his travel time calculations. To local leaders in Indiana and Alabama, he expressed his "considered personal judgement that for reasons of logic, the Board cannot escape approving the pending contract and making it applicable throughout the industry."[78]

For thirty-three days the NWLB pondered the second Illinois contract. Each passing day added to the sense of impending crisis as the October 31 strike deadline drew near. A series of major mine disasters further embittered miners against the shabby treatment they felt they had received from the government. In late September, alone, twelve miners were killed in an explosion in Harlan County, Kentucky; fourteen died in a blast at Minersville, Pennsylvania; and twenty-seven died and seventeen others were seriously maimed in a disaster near Birmingham, Alabama. The dead from this last explosion left behind one hundred and fifteen dependents.[79]

The government continued to return the mines to their private owners, relinquishing the last 1,700 pits on October 13. Beginning in Alabama, a wave of scattered wildcat protest strikes spread through Indiana, Kentucky, Ohio, and Pennsylvania and involved upwards of 90,000 miners. On October 16, Lewis joined with the NWLB in ordering the striking miners back to work, but few of the wildcatters obeyed. The UMW president now found himself in the awkward position of becoming a tail on the rank-and-file's kite. As his followers grew more militant, Lewis worried that firm action against wildcat strikes might alienate the UMW membership. Yet he feared another strike, for he realized that the NWLB was prepared to destroy the union. Fortunately, enough miners remained at work to preclude vigorous government action.[80]

On October 26, the NWLB issued its decision on the second Illinois contract. By a vote of seven to five the Board rejected the agreement, contending that its portal-to-portal pay provisions still violated the government's anti-inflation program. Perhaps aware that their actions created a new crisis for the nation, the Board's majority went on to spell out an acceptable settlement. They consented to payment on an eight and one-half hour day from portal to portal in place of the old seven-hour day excluding travel time. By their calculations, however, the miners would be entitled to $8.125 a day, and not the $8.50 figure embodied in the second Illinois contract.[81]

Lewis kept his own counsel in the days immediately following the Board's decision. Meanwhile the number of miners engaged in wildcat strikes dramatically increased, leading Lewis to attempt what Davis graciously characterized as "a sincere endeavor to end local stoppages, but without success." As a result of the wildcat strikes, on October 28, the NWLB once again referred the coal crisis to Roosevelt for action. In doing so, Davis directed the President's attention to the Board's proposed solution to the controversy and then reminded the Chief Executive that "the issue is the same clear one which it has always been since the beginning of the coal controversy; namely, shall the wage stabilization policies of the Government be applied and enforced irrespective of the displeasure of any group toward these policies."[82]

Roosevelt's public reply to Davis exposed a softening of the President's hitherto intransigent anti-Lewis position, for the urgency for coal constituted a stronger theme in Roosevelt's response than the need to preserve government authority and maintain the stabilization program. Although unable to resist rhetorical rebukes of Lewis, the President was generally firm but conciliatory toward the UMW and "the patriotic American miners." For the first time in the nine-month dispute, he extended to the union the courtesy of not instituting action until the Policy Committee met and evaluated the situation and he felt confident that, when the committee gathered, it would see "the substantial increase in benefits the Board's proposal offers" and would consent to a contract along those lines. To make the NWLB proposal even more attractive to the miners, he asked Davis to consider the wisdom of announcing that the NWLB "has no objection to the insertion of a clause in the contract that in no case shall a miner receive for a day's work less than he would have received for his productive work at the straight time hourly rate under the old contract." Having waved a carrot, Roosevelt ended his letter by threatening to use a stick: "But if I am mistaken and the miners do not accept the Board's proposals, I shall take decisive action to see that coal is mined."[83]

Roosevelt was mistaken. At dawn on Monday, November 1—hours before the UMW Policy Committee would convene to consider the President's plea— 530,000 bituminous and anthracite miners again went on strike. They walked out voluntarily, Lewis would argue in a 1944 *Collier's* article on the coal dispute. "It was the unanimous protest of men who were tired of serving as guinea pigs for Washington's campus theorists, and sick of sabotage and double-crossing. More than that, it was the answer of the rank and file to the repeated charge that they were not behind their elected leaders, and that our demands were 'purely political,' put forward by me to embarrass and harass the Roosevelt Administration."[84]

Roosevelt probably rejected Lewis's self-serving interpretation of the walkout, but he did recognize that rank-and-file militancy could disrupt the war effort for many months to come. He brooded over the situation all day and then at 8:00 P.M., November 1, again ordered Ickes to place the mines under government control. This time he directed the Secretary to negotiate a contract with the UMW to prevail for the duration of the seizure. In order not to undermine the Board totally, however, he insisted that the contract be in accord with the NWLB's ruling on the second Illinois agreement, and that the final document be presented to the Board for its approval. Roosevelt probably recognized that the NWLB could scarcely afford to reject a contract to which a representative of the government was a party.[85]

Lewis and Ickes wasted no time in entering into negotiations. After two days of talks they announced on November 3 the signing of a Memorandum of Agreement and the return of the miners to work. On the following day the UMW Policy Committee approved the agreement by acclamation and joined Lewis in greeting Ickes warmly.[86]

In essence the Lewis-Ickes agreement made the terms of the second Illinois contract approved by the War Labor Board applicable to the entire bituminous industry. On the critical issue of portal-to-portal pay, they used as a base the Board's proposal of $8.125 for a day of 7.75 hours at the face and 3/4 hours travel-time. Then they reduced the thirty-minute lunch period to fifteen minutes and applied the other fifteen minutes to production time. As compensation for this adjustment, they agreed to pay the miners another .375 cents, bringing the basic daily wage to the $8.50 figure Lewis had sought in the rejected second Illinois contract.[87]

The Lewis-Ickes agreement settled the coal dispute. With its signing, the controversy no longer competed day after day with battle accounts as front page news, although until the spring of 1944 aspects of the controversy would occasionally make headline stories. The heightened frustration of the rank and file, for instance, resurfaced a few days after the contract signing when thousands of miners walked out in protest against Roosevelt's failure to decree time-and-one-half holiday pay for work on Armistice Day. The Secretary gained a new antagonist in Lewis, who, now that he had his contract, hounded Ickes to uphold his end of the arrangement, and in general tried to make government management of the mines so unpleasant that the Administration would welcome a resumption of private ownership.

The reversion of the mines from government to private hands took several more months. While the northern operators dutifully negotiated a contract with the UMW paralleling the Lewis-Ickes agreement by December 17, the southerners refused until mid-1944 to come to terms with the union, and the National War Labor Board delayed approving the northern contract until May 29, 1944. The northern mines finally reverted to their private owners on May 31, 1944, while the southern pits were returned in piecemeal fashion as the year progressed.

Lewis showed signs of strain as the coal dispute came to its protracted conclusion. Although *The New York Times* and other papers cursed him as the victor, he knew that he had fallen far short of his original goals. The "Little Steel Formula" and the NWLB had not been smashed. A miner working eight hours a day, six days a week under the 1941 contract would have made $54.50 according to calculations by economist Colston E. Warne. The same miners working the same amount of time under the Lewis-Ickes agreement of 1943 would have earned $57.06. For this small gain Lewis and the miners had earned the enmity of the American people.[88]

For years to come the UMW would be condemned for disrupting the war effort. Lewis, it seems, had so convinced himself of the rectitude of his policy that he refused to contemplate such criticism. From one perspective, he was right. Despite the dramatic pictures of impending doom painted by Roosevelt with each coal walkout, Lewis always realized that the nation faced no immediate peril.

After Lewis-Ickes signed the agreement the government contended that the country lost 17,000,000 tons of coal because of the work stoppages, scarcely threatening when compared to a total production of around 600,000,000 tons is difficult to establish. In another sense the coal crisis did obstruct the conduct of the war. A response to discontent, it generated even more discontent. In terms of war-time national solidarity, the dispute was disruptive. Most directly, the miners' example encouraged workers in other industries to resist wartime controls. Similarly, thousands of men and women 'on the street' began to wonder in an uninformed way about a government that seemed to let the miners bully it. Equally important, the coal crisis forced the country's leaders to turn some of their attention away from winning the war and toward settling a domestic dispute.

Finally, the labor and liberal communities criticized Lewis and the miners for provoking a new wave of anti-unionism. Clearly the 1943 coal strikes intensified the anti-union trend. Lewis's actions were in fact partly a response to the government's antilabor drift. He chose to challenge the trend and he lost. Murray, Hillman, Dubinsky, Green and others preferred to appease the conservative forces. The miners' militancy in 1943 makes it impossible to determine whether the labor moderates' strategy would have succeeded.

The Lewis' Pine Island,
Florida, vacation home

In the living room of his
Alexandria home, 1953
*(State Historical Society of
Wisconsin)*

At the West Frankfurt, Illinois mine disaster
*(State Historical Society of Wisconsin,
World Wide photo)*

(Below right) ———→
Elder labor statesman in UMW
conference room, c. 1955-1959
*(State Historical Society of
Wisconsin)*

(Top left)
With Samuel Eliot Morison (far
left) and J. Russell Wiggins at
Monticello, 1954
*(State Historical Society of
Wisconsin; photo by Bob
Tenney, Charlottesville (Va.)
Daily Progress)*

(Center)
With Manuel Arburan and Jaime
Jerre y Benyto in Madrid, 1956
*(State Historical Society of
Wisconsin)*

W. A. Boyle and Thomas Kennedy (left) and
John Owens (right) at Lewis' retirement
announcement, 1959
*(State Historical Society of Wisconsin; photo
by Chase Studios Ltd., Washington D.C.)*

With Kathryn at his formal retirement dinner
after forty years service as UMW president,
1960
(State Historical Society of Wisconsin)

CHAPTER 19
Contempt, 1944-1946

During World War II, Americans focused their hostility on leaders and movements rather than the people of enemy nations. They despised Hitler and Nazism, Mussolini and Fascism, but not all Germans and Italians. When the World War ended and the Cold War erupted, this pattern was transferred to Stalin and the Communists.

On the homefront many citizens manifested a similar hostility toward labor leaders and unionism. Although such animosity had long prevailed in America, it became particularly intense as a result of the 1943 coal strikes and other wartime labor disruptions. Each day of the war further eroded the public's sense of tolerance and fair play. The end of the conflict aggravated the already strained spirit of national unity, and the tensions of reconversion—inflation, shortages, dislocations, and labor unrest—intensified public rancor toward assumed "enemies" within our borders.

John L. Lewis was a key target in the assault on organized labor. Throughout the war and postwar years, numerous news magazine articles, often with loaded captions, fired the public's rage: "Lewis the Dictator" (*New Republic*, 1941), "John L. Lewis's Commandos" (*Nation*, 1942), "John's Vengeance" (*Time*, 1942), "Lewis grasps for new power" (*Newsweek*, 1946), "John L.'s Coup" (*Newsweek*, 1946), and "Cunning John" (*Time*, 1948). On May 29, 1946, *Newsweek* featured his face on its cover with the lead "Lewis: The Power to Paralyze." Most newspapers concurred in the Hudson, Massachusetts *Sun*'s characterization of him as a labor racketeer and the Washington *Post*'s condemnation of his "holdup methods" and "rule-or-ruin technique." The coverage awarded Lewis in Wellington Roe's 1948 censure of trade union officialdom, *Juggernaut*, suggests his stature as the archetype of tyrannical labor leadership. Roe devoted nine chapters totaling one hundred seventeen pages to an expose of "Old Ironjaw, The Eyebrow," and only one chapter of fifteen pages on James Caesar Petrillo of the Musicians, one chapter of thirteen pages on William L.

Hutcheson of the Carpenters, and two chapters totaling thirty-four pages on the leaders of the "Big Five" railroad brotherhoods.[1]

One group even branded Lewis a Nazi collaborator. Special Assistant Attorney General O. John Rogge spearheaded this attack when he gave syndicated columnist Drew Pearson a story linking Lewis to Nazi efforts to defeat Roosevelt in 1940. In a lecture at Swarthmore College in the fall of 1946 Rogge repeated his accusations, elaborating on Lewis's connections with oil promoter and German informant William Rhodes Davis and the latter's efforts to persuade Roosevelt to consider a Goering peace plan. Rogge's evidence established little more than that the Germans recognized that Lewis's anti-Roosevelt politics coincided with their interests prior to the United States' entrance into the war. Although the Special Assistant Attorney General also listed Senator Burton K. Wheeler, Vice President John N. Garner, President Herbert Hoover, and Postmaster General James Farley as men whom the Wilhelmstrasse saw as having views coinciding with Nazi designs, *The New York Times* headlined its account: "Rogge ties Lewis to Nazis in Politics." As a result of the Swarthmore College lecture, Attorney General Tom Clark dismissed Rogge from the Justice Department for disclosing confidential material. For people who wanted to believe Rogge, his dismissal implied that his charges had validity.[2]

Although most Americans found Rogge's allegations extreme, many influential persons perceived Lewis as a diabolical figure. John Brophy believed him a participant in "a conspiracy on the part of American Firsters, composed of certain business, financial and political interests" intent on driving the New Dealers out of Washington.[3] "John L. Lewis is an enemy," James G. Patton of the Farmers' Union warned Roosevelt. "He is a confessed believer in the dismal doctrines of Hooverism; he believes war-time inflation is inevitable; he has proposed an alliance of laborers and farmers, not to prevent war profits, but to divide and share the poison fruit of inflation. Consciously or unconsciously, he is an ally of reactionaries and defeatists."[4] "You are right in saying," the President replied, "that John L. Lewis fundamentally believes in the dismal doctrines of *Hooverism*."[5] The *Times of London* characterized Lewis as a "political opportunist of the most callous kind—a man whom the Russians would describe as suspended halfway between fascism and the Second International."[6] The veteran labor reporter Louis Stark tagged him "The Warwick of the House of Labor" for his delight in "manipulating men, initiating maneuvers, and above all, engaging in the hurly-burly of the fight." Like others, Stark saw Lewis as "imperious and dominating" and as "craving power for its own sake and for what may be accomplished through it. . . ."[7]

No matter how uncomplimentary the press and opinion makers were toward Lewis, their accounts also contained an underlying sense of awe. Professional journalists helped create a myth of the invincible Lewis by crediting him with victories in situations that were actually compromises or defeats. Despite the past performances of District 50, reporters phrased announcements of drives to organize dairy farmers, chemical workers, steamship hands, and the ticket-takers on the Long Island Railroad as inevitable Lewis successes. At times they let their imaginations run wild in fathoming his motives, and they forgot all the sociology they knew when they claimed that the UMW president only needed to nod and subservient miners would execute his unspoken will.

Lewis consciously fostered his awesome image as an additional source of power. When cameras clicked he would wear a scowl that often vanished as soon as the photographing was over. He adroity cultivated reporters, calling them by first names, occasionally joshing with them over their stories, and staging exciting press conferences. Before them, he ranted against employers, other labor leaders, and politicians in an intentional effort to picture all men of prominence as his enemies. An aura of secrecy cloaked his public personality, adding a sense of intrigue to his actions. ''Questions as to the motive will be purely speculative,'' he taunted reporters as he made one dramatic announcement. ''Some philosopher has said the pursuit of motives is the most elusive task in all the world. . . .''[8]

The sparsity of news coverage on Lewis's private life also served to remove from public view many of his human qualities. In the 1940s Lewis was a major news figure but not a national social celebrity. Consequently, the public came to know the Lewis who flaunted Shakespeare and not the man who read mystery novels and loved western movies. They knew the belligerent and accusative Lewis, but not the charming raconteur at cocktail parties occasionally attended by the very men he publicly ridiculed. They were told of the pugnacious man engaged in an unceasing war on society, and not of the relaxed figure driving along wooded Virginia roads, fishing off the Gulf Coast of Florida, or journeying cross-country for extended vacations at a Wyoming dude ranch. The public Lewis radiated energy. The private Lewis progressively limited his socializing and took extended periods of rest in order to conserve the strength of his aging frame.

When the drama of 1943 closed, Lewis recognized his isolation from the controlling circles of power in the country. Abandoned by most liberals and moderates, he increasingly cultivated the support of those who opposed Roosevelt, the New Deal, and Washington's conduct of the war. Some of these ties extended back to pre-war days and were social as well as political. Alf Landon, Alice Roosevelt Longworth, Walter A. Jones, David I. Walsh, and—as Joseph Guffey divulged to the President's staff—''a few other reactionaries'' all came to Lewis's home as guests. Beginning in 1941, the miners' chief engaged in intimate meetings with Paul Palmer, the political advisor to De Witt Wallace, right-wing owner of the *Reader's Digest*.[9]

Now without strong liberal or radical influence as a ballast, Lewis became deeply entwined in conservative politics. In the spring of 1944 he corresponded and met with Herbert Hoover. The parties purposely concealed ''the subject'' in their letters, but most likely Lewis was exploring the possibilities of Hoover or someone with similar views running for the presidency in the forthcoming campaign.[10] When the Lewis-Hoover machinations produced no results, Lewis expended his political energies denouncing Roosevelt. Although he did not personally endorse Thomas Dewey in 1944, as did editor K. C. Adams in the UMW *Journal*, he praised the Republican candidate as "a firm believer in equal justice, fearless and courageous action."[11] Lewis sought more than a G.O.P. victory. As Elliot Janeway of *Fortune* noted, the miners' chief considered most Republicans "egregious blunderers" and supported their cause solely to improve his own hand.[12]

Lewis also maneuvered to tighten his connections in a business community that was dividing over prospective post-war economic policies. His own desire to weaken the political influence of United States Steel and other offspring of the House of Morgan coincided with that of Cleveland industrialist and financier Cyrus Eaton.[13] Similarly, his interest in protecting the domestic market for coal led to collaboration with H. L. Derby of the American Cyanide and Chemical Corporation and Joseph A. Brown of the Chemical Bank, both of whom feared that the newly created International Bank for Reconstruction and Development might enable England eventually to invade American markets.[14]

More than supportive businessmen, Lewis and the UMW most needed allies within the labor movement. Yet Lewis would have nothing to do with the CIO, which he considered sycophantic to the Roosevelt Administration. He viewed the AFL as less subservient, and pressured it to act on the UMW's application for reaffiliation which had been pending since May, 1943. In August 1943, the AFL Executive Council divided evenly on the petition, with William Green refusing to cast the deciding vote. Two months later the AFL convention instructed the Council to continue exploring the terms for the UMW's readmission. Despite intensive pressure from Lewis, the Council haggled over the issue at its January, 1944 session and then postponed decisive action until its May gathering.

By the time of the spring meeting, Lewis sensed that the AFL would refuse the UMW immediate readmission. Daniel Tobin and other council members close to the White House wanted to wait until after the presidential election before strengthening anti-administration forces in the Federation. A number of council members also had qualms over Lewis's imperial tendencies. For one thing, UMW District 50 contested the jurisdictions of over thirty AFL unions. Although Lewis was unwilling officially to settle jurisdictional disputes before reaffiliation, he promised Green that he would be "reasonable," and apparently even volunteered eventually to disband all divisions of District 50 except the Chemical and By-Product Coke Workers. Nonetheless, Lewis's designs on the chemical industry—one of the fastest growing sectors of the wartime economy—made several council members uneasy. While they were unwilling themselves to launch an aggressive organizing drive in this area, they feared that Lewis would unionize the industry and, then, as the head of a multimillion member organization, dominate the AFL.[15]

Consequently, on May 8, the Executive Council cautiously invited the Miners to return to the AFL with its 1936 jurisdiction. For months, Lewis had made clear that the UMW would only reaffiliate "as it is." Angered by the AFL's terms, he immediately penned a blistering letter to Green accusing the council members of having "constantly muttered and mumbled and indulged in fearsome incantations over the fallacious and hoary question of jurisdictional rights." "The members of the Executive Council," he charged, "by their dishonorable intrigue have permitted the American Federation of Labor to become the puppet of a political organization, and, in fact, to achieve the status of a political company union."16

Spurned by the AFL, Lewis found his domain in the labor movement confined for the next two years to the miners' union and its all-inclusive District 50. In 1941, Lewis had revitalized the District as part of his mounting challenge to the CIO. For a time labor commentators predicted that the catchall unit would become the core of a third mass labor organization. In March 1942, Kathryn Lewis, the District's secretary-treasurer, fed this prognosis by announcing an organizing drive among the three million workers in the dairy industry. Some Americans viewed the campaign as an example of Lewis's pathetic effort to regain his lost labor kingdom. A large segment of the public, however, shared New York Governor Thomas Dewey's nightmare that with the nation's dairy farmers behind him, the "frustrated" Lewis would control "the most staggering slush fund" as well as "the food supply of the nation." "By such a throttlehold on the lifeblood of the nation," portended Dewey, Lewis "would be in a position to dictate America's destiny."

Such alarm distorted the actual threat posed by the dairy industry drive and even the entire sphere of District 50 activities. Although between December, 1940, and June, 1943, the UMW invested three million dollars in the district and had several hundred organizers in the field, by the latter date the subdivision paid per capita dues to the parent organization on only 48,000 members. As a third force in the labor movement, District 50 flopped.17

Ironically, District 50 actually gained its greatest strength after the dairy drive soured and the UMW leadership abandoned the concept of recreating a second CIO. Instructed by Lewis to disregard jurisdictional lines, District 50 organizers signed up workers in a variety of unrelated industries. By 1948, "50" had a membership estimated upward of 200,000, and included in its ranks clam diggers, taxi drivers, dairy farmers, pool parlor employees, and railroad ticket-takers. It had locals in pulp and paper mills, gas plants, bus lines, construction projects, ladies' and men's garment shops, as well as plants making or processing drugs, rubber, fish, and steel. Until the Taft-Harley Act outlawed his efforts, Lewis attempted to enroll mine foremen in the District's United Clerical, Technical, and Supervisory Workers Union. The District also made inroads among chemical employees, although it failed to establish the supremacy in the industry that Lewis desired.

Although far from a substitute for AFL membership, District 50 nonetheless provided Lewis with an instrument to harass his enemies. Rather than unionize an entire industry, District 50 organizers concentrated their efforts at critical points from which Lewis was able to negotiate concessions from employers or labor leaders whose unions had jurisdiction in that field. This strategy also enabled Lewis to magnify his national influence. In the hyperbolic words of Wellington Roe, by 1948 Lewis could "cripple transportation in New York City's suburban area, shut off gas in Boston, halt the production of nylon wearing apparel, disrupt the huge Du Pont chemical empire, tie up the Port of Philadelphia, halt traffic on a dozen railroads and generally raise hell in more than a score of other important industries."[18]

During the summer and fall of 1944, Lewis confronted a challenge to his authority within the Mine Workers' Union. Occurring at a time when rank-and-file militancy continued to disrupt the coal industry by wildcat strikes, the uprising blended extensive membership protest against the internal operations of the union with a power play by one of Lewis's trusted lieutenants.

In rebuilding the UMW in 1933, Lewis had subverted democracy by imposing provisional governments on most of the new and revitalized districts. At the time, many members had expected that they would be permitted self-government after the union achieved stability. Lewis's design moved in the opposite direction, however, until by 1944 twenty-one of the UMW's thirty-one districts were run by officers named by him. On the International Executive Board, Lewis, Kennedy, and O'Leary transacted business with sixteen appointed members casting 287.5 roll-call votes against only ten elected members with a voting strength of 72.5.

At every convention after 1934, a small but bold band of delegates had unsuccessfully challenged the policy of "provisionalism." To keep the situation under control, Lewis often treated the issue in his Officer's Report rather than allow it to be aired in the form of resolutions from local unions. Nonetheless, the pressures for self-government compelled Lewis to guide through the 1938 convention a farcical system of partial autonomy, under which, if the International Executive Board concluded that a provisional district demonstrated sufficient maturity, the district members would be allowed to adopt a constitution, hold conventions, and elect officers—except for the important posts of district president and secretary-treasurer. So protective was Lewis of his authority, that over the next six years only two districts achieved partial autonomy: the inconsequential "2," and District 6 of Ohio under the dominance of John Owens.[19]

At each UMW convention, Lewis would lecture "misguided" delegates on the evils of autonomy. His harangue gained a new edge in 1944 when he contended that the trend toward one national wage agreement made centralization imperative. Nonetheless, in his forty-five minute discourse that year he repeated all his old sophistries. Self-government would give rise to incompetence, inefficiency, corruption, and political maneuvering, while provisionalism provided a mechanism for the nationally elected officers to train talented young men in the business principles and methods of unionism.[20]

One of the talents promoted by Lewis under provisionalism was Ray Edmundson. In 1931, while president of a UMW subdistrict in southern Illinois, he had helped organize the renegade Miners' Rank and File Union. Lewis quickly smashed this opposition group, but took no action against Edmundson who eventually regained the presidency of his subdivision. In the war between the Progressive Mine Workers and the UMW, Edmundson obtained a reputation as a gunman, a bullet wound in the neck, and the attention of Lewis. Needing someone who could keep the rebellious Illinois miners in line, in 1935 the UMW president appointed Edmundson head of provisional District 12.

For the next nine years Edmundson proved a faithful Lewis lieutenant. At the Mine Workers' 1938 and 1940 conventions, for instance, he served as secretary of the Committee on the Officers' Reports where he championed Lewis's views on autonomy and self-government. In all things, he sought to emulate his chief. He affiliated with the same local in Springfield as Lewis; dressed in similar fashion (although he reportedly included a gun among his undergarments); and lived in a house next to Lewis's mother which he purchased from the UMW president. On the speaker's platform, he imitated Lewis in tone, gesture, facial expressions, and oratorical tricks, although his vocabulary and use of the language fell short of the master's. "[I]f Hollywood ever plans a movie on the life of John L. Lewis," Edward A. Wieck contended, "the director would miss a trick if he failed to get Edmundson to play the part."[21]

In 1942, Lewis bypassed Edmundson in selecting a successor to Philip Murray as UMW vice president. Edmundson dated his troubles with Lewis, however, to the 1943 coal crisis when he criticized Lewis's policy and turned to Secretary of the Interior Ickes and others in the Administration for support. Apparently, Lewis tolerated this defiance until the spring of 1944 when he moved to reduce the staff and income available to Edmundson. The latter recognized the scenario—having played a key role in undermining Murray—and on April 17 prepared his resignation as head of District 12 and director of the Illinois division of District 50, to be effective on May 15.

Rather than surrendering, Edmundson was simply selecting his own field of battle and enlisting his troops. After taking a job in a mine to demonstrate his links to the rank and file, he proceeded to broadcast across the coal fields his conversion to the cause of district autonomy and self-government. He cunningly focused on issues that dealt solely with Lewis's stewardship and the internal policy of the union. The UMW president would not be able to transform the dispute into an attack on Roosevelt, Communists, or southern coal operators as he often did when challenged about his wage policies or political positions. Nor could Lewis obfuscate the issue, for he had trumpeted his defense of provisionalism throughout the union. Despite the merit of some of Lewis's arguments, the nation's commitment to democratic principle would align public opinion against him. And most importantly, from Edmundson's perspective, a large number of miners otherwise sympathetic to Lewis disapproved of his "provisionalism." He knew well that coal miners had a long tradition of progressive trade-unionism, that socialist and radical tendencies were as much a part of the UMW's heritage as Lewis's autocratic "business unionism."

In late April, the Illinois local to which Edmundson and the absent Lewis both belonged joined two others in issuing a call for a statewide conference in Springfield on June 4 to compose demands for the restoration of district self-government. The call listed Edmundson as "temporary vice chairman," but when more than one hundred delegates gathered, he dominated the meeting. Among other activities, he served as vice chairman of a committee which called for a larger conference to convene in Cincinnati on July 2.22

Almost eighty delegates from thirteen districts east of the Mississippi River attended the Cincinnati gathering. Some had been sent by their locals, while others possessed no formal credentials. Again, the call listed Edmundson only as vice chairman, but he presided over most of the sessions and clearly led the movement. Under his guidance the delegates approved a series of resolutions and established mechanisms for propagating their message throughout the union before the UMW's fall 1944 convention. Two weeks earlier, on June 25, Edmundson had announced his candidacy against Lewis in the December elections. Although he did not seek an endorsement from the Cincinnati delegates, he linked his cause to theirs.23

Some mystery surrounded the financing of the autonomy movement and Edmundson's campaign for the union's presidency. Both were well polished efforts with no visible means of support. The necessarily small contributions from rank-and-file sympathizers could not conceivably have covered the cost of even the autonomy movement's professionally produced publications, which included a paper, *The Voice*, carrying Edmundson's name on the masthead as publisher but listing no editor. Edward Wieck, investigating the movement for the Russell Sage Foundation, could offer only rumors concerning the sources of financing. Edmundson may have drawn from his own investments, which included several movie theaters. The behavior of Phil Murray, Wieck felt, failed to corroborate stories that assistance was coming directly from that source, but he gave weight to speculation that PAC* or other friends of Roosevelt were providing funds.24

Publicly, Lewis and his followers ignored the autonomy movement and Edmundson's candidacy, with the UMW *Journal* failing to inform its readers of the challenge. Behind the scenes, however, Lewis's agents scouted the Cincinnati conference and applied pressure on other District twelve officers to prevent a mass resignation in support of Edmundson. Above all, they took the necessary steps to assure their boss of an unqualified triumph at the upcoming UMW convention.

---

*The new political arm of the CIO headed by Sidney Hillman and dedicated in 1944 to Roosevelt's reelection.

Labor reporters, knowing well the effectiveness of the UMW machine, speculated more on Lewis's plan of attack than on the outcome of the challenge. With the situation promising an exciting show, in mid-September over twenty-five correspondents journeyed to Cincinnati to crowd around the convention press table which two years earlier had been used by about eight.[25]

On the eve of the convention, as a preliminary to the main event, provisional president William Blizzard of West Virginia led a band of bruisers in breaking up an autonomy movement caucus called by Edmundson and attended by three to four hundred persons. The next day, September 12, Lewis convened the gathering in a hall often used for prize fights. He warmed up by throwing his customary rhetorical punches at Roosevelt and then squared off against Edmundson. "There isn't any mincing, lackadaisical, lace-painted gigolo going to dethrone John L. in his own convention," he sneered.[26]

The entire proceedings demonstrated Lewis's command over the structure of the union, if not all its members. The delegates mechanically approved committee recommendations on resolutions, referred to only by number, so fast that reporters were unable to look them up in the resolution booklet and record the action. So controlled was the gathering that although wartime regulations imposed an eight day limit to the convention, it could not even consume that amount of time and adjourned a day early. In those seven days, the 1944 convention actually met for only twenty-two hours, as compared to thirty-five hours and fifty-five minutes for the seven day 1942 gathering or forty and one-half hours for the seven day convention in 1934. One reason for the brevity was that Lewis had apparently ordered the secondary officers to abstain from their usual round of speeches. For public appearance, this was to be a convention where the rank and file spoke.[27]

Under such manipulated conditions Lewis easily eliminated Edmundson and defeated the autonomy challenge. First, some Lewis supporters challenged Edmundson's right to serve as a delegate, a tactic which allowed the Lewis-appointed credentials committee to delay hearing the case until after the convention had disposed of the autonomy issue. Lacking their leader, the self-government forces proved ineffective in their opposition to the Resolutions Committee's anti-autonomy report. The entire debate on the issue lasted a mere two hours, with twelve speakers favorable to autonomy and twenty opposed. When the standing vote was taken, only one hundred of the 2728 delegates made known their objections to provisionalism. The convention then found Edmundson ineligible to be a delegate, which inspired Lewis to decree a constitutional ruling barring his opponent from seeking union office. No delegate appealed the decision of the chair. Later, Edmundson asked the federal courts to reinstate him on the ballot, but Judge T. Alan Goldsborough declared that he had no jurisdiction in the matter.[28]

Not satisfied with thrashing his opponents, Lewis proceeded to magnify his victory. Without advance notice, his functionaries proposed and the delegates dutifully approved changes in the union's constitution. National union elections and constitutional conventions in the future would be held only at four year intervals, with smaller policy conventions occurring in the biennial off-years. Indeed, the only area in which Lewis did not achieve his will was in the field of political action. Recognizing that many miners still esteemed Roosevelt, Lewis settled for a "statement" critical of the Administration's labor policies.[29]

Lewis's reluctance to force his anti-Roosevelt politics on the convention suggests that he could not have thwarted the autonomy movement so easily had a sizeable number of miners been deeply committed to the cause. District self-government was essentially a pre-Depression tradition in the UMW, but the majority of union members had affiliated after 1932. As old timers died off or left the union, the cause of autonomy faded. For newer recruits, Lewis's accomplishments on wages, hours, and working conditions offset the never-experienced right to vote for district officers. Lewis knew this and paid close attention to his members' material complaints. A number of the demands he would make during the 1945 and 1946 contract negotiations, for example, were variations of resolutions concerning wage policies adopted at the 1944 autonomy conference in Cincinnati. Lewis, as usual, also knew when to forgive. Faced with a hostile political and economic environment, he saw the need for harmony in the union and so within a year enabled Edmundson to rejoin the flock—and eventually appointed him a regional director of District 50.[30]

In 1945 Lewis's disaffection with government interference in Labor relations intensified as he found himself repeatedly restricted in his efforts to transfer a larger share of the coal industry's war-stimulated profits to the men who worked in the mines. Bituminous negotiations opened in March with the country facing its most serious coal shortage in years, causing the government to order brown-outs to conserve fuel. A war-weary public, sensing victory near, clamored for the Administration to wield its power if the miners chose to strike. Since the coal industry had learned during the past two years that it could prosper with its properties technically seized, Lewis lacked even the option he exercised in 1943 of sitting tight as the operators fretted under government control.

Three days before negotiations commenced, Lewis sought to gain some leverage by filing with the proper agencies notification that a labor dispute existed. Under the Smith-Connally Act, this move compelled the National Labor Relations Board to conduct a poll of the union's membership after thirty days to see if they actually wanted to strike in the midst of war. When balloting took place on March 28, the miners voted in a ratio of six to one in favor of shutting down the coal fields unless granted their demands. Lewis's adroit use of a law meant to restrict him incensed his enemies.

The suspense surrounding this maneuver actually masked Lewis's sober stand. Recognizing the union's weak bargaining position, his demands fell within the government's anti-inflation guidelines. At a closed meeting of the UMW Policy Committee on February 28, for instance, Lewis proposed that instead of a wage increase the union should demand a royalty of ten cents a ton on coal mined to be placed in a trust fund for a welfare program. Such a demand, he contended, would be neither inflationary nor violate the "Little Steel Formula."[31]

The royalty-welfare demand, when presented by Lewis at the opening bargaining session, caught the operators by surprise. Given the favorable bargaining position in which they found themselves, the operators saw little reason to yield on such an unusual request and stalled in negotiations until the old contract expired. Lewis, recognizing the moment as inauspicious for any job action, begrudgingly agreed to a contract extension and diluted the UMW's demands.

Finally, on April 11, the union and the operators reached a settlement based on a compromise proposed by Labor Secretary Perkins. Under this agreement a miner making $57.06 working nine hours a day, six days a week under the 1943 contract now would earn $63.50 for the same amount of time. Most of the gain resulted from establishing overtime pay for work after seven hours daily. The agreement led *The New York Times* to proclaim that Lewis had "won another notable victory. . . ." The miners' president and the UMW *Journal*, however, simply viewed the contract as the best settlement possible under disadvantageous conditions.[32]

The factors working against the UMW in the bituminous talks also restricted the union in the anthracite bargaining. When contract negotiations began in early April, the union sought for the hard-coal diggers the gains won by bituminous workers under the 1941 and 1943 agreements, including travel time pay. Again Lewis filed notification of a labor dispute under the Smith-Connally Act, and in the resulting NLRB poll the anthracite miners indicated their determination to strike if their demands were not met.

When the old contract expired at the end of April, 72,000 anthracite miners adhered to the union's tradition of not working without a contract. Confronted with the strike, the Administration seized the mines on May 4, but the workers defied the government by continuing their walkout. Since Lewis had not officially ordered the wartime stoppage, Attorney General Francis Biddle could find no violation of the Smith-Connally Act. The stalemate finally broke when the Supreme Court ruled in favor of portal-to-portal pay for bituminous miners and by implication strengthened Lewis's case for the same provision for hard-coal men. On May 20, union officials and anthracite operators agreed to a contract that reduced substantially the disparity in labor standards between the two segments of the industry.

As with the bituminous contract, Lewis and the UMW *Journal* announced the agreement to the union's members in rather unexuberant language. Editorial writers, however, fumed about the results. In the eyes of Merlo Pusey of the Washington *Post*, the government had "humiliated itself once more before John

L. Lewis and virtually invited other union leaders to apply his rule-or-ruin techniques.'' "[I]nflation and Lewis have won another victory," stated *The New York Times*.33

In the fall of 1945, Lewis again challenged the bituminous operators, and this time suffered unmistakable defeat. For several years he had been interested in organizing the managerial personnel around the mines. When the National Labor Relations Board upheld a foreman's right to join a union in March, 1945, Lewis instructed District 50's United Clerical, Technical, and Supervisory Workers Union to accelerate its recruiting. On September 21, less than three weeks after Japan surrendered, a strike commenced among supervisory employees seeking recognition which eventually idled over 200,000 miners. The operators, viewing unionization of foremen as "an attempt to rob the employers of every vestige of control of their operations and properties," vowed to "fight to the last ditch." Lewis had conceivably anticipated such oppostion, but had calculated that the government would seize the mines and open the way for him to manipulate a victory. Seizure, however, was not forthcoming. As winter approached and the nation's coal supply dwindled, the public's indignation against the miners increased. Recognizing that to push the issue further would bring calamity upon the union, on October 17 Lewis called off the strike. "Future efforts to abate this controversy," a chagrined Lewis informed his membership, "will be resumed at a later more appropriate date."34

The restraints and setbacks Lewis experienced in 1945 increased his apprehensions about the postwar reconversion period. Like many Americans, he feared that the economic dislocations associated with demobilization would plunge the nation into a post-war recession, perhaps even a rerun of the Great Depression. The end of overtime work, he envisioned, would drastically reduce the wage earner's take-home pay, and the return of millions of GI's to civilian life would produce widespread unemployment. Impressed by technological advances made during the war, he also dreaded an increased maldistribution of wealth unless all sectors of society shared in the economic gains derived from greater productivity through science. To protect workers against a foreboding future, Lewis believed it imperative that the government lift all restrictions on organized labor and collective bargaining.

Lewis forcefully presented his views at President Truman's Conference of Labor and Management in November, 1945. When the CIO delegates supported Truman's proposal to tie wage increases to the cost-of-living, Lewis accused them of seeking to impose upon labor a new economic straitjacket to replace the "Little Steel Formula." Recognizing that such measures froze workers into a fixed position in society, he expressed his opposition to any program "that bound labor to a cost-of-living formula, giving labor a chance to advance its wages only as the price of milk, children's shoes or straw hats advanced." "What Mr. Murray and the C.I.O. are asking for," he warned, "is a corporate state, wherein the activities of the people are regulated and constrained by a dictatorial government. We are opposed to the corporate state."[35]

Lewis also assailed the idea made popular by Walter Reuther of linking wage increases to a business's "ability to pay." "I don't want to see the company's books," Lewis declared. "They might prove inability to pay. So what? We can't submerge our standard wage because of inability to pay. It's the constant pressure of trade unions that compels some employers to work out more economical and more efficient ways of doing things. Why should we be 'reasonable' and subsidize their inefficiency."[36]

Lewis's apprehension over the fate of labor in the reconversion era, combined with his need for allies, led him once again to seek affiliation with the AFL. Overlooking his 1944 attack on the Federation's Executive Council for "servility to the Roosevelt Administration," he now told a radio interviewer that the AFL "stands against collectivism and against the centralization of controls in government. It does not constantly depend upon the government to make all decisions affecting the policies of organized labor."[37] In December 1944, Green had approached Lewis about rejoining the AFL, but negotiations had collapsed when the UMW president insisted on an Executive Council seat as a condition for merger. "As I remember the Good Book," declared one Council member, "the prodigal son does not make it a condition of his return that they kill the fatted calf. First he returned and then the calf was killed."[38]

A year later, in January 1946, Lewis's chances of gaining a council seat improved when a vice-presidency fell vacant. Seizing the initative, Lewis dashed off a message which he had hand-delivered to Green, announcing his renewed interest in reaffiliating. After a week had passed without formal reply, he sent Green another letter, this time enclosing a check for $9,000 to cover the UMW's first month's dues.[39]

The arguments previously employed against the UMW had lost much of their impact when the AFL Executive Council took up the subject at its winter meeting. The 1944 Federation convention had chartered a chemical workers' union which now had official jurisdiction in that field. With the death of Roosevelt and the succession of Truman to the Presidency, Daniel Tobin and other AFL Democrats seemed to lose influence at the White House to men from the CIO, and most members of the council resented the Administration's practice of basing its labor policies on developments in the CIO-dominated auto and steel industries. Concerned over the future of collective bargaining, the Council members concluded that Lewis's position on that issue was now more important than the jurisdictional problems posed by District 50.

On January 24, the Council readmitted the UMW to the AFL and elected Lewis Thirteenth Vice President. Delighted, the miners' leader joined his new colleagues in Miami, where he melodramatically handed Green back his UMW membership which he contended had been secretly maintained in good standing since the break in 1936. "These boys have been my friends and I didn't know it," a touched Green declared.[40]

For all Lewis's preparations, he was still ill-prepared for the tensions which gripped America in the reconversion era. Ironically, a people who had just emerged supreme from a devastating world conflict, now questioned the stability of their own institutions and way of life. In late-1945 and 1946, many Americans became traumatized over the wave of strikes that swept the nation as workers, having established a remarkably low wartime strike record, now sought to recoup the sacrifices they had made. In November 1945, two hundred thousand General Motors employees walked out of their plants. Two months later, 300,000 meat packers and 180,000 electrical workers struck, and were followed shortly thereafter by 750,000 steelworkers. In all, 4,630 work stoppages, involving 5,000,000 strikers, and totaling 120,000,000 idle work-days occurred in the twelve months following Japan's surrender. While little physical violence characterized these stoppages, they generated violent emotions as middle- and upper-class Americans feared that unions would disrupt their economic security.

In perspective, the postwar labor struggles involved far more than simple disputes over immediate union demands. Rather, they constituted the first peacetime test of the new alignment of social, economic, and political forces that had come into being during the Great Depression and World War II. At the heart of the labor unrest and the government's, employer's, and public's response lay the issue of the role of workers and their unions in the postwar era. Unfortunately for organized labor, the mainstream of national sentiment as well as the policies of the Truman Administration were in accord with industry's efforts to establish limits to trade-union power.

Within this context, on March 2, 1946, the nation prepared for another coal crisis as Lewis notified the bituminous operators that he desired to reopen negotiations, and informed federal authorities that a labor dispute existed. When the wage conference convened on March 12, Lewis surprised everyone by laying before the operators loosely defined "negotiable suggestions" instead of "demands." Along with recommending the creation of a welfare fund, he proposed a wage increase of an unspecified amount, various improvements in the miners' working and living conditions, and recognition of the foremen's union. Journalists covering the session considered his two hour opening speech "mild," noting the lack of attacks on the Truman Administration and the absence of a strike threat. They paid too little attention to Lewis's dramatic recital of the record of miners killed and injured.

Throughout the subsequent controversy, Lewis proved unable to convince the public of his sincerity on the issues of health and safety. From the outset, most reporters interpreted his actions as a crusade to destroy federal wage-price policies, and, in the process, to show-up Philip Murray who had just won a wage increase for his steelworkers. Lewis's lack of credibility was partly of his own making. His passion for maneuvers, plotting, and secret dealings over the years had created the image of an opportunistic, cunning, power-hungry man of few principles. Recalling past episodes, journalists came to suspect his altruistic demands as facades for baser goals. This characterization had merit; but when taken to an extreme, it denied Lewis's humanity. In his personality the base and the noble blended.

Contrary to popular notions, Lewis's interest in promoting health care and mine safety had a long history. In the 1941 coal negotiations he had demanded that workers have a voice in the management of health programs financed by deductions from their pay; and in 1945 he had raised the issue of a union-run health and welfare fund. His position on mine safety was even stronger. "Lewis has never kept quiet on this matter for long at a time since the adoption by the 1938 convention of a resolution calling attention to the continued high accident rate in coal mines," noted Edward Wieck, author of *Preventing Fatal Explosions in Coal Mines.*[41]

In retrospect, it seems that Lewis first turned to the issues of safety and health in the late 1930s and early 1940s, using them as a means to embarrass Roosevelt and the operators when he could not arouse public sympathy for the miners' economic plight. Yet the more he studied and developed his arguments, the more sincere became his commitment to alleviating these ills. His increased dedication to improving health and pension services for his members coincided with demographic changes among the mining population. In 1940, 50% of the coal diggers were age thirty-two or younger. By 1944 the average age had risen to forty-five, with only 16% of the miners under thirty—one-third of whom had been classified 4-F by the draft. Over 11,000 men age sixty-five or over continued to work in the pits. Lewis's drive for a health and pension fund blended with this new majority of older workers' own anxieties in life.

In session after session of the wage conference, Lewis and his staff dramatically related the dismal details of a UMW investigation into mining accidents, health care, insurance programs, state compensation laws, sanitary facilities in mining camps, and a variety of similar subjects. Bristling under these accusations, the operators charged Lewis with "filibustering" and tried to focus the conference on more traditional subjects. To Lewis's demand for improved company housing, O'Neill snapped that he had come to negotiate a contract and not to act "as a sanitary expert." Throughout the haggling, Lewis refused to talk of wages or hours until the operators agreed "in principle" to a health and welfare fund. And when asked about the cost of the fund, he would reply: "Make me an offer."[42]

On April 1, with the conference making little progress and the old contract expired, the miners struck. Negotiations continued for ten more days before Lewis finally tired of the operators' repetition of "noes." After scribbling his thoughts on a scrap of paper, he rose and presented to the negotiators an expression of his indignation and a revelation of his self-righteous cast of mind:

> For four weeks we have sat with you; we attended when you fixed the hour; we departed when weariness affected your pleasure.
>
> Our effort to resolve mutual questions has been vain; you have been intolerant of suggestions and impatient of analysis.
>
> When we sought surcease from blood-letting, you professed indifference. When we cried aloud for the safety of our members you answer—Be content—'twas always thus!'
>
> When we urged that you abate a stench you averred that your nostrils were not offended.
>
> When we emphasized the importance of life you pleaded the priority of profits; when we spoke of little children in unkept surroundings you said—Look to the State!
>
> You aver that you own the mines; we suggest that, as yet, you do not own the people.
>
> You profess annoyance at our temerity; we condemn your imbecility.
>
> You are smug in your complacency; we are abashed by your shamelessness; you prate your respectability; we are shocked at your lack of public morality.
>
> You scorn the toils, the abstinence and the perils of the miner; we withhold approval of your luxurious mode of life and the nights you spend in merriment.
>
> You invert the natural order of things and charge to the public the pleasures of your own indolence; we denounce the senseless cupidity that withholds from the miner the rewards of honorable and perilous exertion.
>
> To cavil further is futile. We trust that time, as it shrinks your purse, may modify your niggardly and anti-social propensities.[43]

"John L. Lewis did a 'Gromyko' at today's joint coal conference," is how the *New York Times* described his termination of the talks.[44]

For the next nineteen days the nation burned away its coal reserves while little progress was made to resolve the crisis. Finally, on March 29, the government acted, with Secretary of Labor Schwellenbach bringing the parties together for renewed negotiations. The times were inauspicious for a settlement. The wave of antiunionism that was sweeping the nation encouraged the operators' intransigence. On Capitol Hill, legislators debated the Case Bill with its provisions restricting strikes. Simultaneously, Representatives A. Willis Robertson and Howard Smith, both of Virginia, raced to receive credit for introducing legislation that would outlaw health, welfare, and retirement funds financed through employer contributions. In the Senate, Illinois's Scott Lucas warned that the month-old coal strike could "easily become an insurrection against the government. . . . The truth of the matter is," he asserted, "that this is a political strike waged by John L. Lewis for the purpose of obtaining more power."[45]

By the second week in May the nation's coal supply had fallen dangerously low, causing the steel industry to cut production almost in half and Detroit auto plants to close. The Office of Defense Transportation clamped a tight embargo on rail freight and reduced passenger train service 25%. Harry Truman dimmed the lights in the White House, and New York's Great White Way lost its glow.

The public's rage, the threat of punitive legislation, and the urgency of the situation affected Lewis. He also knew that the railroad trainmen and engineers were planning a strike that would disrupt the delivery of coal anyway. He thus calculated that a temporary halt to the miners' walkout might placate public and legislative opinion without sacrificing the union's strategic position. After leaving a conference with President Truman on May 10, Lewis announced that in order to protect the nation's health and safety, the miners would return to work until May 25. At the same time, a White House source indicated that the operators had finally agreed "in principle" to a health and welfare fund.[46]

In the days that followed, the operators squirmed out of their commitment. Consequently, on May 16 Lewis and Charles O'Neill informed the president that negotiations had collapsed and that further talks were futile. Both parties rejected a presidential request that they resort to arbitration. Faced with a deteriorating situation, on May 21 Truman ordered Secretary of the Interior J. A. Krug to seize the mines and negotiate an agreement with the union on "the terms and conditions of employment for the period of the operation of the mines by the government."[47] Once again, and perhaps not without design, Lewis found himself in a position similar to one he had been in in 1943, when he had achieved portal-to-portal pay through an accord with Ickes.

Lewis maintained constant pressure on the government during the ensuing negotiations. By refusing to call a Policy Committee meeting, he assured a resumption of the walkout once the two-week truce ended. Meanwhile, Krug and his staff interviewed various experts on existing health and welfare funds, and apparently they grew sympathetic to the idea. Finally, on May 29 President Truman looked on as Krug and Lewis signed an accord that sent the miners back to work.

The Lewis-Krug agreement provided miners with a welfare and retirement fund jointly supervised by the union and the government. Initially, the government had planned to finance the fund out of a tax on the industry's payroll, but at the request of the operators this was changed to a five-cent royalty on every ton of coal mined. A second medical and health fund was also established, to be administered solely by the union and financed by the companies depositing moneys previously deducted from the miners' wages for company-run medical and health programs. Along with these achievements, the union won an 18.5-cent-per-hour wage increase, an increase in vacation pay to $100, an agreement to accept the NLRB's pending ruling on the issue of the right of foremen to unionize, and a promise that a federal mine safety code would be formulated and applied as the standard while the mines were under government control.[48]

*　　*　　*

For the next month, Lewis labored to tie up the loose ends of his accomplishment in the Lewis-Krug agreement. The anthracite miners went on strike two days after the bituminous agreement was signed to attain similar objectives. On June 8 the UMW and the hard-coal operators reached an agreement that established a jointly managed welfare fund. But Lewis failed to negotiate an agreement covering mine foremen and grew perturbed as Krug's staff delayed formulating and putting into effect a federal coal mine safety code.[49]

The strain of continual battle began to show on Lewis, who had aged considerably during the war years. At sixty-six he tired more easily and occasionally appeared to catnap or at least daydream of time gone by. His world-famous eyebrows grew bushier than ever. His eyes had assumed a cavernous quality; his face became a study of lines and clefts. His hair—now almost white—was no longer kept well groomed; and as it grew longer and became wavier and more unruly, it at times resembled a lion's mane.

For six weeks in the summer of 1946 Lewis escaped the tensions of Washington and journeyed west by car to a Wyoming dude ranch. Along the way he visited various UMW locals, patching up small differences and touching base with the rank and file.

Lewis was back in Washington performing his duties on September 11 when the government assembled the operators and the union. The administration hoped that the parties could now reach an agreement enabling the government to return the mines to their private owners. But the southern operators still refused to accept the welfare and retirement fund or the inclusion of a safety code within a contract. With the parties remaining poles apart, Lewis moved that the sessions be adjourned until after the union's scale and policy convention, scheduled to begin on October 1.[50]

Four days before the gathering, Lewis suffered an acute attack of appendicitis and underwent an operation at the Johns Hopkins Hospital in Baltimore, at least according to reports in the newspapers. Actually, Lewis may have suffered a coronary thrombosis, a fact that he wanted to hide to preserve his image of strength. Although Tom Kennedy publicly quipped that "the only thing Lewis ever lost has been his appendix," Jett Lauck recorded in his diary that the labor leader was actually in Emergency Hospital in Washington, where doctors kept him as quiet as possible and refused to allow him any visitors for several days.[51]

Whatever the case, the UMW scale and policy convention went all out to pay tribute to its recuperating leader. The delegates approved his birthday as a new holiday demand for the soft-coal industry and voted him and other officers another pay increase. Reports of these actions pleased Lewis as he lay in bed. Confined, with little to do, he perhaps pondered future victories.

On October 21, a still recuperating Lewis shocked the nation by demanding that Secretary of the Interior Krug negotiate a new contract with the union. He claimed the right to do so under the contract reopening provision of the 1945 accord, which he maintained had been carried forward into the Lewis-Krug agreement. Under this provision, either party could serve notice that it wanted talks resumed within ten days. After fifteen days of negotiations, the party could then inform its opposite that the contract would expire in five more days. If the other party refused to reopen talks, the contract was canceled.[52]

The announcement of Lewis's action set journalists and editorial writers to speculating on the meaning of this latest move. Was Lewis gluttonously seeking greater gains from the government, they asked, or was he pressuring the operators to come to terms with the union before the government granted the miners more concessions? Years of Lewis-watching had convinced reporters that hidden meaning lay behind the timing of this latest move. Some felt Lewis sought to embarrass Truman and the Democrats on the eve of the 1946 congressional elections. Others envisioned an attempt to steal Philip Murray's thunder by winning a sizable advance while the CIO held its convention. Almost all commentators concurred that Lewis hoped to execute whatever he planned before the adjourned Congress reconvened and passed pending antilabor legislation.

In responding to Lewis's letter, Krug and Coal Mines Administrator N. H. Collisson insisted that the agreement signed in May prevailed for as long as the government controlled the mines; and like the miners' chief, they pointed to a clause in the contract that seemed to justify their view. Although unwilling to reopen negotiations, they informed Lewis that they would meet with representatives of the UMW and discuss any problems that arose.[53]

As the days passed and the November 1 deadline neared, the president and others in the administration began to reconsider Krug and Collisson's initial replies. Around October 26, Attorney General Tom Clark reportedly presented to Truman an "informal" interpretation of the Lewis-Krug agreement, which upheld the UMW president's views. Secretary of Labor Schwellenbach and War Mobilization and Reconversion Director Dr. John R. Steelman both counseled the president to reopen negotiations. With Truman heeding this new advice, on October 27 Krug resentfully informed Lewis that his staff would meet with UMW representatives. Lewis accepted this as an acknowledgment of the validity of his interpretation of the existing contract.[54]

On November 1, Coal Mines Administrator Collisson and his associates assembled with a delegation from the UMW. Secretary Krug was in the West on an "inspection tour" of the type cabinet members frequently take before elections. Because only Interior Department underlings attended, Lewis sent his own lieutenants while he stayed behind in his office. Naturally, the ensuing sessions accomplished little until, on November 11, both Krug and Lewis appeared. Ready for business, Lewis spelled out a series of proposals calling for a reduction in hours, a sharp increase in hourly wage rates, a hike in the amount of the royalty paid into the welfare and retirement fund, recognition of the foremen's union, and other demands.[55]

While the Department of Interior's staff analyzed the union's demands, Krug mapped out a plan to thwart Lewis's challenge to government authority. In this effort he was, ironically, aided by the reverses suffered by the administration on Election Day, when the voters turned both houses of Congress over to Republican control. Disturbed by this setback, Truman began paying closer attention to General Counsel Clark Clifford and others who advised an aggressive stand against Lewis as a means of improving his prestige.[56]

By the evening of November 12, Krug had plotted his strategy. "The Government," he informed the president, "must now chose between two major alternatives: Reaching a new agreement with Lewis or forcing him into negotiations with the operators." Krug opposed the first course. "It would be uniformly interpreted in all quarters as another surrender to Lewis. It would be Government sponsorship of a second round of inflationary wage increases. . . . It would, finally, postpone for an indefinite period the time when the Government might get out of the coal business." The better approach, Krug recommended to the president, was to "accept perhaps an even chance of an immediate coal strike" and exert pressure on the union to negotiate with the operators. This course would avoid "the even greater disaster of a second Government-sponsored wage increase in the coal mines," and it would "put the Government in a position where it has an aggressive program rather than a numbed acquiescence in whatever Lewis should really insist upon."

The secretary's plan was first to gain the consent of the operators and then to inform Lewis that although the government would not negotiate, it would agree to return the coal mines within sixty days of the UMW's resumption of talks with the private operators. Krug recognized the strong possibility "that Lewis will refuse to accept the proposal, denounce it as a breach of faith, and declare the contract with me void." Nonetheless, he counseled Truman to accept this risk

> and trust to the coming of Christmas and a fear of the new Congress to make it a shorter strike than would otherwise be the case. I am advised by the Attorney General in this connection that the existing Krug-Lewis agreement is binding for the duration of Government possession and such a strike would be in violation of the contract. I believe, also, that Lewis would be in a thoroughly untenable public position if he struck against the Government simply because it insisted that he discuss his wage demands with the operators, and that we should exploit this by full public explanation, including a radio address by you (or by me, if you preferred) as well as press statements.[57]

On Wednesday, November 13, Krug began executing his scheme. That morning Lewis received a call from the secretary requesting a private meeting. He willingly agreed but insisted that first the joint negotiators should meet and hear the government's response to the union's proposals. When the negotiators gathered at midday, Krug announced that at a morning meeting with operators, they had indicated their willingness to resume contract talks with the union. Lewis became incensed, criticized the secretary for dealing with a party that had no standing under the prevailing agreement, and stormed back to his office without keeping the planned private conference with Krug. When tempers cooled and the two men finally met in the late afternoon, Lewis heard out the secretary on his sixty-day plan for bargaining between the union and the operators. At another session the following morning, Krug presented him with the proposal in writing. That afternoon Attorney General Clark provided Krug with a "formal" opinion upholding the secretary's stand that the Lewis-Krug agreement prevailed for as long as the government possessed the mines.[58]

Reportedly against the advice of his attorney Welly Hopkins and his brother Dennie, on the morning of November 15 Lewis rejected Krug's proposal. "You now, at the last hour, of the last day, yield to the blandishments and soothing siren voice of the operators and seek to place the United Mine Workers of America and its members between Scylla and Charybdis," he berated the secretary. In line with Krug's strategy, at 2:30 in the afternoon the president sought to mobilize public opinion with a press release describing Krug's proposal as "fair and equitable" and calling on the mine workers to reconsider their stand. Informed of this move, Lewis officially notified the Secretary of the Interior that in line with the UMW's interpretation of the contract reopening provision, the Lewis-Krug agreement would terminate at midnight November 20.[59]

While Lewis kept silent, Truman, Krug, Clark Clifford, and Tom Clark spent the next forty-eight hours plotting the government's next move. During their deliberations, they persistently referred to the events of 1919: the Anderson injunction, the citation of Lewis and his colleagues for contempt, and the UMW acting president's surrender with the declaration, "we cannot fight our Government." Finally, on the afternoon of November 17, a White House spokesman informed the press of Truman's orders to "fight John L. Lewis on all fronts." "It is not that the President is spoiling for a fight with Mr. Lewis," another source told reporters. "It is as simple as ABC's, however, that the Administration must find out sometime whether the power of Mr. Lewis is superior to that of the Federal Government."[60]

Administration officials moved quickly to dramatize the crisis. Although the nation possessed a reasonably substantial thirty-seven-day coal supply, the Solid Fuel Administration froze all bituminous coal in transit or storage, and the Office of Defense Transportation ordered railroads to curtail the use of coal. Amidst government forecasts of a critical coal crisis, Truman and his family journeyed to Key West, Florida, for a vacation. This gesture both communicated to the public the president's confidence that the situation was under control and implied that Lewis no longer rated the chief executive's personal attention. Over the next several days, Truman slept late, took prebreakfast swims, lounged in the sun, and conspicuously read Harold Lamb's *Alexander of Macedon*. "The President is a bear for battle tactics," an aide emphasized to reporters. Behind this front, Truman kept close watch over developments in Washington.[61]

On November 18, Judge T. Alan Goldsborough approved Attorney General Clark's application for a temporary injunction against the union and its officers. In essence, the injunction instructed Lewis and his staff to cease giving effect to the November 15 notice of termination of the Lewis-Krug agreement. Apparently Goldsborough agreed with Clark that given the union's no contract-no work policy, the notice constituted "in fact and in effect" a strike call.[62]

Lewis remained silent as the deadline established in the termination notice drew near. News of the injunction provoked 33,000 miners to strike prematurely, and when midnight, November 20, passed without word from UMW headquarters, the entire bituminous industry closed. "There was no excitement, no disorder, no picketing as the men streamed out of the pits into the icy darkness," A. H. Raskin noted.

In the nation at large, however, memories of the disruptive spring coal strike blended with administration projections of doom to generate a state of panic. After only one day of the walkout, even the normally restrained *New York Times* bore dramatic headlines: "25,000,000 MAY BE IDLE IF COAL STRIKE IS PROLONGED." Historians rose up in anger when a Washington bureaucrat announced plans to turn out the floodlights illuminating the Capitol dome. Despite the demands of the Civil War, the Committee on American History argued, Lincoln ordered construction on the dome continued so that it might one day stand as "a symbol of the continuity and permanence of the United States. And now," they asked, "are we going to darken it for John L. Lewis?"[63]

Perhaps realizing that he had gone too far, Lewis began searching for a way to avert a calamity. Apparently, he paid $16,000 to Henry W. "the Dutchman" Grunewald, an unsavory FBI agent turned private snoop, to probe into Judge Goldsborough's past and personal life. Lewis also sought the aid of Cleveland industrialist Cyrus Eaton and Harry Moses of Frick Coal in arranging some agreement with the operators whereby he could end the strike in a manner other than surrendering to the government. With the miners back at work, Averell Harriman and other Lewis friends might possibly convince the administration to drop any contempt charges against him or the union. Although Eaton gained the support of Edward Burke for a settlement, the maneuver collapsed in face of opposition from I. F. Frieberger, chairman of the board of the Cleveland Trust Company, which controlled James D. Francis's Island Creek and Pond Creek Pocahantas coal companies. Burke's willingness to save Lewis led the Southern Coal Operators' Association to force his resignation as spokesman for the group.[64]

On November 25, Lewis appeared in federal district court to show cause why he and the UMW should not be held in contempt of court. During the several days of hearings, he tried to project an image of confidence and good humor, but occasionally the mask fell, disclosing a tired, pale, and frustrated figure. Heading for lunch one day, he became vexed at a photographer trying to take a close-up and swung at him with the cane he usually twirled. Inside the courthouse, Lewis's legal staff contended that Goldsborough's injunction had no force because it violated the

Clayton and Norris-LaGuardia acts. But on December 3 Judge Goldsborough ruled Lewis and his union guilty of civil contempt of court. Sensing that imprisonment might make Lewis a martyr, the Justice Department requested that the criminal proceedings be dropped.[65]

Early the next morning, a dour Lewis accompanied by his legal retinue arrived at the courthouse. For an hour or two they moved from one conference room to another as Judge Goldsborough sought a formula that would bring peace to the coalfields. Finally, word arrived from the White House that the government would talk with Lewis only after the miners returned to work. Faced with a choice of surrender or defeat, Lewis chose the latter and marched into the courtroom, where the judge fined the UMW $3,500,000 and its president $10,000. Lewis's lawyers initiated an appeal to the Supreme Court.[66]

The nation now waited to see if the vanquished Lewis would yield and send the miners back to work. The pressures upon him were great. Each day the strike continued could cost the union an additional fine of $250,000. The president, moreover, had scheduled a news conference for Sunday evening. At 2:00 P.M., Saturday, December 7, Lewis summoned reporters and dramatically called off the strike. He was doing so, he informed the press, to protect the nation from a coal shortage and to enable the Supreme Court to consider his appeal free from pressure.[67]

Shortly thereafter Lewis vanished to "somewhere in Florida," where, until mid-February 1947, he nursed his ailing health and wounded pride. On March 6, the Supreme Court upheld the convictions of Lewis and the union. Desiring not to be excessively punitive, the justices reduced the UMW's fine to $700,000 but sustained the $10,000 penalty against Lewis. Pleading poverty, Lewis used union funds to pay his fine. On March 19, he obeyed the Supreme Court and officially withdrew his contract termination notice of November 15. At the same time, he raised the specter of a future strike.[68]

The defeat of Lewis and the UMW produced a sensation similar to the trouncing of a neighborhood bully. Whereas on December 2 the editors of *Time* had captioned the raging crisis a "Battle of Titans," two weeks later they mocked Lewis's capitulation as a petty drama starring "Horatius and the Great Ham." In Virginia, an emboldened state corporations commission grasped the moment to initiate legal proceedings against Lewis and the union for "selling" memberships without a permit and had a state process-server dramatically nail a summons on the door of his Alexandria home. Even the "Possum Club" of Polk County, Arkansas, joined in the taunting by crating up and shipping Lewis the ugliest and scrawniest critter they could find.[69]

The outcome of the coal crisis provided the Truman administration the boost it desperately needed. As Truman's first major domestic triumph, the coal victory restored, in the words of Robert Allen and William Shannon, "a dash of vigor to the flabby spiritual tone of the executive office.'' It also marked Truman's emergence from the shadow of Roosevelt. ''There was a big difference in the Old Man from then on,'' Clark Clifford recalled. ''He was his own man at last.''[70]

The significance of the coal crisis transcended the humiliation of Lewis or the restoration of Truman's prestige. At times obscured by the dynamics of personalities and the maneuvering for advantage, the crisis focused on the power of the federal government over a private institution. Truman and Krug contended that the government could compel the UMW to negotiate a contract with the operators who, after the mines were seized, lacked any legal standing in the industry. Lewis repudiated such federal authority and insisted that the only time the union could be compelled to deal with the operators was when the government returned the mines to their private owners. He also asserted that when the government seized property and entered into an agreement with the workers, it could not then subsequently amend that agreement under the cloak of sovereignty. In issuing his injunction, Judge Goldsborough gave implicit sanction to Truman's rejection of Lewis's argument. The resulting contempt hearings—centering on the question of whether Lewis and the union violated a valid injunction—merely skirted the larger issue of the government's power in dealings with private organizations. Like so many developments in the realm of governmental authority, this issue was settled by political power rather than judicial decision.

CHAPTER 20
Opposed on All Fronts, 1947-1950

Lewis's conviction for contempt in the fall of 1946 brought into full public view the feud between the UMW chief and the Truman administration. For the next several years, the nation listened as the protagonists hurled undignified insults at one another. The president personally labeled Lewis a "headline hunter," and when someone jestfully suggested that he appoint the labor leader ambassador to Moscow, Truman publicly quipped that he would not make that man chief dogcatcher of this country.[1] Lewis, in turn, pronounced Truman "totally unfitted" for the presidency. "His principles are elastic and he is careless with the truth," the labor leader snarled. "He has no special knowledge on any subject. And he is a malignant, scheming sort of an individual who is not only dangerous to the United Mine Workers of America but dangerous to the United States."[2]

Although the conflict between the UMW and the administration flowed inevitably from substantial disagreements over reconversion policy, responsibility for transforming economic differences into ad hominem personal attacks falls primarily upon the White House. Truman's animosity toward the miners' chief ran deep, because of a temperamental inclination to treat challenges to his administration as personal affronts. Yet although his contempt for Lewis may have been impulsive, his actual exchanges with the UMW head betrayed calculation. After the Democrats' setback in the congressional elections of 1946, Truman recognized that he had to attract voters away from the increasingly antiunion Republicans while keeping the bulk of organized labor in his camp. In such a situation, Lewis served Truman's purposes. The labor leader had been damned since 1943 by much of the press and the populace; classified publicly as a Republican (although many GOP politicos fought him tooth-and-nail); and held in suspicion and contempt by numerous other labor leaders. By assailing Lewis, Truman intended to placate those threatened by union power without unduly antagonizing his important labor backers.[3]

The Truman-Lewis feud differed considerably in tone and style from the previous Roosevelt-Lewis quarrel. Although FDR had harshly vilified Lewis in private, he had muted his public criticisms of the miners' chief. With proper presidential obliqueness, Roosevelt seldom, if ever, publicly condemned Lewis by name. Truman lacked equal sensitivity to the dignity of the presidency and joyfully engaged in insults. During the 1948 presidential campaign, Attorney General Tom Clark joined Truman in one crowd-pleasing put-down of the miners' chief. In introducing the president to a Dallas audience, Clark referred to Truman as the man who brought the law down on Joe Louis. "You gave me too much credit, Tom," the folksy Missourian replied. "It wasn't Joe, it was John Lewis that I stopped in the Federal Courts."[4]

In truth, Lewis respected the office of the chief executive far more than did its occupant, and in responding to Truman's attacks he either worded his rejoinder so as to separate the man from the office or directed his fire at some other members of the administration. In rebuttal to Truman's quip that he would not make Lewis national dogcatcher, for instance, the labor leader more civilly replied: "The President could ill afford to have more brains in the Dog Department than in the Department of State, and from this standpoint, his remarks to you are eminently justified."[5]

Although exchanges between Truman and Lewis filled the headlines, Lewis actually considered Secretary of the Interior Julius A. Krug the administration villain. This animosity derived in part from Krug's role in the UMW's 1946 conviction for contempt of court. But it also stemmed from Lewis's belief that the secretary was insensitive to the miners' welfare and unconcerned with the health of the coal industry. In the spring of 1947, Lewis seized upon the Centralia disaster as a means of publicly dramatizing his case against Krug.

The Secretary of the Interior still controlled the nation's bituminous mines when, on March 25, 1947, an explosion at the No. 5 colliery of the Centralia Coal Company in Illinois killed 111 men. Twice in the previous six months federal inspectors had visited the mine and had found it in violation of the Federal Mine Safety Code. On their last visit, occurring but five days before the explosion, they had noted roughly fifty code violations, including inadequate rock dusting and ventilation—both important causes of mine explosions. Although the Lewis-Krug agreement provided that the Secretary of the Interior "or his representative shall take immediate action to cause all employees to be removed from the unsafe area until any imminent and serious danger is removed," this was not done. Nor did the local union's safety committee exercise its right to urge various officials to close the pit.[6]

In the aftermath of the Centralia tragedy, Lewis called a week-long work stoppage as a memorial to the victims. Apparently prodded by this move, a House of Representatives subcommittee initiated hearings on the catastrophe, which Lewis attended on April 3. In his testimony, Lewis expounded upon both the inadequacies of prevailing laws and the failure of government agencies to execute their responsibilities even when they possessed authority. Of the 3,345 mines inspected in 1946, he related, only two fully complied with the safety code. Moreover, the 1,723 mines inspected during the period of government seizure averaged twenty-seven violations each. Lewis used such data to initiate a vindictive attack on Secretary Krug, to whom he assigned major responsibility for the disaster. He harped on the fact that the UMW's agreement with Krug made him "the exclusive agency" charged with enforcing the Federal Mine Safety Code and correcting all violations. The dead bodies at Centralia, Lewis stressed, proved that the secretary had failed to meet this moral and legal duty. Accusing Krug of "criminal negligence," Lewis called for his removal from office.[7]

Lewis's charges against Krug were exaggerated, but their spirit was not completely erroneous. Although the number of mining fatalities declined during the government's operation of the collieries, Krug did not attempt fully to enforce the safety provisions of the Lewis-Krug agreement. To do so would have meant at least the temporary shutdown of much of the industry. After the Centralia disaster, moreover, the secretary behaved like a professional bureaucrat. In one self-serving act, he sought to undermine Lewis by choosing the moment when the union leader was testifying before the congressional subcommittee to order 518 mines closed until made safe. His remarks at the cabinet meeting the next day centered on ways to thwart Lewis's accusations rather than the actual disaster or the need for better mine safety legislation. If Lewis distorted reality when he blamed the secretary, Krug proved equally opportunistic when he denied all responsibility and instead criticized the men who died for working in an unsafe mine.[8]

Lewis's denunciation of Krug over the Centralia tragedy coincided with a battle between the two men over the directorship of the Bureau of Mines. Two weeks before the tragedy the secretary had convinced Truman to nominate for the post Dr. James Boyd, dean of the Colorado School of Mines. Boyd's background in metal mining suited the administration's concern with developing stockpiles of vital minerals. Yet Congress had also charged the bureau with promoting the coal industry and protecting miners' lives. Because the special nature of bituminous mining made it more hazardous than other types of underground digging, some knowledge of the industry seemed desirable on a director's part. Until his nomination, however, Boyd had never ventured down a coal shaft. This fact alone would have warranted Lewis's opposition to Boyd's selection, but Krug added insult to injury by failing to follow the customary form of soliciting the UMW president's advice.[9]

With the public's conscience pricked by the dead at Centralia and Lewis exercising what political clout remained to him, the Senate recessed in July 1947 without acting on Boyd's nomination. During the break, Truman appointed Boyd interim director in the belief that the Senate would approve the nomination once it reconvened. Yet for another year and a half Lewis mobilized enough political support to stall confirmation. In this campaign he received the quiet assistance of Undersecretary of the Interior Oscar Chapman, who aspired to Krug's post and kept Lewis's friend Josephine Roche informed of the secretary's moves. As a result of the stalemate in the Senate, Truman cooled to the nomination in late 1948 and tried to convince Boyd to accept an appointment as an atomic energy commissioner. Both the nominee and his backer, however, wanted to fight Lewis to the finish. In lobbying for Boyd, Krug promised senators the beneficences of the Interior Department in return for their support, and in an incident probably related, Department of the Interior officials dismissed Lewis's brother-in-law, C. Herbert Bell, from his post as head of the Bureau of Mines' fuel requirement unit. In the end Krug won, for on March 22, 1949, the Senate finally confirmed Boyd. Lewis dramatized his defeat by calling a two-week memorial stoppage, which also served a second purpose of reducing the extensive coal supply then above ground.[10]

At the same time he was jousting with Fair Dealers in the White House, Lewis vied with conservatives in Congress. Since the formative days of the CIO, Republicans and southern Democrats had united to seek stringent regulation of organized labor. In this campaign, they pointed to John L. Lewis as the personification of the evils they wished to extirpate, and when the miners struck in 1943, they capitalized on public anxiety to pass the Smith-Connally act. In the reconversion era, the conservatives vowed to replace this ill-conceived measure with new legislation. The UMW's battle with the government in late 1946 in conjunction with the most massive strike wave in United States history stimulated public support behind their antiunion drive.

Lewis viewed the cry for revised labor legislation as part of the nation's unhealthy drift toward government bureaucratization in its search for stability. The central issue, he lectured senators in a statement redolent of Samuel Gompers, was whether the country ought "to trade liberty for security." "Certainly," he scolded, "when industry and finance in this country call upon legislative instrumentalities of the government to enact laws to restrain labor and neutralize its strength, they are guilty of the first step toward creating a corporate or absolute state. In the end, the activities of all citizens would be regulated and a regimentation of all groups would be necessary to a maximum degree."[11]

During the fall of 1946, Lewis intended to dilute the antilabor trend by throwing his union's backing behind congressional candidates opposed to new legislation, himself personally campaigning for Burton K. Wheeler. The defeat of the Montana senator, as well as a number of other prounion politicians, alerted Lewis to labor's impending legislative fate.

As could have been expected, Lewis first maneuvered to protect the UMW against any adverse legislation. With the government's authority to manage the collieries expiring on June 30, 1947, the coal mine administrator summoned all parties to private contract bargaining beginning on April 29. Lewis treated these negotiations both as an opportunity to demonstrate the superiority of free collective bargaining over government intervention and as a chance to write into the contract clauses circumventing some of the restrictions on unionism being considered by Congress. Throughout May and early June, Lewis acted in conciliatory fashion, presenting the operators with "proposals" rather than "demands." All the while he delayed serious bargaining until he was certain of the fate of the Taft-Hartley bill. The boom prosperity of the coal industry put most operators in a generally cooperative mood, for they realized their bonanza would end if the miners struck once the government relinquished the mines. Finally, after Congress passed the Taft-Hartley act over Truman's veto, on June 23, Lewis started conferring privately with Benjamin Fairless of U.S. Steel and George M. Humphrey of Hanna Coal and the National Steel Corporation, both of whom wished to avoid a coal strike, which would disrupt their iron and steel interests. After a few days, Charles O'Neill and Harry Moses of the operators' conference joined them, and out of these talks evolved a new national agreement, which all segments of the industry approved by mid-July.[12]

The 1947 contract represented a solid achievement for both the miners and the union. The wage, hour, and fringe benefit costs of the agreement averaged out to an increase per man of $3.00 a day, raising the basic daily wage to $13.05. The agreement also reduced the standard workday from nine to eight hours and lengthened the paid lunch period to half an hour. Most important, the operators agreed to establish a welfare and retirement fund comparable to the one created by the Lewis-Krug agreement.

In addition to providing improved physical benefits for the workers, the contract contained provisions designed to protect the union from the Taft-Hartley law. With astute timing, Lewis had negotiated the agreement subsequent to the enactment of the Taft-Hartley bill but prior to the effective date of certain of its sections. This would enable him, he hoped, to place in the contract conditions that, if executed a few days later, would have been illegal. As a move to prevent civil suits against the union for unauthorized work stoppages as mandated by the Taft-Hartley act, the new coal agreement was to apply to miners only "during such time as such persons are willing and able to work." The contract also stipulated the negotiators of the next agreement in an attempt to avert the provisions of the new law that made it an unfair labor practice for a union to interfere with an employer's choice of a collective bargaining representative. Likewise, a clause found in earlier contracts imposing penalties on the union for wildcat strikes was omitted from the new document out of concern that Taft-Hartley would weaken the UMW leadership's ability to exert discipline over the rank and file.[13]

The achievement of a new coal contract enabled Lewis to direct his energies toward undermining that "despotic, damnable, reprehensible, unwholesome, vicious slave statute," the Taft-Hartley act. For several years he would be among the most outspoken foes of the measure, just as the law would be used most effectively against Lewis and his union. Unlike other labor leaders who privately preferred to amend the statute's more reprehensible features, Lewis was commited to repeal of the act.

Perhaps intoxicated by his own reputation as a strategist, Lewis believed he had found a tactic to debilitate the law. The act required labor officials to file affidavits affirming that they were not members of the Communist party or of any organization supporting it in order for their unions to utilize the services of the National Labor Relations Board. Lewis's strategy called for labor leaders collectively to refuse to file the requested affidavit and to forego the blessings of the NLRB. He recognized that this scheme would not abolish Taft-Hartley, and he realized that many smaller unions might suffer without NLRB support. But he maintained that it was ideologically inconsistent for the labor movement to oppose the measure while union leaders executed optional action under the law so that their organizations could receive the act's benefits. He also felt that by forcing the NLRB into a position where it served only the employers, "the sense of fair play of the American people" would be aroused, and they would demand Taft-Hartley's repeal.[14]

When the NLRB ruled, in the fall of 1947, that all officers of the A.F. of L. had to file anti-Communist affidavits for the organization's federal locals to enjoy the privileges of the board, Lewis—one of the fifteen vice-presidents—refused to comply. To circumvent his refusal, the other officers proposed an amendment to the Federation's constitution that technically demoted the vice-presidents to the status of council members and reclassified the president and secretary-treasurer as the sole officials of the organization.

When the proposed amendment came before the October 1947 A. F. of L. convention, Lewis subjected it to some of his finest oratory. " 'Thou shalt not muzzle the ox that treadeth out the corn'," he preached:

> So runs the Scripture.
> But the Congress of the United States designated 15,000,000 workers in this country, organized into one form or another of unions, as being cattle that treadeth out the economic corn of our country, and the Congress placed an economic muzzle on each of you. What are you going to do about it? Oh, I see. You are going to change our Constitution. God help us!

For the next half hour Lewis treated the delegates to a scorching diatribe against the Taft-Hartley act—"the first ugly, savage thrust of Fascism in America"—and the failure of the A. F. of L. leaders to do their duty to the membership. "I am reminded of the Biblical parable," he intoned, "Lions led by asses." He condemned the proposed amendment as a subterfuge because all persons involved recognized that the council members would still exercise power. "You know," he snapped, "to me that smacks of the Communist technique, to lie to escape responsibility." At the conclusion of his speech he refused to be a candidate for the "debased" board if the delegates approved the amendment.

> Perhaps that makes no difference; perhaps you will say "John Lewis is trying to hold a gun to the head of the convention."
> That is not true. I don't think anyone can hold a gun to the head of this conven-

tion. . . . As far as that is concerned, on this particular issue, I don't think that the Federation has a head. I think its neck has just grown up and haired over.[15]

Lewis's parting sarcasm amounted to an admission that he had failed to sway the delegates, who promptly passed the amendment. True to his word, Lewis declined to be a member of the reconstituted council, and, indeed, he resolved that the time had arrived for the UMW again to depart from the Federation. On October 21, he issued an executive memorandum instructing all district and international officers to refrain from making any more dues payments to the A. F. of L. or its affiliated state units. No doubt the UMW would have quickly separated from the Federation had Lewis not been hospitalized in San Francisco for two weeks following the convention. Although the newspapers claimed he was only undergoing a checkup and enjoying a rest, the death of UMW vice-president John O'Leary on October 27 undoubtedly combined with the tensions of the A. F. of L. convention to shake Lewis's aging frame and weakened heart. As it was, six weeks passed before Lewis consulted with his executive board on December 12, after which he scribbled in pencil a memo to the Federation's president:

> Green, AFL
> We disaffiliate
> Lewis [16]

The failure of the Federation to follow Lewis in his grand design was the most prominent, but not the sole, reason for the UMW's departure. In discussing the situation with his executive board, Lewis complained of the political fund set up by the Federation to finance a campaign against supporters of the Taft-Hartley act. It troubled him that the miners would be assessed $600,000 but would have no control over the fund's use. He also smarted at the antipathy George Meany, Daniel Tobin, and some of the other Federation leaders had displayed toward him and his union. Finally, Lewis believed that a number of A. F. of L. affiliates planned to utilize the Taft-Hartley act to dismantle District 50 and the United Construction Workers. "It adds up to this," he maintained, "that in my judgment it is futile for us to attempt to exercise at this present time any further effective influence in the American Federation of Labor."[17]

Lewis's fight to repeal the Taft-Hartley act persisted after the miners left the A. F. of L. In the elections of 1948, he directed the UMW's opposition to legislators who had voted for the measure, and in 1950 he worked hard to thwart Ohio Senator Robert Taft's bid for reelection. As a result of the UMW's 1948 campaign, forty-one congressmen and six senators residing in coal mining areas who had supported the Taft-Hartley bill were defeated for reelection, and in 1950 two of the four Ohio counties lost by Senator Taft were heavily populated by UMW members. The series of defeats that the UMW experienced in the late 1940s and early 1950s reinforced the aging labor leader's ideological disposition against federal action and led him to recommend to a Senate committe in 1953 the repeal not only of the Taft-Hartley law but of the Wagner Act as well. "This would give to this country, its employers and employees," he argued, "an opportunity (in light of our joint experiences under both Wagner and Taft-Hartley) to practice for a season true, free and genuine collective bargaining without government interference, free from the brooding shadows which presently hover over all bargaining tables."[18] As Samuel Gompers four decades earlier had opposed state intervention because he feared that government favored employers, Lewis by the 1940s was convinced that another historical cycle had begun: that the federal government which had stimulated trade unionism during the 1930s now preferred to protect corporate interests.

By 1948, Lewis and the UMW confronted opposition on all fronts. Press and public opinion clearly aligned against them, with story after story portraying Lewis as a national ogre. The labor leader's relations with the Truman administration, moreover, had soured so badly that he lacked even meaningful influence with the Bureau of Mines, an agency important to the union's day-to-day business. A conservative Congress, through the Taft-Hartley act, sought to paralyze militant unionism as represented by the UMW. And Lewis's and the union's conviction for contempt in 1946 seemed to indicate to them that the courts were willing to help Congress in its drive. Even the A. F. of L., after the 1947 convention, joined the CIO in criticisms of Lewis. Naturally, the coal operators utilized prevailing sentiment in resisting the miners' demands.

In the spring of 1948, another in the decade-long series of labor-management crises erupted in the coal industry. This dispute and the others that followed over the next two years were vividly colored by the Truman-Lewis feud and the efforts of operators and government officials to apply the Taft-Hartley act to the UMW. Yet although frequently obfuscated by clashes of personalities and assertions of legal rights, monetary issues were at the core of these disputes, with the fate and scope of the welfare and retirement fund the primary source of contention.

In 1946, the operators' opposition to a welfare fund had caused a strike, which precipitated the government's seizure of the mines. The subsequent Lewis-Krug agreement established a welfare and retirement system for the period that Washington controlled the collieries. When it came time, in 1947, for the mines to revert to their private owners, the operators found themselves unable to repudiate a program that the government had apparently legitimated, and so they begrudgingly agreed to a welfare fund. At the time, they preferred to negotiate the details of the program at the bargaining table, for they feared that if they delegated the task to the fund's trustees, Lewis would successfully impose obligations that would compel operators to increase the amount of their contributions. Yet rather than force a confrontation and strike during a time of high profits, the industry's negotiators yielded to Lewis. Nonetheless, they still planned to restrict the scope of the fund through litigation under the Taft-Hartley act, by congressional legislation to regulate such programs, and by encouraging their trustee to act obstinately in conducting the fund's business.

For months the three trustees—Ezra Van Horn for the operators, Lewis for the union, and Thomas E. Murray as the neutral member—failed to agree on a program to activate the fund. Lewis proposed one plan that would provide all miners with twenty years of service at age sixty with an annuity of $1,200, but both Murray and Van Horn rejected it as actuarially unsound. Van Horn also contended that although Lewis's plan made all union members eligible for benefits, the Taft-Hartley act limited eligibility to the employees of firms actually under contract. In an effort to develop an acceptable program, Murray proposed that $20 million of the fund be allocated to providing pensions of $1,200 yearly on a priority basis to miners who retired at age sixty or more after July 1, 1942, with twenty years' service. This formula pleased neither Lewis nor Van Horn, the former because he felt all elderly miners meeting the service requirement should receive pensions, the latter because he felt the scheme violated the Taft-Hartley act. Van Horn never proposed a plan of his own, which gave some credence to Lewis's charge that he was practicing obstructionism.[19]

On January 16, 1948, after seven months of stalemate, Murray threw the fund into a crisis by resigning his trusteeship. Neither Lewis nor Van Horn was about to approve a new neutral trustee if any likelihood existed that the person would support the other side on the pension issue. Yet without a third trustee, Van Horn needed only to sit tight to paralyze the welfare and retirement program. The UMW would then be forced to negotiate the details of the fund as part of the next wage agreement.

Lewis, seeking to break the chains in which he seemed bound, wrote Benjamin Fairless and George Humphrey asking them to help settle the pension dispute. Lewis clearly intended to compel Fairless and Humphrey publicly to admit their central position in the coal industry. Both men recognized Lewis's objective and rejected his overture with the argument that they lacked authority. Thwarted on this front, Lewis next resorted to veiled threats by warning all signatories to the 1947 agreement that the UMW "reserves the right at will to take any independent action necessary to the enforcement of the contract."[20]

Over a month passed, during which the operators made no gestures toward activating the fund. Angered at their intransigence and determined not to allow the issue to go before the next wage conference, Lewis circularized the union's membership on Friday, March 12. "For eight months," he asserted, "the Bituminous Coal Operators, through their trustee . . . have dishonored the 1947 Wage Agreement and defaulted under its provisions affecting the Welfare Fund." The remainder of the circular consisted of diatribes against the Taft-Hartley act and the employers' greed, with Lewis implying that the UMW would take action to force the operators "to honor their agreement." When a reporter asked Lewis if his comments alluded to a strike, he dismissed the question as being "more or less hypothetical."[21]

To miners wanting the benefits of the welfare and retirement fund, Lewis's choice of the words "dishonored" and "defaulted" carried more than hypothetical implications. On Sunday, March 14, 200,000 miners commenced an "unofficial" strike, which by Tuesday closed a substantial portion of the bituminous coal industry. Lewis insisted that the Taft-Hartley act was inapplicable in this situation, because he had not ordered the strike and the law guaranteed the right of individuals to act on their own. He also contended that the walkout did not violate the union's 1947 contract, because the document clearly stipulated that its provisions applied to the miners only when they were "willing and able" to work.[22]

Both the mine owners and the government required a few days to respond to the shutdown. On March 20, trustee Ezra Van Horn, in the first of several trips to the courthouse, requested the bench to intervene in the dispute by appointing the third, neutral trustee.[23] On that same day, Cyrus S. Ching, director of the Federal Mediation and Conciliation Service, requested a meeting with representatives of the operators and the union for Monday, March 22. Lewis interpreted Ching's act as a perfunctory move required by law before the administration could act under Taft-Hartley. Moreover, he viewed the composition of the proposed meeting as supporting the operators' fantasy that no central figures, such as Fairless or Humphrey, spoke with finality on coal industry policy.[24]

Probably to ward off adverse public criticism, Lewis nonetheless sent a delegation of lesser UMW officials to confer with Ching and the operators. At the gathering, the conciliation chief proposed that the miners resume work while a fact-finding board studied the controversy. As could have been expected, the UMW delegation rejected Ching's "grotesque offer" because it called for a resumption of production before the grievance was settled.[25]

Within hours after Ching's mediation efforts collapsed, President Truman created a board of inquiry to determine whether the coal crisis warranted an eighty-day Taft-Hartley injunction. Truman appointed to the board Dr. George W. Taylor, professor at the University of Pennsylvania and a former member of the War Labor Board; Mark Ethridge, publisher of the Louisville *Courier-Journal* and *Times* and a troubleshooter for the United Nations; and, as chairman, Judge Sherman Minton, former senator from Indiana and a close friend of Truman.

Setting to their task with determined swiftness, the three men wired Lewis on the morning of their first day of business, Friday, March 26, and requested his testimony that afternoon. Lewis received the telegram ten minutes before they had scheduled him to appear. Annoyed, he informed the board that he needed the weekend to consider all the legal questions involved, including whether he had to testify.

After pondering the issue Saturday and Sunday, Lewis stayed away from the board's Monday morning meeting and instead sent Chairman Minton a blistering letter:

Sir:

My disinclination to attend falls substantially into two categories:

1. *The Law*:

No action has been taken by this writer or the United Mine Workers of America, as such, which would fall within the purview of the oppressive statute under which you seek to function. Without indulging in analysis, it is a logical assumption that the cavilings of the Bar and Bench in their attempts to explicate this infamous enactment will consume a tedious time.

2. *Prejudice*:

Two members of your Board are biased and prejudiced and in honor should not serve. They are Ethridge and Taylor. Since the inception of this imbroglio, Ethridge has published biased and prejudicial editorials and special articles deleterious to this union and this writer in a newspaper controlled by him.

Taylor for years has been an Administrative hangeron in Washington, and he has never lost an opportunity to harass and persecute this Union and this writer. He is inherently incapable of determining the distinction between a fact and scruple.

In attendance is Ching, a truly remarkable man, who sees through the eyes of United States Rubber.[26]

Upon receiving Lewis's letter, Minton subpoenaed the UMW leader to appear before the board at 2:00 that afternoon. Despite Minton's warning of "fail not at your peril," Lewis refused to show. That night federal marshalls appeared at Lewis's home in Alexandria and ordered him to explain in court the next morning why he had ignored Minton's summons. At the Tuesday court session, the judge overruled Lewis's arguments and directed him to testify before the board that afternoon.

Recognizing the futility of further resistance, Lewis made the requisite appearance. In his testimony, offered "under the compulsion of a court order," he criticized the "mentally bound die-hards" among the operators, including "no plan Van." He also rejected responsibility for the walkout that followed his March 12 circular. His testimony consumed only thirty minutes and contained nothing not already known by the board.[27]

On Wednesday, March 31, the board of inquiry submitted its report to Truman. In it, the board exploited all the weak points in Lewis's position while neglecting his charges against the operators. The report failed to mention, for instance, that in an eight-month period Van Horn had failed to propose any pension plan to the other trustees. On the crucial point of whether the dispute came under the provisions of the Taft-Hartley act, the board members found in the affirmative. "The stoppage of work," they concluded, "followed so closely upon the receipt of the letter [of March 12 from Lewis to the membership] as to constitute cause and effect. This was more than a coincidence."[28]

After considering the report for two days, on April 3 Truman instructed Attorney General Tom C. Clark to seek an injunction under the Taft-Hartley act. Clark went immediately to Judge Matthew F. McGuire, who ordered Lewis to "instruct forthwith" the idle soft-coal miners to return to work. In a second injunction, the judge also directed the UMW to resume negotiatons with the operators on the pension issue.[29]

The injunctions placed Lewis in a delicate position. To recognize them as valid would weaken his legal challenge to the Taft-Hartley act (as well as relieve the pressures on the operators to seek a settlement). Yet he knew that to ignore the orders would result in the union and himself being convicted of criminal and civil contempt of court. In an effort to escape this predicament, on April 3 he again circularized the union membership. For the most part, his message chronicled the events in the dispute, although it did not mention the injunctions issued that morning. Throughout, Lewis advanced the argument that because he had not officially called the strike, he lacked the authority to terminate it. "I . . . now repeat," he closed, "that you are not now under, and have never been under, any orders, directions or suggestions, expressed or implied, from me or any of the union officers to cease work or to continue to cease work in protest to the present dishonoring (as we see it) of the 1947 Contract."[30]

As could have been expected, the coal miners did not return to work, nor did the Truman administration view Lewis's circular as compliance with the injunctions. On Wednesday, April 7, Judge T. Alan Goldsborough, acting on a petition from the attorney general, ordered Lewis and the United Mine Workers to show cause on the following Monday why they should not be found in contempt for failing to call off the strike.

Fears of a repeat of 1946 now mounted for Lewis, as he searched for a way to avert the impending verdict. To fulfill Judge McGuire's second order, he delegated a squad of lieutenants to bargain with the operators. Meanwhile, he spent the weekend struggling to extricate himself from his legal predicament by playing presidential primary politics.

Lewis reportedly utilized the good offices of Alf M. Landon to contact the speaker of the House of Representatives, Joseph W. Martin, about arranging a settlement to the coal dispute. Martin hoped to win the 1948 Republican presidential nomination as a compromise candidate, and apparently he envisioned settling the coal crisis as a coup that would give him national recognition. The exact details of the negotiations among Martin, Lewis, and possibly Van Horn are unclear, although it seems that some planning occurred before the fund's two trustees dramatically entered the speaker's Capitol Hill office on Saturday afternoon. Thirteen minutes later, the three men emerged to announce to waiting newsmen that both Lewis and Van Horn had accepted Martin's suggestion of New Hampshire Senator Styles Bridges as the fund's new neutral trustee.[31]

On Monday morning the trustees approved a "tentative" solution, which Bridges proposed for the pension crisis. The senator and Lewis voted for the plan, although Van Horn rejected it. "The Mine Workers," Lewis noted "understand that the coal operators are still against the pensions." Bridges's compromise supported Lewis over Van Horn on the issue of eligibility, but it was far less generous in its benefits than Lewis had desired. Under the plan, an annuity of $1,200 would go to "those members of the UMWA who attain the age of 62 years and complete 20 years in the coal industry on or after May 29, 1946." Clearly the older members of the union would have been better off had Lewis accepted Thomas E. Murray's proposal, offered months earlier, which established July 1, 1942, as the eligibility date. True to form, however, Lewis announced the settlement as a glorious union victory and wired all bituminous locals: "Pensions granted. The agreement is now honored." Lewis then set off for court to answer to the contempt charges.[32]

Judge Goldsborough proved unresponsive to the argument that Lewis and the union had purged themselves of the contempt charges by settling the pension dispute that morning, and he ordered the accused to stand trial. After several days of proceedings, a "gray and grimvisaged" Lewis listened as the judge ruled the UMW and its president guilty. On April 20, Goldsborough fined the union $1,500,000 and Lewis $20,000—double the penalty imposed on them in 1946. Seeking to avert further court action, Lewis wired all bituminous district presidents instructions to "convey to each member my wish that they immediately return to work." This gesture still did not satisfy Judge Goldsborough, who granted the government's petition for an eighty-day injunction despite the union's insistence that the dispute had been settled.[33]

To the contrary, the pension fight continued. At the very moment that Judge Goldsborough was issuing the eighty-day injunction, Ezra Van Horn was in another courtroom filing a petition to suspend the Bridges pension plan until the courts determined its validity. Then, a week later, while a judge considered Van Horn's request, Lewis and Bridges voted to activate the fund and named the miners' leader as administrator and his friend Josephine Roche as director. To nullify this action, Van Horn notified all banks serving as depositories for the fund that the removal of monies without his signature would be at their risk. Again, Lewis saw his goals frustrated. At this point, the pension issue became inextricably involved with the 1948 contract negotiations.[34]

In passing, it should be noted that Speaker Martin's role in the dispute actually hurt his presidential chances. His opponents, with the aid of some blundering remarks by the speaker himself, easily argued that a man who would deal with Lewis should not be trusted around Stalin or the devil.[35] It should also be noted that observers were initially baffled by conservative Senator Bridges's close collaboration with Lewis during his tenure as a trustee. In the nine meetings he attended prior to August 1949, the senator voted on twenty-eight disagreements between Van Horn and Lewis and sided with the miners' chief on each one. No doubt part of the reason for such a meeting of minds derived from Lewis's support of a yearly salary of $35,000 to the fund's public and management trustees. In 1948, Bridges received an additional $12,000 for some mysterious legal advice. Naturally, Lewis refused any recompense for his own work as a trustee.[36]

*   *   *

On April 30, less than two weeks after the six-week pension strike ended, Lewis notified the bituminous operators that the 1948 contract talks would begin on May 18. This action permitted him legally to call a strike at the expiration of the 1947 contract on June 30. Indeed, the probability of a work stoppage seemed high, for this would be the first agreement written since the Taft-Hartley act went into force and the operators wanted to restrain the union. Moreover, the contentious pension issue remained unsettled.

Even before the wage conference began, the union and the operators fought over the role of the Southern Coal Producers' Association in the coming talks. In negotiating the 1947 contract Lewis had insisted on a clause making the signatories of that agreement the conferees for negotiating the next. By this move he sought to exclude the SCPA from further contract talks, because it did not sign the 1947 agreement, although its members did.

In the weeks prior to the 1948 talks, all the constituent members of the southern association informed Lewis that they now wished the SCPA to represent them. He replied to each that this was not permissible under the prevailing agreement. Nonetheless, the southerners insisted, and when the conference began on May 18, the parties adjourned the session abruptly rather than debate the SCPA issue. On the next day the conference collapsed outright when the UMW refused to seat the SCPA and the operators refused to negotiate without it.[37]

The southerners promptly appealed to the NLRB's general counsel to initiate legal action against Lewis and his union. In turn, the counsel petitioned Judge Goldsborough for a temporary injunction requiring the union to bargain with the southern association while the board considered the case. On June 4, when Goldsborough signed the injunction, he also lectured Lewis on his misuses of power, flinging at him one of Cicero's orations: "It is your boundless audacity, O Catiline."[38]

On Monday, June 7, the 1948 national wage conference began anew, with the SCPA in attendance and Lewis moaning about being there "only through duress." He now insisted that the operators "honor" the welfare and pension provisions of the 1947 contract as a "condition precedent" to a new agreement. Under pressure, the operators finally offered a pension plan, but its terms were clearly unacceptable to the union. For a week the talks rambled on. Then, on June 15, the northern and western operators declared the sessions "futile" and walked out of the conference.[39]

Within hours, Federal Mediation and Conciliation Director Ching requested both sides to meet with him the next day, as the administration began to move through the steps for an eighty-day injunction. By June 19, Ching had referred the deadlock to Truman, who proceeded to name a board of inquiry to investigate the dispute. The nation tensed for another showdown between Lewis and the courts.

Then, the unexpected happened. On June 22, Justice Goldsborough upheld the legality of Bridges's pension plan and dismissed the suit filed by Trustee Van Horn. In his decision, Goldsborough concurred with Lewis that all members of the union could be covered by the fund and not just employees of the signatories of the 1947 contract. He also supported Lewis's contention that the business of the fund required only a majority vote of the trustees. Goldsborough's ruling undermined the operators' case against the fund, leading them promptly to seek a truce. Within forty-eight hours the commercial operators and the union agreed on a new contract granting the miners a dollar-a-day increase and doubling to twenty cents the operators' payments to the welfare and retirement fund.[40]

Only the captive mine operators refused to concur in the new contract. They contended that signing would place them in violation of the Taft-Hartley act because the agreement contained a union-shop provision. According to the law, they pointed out, a majority of the workers had to approve the union shop in an election supervised by the NLRB. The rub was that Lewis could not request an NLRB election, because he had refused to file a non-Communist affidavit. This stalemate caused a week-long shutdown in mid-July, until Goldsborough developed a compromise to prevail while the NLRB considered the case.[41]

For eight months, labor-management strife in the coalfields subsided. The board of inquiry appointed by Truman declared the 1948 contract dispute settled and adjourned. During the summer, Josephine Roche assembled an administrative staff for the welfare and retirement fund, and on September 9, Lewis ceremoniously handed the first pension check to sixty-two-year-old Horace Alinscough, of Rock Springs, Wyoming. Along with boastful stories on the benefits of the fund, the UMW *Journal* contained curses directed at the Taft-Hartley act and criticisms of Harry Truman. These themes also dominated the UMW's October 1948 convention, which for the most part was uneventful. In December, the membership confirmed Lewis's promotion of Tom Kennedy to the deceased O'Leary's post as vice-president and John Owens to the position of secretary-treasurer. With these men running headquarters, Lewis journeyed to Pine Island, Florida, for his now annual winter rest.

The routine nature of union life during these months veiled a growing awareness by leaders of labor and management of the changing fortunes of the coal industry. From reports for the first quarter of 1949, they learned that coal production had fallen 11.4% from the same period the year before and that prices had declined substantially. Actually, some observers had noted signs of the industry's waning prosperity toward the end of World War II, as diesel engines replaced coal-burning steam locomotives and homeowners converted their coal-burning furnaces to cleaner and more convenient fuels. For a while, the export of coal to a devastated Europe more than offset the deterioration of domestic markets. The year 1947 proved the most productive year in the industry's history, with 77 of the 688 million tons mined being sold abroad. As coal production in the Old World recovered, however, New World producers felt the impact of the black substance's relative decline as a major energy source.[42]

Again, as in the 1920s, the operators attempted to stimulate the demand for coal by maintaining production levels while cutting costs to reduce price. And because labor costs still constituted a sizable percentage of total operating budgets, mine owners eyed these expenses as items to trim. In particular, their gaze fell upon the multimillion-dollar welfare and retirement fund, which, under the 1948 contract, drained from their purses twenty cents for each ton of coal dug. After exploring the problem at a meeting in early April 1949, the Southern Coal Producers' Association concluded that the forthcoming bargaining conference would need to be the "toughest wage negotiations since 1933."[43]

When the United Steelworkers of America declared in May that they would seek a medical and pension program that year, the steel industry also gained an interest in curtailing the miners' welfare and retirement fund. As had been the case on the issues of wages, union recognition, and the union shop in prior years, the steel industry's policy makers feared that they could not grant the steelworkers fewer benefits than their captive miners. Consequently, throughout 1949, steel's captive mine operators encouraged the commercial mine owners to resist the union and sought to delay formulation of a new coal contract until after the settlement of the steelworkers' pension dispute.[44]

The Southern Coal Producers' Association made the first move in the coal drama of 1949-1950 when, in May, it summoned the UMW to separate contract negotiations. Compelled to comply by a previous court ruling, Lewis insisted that the talks be held in Bluefield, West Virginia, away from the political influences of Washington and in a community whose lack of renown communicated his contempt for the association. From the start of the conference, on May 25, Lewis refused to make demands and cunningly asserted that he would consider any improvements the operators wished to suggest in the prevailing contract. Because the SCPA branded the 1948 agreement "inequitable, illogical and unworkable," the improvements it proposed froze, restricted, or eliminated many of the contract's provisions.[45]

On June 8, the southerners demanded from the union a continuation of the 1947 hourly and tonnage rates, no limits on running time, restrictions on paid vacations, and the elimination of the paid lunch period. They also stated their opposition "to the present scope of the Welfare Fund provisions," without elucidating their alternative. The main point the operators dramatized, however, was the need to curtail the union's ability to call memorial periods and to eliminate from the contract the "willing and able" clause under which strikes had been justified in the past.[46]

As a blunt response to the SCPA's proposals and as a means of reducing the fifty-six day stockpile of coal, Lewis ordered an industrywide "stabilizing period of inaction" to run from June 13 to June 20. Lewis timed the "stabilizing period" well, for when it ended the miners would return to work for one week before vacationing from June 25 to July 5. Lewis's audacity appalled the nation.[47]

Because the SCPA had compelled the UMW to enter separate negotiations, Lewis decided further to divide the bituminous industry; on May 18 he notified the captive mine operators of his desire to begin contract talks. On May 23 Lewis held the first of eleven sessions with Harry Moses and his associates.[48]

Lewis waited until late June before initiating negotiations with the northern and western commercial operators at White Sulphur Springs, West Virginia. This group represented over 55% of the nation's annual tonnage and dominated the industry. Under the leadership of George Love, of Pittsburgh Consolidation Coal Company, moreover, it frequently aligned with the steel corporations. Over the ensuing months, Lewis haggled with this group while UMW Secretary-Treasurer John Owens dealt with the South. At the northern negotiations Lewis continued the bargaining posture that he had assumed with the SCPA.[49]

From July 1 to mid-September, participants in the three conferences parleyed without notable progress. In the words of a government observer at the SCPA talks, it was "fencing rather than bargaining."[50] When the old contract expired on June 30, Lewis broke the union's traditional policy of "no contract, no work," and instead imposed a three-day workweek on the industry. Several considerations led him to this action. First he recognized that a strike when excessive amounts of coal lay above ground would do little to speed deliberations. By instituting a three-day week, he intended to reduce coal stockpiles so that if the miners struck later, their walkout would have an effect. Second, the three-day week enabled Lewis to exert extra pressure on the steel industry, which, unable to obtain enough coal with the captive mines working a shortened week, would have to increase purchases from commercial operators, thus raising the industry's costs. Third, the three-day week provided union members with predictable and equitable employment until the demand for coal revived. And finally, by ordering the three-day week, Lewis usurped the operators' control over their property. In a sense, he was telling them that if they insisted on interfering in his management of the welfare and retirement fund, he would interfere with their management of the mines.[51]

The southern operators responded to the three-day week by withholding payments to the welfare and retirement fund on coal mined after June 30. By mid-September, their failure to pay, combined with the reduced income to the fund owing to the three-day week, placed the welfare and pension programs in jeopardy. Consequently, on September 16 the board of trustees halted the disbursement of benefits. Van Horn opposed this action and, resigned from the board. On September 19, after being informed that the "default" of the southern operators had forced a suspension of welfare and pension payments, miners across the bituminous fields commenced a work stoppage that lasted, in most places, until November 9.[52]

In late September, public opinion became aroused over the steel industry's disregard for a presidential fact-finding board's recommendations for settling the steelworkers' pension dispute. Seizing upon this outcry, Lewis sought to improve his case with the public by harping on the steel industry's influence in the coal negotiations. "Love is the agent of Steel master George Humphrey," he asserted at one press conference. "Obviously Humphrey would not permit his agent, Love, to come to any agreement on any issue that would prejudice the controversy in steel."[53] To dramatize the connection between coal and steel, Lewis proposed that the A. F. of L. and the UMW form a defense fund for use by the striking United Steelworkers of America.[54]

In a counterattack, the operators lashed out at the UMW president. "What the coal industry needs," George Love snarled to reporters, "are more customers and less Lewis strikes." Such words betrayed Love's increasing frustration in bargaining with the union. On October 21, after listening to the UMW once again reject their offer to renew the 1948 contract without certain provisions, Love and his delegation bolted the conference. Two weeks later, the SCPA also broke off talks with the union.[55]

Until the collapse of the wage conferences at White Sulphur Springs and Bluefield in late October, the national government had involved itself little in the dispute. Now, Federal Mediation and Conciliation Director Cyrus Ching felt it time to take a more active role. First, he met separately with Lewis and representatives from each of the three groups of operators. Then, on November 8, he summoned all disputants to his Washington office on November 10. Lewis received the summons in Chicago, where he was meeting with the UMW Policy Committee, and became peeved at the conciliation director's presumption that he need but set the hour and all parties would obey. Consequently, on November 9, an angry Lewis guided through the Policy Committee a resolution ending the strike until December 1. He then wrote Ching that he would be busy until November 14 securing maximum resumption of coal production and could not meet the conciliation director until then. Ching dropped the whole idea of a joint conference. Instead, on November 16, he recommended to Truman the formation of a fact-finding board similar to the one that had already proved less than successful in the steelworkers' pension dispute. For the time being, the president shelved Ching's plan and informed newsmen that he would invoke the Taft-Hartley act if he decided to intervene, but he would do so only in the event of a national emergency.[56]

The coal dispute, having simmered along for six months, began to boil in early December. After the steel corporations settled the pension dispute with the steelworkers in November, the captive mine operators indicated a willingness to talk seriously with the UMW. So, too, did George Love, of the northern commercial operators, who on December 28 proclaimed his readiness to effect a welfare and retirement plan with the miners "equal to the program which settled the recent steel strike." Because the steelworkers' settlement was inferior to the miners' current arrangement, Lewis ignored Love's offer. To make Lewis more cooperative, the SCPA, backed by the captive and northern operators, filed with the NLRB unfair labor practices charges against the UMW and pleaded for an injunction.[57]

Provoked by the operators' actions, groups of miners participated in a series of work stoppages. The union labeled these walkouts "spontaneous strikes," although they had about them an element of strategy in that they cut most acutely into the steel industry's coal supply. During the first week in January, 15,000 captive miners in Illinois struck. As these men returned to work, the employees of George Love's Pittsburgh Consolidation and Harry Moses' Frick Coal companies instituted an "unauthorized walkout." Regardless of the behind-the-scenes influence union officials may have exerted over the early phase of the walkouts, by January 11 the wildcat strikes had developed a momentum of their own, with the 66,000 participants disregarding Lewis's instructions to return to work.[58]

The wildcat strikes led to increased pressures for federal intervention. The northern and captive operators, perhaps hoping to transform the scattered walkouts into a single nationwide strike that would force Truman to invoke the Taft-Hartley act, joined the SCPA in withholding royalty payments to the miners' welfare and retirement fund. On January 19, moreover, the NLRB's general counsel, acting on the operators' unfair labor practices charge, asked the district court to issue an injunction compelling the miners to resume work and the union to resume negotiations with the operators.[59]

Lewis searched vigorously for a way to checkmate both the possible court injunctions and imminent action by the White House. Seizing up George Love's publicity-oriented overture to renew negotiations, Lewis accepted and cornered the operators into renewing talks on February 1.[60]

Even before the parties met, Truman assured the collapse of the conference. On January 31, he sent identical telegrams to Lewis and the operators outlining his solution to the dispute. His proposal resembled the recommendation made by Ching on November 16 and was based upon the procedures followed during the steelworkers' pension crisis. The president asked the miners to return to work for seventy days while an all-citizen fact-finding board investigated the issues. At the end of this period, the disputants would consider the board's recommendations, although they were not bound to accept them. This procedure favored the operators, for it guaranteed them full coal production during the peak winter season without requiring from them any sacrifice. The union, however, would lose whatever strategic advantage it had won through its tactics to reduce coal stockpiles. In light of the recent steelworkers' settlement, moreover, the board's report could be expected to lean toward the operators' side. The president, when making the proposal, gave the disputants until Saturday, February 4, to reply.[61]

The operators consequently found little reason to talk with the union unless they could attain even better terms than a fact-finding board might recommend. Therefore, on February 2, after the UMW had refused to continue the current wage scale and to give up the "willing and able" clause, the operators walked out of negotiations and accepted Truman's plan.[62]

Lewis now faced a critical decision. The failure of the wildcat strikers to obey his January 11 return-to-work order convinced him that he would not be able to appease Truman and the public by having coal production resumed on Monday. He had either to accept the president's proposal or to face a Taft-Hartley act injunction. If he accepted the president's plan, he knew that public pressures would make it difficult for the UMW to reject the fact-finding board's recommendations. To do so, moreover, would simply result in Truman then invoking the hated labor law. Turning down the president's proposal would just lead Truman immediately to seek a Taft-Hartley injunction. Forced to choose between voluntary surrender and compulsory defeat, Lewis chose the latter and, on Saturday, February 4, rejected the president's plan.[63]

By Monday, February 6, the operators' withholding of pension payments had transformed the month-old series of wildcat strikes into a national walkout. This development and Lewis's rejection of the president's proposal led Truman to create a board of inquiry to investigate the need for an eighty-day injunction. The board's report criticized the collective bargaining tactics of the disputants and confirmed that the dispute now posed a danger to the nation's welfare.[64]

Within hours after receiving the report, the administration obtained from Judge Richard B. Kleech an injunction directing the miners to return to work and the union to resume talks with the operators. At the same time, Judge Kleech upheld the operators' contention that some of the UMW's demands constituted unfair labor practices under the Taft-Hartley act. In a second injunction, he instructed the union negotiators to cease demanding a union shop, the extension of the "willing and able" and "memorial period" clauses, or a welfare program limited to union members.[65]

Lewis, desiring to avoid a repeat of his contempt convictions of 1946 and 1948, immediately ordered an end to the strike. His words, however, failed to move the coal diggers off the picket line, committed as they were to the union's program and annoyed by the operators' obstinance and the government's intervention. Nor did they heed his second directive, issued a week later, "to cease forthwith all stoppages and return to work without delay."[66]

When it became clear that the miners would not return to work, the Truman administration debated its next course of action. Comforted by new statistics from the Bureau of Mines that revealed that the danger of a coal shortage was not as imminent as earlier portended, the president decided to use the crisis to demonstrate to the nation the unworkability of the law. On Monday, February 20, the Justice Department obtained from Judge Kleech an order directing the UMW to show cause why it should not be held in contempt. Significantly, the judge refused to name Lewis in the citation. After considering the case for two weeks, on March 2 Kleeck ruled that the government had failed to prove the UMW in criminal or civil contempt of court, despite the fact that most of the membership was still on strike.[67]

The not-guilty verdict created the preconditions for a rapid settlement of the nine-month dispute. With the miners having successfully frustrated a Taft-Hartley injunction, Truman immediately asked Congress for authority to seize the collieries. Both the union and the operators viewed Truman's plan with alarm. Under the proposal, the miners would be forced to work under the terms of the 1948 contract, and the operators would have their profits regulated by a specially established board. Above all, both union and management objected to the further interjection of government into their affairs.[68]

Undermining Truman's seizure plan now became more important to the disputants than the differences between them. Within hours of the president's petition to Congress, they announced the settlement of major points in contention. Two days later, on March 5, they signed the National Bituminous Coal Wage Agreement of 1950, leading Congress readily to abandon Truman's seizure proposal.

The new agreement, signed after ten months of conflict, constituted a compromise. The operators received reassurance that the union would respect their right to control their facilities and that labor and management would work together to reduce the extent of government involvement in industry affairs. In line with the arrangement, the contract lacked the "willing and able" provision found in the 1948 agreement. In return, the operators agreed to cooperate with the union in administering the welfare and retirement fund. Most particularly, they consented to replacing Senator Styles Bridges as the neutral trustee with Lewis's faithful friend Josephine Roche. This move guaranteed that the fund would always reflect Lewis's will. The operators also agreed to pay their employees an extra seventy cents a day and to increase their contribution to the welfare and retirement fund from twenty to thirty cents per ton.[69]

The most important aspect of the 1950 contract, however, was its spirit, rather than its content. "We have had a good fight, but we are all glad it's over," George Love informed newsmen after the signing. "This two-and-one-half year Contract gives the industry its first real opportunity for stability in the last decade." Lewis concurred in Love's assessment, adding that the new agreement provided "assurance that for a substantial period of time the industry can abate its labor warfare and apply itself—both management and labor—to the constructive problems of producing coal in quantity for the benefit of the American economy at the lowest possible cost permitted by modern techniques."[70]

The abrupt termination of the 1949-1950 coal dispute also concluded many years of turbulence in the mining industry. In announcing the settlement, Lewis described the 1949-1950 struggle as "a sort of 'Marengo' campaign," in reference to the drawn-out battle on the plains of Marengo, Italy, in 1800, which culminated in a victory for Napoleon over the Austrians. Actually, Lewis's erudite parallel was ill-conceived. He had not triumphed over the operators and firmly established his empire. Rather, the warring parties settled their differences when they realized that while they fought, outside powers were weakening the kingdom of coal. The rise of competitive fuels, the threat of intensified and continuous government intervention in the industry, and the increase in small "gopher hole" nonunion mines led the combatants rapidly to become allies. Although Lewis would remain president of the UMWA for another decade, he had led his last great strike. The public's symbol of an irresponsible union leader now began to transform himself into a labor executive.

CHAPTER 21
A Prisoner of Change, 1950-1960

Aging is a painful process in America. In a culture dominated by the middle-aged but enamored with youth, the elderly serve as passive spectators to the game of life. After decades of active participation in society, they confront the depressing realization that the day belongs to a younger generation set on remodeling anew the world older people helped to create. This phenomenon, affecting in one way or another all senior citizens, is perhaps most disturbing to those who once occupied center stages in national affairs. Long accustomed to exercising great power, they must adapt to their fading influence.

For John L. Lewis, the 1950s was the period of trial. The decade began with the sixty-nine-year-old union boss leading a major strike that he did not foresee as his last. His name still evoked editorial criticism; his actions continued to warrant presidential attention. Yet with coal's declining importance and his own increased isolation from the labor movement, Lewis gradually came to sense the ending of an era. At first, he responded by trying to recapture some of his old dash through attempting to unify labor and to smash the Korean War Wage Stabilization Board. Unable to regain past glories, he spent the remainder of the decade establishing himself as a coal industry statesman, a labor executive, and a noble humanitarian. In doing so, as often had been the case in the past, Lewis tarnished his golden ends by his choice of base means.

Each year during the 1950s, Lewis witnessed the passing of family members, associates, and adversaries, and he also experienced failing health. Sorrowfully, too, he experienced frustration as the new generation in power treated his cherished values as outdated. By 1958, he had concluded that the time had come for new leadership to develop in the UMW, and two years later he voluntarily abdicated his throne. Such action was unprecedented among labor leaders of his stature: Samuel Gompers, William Green, Phil Murray all died in union office, and George Meany seems determined to do likewise. It is a measure of the change Lewis underwent that he, whose life centered so much on amassing power, considered relinquishing it to others.

*   *   *

Few events communicated as clearly to Lewis his waning importance as did the reunification of the A. F. of L. and CIO without him. Even before his dramatic break with the CIO in 1942, he had dreamed of being the person who would reunite the two federations. In the mid-1940s he strove to attain a position with the A. F. of L. from which to lead a unity movement. The success of Daniel Tobin, George Meany, and others in rejecting Lewis's strategy, however, contributed to his decision to disaffiliate from the federation in 1947. Two years later, he again indicated his eagerness to rejoin the A. F. of L. on certain conditions, but the federation's executive council unanimously rejected his bid.[1]

After this spurning, Lewis abandoned attempts to lead a merger movement from within one of the houses of labor and instead sought to create a new vehicle for unity independent of the two federations. In approaching other unions for alliances, moreover, he placed increasing emphasis on the UMW's financial might, for the decline of the coal industry had weakened his former arguments concerning the miners' numerical and strategic strength. Lewis unveiled his new unity approach on October 14, 1949, in the midst of the United Steelworkers' long strike against U.S. Steel (and while the mine workers were grappling with the operators). In a letter to William Green, he proposed that nine international unions in the A. F. of L. join with the UMW in each making available to the steelworkers $250,000 a week until they were victorious. Since the USWA had not asked for help, the A. F. of L.'s leadership disregarded Lewis's scheme.[2]

Undaunted, Lewis continued to try to purchase an alliance. In March 1950, he offered Walter Reuther a loan of $1 million for use by the United Automobile Workers in its struggle against the Chrysler Corporation. When Reuther rejected this bait, the miners' chief suggested to Phil Murray that the steelworkers and the UMW form "a mutual aid pact for common defense," but Murray proved uninterested in working with his former boss. In April Murray proposed a committee representing all organized labor to work for organic unity. Seizing the opening, Lewis accepted the plan, but the leaders of the A. F. of L. and CIO consciously excluded him from the ensuing conferences that summer. Isolated from the labor movement, Lewis clung to his idea of a financial aid pact as a prelude to unity and reiterated his plan in a major speech before a large autoworkers' local in July 1951.[3]

In the fall of 1952, Lewis and William Green were again exploring the possibility of the UMW rejoining the A. F. of L., when the federation's president died. His successor, George Meany, seldom agreed with Lewis, so they never resumed the discussions. Nor did Walter Reuther's advancement to the presidency of the CIO after Phil Murray's death improve Lewis's chances for an accommodation on that front. Indeed, during the 1950s Reuther was one of Lewis's pet aversions. The UMW president loved to taunt the autoworkers' head for his former socialism, his fascination with "big" ideas, and his use of "fancy" phrases, which Lewis contended Reuther "had evidently picked up while idling away a few hours in the public library."[4] Because Lewis was unable to deal with the new spokesmen for the A. F. of L. or CIO, he now sought to bring together those union heads who felt slighted in the transfer of power.

For help in this matter, he called upon David B. Charnay, the head of the Allied Public Relations Association, which the UMW had been employing since the late 1940s to improve its public image. Following Charnay's advice, in late December 1953 Lewis threw UMW support behind the International Longshoremen's Association (recently expelled from the A. F. of L. for corruption) in its fight to win a representation election against the federation for control over the work at the Port of New York. As a former reporter for New York's *Daily News*, Charnay knew how to leak information to newsmen in such a way that the ILA's victory bolstered Lewis's sagging reputation as a force in the labor movement.[5]

Charnay next turned to lining up allies for Lewis. One natural candidate was another of Charnay's clients, Dave Beck, president of the million-member International Brotherhood of Teamsters, who feared losing his union's independence and jurisdiction in the possible A. F. of L.-CIO merger. David McDonald, the new head of the United Steelworkers, seemed another potential ally, as he was brooding over his union's declining influence in the CIO since Walter Reuther took the helm.

After some preliminary maneuvering, on April 30, 1954, Charnay set up the first in a series of luncheon meetings involving Lewis, McDonald, and Beck and released enough publicity to create some concern within the two houses of labor that a third dwelling might be built. Lewis hoped that the talks either would lead to the formation of a new federation or would scare the leaders of the A. F. of L. and CIO into inviting him to their unity negotiations. Neither Beck nor McDonald, however, shared such desires. For them, the "Lew McBeck" discussions were part of a strategy to enhance their own influence within their respective federations. The only matter on which they actually intended to cooperate with Lewis was the upcoming election for governor of Pennsylvania. McDonald passionately hated the UMW president for his treatment of Murray, while Beck was peeved at Lewis for allowing District 50 to invade teamster union territory. Both men represented larger memberships than Lewis, and neither needed UMW money. By the end of 1954 Beck and McDonald discarded Lewis and excluded him from future luncheons.[6]

When, in 1955, it became clear that the A. F. of L. and CIO would reunite without the miners, Lewis was outwardly critical but inwardly hurt. Appearing on CBS's "Face the Nation," he grumbled about the UMW being "stipulated" out of the talks and characterized the unity arrangements as "particularly unfortunate" since they placed in "a small group of men in the merged organization, the sovereignty and jurisdiction and the welfare of all the lesser unions in both groups. . . . They may merge," he wailed at one point in the interview, "but, when the strains and stresses of the human compulsion that affects those organizations are made manifest after the merger, I greatly fear that the new merger will part like the rope of sand that it is.''[7]

Whatever the merits of his criticisms of the merger, Lewis could not repress his personal feelings for long. On November 30, 1955, in the petty manner in which he customarily responded to slights, Lewis instructed John Owens to demand repayment of $1,685,000 that he contended the UMW had loaned the CIO back in the 1930s. Only resentment can explain the resurrection of a dead issue. Upon receiving Owens's message, James Carey wrote back directly to Lewis: ''The CIO owes you no money.'' And then, with cutting sarcasm, he added: ''You have achieved the momentary ripple of publicity which you sought to relieve the boredom of your isolation from the democratic labor movement.''[8]

Lewis's loss of national prominence involved far more than his isolation from the labor movement. From beginning to end, his career was shaped by the fortunes of the coal industry—and in the years following World War II, the black diamond's importance as a national energy source dwindled. Intense competition from oil, natural gas, and hydroelectricity rapidly reduced the anthracite industry to slow death and placed bituminous producers in grave economic straits. Whereas in 1940 coal had constituted 30.3% of the fuel energy consumed in this country, by 1964 it had dropped to 23.1%. More significantly the decline in coal markets was absolute as well as relative. From a high of 688 million tons of coal produced in 1947, output fell to 516 million tons in 1950 and then to 392 million tons in 1954. Although some improvement occurred in the late 1950s, the industry did not regain production levels until the 1960s.[9]

The operators, plagued by intense competition for a declining market, sought to protect profits by cutting labor costs. For most large and middle-sized companies, increased productivity through mechanization accomplished this end. Although machines had been introduced into mining as early as the 1890s, the pace of modernization accelerated during World War II. By 1950, mining technology had changed greatly from what it had been when Lewis first went underground. Coal was no longer dug with picks, the traditional symbol of the trade. Now miners participated in a highly mechanized operation or, as Harry Moses described it in 1952, ''the only assembly-line mass production industry carried on underground.''[10] Various power-driven machines cut the black rock from the seam, loaded it onto shuttle cars, and transported it to the surface. In the most modern collieries even this equipment had been outmoded by the continuous mining machine, which coordinated the entire operation. Strip-mining, moreover, which produced only 1% of the total tonnage when Lewis first became a national union officer, by the mid-1950s accounted for nearly one quarter of the annual output and seemed likely to grow.[11]

Coal companies could also cut labor costs by operating on a nonunion basis. The demand for coal during World War II, followed by the emergence of the Tennessee

Valley Authority as a major coal consumer, fostered hundreds of small mines in traditionally antiunion areas of Kentucky and Tennessee. Unable or unwilling to mechanize fully, these marginal mines generally resorted to nonunion production in order to win a competitive advantage. Even if a nonunion operator granted his employees the UMW wage, he still realized tremendous savings by escaping royalty payments to the welfare and retirement fund. And without the UMW to police safety practices, small nonunion operators could reap further cost savings, because the federal mine laws did not apply to companies with fewer than sixteen employees. The government also bolstered nonunion mines through the coal purchasing policies of the TVA, which granted contracts to the lowest bidder. TVA policy disregarded the amount of coal each operator could supply, the wage rates and benefits paid by the contractors as compared to the prevailing standards, or the effect of such a policy on the industry. Hence, the number of nonunion mines grew until, by the early 1960s, they accounted for almost 25% of the annual coal production.

Such economic changes in the coal industry weakened the United Mine Workers of America, whence Lewis drew his strength. The increase in productivity, the decline in markets, and the rise of nonunion pits interacted to reduce the size of the work force Lewis represented. Whereas in 1945, 400,000 UMW members dug coal, a decade later this figure fell by half. For the families of unemployed coal diggers, this translated into a life of poverty in Appalachia; for Lewis and his organization, it meant a decline in stature in an era of million-member unions.

More ominous from an institutional perspective was the union's loss of its strategic position in the economy. With coal's waning importance and the industry's tendency to exceed demand, a miners' strike no longer immediately threatened the nation's well-being. Coal disputes could continue for months or even a year before arousing alarm. In fact, now they actually hurt the union, for they forced coal consumers to seek alternative fuels. The situation struck Lewis as a replay of the 1920s and as proof of his cyclical theory of history. Clearly the economics of coal demanded a new mode of action from the UMW and its chief.

The operators, not the union, however, pioneered in adapting to the new conditions. Coal's decreased proportion of the energy market, the rise of price-cutting nonunion producers, the disruptive impact of strikes on markets, and the constant threat of government intervention all caused leading operators to recognize that they could not allow the contentious pattern of labor relations to prevail and still operate profitably. And reinforcing this awareness were the realities of the markets that the industry struggled to maintain. During the 1950s, electric power companies became the foremost consumers of coal, with the steel industry occupying second place. By 1957, these two industries burnt over 60% of domestic coal output. Because both required steady deliveries of the mineral and electrical utilities possessed the capability of switching to other fuels, both industries demanded multiyear contracts with operators, again reinforcing the need for labor peace and predictable production in the coalfields.

The rise of new leadership among the operators facilitated the implementation of a new approach to labor relations. In place of the melodramatic Charles O'Neill and the dour Ezra Van Horn—veterans of two decades of warfare with Lewis—emerged genial but forthright George Love. A Pennsylvania blue blood replete with a Princeton degree, Love had entered the coal business in 1926 after a brief career as an investment broker. Skilled at high finance and corporate administration, he sought to create a prosperous coal industry through "far sighted" management. "We had a dream," Love told a writer for *Fortune* magazine. "The trouble with the coal industry was that it was fragmentary in its organization, and wasteful in its technology. We reasoned . . . that if we could get our hands on enough properties, we could close down or sell off the bad mines, [and] exploit only the good ones."[12] Following this plan, in 1945 Love merged three large firms into the Pittsburgh Consolidation Coal Company. The new colossus, popularly known as Consol, was the world's largest commercial producer of bituminous coal. As president of this giant—and with the behind-the-scenes aid of Secretary of the Treasury George Humphrey, whose business connections linked Consol to the captive mines—Love dominated the coal industry during the 1950s.

The strikes of the postwar era, culminating in a long, bitter struggle in 1949-1950, threatened Love's plans for the industry. After studying the subject, Love concluded that such strife stemmed as much from the way the parties engaged in collective bargaining as it did from clear conflicts of interest between labor and management. The employers, he noted, lacked sufficient unity, which meant that too often a small band of obstinate producers provoked a strike that threatened the best interests of a majority of the firms. The designation of a fixed expiration date for each contract also promoted needless strife, because Lewis, responding to rank-and-file pressures, felt compelled to make demands regardless of the health of the industry. The practice of conducting negotiations at public joint mass meetings transformed collective bargaining into a spectator sport in which both parties broadcasted half-truths, vilified their adversaries, and locked themselves into untenable positions in an effort to enlist the power of public opinion. Inevitably, such conduct led to government intervention and the settlement of the industry's economic problems on a political basis or at the whim of a judge.[13]

In July 1950 Love initiated a major step toward restructuring labor relations in the industry by organizing the Bituminous Coal Operators' Association (BCOA). Essentially an alliance among northern commercial operators and the captive mines, BCOA was headed by U.S. Steel's Harry Moses, although Love remained its guiding spirit. He personally controlled 52 of the 110 votes cast at its meetings, and, if necessary, he could call upon his friend Moses for 19 more. The new association accounted for roughly 50% of the coal mined in the country and out-produced its southern counterpart, SCPA, by better than two to one. Such strength enabled BCOA to shape policy for the remainder of the industry. Love intended to use his association to persuade the country's coal operators that strikes were ruinous and should be avoided, that the government and public should be eliminated from dealings with the union, and that labor and management should work together to solve mutual problems in a businesslike way.[14]

BCOA's leadership faced a major task—convincing Lewis of the operators' commitment to developing more harmonious relations with the union. Fortunately for them, Lewis had no ideological qualms about collaboration and was well practiced at it. Moreover, he, too, sought a way to cope with the political, economic, and technological forces that concerned the mine owners. In particular, Lewis, as much as any employer, sought to minimize government intervention in the industry. Yet Lewis approached BCOA cautiously. After three decades of bickering with coal barons, the aging labor leader doubted their ability to adopt a new attitude toward the union. Most particularly, he remembered the breakdown of cooperation in the 1920s, when the coal industry faced a similar economic plight. Thus, he initially treated Love's labor strategy as a delicate, temporary arrangement dictated by external forces. It was not until the middle of the decade that he abandoned circumspection and became an apostle of the "new look."

Lewis first tested Love's labor relations system in December 1950. Although the March 1950 agreement still had almost a year to run, Lewis nonetheless indicated to Moses of BCOA and Moody of SCPA his desire for a new contract. Clearly, the UMW sought an advance in wages in anticipation of the national government imposing controls to curtail inflation during the Korean War. Through December and early January, Lewis, Moses, and Moody engaged in a new style of casual, quiet negotiations, with no fanfare, no public spectacles, and no meddling by "bureaucrats." Few people even knew of the contract talks, least of all the miners. Despite appearances, however, Lewis played his old game of pitting the South against the North and also kept the threat of a strike always present. Finally, on January 18, a surprised public learned that the parties had reached a new accord, which gave coal diggers $1.60 more a day in pay. Thus far, Lewis indicated to the press, he was satisfied with BCOA's performance.[15]

Yet the operators still had not won Lewis's full confidence. He respected the 1951 accord until mid-1952, when he again notified them that he wished to formulate a new agreement. And in the ensuing negotiations, he applied steady pressure, including a "memorial" work stoppage to reduce coal stockpiles. When, on September 10, BCOA rejected the terms of an agreement arranged by Lewis and Moses, the mine workers' president threatened to disrupt the association. All nonmembers of BCOA, he proposed, could continue producing coal when the present contract expired, if they agreed to accept any new accord once negotiated. Attracted by the prospect of large profits while much of the industry lay idle, a number of BCOA members indicated their intention of becoming independent. Soon Love and the other major operators, fretting that labor relations would revert to the old, turbulent pattern if BCOA collapsed, acquiesced to the original Moses-Lewis terms. The 1952 agreement, signed by BCOA on September 29 and by SCPA the next day, provided miners with a wage increase of $1.90 a day and added ten cents more a ton in royalty payments to the welfare and retirement fund. [16]

Before the 1952 contract could be implemented, however, it required the approval of the Wage Stabilization Board that Truman had established to combat inflation during the Korean War. Since the start of the Asian conflict, Lewis had opposed government controls, and now he had an opportunity to press his point. Although he may not have demanded a substantial wage increase primarily to test Truman's economic program, and while some of his arguments possessed considerable merit, Lewis's behavior in the ensuing events betrays a pathetic attempt to recapture his World War II notoriety. His battle against Washington "bureaucrats," moreover, sorely tested BCOA's commitment to ameliorating union-management relations and to eliminating government interference in the industry. The association's willingness to cooperate, and even to do his bidding, helped convince Lewis that a new era of labor policy had truly dawned.

On October 1, the operators alone submitted the new contract to the Wage Stabilization Board for its approval. During the next two weeks, the board, headed by Archibald Cox, asked Lewis for supporting evidence and also to send representatives to a conference on the matter. The miners' chief responded with silence.[17]

Spurned by Lewis, the Wage Stabilization Board released its eight-to-four decision on October 18. The majority, composed of all the public and industry members, approved $1.50 of the $1.90-a-day wage increase, but it denied the additional forty cents on the ground "that it is inconsistent with the economic stabilization program." The miners' hourly wage rates and annual earnings, they contended, compared favorably with employees in manufacturing industries and did not warrant special treatment. Perhaps anticipating trouble over their decision, the board majority stressed the need for compliance to ensure national unity in the face of danger. "It must be our hope," they wrote, "that the sound common sense of the coal miners and the wisdom of their leaders will lead them to share in the national endeavor to remain strong and free. For both the miners and their leaders must know that freedom—their freedom—cannot long survive when the supremacy of law is challenged by naked power."[18]

In their minority report, the four labor representatives expressed indignation at the majority for clouding the case with "pious homilies of democracy and equality." In the minority view, the mine workers deserved more than the forty cents in dispute, for in negotiating the contract the union had accepted higher pay in lieu of added fringe benefits that its members would have been allowed under the stabilization program.[19]

The WSB's decision angered the workers in the coalfields. As soon as they heard the news, miners walked out of the pits without Lewis's formal approval. Disturbed by these shutdowns, Harry Moses reminded Lewis that BCOA "unilaterally and without reservations has urged the Wage Stabilization Board to approve the $1.90 increase called for in this agreement." The association's willingness to pay the full amount "is restrained only by the legal limitations imposed by the Board." In light of such cooperation, Moses pleaded, could not Lewis urge the miners to return to work?[20]

The UMW president replied to Moses with his customary purple prose. Yet in the year 1952 this language struck many observers as antiquated. "We have a contract," Lewis wrote.

> It is with your Association. It is complete. It speaks for itself. You signed it. It was negotiated in the American way—through collective bargaining. It is as pure as a sheep's heart.
>
> Now comes the attempt to dismember it. Four agents of the National Association of Manufacturers, aided by a professor from the Harvard Law School and his timid trio of dilettante associates, form a cabal to steal forty cents a day from each mineworker.
>
> Naturally miners resent such attempted thievery. Miners are people, Mr. Moses. They have children. Children need milk. The forty cents would buy milk each day. You of all men should know that the mine-workers will fight to protect the milk supply of their families.[21]

Despite asserting that the operators were the "sole petitioner and plaintiff" in the dispute, Lewis joined Moses on October 24 in requesting the economic stabilization administrator, Roger L. Putnam, to review the case. They based their appeal on two points. First, they contended that the miners should receive the higher pay, because they had not received added fringe benefits. Second, they asserted that the total contract should be approved, because it ensured "the maintenance and furtherance of the American way of life." "The principal contribution to the stabilization policy that this contract makes, . . ." Lewis and Moses jointly maintained, "is the fact that agreement was reached, after concessions on each side, without a shutdown in the industry. Failure of approval by competent authority defeats this purpose."[22]

As the coal walkout provoked public discontent only weeks before a presidential election, Harry Truman summoned Lewis and Moses to the White House on October 26. There they explored the issue, with Moses no doubt repeating his belief that the government's policy threatened the new, harmonious labor relations in the coal industry. After the conference, the president announced to the press that Putnam would give "serious and prompt" consideration to the case and that in the meantime Lewis would order the miners back to work.[23]

Truman's order to review the WSB decision clearly distressed Roger Putnam. A large segment of the population, weary of the "police action" in Korea, found much to criticize about the administration's "partial" domestic economic control program. Such displeasure had risen noticeably in the summer of 1952, following Truman's submission to the steel industry's price increase demands after the Supreme Court had ruled his seizure of the mills illegal. With the steel fiasco having exposed publicly the rickety structure of wage and price controls, Putnam now feared that the coal case would bring the teetering framework tumbling down.[24]

Consequently, Putnam delayed any action until after the November elections, suggesting that he intended to equivocate until a new administration took over. Lewis, having been promised by Truman a "serious and prompt" review, became infuriated when the economic stabilization administrator called for additional hearings after twenty-three days of procrastination. In his testimony, Lewis uttered barely veiled threats of a strike but still failed to budge Putnam. By then, the stabilization administrator had concluded that if forced to rule on the case, his verdict would be against the union.[25]

By the end of November, the coal situation became a major headache for Truman. On the one hand, the majority of the wage stabilization board, the administrator of the Economic Stabilization Agency, and the director of defense mobilization all endorsed the WSB's rejection of the forty-cent increase. To ignore their advice would emasculate what remained of Truman's economic control program. On the other hand, the director of the Federal Mediation and Conciliation Service warned the president of the likely adverse consequences if Putnam sustained the board's decision, and he urged Truman personally to approve the 1952 contract.[26]

On December 3 Truman, fully aware that the "buck" stopped with him, ordered Putnam to reverse the WSB's ruling and to approve the disputed forty cents. "The decision in this case must not only recognize the importance of continuing stabilization as an effective program," he informed the administrator, "but must also face up to problems completely apart from stabilization which are involved in the transition from this Administration to its successor." In particular, Truman feared that if the WSB's decision stood, the resulting coal strike—although adversely affecting some segments of the economy—would not immediately constitute a national crisis in which he could act under law. "Such an emergency would arise at just about the time my successor took office," he declared. "I am not willing to take an action that will create such a crisis for my successor."[27]

Truman's order to uphold the 1952 coal contract terminated the economic control program, as Chairman Archibald Cox and all industry members of the wage stabilization board resigned in protest. Lewis, of course, was pleased with his victory and ranked it as "one of the greatest triumphs of our Union." An even more exuberant K. C. Adams rejoiced: *"The UMWA victory is truly a victory for all American labor."* Yet in truth Lewis had slain no giant but had simply kicked a dying dwarf. Truman's action had disclosed that the government would not hold the line against labor when corporate interests desired otherwise. By December it was clear that the control program would end as soon as Eisenhower assumed the presidency.[28]

*   *   *

The Bituminous Coal Operators' Association's support of Lewis in his battle against controls stimulated cooperation between the union and the large producers. Henceforward, the UMW chief spoke more and more of partnership for the good of the industry and less and less of labor-management conflict. He allowed the 1952 contract to remain in force until 1955 and requested a new accord only when coal's financial fortunes seemed to improve. Although the ensuing negotiations involved months of shadowboxing between Lewis and Moses, the prospect of a strike was absent. By late 1956, labor relations had become so "normalized" that Tom Kennedy negotiated that year's agreement without Lewis's aid. Likewise, the 1958 contract talks, the last Lewis participated in, lacked any excitement whatsoever—a far cry from the hectic scene that had existed when he took over the union almost four decades before.

Lewis publicly justified collaboration as necessary for the preservation of "free enterprise" capitalism and free collective bargaining. Yet when translated from ideology to actuality, Lewis's and the large operators' plan was simply to promote the profitability of an industry in whose future both workers and owners had a stake. Despite odes to unrestrained competition, the union president, like the robber barons of his youth, freely called upon the government for special favors. Among other things, he solicited a tariff on residual oil, a foreign aid program that promoted coal exports, and a floor under the wages paid to miners producing coal sold to the TVA. His pet cause was the establishment of a federal fuel policy to "determine the line of demarcation for the uses of the liquid and solid fuels of this country."[29]

The UMW and the large operators built their marriage on economic necessity, not interclass love. Management conceded to labor a series of agreements that the union's officials viewed as "equal, if not better than any wage contract now in existence anywhere in the world."[30] By 1958, working UMW members earned between twenty-three and twenty-seven dollars a day. The operators also provided them with improved vacation benefits and, from 1952, paid forty cents on each ton of coal mined to the welfare and retirement fund, which they left Lewis free to administer.

Further, BCOA worked with the union in securing from the government various policies of direct benefit to the miners but also advantageous to the large operators. In the late 1950s, for instance, they jointly agitated for a stricter mine safety law. Indeed, here was a classic case of "corporate liberalism," for although the overt purpose of the law was to save miners' lives, the covert aim was to force small companies out of business by imposing on them the same expensive safety standards required of larger producers.[31]

Finally, in return for the union's cooperation, the large operators granted Lewis a role in determining industry policies. In the early and mid-1950s, for instance, the miners' chief fervently argued that the industry could offset the loss of domestic markets by active foreign trade. Then, in 1956, leading mine owners and representatives of coal-carrying railroads joined with him in advancing his plan and formed the American Coal Shipping Company. Symbolizing his new standing as a constructive force in the industry, Lewis spoke for the new company—one-third owned by the UMW—when it applied to the federal government for use of thirty "mothballed" Liberty ships to transport coal throughout the world.[32]

Lewis's ultimate recognition by the operators as an industry statesman came on May 5, 1958, when, for the first time in his life, he addressed many of his former bargaining foes at the coal convention of the American Mining Congress. In introducing Lewis, George M. Humphrey—former secretary of the treasury, chairman of National Steel, and a behind-the-scenes power in the bituminous industry—proclaimed his "great respect and admiration" for the UMW president and knighted him "a friend of coal." Lewis, in his speech, called for the creation of a body that would coordinate the policies of the various coal interests so that the industry could confront the government and the public with a united front. In less than a year, his idea became reality as coal operators, the union, thirty-two coal-carrying railroads, seven power companies, and a number of mine equipment manufacturers formed the National Coal Policy Conference. Appropriately, George Love, the proponent of the new system of labor relations, became the group's first chairman, with Lewis, the system's most important convert, succeeding him in 1962.[33]

The UMW, of course, had to reciprocate for the blessings bestowed on it by the operators. Most obviously, Lewis assured management that work stoppages would not disrupt production, and throughout the decade he dealt harshly with wildcat strikes. He also vowed to avoid actions that might provoke government interference in the industry. Finally, he consented to use the union's resources to advance the industry's productivity, to find new markets for coal, and to eliminate nonunion mines. Because Lewis believed that the miners' standard of living could advance only if the coal industry prospered, he did not perceive any of these activities as injurious to his members' interests.

This was certainly his reasoning on the issue of mechanizing the mines. "We've encouraged the leading companies in the coal industry to resort to modernization in order to increase the living standards of the miner and improve his working conditions," Lewis told an interviewer for *U.S. News & World Report*.[34] Failure to mechanize, he maintained, would have meant intense pressures from the operators to reduce the miners' wages. Greater productivity through machines assured high wages by reducing the labor costs involved in extracting each ton of coal.

To be sure, modernization made large numbers of miners technologically unemployed and caused the union's roster to shrink. Yet, this phenomenon never vexed Lewis. "The United Mine Workers of America has never undertaken to oppose modernization or progress from the standpoint of compelling the retention of uneconomic employment in the industry," he contended. "From a policy standpoint, it is immaterial to us whether the Union has a million or a half million members."[35] (Actually, by then, the issue was 200,000 or 100,000 members.)

Lewis so prided himself on being an economic realist and so much believed that the primary goal of unionism was higher and higher pay that he never truly grasped what modernization meant to the unemployed coal digger. When questioned on the fate of the technologically displaced miners, he replied with the economist's formula of individuals being reabsorbed into the economy rather than with a realist's picture of the squalor and degradation of Appalachia. The young, he envisioned, would go off to Pittsburgh or Detroit to work in steel or autos, while the old would live pleasantly on Social Security and their UMW pension checks. He knew this was not true, but he seemed unable to force himself to admit that the union had become a prisoner of conditions under which some members had to suffer so that others would prosper. He made a few weak efforts to do something about the problem, mainly authorizing District 50 to organize factories, stores, and highway construction projects in the coalfields in hope of providing jobs for displaced miners. Yet these efforts were never successful, leading Lewis, the opponent of "creeping socialism," increasingly to suggest that displaced miners seek relief from the state.

As a concomitant of mechanization, the large operators urged Lewis either to organize or drive out of business the rising number of nonunion mines. The advantages of mechanization—low labor cost per ton yet high daily wages—could only benefit the large operators and working UMW members if other producers could not attain the same result—low price per ton—by simply working on a nonunion basis. In June 1953, BCOA spokesman Harry M. Moses, disturbed by nonunion competition, publicly criticized the UMW for failing to organize the entire industry. He attributed part of this shortcoming to Lewis's refusal to sign the Taft-Hartley non-Communist affidavit, which would permit the UMW to participate in NLRB elections.[36]

By Moses's estimate, in 1953 20% of the working miners were not UMW members, and the percentage promised to rise. Nonunion miners could be found throughout the coalfields, but they were concentrated in Kentucky and Tennessee. Here, the Tennessee Valley Authority, rapidly becoming the nation's largest consumer of coal, encouraged the development of hundreds of "truck" mines, whose aggregate annual production added up to a sizable tonnage. Prior to 1947, Lewis had used the NLRB's procedures to organize the area, only to find that antiunion sentiment and pressures from operators made this approach futile. In the hills of Harlan County and Middlesboro, Kentucky, as well as LaFollette, Tennessee, the refrain of "Which Side Are You On?"—written during miners' struggles of the 1930s—still exemplified reality and not nostalgia.

Finally, Lewis instructed his field staff to organize the area "and damn the law suits. We'll take care of them." [37] There soon followed a reign of violence against persons and property—a labor guerrilla war. From the late 1940s on, people were killed, property was destroyed, and threats and intimidations abounded. Union miners, fighting for their livelihood, resorted to the strong-arm tactics that had been used against them not many years before. And the nonunion operators met force with force. Unlike the 1930s, however, liberals and radicals now viewed the union as the giant monopoly and sided with the price-cutting, non-union operators, whom they treated as simply little guys trying to make good. [38]

Lewis apparently made a point of keeping poorly informed about events in Kentucky and Tennessee. He wanted to become known as a labor statesman and so turned the "embarrassing" problems of the union over to his assistant, William Anthony "Tony" Boyle. Boyle was already familiar with "rough stuff" from his tenure as president of the Montana coal miners prior to 1948. Now, as assistant to the UMW president, he executed a host of ill-defined, covert duties. Some may have been ordered by Lewis; others, Boyle may have taken on his own initiative in order to impress his boss with his right to become heir apparent. Increasingly, Boyle's chief contact in Kentucky and Tennessee became District 19's secretary-treasurer, Albert E. Pass. Pass, in turn, communicated orders to the district's field representatives, one of whom was William J. Prater. In the 1970s, all three men would be convicted for participating in the murder of "Jock" Yablonski. [39]

The real union terrorists consisted of a gang of local miners known as "the Jones Boys" and a band of men from Illinois and Indiana angered at the nonunion operators stealing their markets. Both groups roamed the countryside in armies that at times numbered in the hundreds. They would converge on a nonunion operation, march the miners out of the colliery at gunpoint, and then coerce them to join the union. If the mine owner continued to operate on a nonunion basis, some of his equipment might be dynamited or the truckers who hauled his coal to market would be intimidated by a few rifle shots. [40]

One obstacle to understanding the labor violence of the 1940s and 1950s is that so much of what happened is recorded in the form of lawyers' accusations and so little in documented facts. Take, for instance, the suit brought against the union by one Charles Minton. The plaintiff, a UMW field representative, sought $350,000 in damages because, he claimed, he had been fired from his job when he refused to kill two mine owners. Minton admitted blowing up the Gladeville Coal Company's mine substation and arranging other dynamiting activities against the mine. The company, however, would not surrender to the union, so one day, Minton alleged in his complaint, he was summoned to a meeting with "Tony Boyle, agent extraordinary of the UMWA and personal agent of John L. Lewis, in Knoxville, Tennessee." At the meeting, Boyle reportedly told Minton "that he had been selected for the purpose of murdering one C. P. Fugate and one Harry L. Turner, owners of the Gladeville Coal Company." Minton refused, whereupon, he declared in his suit, "his star was lessened in the esteem of the UMWA." Despite the fascination Minton's story must have had for Lewis's enemies, no prosecutions flowed from the complaint for lack of corroborative evidence. The union quietly settled the case by paying Minton $45,000. [41]

By 1959, the mounting number of lawsuits against the union and the adverse publicity they generated finally led Lewis to order most of the "rough stuff" stopped. He now felt that he could eliminate the nonunion producers through the Protective Wage Clause of the 1958 contract. This provision, which prohibited unionized firms from allowing unorganized collieries to use their services, hindered "truck" mines from marketing their coal and in sidestepping the requirements of the Walsh-Healey Act.* Eventually, the propriety of the Protective Wage Clause would be challenged in court, but then legalisms did not bother Lewis.[42]

One of the most significant legacies Lewis would pass on to Boyle was an acceptance of lawlessness, of which a willingness to use violence was the most extreme manifestation. Lewis's disregard for the legal rules of society stemmed from witnessing throughout his life the triumph of power over principles. He had experienced the "justice" of the Lever Act, had been a defendant in the Hitchman Coal Company Case, and had watched Little Steel and Henry Ford repudiate their obligations under law. Twice he had been found guilty of contempt of court for actions that had been permitted even in the midst of World War II. And now, under the Taft-Hartley act, various operators were harassing the union by filing a host of unfair labor practices charges simply as a collective bargaining technique. In short, for Lewis, too much familiarity with the law had bred contempt.

Lewis, in fulfilling the UMW's obligations to the operators and, indeed, in endeavoring to extend his influence throughout the economy, increasingly resorted to using his organization's financial might. No longer could he act as spokesman for the toiling masses, as he had in the 1930s. Nor could he command attention, as he had through most of the 1940s, by threatening to paralyze the national economy with a miners' strike. The diminished place of coal in the national economy, the changed nature of the industry itself, and the UMW's isolation from the larger labor movement all served to transfer the union's source of power from its membership to its treasury. And, as the UMW's strength flowed solely from its purse, its values and structure changed. Lewis, at times unintentionally and unknowingly, acted to transform the UMW's primary concern from the welfare of its membership to the preservation of its treasury.

This process was most apparent on the issue of mechanization. Lewis promoted modernization principally because he felt it better for the industry to support 200,000 well-paid miners than 500,000 destitute ones. Yet his arrival at this policy was eased by the realization that the UMW's strength would not suffer with a decline in membership. Lewis recognized that increased productivity would actually increase the income of the welfare and retirement fund, because it was based on a per ton royalty and not a payroll tax. Moreover, he knew that well-paid miners could afford higher dues and assessments than poorer men. And finally,

*The Walsh-Healy Act required workers for firms under government contract to receive the prevailing, usually union, wage.

506 ● JOHN L. LEWIS

even if fewer miners worked, the union would still retain control of all the jobs in and around the mines. Modernization, in short, did not threaten the UMW's power base.

Lewis, of course, had long dabbled in business. Among other things, he had engaged in grain sales in the 1900s, launched a ''labor bank'' in the 1920s, and formed the Lewmurken Corporation in the 1930s to support the sagging businesses of his friends. He long had invested both the union's and his own money in the stock market with great skill. Since moving the union's headquarters to the nation's capital, the UMW had quietly purchased an impressive array of downtown real estate. Beginning with the University Club Building at 15th and I streets, for which the union paid $275,000, it went on to acquire 1453 K Street for $600,000; the Insurance Building at 15th and I for $1 million; and finally, in 1949, the eleven-story Chandler Building at 1427 I Street for $550,000. All in all, then, his entrepreneurial activities of the 1950s merely expanded and elaborated his earlier business endeavors.[43]

With the establishment of the welfare and retirement fund in the late 1940s, Lewis gained access to a multimillion-dollar treasury that he decided to invest in the banking business. This decision was perhaps inevitable, given his personal fascination with high finance, the counseling of such friends as Cleveland tycoon Cyrus Eaton, and his belief that financiers controlled the economy. In the 1960s, Secretary-Treasurer John Owens would inform convention delegates that the union purchased a bank because the establishment where the UMW kept its funds repeatedly insulted Owens by asking for identification each time he cashed a check. Although an apt tale for individuals angered by the impersonality of the times, it was not the real explanation for the union's actions. Closer to the truth was Lewis's contention that he saw no reason why the welfare and retirement fund should sit in other people's banks and not be put to work for the union. In this exploit, as well as in his other entrepreneurial activities, Lewis was not seeking personal financial profit but rather trying to strengthen the union and, consequently, his own position of power. Unfortunately, activities advantageous for the institution were not necessarily beneficial to the membership.

Apparently, in the spring of 1949, Lewis employed the investment firm of Johnston, Lemon and Company secretly to purchase for the UMW controlling interest in the National Bank of Washington. By April, the firm had completed the arrangements. Over the next thirteen months the union transferred the welfare and retirement fund into the bank's vaults, which increased the institution's total deposits from $22,610,346 to $83,676,875. By June 1950, the National Bank had become fourth largest among nineteen banks in the city. Even then, Lewis refused to acknowledge his connection to the institution, although he had personally chosen Barnum L. Colton to be the bank's president and his brother Dennie and UMW attorney Welly K. Hopkins sat on the board of directors. In 1956 they would be joined by Lewis's son, John Jr., and then later by the comptroller of the welfare and retirement fund, Thomas Ryan, in an appointment that raised seriously the issue of conflict of interest.[44]

The scope of the UMW's banking activities, as with most of its financial adventures, increased as Lewis became further isolated from the labor movement. Shortly after the A. F. of L. and CIO made known their merger plans, Lewis directed the National Bank to outbid all competitors for controlling interest in the Hamilton National Bank. This accomplished the National Bank of Washington subsequently absorbed the Liberty National Bank and the Anacostia Banks so that by 1964 it was the second largest bank in Washington, with eighteen units and total assets of $432 million. By 1964, Secretary-Treasurer John Owens proudly boasted that the union's $23 million investment in bank stocks over the previous fourteen years was worth $72 million.[45]

The deposits in the National Bank of Washington provided Lewis with tremendous financial leverage. Full details on the actual use of the bank's resources are unavailable, but it is clear that the institution responded to Lewis's will. It made loans to coal operators wishing to modernize their properties, and it bought heavily in the electric power field, where it then used its position to convince companies to burn union coal. Like all financial institutions, moreover, it made loans to people of influence when the need arose. Perhaps because of the possibility of government scrutiny of the bank's affairs, in delicate situations Lewis generally relied directly on the UMW treasury.

The UMW hierarchy intentionally cloaked the disposition of the union's monies. With unintended irony, John Owens told the 1960 convention delegates: "We differ from other labor unions in this country. We haven't publicly bragged about the resources of our Union." More accurately, the leadership mystified its financial activities. For years, the officers had reported the union's assets at approximately $30 million. Then the passage of the Labor-Management Reporting and Disclosure Act in 1959 compelled them to reevaluate the organization's worth at more nearly $110 million. This dramatic disclosure, combined with a series of legal cases, created enough of a stir among the membership and the press to force the officials to offer more detailed information on the UMW's financial empire.[46]

At the 1960 convention, John Owens presented a murky report on the union's financial resources that named names and cited figures, at least, even if it did not measure up to the standards of intelligible accounting. Owens made clear that he was speaking for "Mr. Labor Leader himself, who has so ably guided and directed me in whatever I have done, in whatever we have accomplished." According to Owens, the $21,646,174.72 tied up in the National Bank of Washington was the union's largest outright investment. Next came Lewis's 1951 investment of $9,421,518.45 in securities of the coal-carrying Chesapeake and Ohio Railway, which was managed by his close friend and economic counselor Cyrus Eaton. "I am only sorry to report to you," Owens gloated to the delegates, "that we have made just a few million dollars out of that investment for which no coal miner worked in the coal mines.'' Finally, since 1956, when the union allied with business interests to sell coal abroad through the American Coal Shipping Corporation, Lewis invested $8,346,489 into that venture and, through it, into the Bull Steamship Line.[47]

By 1960 such outright investments amounted to a sum conservatively estimated by Owens to be $17,688,329; but the union's secretary-treasurer reported a far larger amount—$56,743,337—tied up in loans and notes receivable. Since 1950, Lewis loaned union money to several parties, unnamed by Owens, who offered as collateral stock in such enterprises as the Tampa Electric Company, the Union Electric Company of Missouri, the Illinois Central Railroad, the Cleveland Electric Illuminating Company, and the Tri-Continental Corporation (Eaton Investment Company). Each of these firms was linked to the coal industry in one way or another. The loans did more than advance the industry, however, for according to Owens the union itself received $14,623,200 in ''profits and dividends'' over the decade from these deals.[48]

The most opaque section of Owens's report concerned the UMW's financial ties with actual mining properties. With great warmth, he told of advancing $5,200,000 to the Coaldale Mining Company in an effort to keep at least one segment of the decaying anthracite industry alive. He also defended the union's $26 million investment in the West Kentucky and Nashville Coal Companies. Yet on all other arrangements he was incredibly fleeting, asserting something about bringing stability to the Pittsburgh Midway properties and blurting out that the union had attained mines in Kansas under contract. ''We brought about hundreds and thousands of other tons of production on which men are receiving the wage scale, and the 40 cents a ton is going into the Welfare and Retirement Fund,'' he concluded without further elaboration.[49] Nonetheless, he had said enough to substantiate the New York Times' conclusion that the United Mine Workers was the ''wealthiest union in the land.''[50]

One reason Owens said as much as he did was the increasing publicity given to Lewis's collaboration with Cyrus Eaton. Lewis and Eaton first became friends in the 1940s, when they discovered that they shared a desire to stabilize the coal industry, a fascination with financial power, and a love of classical lore. Gradually, the Nova Scotia-born, Rockefeller-trained capitalist became Lewis's unofficial financial consultant, instructing the labor leader in his specialty, the art of ''leverage.'' The UMW's purchase of the National Bank of Washington met with Eaton's full approval, for the institution proved of great value to the two men as they united to strengthen their respective empires.

Perhaps while dining at Eaton's luxurious Northfield, Ohio, estate early in 1951, Lewis directed the conversation to the Tennessee Valley Authority's construction of a series of giant coal-fired power plants. Eaton and Lewis, as shrewd businessmen, recognized that the Authority would probably be one of the few expanding markets for the ailing coal industry. Yet the coal-purchasing policies of the TVA actually disrupted the stability of the industry by encouraging the rise of small, nonunion, marginal mines in Kentucky and Tennessee.

As Eaton's English butler cleared the table, Lewis perhaps recapitulated the UMW's efforts to organize that area, including the bloody struggles in Harlan County in the 1920s and 1930s as well as the more recent strife around Sparta, Tennessee. Finally, he dwelt upon the West Kentucky Coal Company, one of the largest nonunion firms, which, because of its competitive advantage, worked a full six-day week when unionized collieries produced on a three-day basis. In 1949, miners from as far away as Illinois and Indiana converged on the West Kentucky Coal Company mines and even resorted to force, but they still failed to organize the property.

At this point, the capitalist perhaps interrupted his union friend to advise him to use the union's financial might instead of mineworkers' muscles. He then outlined a plan whereby the UMW would lend him money from its treasury and its bank with which he could gain controlling interest in the West Kentucky property. Once in control, Eaton would direct the company to recognize the union, which would mean more members for the organization and more royalties for the welfare and retirement fund. Next, the union would provide more money so that the company could purchase the latest mine equipment. Fully mechanized, West Kentucky Coal would exert pressure on its competitors either to modernize and go union or be driven out of business. Because the union would benefit substantially from his proposal, Eaton demanded liberal credit arrangements.

Regardless of the actual circumstances under which the two men mapped out their plan, in 1951 Lewis lent Eaton about $6 million from the National Bank and the UMW treasury. The union also purchased West Kentucky stock and assigned its proxy to Eaton. By 1953, the Cleveland industrialist had become chairman of the company's board of directors, and shortly thereafter West Kentucky Coal finally recognized the union. More UMW money, funneled through Eaton, enabled the company to improve its competitive position and attain an ever larger share of the TVA's business. During its first few years, the venture looked so promising that in 1955 Lewis provided Eaton with at least another $7 million in order to purchase the Nashville Coal Company, another large nonunion coal mining and sales operation. Together West Kentucky and Nashville produced 12,500,000 tons of coal annually, which, when combined with the output from other properties controlled by the Cleveland industrialist and the union in 1960, made the Eaton-Lewis empire the third-largest bituminous producer in the country.[51]

Lewis and Eaton collaborated in other business ventures, particularly in investing in electrical utility stocks. Some of these power companies, such as Tampa Electric, also purchased West Kentucky and Nashville Coal. Of all the UMW's investments, however, the involvement in coal mining properties placed the union in the most awkward position. In seeking to create a healthy industry through modernization and consolidation, Lewis had to drive out of business all marginal properties regardless of their union standing. And in the area of the TVA, the union-backed West Kentucky and Nashville companies enforced the rules of competition, often to the detriment of UMW members employed at small mines. When, in the autumn of 1955, union and nonunion miners from the small collieries of the Sequatchie Valley struck for higher pay, the West Kentucky Coal Company moved in and captured the business of the area's main consumer—the TVA's Willow Creek steam plant—and in the process broke the strike.[52] More frequently, the union-backed coal companies combined with other large operations to force marginal, unionized mines first into a nonunion status and then completely out of business. Although slight rumbles of discontent over these activities could be heard in the 1950s, it would not be until after Lewis retired in 1960 that the full story of such business manipulations would unfold and tarnish his waning years.

Privately, Lewis enjoyed his standing as the head of a great financial empire and gloated when a tycoon such as Eaton referred to him as "the giant in Washington who has been my silent but stalwart coadjutor."[53] With his belief in capitalism, free enterprise, and the myth of the self-made man, Lewis's financial adventures proved to him that he had indeed made it—albeit with mineworkers' money.

Of all his activities in the 1950s, Lewis wanted to be remembered most for his work with the sick and the aged, the orphaned and the lame through the welfare and retirement fund. He was truly dedicated to ameliorating the conditions of the miners; but he also wanted to build a monument to himself. Much of his correspondence with Josephine Roche, the fund's director, concerned publicity given the endeavor, and throughout the decade he proved unusually vigilant in challenging criticisms of the program. Subconsciously, it seems, the elderly general of labor sought to emulate the senior captains of industry who engaged in philanthrophy in their declining years.

Revealingly, the business-oriented Lewis automatically defended his great humanitarian venture by equating workers and machines. "The Fund is predicated upon the principle," Lewis proclaimed, "that the cost of maintaining the manpower in the industry in a workable and healthful condition so that service can be rendered to the industry and the public, is just as much a part of the cost of production as lubricating oil, as mule feed, as steel rails, as taxes, or any other items that enter into the cost of production."[54]

In establishing the details of the fund Lewis allowed his idealism to transcend that practical hard-headedness for which he was known. He refused, for instance, to heed actuary reports that recommended the creation of a large trust fund to guarantee the promised benefits for the lifetime of the recipient. Rather, he insisted on his own pay-as-you-go scheme, in which benefits came directly out of income. Though this approach permitted workers to receive higher monthly payments, it also tied the program's future to fluctuations in the industry. Again, he refused to follow the customary procedure of first determining the amount of money available and then dividing it among the beneficiaries. Instead, he insisted on a liberal benefit program and expected to wrest from the operators the money needed to cover the costs through his collective bargaining skills. As a result of these decisions, the welfare and retirement fund was a noble venture fated for financial troubles.

To cover the cost of benefits and to meet inflation, Lewis successfully increased the royalty paid per ton of coal from five to forty cents between 1946 and 1952. For the fiscal year ending June 30, 1952, the fund earned $126,504,000 and expended $126,338,000. Roughly 40% of this money flowed out as payments to 38,690 pensioners. Under the provisions prevailing at that time, a retired union miner received $100 a month at the age of sixty if he had put in twenty years of service in the industry, regardless of his income from other sources. In comparison with similar pension programs, the UMW's was quite generous, partly to encourage older miners to retire in order to reduce the extent of technological unemployment.[55]

The welfare aspects of the fund, which accounted for some 55% of the expenditures in fiscal 1952, consisted of two small programs—Rehabilitation & Maintenance Aid Cash Benefits, and Aid to Widows, Dependent Children and Orphans—and the much larger medical and hospitalization program. By 1956, ten years after the establishment of the fund, over 75,000 retired miners had received pensions and almost 40,000 widows and orphans had obtained some form of aid. The fund's hospital and medical program had enabled 600,000 patient cases to benefit from over 7 million days of hospitalization and 6 million visits by physicians. In addition, the fund financed some 400,000 office consultations for beneficiaries by specialists and outpatient clinics.[56]

The high quality of the medical treatment and hospital care provided to beneficiaries earned awards for the fund from the president's Committee on Employment of the Physically Handicapped in 1951 and 1954, from the National Rehabilitation Association in 1957, and from Goodwill Industries in 1960. In 1956, the fund received the Albert Lasker Award, the most prestigious honor in the public health field, in part because of the impetus it gave to the speciality of physical medicine. That same year, Senator Paul Douglas's subcommittee on labor investigated the fund and stamped it honest and well administered and ranked the medical program as outstanding.[57]

Lewis took particular pleasure from praise of the fund's low operating costs—roughly 3% of expenditures each year. He strove for administrative efficiency in part to prove the superiority of an industry-run "free enterprise" welfare system over "socialized" government operations. But more important, efficiency was dictated by the necessity of making Lewis's pay-as-you-go scheme work under the adverse conditions facing the coal industry in the 1950s. In the fiscal year 1952, for instance, the fund took in only $166,000 more than it expended in benefits, and the next year it actually went into the red by spending $7,500,000 more than it received. The difference came from the $100 million the fund kept in reserve,

512 • JOHN L. LEWIS

which was not enough to meet benefit payments for a year if all income stopped. Indeed, Lewis was lucky that the operators had insisted back in 1946 that the fund be financed by a royalty on tonnage mined rather than the more common methods of a per capita tax or a percentage of the payroll. Although coal production dropped substantially in the 1950s, the decline in the number of miners working and the industry's labor costs were even more dramatic because of mechanization.[58]

Clearly, economic realities demanded a revision of Lewis's expectations of the fund. In 1951 and 1952, the fund had tried to provide dental care for its beneficiaries but had to drop it as too expensive. For the same reason it stopped assuming the cost of thousands of tonsil and adenoid operations for miners and their children. The failure of revenues to cover costs in 1953 led Lewis and his associates on the board of trustees to tighten the eligibility requirements for pensions from any union miner over sixty with over twenty years in the industry to any UMW member who accrued twenty years of service within the thirty years prior to his application for a pension. Until the trustees reversed this rule in 1965, it created injustice in some unique cases involving old-timers and long-disabled individuals, which Lewis and his associates seemed too inflexible to correct. For the most part, however, the new rule assured those miners who had spent their lives in the industry and had fought with the union in the 1930s and 1940s first access to the funds.[59]

In 1954 the trustees again cut the number of beneficiaries in order to enable expenditures to balance receipts. By rewriting the eligibility rules, they denied 30,000 disabled miners and 24,000 widows and children further benefits from the fund. The inclusion of these unfortunates in the first place dramatized Lewis's idealistic attempt to have the fund alleviate all suffering linked to coal. Their exclusion demonstrated the inadequacies of his industry-financed "free enterprise" system. Such retrenchment enabled the fund to meet expenses for the next few years, but by 1958 it was again operating at a deficit, leading the trustees to reduce benefits further in the early 1960s.[60]

As part of an effort to reduce costs, the fund abandoned its initial policy of allowing beneficiaries free choice of physicians and hospitals. This practice, Dr. Warren F. Draper, the fund's medical director, complained in 1955, led to "unnecessary hospitalization, undue length of stays, unnecessary procedures, unqualified physicians, failure to use specialists," and essentially "the subsidizing of a gravy train." Despite strong opposition from the American Medical Association, the fund began certifying certain doctors and hospitals as eligible to take part in the miners' medical program. As a result, total medical care expenditures decreased 13%, hospital admission rates dropped 16%, days of hospital care decreased 17%, and medical care per beneficiary costs declined 12%.[61]

Lewis's critics felt that he should have solved the fund's financial problems with transfusions from the UMW's treasury. They saw little reason for the union to make loans to the longshoremen's union or purchase stock in coal and power companies when the fund reduced benefits to the miners. Lewis contended that the

Taft-Hartley and other laws prohibited the intermingling of the two treasuries, although occasionally he funneled UMW money to operators so that they could pay it back in the form of royalties to the fund. For the most part, however, he felt that it was best to invest the union's resources in building up the strength of the industry, which would eventually improve the fund's position.

Actually, during the 1950s most union members overlooked the fund's retrenchment policies and continued to praise Lewis. At the 1956 convention, for instance, a delegate from Gary, West Virginia, resolved that the union begin building a monument to Lewis. John L. humbly ruled the motion out of order. But he had already executed its spirit by spending almost $30 million from the welfare and retirement fund on the construction of ten hospitals. The chain ran through Virginia, West Virginia, and Kentucky and brought high-quality medical and health service to an area pitifully lacking such care.[62]

The dedication of the hospitals in 1956 was a momentous occasion for the seventy-six-year-old union leader. He saw the project as proof of his commitment to the miners and as the crowning achievement of his long career. For weeks prior to the ceremony he fretted over the arrangements and worried whether various dignitaries would come. The UMW even hired a special train to convey the guests from Washington to Beckley, West Virginia, where the dedication occurred. There, on a drizzly June 2, a crowd of thousands participated in Lewis's moment of glory. And before them stood a well-equipped brick-and-glass building that gave the sense of having been constructed around a portrait of John L. Lewis.[63]

At the dawn of the decade, Lewis had few reasons to feel generationally out of date. While new faces appeared, individuals with whom he had interacted for years still held key positions in the nation's social, political, and economic life. As time passed, the old faded away and a new generation emerged. The Republicans who took over Washington in 1953, for instance, were neither personally nor ideologically akin to the GOP leaders Lewis had related to for most of his career. He now felt more comfortable with old-timers from the party of Roosevelt—Alben Barkley, Oscar Chapman, Averell Harriman, and even Harry Truman—and apparently voted Democratic in presidential elections for the rest of his life. And in the coal industry such men as George Love and Martin Fox replaced such longtime adversaries as Charles O'Neill, Ezra Van Horn, Harry Moses, and Major William W. Inglis. Lewis watched the most sweeping transition in leadership occur within the labor movement. Here, Daniel Tobin, William L. Hutcheson, Matthew Woll, John Frey, George Berry, and others of their breed—men who had dominated unionism for nearly a half century—passed from the scene. If Lewis had been allowed to rejoin the executive board of either the A. F. of L. or CIO in 1950, a majority of his associates would have been men with whom he had worked in the turbulent 1930s. By 1960, this would not have been the case.

The deaths of William Green and Phil Murray in 1952 had particular meaning for Lewis. So much of his career had involved these two men, first in their roles as his faithful lieutenants and then as heads of the national federations that Lewis alternately courted and cursed. Since the mid-1940s, the miners' chief had rekindled a personal fondness for Green. When Green died, he felt real sadness, and at the next miners' convention he magnanimously listed the A. F. of L. president as among the UMW's "Departed Brothers." Lewis proved unable to make a similar gesture for Phil Murray and to the end could not forgive the CIO chief for his "betrayal."[64]

Perhaps Lewis could control the psychological sense of aging as long as his mother survived, but on January 12, 1950, Ann Louisa Lewis passed away at the age of ninety-one. For two years she had been in poor health. Then, in September 1949, she fractured her hip and, while confined, contracted pneumonia. Throughout that autumn, Lewis pushed himself to his own physical limits, dividing his time between his ailing mother in Springfield, Illinois, and the prolonged coal negotiations in White Sulphur Springs, West Virginia. On such pretexts as fetching a newspaper, he would abruptly leave the bargaining table and would not return for up to ten days. Driving the long trip alone, he was ticketed for speeding and illegal passing on at least one occasion. On another trip he arrived in Springfield at 1:00 A.M. only to discover that a convention had taken over all the sleeping accommodations in town. Utterly exhausted, he spent the night on a cot in a banquet hall, where unknowing employees continually interrupted his rest. When his mother finally died, in January, the coal situation was at such a critical state that he had little time—physically or emotionally—to adjust to his loss.[65]

Time also took a heavy toll of other members in his circle of family and faithful associates. A little more than a month after his mother's death, he received the tragic news that his brother, Tom, painfully ill for an extended period, had ended his suffering by suicide.[66] During the decade, many of Lewis's "union brothers" also passed away. No longer could he call upon W. Jett Lauck for advice or be entertained by the sarcasm of K. C. Adams. Gone, too, were William Sneed, Sam Caddy, O. E. Gasaway, William Brennan, Frank Hefferly, John T. Jones, William Blizzard, A. T. Pace, and other fellow union warriors.

For Lewis, the deaths of family, associates, and adversaries constituted one part of the totality of experiences that ultimately led him to recognize the passing of his era. On another level, he increasingly feared that the American people no longer revered his generation's values and principles. True, since his break with Roosevelt he had been protesting the direction in which the country seemed headed; but now, in the 1950s, his cry approached a lament: "Can we keep this nation of ours?" he asked. "Can we retain free enterprise? Can we offset and resist the rising, threatening tide of world Communism? Can we resist the tendency in a Republic such as our own, to adopt the device of the more absolute forms of government, seeking to justify ourselves in so doing that we are saving the basic concepts of the Republic?"[67]

Persistently he mourned the fact that he could "see changing the character of my country before my eyes. . . . There is a trend now toward the acceptance of the use of force to regulate the affairs of freemen,'' he bemoaned, ''which is danger-ous—dangerous to all it effects and dangerous to the future of the nation. . . . [T]he whole concept of our public life,'' he told congressmen in 1953, ''is based upon free enterprise, liberty of the citizen, tolerance for each other's viewpoint, and due regard for the rights of all. Have we lost confidence in that?'' To the same group six years later, he queried: ''Whither are we drifting?''[68]

Most disturbing to Lewis was the tendency of the government to investigate and regulate unions. To him, the McClellan committee was but ''a re-establishment of the principle of the star chamber of the Tudor and Stuart kings—with a slight touch of the Spanish Inquisition.''[69] He contended that there were enough laws on the books to punish wrongdoing by labor leaders and that efforts to attain special legislation constituted nothing more than a drive to taint and cast aspersions upon the labor movement. Lewis's opposition to the Landrum-Griffin act and other measures rested upon his vision of a pluralistic society of voluntary associations threatened by the rise of the corporate state. ''I do not believe,'' he told Senator John F. Kennedy's subcommittee on welfare funds, ''that the Republic, through its central powers, can regulate those voluntary associations either in whole or in part without of necessity expanding its powers as a central government to the point where it will become a police state in truth and in fact.''[70]

Yet although opposed to government regulation of labor unions, he also rejected the idea that the organizations themselves should police the honesty of their officers. He viewed unions as simply vehicles to attain better physical conditions for their members. ''The question of sin and morality and the hunting down of sin and immorality and its eradication,'' he declared, ''is not an enterprise within the purview of the province of labor unions and the members of those labor unions didn't pay in their money—whatever it may be for membership—to have it used for that kind of a purpose.''[71] The essence of this argument would be repeated by Tony Boyle years later to explain why he failed to probe into his lieutenant's involvement in ''Jock'' Yablonski's death.[72] Like the nullification and state's rights doctrines of John C. Calhoun, Lewis's philosophical construct of a pluralis-tic republic could be twisted to self-serving purposes.

It now made little difference what Lewis believed, however, for few people outside of the miners' union paid attention to him. Senators would flock into a committee room to gaze at him as they would a museum piece; he was a living bit of history and a great theatrical show. In the midst of one hearing, Congressman Carroll Kearns praised him for being ''the Lionel Barrymore of the labor move-ment.''[73] More and more, he was the recipient of patronizing courtesies granted elders rather than the blunt respect offered to a person of power. His appointment to Eisenhower's Citizens Advisory Committee on Foreign Aid was just such a gesture, for it was known that his health and age would limit Lewis's role.

As a response to aging, Lewis, under the coaxing of Josephine Roche, sought to forge closer bonds with his children and their offspring. In the mid-1940s, Kathryn had made another attempt to escape her father's domination by moving to an isolated cottage near Scarborough-on-Hudson in New York. By the early 1950s, however, she was again by his side. Together they took a South American vacation in 1952, and John L.—in his fatherly way—appointed her UMW specialist for foreign labor relations. As his administrative assistant for the rest of the decade, she saw her job as protecting him from others. In public she always referred to him as "Mr. Lewis"; few people ever heard her call him "father."[74]

A far wider gap separated Lewis and his son, although it was closed somewhat by the young psychiatrist's attentiveness during his father's wave of heart attacks in the 1940s. In June 1948 John L. was delighted when he became a grandfather for the second time and disrupted a negotiating session to celebrate. Lewis's interest in building hospitals and medical facilities might in part have been an attempt to win his son's favor. In 1956, he did appoint John Jr., to the board of directors of the National Bank of Washington. Despite such overtures, however, the distance between the house on Orinoco Street in Alexandria and the son's residence near Baltimore remained greater than one of mere miles.[75]

By 1958 Lewis began to speculate about whether he should retire. "The time has come now," he informed Martin Agronsky of NBC-TV, "for other leadership to develop."[76] The realities of his isolation in the labor movement, the weakening of his union, the decline of the coal industry, and the obsolescence of his politics all weighed heavily on his mind. Retirement, too, could be that ultimate gesture to certify that his aim in life was not simply amassing and holding power. And by stepping down, Tom Kennedy could end his own career as UMW president as a reward for faithful service. More directly, Lewis confronted the condition of his health, for in 1955 he had entered Emergency Hospital in Washington with another heart attack, and in 1957 poor health had forced him to cut short a world tour as a member of Eisenhower's commission to investigate foreign aid programs.

Then in January 1959, another heart attack sent him back to Georgetown Hospital. He spent three weeks there and several more recovering in Alexandria. Lewis could have retired then, but apparently he wanted to stay in office a little longer, perhaps in order to match Samuel Gompers's forty years as a leader in the labor movement. Finally, on December 15, 1959, Lewis informed the membership of his intent to resign soon after the beginning of the new year.[77]

Over the next few weeks, Lewis received a flood of messages from both the nation's high and mighty and meek and lowly expressing their appreciation for the things he had done over the years. From rank-and-file miners came hand-scrawled notes filled with personal references to what he meant to them. "I have never been ask [sic] to write a letter that tuched [sic] my heart as much as this one," wrote a coal digger from Pennington Gap, Virginia:

> They ask me, and by a vote of 100 per cent, to write *you* and express our *heart felt appreciation to you* for what a soilder [sic] *you have been for Our organization*. We

know there is no other man who can *speak with so much influence* for labor as you have in the past 28 years.

My little Local 6374 in Va has been in action since 1933 June, which you will remember up to *that time we were in Slavery* in the Va coal mines. . . .

Now Mr. Lewis we are so very sorry to give you up. But we under stand and as great as you are, and as great as you have been to our Organization we will *always miss you* at the front.

Now we agree that Mr. Kennedy is the man to be put in your place. He is a *firm and solid* union man and has experience under you long enough that *we all have faith in Him—and* if any thing should happen to him, for me *I would want your Brother* there in Washington, D.C. in charge of the *Bank.*

Now for me and my wife we want to thank *you* from our hearts for the Hospitals, Pensions, and for bringing us out of slavery. I guess the Welfare fund has spent *six or seven* thousand dollars on Mrs. Wallen and about $800.00 on me. . . .

Now I know there is no miner any more thankful than I am for our organization in this U.S.A.

Now Mr. Lewis we hope you the very best of health, and many more years to stand by us.[78]

Moving as such letters were, Lewis took greater satisfaction in praise from the power elite. Among the tributes he prized most was one from Herbert Hoover, which he never made public, although George Love begged him to. ''From some experience in public affairs relating to coal,'' the former president wrote, ''I know your life has been one of stout support of the miners' interests. And during all your long years you upheld private enterprise in the industry; you supported the installation of every labor-saving device and the elimination of feather-bedding; and you insisted upon constantly greater safety measures. That is statesmanship.''[79]

CHAPTER 22
Twilight and Darkness, 1960-1969

On January 14, 1960, John L. Lewis retired as UMW president. The union marked the occasion with some ceremony, but not with the pomp and pageantry reporters had anticipated. Even Lewis's speech at the dinner in his honor was "without histrionics and, for him, quiet."[1] He talked on future challenges facing organized labor and offered his listeners few reminiscences and no introspection. The entire day's activities emphasized that although Lewis was retiring from formal leadership in the union, he intended to remain active in coal industry affairs for some time to come.

The official transfer of power from Lewis to Thomas Kennedy occurred at an afternoon meeting of the UMW executive board. For years various union politicos, including W. A. "Tony" Boyle and Joseph A. "Jock" Yablonski, had courted Lewis in hopes of becoming his successor. Yet contrary to journalistic opinion, Lewis had no understudy as heir apparent. The order of succession at his retirement followed bureaucratic lines. Seventy-three years old, Vice-President Kennedy automatically moved into the presidency. Secretary-Treasurer John Owens declined the vacant vice-presidential post, however. Unaware that Kennedy had cancer and would die shortly, Owens saw no reason to master new duties at the age of seventy. Consequently, the vice-presidency went to the next person in line, Lewis's assistant W. A. "Tony" Boyle. The executive board sanctioned this arrangement and then appointed Lewis to the new position of president emeritus with an annual pension of $50,000.[2]

For the first few years of retirement, Lewis played an active but diminished role in coal industry affairs. Occasionally he would enter the public spotlight, as when, on June 25, 1962, he made an unexpected appearance at the Conference on Coal Recovery and blamed the Eisenhower and Kennedy administrations for the industry's ills. For the most part, however, Lewis conducted his activities out of the public's view. In consultation with Cyrus Eaton, he continued to oversee the UMW's far-flung financial empire with, for instance, the two men exploring ways to compel the Cleveland Electric Illuminating Company to purchase union coal.[3]

518

Lewis also spent time consulting with the UMW's legal staff on several antitrust suits challenging the labor relations system developed in the 1950s. In the Pennington-Phillips Brothers case and similar actions, small unionized operators contended that the union conspired with the large members of BCOA to impose the forty-cents-per-ton royalty upon the industry in order to drive marginal mines out of business. The large operators were not hurt by the royalty payments, the plaintiffs claimed, because the UMW made sure that they could modernize their properties with loans from the National Bank of Washington. Other cases, such as *Tennessee Consolidated Coal Company* vs. *UMWA*, challenged the union-owned Western Kentucky Coal Company's role in suppressing competition. For years such antitrust suits went through appeals and retrials without receiving clear decisions. The adverse public criticism they generated and the prospect of further law suits, however, led the union, through Cyrus Eaton, to divest itself of the West Kentucky Coal Company in September 1963.[4]

Lewis's primary responsibility in the 1960s was as chairman of the welfare and retirement fund, a post he held until his death. Although the fund's staff assumed greater discretion as Lewis grew more decrepit, the octogenarian dictated the program's basic policies. His decisions displayed increasing insensitivity, poor judgment, and manipulation, yet neither Josephine Roche, the neutral trustee, nor Henry G. Schmidt, the operators' representative, challenged his verdicts. As a consequence, the fund that Lewis had once envisioned as a monument to his humanitarianism became a symbol of dictatorial rule.

Throughout the 1950s and early 1960s, the depressed state of the coal industry greatly reduced the fund's income. By 1961 royalties amounted to only $114 million—the smallest figure in the program's history. At the same time, the number of pensioners had reached a record 66,759, forcing the fund to expend nearly $16.5 million more than it received. In meeting this crisis, the UMW refused to demand a larger per ton royalty from the operators out of fear of both placing unionized mines at a greater competitive disadvantage and driving marginal producers to a nonunion status.[5]

Consequently, Lewis sought to solve the fund's financial problems by cutting expenditures. In mid-1960 the trustees revoked the medical and hospital coverage of all miners unemployed for more than a year. At the same time, they denied coverage to working UMW members if their employers had not signed the national wage agreement. A few months later, in December 1960, the trustees reduced pension payments from $100 to $75 a month. Again, in 1962, they canceled the health cards of miners employed by operators making only token royalty payments. This last policy generated a wave of wildcat strikes against the reneging companies and a letter to Lewis from his brother Raymond, president of District 17, criticizing him for arbitrary and illegal action.[6]

Lewis also put the fund's ten ''Miners'' hospitals up for sale in order to free the millions of dollars tied up in noninterest-bearing mortgages for income-generating investments. Apparently, he lost interest in the hospitals when declining employment in the coal industry reduced the proportion of miners as patients. The failure of the local communities served by the hospitals to purchase them caused the welfare and retirement fund to consider closing the facilities. Fortunately, the United Presbyterian Church became interested in medical care in Appalachia and, with federal money allocated directly by President Kennedy, purchased eight of the ten centers in 1964. The fund eventually closed the other two and, in the entire transaction, lost about half of its $27 million investment in the chain.[7]

By the mid-1960s, the growing demand for electrical energy improved coal sales and generated larger royalties for the fund. Some of this money went toward improved benefits for miners, but Lewis also enlisted it in the UMW's battle against nonunion coal. In February 1965, for example, the trustees raised pensions, previously cut from $100 to to $75, to $85 a month. They could have restored the full amount but instead decided to lower the qualifying age from sixty to fifty-five to encourage older unemployed miners to retire rather than to take jobs at nonunion pits. In another attempt to reduce the work force available to nonunion operators, the trustees ruled that a miner's last year of work had to be in a union colliery in order for him to qualify for a pension. This policy harshly punished those old-timers who had labored years in organized mines only to be forced by the vicissitudes of age to accept nonunion employment.[8]

Under Lewis's domination the insensitivity, manipulation, and mismanagement apparent in the fund's benefit programs also characterized its investment policies. The fund lost nearly $4 million, for example, when the trustees sold almost $46 million worth of government securities prior to their maturity date. Lewis and his associates argued that they had accepted this loss in order to obtain capital for investment in higher-yield ventures. Yet if the trustees wanted capital, they could have tapped the fund's general checking account, which contained millions of dollars not earning interest. Indeed, from 1961 to 1967 the nonyielding deposits in the general account climbed from $12 million to $72 million, or 44% of the fund's resources. The UMW-owned National Bank of Washington, where the fund did its business, had use of this money at no cost, giving rise to suspicion.[9]

Although Lewis remained a trustee until his death, he no longer seemed to view the fund as the crowning accomplishment of his career. Rather, he took greater pride in his role in initiating the National Coal Policy Conference (NCPC) to coordinate the industry's affairs and was elated at becoming NCPC chairman in 1962. To Lewis, attainment of this post symbolized his arrival as a peer of the Captains of Industry.

For several months Lewis served as the spokesman for coal in demanding benefits and subsidies from the government equal to those provided other fuels. Surgery and prolonged hospitalization in late 1962, however, curtailed Lewis's work as NCPC chairman. And then, on January 19, 1963, while he recuperated, his longtime associate and successor as UMW president, Thomas Kennedy, died of cancer. Kennedy's death symbolized to Lewis the departure of all his old comrades and the end of the UMW that he knew best. These thoughts, along with his erratic health, led Lewis significantly to reduce his activities.

On April 3, 1963, when Lewis retired as NCPC chairman, the conference honored him with a luncheon. Throughout the proceedings businessmen sang his praises. Joseph P. Routh, chairman of Pittston Company, for instance, ranked Lewis's two greatest achievements as promoting modernization and initiating the National Coal Policy Conference. "[I]t was only because of this great man," Routh conceded, "that this industry survives today."[10]

Accepting such praise graciously—indeed, concurring in it—Lewis uttered thoughts appropriate as one relinquishes power. This occasion, and not the 1960 UMW ceremonies, marked Lewis's retirement from a central role in the coal industry. "The shadows are gathering on all of us," he philosophized. "We only make such contributions as we can while we are here." As if granting absolution, he disclaimed any animosity toward those operators who fought him so viciously prior to 1950. "They moved as they saw the light," he conceded. "They acted within the limitations that were upon them as so do we now."[11]

Although Lewis proved able to announce the end of his era, he still seemed incapable of evaluating his life or fathoming his personality. When the members of the NCPC presented him with a painting of himself, he thanked them for the gift. "I value this portrait," he said. And then looking down at his likeness, he added: "although I am going to have a hard time reading all the facets of his character."[12]

During his first few years of retirement, Lewis vacationed in the West and in Florida and journeyed to New York City to be with Kathryn, who was under psychiatric care. He also collected numerous honors that had evaded him during his active career. It was as though proper society chose to wait until the volcanic man became inactive before offering him the homage paid most prominent individuals earlier in their lives. Lewis did not receive his first honorary degree, for example, until 1957, when the University of West Virginia granted him an LL.D. Three years later Georgetown University made him a "Doctor of Humane Letters, *honoris causa*," but not commencement speaker. No other university came forth with similar recognition, although in 1966 Buena Vista College, observing its seventy-fifth anniversary, gave Lewis one of seventy-five Honor Iowans' Awards.[13]

Some tributes clearly amused Lewis. Upon receiving the Freedom Medal from President Lyndon Johnson in 1964, the elderly labor leader chuckled, "So they gave me a medal for doing all those things they fought me for doing all those years."[14] Even more irony lay behind his acceptance of the Eugene V. Debs Award in 1965. Not only had Lewis opposed Debs when the socialist was alive, but in 1962 he forbade the UMW from participating in a memorial to the man.

Now, perhaps moved by a vain drive to accumulate recognition, Lewis took the award and forwarded fifty dollars to the Debs Foundation.[15]

Because of Lewis's status as the nation's senior labor statesman, his office became a stop for most foreign labor dignitaries touring the country in the 1960s. The Kennedy administration, moreover, solicited Lewis's participation in an international lecture series that constituted part of the government's new emphasis on cultural diplomacy. Lewis, who considered economics the foundation of foreign affairs, rejected the invitation. "I cannot believe," he replied, "that a cultural program, however virtuous and well managed, will be a controlling factor in the adjustment of these world-wide problems. In addition," he jibed, "I would perhaps be a little out of character in lecturing on a subject ["The Concept of Freedom"] on which, heretofore, I had not been recognized as an authority."[16]

When not traveling, Lewis resided in his Alexandria house, where the black couple who had served him for many years continued to wait upon his needs. On weekdays he would be chauffeured to the UMW building, where he would spend a few hours in his sixth floor office. Actually, his quarters consisted of a suite of rooms filled with overstuffed leather sofas and chairs, with mementos decorating the walls and a wagon-wheel chandelier obtained during one of his western vacations hanging above his desk. At noon, Lewis usually strolled to the Sheraton-Carlton Hotel, occasionally with company, but most often alone. Several times in the 1960s George DeNucci, an old Ohio labor organizer, entered the Carlton's dining room and noticed John L. Lewis, "Tony" Boyle, and John Owens each eating in isolation.[17]

After lunch, Lewis occasionally granted an audience to a reporter, foreign labor dignitary, or old acquaintance. He could be quite charming and generally treated his guests to a delightful time. Labor reporter John Herling enjoyed one such interview in late 1963, which he reported in his skillful style. Herling anxiously waited in the sixth floor anteroom for a few minutes before the aging labor giant strolled out of his office with his hand extended. "His look is sharp and seems to fold back on itself," Herling recalled.

> He looks you over and, as you return the look, he seems to be trying to guess your thoughts about him.
>
> "It must be a dull day on the rialto that brings you to this humble abode," he rumbles softly. It's an old line of his and he utters it with relish. Then he settles back in an armchair. He stares at you and you stare back, faint-heartedly. His eyes, always deep, now seem more cavernous. His eyebrows grow hugely. They flare out luxuriantly. He picks up a long cigar, bites the end, lights up, and waves it like a scepter.
>
> "How are all your heroes?" he says derisively. "Heroes?" I reply defensively, bristling a little, "Whom do you mean?" Then he mockingly intones the names of several great and near great—in and out of the labor movement. After he gets through with this elephantine caper, I say: "Mr. Lewis, you do yourself an injustice. You know, sir, even those who are reluctant to admit it consider you something rather

special. They are only great. You are most great, you are maximus.'' We are trading extravagances. His eyes light up.

"Aha," says Mr. Lewis, "we know you as being most gracious, even though you are not always perceptive." To which I reply, "On this subject of yourself, you can hardly be objective. By profession, I can only tell the truth."

He waves, as if granting that this round must end somewhere. And then, as is his wont, he interviews you. He asks you a question, and doesn't always wait for your inadequate answer. Most of his questions are rhetorical. They punctuate the reality around you and the world beyond. His talk is filled not only with generalizations about men and motives, but like a cigar wrapper, it encloses layers and layers of detail.[18]

Most interviewers left a session with Lewis convinced that he no longer coveted power. "I'm out of the front line now," he told Edward Folliard of the Washington *Post,* who found Lewis's associates commenting on how benign he seemed. "He knows his heyday is past," one UMW aid remarked, "and sees little value in getting into newspaper scraps with other labor leaders." Quite simply, observed Fred Perkins of the Scripps-Howard chain, "he doesn't seek the spotlight." When John Herling asked him if he intended to renew the sense of urgency in the labor movement, Lewis straightened himself up. "I?" he asked, "I? . . . The arena and the welkin are now for others." Then, abruptly, he intoned: "Mr. Herling, how many blocks of seven years do you think one man has to give?"[19]

People continually prodded Lewis to write his memoirs, and several publishers offered him lucrative book contracts. But Lewis unhesitatingly rejected such pressures. Infrequently, he would reminisce with reporters, but even these talks were not for repeating. When Walter Cronkite's "Twentieth Century" prepared a television special on Lewis, the aging labor leader refused to participate in the production. Lewis cooperated even less with professional scholars and refused to take part in the Columbia Oral History Project. He mocked "Thus is history made" when informed of the State Historical Society of Wisconsin's acquisition of the Adolph Germer Papers, and he felt no call to preserve his own records for posterity. Students of the past approaching him for an interview almost always met a negative reply. "[T]he moving finger has made a record," he wrote to one scholar. "It is available in every library and newspaper morgue across the land. Not all my 'piety nor wit shall lure it back to cancel half a line, nor all your tears wash out a word of it'."[20]

Lewis undoubtedly recognized that it had been his own "moving finger" that had "made the record" through his control over everything the UMW put into print. Understandably, Lewis displayed a love for history but suspicion for historians. Although he avidly read *American Heritage* and prided himself on being a student of classical culture, he also doubted that the "true" past could be recreated. Himself devious, he believed that all historical actors maneuvered in secret and conspiratorial ways that historians could never penetrate. Nor did he like to have his own mysteries probed by someone he could not dominate, for

Lewis characteristically sought to control all events in which he participated, even those that had already occurred.

At night and on weekends, Lewis engaged in little socializing, partly to preserve his waning strength and partly because he found cocktail parties to be "an abomination." He preferred spending his evenings at home reading a novel or article on business and listening to the radio. Josephine Roche kept a lookout for literature that would strike his fancy, and on one occasion she made him a gift of Victor Hugo's *Les Miserables*. He also combed through the fifteen-volume, 1793 edition of Shakespeare's works presented to him by the National Coal Policy Conference. After finishing a book, Lewis occasionally wrote Josephine Roche an appraisal of the work. David Demarest Lloyd's *Spend and Survive,* for example, failed to make a good impression on the labor leader: "Much of it is elementary in nature and designed to impress the uninformed."[21] At his suggestion, Roche would read various volumes, only to concur in his assessment. "As you said," she wrote him after perusing Walter Galenson's *The CIO Challenge to the AFL,* "there is a vast amount of more or less factual data totally lacking in any perception or realization of all that was, and is, back of fact."[22]

Josephine Roche became Lewis's most comforting friend during his retirement years. In addition to looking after most of the routine welfare and retirement fund business that came across Lewis's desk, Roche provided the octogenarian with cheerful companionship that brightened his otherwise lonely existence. In the last few years of his life, when infirmities often kept him confined to his Alexandria home, Roche served as both a link and a protective buffer between the fading Lewis and the outside world.

Among other things, Roche helped satisfy Lewis's almost insatiable desire for worship. He thrived on adulation and purposely sent her the eulogistic correspondence he received in order to evoke her praise. "More deeply appreciated than I can express," she effused on one occasion:

> is your thoughtfulness in letting me read this remarkable "day's grist" which records the overwhelming evidence of your profound and lasting achievements for your members, the industry and the national economy. In these days when we seem straying so far as a nation from what some of us feel this country is and stands for [,] you cannot fail to have a sense of reassurance as to its continuing basic soundness from this testimony coming to you from its every segment—your members, your pensioners, your countless friends among the outstanding national, financial and industrial leaders. . . .
>
> Thank you most sincerely for the privilege you have given me.[23]

Like Roche, Cyrus Eaton heaped unqualified acclaim on his old friend. When the labor leader extended Eaton birthday greetings in 1964, the Cleveland financier lauded: "To be the recipient of such generous praise from one of the world's great citizens of all times gives me new inspiration for the busy years ahead."

"The pride of my own 84 years," Eaton extolled on Lewis's eighty-eighth birthday, "is my long and cherished friendship with history's greatest labor statesman."[24]

Lewis thought that such formality and pomposity communicated deep affection. Yet in reality, Lewis's Victorian stiffness tended to hinder warm interaction with those he loved. He gloated over his grandson, Tom, for example, but corresponded with the youngster in business letter format, including a colon following the salutation and "Sincerely yours."[25] Formality also stood between John L. and his daughter Kathryn, who, while emotionally tied to him, seemed unable to penetrate his defenses and share his innermost life. Ever since the 1930s, she had been either working intensely by his side or fleeing from his domination. Frustrated, in the early 1960s Kathryn again sought to end her submissiveness to her father and fled to New York, where she underwent treatment for depression. Then, mysteriously, on January 7, 1962, she died at the age of fifty in Wickersham Hospital. The newspapers gave no details although the death certificate claimed natural causes. Her death deeply grieved Lewis, who had tried to be a good father even if he did not know how. As always, he kept his sorrow to himself.[26]

A few weeks after Lewis suffered the loss of Kathryn, Alma Dennie Lewis died. Of all the Lewis brothers, Dennie had fought longest by John L.'s side and had remained the most faithful. "Denny [sic] called his brother 'The Boss'," Len De-Caux recalled. "Loyalty to him came first, and he liked to stress an almost carbon-copy subordination."[27] Lewis lost other members of his family over the next few years: his sister Hattie on January 18, 1963; his brother Howard on April 5, 1968.

The remaining relatives proved unable or unwilling to meet Lewis's emotional needs. Most painful to the aging leader, his son, John Jr., continued to have little to do with him and kept the grandchildren from visiting the old man too frequently. Lewis spent the last years of his life almost isolated from his offspring when his son moved his family from Baltimore to Milwaukee. John L.'s brother Raymond, moreover, showed few indications of affection for his brother and at times criticized him harshly. But for Josephine Roche and a few other UMW staff members, Lewis would have been depressingly lonely in his declining years.

W. A. "Tony" Boyle's ascent to the UMW presidency in 1963 placed the retired Lewis in an awkward position. Although Boyle had served as Lewis's assistant, the new president enjoyed no special rapport with the elderly labor leader. The UMW patriarch kept Boyle, as he did all his lieutenants, at a social distance, and he could not envision anyone adequately replacing him as head of the union. Yet publicly, the president emeritus supported his former assistant, occasionally with kind words but most often with silence. After Boyle took over the union, Lewis avoided involvement in UMW affairs except for welfare and retirement fund business and even failed to attend the miners' 1964 convention. In a sense, the aged Lewis became subject to the code of loyalty he had originated, for now Boyle expected him to suppress his personal opinions just as for decades Lewis had demanded the same from others. No longer wanting to play union politics and in erratic health, Lewis quietly concurred in this policy.

Boyle needed Lewis's acquiescence in order to strengthen his control over his inherited union. The new president's origins in the remote Montana coalfields and his ascension through a nonelected staff position resulted in his lacking significant support among the miners. Clearly, if Lewis had intended Boyle to be his heir apparent he would have done more to strengthen his assistant's ties with the rank and file. As it was, Boyle recognized that his claim to the presidency rested on his image as Lewis's protégé, and he consciously manipulated the labor giant's charisma to win the miners' acceptance. In 1964, for example, bituminous miners, angered at not receiving a wage increase in six years, forced the union to negotiate a new contract. When Boyle returned to the miners with the agreement he had negotiated, he was fearful that they would turn it down. In order to win their support, therefore, he emphasized that although Lewis had not participated in the actual bargaining, he had followed the negotiations closely and had advised Boyle on every move.[28]

In another effort to capitalize on the miners' allegiance to Lewis, on June 12, 1963, the executive board elected John L.'s brother Raymond UMW vice-president. Although this might have pleased union members in the coalfields, it caused Boyle alarm. As an official in District 17, Raymond had exercised family liberties and harshly criticized his brother. He now felt little reason to submit to Boyle, and perhaps he even thought of obtaining the union presidency for himself. All was not harmony between the two men, with on at least one occasion Raymond charging Boyle with acting unconstitutionally. Soon after the episode, Raymond received a letter from George Titler, Boyle's strongest ally and head of the union's violent southern West Virginia district. "What would John L. Lewis have done with a maverick of your ilk?" Titler asked. "The answer is simply: a kick in the pants with a hard-toe shoe."[29] Faced with such blunt opposition—and apparently unable to enlist his brother's backing—Raymond Lewis resigned the vice-presidency in November 1965.

By the late 1960s, the decay of the UMW under Boyle began to disturb Lewis. He felt sadness at seeing his kingdom weakened by a rank-and-file revolt from within and legal challenges from without. The appointment of Boyle, he reportedly told intimates, was "the worst mistake I ever made."[30] Perhaps old age and cognitive dissonance prevented Lewis from recognizing his responsibility for the state of union affairs. Lewis, not Boyle, had initiated collaboration with large operators, "sweetheart contracts," and the drive to wipe out marginal and nonunion mines. He had created the UMW's financial empire and repressed rank-and-file democracy. And as chairman of the welfare and retirement fund, Lewis was responsible for most of the manipulations and misdeeds condemned in Judge

Gerhard Gesell's 1971 decision in *Blankenship* vs. *Boyle*. In short, entrepreneurism, despotism, and a contempt for the law ranked high among the legacies the ancient leader passed on to his successors. "The conduct and policies of John Llewellyn Lewis" Joseph Finley rightly concludes, "led directly to the miseries of the United Mine Workers of America in the decade of the 1970s."[31]

Given Lewis's character, however, he probably privately criticized Boyle not for his policies (because most of them were the retired labor leader's own) but for Boyle's ineptitude at running the union. At the 1964 and 1968 conventions, Boyle proved incapable of capturing delegate support through empathy or of yielding graciously to the membership on a few minor points. Lacking Lewis's political skills and petrified of losing control of the union, Boyle did everything heavy-handedly, from transforming the UMW *Journal* from a subtle to a blatant house organ to allowing an army of his supporters indiscriminately to intimidate convention-goers. Boyle also lacked Lewis's insight into the miners' minds, and consequently could not satisfy their emotional needs. When, on November 20, 1968, an explosion at the Consolidation Coal Company's No. 9 mine near Farmington, West Virginia, killed seventy-eight men, Boyle did not understand what the bereaved relatives psychologically needed to hear. "As long as we mine coal," he told them, "there is always this inherent danger." And then he added that Consolidation Coal was "one of the best companies to work with as far as cooperation and safety are concerned."[32] Clearly, in the same situation, Lewis, concealing his personal beliefs, would have shouted at the operators for their greed and insensitivity and at the government for its failure to enforce the law.

The Farmington disaster and Boyle's cold response to it transformed the disjointed and weak opposition to his regime into an increasingly stronger and purposeful revolt. The rebellion leaders recognized that a Lewis endorsement of their cause would help wean the rank and file from its traditional loyalty to the incumbent administration. On May 22, 1969, therefore, consumer and safety crusader Ralph Nader sent Lewis a letter, which he also released to the press to make sure that its contents reached the average miner. In this letter, Nader charged Boyle with trying to oust Lewis from the chairmanship of the welfare and retirement fund and called upon the eighty-nine-year-old labor giant to lead a rank-and-file revolt against his "incompetent" and "authoritarian" successor.[33] Through his letter, Nader cleverly attempted to link Lewis and the rebellion in the miners' minds, even though the consumer advocate did not really expect the enfeebled labor leader to reply. The letter created consternation at the UMW's headquarters, with Boyle's supporters wanting Lewis to lash out at Nader for breeding division within the union. But Lewis refused to cooperate. "They built that cesspool over there," he reportedly remarked to Josephine Roche. "Let them drown in their own slime."[34]

When Joseph "Jock" Yablonski decided to challenge Boyle for the UMW presidency, he thought that he stood a chance of winning Lewis's support. In the 1950s, as a devoted Lewis lieutenant, Yablonski had earned some of the patriarch's strongest praise. "He's my right-hand man," Lewis had declared. "Whenever I have trouble in the coal fields, I need him." On May 25, 1969, three days before he formally announced his candidacy, Yablonski telephoned Lewis at his home in Alexandria and asked for an appointment. Lewis was too ill to see visitors but suggested that the insurgent approach him at another time. A few days later, on June 1, Yablonski talked to Lewis's confidant Josephine Roche and learned that she, at least, enthusiastically greeted his candidacy. Encouraged by this news, Yablonski called Lewis in Alexandria. The enfeebled labor leader still could not receive visitors but suggested that they meet the following week. Yablonski interpreted Lewis's willingness to confer as a favorable sign.[35]

Lewis's meeting with Yablonski never occurred. On Sunday, June 8, the labor giant entered Washington's Doctors Hospital with acute internal bleeding from some unknown cause. Three days later, on June 11, 1969, John L. Lewis died.

Just as Lewis had spent his life hiding his personal affairs from the public, so now his family kept the details of his death private. Doctors performed an autopsy but, obeying the family's wishes, made no report to the newspapers. The family also declined a public funeral service and requested that mourners send donations to the welfare and retirement fund instead of flowers. Lewis's body was cremated in Washington and then entombed in Springfield, Illinois.

Miners across the coalfields felt a genuine loss at Lewis's death and for four days remained away from work in a memorial to their fallen leader. W. A. "Tony" Boyle might also have been saddened, but he seized upon the miners' moment of grief to remind them again that he was the great man's protégé. For Yablonski, Lewis's death was a great political blow. Other labor leaders and politicians uttered expected eulogies, with even David McDonald, one of the most passionate Lewis-haters, admitting that "in the field of labor he was the greatest Roman of them all."[36] Most Americans, however, reacted to Lewis's death with mild curiosity rather than grief. From many came the telling words: "I thought he was already dead."

In ending his 1949 biography of Lewis, Saul Alinsky predicted that the great man's passing would mark "the end of an era." It would be a highly emotional event, he forecasted, for "until that time, today, as before, and to the end, Lewis will continue as the incredible earthquake beneath our economy." "America will sigh with relief," Alinsky concluded, "and yet America will sorely miss him."[37]

When Lewis died two decades later, the *New York Times* recalled Alinsky's words and tried to explain why they failed to come true. "The death of the most dynamic, the most constructive, and surely the most colorful of American trade union chiefs," the paper editorialized, "has aroused no such emotions—for the simple reason that Lewis's era has since long passed; for fifteen years, at least, he and his works have belonged to history. To say this is in no way to belittle the founder of the C.I.O., but to comment, rather, on the swiftness with which history moves in these times, rendering big men and bigger movements 'irrelevant' to the young and nostalgic even to the middle-aged."[38]

The *Times* accurately expressed the popular mood but too quickly forecasted the future. The meaning of the past is invariably shaped by the present. At the time of Lewis's death events were unfolding that would give his life renewed meaning.

On December 30, 1969, Joseph A. "Jock" Yablonski, his wife, and his daughter retired for the night. . . .

Abbreviations for Notes

ALHUA, WSU	Archives of Labor History and Urban Affairs, Wayne State University
COHC	Columbia University Oral History Collectioin
CUA	Catholic University of America
D.J.	Department of Justice
D.L.	Department of Labor
FDRL	Franklin D. Roosevelt Library
JLL	John L. Lewis
L.C.	Library of Congress
N.A.	National Archives
NRA	National Recovery Administration
NWLB	National War Labor Board
NYT	The New York Times
PSULA	Pennsylvania State University Labor Archives
SHSW	State Historical Society of Wisconsin
UMWAA	United Mine Workers of America Archives
UMWJ	United Mine Workers Journal
U.S.M & CS	United States Mediation and Conciliation Service
UVL	University of Virginia Library
UWVa.L	University of West Virginia Library

Notes

NOTES TO CHAPTER 1

1. Allan G. Bogue, *From Prairie to Corn Belt* (Chicago, 1963), pp. 4-5, 287.

2. Eric J. Hobsbawm, *Industry and Empire: An Economic History of Britain since 1750* (London, 1969), p. 256.

3. Manuscript Population Schedule, 1880 Federal Census, Lucas Township and Cleveland Township, Lucas County, Iowa, N.A.

4. E. J. Hobsbawm, *Industry and Empire*, pp. 253-256; Marcus Lee Hansen, *The Atlantic Migration, 1607-1860* (New York, 1961 ed.), pp. 142-143.

5. Richard Carwardine to Melvyn Dubofsky, June 14, 1974; clippings from *Western Mail*, n.d. (Jan. 1937?); UMWJ, Mar. 15, 1919, p. 11.

6. UMWJ, Mar. 15, 1919, p. 11; for typical migratory patterns of British immigrant miners in the United States, see John Brophy, *A Miner's Life,* ed. John O. H. P. Hall (Madison, Wis., 1964), Chs. 3-8, and Wyndham Mortimer, *Organize! My Life as a Union Man* (Boston, 1971), Ch. 2.

7. Press clippings, *Western Mail,* n.d. (Jan. 1937?), courtesy of Richard Carwardine.

8. Press clippings, *Western Mail,* n.d. (Jan. 1937?); Richard Carwardine to Melvyn Dubofsky, June 14, 1974; JLL Papers (microfilm copy), SHSW, Reel 1; E. J. Hobsbawm, *Industry and Empire*, p. 253.

9. John L. Lewis to Wally Jenkins, July 5, 1922, UMW Archives, JLL M.A. File.

10. Manuscript Population Schedule, 1880 Federal Census, Lucas Township and Cleveland Township.

11. *History of Lucas County, Iowa* (Des Moines, 1881), pp. 608-609, 611-615.

12. George Korson, *John L. Lewis: Young Militant Labor Leader* (Indianapolis, 1970), pp. 25-37; Edward G. Hartmann, *Americans from Wales* (Boston, 1967), pp. 139-155.

13. On Mormonism and John Watkins, see *History of Lucas County,* p. 610; Frances Perkins, COHC, V. 8, p. 365; E. G. Hartmann, *Americans from Wales*, pp. 73-75.

14. *History of Lucas County*, pp. 612-614; UMWJ, Apr. 15, 1940, p. 6, Feb. 1, 1941, p. 7.

15. Manuscript Population Schedule, 1900 Federal Census, Whitebreast Township, Lucas County, Iowa, N.A., reports Thomas H. Lewis as unnaturalized.

16. Olive Osborne Lanhart to John L. Lewis, Jan. 8, 1943, UMW Archives, JLL M.A. File.

17. The Watkins household is so reported in Manuscript Population Schedule, 1880 Federal Census, Lucas Township.

18. *Ibid.*; *History of Lucas County*, pp. 610-615.

19. *Journal of United Labor* (May 13, 1880).

20. UMWJ, Mar. 1, 1950, p. 4; Lucas *Ledger*, Jan. 20, 1887.

21. Saul D. Alinsky, *John L. Lewis: An Unauthorized Biography* (New York, 1970 ed.), p. 15; UMWJ, Mar. 15, 1919, p. 11.

22. Chariton *Democrat-Leader*, Mar. 16, May 11, and Oct. 26, 1882.

23. *Proceedings 1882 Convention,* Knights of Labor, p. 383; *Proceedings 1883 Convention,* Knights of Labor, p. 535.

24. Barbara Snedden to Melvyn Dubofsky, Feb. 27 and Mar. 24, 1976.

25. They seemed to form a part of that huge mass of American workers who moved so frequently, lived transient lives, and, hence, seemed invisible to those who prepared the era's city directories and gathered its vital statistics. See Stephan Thernstrom, "Working Class Social Mobility in Industrial America," paper delivered at Anglo-American Colloquium of the British Society for Labor History, London, 1968; *idem., The Other Bostonians* (Cambridge, Mass., 1973), pp. 220-232; J. Brophy, *A Miner's Life,* Chs. 3-8; W. Mortimer, *Organize!,* Ch. 2.

26. Lucas *Ledger*, Jan. 20, 1887.

27. Olive Osborne Lanhart to John L. Lewis, Jan. 8, 1943, UMW Archives, JLL M.A. File; UMWJ, Feb. 1, 1962, p. 6.

28. A. G. Bogue, *Prairie to Corn Belt,* pp. 182-187.

29. Ms. Lida L. Greene, Librarian, Iowa State Historical Department, to Melvyn Dubofsky, Jan. 10 and Feb. 16, 1976; Barbara Snedden to Melvyn Dubofsky, Feb. 27 and Mar. 24, 1976.

30. Computed from Manuscript Population Schedule, 1900 Federal Census, Whitebreast Township.

31. For a portrait of coal mining life in Iowa, see Cynthia J. Johnson, "A New Life: The Iowa Coal Mines," *Palimpset,* 56 (Mar.-Apr. 1975), 56-64.

32. For Lewis's childhood playmates and games, see Olive Osborne Lanhart to John L. Lewis, Jan. 8, 1943, and Lewis to Lanhart, Jan. 14, 1943, UMW Archives, JLL M.A. File.

33. Manuscript Population Schedule, 1900 Federal Census, Lucas Township and Cleveland Township.

34. *Ibid.,* Whitebreast Township.

35. Gerald G. Baker to John L. Lewis, Apr. 21, 1966, UMW Archives, JLL M.A. File.

36. UMWJ, July 1, 1924, pp. 8-12, and Aug. 15, 1941, p. 11.

37. Gerald G. Baker to John L. Lewis, Apr. 21, 1966, UMW Archives, JLL M.A. File.

38. Myrta Nickey, Oral History Transcript, p. 5, Sangamon State University, Oral History Project (Springfield, Ill.); S. D. Alinsky, *Lewis,* pp. 18-19; UMWJ, Mar. 1, 1921, p. 4; Adolph Germer to James J. Leary, July 21, 1948, Leary to Germer, July 28, 1948, and Germer to Leary, July 30, 1948, Adolph Germer Papers, Box 11, SHSW.

39. S. D. Alinsky, *Lewis,* p. 19.

40. *Ibid.,* p. 18.

41. Norman F. Baker to John L. Lewis, Nov. 2, 1946, with enclosures, JLL Papers (microfilm copy), Reel 1.

42. *Ibid.*; Manuscript Population Schedule, 1900 Federal Census, Lucas Township; M. Nickey, Oral History Transcript, pp. 2-3; *Iowa State Gazeteer and Business Directory* (Chicago, 1891), VI, 1573; *The Alumni of the College of Physicians and Surgeons* (c. 1928-1929), deposited in the University of Iowa, Division of Alumni Records, Iowa City, Iowa; *Iowa Medical Journal,* I (Feb. 1896), 635; Tom M. Throckmorton and Tom B. Throckmorton, "The History of Medicine in Lucas County," *The Journal of the Iowa State Medical Society,* XXIV (Feb. 1934), 120.

43. S. D. Alinsky, *Lewis*, p. 17; on Myrta's education at Drake University, Z. Moore to Melvyn Dubofsky, Oct. 28, 1975, and Nancy Clark to Melvyn Dubofsky, Apr. 20, 1976.

44. See pp. 294-295; Nickie (?) to Josephine Roche, May 20, 1955, Josephine Roche Papers, Box 25, University of Colorado Library.

45. S. D. Alinsky, *Lewis*, p. 20; cf. G. Korson, *John L. Lewis*, pp. 165-167.

46. John L. Lewis to A. L. Deibel, July 22, Aug. 21, Sept. 11, and Oct. 16, 1908, and Mar. 22 and June 7, 1909; John L. Lewis to Oscar H. Winn, Feb. 10 and Mar. 5, 1913, JLL Papers (microfilm copy), Reel 1.

NOTES TO CHAPTER 2

1. Saul D. Alinsky, *John L. Lewis: An Unauthorized Biography* (New York, 1970 ed.), pp. 20-21, for the legend's core.

2. *Illinois Coal Reports, 1906-1910* (Springfield, Ill., 1920) (7th District, 1906-1909; 6th District, 1910, 1920).

3. Newton Bateman and Paul Selby, eds., *Historical Encyclopedia of Illinois*, Vol. II, *History of Montgomery County*, ed. Alexander T. Strange (Chicago, 1918), p. 877; "Testimony of Angelo Corradini," in John R. Schaefer and Henry Meyer to Frank Farrington, Sept. 12, 1918, Adolph Germer Papers, Box 1, File 3, SHSW; "Testimony in the Matter of the Misappropriation of Funds of Local Union No. 1475, Panama, Illinois," John H. Walker Papers, Box 59, University of Illinois Historical Survey.

4. The UMW conventions from 1916 to 1930 offer much evidence of the deferential and symbiotic relationship that existed between union leaders of American and British birth (and Protestant faith) and immigrant miners from the south and east of Europe of the Catholic faith.

5. N. Bateman and P. Selby, *Historical Encyclopedia*, p. 877.

6. *Ibid.*

7. For the full ramifications and mechanics of the Panama "scandal," see John R. Schaefer and Henry Meyer to Frank Farrington, Sept. 12, 1918, Adolph Germer Papers, Box 1, File 3, SHSW. A copy of the same report can also be found in the John H. Walker Papers, Box 59, which also contains the following relevant correspondence on the scandal: James Hicks to Walker, Nov. 13, 1918; Hicks to Walker, two letters, n.d.; William J. Sneed to Walker, Nov. 23, 1918; Walker to Sneed, Nov. 30, 1918; Hicks to Walker, Jan. 14, 1919, with enclosures, all in Box 872. Walker to J. G. Brown, Aug. 16, 1921, with enclosures, Box 59.

8. See note 7 above.

9. William Green to John L. Lewis, Dec. 22, 1909, and Green to Lewis, Dec. 21, 1910, JLL Papers (microfilm copy), SHSW, Reel 1.

10. See especially S. D. Alinsky, *Lewis*, pp. 21-22.

11. William Green to John L. Lewis, Dec. 21, 1910, JLL Papers (microfilm copy), SHSW, Reel 1.

12. *Proceedings 1911 Convention*, UMWA, as reported in the UMWJ, Feb. 1, 1912, pp. 2-3, and Feb. 8, 1912, p. 2. Contrary to Saul Alinsky's assertion that industrial unionism was the crucial issue at the 1911 convention (*Lewis*, p. 22) and that the UMW directly challenged Samuel Gompers's philosophy of trade unionism, it was John Mitchell's membership and salaried position in the National Civic Federation—an organization of industrialists, labor leaders, and public figures committed to "responsible" labor rela-

536 • NOTES

tions—that dominated convention debate. If Lewis learned anything from this experience, it was that the charge of "class collaboration" was the most effective weapon union insurgents could use against incumbents.

13. John P. White to Samuel Gompers, Oct. 21, 1911, JLL Papers (microfilm copy), Reel 1.

14. Samuel Gompers to John L. Lewis, Oct. 21, 1911; John P. White to Lewis, Oct. 22, 1911; Lewis to Gompers, Oct. 23, 1911, *ibid.*; Gompers to Lewis, Oct. 23, 1911, Gompers Letterbooks, L.C.

15. The travel diaries are in the JLL Papers (microfilm copy), Reel 2. The following description and analysis of Lewis's life as an A. F. of L. organizer are drawn from the diaries.

16. Samuel Gompers to John L. Lewis, Dec. 27, 1911, Gompers Letterbooks, L.C.

17. Mrs. Doris Bell to Melvyn Dubofsky, Feb. 2, 1976.

18. *Proceedings 1919 Convention*, UMWA, pp. 728-729.

19. 1912 travel diary, entries for weeks of June 1-15.

20. Entries in the period in the 1915 travel diary.

21. Lewis to A. W. McIntyre, Oct. 2, 1920, UMW Archives, JLL M.A. File.

22. J. J. Keegan to Samuel Gompers, Oct. 11, 1912; Gompers to Keegan, Oct. 14, 1912; Keegan to Gompers, telegram and letter, Oct. 15, 1912, A. F. of L. Papers, Office of the President, File A, Box 17, SHSW.

23. Memorandum by R. Lee Guard, July 14, 1916, *ibid.*, Box 22; Samuel Gompers to John L. Lewis, Nov. 19, 1916; Lewis to Gompers, Nov. 20 and 21, 1916; Gompers to William B. Wilson, Nov. 23, 1916, *ibid.*, Box 23.

24. S. D. Alinsky, *Lewis,* pp. 23-24.

25. Samuel Gompers to John L. Lewis, Sept. 19, 1917, and Lewis to Gompers, Sept. 21 and 22, 1917, A. F. of L. Papers, Office of the President, File A, Box 28.

26. Samuel Gompers to John L. Lewis, Dec. 31, 1915, and Oct. 13, 1916, Gompers Letterbooks, L.C.; Gompers to Lewis, Feb. 24, 1916, A. F. of L. Papers, Office of the President, File A, Box 22.

27. "Mercenary or Trade Unionist," Feb. 17, 1912, and original undated typescript in JLL Papers (microfilm copy), Reel 1.

28. Notarized Affidavit of Fred Reilly, dated Jan. 7, 1918, UMW Archives, Elections File; Walker later made similar charges concerning the 1918 election, asserting that K. C. Adams had hired someone to forge telegrams. Walker, however, may have confused dates and union elections. *Proceedings 1921 Convention*, UMWA, p. 701.

29. *Proceedings 1916 Convention*, UMWA, pp. 329-330, 333, 464, 1006-1007.

30. *Ibid.*, pp. 232-233, 720-721.

31. UMWJ, Nov. 9, 1916; Feb. 8, 1917, p. 5, for election results.

32. Samuel Gompers to John L. Lewis, Nov. 15, 1916, Gompers Letterbooks, L. C.; Lewis to Gompers, Nov. 18, 1916, and enclosed letter to unknown recipient from Tom Wilson, n.d., UMW Archives, Elections File.

33. John P. White to John L. Lewis, Jan. 23, 1917, and Lewis to White, Jan. 31, 1917, JLL Papers (microfilm copy), Reel 1. For Lewis's resignation from the A. F. of L., see Frank Morrison to Lewis, Feb. 10, 1917, and Gompers to Lewis, Feb. 17, 1917, *ibid.*

34. On UMW membership see William Green's report in *Proceedings 1921 Convention*, UMWA, pp. 206-207.

35. Melvyn Dubofsky, *Industrialism and the American Workers 1865-1920* (New York, 1975), pp. 111-115.

36. UMWJ, July 20, 1916, pp. 11-12, July 27, 1916, p. 5, Mar. 29, 1917, p. 4, Apr. 19, 1917, p. 4, June 7, 1917, p. 4; entries in travel diary for Feb. 15, Apr. 10-17, June 19-20, June 26-27, Aug. 27, 1917, JLL Papers (microfilm copy).

37. UMWJ, Apr. 5, 1917, p. 8.

38. The UMW Archives, JLL M.A. File contain an Al Hamilton-Lewis correspondence file that reveals the friendship but lacks documents concerning the official, or "business," relationship.

39. John H. Walker's correspondence for the years 1918-1921 is filled with references to the Lewis-Hamilton connection as the source of all union corruption. See especially two letters from Walker to Heber Blankenhorn dated Nov. 11, 1920, John H. Walker Papers, Box 9; cf. John Brophy, *A Miner's Life,* ed. John O. H. P. Hall (Madison, Wis., 1964), pp. 134-136.

40. Re union contract in the Fairmont Field, West Virginia: "Much credit is due Mr. Hamilton, who acted as Chairman of the Joint Conference and spokesman for the operators, in advancing his liberal view on complete recognition. He assuredly worked like a trojan to secure the consummation of this agreement." John L. Lewis to H. J. Straub, editor, *Coal Trade Bulletin,* Sept. 21, 1918, UMW Archives, JLL M.A. File.

41. Samuel Gompers to John L. Lewis, Aug. 17, 1917, Gompers Letterbooks, L. C.

42. Travel diary, 1917, entries for Sept. 6 and 8, 1917, JLL Papers (microfilm copy). Mrs. Doris Bell to Melvyn Dubofsky, Feb. 2 and Mar. 12, 1976.

43. Mrs. Doris Bell to Melvyn Dubofsky, Feb. 2 and Mar. 12, 1976.

44. NYT, Oct. 26, 1917, p. 14; UMWJ, Jan. 17, 1918, p. 18; cf. J. Brophy, *A Miner's Life*, p. 150.

45. Samuel Gompers to John L. Lewis, Feb. 14, 1918, Gompers Letterbooks, L. C.; John Brophy Diary, May 31 and June 2, 1918, John Brophy Papers, CUA.

46. John L. Lewis to H. J. Straub, Sept. 21, 1918, UMW Archives, JLL M.A. File; William Green to John Walker, Sept. 10, 1918, Walker Papers, Box 60; UMWJ, Aug. 1, 1918, p. 10, and Feb. 15, 1919, p. 9.

47. John H. Walker to Joe Roebuck, Dec. 4, 1918, John H. Walker Papers, Box 7; see also Walker to G. M. Carroll, Oct. 18, 1918, and many other letters in *Ibid.*, Box 7.

48. UMWJ, May 15, 1919, p. 3, and Feb. 15, 1920, pp. 5-6.

49. Frank Farrington to Senator Rush D. Holt, Feb. 17, 1937, A. F. of L. Papers, Office of the President, File C, Box 3.

50. James Lord to Adolph Germer, Oct. 14, 1951, Adolph Germer Papers, Box 13.

51. *Proceedings 1918 Convention*, UMWA, pp. 44-85, 496-498, 665-666.

52. Samuel Gompers to John L. Lewis, Sept. 19, 20, and 22, 1919, Gompers Letterbooks, L. C.

NOTES TO CHAPTER 3

1. Matthew Josephson, *Sidney Hillman: Statesman of American Labor* (New York, 1952), pp. 190-193.

2. Melvyn Dubofsky, *Industrialism and the American Worker, 1865-1920* (New York, 1975), pp. 127-129.

3. Warren G. Harding to F. E. Scobey, Oct. 25, 1919, and Nov. 3, 1919, Warren G. Harding Papers (microfilm copy), Reel 21, Ohio Historical Society.

4. *Proceedings 1919 Convention*, UMWA, pp. 75-76.

5. Much of the information that follows has been inferred from Lewis's 1919 travel diary, JLL Papers (microfilm copy), SHSW.

6. James Robb, Oral History Transcript, p. 22 and *passim,* SWOC File, PSULA; also see p. 295.

7. See pp. 295-296.

8. K. C. Adams, "Demands of Bituminous Miners Born as Result of Political Scheme of Ambitious Men in Organization" (Indianapolis, Oct. 19, 1919).

9. *Ibid.*

10. *Proceedings 1919 Convention*, UMWA, pp. 22-23.

11. *Ibid.*, pp. 392-394, 868-870.

12. *Ibid.*, pp. 76-79.

13. *Ibid.*, pp. 951-953.

14. *Ibid.*, pp. 438-456, 514-521, 549-557, 560.

15. *Ibid.*, pp. 727-729, 888-889.

16. *Ibid.*, pp. 876-881.

17. *Ibid.*, p. 528.

18. *Ibid.*, pp. 54-55, 340-344.

19. *Joint Conference of Coal Operators and Coal Miners of the Central Competitive Field* (Buffalo, New York, Sept. 1919), pp. 164, 183; UMWJ, Oct. 15, 1919, pp. 3-5. For reasons behind operators' resistance to wage increases, see Barbara M. Brockmeier, "Government Intervention and Union Politics: The 1919 Coal Strike" (M. A. Thesis, Ohio State U., 1974), pp. 8-14.

20. William B. Wilson to John L. Lewis, Oct. 14, 1919, Oct. 17, 1919, D/L, R.G. 174, Box 207, N.A.

21. Thomas T. Brewster to William B. Wilson, Oct. 17, 1919; F. W. Lukins to Wilson, Oct. 16, 1919, *ibid.*

22. Edward S. McGraw to Tom Connally, Nov. 1, 1919, *ibid.*, encloses a brief summary of the proceedings of the October 21-24 conference. Cf. *Proceedings 1919 Convention* (Reconvened Session, Jan. 5-7, 1920), UMWA, p. 18.

23. For a version of cabinet policy and federal intervention in the dispute that is marginally different, that deflates Woodrow Wilson's role—because of the president's illness—and that neglects the pre-October 25 negotiations, see Stanley Coben, *A. Mitchell Palmer: Politician* (New York, 1963), pp. 177-178.

24. NYT, Oct. 27, 1919, p. 1; *Proceedings 1919 Convention* (Reconvened Session, Jan. 5-7, 1920), UMWA, p. 18.

25. NYT, Oct. 27, 1919, p. 1.

26. J. H. Tumulty to William B. Wilson, Oct. 29, 1919, D/L, R.G. 174, Box 207, N.A.

27. NYT, Oct. 31, 1919, p. 1; *Proceedings 1919 Convention* (Reconvened Session, Jan. 5-7, 1920), UMWA, pp. 18-19.

28. Samuel Gompers to John L. Lewis, Oct. 29, Oct. 31, and Nov. 7, 1919, Gompers Letterbooks, L.C.

29. Samuel Gompers to John L. Lewis, Dec. 15 and 30, 1920, *ibid.*; UMWJ, Feb. 1, 1921, pp. 7-8.

30. K. C. Adams, "Demands of Bituminous Miners"; Frank Burke, "Memorandum for Judge Ames," with enclosures, Nov. 17, 1919, D/J, R.G. 60, File 16-130-13, N.A.

31. D/J, R.G. 60, File 16-130-13, and D/L, R.G. 174, Box 207 contain evidence revealing the full scope of the government's antistrike activities.

32. Samuel Gompers to John L. Lewis, Nov. 10, 1919, Gompers Letterbooks, L.C.; NYT, Nov. 10, 1919, p. 1.

33. Adolph Germer to John Gibson, Apr. 1 and 22, 1947, Adolph Germer Papers, Box 28, SHSW. Cf. John H. Walker to Dan Tobin, July 1, 1921, and Tobin to Walker, July 2, 1921, John H. Walker Papers, Box 10, University of Illinois Historical Survey, Springfield.

34. NYT, Nov. 11, 1919, p. 1, Nov. 12, 1919, p. 1; *Proceedings 1919 Convention* (Reconvened Session, Jan. 5-7, 1920), UMWA, p. 19; UMWJ, Nov. 15, 1919, pp. 3-5.

35. Memorandum, Nov. 13, 1919, Royal Meeker, D/L, R.G. 174, Box 207.

36. "Conference of Representatives of Coal Operators and the United Mine Workers of America, Called by Honorable William B. Wilson, Secretary of Labor," Nov. 14, 1919, *ibid*.

37. H. A. Garfield to Woodrow Wilson, Dec. 5, 1919, *ibid*. Cf. B. M. Brockmeier, "Government Intervention," pp. 8-11.

38. "Memorandum to the Secretary of Labor Relative to His Position on the Coal Strike," n.d., D/L, R. G. 174, Box 207.

39. *Ibid*.; *Proceedings 1919 Convention* (Reconvened Session, Jan. 5-7, 1920), UMWA, pp. 19-20.

40. A. Mitchell Palmer to Chamber of Commerce, Moberly, Mo., Dec. 1, 1919, D/L, R.G. 174, Box 207.

41. NYT, Nov. 29, 1919, pp. 1-2; *Proceedings 1919 Convention* (Reconvened Session, Jan. 5-7, 1920), UMWA, p. 20; for President Wilson's actual noninvolvement in these negotiations, see S. Coben, *Palmer*, pp. 181-183.

42. NYT, Dec. 7, 1919, pp. 1, 3; *Proceedings 1919 Convention* (Reconvened Session, Jan. 5-7, 1920), UMWA, pp. 20-21.

43. William B. Wilson to John L. Lewis, Dec. 8 and 9, 1919, D/L, R.G. 174, Box 207.

44. NYT, Dec. 11, 1919, pp. 1-2; Notice from UMW to Officers and Members, Dec. 11, 1919, William Mitch Papers, PSULA; *Proceedings 1919 Convention* (Reconvened Session, Jan. 5-7, 1920), UMWA, pp. 21-23; UMWJ, Dec. 15, 1919, pp. 3-8.

45. Saul D. Alinsky, *John L. Lewis: An Unauthorized Biography* (New York, 1970 ed.), p. 34.

46. *Proceedings 1919 Convention* (Reconvened Session, Jan. 5-7, 1920), UMWA, p. 148.

47. John L. Lewis to A. Mitchell Palmer, Dec. 11, 1919; Palmer to Lewis, Dec. 15, 1919; Lewis to Palmer, Dec. 16 and 18, 1919; Dan W. Simms to C. B. Ames, Dec. 23, 1919, all in D/J, R.G. 60, File 16-130-29.

48. See *Ibid*., File 16-130-26; UMWJ, Apr. 15, 1920, pp. 5, 8.

49. *Proceedings 1919 Convention* (Reconvened Session, Jan. 5-7, 1920), UMWA, pp. 146-156.

50. *Ibid*., pp. 157-159.

51. John L. Lewis to William B. Wilson, Jan. 20, 1920; Wilson to Lewis, Jan. 22, 1920; Lewis to Wilson, Feb. 6, 1920, D/L, R.G. 174, Box 207; UMWJ, Jan. 1, 1920, pp. 3, 5, 8, Feb. 1, 1920, pp. 3, 5, 8, Apr. 1, 1920, pp. 4-5, 11-13.

52. NYT, July 28, 1920, p. 24, Aug. 5, 1920, p. 15.

53. Cunningham to William B. Wilson, Aug. 19, 1920, United States Conciliation and Mediation Service, R.G. 280, File 170/1215, Federal Records Center, Suitland, Md.; *Proceedings 1921 Convention*, UMWA, pp. 64-69; Woodrow Wilson to John L. Lewis, Aug. 2, 1920, JLL Papers, SHSW; UMWJ, Aug. 15, 1920, pp. 3-4, Sept. 1, 1920, pp. 3-4; *American Coal Miner* (Aug. 20, 1920), pp. 7-10.

54. John H. Walker to William H. Short, Mar. 16, 1920, Walker Papers, Box 9.

55. John H. Walker to James Ritchie, Oct. 12, 1920; Walker to Heber Blankenhorn, Nov. 1 (three letters) and Nov. 3, 1920, *ibid*., Box 9.

56. John L. Lewis to A. W. McIntyre, Oct. 2, 1920, UMW Archives, JLL M.A. File.

57. On this point see Warren Van Tine, *The Making of the Labor Bureaucrat* (Amherst, Mass., 1973), pp. 115-137.

58. John L. Lewis to John H. Walker, Mar. 26, 1920; Walker to Lewis, Mar. 30, 1920; Lewis to Walker, Apr. 5, 1920; Walker to Lewis, Apr. 9, 1920; Lewis to Walker, Apr. 12, 1920; Walker to Lewis, Apr. 29, 1920; Lewis to Walker, May 5, 1920; Walker to Lewis, May 8, 1920; Walker to Lewis, June 2, 1920; Walker to Lewis, June 3, 1920, with enclosures; Walker to John P. White, June 29, 1926 and White to Walker, July 5, 1916;

Lewis to J. E. Fenwick, Nov. 12, 1920; Walker to Lewis, Dec. 7, 1920, all in John H. Walker Papers, Boxes 8-9.

59. James Malone and Frank Doblin to John L. Lewis, Sept. 14, 1920; Lewis to Robert H. Harlin, Sept. 18, 1920; Harlin to Lewis, Sept. 23 and 24, 1920, *ibid.*, Box 9.

60. Ellis Searles to E. J. Costello, Nov. 30, 1920, UMW Archives, JLL M.A. File.

61. On the Alabama strike see Van A. Bittner to John L. Lewis, Oct. 22, 1920; Lewis to Woodrow Wilson, Oct. 24, 1920; Bittner to Lewis, Oct. 26 and 28, 1920; Robert Harlin to Oscar Davis, Dec. 11, 1920; Bittner to Harlin, n.d.; Lewis to Bittner, Jan. 28, 1921; David McCrossie and Jonah F. Hall to Lewis, Aug. 31, 1921, all in Van A. Bittner Papers, WVa.UL; Harlin to John H. Walker, Oct. 4, 1920, John H. Walker Papers, Box 9; Harlin to William Mitch, Dec. 11, 1920, William Mitch Papers; *Proceedings 1921 Convention*, UMWA, pp. 107-110.

62. Alex Howat to John H. Walker, Dec. 30, 1920, John H. Walker Papers, Box 9; John L. Lewis to William Mitch, Nov. 19, 1920, and Mitch to Lewis, Dec. 27, 1920, William Mitch Papers.

63. John L. Lewis to William Mitch, Jan. 8, 1921, William Mitch Papers; John H. Walker to Peter Grant, June 10, 1921, John H. Walker Papers, Box 10; UMWJ, Feb. 15, 1921, p. 5.

NOTES TO CHAPTER 4

1. John L. Lewis to Warren G. Harding, Oct. 17, 1920, Warren G. Harding Papers (microfilm copy), Reel 39, Ohio Historical Society.

2. C. J. Jarvis to Warren G. Harding, "Recommendations for Appointments, 1920-1921," *ibid.*, Reel 128; James J. Davis to Warren G. Harding, Oct. 24, 1921, *ibid.*, Reel 140; Harding to John L. Lewis, Mar. 28, 1921, JLL Papers (microfilm copy), SHSW.

3. Carolyn Grin, "The Unemployment Conference of 1921," *Mid-America*, LV (Apr. 1973), 83-107; Robert K. Murray, *The Harding Era* (Minneapolis, 1969), pp. 231-234; Robert H. Zieger, *Republicans and Labor, 1919-1929* (Lexington, Ky., 1969), pp. 90-97.

4. NYT, Oct. 12, 1921, pp. 1, 6; E. M. Poston to Herbert Hoover, Feb. 22, 1929, Pre-Presidential Cabinet Appointments, Box 30, Herbert Hoover Papers, Hoover Library, West Branch, Iowa; UMWJ, Nov. 1, 1921, pp. 3-5.

5. Philip Taft, *The A. F. of L. in the Time of Gompers* (New York, 1957), pp. 254-255.

6. John L. Lewis to William Mitch, May 25, 1921, William Mitch Papers, PSULA.

7. John L. Lewis to Basil M. Manly, May 28, 1921, with enclosures, UMW Archives, JLL M.A. File.

8. John L. Lewis to K. C. Adams, May 28, 1921, *ibid.*

9. Isadore Lubin, COHC, p. 164; Edwin A. Lahey, COHC, p. 94.

10. NYT, June 21, 1921, pp. 1-2, June 22, 1921, p. 6.

11. John L. Lewis to Adolph Germer, two telegrams, June 21, 1921, Adolph Germer Papers, Box 27, University of Illinois Historical Survey.

12. P. Taft, *AFL in Time of Gompers*, pp. 367-368; Memorandum, n.d., UMW Archives, JLL Files; John H. Walker to Frank Farrington, July 1, 1921, John H. Walker Papers, Box 10.

13. John L. Lewis to John Brophy, June 24, 1921; Thomas Kennedy to Brophy, June 24, 1921; Brophy to Kennedy, June 25, 1921; Lewis to Brophy, June 27, 1921; Brophy to

Lewis, June 24, 1921; Brophy to Robert Harlin and Frank Farrington, June 25, 1921, John Brophy Papers, Box A5-1, CUA.

14. NYT, June 23, 1921, p. 16.

15. P. Taft, *AFL in Time of Gompers*, pp. 367-388; *Proceedings 1921 Convention*, AFL, pp. 449-459.

16. John L. Lewis to Van A. Bittner, July 9, 1921, Van A. Bittner Papers, Series 1, Box 6, WVa.UL.

17. Samuel Gompers to John L. Lewis, September 20, 1921, Gompers Letterbooks, L.C.

18. *Proceedings 1921 Convention*, UMWA, pp. 93-94, 850-855.

19. Saul D. Alinsky, *John L. Lewis: An Unauthorized Biography* (New York, 1970 ed.), p. 42.

20. Irving Bernstein, *The Lean Years: A History of the American Worker, 1920-1933* (Boston, 1960), p. 122.

21. Hywel Davies, "Special Report to the Secretary of Labor," Aug. 12, 1921, D/L, R.G. 280, Box 140, File 165/186A, N.A.

22. See p. 63.

23. Winthrop D. Lane, *Civil War in West Virginia* (New York, 1969 ed.), p. 122 and *passim*.

24. *Ibid.*; "West Virginia Coal Fields," *Senate Report 457, Serial Set 7950; Struggle in the Coal Fields: The Autobiography of Fred Mooney*, ed. J. W. Hess (McLain, West Va., 1967).

25. "West Virginia Coal Fields," *Senate Report 457, Serial Set 7950*; Colonel W. A. Bethel, Judge Advocate, Memorandum for Mr. Herron, Subject: Recent Disturbance in West Virginia, Nov. 15, 1921, D/J. R.G. 60, File 16-130-83, Sec. 4, N.A.; James M. Wainwright to Attorney General Harry Daugherty, Feb. 28, 1922, *ibid.*; for an analysis of the conflict and its aftermath see, Daniel P. Jordan, "The Mingo War: Labor Violence in the Southern West Virginia Coal Fields, 1919-1922"; David A. Corbin, "Frank Keeney Is Our Leader and We Shall Not be Moved: Rank-and-File Leadership in the West Virginia Coal Fields"; and Richard Lunt, "The Struggle against the Law to Organize the Coal Fields of West Virginia," all unpublished papers delivered at the Southern Labor History Conference, Atlanta, Georgia, April 1-3, 1976.

26. Elliott Northcott to the Attorney General, Dec. 18, 1922, D/J, R. G. File 16-130-83, Sec. 4.

27. Hitchman Coal and Coke Company v. Mitchell, *245 U.S. 229*, pp. 232-258.

28. The UMWJ for the years 1920-1922 and the president's and secretary-treasurer's reports to the 1921 UMW convention are replete with instances of judicial repression.

29. United Mine Workers *et al*. v. Coronado Coal Company *et al*., *259 U.S. 344* (1922); Coronado Coal Company *et al*. v. United Mine Workers *et al*., *268 U.S. 295* (1925); Stanley I. Kutler, "Chief Justice Taft, Judicial Unanimity, and Labor: The Coronado Case," *The Historian*, XXIV (Nov. 1961), 68-83; Charles O. Gregory, *Labor and the Law* (New York, 1946), pp. 212-218; I. Bernstein, *Lean Years*, pp. 203-204.

30. Statement of UMW Expenses, Feb. 1, 1920, to Dec. 1, 1930, UMW Archives.

31. William Green to John L. Lewis, June 3, 1921, A. F. of L. Papers, Office of the President, File B, Box 3, SHSW.

32. Statement of UMW Expenses, UMW Archives.

33. John L. Lewis to All International Officers and Field Workers, June 28, 1921, Van A. Bittner Papers; Lewis to John Hessler and William Mitch, July 2, 1922, William Mitch Papers.

34. Hywel Davies to Secretary of Labor, Aug. 12, 1921, D/L, R.G. 280, Box 141, File 165/186A.

35. Herbert Hoover to Attorney General Harry Daugherty with enclosed unsent telegram of Oct. 13, 1921, Oct. 14, 1921, D/J, R.G. 60, File 16-130-183, Sec. 3.

36. *Proceedings 1921 Convention*, UMWA, pp. 92-93, 1198-1200; *Proceedings 1921 Reconvened Convention*, UMWA, pp. 90-122.

37. *Proceedings 1921 Convention*, UMWA, p. 862.

38. *Proceedings 1921 Reconvened Convention*, UMWA, p. 191.

39. NYT, Feb. 2, 1922, p. 19, Feb. 3, 1922, p. 14.

40. *Ibid.*, Feb. 23, 1922, pp. 1, 6.

41. *Ibid.*, Feb. 24, 1922, p. 12.

42. *Ibid.*, Apr. 4, 1922, pp. 1, 4.

43. Ellis Searles, "Giving Stability to the Coal Industry," *Review of Reviews*, 65 (June 1922), 639-642.

44. For a different interpretation of Harding administration policy in the coal strike—one that emphasizes its impartiality—see R. K. Murray, *The Harding Era*, pp. 242-244, and R. Zieger, *Republicans and Labor,* pp. 114-117.

45. "Consumer Coal Shortage," 1922, Harding Papers, Reel 140.

46. Herbert Hoover to John L. Lewis, June 11, 1922, and June 14, 1922, Herbert Hoover Papers, Pre-Presidential, Commerce, Box 355.

47. The following account is based largely on Paul M. Angle, *Bloody Williamson: A Chapter in American Lawlessness* (New York, 1952), pp. 3-27.

48. *Ibid.*, pp. 28-43.

49. Interview with John L. Lewis, Atlantic City, July 8, 1923, Calvin Coolidge Papers, Series I, Case 175, Reel 88, L.C.

50. Warren G. Harding to John L. Lewis, June 28, 1922, and Lewis to Harding, June 29, 1922, Harding Papers, Reel 184; NYT, June 26, 1922, p. 1, June 27, 1922, p. 1, June 29, 1922, p. 1, July 2, 1922, p. 1, July 7, 1922, p. 19; UMWJ, July 1, 1922, p. 9.

51. NYT, July 11, 1922, pp. 1, 16; R. K. Murray, *The Harding Era*, p. 246; R. Zieger, *Republicans and Labor,* pp. 124-125.

52. NYT, July 16, 1922, pp. 1, 3; John Brophy, *A Miner's Life,* ed. John O. H. P. Hall (Madison, Wis., 1964), pp. 189-190; UMWJ, July 15, 1922, pp. 3-5.

53. Memorandum on Bituminous Negotiations, July 26, 1922 (?), D/L, R.G. 280, File 165/411.

54. NYT, July 18, 1922, pp. 1, 3, July 19, 1922, p. 1; R. K. Murray, *The Harding Era*, pp. 246-248; R. Zieger, *Republicans and Labor*, pp. 126-128.

55. John L. Lewis to Adolph Germer, Aug. 4, 1922, Adolph Germer Papers, Box 27.

56. NYT, Aug. 8, 1922, pp. 1-2.

57. Heber Blankenhorn, *The Strike for the Union* (New York, 1969 ed.), pp. 151-153; NYT, Aug. 11, 1922, pp. 1-2, Aug. 15, 1922, p. 1, Aug. 16, 1922, pp. 1, 3; Thomas H. Watkins, "The Armistice in the Coal Fields," *Current History*, XV (Nov. 1922), 213-217.

58. NYT, Aug. 16, 1922, pp. 1, 3; cf. Ellis Searles, "The Victory of the Coal Miners," *Current History*, XV (Nov. 1922), 182-221; UMWJ, Aug. 15, 1922, pp. 3-5, 14.

59. John Brophy, Diary, Jan. 22, 1923, John Brophy Papers.

60. *Literary Digest*, Sept. 23, 1922, p. 72; *American Coal Miner*, Sept. 1922, p. 12.

61. John L. Lewis to William Green, Sept. 11, 1922, A. F. of L. Papers, Office of the President, File B, Box 3.

62. Heber Blankenhorn, *Strike for the Union*, pp. 152-172, esp. pp. 151-153, 166-167; J. Brophy, *A Miner's Life*, pp. 190-196.

63. L. G. Ball to John L. Lewis, C. F. Keeney, and John Brophy, Aug. 24, 1922; Lewis to Brophy, Aug. 26, 1922; Lewis to Brophy, Sept. 6, 1922; Lewis to Brophy, Sept. 11, 1922; Lewis to Brophy, Sept. 14, 1922; Lewis to Brophy, Sept. 20, 1922; Brophy to

Lewis, Sept. 21, 1922, all in John Brophy Papers, Box A5-1; cf. J. Brophy, *A Miner's Life,* pp. 194-195.

64. J. Brophy, *A Miner's Life,* p. 192; H. Blankenhorn, *Strike for the Union*, pp. 166-167.

65. John L. Lewis to Adolph Germer, Aug. 4, 1922, Adolph Germer Papers, Box 27.

66. Herbert Hoover and James J. Davis to John L. Lewis, Sept. 29, 1922; John L. Lewis to James J. Davis, Oct. 4, 1922; Thomas K. Maher to James J. Davis, Oct. 4, 1922, all in D/L, R.G. 280, File 165/411; R. Zieger, *Republicans and Labor*, pp. 218-220.

67. *Report of the United States Coal Commission, Five Parts* (Washington, 1925); E. E. Hunt, *What the Coal Commission Found* (Baltimore, 1925).

68. T. H. Watkins, "The Armistice in the Coal Fields," pp. 213-217; E. Searles, "Victory of the Coal Miners," pp. 218-221.

69. W. H. Rodgers to Hugh L. Kerwin, Jan. 4, 1923, and Transcript of Long-Distance Telephone Call, Rodgers to Kerwin, Jan. 5, 1923, D/L, R.G. 280, File 165/411; NYT, Jan. 25, 1923, p. 7.

70. Ellis Searles to John Brophy, Apr. 13, 1921, John Brophy Papers, Box A5-1.

71. Memorandum to John L. Lewis, dated Oct. 5, 1921, *ibid.*; J. Brophy, *A Miner's Life*, p. 160.

72. Copy in William Mitch Papers.

73. Box 5A-1, the John Brophy Papers, contains an extensive file of correspondence that details the financial, ideological, and personal relationships among Brophy, the Nationalization Research Committee, and the New York intellectuals; J. Brophy, *A Miner's Life*, pp. 163-165. John Brophy, "The Miners' Program," *New Republic* (Aug. 9, 1922), pp. 297-298.

74. John Brophy to William Mitch, Jan. 11, 1923, William Mitch Papers; John Brophy, Diary, Jan. 21, 1923, John Brophy Papers; J. Brophy, *A Miner's Life*, p. 170.

75. See J. Brophy, *A Miner's Life*, pp. 170-171.

76. Norman Thomas, Open Letter to John L. Lewis, copy in William Mitch Papers; cf. J. Brophy, *A Miner's Life*, p. 171.

77. John L. Lewis to William Mitch, Jan. 30, 1922, William Mitch Papers.

78. William Mitch to John Brophy, Feb. 3 and 9, 1923; Lewis to Mitch, Feb. 10, 1923, William Mitch Papers; J. Brophy, *A Miner's Life*, pp. 173-174.

79. John Brophy to William Mitch, Feb. 13, 1923, John Brophy Papers, Box A5-1.

80. NYT, Feb. 25, 1923, II, 1-2.

81. Philip Murray to John L. Lewis, Mar. 15, 1923, UMW Archives, JLL M.A. File.

NOTES TO CHAPTER 5

1. 1923 Passport for Mr. and Mrs. John L. Lewis, JLL Papers (microfilm copy), SHSW.

2. Warren Van Tine, *The Making of the Labor Bureaucrat, 1870-1920* (Amherst, Mass., 1973).

3. Photographs, JLL Papers, Reel 4.

4. Gardner Jackson, COHC, pp. 728-735.

5. Bill of Sale, Aug. 9, 1920, Springfield Granite and Marble Company, JLL Papers, Reel 3.

6. Among other items and account books in the JLL Papers, see Fred J. Cooper to

Mrs. John L. Lewis, Jan. 17, 1928; R. L. Schmidt Co. to Mrs. Lewis, Apr. 24, 1929; Samuel Shapiro to Mrs. Lewis, Aug. 11, 1936; L. E. Seibert to Kathryn Lewis, Sept. 4, 1936; J. K. Fletcher, Ltd., to Mrs. Lewis, Sept. 26, 1936, Reel 3.

7. Membership certificates, *ibid.*

8. Lee Pressman, COHC, p. 185.

9. R. J. Thomas, COHC, No. 5, p. 15.

10. Cyrus Ching, COHC, pp. 564-567, 706-718.

11. Harriman Correspondence File, UMW Archives, JLL M.A. File; John L. Lewis to Thomas Kennedy, Apr. 23, 1929, *ibid.*; Box 39 of the W. Jett Lauck Papers contains a large correspondence concerning Lauck's loans from the Harriman National Bank between the years 1923 and 1938, W. Jett Lauck Papers, Alderson Library, UVL.

12. Jacob Harriman to John L. Lewis, May 17, 1934; Leonard Oberweis to Lewis, May 28, 1934; J. Harriman to Lewis, June 1, 1934, UMW Archives, JLL M.A. File.

13. John L. Lewis to John Riddle, Sept. 27, 1933, *ibid.*; Newton Todd to John H. Walker, Apr. 16, 1930, Adolph Germer Papers, Box 1, SHSW; *Coal Age* (Oct. 18, 1923), p. 604.

14. NYT, Jan. 18, 1923, p. 5, June 27, 1923, p. 30, June 29, 1923, p. 3, June 30, 1923, pp. 1, 3.

15. *Literary Digest*, Sept. 29, 1923, pp. 5-7; UMWJ, Sept. 15, 1923, p. 23, for first article of six-part series on Communist threat.

16. George G. Moore to John L. Lewis, July 12, 1944, UMW Archives, JLL M.A. File.

17. John L. Lewis to W. Jett Lauck, Apr. 16 and 30, 1926, W. Jett Lauck Papers, Box 39.

18. John L. Lewis to William Green, May 28, 1923; Green to Lewis, June 4, 1923; Lewis to Green, May 24, 1924; Green to Lewis, June 2, 1924, all in A. F. of L. Papers, Office of the President, File B, Box 3, SHSW.

19. John L. Lewis to William Green, Aug. 1, 1924; Green to Lewis, Aug. 29, 1924; Lewis to Green, Aug. 30, 1924, *ibid.*

20. William Mitch to John L. Lewis, Sept. 13, 1924: Lewis to Mitch Sept. 20, 1924; Searles to Mitch, Sept. 22, 1924; Mitch to Searles, Sept. 23, 1924; Mitch to W. D. Van Horn, Sept. 23, 1924; Searles to Mitch, Sept. 24 and 26, 1924; Mitch to Searles, Oct. 3, 1924, all in William Mitch Papers, PSULA.

21. NYT, June 15, 1924, p. 14, June 20, 1924, p. 5; UMWJ, July 1, 1924, pp. 3-4.

22. UMWJ, Aug. 1, 1923, pp. 3-4.

23. JLL Papers, Reel 1.

24. Interview with John L. Lewis at Atlantic City, July 8, 1923, Calvin Coolidge Papers, Series 1, Reel 88, L.C.; Robert H. Zieger, *Republicans and Labor, 1919-1929* (Lexington, Ky., 1969), pp. 137n, 146-148; R. H. Zieger, "Senator George Wharton Pepper and Labor Issues in the 1920's," *Labor History*, IX (Spring 1968), 163-170.

25. Interview with John L. Lewis, Coolidge Papers; R. H. Zieger, *Republicans and Labor*, pp. 147ff.

26. R. H. Zieger, *Republicans and Labor*, pp. 147ff, and "Pinchot and Coolidge: The Politics of the 1923 Anthracite Crisis," *Journal of American History*, LI (Dec. 1965), 566-581; see the extensive correspondence in Calvin Coolidge Papers, File 175.

27. Interview with John L. Lewis, Calvin Coolidge Papers.

28. John L. Lewis to K. C. Adams, July 31, 1923, UMW Archives, JLL M.A. File.

29. Donald Markle to Lewis, Nov. 18, 1927; Lewis to Markle, Nov. 30, 1927, *ibid.*

30. NYT, Aug. 28, 1923, p. 1; R. H. Zieger, *Republicans and Labor*, pp. 152-154.

31. NYT, Sept. 8, 1923, p. 1; R. H. Zieger, *Republicans and Labor*, pp. 154-157.

32. General Circular Letter No. 51, Apr. 17, 1924, Winding Gulf Operators' Association, Beckley, West Virginia, D/L, R.G. 174-167, File 893, N.A.

33. *Report of the United States Coal Commission,* "Part III, Bituminous" (Washington, 1925); Walton H. Hamilton and Helen R. Wright, *A Way of Order for Bituminous Coal* (New York, 1928); Waldo E. Fischer and Charles M. James, *Minimum Price-Fixing in the Bituminous Coal Industry* (Princeton, N. J., 1965), pp. 5-19.

34. Box 39 of the W. Jett Lauck Papers contains the substantial Lauck-Lewis correspondence concerning the reorganization of the coal industry.

35. F. E. Herrimann to John L. Lewis, July 30, 1923, UMW Archives, JLL M.A. File.

36. On Hoover's basic labor policies see R. H. Zieger, *Republicans and Labor*, pp. 65-67, 87-88, 227-234, 236-247.

37. John Brophy remarked on several occasions that Lewis always worked privately with someone behind the scenes, either among the operators or in the federal government. Scrap Note, n.d., Box A5-34, John Brophy Papers, CUA.

38. F. E. Herrimann to John L. Lewis, Dec. 18, 1923 and Lewis to Herrimann, Dec. 20, 1923, UMW Archives, JLL M.A. File.

39. George G. Moore to John L. Lewis, July 12, 1944, *ibid.*; NYT, Apr. 20, 1924, IX, 7.

40. John L. Lewis to Herbert Hoover, Feb. 4, 1924, with enclosures; Hoover to Lewis, Feb. 7, 1924, Herbert Hoover Papers, Commerce-Coal, Box 355, Hoover Library; Memorandum, Hoover to President Coolidge, Feb. 5 or 6, 1924, Calvin Coolidge Papers, Series 1, Case 175, Reel 89; cf. R. Zieger, *Republicans and Labor,* pp. 228-230.

41. *Financial World*, Feb. 9, 1924, clipping, JLL Papers, Reel 2.

42. International Policy Committee Statement, Feb. 19, 1924, and Inter-State Agreement, Feb. 19, 1924, Herbert Hoover Papers, Commerce-Coal, Box 355; UMWJ, Mar. 1, 1924, pp. 3-4.

43. Herbert Hoover to John L. Lewis, Feb. 20, 1924, Herbert Hoover Papers, Commerce-Coal, Box 355; Hoover to Calvin Coolidge, Feb. 20, 1924; Coolidge to Michael Gallagher, Feb. 29, 1924; Coolidge to Lewis, Feb. 29, 1924; Lewis to Coolidge, Mar. 7, 1924, Coolidge Papers, Series 1, Case 175, Reel 89.

44. NYT, Apr. 20, 1924, IX, 7.

45. Herbert Hoover to John L. Lewis, Mar. 7, 1924; Lewis to Hoover, Mar. 14 and Apr. 10, 1924, Herbert Hoover Papers, Commerce-Coal, Box 355.

46. Commerce Department, *12th Annual Report* (Washington, 1924), pp. 13-14, cited in Morton Baratz, *The Union and the Coal Industry* (New Haven, 1955), p. 60. On the general meaning of the Jacksonville agreement see Edmond M. Beame, "The Jacksonville Agreement: Quest for Stability in Coal," *Industrial and Labor Relations Review,* VIII (Jan. 1955), 195-203.

47. John L. Lewis to K. C. Adams, Aug. 29, 1924, UMW Archives, JLL M.A. File.

48. *Ibid.*; Jacob M. Harriman to Earl E. Houck, Apr. 28, 1924, JLL Papers, Reel 1; *American Coal Miner* (March 1924), pp. 2-3.

49. Joseph Pursglove to John L. Lewis, Nov. 24, 1924, and Lewis to Pursglove, Nov. 27, 1924, UMW Archives, JLL M.A. File; NYT, Nov. 13, 1924, p. 23, Nov. 19, 1924, p. 35, Nov. 20, 1924, p. 25.

50. Ewing R. Emerson to Bascom Slemp, Mar. 19, 1924; John L. Lewis to Calvin Coolidge, Mar. 19, 1924; Lewis to Senator James Watson, Mar. 19, 1924; James Watson to Coolidge, Mar. 19, 1924; B. Slemp to Lewis, Mar. 20, 1924; J. Watson to Coolidge, Mar. 22, 1924, all in Calvin Coolidge Papers, Series 1, Case 209G, Reel 102.

51. F. E. Taplin to Joseph Pursglove, n.d.; Ellis Searles to Pursglove, Nov. 7, 1924; Pursglove to J. L. Lewis, Nov. 18, 1924; Lewis to Pursglove, Nov. 27, 1924, UMW Archives, JLL M.A. File.

52. Florence Thorne, COHC, p. 93.

53. George G. Moore to John L. Lewis, July 12, 1944, UMW Archives, JLL M.A. File.

54. Florence Thorne, COHC, p. 93.

55. John L. Lewis to William Mitch, Jan. 5, 1925, William Mitch Papers; Lee Hall to Lewis, Jan. 5 1925, UMW District 6 Papers, Box 2, File 4, Ohio University Archives; UMWJ, Jan. 1, 1925, p. 11; Jan. 15, 1925, p. 6.

56. UMWJ, Feb. 1, 1925, p. 17.

57. Press Clippings and Leaflets, JLL Papers, Reel 1.

NOTES TO CHAPTER 6

1. Oscar Ameringer to John H. Walker, Mar. 15, 1921; Ameringer to Alex Howat, Mar. 15, 1921, Adolph Germer Papers, Box 9, SHSW.

2. Frank Farrington to John L. Lewis, Feb. 11, 1921; Lewis to Farrington, Feb. 15, 1921; Farrington to Lewis, Feb. 18, 1921; Lewis to Farrington, Feb. 25, 1921; Farrington to Lewis, Mar. 8, 1921, UMW Archives, JLL M.A. File; UMWJ, Oct. 15, 1920, pp. 3-5.

3. Philip Taft, *The A. F. of L. in the Time of Gompers* (New York, 1957), pp. 411-413; *Official Statement of the UMWA Executive Board in re the Kansas Controversy* (Indianapolis, Dec. 6, 1921); *Proceedings 1921 Convention,* UMWA, pp. 603-640, 980-995.

4. NYT, Aug. 16, 1921, p. 24, Aug. 17, 1921, p. 15.

5. *Proceedings 1921 Convention*, UMWA, pp. 1000-1001.

6. *Ibid.*, pp. 516-517, 523.

7. *Ibid.*, p. 592.

8. *Ibid.*, pp. 606, 608-610, 618, 627.

9. *Ibid.*, pp. 627-629, 631, 635-636, 640-641, 995.

10. *Ibid.*, pp. 832-833.

11. NYT, Sept. 29, 1921, p. 20, Oct. 14, 1921, p. 5; UMWJ, Nov. 1, 1921, p. 7.

12. NYT, Oct. 14, 1921, p. 5.

13. Van Bittner to John L. Lewis, Nov. 5, 1921, Van A. Bittner Papers, Series I, Box 6, WVUL; UMWJ, Dec. 1, 1921, pp. 3-4.

14. P. Taft, *AFL in Time of Gompers*, pp. 414-415.

15. NYT, Jan. 15, 1922, p. 13.

16. *Proceedings 1921 Reconvened Convention*, UMWA, pp. 27-40.

17. *Ibid.*, pp. 41-51.

18. NYT, Feb. 18, 1922, p. 9.

19. *Proceedings 1921 Reconvened Convention,* UMWA, pp. 84-88.

20. *Ibid.*, pp. 188-191.

21. NYT, Feb. 18, 1922, p. 9, Feb. 19, 1922, pp. 1, 9, Feb. 20, 1922, p. 5.

22. John L. Lewis to William Mitch, Apr. 19, 1922, William Mitch Papers, PSULA.

23. Van A. Bittner to Phillip Murray, Mar. 1, 1923, Van A. Bittner Papers, Series I, Box 7; see also John L. Lewis to Bittner, Apr. 29, 1922; George Peck to Bittner, Nov. 7, 1922; James T. Skahan to Bittner, Nov. 20, 1922, *ibid.*

24. Powers Hapgood to Dearest Mother and Father, Aug. 16, 1922, Powers Hapgood Papers, Lilly Library, Indiana University. Brophy does not even mention this incident in his *A Miner's Life*, ed. John O. H. P. Hall (Madison, Wis., 1964).

25. "Minutes of Progressive International Conference of the United Mine Workers of America," Powers Hapgood Papers.

26. Frank Farrington to John L. Lewis, May 21, 1923, copy in Gompers Letterbooks, L.C.

27. John L. Lewis to Frank Farrington, May 25, 1923; Samuel Gompers to Farrington, May 31, 1923; Farrington to Gompers, June 8, 1923; Farrington to Alex Howat, June 13, 1923; Gompers to Executive Council, Document No. 100, June 16, 1923, *ibid.*

28. "Minutes of Progressive Conference," pp. 5, 11.

29. John Brophy to Arthur Gleason, June 26, 1923, John Brophy Papers, Box 5A-1, CUA.

30. John L. Lewis to John Brophy, July 11, 1923, *ibid.*

31. John Brophy to Arthur Gleason, July 12 and 26, 1923, *ibid.*

32. John L. Lewis to Adolph Germer, Aug. 13, 1923, Adolph Germer Papers, Box 27.

33. Father to Powers Hapgood, Nov. 1, 1923, Powers Hapgood Papers.

34. *Proceedings 1924 Convention*, UMWA, pp. 623-688; NYT, Jan. 30, 1924, p. 21, Jan. 31, 1924, p. 19.

35. *Proceedings 1924 Convention*, UMWA, pp. 855-856; NYT, Feb. 3, 1924, p. 1.

36. NYT, Feb. 3, 1924, pp. 1, 16.

37. Memorandum of Agreement between Peabody Coal Company and Frank Farrington, with Enclosed Letter of Resignation, UMW Archives, JLL M.A. File.

38. Frank Farrington to Peabody, Aug. 1, 1926, *ibid.*

39. NYT, Aug. 28, 1926, p. 19, Aug. 29, 1926, p. 18, Aug. 31, 1926, p. 20.

40. Edward A. Wieck, "Frank Farrington, Essay Based on Interview with Farrington," Apr. 1948, E. A. Wieck Papers, Box 13, ALHUA, WSU.

41. Farrington admitted as much in his interview with Wieck, *ibid.*, pp. 1-6.

42. Powers Hapgood to Mother and Father, June 20, 1926; Hapgood to Mother and Father, July 5, 1926, Powers Hapgood Papers.

43. Powers Hapgood to Mother and Father, July 10 and 26, 1926; Albert Coyle to Hapgood, Aug. 4, 1926, *ibid.*

44. "Open Letter of August 6, 1926"; "Save the Union," Open Letter, Sept. 24, 1926, and John Brophy, *A Larger Program for the Miners' Union*, Nov. 8, 1926, all in John Brophy Papers, Box A5-2.

45. J. Brophy, *A Miner's Life*, pp. 210-211. In his treatment of the 1926 union election Brophy does not even mention the role of Communists.

46. NYT, Oct. 13, 1926, pp. 1, 3; UMWJ, Nov. 1, 1926, pp. 3, 5, 7.

47. NYT, Oct. 16, 1926, p. 7; see also Powers Hapgood to Mother, Oct. 18, 1926, Powers Hapgood Papers; Powers Hapgood to Officers and Members of District 2, Oct. 20, 1926, John Brophy Papers, Box A5-2.

48. District 2, Executive Board to Membership of UMWA, n.d., John Brophy Papers, Box A5-2.

49. For charges of vote-stealing and some of the supporting evidence, see Powers Hapgood to Evelyn, May 2, 1927, Powers Hapgood Papers; "John Brophy Appeals for Honesty and a Square Deal," May 28, 1927, John Brophy Papers, Box A5-2; for some countervailing evidence, see James Robb, Oral History Transcript, p. 7, SWOC Collection, PSULA.

50. Powers Hapgood to Evelyn, May 2, 1927, Powers Hapgood Papers.

51. *Proceedings 1927 Convention*, UMWA, pp. 269, 311-343, 345-346.

52. *Ibid.*, pp. 286-287.

53. *Ibid.*, pp. 75, 218-226, 199-200.

54. *Ibid.*, p. 206.

55. *Ibid.*, p. 304.

56. *Ibid.*, pp. 212-214.

57. *Ibid.*, pp. 234-235.

58. *Ibid.*, p. 452.

59. John L. Lewis to Van Bittner, with enclosure, June 7, 1927, Van A. Bittner Papers, Series I, Box 7; Hugh D. Friel to Hugh L. Kerwin, Mar. 25, 1928, D/L, R.G. 280, File 170/3918, N.A.; NYT, Apr. 22, 1928, II, 1.

60. NYT, Sept. 10, 1928, p. 25.

61. James Mark *et al.* to Peter P. Patrick, May 4, 1928; Patrick to John Brophy, May 7, 1928; Brophy to Patrick, May 10, 1928, John Brophy Papers, Box A5-2.

62. John L. Lewis to Thomas Kerr, Jan. 21, 1929; Percy F. Tetlow to Lewis, Aug. 2, 1929; Lewis to Tetlow, Aug. 8, 1929, UMW Archives, JLL Files.

63. William Dalrymple to William Mitch, July 5, 1928, and Mitch to Dalrymple, July 7, 1928, William Mitch Papers.

NOTES TO CHAPTER 7

1. "Bituminous Coal," n.d., D/L, R.G. 280, N.A.

2. *Ibid.*

3. *Proceedings 1927 Convention*, UMWA, p. 75.

4. Philip Taft, *The A. F. of L. from the Death of Gompers to the Merger* (New York, 1959), pp. 17-18; cf. *Proceedings of the 41st Annual Convention of the Ohio State Federation of Labor* (1924), p. 37.

5. UMW Financial Report, 1920-1930, UMW Archives, JLL Files.

6. Lewis to K. C. Adams, Aug. 29, 1924, *ibid.*, M.A. File.

7. J. W. Blower to Joseph Pursglove, Nov. 6, 1924; Pursglove to John L. Lewis, Nov. 18, 1924, *ibid.*

8. *Cushing's Survey*, Feb. 19, 1925, in Herbert Hoover Papers, Commerce-Coal, JLL, Box 183, Hoover Library.

9. *Ibid.*; C. P. White to Herbert Hoover, Feb. 26, 1925, *ibid.*

10. *Cushing's Survey,* Feb. 19, 1925; James J. Davis, Confidential Memorandum on the Coal Mining Situation, Mar. 10, 1925, Calvin Coolidge Papers, Series I, Case 175, Reel 89, L.C.; C. P. White, Memorandum for Herbert Hoover, Apr. 3, 1925, Herbert Hoover Papers, Commerce-Coal, Miscellaneous, Box 346.

11. C. P. White, Memorandum, Apr. 3, 1925.

12. Felix Morley in New York *Sun*, May 16, 1925, clipping in *ibid.*, Coal-JLL, Box 355.

13. *Ibid.*

14. On general federal labor policy, see Robert H. Zieger, *Republicans and Labor* (Lexington, Ky., 1969), pp. 216-247.

15. Fred Mooney to William Green, Jan. 31, 1925, A. F. of L. Papers, Office of the President, File C, SHSW.

16. *Cushing's Survey*, Feb. 19, 1925.

17. See Interstate Commerce Committee, United States Senate, 70th Congress: 1st Session, on S.R. 105 to Investigate Conditions in the Coal Fields of Pennsylvania, West Virginia, and Ohio, Feb. 10, 1928.

18. Harold Phelps Stokes to John L. Lewis, June 22, 1925, Herbert Hoover Papers, Commerce-JLL, Box 355.

19. Saul D. Alinsky, *John L. Lewis: An Unauthorized Biography* (New York, 1970 ed.), p. 368.

20. *The Miner's Fight for American Standards* (Indianapolis, 1925), pp. 12, 15, 38-39, 40-41, 52, 93.

21. *Ibid.*, pp. 110 and *passim.*

22. *Ibid.*, pp. 188-189.

23. *Ibid.*, pp. 40-41, 93, 110, 179-180, and *passim.*

24. NYT, June 21, 1925, IX, 15, Aug. 16, 1925, II, 2.

25. *Ibid.*, July 1, 1925, pp. 1, 6, July 2, 1925, p. 4; Harold K. Kanarek, "Disaster for Hard Coal: The Anthracite Strike of 1925-1926," *Labor History*, XV (Winter 1974), 44-45.

26. Donald Markle to John L. Lewis, Nov. 18, 1927, and Lewis to Markle, Nov. 30, 1927, UMW Archives, JLL M.A. File.

27. On the collapse of negotiations, see "Anthracite Strike," D/L, R.G. 280; John J. Leary, Jr., to Herbert Hoover, Aug. 12, 1924, Hoover Papers, Commerce-Coal-JLL, Box 183; Robe Carl White to Everett Sanders, Aug. 3, 1925, Calvin Coolidge Papers, Series I, Case 175, Reel 88; UMWJ, Aug. 15, 1925, pp. 3-4, 17.

28. John J. Leary, Jr., to Herbert Hoover, Aug. 12, 1924, Herbert Hoover Papers, Commerce-Coal-JLL, Box 183.

29. John L. Lewis to K. C. Adams, Aug. 24, 1925, UMW Archives, JLL M.A. File.

30. On the strike see H. Kanarek, "Disaster for Hard Coal," pp. 44-62.

31. Robe Carl White to Everett Sanders, Aug. 5 and 11, 1925; James J. Davis, Memorandum, Sept. 14, 1925, Calvin Coolidge Papers, Series I, Case 175, Reel 89.

32. NYT, Sept. 26, 1925, p. 1, Sept. 27, 1925, pp. 1, 21; Paul Wooton to Harold Phelps Stokes, with enclosure, Sept. 25, 1925; UMW Press Release, Sept. 26, 1925; and C. P. White, Memorandum for Herbert Hoover, Sept. 28, 1925, Herbert Hoover Papers, Commerce-Coal-JLL, Box 346.

33. E. E. Hunt, Memorandum to Hoover, Sept. 28, 1925, Herbert Hoover Papers, Commerce-Coal-JLL, Box 346.

34. R. Zieger, *Republicans and Labor,* pp. 236-237.

35. *Ibid.*, pp. 240-241; NYT, Nov. 23, 1925, pp. 1, 3; UMWJ, Dec. 1, 1925, p. 8, Mar. 15, 1928, p. 13.

36. Herbert Hoover to Calvin Coolidge, three letters and enclosure, Nov. 25, 1925; Hoover to Andrew Mellon, Nov. 25, 1925; Hoover to Coolidge, Nov. 27, 1925, with enclosed memorandum; Eugene McAsuliffe (president, Union Pacific Coal Company) to Hoover, Nov. 28, 1925, all in Herbert Hoover Papers, Commerce-Coal-JLL, Box 355; NYT, Nov. 23, 1925, pp. 1, 4, Nov. 24, 1925, pp. 1, 10; R. Zieger, *Republicans and Labor,* pp. 241-243.

37. John J. Leary, Jr., to Herbert Hoover, Nov. 27, 1925, Herbert Hoover Papers, Commerce-Coal-JLL, Box 183.

38. *Ibid.*, and John J. Leary, Jr., to Herbert Hoover, Dec. 2, 1925, *ibid.*; "Anthracite Strike," D/L, R.G. 280; W. Jett Lauck to John L. Lewis, Dec. 31, 1925, and Lewis to Lauck, Jan. 2, 1926, W. Jett Lauck Papers, Box 39, Alderson Library, UVL.

39. NYT, Feb. 13, 1926, pp. 2-3.

40. "Anthracite Strike," D/L, R.G. 280; H. Kanarek, "Disaster for Hard Coal," pp. 57-58.

41. Cited in H. Kanarek, "Disaster for Hard Coal," p. 61.

42. NYT, Jan. 24, 1927, p. 19.

43. John L. Lewis to F. E. Herrimann, Feb. 6, 1926, UMW Archives, JLL M.A. File.

44. Union and Operator Bargaining Proposals, n.d., D/L, R.G. 280, File 170/3918; NYT, Feb. 16, 1927, p. 12, Feb. 18, 1927, p. 15, Feb. 23, 1927, pp. 1 and 18, Feb. 27, 1927, p. 28; UMWJ, Mar. 1, 1927, pp. 3-5, 8-11.

45. J. Joseph Huthmacher, *Senator Robert Wagner and the Rise of Urban Liberalism* (New York, 1968), p. 64; James F. Dewey to Hugh L. Kerwin, Apr. 19, 1927, D/L, R.G. 280, File 170/3918; 70th Congress: 1st Session on S.R. 105 to Investigate Conditions in the Coal Fields of Pennsylvania, West Virginia, and Ohio.

46. Memorandum for Secretary Davis, D/L, R.G. 280.

47. Memorandum for Secretary Davis on Pittsburgh Conference, Nov. 14-15, 1927, *ibid.*; P. Taft, *AFL from Death of Gompers*, p. 16; UMWJ, Dec. 1, 1927, pp. 3-5, 8-14.

48. Memorandum of Recent Coal Conference, Dec. 9-15, 1927, D/L, R.G. 280; undated report (1927?) in *ibid.*, File 170/3918A; NYT, Nov. 22, 1927, pp. 1-2; P. Taft, *AFL from Death of Gompers*, p. 16.

49. Davis's three telegrams of Dec. 9, 12, 13, Lewis's reply of Dec. 10, and the operators' responses are all in D/L, R.G. 280, File 170/3918. Cf. NYT, Dec. 10, 1927, p. 9, Dec. 11, 1927, p. 28.

50. F. E. Taplin to James J. Davis, Dec. 10, 1927, D/L, R.G. 280, File 170/3918.

51. Morrow to James J. Davis, Dec. 12, 1927, *ibid*.

52. *Ibid*.

53. Memorandum of Recent Coal Conferences, Dec. 9-15, 1927; Memorandum on Dec. 13-15, 1927, conference; Remarks by James J. Davis at the opening of the conference between the representatives of the United Mine Workers and the operators, Dec. 13, 1927; Press Release of Dec. 13, 1927; Press Releases of Dec. 13, 14, 15, 1927, all in *ibid.*; NYT, Dec. 14, 1927, p. 52, Dec. 15, 1927, p. 32.

54. F. E. Taplin to James J. Davis, Dec. 22, 1927, D/L, R.G. 280, File 170/3918B.

55. Ivan A. Boucher to James J. Davis, Dec. 21, 1927, *ibid*.

56. James J. Davis to John A. Topping, Dec. 23, 1927, and Topping to Davis, Dec. 28, 1927, *ibid*.

57. W. Jett Lauck Papers, Box 39; UMWJ, Aug. 1, 1928, p. 3.

58. Speech and Pamphlet in JLL Papers (microfilm copy), SHSW.

59. Dan G. Smith to John L. Lewis, Dec. 13, 1928, *ibid*.

60. See correspondence in Herbert Hoover Papers, Pre-Presidential File, Cabinet Appointments: JLL, Box 30, especially Harriman to Hoover, Jan. 18, 1929, and E.N. Foss to Hoover, Jan. 18, 1929. Also see Lauck to Hoover, Feb. 9, 1929.

61. W. Jett Lauck to John L. Lewis, Feb. 2, 1929; Lewis to Lauck, Feb. 8, 1929; Lauck to Lewis, Feb. 11, 1929, W. Jett Lauck Papers, Box 39.

62. E. M. Poston to My Dear Hoover, Feb. 22, 1929, and Hoover to My Dear Poston, Feb. 26, 1929, Herbert Hoover Papers, Pre-Presidential File, Cabinet Appointments: JLL, Box 30.

63. *Cushing's Survey*, Feb. 19, 1925.

64. John L. Lewis to Tom Moses, July 28, 1927, UMW Archives, JLL M.A. File.

NOTES TO CHAPTER 8

1. George Korson, *Coal Dust on the Fiddle* (Hatboro, Pa., 1965), pp. 177-178.

2. Irving Bernstein, *The Lean Years* (Boston, 1960), pp. 358-366; Malcolm H. Ross, *Machine Age in the Hills* (New York, 1933); Malcolm Brown and John Webb, *Seven Stranded Towns: A Study of an American Depressed Area* (New York, 1971 reprint).

3. UMW Financial Statement, 1920-1930, UMW Archives, JLL Files.

4. On these developments see John L. Lewis to Lee Hall and G. W. Savage, Apr. 25, 1929, UMWA District 6 Papers, Box 4, File 6, Ohio University Archives; and James Robb, Oral History Transcript, II, 19-20, SWOC Collection, PSULA.

5. John H. Walker to B. M. Flaherty, Aug. 8, 1928; Walker to John L. Lewis, Aug. 10, 1928; Lewis to Walker, Aug. 14, 1928; Walker to Lewis, Aug. 15, 1928; Lewis to

Walker, Aug. 16, 1928; Walker to Lewis, Aug. 17, 1928, John H. Walker Papers, Box 4, University of Illinois Historical Survey.

6. Frank Farrington, *The Wrecking of the Miners' Union* (Springfield, Ill., n.d.), in the Adolph Germer Papers, Box 23, SHSW.

7. James Sneddon to A. D. Lewis, June 3, 1929, and A. D. Lewis to Sneddon, June 6, 1929, *ibid.*, Box 1.

8. *Proceedings 1930 Convention*, UMWA, pp. 170-173; cf. I. Bernstein, *Lean Years*, p. 367, and Lorin Lee Cary, "The Reorganized United Mine Workers of America," *Journal of the Illinois State Historical Society*, 66 (Autumn 1973), 246-247.

9. *Proceedings 1930 Convention*, UMWA, pp. 78-87; UMWJ, Oct. 1, 1929, pp. 3-5, Oct. 15, 1929, pp. 3-7. For somewhat different versions of events, see I. Bernstein, *Lean Years*, p. 367; L. Cary, "The Reorganized," pp. 246-247.

10. John Brophy to Oscar Ameringer, Oct. 25, 1929, John Brophy Papers, Box A5-2, CUA.

11. William Mitch to William Green, Nov. 8, 1929, William Mitch Papers, PSULA.

12. L. Cary, "The Reorganized," p. 247; UMWJ, Nov. 1, 1929, pp. 3-4, Nov. 15, 1929, pp. 3-5, Dec. 1, 1929, pp. 3-5, 10.

13. Frank Farrington to Joe Allison, Jan. 28, 1930, Adolph Germer Papers, Box 1; cf. UMWJ, May 1, 1930, pp. 8-9.

14. Alexander Howat to John O'Leary *et al.*, Oct. 27, 1928, John H. Walker Papers, Box 44; cf. *Proceedings 1930 Convention*, UMWA, pp. 182-183.

15. Adolph Germer to James O'Neal, Apr. 15, 1931, Adolph Germer Papers, Box 1; L. Cary, "The Reorganized," pp. 247-248; I. Bernstein, *Lean Years,* p. 368.

16. Adolph Germer to James O'Neal, Apr. 15, 1931, Adolph Germer Papers, Box 1.

17. Alex Howat *et al.* to John L. Lewis *et al.*, Feb. 26, 1930, *ibid.*; I. Bernstein mistakenly dates the compromise proposal after the founding of the RUMWA at the Springfield convention, *Lean Years,* p. 370.

18. Copy of Insurgents Official Convention Call, in John H. Walker Papers, Box 24.

19. John L. Lewis to W. Jett Lauck, Mar. 27, 1930, W. Jett Lauck Papers, Alderson Library, UVL.

20. *Proceedings 1930 Convention*, UMWA, pp. 78-94, 169-184, 397-399.

21. *Ibid.*, p. 467.

22. *Ibid.*, p. 570.

23. *Ibid.*, pp. 474-477, 484-485, 487.

24. *Ibid.*, pp. 684-686.

25. Adolph Germer to James O'Neal, Apr. 15, 1931, Adolph Germer Papers, Box 1; L. Cary, "The Reorganized," pp. 250-251.

26. John Brophy to Mr. Andrews, Mar. 15, 1930; Brophy to Patrick McDermott, Mar. 15, 1930; and Brophy to Powers Hapgood, Mar. 26, 1930, John Brophy Papers, Box A5-3; *Proceedings RUMWA*, pp. 172-247. L. Cary, "The Reorganized," pp. 249-251.

27. *Proceedings RUMWA,* pp. 172-247, 335-345, 373-399; L. Cary, "The Reorganized," pp. 249-251. Remarkably, Oscar Ameringer, one of the leading insurgents, scarcely mentions the convention or the union struggle in Illinois in his autobiography, *If You Don't Weaken* (New York, 1940).

28. Adolph Germer to Norman Thomas, Mar. 21, 1931, Adolph Germer Papers, Box 27; Germer to James O'Neal, Apr. 15, 1931, Box 1; Thomas Kennedy to Steve Toth, Apr. 1, 1930, Box 1; Financial Reports for RUMWA, Box 23; the John H. Walker Papers have full and accurate membership reports for the RUMWA. See Walker to Kennedy with enclosure, Mar. 9, 1931, Box 29; also see Boxes 30 and 32.

29. Alex Howat to A. J. Muste, Mar. 24, 1930; Alex Howat to Arch B. McCallum, Mar. 24, 1930, Adolph Germer Papers, Box 1; John J. Watt to Howat, Oct. 24, 26, 31,

1930, *ibid.*; Howat to Joe Vincent, Sept. 19, 1930, *ibid.*; on Farrington, see UMWJ, May 1, 1930, pp. 8-9.

30. Germer employed "spies" to check on Howat and kept records of their reports, Germers Papers, Box 1; Germer's diary for the period is filled with unflattering references to Howat and his drinking habits, Box 24.

31. "Whiskey Breath," n.d., *ibid.*, Box 27.

32. Germer's papers are filled with copies of correspondence between Howat and his supporters. See also Germer Memoranda, dated Sept. 15-Oct. 12, 1930, Box 1; Tom Tippett to Howat, Aug. 18, 1930, *ibid.*; and comments in Germer's Diary for 1930, Box 27; cf. Germer Memorandum, Sept. 28, 1930, John H. Walker Papers, Box 26.

33. NM Leaflets in Adolph Germer Papers, Box 1.

34. John H. Walker to Victor A. Olander, Apr. 9, 1930; William Green to Olander, Aug. 5, 1930; Walker to Olander, Aug. 26, 1930 and Nov. 11, 1930; Olander to Walker, Nov. 8, 1930, John H. Walker Papers, Box 44; P. Taft, *The A. F. of L. from the Death of Gompers to the Merger* (New York, 1959), pp. 18-20.

35. George W. Lewis to John L. Lewis, Jan. 31, 1931, UMW Archives, JLL M.A. File.

36. Germer Diary entries for Apr. 9, 18, 19, July 3, 1930, Adolph Germer Papers, Box 24; McAlester Coleman, *Men and Coal* (New York, 1943), pp. 141ff; L. Cary, "The Reorganized," pp. 253-254.

37. John H. Walker to Joseph Claypool, July 15, 1930, A. F. of L. Papers, Office of the President, File B, Box 3, SHSW; Germer Diary, July 31, Aug. 1, 1930, Adolph Germer Papers, Box 24.

38. NYT, Sept. 6, 1930, p. 16.

39. Many of the legal papers, writs, injunctions, and court orders can be located in the Adolph Germer Papers, Box 23.

40. The Edwards ruling can be found in *ibid.* and also UMWJ, Mar. 15, 1931, pp. 8-10; cf. L. Cary, "The Reorganized," pp. 264-265.

41. Alex Howat to Floyd E. Thompson, Mar. 1, 1931, Adolph Germer Papers, Box 1; L. Cary, "The Reorganized," pp. 264-265.

42. Adolph Germer to Norman Thomas, Mar. 21, 1931, Adolph Germer Papers, Box 27; Germer to James O'Neal, Apr. 15, 1931, *ibid.*, Box 1.

43. Norman Thomas to Adolph Germer, Mar. 18, 1931, *ibid.*, Box 27.

44. Adolph Germer to Norman Thomas, Mar. 21, 1931, *ibid.*; Germer to James O'Neal, Apr. 15, 1931, *ibid.*, Box 1; L. Cary, "The Reorganized," pp. 266-268.

45. Adolph Germer had an informant at the Saint Louis meeting who provided him with detailed information. See notes on the Saint Louis Meeting, Mar. 17-22, 1931, Adolph Germer Papers, Box 1; Germer to James O'Neal, Apr. 15, 1931, *ibid.*; Germer Diary, Mar. 17, 18, 22, 1931, *ibid.*, Box 24.

46. Convention Call, *ibid.*, Box 23.

47. Copy of Lewis's remarks to the IEB, June 12, 1931, William Mitch Papers.

48. NYT, July 27, 1931, p. 11.

49. John H. Walker to William Green, Nov. 29, 1937, A. F. of L. Papers, Office of the President, File C, Box 31; John L. Lewis to Officers and Members of all Local Unions of District 12, William Mitch Papers.

50. The doggerel is in John H. Walker to William Green, Nov. 29, 1937, A. F. of L. Papers, Office of the President, File C, Box 31; I. Bernstein, *Lean Years*, pp. 373-374.

51. I. Bernstein, *Lean Years*, pp. 373-374; John H. Walker to William Green, Nov. 29, 1937, A. F. of L. Papers, Office of the President, File C, Box 31; Walker to Robert McCormick, Nov. 7, 1937, *ibid.*

52. On the progressives, see Harriet D. Hudson, *The Progressive Mine Workers of*

America: A Study in Rival Unionism (Urbana, Ill., 1952); Adolph Germer to Ernest Doerfler, Sept. 22, 1932, Adolph Germer Papers, Box 1; Germer to Gerry Allard, Jan. 3, 1933, *ibid.*; Henry Hauser to Germer, Mar. 19, 1933, *ibid.*, Box 27.

53. John H. Walker to William Green, Nov. 29, 1937, A. F. of L. Papers, Office of the President, File C, Box 31.

54. Strike Activity in the Coal Industry, Jan. 20, 1947, D/L, R.G. 174, Box 71, N.A.

55. Harold W. Houston to Adolph Germer, Mar. 26, 1931, Adolph Germer Papers, Box 27; C. Frank Keeney to Germer, Mar. 26, 1931, *ibid.*, Box 1; Germer to Keeney, Mar. 31, 1931, *ibid.*; Helen G. Norton, "Feudalism in West Virginia," *Nation* (Aug. 12, 1931), pp. 154-155; Edmund Wilson, "Frank Keeney's Coal Diggers," *New Republic* (July 8, 1931), pp. 195-199, and "Frank Keeney's Coal Diggers: II," *ibid.* (July 15, 1931), pp. 229-231.

56. Theodore Draper, "Communists and Miners, 1928-1933," *Dissent* (Spring 1972), pp. 371-375.

57. *Ibid.*, pp. 375-392; I. Bernstein, *Lean Years*, pp. 377-381, 385-389; Tony Bubka, "The Harlan County Coal Strike of 1931," *Labor History*, XI (Winter 1970), 41-57.

58. NYT, Aug. 29, 1930, p. 2, Oct. 6, 1930, p. 14; George Akerson to John L. Lewis, Aug. 22, 1930; Lewis to Akerson, Aug. 26, 1930, Herbert Hoover Papers, President's Secretary File, Box 565, Hoover Library; W. Jett Lauck to Lewis, Nov. 6, 1930; Lewis to Lauck, Nov. 11, 1930, Lauck Papers, Box 39.

59. John Brophy, COHC, pp. 623-625.

60. Memorandum dated June 11, 1931, Hoover Papers, PSF, Box 565.

61. F. E. Taplin to Herbert Hoover, June 27, 1931, D/L, R.G. 280, File 165/944, N.A.; see also H. W. Showalter to R. P. Lamont, July 22, 1931, and R. H. Sherwood to Sidney A. Hale, Aug. 28, 1931, *ibid.*

62. Herbert Hoover to John L. Lewis, June 29, 1931, Hoover Papers, PSF, Box 565.

63. NYT, July 14, 1931, p. 14.

64. Transcript of Conference, July 14, 1931, D/L, R.G. 280, File 165/944; NYT, July 15, 1931, p. 5.

65. W. N. Doak to James C. Chaplin, Sept. 5, 1931, D/L, R.G. 280 File 165/944A; UMWA, Memorandum, Aug. 20, 1931, William Mitch Papers; John L. Lewis to W. Jett Lauck, Aug. 12, 1931, W. Jett Lauck Papers, Box 39.

66. W. Jett Lauck to John L. Lewis, Aug. 26, 1931, W. Jett Lauck Papers, Box 39.

67. John L. Lewis to W. Jett Lauck, Aug. 31, 1931, *ibid.*

68. W. Jett Lauck to John L. Lewis, Sept. 4, 1931, *ibid.*

69. Press Release, Sept. 7, 1931, William Mitch Papers; NYT, Sept. 8, 1931, p. 4.

70. W. Jett Lauck to John L. Lewis, Oct. 20, 1931, Nov. 30, 1931; Lewis to Lauck, Nov. 30, 1931, W. Jett Lauck Papers, Box 39.

71. Henry Warrum to W. N. Doak, Dec. 14, 1931, *ibid.*, Box 232; W. Jett Lauck to John L. Lewis, Feb. 18, 1932, Box 39; Lewis to Lauck, Feb. 22, 1932, *ibid.*; Lewis to Lauck, Feb. 27, 1932, *ibid.*; Lauck to Lewis, Feb. 29, 1932, *ibid.*; UMWJ, June 15, 1932, pp. 3-5, 13-19.

72. Lawrence Richey to John L. Lewis, Oct. 21, 1932, Herbert Hoover Papers, PSF, Box 565; Phil Murray to William L. Hutcheson, Sept. 13, 1932, and Hutcheson to Murray, Sept. 16, 1932, John Brophy Papers, Box A5-3.

73. William H. Crawford to Louis Howe, n.d. (1932), Roosevelt Papers, Democratic National Committee, Box 405, FDRL.

74. W. Jett Lauck to John L. Lewis, Oct. 10, 1932; Lewis to Lauck, Nov. 14, 1932, W. Jett Lauck Papers, Box 39; UMWJ, Sept. 15, 1932, pp. 3-4, for Lewis's call in a national radio speech for national economic planning.

75. John L. Lewis to W. Jett Lauck, Nov. 17, 1932, and Lauck to Lewis, Nov. 21, 1932, W. Jett Lauck Papers, Box 39.

76. NYT, Nov. 27, 1932, p. 2, Dec. 2, 1932, p. 18.

77. Memorandum #1 to Lewis *in re* Statement to Finance Committee of United States Senate, Feb. 17, 1933, W. Jett Lauck Papers, Box 231; UMWJ, Mar. 1, 1933, pp. 3-4.

NOTES TO CHAPTER 9

1. Arthur M. Schlesinger, Jr., *The Coming of the New Deal* (Boston, 1959), pp. 2-3.

2. UMWJ, Mar. 1, 1933, pp. 3-4.

3. Raymond Moley to Marvin McIntyre, Mar. 21, 1933, FDR Papers, OF 175, Roosevelt Library; NYT, Mar. 28, 1933, p. 3; Irving Bernstein, *Turbulent Years* (Boston, 1970), pp. 27-31; J. Joseph Huthmacher, *Senator Robert F. Wagner and the Rise of Urban Liberalism* (New York, 1968), pp. 146-150.

4. NYT, June 2, 1933, p. 4; UMWJ, June 15, 1933, pp. 8-9.

5. A. M. Schlesinger, Jr., *Coming of the New Deal*, p. 23.

6. Saul D. Alinsky, *John L. Lewis: An Unauthorized Biography* (New York, 1970 ed.), pp. 67-71; I. Bernstein, *Turbulent Years*, pp. 40-41, picks up Alinsky's "story" and lends credence to it.

7. There is absolutely no evidence in the UMW Archives, the union's convention proceedings, its journal, or the papers of Lewis's friends and associates that indicates any factual basis for Alinsky's story. Indeed, as the following chapter on the origins of the CIO should suggest, Lewis, as late as the summer of 1935 (perhaps even later), had not given up hope that the A. F. of L. could be converted to his organizing program.

8. Burchel Baker to Adolph Germer, Feb. 14, 1933, and George L. Mercer to Germer, Feb. 23, 1933, Adolph Germer Papers, Box 27, SHSW.

9. Van A. Bittner to William Mitch, June 23, 1933, William Mitch Papers, PSULA; untitled, undated report on the UMW organizing campaign of 1933 in Edward A. Wieck Collection, Box 12, ALUHA, WSU; cf. I. Bernstein, *Turbulent Years*, pp. 41-42.

10. See, for example, John Brophy, COHC, pp. 505-506.

11. E. Wieck Report.

12. *Ibid.*

13. L. Epperly to Justus Collins, July 21, 1923, Justus Collins Collection, Series I, WVa.UL.

14. E. Wieck Report.

15. *New Republic,* Aug. 16, 1933, p. 5.

16. Hugh Johnson to John L. Lewis, Dec. 30, 1933, and Aug. 10, 1935, JLL Papers (microfilm copy), SHSW; on Johnson see I. Bernstein, *Turbulent Years*, pp. 43-44, and A. M. Schlesinger, Jr., *Coming of the New Deal*, pp. 105-106.

17. Transcript of Coal Code Hearing, Aug. 9-10, 1933, pp. 24, 36-41, 360, D/L, R.G. 9, File 702/4S, N.A.

18. On this point see the *Nation,* Aug. 16, 1933, pp. 176-177, Aug. 23, 1933, pp. 205-206.

19. Louis Stark to Franklin D. Roosevelt, FDR Papers, OF 175, Coal, Box 1.

20. *Ibid.*

21. Gifford Pinchot to Franklin D. Roosevelt, Sept. 5, 1933, *ibid.*

22. Unsigned, anonymous report, Sept. 6, 1933, *ibid.*

23. Gifford Pinchot to Franklin D. Roosevelt, Sept. 12, 1933, *ibid.*

24. UMWJ, Aug. 15, 1933, pp. 4-5, 14, Sept. 1, 1933, pp. 8-9, Sept. 15, 1933, pp. 9-11; I. Bernstein, *Turbulent Years*, p. 45.

25. William Taylor to John L. Lewis, Sept. 19, 1933, UMW Archives, JLL M.A. File; for the Brubaker comment see I. Bernstein, *Turbulent Years*, p. 45.

26. George Korson, *Coal Dust on the Fiddle* (Hatboro, Pa., 1965), pp. 301-305.

27. *Proceedings 1930 Convention*, UMWA, p. 686; John Brophy, COHC, pp. 597-600.

28. On Moses, see Tom Moses File, UMW Archives, JLL, M.A. File; on Taylor, see I. Bernstein, *Turbulent Years*, pp. 46-48.

29. Myron Taylor to Franklin D. Roosevelt, Oct. 3, 1933, with enclosures, FDR Papers, OF 175, Coal, Box 1; E. Wieck Report; I. Bernstein, *Turbulent Years*, pp. 49-53.

30. Hugh S. Johnson to Franklin D. Roosevelt, Oct. 1, 1933; Roosevelt to Johnson, n.d. (probably Oct. 1, 1933); and Johnson to Roosevelt, Oct. 2, 1933, FDR Papers, OF 175, Coal, Box 1.

31. Gifford Pinchot to Franklin D. Roosevelt, Oct. 1, 1933, *ibid*.

32. Franklin D. Roosevelt to Myron Taylor, Oct. 4, 1933, *ibid*.

33. Myron Taylor to Franklin D. Roosevelt, Oct. 6, 1933; Tom M. Girdler *et al*. to Roosevelt, Oct. 6, 1933, *ibid*.

34. Nathan L. Miller to Franklin D. Roosevelt, Oct. 10, 1933; T. M. Girdler *et al*. to Roosevelt, Oct. 10, 1933, all in Press Release of Oct. 12, 1933, *ibid*.; Philip Murray to Thomas Moses, Oct. 12, 1933; Moses to Murray, Oct. 13, 1933; Murray to Moses, Oct. 13, 1933; Moses to Murray, Oct. 16, 1933; Myron Taylor to Roosevelt, Oct. 16, 1933; and W. A. Irvin to Roosevelt, Oct. 16, 1933, all in *ibid*.

35. Donald R. Richberg to Marvin McIntyre, Oct. 18, 1933, and Franklin D. Roosevelt to Myron Taylor and W. A. Irvin, Oct. 19, 1933, *ibid*.

36. I. Bernstein, *Turbulent Years*, pp. 59-60.

37. *Ibid*., p. 60; E. Wieck Report.

38. National Labor Board, Stenographic Report of Hearing in the Matter of Provisions of the Captive Mines of the H.C. Frick Company *et al.*, Jan. 4, 1934, p. 107, National Recovery Administration, R.G. 9, File 702/45.

39. *Ibid*., pp. 5-10, 24-25, 32-33; I. Bernstein, *Turbulent Years*, pp. 60-61.

40. E. Wieck Report.

41. NYT, Oct. 12, 1933, p. 2; *Proceedings 1933 Convention*, A. F. of L., pp. 396-403.

42. *Proceedings 1934 Convention*, UMWA, p. 56.

43. E. Wieck Report.

44. UMWJ, Mar. 15, 1934, pp. 3-5.

45. *Ibid*., Apr. 15, 1934, p. 3.

46. *Ibid*., pp. 3-5, 8-9.

47. Transcript of Hearing, Code of Fair Competition for the Bituminous Coal Industry, Apr. 11, 1934, p. 800, National Recovery Administration, R.G. 9.

48. *Ibid*., pp. 323-368.

49. *Ibid*.

50. William Green to Adolph Germer, Oct. 28, 1933, Adolph Germer Papers, Box 1.

51. John Brophy, "Twenty Years with the CIO," mss., John Brophy Papers, Box A5-41; John Brophy, *A Miner's Life*, ed. John O. H. P. Hall (Madison, Wis., 1964), pp. 238-239.

52. J. Brophy, *A Miner's Life*, pp. 240-241.

53. John Brophy to John L. Lewis, Nov. 7, 1933, and Brophy to Philip Murray, Nov. 7, 1933, John Brophy Papers, Box A5-3; J. Brophy, *A Miner's Life*, pp. 240-242.

54. John Brophy to John L. Lewis, Nov. 7, 1933, John Brophy Papers, Box A5-3.

55. *Ibid*.

56. *Proceedings 1934 Convention* UMWA, p. 316.

57. John L. Lewis to Philip Murray, May 6, 1934, UMW Archives, JLL M.A. File.

58. UMWJ, June 1, 1934, p. 10.

59. The invitations, picture postcards, and receipts for the purchase of antiques are in the JLL Papers (microfilm copy).

60. The first quotation is from David Brody, "Labor and the Great Depression: The Interpretive Prospects," *Labor History,* XIII (Spring 1972), 239; the second is from Len DeCaux, *Labor Radical* (Boston, 1970), p. 230.

61. *New Republic,* Oct. 31, 1934, p. 331.

NOTES TO CHAPTER 10

1. A report that indicates how small a proportion of the total labor force was involved in strikes during the first half of 1934 can be found in a memorandum to the president from Isadore Lubin, Aug. 29, 1934, FDR Papers, OF 407B, Box 10, Roosevelt Library.

2. The most complete and dramatic treatment of the three conflicts is in Irving Bernstein, *Turbulent Years* (Boston, 1970), pp. 217-298.

3. Sidney Fine, *The Automobile under the Blue Eagle* (Ann Arbor, Mich., 1963), pp. 142-181, 213-258.

4. I. Bernstein, *Turbulent Years,* pp. 92-94, 98-102. On steel see Staughton Lynd, "The Possibility of Radicalism in the Early 1930's: The Case of Steel," *Radical America,* VI (Nov.-Dec. 1972), 38-47; for rubber, Harold S. Roberts, *The Rubber Workers* (New York, 1944), pp. 147-150 and Ruth McKenney, *Industrial Valley* (New York, 1968 ed.).

5. Robert S. and Helen M. Lynd, *Middletown in Transition* (New York, 1937), pp. 26-34, 42-44.

6. I. Bernstein, *Turbulent Years*, pp. 298-315.

7. John Frey to W. A. Appleton, Sept. 9, 1935, John Frey Papers, Box 1, File 7, L.C.

8. John L. Lewis to William Green, June 7, 1936, A. F. of L. Papers, Office of the President, File C, Box 1, SHSW.

9. Saul D. Alinsky, *John L. Lewis: An Unauthorized Biography* (New York, 1970 ed.), pp. 64-65, 68-70, 76-80; I. Bernstein, *Turbulent Years*, pp. 352-431, *passim.*

10. Lee Pressman, COHC, pp. 327-328, 353-356.

11. Almost all of Lewis's major speeches and articles during the 1930s were prepared by W. Jett Lauck. List of Speeches and Articles Written for John L. Lewis, W. Jett Lauck Papers, Boxes 262-263, Alderson Library, UVL.

12. NYT, Sept. 3, 1934, p. 3.

13. W. Jett Lauck to John L. Lewis, Oct. 22, 1934, W. Jett Lauck Papers, Box 39.

14. UMWJ, Nov. 15, 1934, pp. 10-14; NYT, Oct. 11, 1934, p. 6.

15. Minutes of Executive Council, Apr. 30-May 7, 1935, A. F. of L., pp. 113-115; *Proceedings 1934 Convention,* A. F. of L., pp. 581-598; I. Bernstein, *Turbulent Years*, pp. 363-368.

16. Cited in I. Bernstein, *Turbulent Years*, p. 366.

17. W. Jett Lauck to John L. Lewis, Oct. 22, 1934, W. Jett Lauck Papers, Box 39.

18. NYT, Oct. 21, 1934, VIII, 3.

19. John L. Lewis to Adolph Germer, Nov. 28, 1934, Adolph Germer Papers, Box 27, SHSW.

20. Minutes of the Executive Council, A. F. of L., Jan. 29-Feb. 14, 1935, pp. 56-58.

21. *Ibid.*, pp. 42, 58-59, 67-69.

22. *Ibid.*, pp. 217-220, 222.
23. *Ibid.*, pp. 191-193.
24. *Ibid.*, pp. 235-237.
25. *Ibid.*, pp. 217-220, 246-247.
26. *Ibid.*, pp. 285-286; cf., Minutes of Executive Council, A. F. of L., Apr. 30-May 7, 1935, pp. 47-49, 57-59.
27. A. Germer Diary, Apr. 23, 1935, Adolph Germer Papers.
28. NYT, May 4, 1935, pp. 1, 16.
29. John Brophy Diary, Apr. 30 and May 1, 1935, John Brophy Papers, CUA; cf. S. Lynd, "The Possibility of Radicalism," pp. 52-55.
30. John Frey to W. A. Appleton, Mar. 21, 1935, Frey Papers, Box 1, File 7.
31. Minutes of Executive Council, A. F. of L., Apr. 30-May 7, 1935, pp. 113-116.
32. *Ibid.*, pp. 136-137.
33. *Nation*, May 22, 1935, p. 589.
34. John Brophy Diary, May 16 and Nov. 10, 1934, John Brophy Papers; John Brophy to James Nelson, Apr. 20, 1935, CIO Papers, Box A7-28, Folder "District 50," CUA; Proceedings of the Conference of the Federal Local Unions in the Gas and By-Product Coke Industries with President William Green of the A. F. of L., July 25, 1935, Edward A. Wieck Collection, Box 13, ALUHA, WSU.
35. Powers Hapgood to Sweetheart, July 24, 1935, Powers Hapgood Papers, Lilly Library, Indiana University.
36. Adolph Germer Diary, Sept. 7, 1935, Adolph Germer Papers.
37. On the passage and significance of federal labor legislation, see I. Bernstein, *Turbulent Years*, pp. 318-351.
38. NYT, Sept. 1, 1935, p. 2, Sept. 2, 1935, p. 2.
39. Len DeCaux, *Labor Radical* (Boston, 1970), p. 207.
40. *Ibid.*, pp. 208-211.
41. *Proceedings 1935 Convention*, A. F. of L., pp. 439, 793-794.
42. "Reminiscences of Heber Blankenhorn," Ch. 14, pp. 6-8, Heber Blankenhorn Papers, Box 9, File 9-2, ALUHA, WSU.
43. *Proceedings 1935 Convention*, A. F. of L., pp. 521-528.
44. *Ibid.*, pp. 534-542; see p. 31.
45. *Proceedings 1935 Convention*, A. F. of L., pp. 542ff.
46. *Ibid.*, pp. 727-729; Edward Levinson, *Labor on the March* (New York, 1956 ed.), pp. 99-117; L. DeCaux, *Labor Radical*, p. 216; I. Bernstein, *Turbulent Years*, pp. 396-397.
47. NYT, Oct. 20, 1935, p. 22.

NOTES TO CHAPTER 11

1. For an overly dramatic version of the breakfast meeting, see Saul D. Alinsky, *John L. Lewis: An Unauthorized Biography* (New York, 1970 ed.), pp. 80-81.
2. John Brophy Diary, Nov. 9, 1935, John Brophy Papers, CUA; John Brophy, *A Miner's Life*, ed. John O. H. P. Hall (Madison, Wis., 1964), pp. 254-255.
3. "Proposed Outline of the Activities of the Committee for Industrial Organization," Nov. 18, 1935, Katherine Pollak Ellickson Papers (microfilm), FDR Papers, Roosevelt Library; J. Brophy Diary, Nov. 18, 1935; J. Brophy, *A Miner's Life*, p. 257.
4. J. Brophy, *A Miner's Life*, p. 258; Len DeCaux, *Labor Radical* (Boston, 1970), pp. 219-220.

5. NYT, Nov. 24, 1935, p. 1.
6. William Green to John L. Lewis *et al.*, Nov. 23, 1935, A. F. of L. Papers, Office of the President, File C, Box 1, SHSW.
7. See, for example, Irving Bernstein, *Turbulent Years* (Boston, 1969), pp. 402-404.
8. John L. Lewis to Sidney Hillman, Nov. 25, 1935, Sidney Hillman Papers, CIO Folder, 1935-1936, Amalgamated Clothing Workers of America Archives, New York.
9. Notes of CIO Meeting, Dec. 9, 1935, K. P. Ellickson Papers; "The Future of Organized Labor," speech transcript, JLL Papers (microfilm copy), SHSW; UMWJ, Dec. 15, 1935, pp. 20-21.
10. Notes of CIO Meeting, Dec. 9, 1935, K. P. Ellickson Papers; Sidney Hillman to John L. Lewis, Nov. 29, 1935, and Lewis to Hillman, Nov. 30, 1935, Sidney Hillman Papers, CIO Folder, 1935-1936.
11. John L. Lewis to Sidney Hillman, Nov. 30, 1935, Sidney Hillman Papers, CIO Folder, 1935-1936.
12. I. Bernstein, *Turbulent Years*, pp. 402-403.
13. H. Fremming to William Green, Nov. 27, 1935; Sidney Hillman to Green, Dec. 12, 1935; David Dubinsky to Green, Dec. 11, 1935; John M. Sherwood to Green, Dec. 16, 1935, A. F. of L. Papers, Office of the President, File C, Box 1.
14. Memorandum from John L. Lewis to CIO Members, Dec. 6, 1935, Sidney Hillman Papers, CIO Folder, 1935-1936.
15. John L. Lewis to William Green, Dec. 7, 1935, A. F. of L. Papers, Office of the President, File C, Box 1.
16. Memorandum of Dec. 6, 1935, Sidney Hillman Papers, CIO Folder, 1935-1936; Notes of CIO Meeting, Dec. 9, 1935, K. P. Ellickson Papers; Green to Lewis, Dec. 9, 1935, Adolph Germer Papers, Box 2, SHSW.
17. John Brophy to Adolph Germer, Nov. 30, 1935; Germer to John L. Lewis, Dec. 8, 1935; Germer to Brophy, Dec. 8, 1935; Powers Hapgood to Germer, Dec. 15, 1935; Germer to Brophy, Jan. 7, 1936, Adolph Germer Papers, Box 2; Powers Hapgood to John Battuello, Dec. 31, 1935, Powers Hapgood Papers, Lilly Library, Indiana University.
18. Notes of CIO Meeting, Dec. 9, 1935, K. P. Ellickson Papers; Press Release, Dec. 10, 1935, Adolph Germer Papers, Box 2.
19. Adolph Germer Diary, Dec. 6, 7, 11, 1935, Jan. 6, 1936; Allan Strachan to Germer, Jan. 7, 1936, and Germer to Strachan, Jan. 8, 1936, Adolph Germer Papers, Box 2.
20. John Brophy to William Green, Jan. 10, 1936, A. F. of L. Papers, Office of the President, File C, Box 1.
21. Report in Sidney Hillman Papers, CIO Folder, 1935-1936.
22. I. Bernstein, *Turbulent Years*, pp. 405-406.
23. Speech Typescript, JLL Papers; UMWJ, Feb. 1, 1936, p. 9.
24. Ruth McKenney, *Industrial Valley*, (New York, 1968 ed.), pp. 248-251.
25. Minutes of Executive Council, A. F. of L., Jan. 15-29, 1936, p. 86.
26. William Green to John L. Lewis, Feb. 7, 1936, A. F. of L. Papers, Office of the President, File C, Box 1; I. Bernstein, *Turbulent Years*, pp. 408-409.
27. Adolph Germer to John Brophy, Jan. 28 and Feb. 2, 1936, Adolph Germer Papers, Box 2.
28. Charles P. Howard later informed Sidney Hillman that he had never before seen Green indicate so much feeling on an issue. Howard to Hillman, Feb. 3, 1936, Sidney Hillman Papers, CIO Folder, 1935-1936.
29. *Proceedings 1936 Convention*, UMWA, p. 11; Sidney Hillman to C. P. Howard,

Feb. 7, 1936, Sidney Hillman Papers, CIO Folder, 1935-1936; *Nation*, Feb. 19, 1936, p. 208.

30. *Proceedings 1936 Convention,* UMWA, pp. 11, 164, 173-179; Sidney Hillman to C. P. Howard, Feb. 7, 1936, Sidney Hillman Papers, CIO Folder, 1935-1936.

31. *Proceedings 1936 Convention,* UMWA, pp. 303-309.

32. *Ibid.*, p. 309.

33. W. Jett Lauck Diary, W. Jett Lauck Papers, Alderson Library, UVL; *Nation,* Feb. 19, 1936, p. 221.

34. John Brophy to Adolph Germer, Feb. 13, 1936, Adolph Germer Papers, Box 2; *Nation* (Feb. 19, 1936), pp. 208, 221.

35. James O'Neal to Adolph Germer, Feb. 3, 1936, Adolph Germer Papers, Box 2.

36. C. P. Howard to Sidney Hillman, Feb. 3, 1936, and Hillman to Howard, Feb. 7, 1936, Sidney Hillman Papers, CIO Folder, 1935-1936.

37. John Brophy to Adolph Germer, Feb. 13, 1936, Adolph Germer Papers, Box 2.

38. C. P. Howard to Sidney Hillman, Feb. 3, 1936, Sidney Hillman Papers, CIO Folder, 1935-1936.

39. Memorandum of Jan. 31, 1936, and Feb. 5, 1936, William Green to John L. Lewis *et al.*, Feb. 7, 1936, A. F. of L. Papers, Office of the President, File C, Box 1.

40. H. C. Fremming to William Green, Feb. 13, 1936; John L. Lewis to Green, Feb. 13, 1936; and Green to Lewis, Feb. 14, 1936, *ibid.*

41. Lewis *et al.* to Green, Feb. 21, 1936, *ibid.*

42. Harrison Committee to John L. Lewis, May 16, 1936; Extract, Minutes of Executive Council, A. F. of L., May 5-20, 1936, both in *ibid.*; Handwritten Notes of Meeting between AFL and CIO Committees, May 19, 1936, K. P. Ellickson Papers; Typewritten Summaries of May 19 Meeting in John Brophy Papers, Box A5-4, and Adolph Germer Papers, Box 3.

43. Extract, Minutes of Executive Council, A. F. of L., May 5-20, 1936, and George Harrison *et al.* to Charles P. Howard, May 20, 1936, A. F. of L. Papers, Office of the President, File C, Box 1.

44. Charles P. Howard to G. M. Harrison, June 1, 1936; David Dubinsky to Harrison, June 1, 1936, *ibid.*

45. *Ibid.*

46. John Brophy to Adolph Germer, June 3, 1936, and Germer to Brophy, June 5, 1936, Adolph Germer Papers, Box 3.

47. Powers Hapgood to John L. Lewis, Mar. 29, 1936, Powers Hapgood Papers; Notes on an Interview with John Brophy, Apr. 15, 1936, Edward A. Wieck Collection, Box 15, ALHUA, WSU; Harold S. Roberts, *The Rubber Workers* (New York, 1944), pp. 150-152.

48. John Chorey, Oral History Transcript, pp. 12-13, SWOC Collection, PSULA.

49. Memorandum to Lewis on Procedure and Policy of CIO, Dec. 17, 1935 (Nathan S. Fine) and Memorandum to Lewis, Jan. 27, 1936 (W. J. Lauck), W. Jett Lauck Papers, Box 164.

50. Draft of letter, Feb. 4, 1936, K. P. Ellickson Papers; John L. Lewis to William Green, Feb. 22, 1936, in Minutes of Executive Council, A. F. of L., May 5-20, 1936, pp. 41-42.

51. Draft of unsent letter in response to Green's letter of Mar. 2, 1936, K. P. Ellickson Papers.

52. AAISTW, Executive Board Minutes, Mar. 26, 1936, pp. 3, 6-8, Louis Leonard Papers, Box 10, PSULA.

53. John L. Lewis and C. P. Howard to M. F. Tighe, Apr. 15, 1936, SWOC Papers, PSULA.

54. Amalgamated Association, Executive Board Minutes, Apr. 22, 1936, p. 4, Louis Leonard Papers.

55. Heber Blankenhorn Papers, Series I, Box 1, ALHUA, WSU.

56. John L. Lewis to Amalgamated Association Officers and Convention Delegates, May 8, 1936, A. F. of L. Papers, Office of the President, File C, Box 2; Minutes of Executive Council, A. F. of L., May 5-20, 1936, pp. 99-100.

57. M. F. Tighe to William Green, May 30, 1938, A. F. of L. Papers, Office of the President, File C, Box 43; Report of Amalgamated Association International Executive Board Meeting, May 30, 1936, SWOC Papers; "The Steel Situation," May 25, 1936, Heber Blankenhorn Papers, Series 1, Box 1, File I-33.

58. Handwritten and also typed notes of the meeting between CIO and Amalgamated Association, June 3, 1936, K. P. Ellickson Papers.

59. Amalgamated Association, Executive Board Minutes, June 8, 1936, p. 1, Louis Leonard Papers.

60. I. Bernstein, *Turbulent Years*, pp. 440-441.

61. A. F. of L. Papers, Office of the President, File C, Box 1.

62. *Ibid.*

63. For examples of such flattery, see Dan J. Tobin to William Green, June 3, 1936, and Harry C. Bates to Green, June 10, 1936, *ibid.*

64. John L. Lewis to William Green, June 7, 1936, *ibid.*

65. Charlton Ogburn to William Green, July 8 and 13, 1936, *ibid.*; P. Taft, *The A. F. of L. from the Death of Gompers to the Merger* (New York, 1959), pp. 155-156.

66. P. Taft, *AFL from Death of Gompers*, p. 156.

67. CIO Executive Board Meeting, July 2, 1936, K. P. Ellickson Papers; cf. John Brophy to William Green, June 23, 1936, A. F. of L. Papers, Office of the President, File C, Box 1.

68. William Green to John L. Lewis, July 16, 1936, A. F. of L. Papers, Office of the President, File C, Box 1; Minutes of Executive Council, A. F. of L., July 8-15, 1936.

69. CIO Executive Board Minutes, typed and handwritten notes, July 21, 1936, K. P. Ellickson Papers.

70. The files of the A. F. of L.'s president's office; File C is filled with such letters, wires, and petitions.

71. John L. Lewis *et al.* to William Green, July 21, 1936, A. F. of L. Papers, Office of the President, File C, Box 1.

72. Sidney Hillman Papers, CIO Folder, 1935-1936.

73. John Frey to W. A. Appleton, Aug. 3, 1936, John Frey Papers, Box 1, File 7, L.C.; Proceedings of the Executive Council in the Matter of Charges Filed by the Metals Trades Department against the Committee for Industrial Organization and National and International Unions Holding Membership Therein (Washington, D.C.), Aug. 3-4, 1936, pp. 307, 318-319, 325, and *passim*; Executive Council Decision in the Proceedings; A. F. of L. Press Release, Aug. 5, 1936; and William Green to John L. Lewis, Aug. 6, 1936, all in A. F. of L. Papers, Office of the President, File C, Box 2.

74. CIO Executive Board Minutes, Aug. 10, 1936, K. P. Ellickson Papers.

75. *Ibid.*

76. On the origins of the cap makers' role as a dual union, see Melvyn Dubofsky, "Organized Labor and the Immigrant in New York City, 1900-1918," *Labor History*, II (Spring 1961), 197-199; cf. Donald L. Robinson, *Spotlight on a Union: The Story of the United Hatters, Cap and Millinery Workers Union* (New York, 1948).

77. Max Danish, *The World of David Dubinsky* (Cleveland, 1957), pp. 45-58, 106-116, 240-250, 284-296, and *passim*; Matthew Josephson, *Sidney Hillman* (New York, 1952), pp. 427-428, 455, 578-579, 600-606.

78. For the Left-Right split in American socialism and its relation to the CIO, see

David Shannon, *The Socialist Party of America* (New York, 1955), pp. 236-245; extensive correspondence between James O'Neal, editor of the *New Leader*, and Adolph Germer scattered through the latter's papers indicates why old-guard socialists were suspicious of Lewis and the CIO; on jealousy to Hillman, see also Jay Lovestone to John Brophy, Oct. 23, 1937, John Brophy Papers, Box A5-6.

79. NYT, Oct. 5, 1936, pp. 1, 17, Oct. 9, 1936, p. 22, Oct. 10, 1936, p. 1; I. Bernstein, *Turbulent Years,* pp. 424-425.

80. NYT, Oct. 7, 1936, p. 23, Oct. 10, 1936, p. 1; I. Bernstein, *Turbulent Years*, p. 425.

81. David Dubinsky to John L. Lewis, Oct. 16 and 17, 1936; Max Zaritsky to Lewis, Oct. 19, 1936, and Zaritsky to Sidney Hillman, Oct. 19, 1936, Sidney Hillman Papers, CIO Folder, 1935-1936.

82. NYT, Oct. 27, 1936, p. 2; *Nation*, Nov. 7, 1936, pp. 536-538, Dec. 5, 1936, pp. 684-686, 688.

83. Notes on CIO Meeting, Nov. 7-8, 1936, pp. 1-4, K. P. Ellickson Papers.

84. Charles Howard to Max Zaritsky, Oct. 24, 1936, Sidney Hillman Papers, CIO Folder, 1935-1936.

85. George Berry to George Harrison, Dec. 8, 1936; Berry to John L. Lewis and Sidney Hillman, Dec. 8, 1936; Harrison to Berry, Dec. 14, 1936; Berry to Lewis and Hillman, Dec. 18, 1936; Lewis to Hillman, Dec. 21, 1936; Lewis to Berry, Dec. 21, 1936, all in *ibid*.

86. John L. Lewis to David Dubinsky, Oct. 19, 1936, and Dubinsky to Lewis, Oct. 20, 1936; Dubinsky to Sidney Hillman, Oct. 20, 1936, *ibid*.

87. Notes on CIO Executive Board Meeting, Nov. 7-8, 1936, pp. 3-5, K. P. Ellickson Papers.

88. *Ibid.*, pp. 1, 3, 5, 7, 18.

89. *Ibid.*, pp. 17-19.

90. *Ibid.*, pp. 7-9, 19.

91. *Ibid*.

92. William Green to C. P. Howard, Nov. 7, 1936; John L. Lewis to Green, Nov. 8, 1936; and Green to Lewis, Nov. 9, 1936, all in Minutes of Executive Council, A. F. of L., Nov. 1936, pp. 6-7.

93. I. Bernstein, *Turbulent Years*, p. 426.

94. Walter Smethurst to William Green, Nov. 11, 1936, A. F. of L. Papers, Office of the President, File C, Box 4.

95. Walter Smethurst to William Green, Nov. 18, 1936, *ibid*.

96. I. Bernstein, *Turbulent Years*, p. 427.

NOTES TO CHAPTER 12

1. David Brody, "Labor and the Great Depression: The Interpretive Prospects," *Labor History*, XIII (Spring 1972), 238.

2. Feb. 19, 1936, p. 208; on early steps to forge a labor-Roosevelt alliance see *Proceedings 1936 Convention*, UMWA, pp. 10-11, 210-211.

3. Notes on CIO Executive Board Meeting, July 2, 1936, Katherine Pollak Ellickson Papers (microfilm), Roosevelt Library.

4. John L. Lewis to George Berry, May 16, 1936, and Lewis to Sidney Hillman, May 16, 1936, Sidney Hillman Papers, Labor's Non-Partisan League File, Amalgamated Clothing Workers of America Archives, New York; UMWJ, Aug. 15, 1936, p. 6.

5. W. Jett Lauck Diary, May 9, 1936, W. Jett Lauck Papers, Alderson Library, UVL.

6. *Ibid.*, May 11, 1936.

7. *Ibid.*, June 22, 1936; NYT, June 23, 1936, p. 12.

8. W. Jett Lauck Diary, June 29, 1936.

9. *Ibid.*, June 29 and July 3, 1936.

10. Typescript of Radio Address, "Industrial Democracy in Steel," JLL Papers (microfilm copy), SHSW; UMWJ, July 15, 1936, pp. 3-6.

11. W. Jett Lauck Diary, July 9, 1936; NYT, July 10, 1936, p. 7.

12. NYT, July 26, 1936, p. 2.

13. W. Jett Lauck Diary, July 26, 1936.

14. NYT, Aug. 9, 1936, IV, 2, 10; cf. Dan Tobin to Franklin D. Roosevelt, Feb. 18, 1936, FDR Papers, PPF 1180, and Tobin to James Farley, Aug. 30, 1936, FDR Papers, OF 300, #7, Roosevelt Library.

15. NYT, Aug. 9, 1936, IV, 10.

16. UMWJ, Aug. 15, 1936, pp. 6-7.

17. Typescript of speech, "Labor and the Future," JLL Papers; W. Jett Lauck Diary, Sept. 6-7, 1936.

18. NYT, Sept. 12, 1936, pp. 1, 4.

19. Typescript, Pottsville, Pa., Speech, JLL Papers; UMWJ, Oct. 1, 1936, pp. 16-19; W. Jett Lauck Diary, Sept. 17, 1936.

20. John L. Lewis to Franklin D. Roosevelt, Oct. 6, 1936, FDR Papers, PPF 3183.

21. UMWJ, Oct. 15, 1936, p. 9, has a schedule of Lewis's campaign speeches; Memorandum for the President from Marvin McIntyre, Oct. 19, 1936, and Memorandum from McIntyre to James A. Farley, Oct. 20, 1936, FDR Papers, OF 290, Box 1.

22. NYT, Oct. 28, 1936, pp. 1, 21.

23. "Miscellaneous—Contributions to Campaign," UMWA Archives.

24. Notes on CIO Meeting, Nov. 7-8, 1936, K. P. Ellickson Papers.

25. NYT, Nov. 5, 1936, p. 1, Nov. 12, 1936, p. 2.

26. *Ibid.*, Nov. 13, 1936, p. 22, Nov. 16, 1936, p. 18.

27. *Ibid.*, Nov. 21, 1936, p. 6; *Nation*, Nov. 14, 1936, pp. 571-572, Dec. 5, 1936, pp. 684-686, 688; *New Republic,* Dec. 23, 1936, pp. 234-236; George L. Berry to Franklin D. Roosevelt, Nov. 11, 1936; Berry to Sidney Hillman, Nov. 11, 1936; Roosevelt to Berry, Nov. 16, 1936; Berry to John L. Lewis and Hillman, Dec. 8, 1936, all in Sidney Hillman Papers, Labor's Non-Partisan League File.

28. Typescript of speech, "Industrial Democracy," JLL Papers; UMWJ, Jan. 15, 1937, pp. 3-4.

29. On the Flint strike, Sidney Fine, *Sit-Down: The General Motors Strike of 1936-1937* (Ann Arbor, Mich., 1969) is a masterful and indispensable history. Much of the material on the strike and its resolution in this book is drawn from Fine.

30. *Ibid.*, pp. 21-22.

31. *Ibid.*, pp. 37-44; Jerold S. Auerbach, *Labor and Liberty: The LaFollette Committee and the New Deal* (Indianapolis, 1966), pp. 99, 207.

32. Adolph Germer to John L. Lewis, Nov. 30, 1936, and Philip Murray to Germer, Dec. 4, 1936, Adolph Germer Papers, Box 3, SHSW.

33. John Brophy to Adolph Germer, Dec. 19, 1936, *ibid*.

34. See Heber Blankenhorn to John L. Lewis, Jan. 4, 1937, Heber Blankenhorn Papers, Series 1, Box 1, File 1-9, ALHUA, WSU.

35. Gardner Jackson, COHC, pp. 666-667.

36. S. Fine, *Sit-Down*, p. 157.

37. *Ibid.*, p. 171.

38. *Ibid.*, p. 201, see also pp. 156-177, *passim*.

39. On Martin see *ibid.*, p. 78 and *passim*; Adolph Germer's Diary (Adolph Germer Papers) for 1936-1937 is filled with deprecatory entries on Martin's behavior.

40. S. Fine, *Sit-Down,* pp. 100-120, 178-198.

41. *Ibid.*, pp. 193-195; Adolph Germer Diary, Jan. 3, 1937.

42. The following account is from S. Fine, *Sit-Down*, pp. 1-11 and NYT Jan. 12, 1937, pp. 1, 12.

43. On Murphy see S. Fine, *Sit-Down,* pp. 148-155; cf. Richard D. Lunt, *The High Ministry of Government: The Political Career of Frank Murphy* (Detroit, 1965), and J. Woodford Howard, *Mr. Justice Murphy* (Princeton, N. J., 1968).

44. *Ibid.*, pp. 247-252.

45. *Ibid.*, pp. 252-254.

46. *Ibid.*, pp. 254-255; Memorandum, Frances Perkins to Franklin D. Roosevelt, Jan. 19, 1937, FDR Papers, PSF (Labor), Box 61.

47. Perkins Memorandum, Jan. 19, 1937, FDR Papers; S. Fine, *Sit-Down*, p. 255.

48. NYT, Jan. 22, 1937, p. 1; S. Fine *Sit-Down*, p. 256.

49. NYT, Jan. 23, 1937, p. 1.

50. See pp. 326-327; Paul W. Ward, "Did John L. Lewis Blunder?" *Nation* (Jan. 30, 1937), pp. 119-120.

51. NYT, Jan. 23, 1937, p. 1.

52. S. Fine, *Sit-Down*, pp. 256-257.

53. John L. Lewis to Stay-In Strikes in Fisher Plant No. 1, c/o Robert Travis, Jan. 22, 1937, Bud and Hazel Simons Papers, Box 1, ALHUA, WSU; NYT, Jan. 23, 1937, p. 1.

54. Transcript of conversation between Adolph Germer and John L. Lewis, Jan. 26, 1937, Adolph Germer Papers, Box 3; S. Fine, *Sit-Down*, pp. 257-259.

55. NYT, Jan. 27, 1937, p. 1.

56. S. Fine, *Sit-Down,* pp. 259-262, 296; NYT, Jan. 27 and 28, 1937, p. 1.

57. S. Fine, *Sit-Down,* pp. 266-271; NYT, Feb. 2, 1937, pp. 1-2.

58. S. Fine, *Sit-Down,* pp. 274-276.

59. *Ibid.*, pp. 278-284, 294.

60. NYT, Feb. 3, 1937, p. 1; Adolph Germer Diary, Feb. 3, 1937; Saul. D. Alinsky, *John L. Lewis: An Unauthorized Biography* (New York, 1970 ed.), pp. 128-129.

61. Adolph Germer Diary, Feb. 3, 1937; Memorandum of Phone Conversation with Governor Murphy, Feb. 8, 1937, FDR Papers, OF 407B, Box 18.

62. S. Fine, *Sit-Down,* pp. 287-288.

63. Memorandum for the President, Feb. 5, 1937; Memorandum for President's Conversation with John Lewis and with Knudsen and Brown; Proposal for General Motors-Lewis Agreement, all in FDR Papers, PSF (Labor), Box 61; S. Fine, *Sit-Down,* p. 289.

64. S. Fine, *Sit-Down*, pp. 289-290.

65. Settlement of General Motors Strike, Feb. 10 (Feb. 25, 1937), Heber Blankenhorn Papers, Series I, Box 1, File 1-37.

66. *Ibid.*

67. *Ibid.*

68. *Ibid.*

69. *Ibid.*

70. Settlement of General Motors Strike, Feb. 10, 1937, Herber Blankenhorn Papers; S. Fine, *Sit-Down*, pp. 302-305.

71. CIO Executive Board Minutes, Mar. 9, 1937, K. P. Ellickson Papers.

72. Settlement of General Motors Strike, Feb. 10, 1937, Heber Blankenhorn Papers.

73. S. Fine, *Sit-Down*, pp. 306, 328.

74. *Ibid.*, p. 327.

75. *Ibid.*, p. 331.
76. I. Bernstein, *Turbulent Years*, pp. 551-554; S. Alinsky, *Lewis*, pp. 149-152; Nicholas Kelley, COHC, *passim*.
77. See pp. 249-250.
78. Notes and Memoranda in W. Jett Lauck Papers, Box 164; I. Bernstein, *Turbulent Years*, pp. 432-473, *passim*.
79. I. Bernstein, *Turbulent Years*, pp. 432-473; Walter Galenson, *The CIO Challenge to the AFL: A History of the American Labor Movement, 1935-1941* (Cambridge, Mass., 1960), considers the CIO-SWOC-U.S. Steel agreement one of the most critical junctures in United Sates economic history, p. 193.
80. Robert R. Brooks, *As Steel Goes: Unionism in a Basic Industry* (New Haven, Conn., 1940), pp. 70-109.
81. "It Happened in Steel," *Fortune* XV (May 1937), 92-94, 176-180.
82. *Ibid.*, pp. 93-94.
83. *Ibid.*, pp. 94, 176; W. Jett Lauck Diary, Jan. 25, 1937.
84. "It Happened in Steel," pp. 176-180; Lee Pressman, COHC, pp. 79, 102; for an impression similar to Pressman's, see Father Charles Owen Rice, Oral History Transcript, p. 6, SWOC Collection, PSULA.
85. "It Happened in Steel," pp. 92-94.
86. Memorandum from Myron Taylor, Sept. 11, 1935, FDR Papers, PPF 423; on captive mines strike, see pp. 397-404.
87. See note 71 above.
88. "It Happened in Steel," p. 179.
89. Staughton Lynd, "The Possibility of Radicalism in the Early 1930's: The Case of Steel," *Radical America,* VI (Nov.-Dec. 1972), 37-64; Len DeCaux, *Labor Radical* (Boston, 1970), pp. 276-285; on SWOC's relatively small membership before the agreement, see L. Pressman, COHC, *passim*.
90. Powers Hapgood to Mary Hapgood, June 16, 1936, Powers Hapgood Papers, Lilly Library, Indiana University.
91. K. P. Ellickson Papers.
92. Report of CIO Director, Mar. 9, 1937, *ibid.*; Notes on Conference with Mr. Howard, Mar. 24, 1937, John Brophy Papers, Box A5-5, CUA.
93. Quoted in W. Galenson, *The CIO Challenge,* p. 29.
94. Memorandum, Ralph Hetzel, Jr., to John L. Lewis, Aug. 31, 1937, K. P. Ellickson Papers.
95. Adolph Germer to Henry Hauser, Oct. 29, 1937, Adolph Germer Papers, Box 4.
96. W. Jett Lauck Diary, Oct. 13-14, 1937.
97. CIO Financial Statement, May 31, 1936, to Sept. 30, 1937, John Brophy Papers, Box A5-5.
98. Pp. 203-205.

NOTES TO CHAPTER 13

1. Amelia Earhart to John L. Lewis, Dec. 4, 1936, JLL Papers (microfilm copy), SHSW; *Nation*, Jan. 22, 1937, p. 7, Feb. 6, 1937, p. 156.
2. NYT, Mar. 16, 1937, p. 1, Aug. 28, 1937, p. 3, Sept. 7, 1937, p. 3, Oct. 5, 1937, p. 1.
3. John Brophy, COHC, p. 606.

4. Gardner Jackson, COHC, pp. 727-728.

5. Lee Pressman, COHC, p. 192.

6. *Nation,* Aug. 15, 1936, p. 199; Louis Adamic, "John L. Lewis: Push to Power," *Forum,* 97 (Mar. 1937), 131-137; Raoul DeRoussy, "John L. Lewis," *Atlantic Monthly,* 159 (June 1937), 652-659.

7. Quoted in Irving Bernstein, *Turbulent Years* (Boston, 1970), p. 387.

8. Louis Adamic, *My America, 1928-1938* (New York, 1938), pp. 385-386; Edward Levinson, *Labor on the March* (New York, 1956 ed.), p. 19; Len DeCaux, *Labor Radical* (Boston, 1970), p. 223, writes of sitting in an auto backseat with Lewis: "The spread of the man was enormous. I didn't really have to shrink to fit in. I just felt shrunken." Previously he had observed, "Lewis tended to shrink his associates."

9. G. Jackson, COHC, p. 755; Alfred Staehle, COHC (McGraw-Hill Project), pp. 68-69; Frances Perkins, COHC, V. 8, p. 389.

10. Saul D. Alinsky, *John L. Lewis: An Unauthorized Biography* (New York, 1970 ed.), pp. 18-19; for another less flattering version, see Art Gramlich, Oral History Transcript, pp. 4-5, Sangamon State University Library, Springfield, Illinois.

11. Cyrus Ching, COHC, p. 564.

12. Marquis Childs, COHC, pp. 60-61.

13. L. Adamic, *My America,* p. 385.

14. L. DeCaux, *Labor Radical,* p. 225.

15. K. Crawford as quoted in James Wechsler, *Labor Baron: A Portrait of John L. Lewis* (Westport, Conn., 1970 ed.), p. 243; McAlester Coleman, *Men and Coal* (New York, 1969 ed.), xi-xiv.

16. S. D. Alinsky, *Lewis,* pp. 4-5; M. Coleman, *Men and Coal,* xi-xiv.

17. M. Childs, COHC, pp. 60-61.

18. E. Levinson, *Labor on the March,* p. 288.

19. John Brophy, COHC, p. 658; Lee Pressman, COHC, p. 185; Myrta Nickey, Oral History Transcript, p. 11, Sangamon State University Library, for Myrta alone calling her husband, Jack.

20. W. Jett Lauck's Diary, W. Jett Lauck Papers, Alderson Library, UVL, in numerous entries suggests the social distance between two otherwise close associates; L. DeCaux, *Labor Radical,* p. 223, comments on Lauck's special place with Lewis.

21. John Brophy, COHC, pp. 624-626.

22. Cyrus Ching, COHC, pp. 564-567; A. Staehle, COHC, pp. 68-69; James M. Landis, COHC, pp. 285, 288.

23. John Brophy, COHC, pp. 609-611.

24. Lee Pressman, COHC, pp. 183-184; for lack of coal mining stories, see M. Nickey, Oral History Transcript, p. 7.

25. Lee Pressman, COHC, p. 189; Marquis Childs, COHC, p. 61.

26. E. Levinson, *Labor on the March,* pp. 285-286.

27. Interview with David Dubinsky, Sept. 21, 1972.

28. *Ibid.*; Interview with Jacob Potofsky, April 18, 1974, A. H. Raskin, June 4, 1974; conversations with Rex Lauck, June-July, 1972.

29. John Brophy, Scrap Note, n.d., John Brophy Papers, Box A5-34, CUA.

30. John Brophy, COHC, p. 628; Gardner Jackson, COHC, pp. 713-714; Lee Pressman, COHC, p. 421.

31. John Brophy, COHC, pp. 636-639; J. David Stern, COHC, p. 58.

32. On Lewis and communism see S. Alinsky, *Lewis,* pp. 152-155; I. Bernstein, *Turbulent Years,* pp. 782-783; Len DeCaux, *Labor Radical,* pp. 260-261, 298-302, 315-322.

33. S. D. Alinsky, *Lewis,* p. 352; I. Bernstein, *Turbulent Years,* p. 554, repeats the story.

34. I. Bernstein, *Turbulent Years*, p. 783.

35. Lee Pressman, COHC, pp. 170-171.

36. L. Adamic, *My America,* pp. 397-401, for Lewis's refusal to discuss philosophical issues.

37. Scrap Note, n.d., John Brophy Papers, Box A5-34.

38. Gardner Jackson, COHC, p. 678; Lee Pressman, COHC, p. 178; L. DeCaux, *Labor Radical*, pp. 241-242.

39. L. Adamic, *My America,* pp. 397-399; John Brophy, COHC, pp. 597-600; Lee Pressman, COHC, pp. 190-192, 353-355; "John L. Lewis Tells of Plans," Press Release, Dec. 20, 1935, A. F. of L. Papers, Office of the President, File C, Box 1, SHSW; Copy of letter, John L. Lewis to Cyrus L. Sulzberger, July 10, 1936, *ibid.*; S. J. Woolf, "John L. Lewis and his plan," NYT, Mar. 21, 1937, VIII, 3, 20.

40. John Brophy, COHC, p. 616; Frances Perkins, COHC, V. 8, p. 396.

41. Alfred Staehle, COHC, pp. 54-55.

42. Cyrus Ching, COHC, p. 567.

43. L. Adamic, *My America*, p. 388.

44. *Proceedings 1938 Convention,* UMWA, I, 172; *Proceedings 1940 Convention*, UMWA, I, 14.

45. Richard Hughes, *The Wooden Shepherdess* (New York, 1973), pp. 191, 314.

46. J. M. Landis, COHC, p. 285, for Sunday tea parties; the John Brophy, Gardner Jackson, and Lee Pressman COHC's all remark about Lewis's personal temperance.

47. John Brophy, COHC, pp. 647-648; Myrta Nickey, Oral History Transcript, *passim;* L. DeCaux, *Labor Radical*, pp. 323-324.

48. Edwin A. Lahey, COHC, p. 94; Lee Pressman, COHC, p. 310.

49. Lee Pressman, COHC, pp. 116-117; Gardner Jackson, COHC, pp. 728-735; L. DeCaux, *Labor Radical*, pp. 323-324.

50. Gardner Jackson, COHC, pp. 728-735.

51. Lee Pressman, COHC, pp. 327-328, 353-354; L. DeCaux, *Labor Radical*, pp. 241-242.

52. The JLL Papers are filled with newspaper clippings on the Alexandria house tour controversy; Gardner Jackson, COHC, pp. 728-735; Frances Perkins, COHC, V. 8, pp. 367-368; Myrta Nickey, Oral History Transcript, p. 14, on home furnishings.

53. Gardner Jackson, COHC, pp. 573-574, 728-735; Frances Perkins, COHC, V. 8, pp. 371-372; L. DeCaux, *Labor Radical*, pp. 323-324.

54. Frances Perkins, COHC, V. 8, pp. 371-372.

55. Gardner Jackson, COHC, pp. 573-574, 728-735; Frances Perkins, COHC, V. 8, pp. 371-372; W. Jett Lauck Diary, Jan. 4, 1940, Oct. 1940, Jan. 6, 1941; John Brophy, *A Miner's Life*, ed. John O. H. P. Hall (Madison, Wis., 1964), p. 281.

56. Gardner Jackson, COHC, pp. 728-735; L. DeCaux, *Labor Radical*, pp. 323-324; interview with A. H. Raskin, June 4, 1974; several notes and letters found in the UMW Archives (dated during the 1940s and 1950s) hint at the emotional distance that separated father and son.

57. Gardner Jackson, COHC, pp. 694-695; Frances Perkins, COHC, V. 8, pp. 367-368.

58. W. Jett Lauck Diary, 1935-1937.

59. Gardner Jackson, COHC, p. 728; Kingman Brewster to John L. Lewis, Apr. 25, n.d., JLL Papers; invitations from Evelyn Walsh McLean were found in *ibid.*, and also in UMW Archives, JLL M.A. File.

60. Clipping from New York *Telegram*, July 7 or 8, 1937, and clipping from unspecified Washington newspaper, Oct. 21, 1937, JLL Papers; Frances Perkins, COHC, V. 8, pp. 367-368.

61. Clipping New York *Telegram* invoices, correspondence, and receipts for antiques and other purchases are in the JLL Papers.

62. Clipping, New York *Telegram*, *ibid.*

63. Memorandum, initialed, J.L.L., K.L., and J.L., M.D., Sept. 28, 1942; Harry Schlatter to John L. Lewis, Dec. 28, 1949; Lewis to Schlatter, Jan. 24, 1950; Lewis to A. J. Treat and Son, Inc., Dec. 17, 1956, all in *ibid.*; L. Adamic, *My America*, p. 388.

64. *Proceedings 1936 Convention*, UMWA, II, 503-504.

NOTES TO CHAPTER 14

1. Cecil Carnes, *John L. Lewis: Leader of Labor* (New York, 1936), pp. 306-307; C. L. Sulzberger, *Sit-Down with John L. Lewis* (New York, 1938), p. 134.

2. Interview with David Dubinsky, Sept. 21, 1972.

3. Extract, Minutes Executive Council, A. F. of L., Feb. 8-19, 1937, A. F. of L. Papers, Office of the President, File C, Box 4, SHSW.

4. W. Jett Lauck Diary, Apr. 16, 1937, W. Jett Lauck Papers, Alderson Library, UVL; for a somewhat different version of the Lewis-Green meetings, see Irving Bernstein, *Turbulent Years* (Boston, 1970), p. 688.

5. Extract, Minutes of Executive Council, A. F. of L., Apr. 19-22, 1937, A. F. of L. Papers, Office of the President, File C, Box 4.

6. I. Bernstein, *Turbulent Years*, p. 689.

7. On A. F. of L. doubts about the CIO proposal and a different version of Lewis's behavior, see *ibid.*, pp. 689-690.

8. Fremming to Morrison, Oct. 16, 1937; Morrison to Fremming, Oct. 16, 1937; Philip Murray to Morrison, Oct. 15, 1937; Morrison to Murray, Oct. 17, 1937, all in A. F. of L. Papers, Office of the President, File C, Box 24.

9. William L. Hutcheson and Frank Duffy to William Green, Oct. 26, 1937; Green to Hutcheson, Oct. 26, 1937; Hutcheson to Green, Oct. 27, 1937; W. Mahon to Green, Oct. 27, 1937; Dan Tobin to Green, Dec. 1, 1937; Green to Tobin, Dec. 2, 1937, all in *ibid.*

10. Copy of CIO Proposal, Oct. 26, 1937, *ibid.*; Report of the A. F. of L. Conference Committee to Executive Council, Feb. 3, 1938, *ibid.*, Box 43; cf. I. Bernstein, *Turbulent Years*, pp. 690-691, and Philip Taft, *The A. F. of L. from the Death of Gompers to the Merger* (New York, 1959), p. 195; UMWJ, Nov. 1, 1937, pp. 3-4, 23.

11. A. F. of L. Press Statement, Oct. 26, 1937, A. F. of L. Papers, Office of the President, File C, Box 4.

12. Statement by Philip Murray, *ibid.*; I. Bernstein, *Turbulent Years*, pp. 691-692; P. Taft, *AFL from Death of Gompers*, pp. 195-196.

13. W. Jett Lauck Diary, Oct. 30, 1937, and Memo to Mr. Lewis, Oct. 30, 1937, W. Jett Lauck Papers, Box 39.

14. Memorandum from John R. Steelman, Weekly Labor Report, Nov. 12, 1937, D/L, R.G. 174, Box 28, N.A.

15. See especially I. Bernstein, *Turbulent Years*, pp. 694-695, and P. Taft, *AFL from Death of Gompers*, p. 198; Walter Galenson, *The CIO Challenge to the AFL: A History of the American Labor Movement, 1935-1941* (Cambridge, Mass., 1960), pp. 41-43; Report of the A. F. of L. Conference Committee to the Executive Council, Feb. 2, 1938, A. F. of L. Papers, Office of the President, File C, Box 43; Notes, Meeting, A. F. of L.-CIO, 11-29-37, John Brophy Papers, Box A5-5, CUA.

16. Notes, Meeting, A. F. of L.-CIO, 11-29-37, John Brophy Papers, Box A5-5.
17. Interview with David Dubinsky, Sept. 21, 1972; P. Taft, *AFL from Death of Gompers*, pp. 196-199; I. Bernstein, *Turbulent Years*, pp. 694-695; W. Galenson, *CIO Challenge*, pp. 41-43; Report of A. F. of L. Conference Committee to Executive Council, Feb. 3, 1938, A. F. of L. Papers, Office of the President, File C, Box 43.
18. W. Jett Lauck Diary, Dec. 21, 1937.
19. Adolph Germer to James O'Neal, May 9, 1938, Adolph Germer Papers, Box 27, SHSW.
20. Max D. Danish, *The World of David Dubinsky* (Cleveland, 1957), p. 115.
21. Bruce Bliven, Jr., "The CIO Comes of Age," *New Republic* (Nov. 30, 1938), pp. 92-93; see *ibid.*, Jan. 4, 1939, pp. 260-261, for controversy generated by Louis Stark's reports in the *New York Times* concerning Communist role at convention; Robert Bendiner, "C.I.O.—From Committee to Congress," *Nation* (Dec. 3, 1938), pp. 590-593; NYT, Nov. 16, 1938, p. 18, Nov. 17, 1938, pp. 1, 21.
22. John Brophy, *A Miner's Life*, ed. John O. H. P. Hall (Madison, Wis., 1964), pp. 280-282.
23. Father Francis J. Haas to Sidney Hillman, Dec. 6, 1938, and George Harrison to Hillman, Dec. 8, 1938, Sidney Hillman Papers, Peace Negotiations File, 1938, Amalgamated Clothing Workers of America Archives, New York; John L. Lewis to Franklin D. Roosevelt, July 12, 1938, and Memorandum Franklin D. Roosevelt to Steven McIntyre, Dec. 27, 1938, FDR Papers, OF 2546, Box 1, 1938-1939, FDR Library.
24. Memorandum, S. T. Early to Rudolph Forster, Feb. 16, 1939; Memorandum, Franklin D. Roosevelt to Early, Feb. 18, 1939; telegram from Early and William Hassett, Feb. 24 and 25, 1939; Roosevelt to William Green, also to Lewis, Feb. 23, 1939, all in FDR Papers, OF 407 (Labor), Box 3; Early to Hassett, Feb. 25, 1939, *ibid.*, File 2546, Box 1, 1938-1939.
25. I. Bernstein, *Turbulent Years,* pp. 699-703; W. Galenson, *CIO Challenge,* pp. 53-54.
26. John L. Lewis to Franklin D. Roosevelt, Feb. 28, 1939, FDR Papers, OF 407 (Labor), Box 3; cf. I. Bernstein, *Turbulent Years*, p. 701.
27. John Brophy Diary, Mar. 4, 1939; Memorandum to John L. Lewis from W. Jett Lauck, n.d., W. Jett Lauck Papers, Box 367, Folder 6; Peace Proposals of the CIO, White House, Conference, Mar. 7, 1939, A. F. of L. Office of the President, File C, Box 28; UMWJ, Mar. 15, 1939, pp. 6-7.
28. W. Jett Lauck Diary, Mar. 7, 1939.
29. Notes on A. F. of L.-CIO Peace Negotiations, 1939, A. F. of L. Papers, Office of the President, File C, Box 4; Statement on A. F. of L.-CIO by Executive Council, A. F. of L., Mar. 22-23, 1939, *ibid.*; Memoranda, Matthew Woll, Apr. 5 and 12, 1939, *ibid.*, Box 24.
30. John L. Lewis, Confidential Memorandum to Members of CIO Executive Board, Mar. 25, 1939, Hillman Papers, Peace Negotiations Folder, 1939; cf. Herbert Harris, *Labor's Civil War* (New York, 1940), pp. 231-236.
31. John L. Lewis to Franklin D. Roosevelt, Oct. 15, 1939, FDR Papers, PPF 5640.
32. New York *Daily Mirror*, Nov. 16, 1939, clipping in A. F. of L. Papers, Office of the President, File C, Box 4; FDR Press Conferences, Transcripts, Nov. 10 and Dec. 19, 1939, V. 14, pp. 294-295, 370-371, FDR Papers.
33. W. Jett Lauck Diary, Jan. 4, 1940.
34. Lee Pressman, COHC, p. 193.
35. David J. MacDonald, Oral History Transcript, p. 11, SWOC Collection, PSULA; Saul D. Alinsky, *John L. Lewis: An Unauthorized Biography* (New York, 1970 ed.), p. 224.
36. Lee Pressman, COHC, pp. 193-194.

37. *Ibid.*, p. 206.
38. *Ibid.*, p. 194.
39. I. Bernstein, *Turbulent Years*, pp. 474-484.
40. *Ibid.*, pp. 485-490; Donald G. Sofchalk, "The Chicago Memorial Day Massacre: An Episode of Mass Action," *Labor History*, VI (Winter 1965), 3-43.
41. NYT, June 22, 1937, pp. 1-2.
42. FDR Press Conferences, Transcripts, V. 9, p. 467, FDR Papers; NYT, June 30, 1937, pp. 1-2; I. Bernstein, *Turbulent Years*, p. 496.
43. Harry Hopkins to Franklin D. Roosevelt, with enclosure, July 2, 1937, FDR Papers, OF 407B, Box 27.
44. I. Bernstein, *Turbulent Years*, pp. 617-623; Matthew Josephson, *Sidney Hillman* (New York, 1952), pp. 416-425.
45. NYT, June 22, 1937, pp. 1, 8.
46. Lee Pressman, COHC, p. 191.
47. On the Bridges-Lundeberg clash see John L. Lewis to Harry Lundeberg, n.d., and "Notes Taken from Atlantic Material: Correspondence between Sailors Union of the Pacific and Mr. Lewis," Sept. 30, Oct. 5 and 15, 1937, John Brophy Papers, Box A5-5; John Brophy, "Twenty Years with CIO," Ch. X, p. 3, *ibid.*; I. Bernstein, *Turbulent Years*, pp. 576-584, 586-589; on the Hollywood events see the extensive correspondence in the John Brophy Papers, Box A5-7; for the conflict between carpenters and CIO woodworkers in the Pacific Northwest, see I. Bernstein, *Turbulent Years*, pp. 624-632.
48. William E. Leuchtenberg, *Franklin D. Roosevelt and the New Deal* (New York, 1963), p. 249.
49. On this point see W. Galenson, *CIO Challenge*, p. 585, and P. Taft, *AFL from Death of Gompers*, pp. 199-200.
50. W. Jett Lauck Diary, Dec. 13, 1937.
51. John Frey to W. A. Appleton, Apr. 13, 1938, and Aug. 1, 1938, John Frey Papers, Box 1, File 8, L.C.
52. Wyndham Mortimer to John Brophy, Sept. 29 and Oct, 1937, John Brophy Papers, Box A5-6.
53. John Brophy to Tucker P. Smith, Oct. 4, 1937, *ibid.*
54. Confidential Memorandum to President Lewis, Nov. 30, 1937, W. Jett Lauck Papers, Box 39.
55. For some of the background to UAW Factionalism, see *Affidavit of John L. Lewis and Appendices*, Feb. 1939, in Henry Kraus Papers, Box 14, ALHUA, WSU; cf. I. Bernstein, *Turbulent Years*, pp. 563-566.
56. Adolph Germer Diary, June 30, Aug. 4, and Aug. 5, 1938; M. Josephson, *Hillman*, pp. 456-457; I. Bernstein, *Turbulent Years*, p. 566; Wyndham Mortimer, *Organize: My Life as a Union Man* (Boston, 1971), pp. 150-162.
57. Homer Martin to John L. Lewis, Jan. 25, 1939, CIO Papers, Secretary-Treasurer's Office, Box 89, ALHUA, WSU; *Affidavit of Lewis*, Kraus Papers, Box 14; I. Bernstein, *Turbulent Years*, pp. 567-569; M. Josephson, *Hillman*, pp. 457-458.
58. Adolph Germer Papers, Box 4.
59. John L. Lewis to Dear Sid, Dec. 2, 1937, Sidney Hillman Papers, UMW Folder.
60. For the salient differences between Lewisites and Hillmanites, see Len DeCaux, *Labor Radical* (Boston, 1970), pp. 328-344, and Lee Pressman, COHC, pp. 91 and *passim*.
61. See John Frey to W. A. Appleton, Aug. 1, 1938, John Frey Papers, Box 1, File 8.
62. Benjamin Stolberg, *The Story of CIO* (New York, 1938); Len DeCaux, *Labor Radical*, pp. 303-311.
63. Adolph Germer Diary, Sept. 12, 1939.

64. Handwritten copy of JLL Press Statement for Immediate Release, Oct. 8, 1939, JLL Papers, SHSW. Oct. 8, 1939, ALHUA, WSU.

65. L. DeCaux, *Labor Radical*, pp. 346-347; W. Mortimer, *Organize,* p. 165; M. Josephson, *Hillman,* pp. 470-471; W. Jett Lauck Diary, Nov. 1, 1939; J. Brophy, "Twenty Years with CIO," pp. 7-8, John Brophy Papers; Matthew Woll to William Green, with enclosures, Nov. 1, 1939, A. F. of L. Papers, Office of the President, File C, Box 24.

66. *Proceedings 1939 Convention,* CIO, 5-6, 106-109; Franklin D. Roosevelt to John L. Lewis, Oct. 11, 1939, FDR Papers, OF 2546, Box 1; Harold L. Ickes to Lewis, Oct. 16, 1939, JLL Papers; interview with Jacob Potofsky, Apr. 18, 1974; M. Josephson, *Hillman*, p. 471.

67. Matthew Woll to William Green, with enclosures, Nov. 1, 1939, A. F. of L. Papers, Office of the President, File C, Box 24.

68. *Ibid.*; Adolph Germer Diary, Oct. 14, 1939; J. Brophy, *A Miner's Life,* p. 282; for a different view of Lewis's anticommunism, one that sees it as shadow, not substance, see L. DeCaux, *Labor Radical,* pp. 347-349.

69. See p. 279; Matthew Woll to William Green, with enclosures, Nov. 1, 1939, A. F. of L. Papers, Office of the President, File C, Box 24.

70. Matthew Woll to William Green, as cited above.

71. W. Jett Lauck Diary.

72. S. D. Alinsky, *Lewis,* p. 212.

73. *Ibid.,* pp. 165, 210, and 161-212, *passim.*

74. I. Bernstein, *Turbulent Years,* pp. 713-714.

75. NYT, Oct. 7, 1938, p. 3.

76. Lee Pressman, COHC, pp. 353, 356.

77. Paul Thompson, *The Edwardians: The Remaking of British Society* (Bloomington, Ind., 1975), pp. 260-262, for Lloyd George and the British crisis.

78. Lee Pressman, COHC, pp. 91, 96-97, 188, 191; L. DeCaux, *Labor Radical*, p. 295.

79. Louis Adamic, *My America, 1928-1938* (New York, 1938), p. 403.

80. S. D. Alinsky, *Lewis,* p. 165.

81. Transcript, Radio Address, "Labor and the Supreme Court," May 14, 1937, JLL Papers; UMWJ, June 1, 1937, pp. 6-7.

82. UMWJ, June 15, 1937, pp. 3-4.

83. Memorandum, Franklin D. Roosevelt to Harold L. Ickes, Feb. 2, 1937, FDR Papers, OF 290, Box 1; Memorandum, Franklin D. Roosevelt to Frances Perkins, Aug. 5, 1937, *ibid.,* PSF, Box 61.

84. NYT, June 23, 1937, p. 1.

85. FDR Press Conferences, Transcript, V. 10, pp. 15, 27, FDR Papers; I. Bernstein, *Turbulent Years,* p. 496.

86. NYT, Aug. 1, 1937, p. 33, Aug. 21, 1937, pp. 1, 4, Aug. 24, 1937, p. 19, Aug. 28, 1937, p. 1.

87. Transcript of Radio Address, "Labor and the Nation," Sept. 3, 1937 (reprinted as CIO pamphlet with same title, Sept. 11, 1937), JLL Papers; UMWJ, Sept. 15, 1937, pp. 3-4; NYT, Sept. 4, 1937, pp. 1, 6.

88. Transcript of Radio Address, JLL Papers.

89. FDR Press Conferences, Transcripts, V, 10, p. 196, FDR Papers.

90. John Brophy, "Twenty Years with CIO," Ch. VII, p. 15, John Brophy Papers.

91. NYT, Sept. 12, 1937, IV, 3.

92. *Ibid.*, Sept. 16, 1937, pp. 1, 15.

93. Rexford Tugwell to Franklin D. Roosevelt, Dec. 14, 1937, FDR Papers, PPF 564.

94. NYT, May 21, 1938, p. 2; UMWJ, Apr. 1, 1938, pp. 3-4, May 15, 1938, pp. 3-4;

Eli L. Oliver to Sidney Hillman, July 29, 1938, enclosing memorandum, John L. Lewis to Oliver, July 23, 1938, Sidney Hillman Papers, Non-Partisan League Folder.

95. NYT, Nov. 13, 1938, pp. 1, 13.

96. UMWJ, Jan. 1, 1939, p. 6, May 15, 1939, pp. 18-19, Aug. 15, 1939, pp. 3-4; Statement of John L. Lewis, May 2, 1938, John Brophy Papers, Box A5-5; Minutes of CIO Executive Board Meeting, June 13-15, 1939, CIO Papers, Secretary-Treasurer's Office, Box 90, ALHUA, WSU; NYT, Nov. 7, 1939, p. 7, for Lewis's endorsement of New Deal.

97. John L. Lewis to Franklin D. Roosevelt, Feb. 7 and May 25, 1939, FDR Papers, PPF 3183; Memorandum for General Watson from K, May 9, 1939, ibid., OF 2546, Box 1.

98. W. Jett Lauck Diary, Dec. 12, 1937.

99. UMWJ, Sept. 15, 1939, pp. 3-5; see folders in Labor's Non-Partisan League File, Box A7b-1, John Brophy Papers, for material on CIO and its relations in 1938-1939 with the American Student Union and American Youth Congress, especially John L. Lewis to Joseph P. Lash, Dec. 22, 1938.

100. Speech at Schuylkill County Fairgrounds, Sept. 19, 1936, JLL Papers.

101. NYT, Mar. 16, 1937, p. 2; UMWJ, Apr. 1, 1937, pp. 10-11; William Taylor to John L. Lewis, Jan. 27, 1938; Lewis to Taylor, Jan. 29, 1938; and Taylor to Lewis, Feb. 1, 1938, UMW Archives, Correspondence File, 1930-1939.

102. NYT, Sept. 7, 1938, p. 10, Sept. 9, 1938, p. 2, Sept. 12, 1938, p. 1, Sept. 27, 1938, p. 6; Ralph Hetzel to Sidney Hillman, July 25, 1938, Sidney Hillman Papers, CIO Folder, 1938; John L. Lewis to Marvin McIntyre, Nov. 6, 1936, FDR Papers, OF 146A; Josephus Daniels to Franklin D. Roosevelt, Sept. 9, 1938, and Lewis to Roosevelt, Sept. 9, 1938, ibid., PPF 3183.

103 S.D. Alinsky, Lewis, pp. 201-203; L. DeCaux, Labor Radical, p. 356; Ladislaw Farrago, The Game of Foxes (New York, 1971), pp. 351-365; Marquis Childs, I Write from Washington (New York, 1942), pp. 174-186; Kenneth Crawford series in PM, Dec. 11, 1940, Apr. 25, 28, 29, 30, and May 5, 1941, and also Saint Louis Post-Dispatch, June 15, 1939, clippings in Adolph Germer Papers, Box 23, File 57. See also Ch. 19, note 2.

104. UMWJ, Sept. 15, 1939, p. 5.

105. Memorandum from A. D. Lewis, Sept. 9, 1939, UMWA Archives, Correspondence File, 1930-1939; Memorandum from Lee Pressman to John L. Lewis, Sept. 11, 1939, ibid.; Memorandum to John L. Lewis on Proposed Labor Policy for War Period, from W. Jett Lauck, Sept. 13, 1939, ibid.; Memorandum for John L. Lewis from Lee Pressman, Oct. 27, 1939, ibid.; CIO Executive Board Minutes, Oct. 6, 1939, CIO Papers, Secretary-Treasurer's Office, Box 90, ALHUA, WSU.

106. Memorandum of Telephone Conversation in UMWA Archives, Correspondence File, 1930-1939.

107. NYT, Oct. 31, 1939, p. 17, Nov. 1, 1939, p. 15; Proceedings 1939 Convention, CIO, pp. 17, 19.

108. UMWJ, Sept. 15, 1939, p. 5.

NOTES TO CHAPTER 15

1. Frances Perkins, The Roosevelt I Knew (New York, 1946), pp. 126-127.

2. Saul D. Alinsky, John L. Lewis: An Unauthorized Biography (New York, 1970 ed.), pp. 194-199; Irving Bernstein, Turbulent Years (Boston, 1969), pp. 717-718; Matthew Josephson, Sidney Hillman (New York, 1952), p. 474.

3. NYT, Jan. 20, 1940, p. 11.

4. Edward A. Lahey, COHC, p. 78.
5. Lee Pressman, COHC, pp. 108, 196.
6. *Ibid.*, pp. 350-352.
7. *Proceedings 1940 Convention*, UMWA, p. 104; see the following chapter, p. 385, for pro-Roosevelt sentiment among UMW rank and file.
8. *Ibid.*, pp. 103-105.
9. *New Republic* (Feb. 12, 1940), pp. 210-211; NYT, Jan. 25, 1940, p. 20.
10. Burton K. Wheeler with Paul F. Healey, *Yankee from the West* (New York, 1962), pp. 135-164.
11. *Proceedings 1940 Convention*, UMWA, p. 118.
12. *Ibid.*, pp. 294-295, 469.
13. NYT, Jan. 28, 1940, pp. 1, 29.
14. *New Republic,* Feb. 12, 1940, pp. 210-211.
15. *Proceedings 1940 Convention*, UMWA, p. 315.
16. Gardner Jackson, COHC, p. 774; for rumors and facts about Lewis's links to a Nazi propaganda campaign to defeat Roosevelt's reelection bid, see Alton Frye, *Nazi Germany and the American Hemisphere, 1933-1941* (New Haven, Conn., 1967), pp. 142-144; Herbert S. Parmet and Marie B. Hecht, *Never Again: A President Runs for a Third Term* (New York, 1968), pp. 256-257, and this book, pp. 331-333.
17. Franklin D. Roosevelt to Frances Perkins, Feb. 1, 1940, Perkins to Roosevelt, Feb. 7, 1940, with enclosure, and George S. Messersmith to General Edwin M. Watson, Jan. 26, 1940, FDR Papers, PSF Box 61 (Labor), Roosevelt Library; J. David Stern, COHC, pp. 57-58.
18. Joseph P. Lash, *Eleanor and Franklin* (New York, 1971), pp. 604-605.
19. *Ibid.*, p. 605; Transcript of Lewis Speech to American Youth Congress, Feb. 10, 1940, JLL Papers (microfilm copy), SHSW, reprinted by CIO as *Jobs, Peace, Unity.*
20. J. Lash, *Eleanor and Franklin,* p. 605.
21. UMWJ, Apr. 15, 1940, pp. 3-6; NYT, Apr. 2, 1940, pp. 1, 4.
22. UMWJ, Apr. 15, 1940, pp. 3-6.
23. *Ibid.*
24. NYT, Apr. 8, 1940, p. 4.
25. FDR Press Conferences, Transcript, V. 15, pp. 102, 120, FDR Papers.
26. *Ibid.*, p. 389.
27. Lee Pressman, COHC, p. 317; cf. S. Alinsky, *Lewis*, pp. 182-184; M. Josephson, *Hillman*, pp. 481-484.
28. NYT, May 30, 1940, p. 9; UMWJ, Aug. 1, 1940, p. 9.
29. Minutes CIO Executive Board Meeting, June 1940, John Brophy Papers, Box A5-8, CUA; UMWJ, July 1, 1940, pp. 6-7.
30. M. Josephson, *Hillman,* p. 485; see Sidney Hillman Papers, File, "John L. Lewis Correspondence and Executive Order, 1940," Amalgamated Clothing Workers of America Archives, New York.
31. John L. Lewis to Sidney Hillman, July 29, 1940; Hillman to Lewis, Aug. 7, 1940, Sidney Hillman Papers, Lewis-Matles File.
32. Typescript, Address to NAACP, June 18, 1940, JLL Papers; Press Release, CIO, June 18, 1940, Herbert Hoover Papers, Post-Presidential Files, John L. Lewis, Hoover Library.
33. NYT, June 20, 1940, pp. 1, 21.
34. Lee Pressman, COHC, p. 380.
35. Herbert Hoover Papers, Post-Presidential Files—John L. Lewis, June 1940, Box 98.
36. NYT, July 3, 1940, pp. 1, 7, July 31, 1940, p. 15.
37. I. Bernstein, *Turbulent Years*, p. 718.

38. W. Jett Lauck Diary, June-August, 1940, W. Jett Lauck Papers, Alderson Library, UVL; Len DeCaux, *Labor Radical* (Boston, 1970), p. 359.

39. UMWJ, Sept. 1, 1940, pp. 12-14.

40. *Ibid.*, Sept. 15, 1940, pp. 6-7; Speech Typescript, JLL Papers.

41. Lee Pressman, COHC, p. 387; W. Jett Lauck Diary, Oct. 1940.

42. S. D. Alinsky, *Lewis,* pp. 176-177.

43. *Ibid.*, p. 180; Lee Pressman, COHC, pp. 117-120; L. DeCaux, *Labor Radical*, pp. 323-324; Lauck makes numerous references in his Diary to Kathryn's hatred of Roosevelt.

44. NYT, Oct. 16, 1940, p. 15.

45. *Ibid.*, Oct. 18, 1940, p. 16.

46. *Ibid.*

47. S. D. Alinsky, *Lewis,* pp. 186-187, alleges that immediately after the Oct. 17 Lewis-Roosevelt meeting both Lewis and Kathryn told him the FBI story.

48. J. Edgar Hoover to Stephen Early, Oct. 31, 1940, FDR Papers, OF 2546, Box 2.

49. S. D. Alinsky, *Lewis*, pp. 186-187; Sidney Fine to Melvyn Dubofsky, May 5, 1975.

50. Rumors and circumstantial evidence that linked Lewis to Nazi and Soviet propaganda and espionage schemes also may have led Roosevelt to place the labor leader under surveillance. See notes 16-17 above.

51. John L. Lewis to John Owens, Oct. 22, 1940, UMW District 6 Papers, Box 6, File 8, Ohio University Archives; FDR Press Conferences, Transcript, V. 16, p. 282, FDR Papers; Memorandum for Roosevelt from E. W. W., Oct. 22, 1940, FDR Papers, PPF 1180.

52. Speech Typescript, JLL Papers; UMWJ, Nov. 1, 1940, pp. 4-6; NYT, Oct. 26, 1940, pp. 1, 12.

53. NYT, Oct. 26, 1940, pp. 1, 12.

54. Herbert Hoover to John L. Lewis, Oct. 25, 1940, Herbert Hoover Papers, Post-Presidential Files, John L. Lewis, Box 98; Harvey Fremming to Lewis, Oct. 1940, Adolph Germer Papers, Box 4, SHSW.

55. Wendell Willkie to John L. Lewis, Oct. 25, 1940, JLL Papers; Mary E. Dillon, *Wendell Willkie, 1882-1944* (Philadelphia, 1952), pp. 217-218.

56. JLL Papers.

57. NYT, Oct. 29, 1940, p. 22.

58. Lee Pressman, COHC, pp. 387-389.

59. Undated handwritten statement, JLL Papers; speech typescript, Nov. 5, 1940, *ibid.*; NYT, Nov. 4, 1940, p. 13, Nov. 5, 1940, p. 20.

60. Transcripts of J. S. Potofsky Radio Speech, Oct. 29, 1940, and Madison Square Garden, Oct. 31, 1940, in personal possession of Jacob S. Potofsky; CIO Council Bulletin, San Francisco Industrial Union Council, Oct. 29, 1940, in Adolph Germer Papers, Box 4.

61. Gardner Jackson to John L. Lewis, Oct. 27, 1940, Adolph Germer Papers, Box 4; M. Josephson, *Hillman*, pp. 488-490; cf. Allan S. Haywood to Paul Schuler, Oct. 28, 1940, and Ralph Hetzel to Alfred Rubino, Oct. 31, 1940, CIO Papers, Labor Non-Partisan League File, Box A76-1, CUA.

62. Powers Hapgood to Mary Hapgood, Oct. 9 and 26, 1940, Powers Hapgood Papers, Lilly Library, Indiana University.

63. James Murray to Franklin D. Roosevelt, Nov. 2, 1940, and Roosevelt to Murray, Nov. 4, 1940, FDR Papers, PPF 2534; Charles H. Bryson to Roosevelt, Nov. 4, 1940, *ibid.*, OF 2546, Box 5.

64. J. Q. Ferguson to Franklin D. Roosevelt, Oct. 25, 1940, *ibid.*, OF 2546, Box 5; Boxes 6 and 7 are also filled with anti-Lewis items.

65. NYT, Nov. 7, 1940, p. 22.

66. John L. Lewis to Ernest A. Dye, Jan. 16, 1943, UMW Archives, JLL M.A. File; NYT, Nov. 6, 1940, p. 4, for story that Lewis voted by absentee ballot.
67. L. DeCaux, *Labor Radical*, pp. 366-367.
68. S. D. Alinsky, *Lewis,* p. 208; *New Republic*, Nov. 4, 1940, pp. 627-628.
69. See, for example, Louis Stark in NYT, Oct. 30, 1940, pp. 1, 15.
70. *Ibid.*; Lewis Press Statement, Oct. 30, 1940, John Brophy Papers, Box A5-8.
71. Morris L. Ernst to Franklin D. Roosevelt, Apr. 7, 1939, FDR Papers, PPF 2841; W. Jett Lauck Diary, Apr. 19, 1939.
72. M.E. Dillon, *Willkie*, pp. 213-214; H. Parmet and M. Hecht, *Never Again,* pp. 233-234. It is this meeting—allegedly arranged by the oil entrepreneur William Rhodes Davis, an associate of Goering and other Nazis—that has been cited as evidence to link Lewis to a German effort to defeat Roosevelt's reelection. Marquis W. Childs, *I Write from Washington* (New York, 1942), pp. 174-175, 182-185, 206-207, for charges that Davis and Nazi money paid for Lewis's Oct. 25 speech. On Willkie's promises to Lewis, see W. Jett Lauck Diary, Jan. 6, 1941.
73. S. D. Alinsky, *Lewis*, pp. 208-209.
74. For Lewis's aversion to communism and third-party politics in the summer of 1940, see Adolph Germer Diary, Aug. 13-14, 1940.
75. UMWJ, Sept. 1, 1940, p. 12.
76. Letters of Oct. 9 and 26, 1940, Powers Hapgood Papers.
77. Harvey Fremming to Adolph Germer, Nov. 9, 1940, Adolph Germer Papers, Box 5; Powers Hapgood to Mary Hapgood, Nov. 11, 1940, Powers Hapgood Papers.
78. M. Josephson, *Hillman*, pp. 491-492; I. Bernstein, *Turbulent Years*, pp. 721-722.
79. M. Josephson, *Hillman*, pp. 492-493; L. DeCaux, *Labor Radical*, pp. 372-373.
80. UMWJ, Dec. 1, 1940, p. 13.
81. Lee Pressman, COHC, p. 310.
82. *Proceedings 1940 Convention*, CIO, pp. 158-165.
83. *Ibid.*
84. *Ibid.*
85. *Ibid.*; Lee Pressman, COHC, p. 393.
86. *Proceedings 1940 Convention,* CIO, pp. 158-165.
87. M. Josephson, *Hillman*, pp. 496-497; L. DeCaux, *Labor Radical*, pp. 375-376.
88. M. Josephson, *Hillman,* pp. 498-502; *Proceedings 1940 Convention,* CIO, pp. 182-192, 266-271.
89. Lee Pressman, COHC, pp. 198-199; S. Alinsky, *Lewis,* pp. 220-222; L. DeCaux, *Labor Radical,* pp. 378-381; NYT, Nov. 20, 1940, p. 1.
90. *Proceedings 1940 Convention*, CIO, pp. 266-271.
91. *Ibid.*, pp. 271-274.
92. Lee Pressman, COHC, p. 357.
93. L. DeCaux, *Labor Radical*, p. 388.

NOTES TO CHAPTER 16

1. Marquis Childs, COHC, pp. 60-61.
2. *Historical Statistics of the United States, Colonial Times to 1957* (Washington, D.C., 1960), pp. 356-359.
3. *Ibid.*, pp. 92-93; *Employment and Earnings Statistics for the United States, 1909-1960* (Washington, D.C., 1961), pp. 12-15.

4. "Strike Activity in the Coal Industry, Jan. 20, 1947," D/L, R.G. 174, Box 71, N.A.

5. National Recovery Administration, *Coal Administration Hearings*, Jan. 4, 1935, pp. 94-97, R.G. 9, Box 7196, N.A.; UMWJ, Jan. 15, 1935, p. 13.

6. NRA, *Coal Code Hearings,* Jan. 4, 1935, pp. 11-15, 78-97, 112-118; UMWJ, Jan. 15, 1935, pp. 12-14.

7. UMWJ, Jan. 15, 1935, p. 14; NRA, *Coal Code Hearings*, Jan. 4, 1935, pp. 379-383.

8. *Proceedings 1936 Convention,* UMWA, I, 23; UMWJ, Mar. 15, 1935, p. 3.

9. James Dewey to Hugh L. Kerwin, May 25, 1935, and Oct. 8, 1935, R.G. 280, File 182/471, N.A.; for President Roosevelt's role, see FDR Papers, OF 175 (Coal), Box 4, Roosevelt Library.

10. See note 9 above.

11. *Proceedings 1938 Convention*, UMWA, pp. 18-26.

12. *Ibid.*, pp. 54-55; UMWJ, June 15, 1936, pp. 5-6; FDR Papers, OF 175 (Coal), Box 4; Waldo E. Fisher and Charles M. James, *Minimum Price Fixing in Bituminous Coal* (Princeton, N.J., 1955), pp. 39-49.

13. See, for example, UMWJ, Mar. 15, 1937, p. 4.

14. *Proceedings 1938 Convention*, UMWA, p. 211.

15. *Ibid.*, pp. 23-26; John L. Lewis to Thomas J. Price, July 18, 1940, UMW District 6 Papers, Box 6, File 8, Ohio University Archives.

16. A whole four-drawer file cabinet in the UMW Archives contains the correspondence and reports Lewis amassed on this issue beginning in the mid-1930s.

17. William A. Taylor to William W. Stafford, Nov. 23, 1938, *ibid.*, JLL, M.A. File.

18. "Bituminous Coal Controversy, March-May, 1939," pp. 1-3, R.G. 280, File 196/1080.

19. Personal Interview, June 4, 1974.

20. UMWJ, Apr. 1, 1939, p. 10; "Bituminous Coal Controversy, 1939," pp. 3-4.

21. UMWJ, Apr. 1, 1939, pp. 10-12; "Bituminous Coal Controversy, 1939," pp. 3-4.

22. Transcript of phone call, James Dewey to Frances Perkins, Apr. 1, 1939, D/L, R.G. 174, Perkins File, Box 32; "Bituminous Coal Controversy, 1939," p. 5; UMWJ, Apr. 1, 1939, pp. 10-12.

23. "Bituminous Coal Controversy, 1939," pp. 5-6; UMWJ, Apr. 15, 1939, p. 3.

24. Transcript of phone call, James Dewey to Frances Perkins, Apr. 6, 1939, D/L, R.G. 174, Perkins File, Box 32; "Bituminous Coal Controversy, 1939," pp. 6-9; W. Jett Lauck Diary, Apr. 18, 1939, W. Jett Lauck Papers, Alderson Library, UVL; UMWJ, Apr. 15, 1939, pp. 3-5.

25. "Bituminous Coal Controversy, 1939," pp. 10-12.

26. John L. Lewis to John R. Steelman, May 7, 1939, R.G. 280, File 196/1080A, Box 725, N.A.; "Bituminous Coal Controversy, 1939," pp. 10-16; UMWJ, May 1, 1939, pp. 3-4, May 15, 1939, pp. 4-5.

27. Transcript of phone call, Frances Perkins to White House, May 10, 1939, FDR Papers, PSF (Labor), Box 61; "Bituminous Coal Controversy, 1939," pp. 18-19.

28. "Bituminous Coal Controversy, 1939", pp. 19-29; Transcript of phone call, John R. Steelman to Miss Jay (Jurkowitz), May 4, 1939, D/L, R.G. 174, Perkins File, Box 32; Memorandum, Gerard D. Reilly to F. Perkins, May 9, 1939, *ibid.*; Memorandum to F. Perkins of Phone Conversation between J. R. Steelman and John L. Lewis, May 17, 1939, *ibid.*; Confidential Memorandum, Steelman to Perkins, May 19, 1939, *ibid.*; W. Jett Lauck, Diary, May 11 and 13, 1939.

29. UMWJ, pp. 3-7.

30. Cited in "Bituminous Coal Controversy, 1939," pp. 27-28.

31. *Proceedings 1938 Convention*, UMWA, pp. 193, 367-368.
32. *Proceedings 1936 Convention,* UMWA, pp. 40-51; *Proceedings 1938 Convention,* UMWA, pp. 71-72; *Proceedings 1940 Convention*, UMWA, pp. 89-90.
33. *Proceedings 1936 Convention*, UMWA, pp. 114-117.
34. *Ibid.* pp. 122-132.
35. *Ibid.*, p. 467.
36. *Ibid.*, p. 132.
37. *Proceedings 1938 Convention*, UMWA, pp. 153-157.
38. *Ibid.*, p. 346.
39. *Ibid.*, pp. 165-166.
40. *Proceedings 1940 Convention,* UMWA, pp. 89-90, 135-141.
41. *Ibid.*, pp. 191-192.
42. *Ibid.*, pp. 201-202.

NOTES TO CHAPTER 17

1. Lee Pressman Interview, COHC, p. 48; UMWJ, Mar. 1, 1941, p. 8.
2. Lee Pressman Interview, COHC, p. 50; *Business Week* (Mar. 8, 1941), p. 14; NYT, Mar. 12, 1941, p. 1.
3. UMWJ, Mar. 15, 1941, p. 6.
4. *Proceedings 1942 Convention*, UMWA, pp. 40-41.
5. NYT, Mar. 14, 1941, pp. 1, 11; NYT, Mar. 31, 1941, p. 1; UMWJ, Apr. 1, 1941, pp. 5-6.
6. NYT, Apr. 1, 1941, p. 1.
7. NYT, Apr. 7, 1941, p. 9; NYT, Apr. 8, 1941, p. 16; NYT, Apr. 11, 1941, p. 14; NYT, Apr. 12, 1941, p. 9.
8. *Proceedings 1942 Convention*, UMWA, pp. 50-54; UMWJ, April 15, 1941, pp. 3-6; NYT, Apr. 19, 1941, p. 1.
9. NYT, Apr. 15, 1941, p. 13, Apr. 17, 1941, p. 18; UMWJ, Apr. 15, 1941, pp. 3-6.
10. UMWJ, May 1, 1941, pp. 5-6.
11. *Ibid.*
12. NYT, Apr. 24, 1941, p. 6.
13. UMWJ, May 15, 1941, pp. 3-6; *Proceedings 1942 Convention,* UMWA, pp. 56-60.
14. NYT, May 1, 1941, p. 17; for pressure by Roosevelt on southern operators, W. Jett Lauck Diary, Apr. 29, 1941, W. Jett Lauck Papers, UVL.
15. UMWJ, June 1, 1941, p. 16.
16. NYT, June 24, 1941, p. 11; *Appalachian Joint Wage Agreement Effective April 1, 1941 to March 31, 1943*, p. 5; Memorandum, Franklin D. Roosevelt to William Davis, June 23, 1941, Roosevelt Papers, OF 290, Box 2, FDRL.
17. UMWJ, July 1, 1941, pp. 3-4; NYT, June 25, 1941, p. 12, July 7, 1941, p. 1.
18. UMWJ, June 1, 1941, p. 16.
19. UMWJ, Apr. 1, 1941, p. 1.
20. NYT, May 1, 1941, p. 18, July 8, 1941, p. 1, July 9, 1941, p. 1.
21. NYT, Aug. 12, 1941, p. 11.
22. NYT, Aug. 6, 1941, p. 6; Len DeCaux, *Labor Radical* (Boston, 1970), pp. 383-385; Saul D. Alinsky, *John L. Lewis* (New York, 1949), pp. 230-232; NYT, Sept. 6, 1941, p. 16, Sept. 26, 1941, p. 9.

23. NYT, Sept. 1, 1941, p. 32; "Fortune Survey: V, Three Men and Two Corporations," *Fortune* (June, 1941), pp. 148, 151.

24. William H. Davis Interview, COHC, pp. 110-111.

25. John L. Lewis to President [Franklin D. Roosevelt], October 25, 1941, RG 202, NDMB, Box 165, Coal File, N.A.

26. John L. Lewis to John Brophy, July 12, 1941, and Lewis to Brophy, July 3, 1941, John Brophy Papers, A5-8, CUA.

27. See, for instance, "John L. Lewis's Rebellion," *Business Week* (Nov. 1, 1941), pp. 15-16; F. Kirchwey, "Lewis's big gamble," *Nation* (Nov. 8, 1941), pp. 444-445. Inevitably, such views creep into historical writing. See Foster Rhea Dulles, *Labor in America,* 3rd ed. (New York, 1966), p. 328; Matthew Josephson, *Sidney Hillman* (New York, 1952), p. 562.

28. S. D. Alinsky, *Lewis,* pp. 238-239.

29. Myron Taylor to President [Franklin D. Roosevelt], Oct. 25, 1941, RG 202, Box 165, Bituminous Coal File, N.A.

30. *Proceedings 1942 Convention,* UMWA, pp. 64-66; "Proposal of United Mine Workers of America to National Defense Mediation Board," Sept. 17, 1941, RG 202, Box 165, Bituminous Coal File, N.A.

31. UMWJ, Nov. 1, 1941, p. 3; NYT, Oct. 22, 1941, p. 22.

32. UMWJ, Nov. 1, 1941, p. 3.

33. *Ibid.,* p. 15; *Proceedings 1942 Convention*, UMWA, pp. 66-68.

34. *Ibid.*

35. UMWJ, Nov. 1, 1941, p. 4; *Proceedings 1942 Convention*, UMWA, p. 68.

36. Myron Taylor to President [Franklin D. Roosevelt], Oct. 25, 1941, RG 202, Box 165, Bituminous Coal File, N.A.

37. John L. Lewis to President [Franklin D. Roosevelt], Oct. 25, 1941, RG 202, Box 165, Bituminous Coal File, N.A.

38. Franklin D. Roosevelt to John L. Lewis, Oct. 26, 1941, Roosevelt Papers, OF 407-B, FDRL.

39. Myron Taylor to President [Franklin D. Roosevelt], Oct. 26, 1941, Roosevelt Papers, OF 407-B, FDRL; U. S. Department of Interior, *Mineral Yearbook, 1941* (Washington, D.C., 1942), p. 819.

40. John L. Lewis to President [Franklin D. Roosevelt], Oct. 27, 1941, Roosevelt Papers, OF 407-B, FDRL.

41. Franklin D. Roosevelt to John L. Lewis, Oct. 27, 1941, Roosevelt Papers, OF 407-B, FDRL.

42. NYT, Oct. 28, 1941, p. 1.

43. Franklin D. Roosevelt to Thomas W. Lamont, Nov. 10, 1941, Roosevelt Papers, OF 407-B, FDRL.

44. Sherman Minton to Franklin D. Roosevelt, Nov. 1941, Roosevelt Papers, PPF 2235, FDRL.

45. *Proceedings 1942 Convention*, UMWA, pp. 72-74; *Time* (Nov. 10, 1941), p. 19.

46. NYT, Oct. 31, 1941, p. 1.

47. *Proceedings 1942 Convention,* UMWA, pp. 75-76; NYT, Nov. 11, 1941, p. 1.

48. UMWJ, Nov. 15, 1941, p. 4.

49. "White House Press Release, November 14, 1941," Roosevelt Papers, OF 407-B, FDRL.

50. UMWJ, Dec. 1, 1941, p. 14.

51. Franklin D. Roosevelt to John L. Lewis, Philip Murray, Thomas Kennedy, Nov. 18, 1941, Roosevelt Papers, OF 407-B, FDRL.

52. "Coal Bulletin," RG 202, Box 166, File "Coal Bulletins," N.A.

53. *Ibid.*

54. *Proceedings 1942 Convention,* UMWA, pp. 79-82; UMWJ, Dec. 1, 1941, pp. 5-6.

55. NYT, Nov. 23, 1941, p. 1; Franklin D. Roosevelt to John L. Lewis, Nov. 22, 1941, and John L. Lewis to President [Franklin D. Roosevelt], Nov. 22, 1941, Roosevelt Papers, OF 407-B, FDRL.

56. *Proceedings 1942 Convention,* UMWA, pp. 82-88. In 1944, the UMWJ published parts of a reported interview with John R. Steelman in which the conciliation chief supposedly stated: "In the captive-mine case it had been decided that John L. Lewis should be licked. William H. Davis, aided and abetted by certain White House advisors, seemed to relish the job. He turned about face, changing the policies already established by the National Defense Mediation Board, and ruled that miners could not have even a union shop. It would give John L. Lewis and his mine workers too much power." The NDMB, Steelman reportedly concluded, "had established the facts, but yielded to political pressure. I merely had the fortitude to put action back of facts." (UMWJ, Nov. 15, 1944, pp. 3, 14). Steelman refuted telling this story. (NYT, Nov. 17, 1944, p. 6).

57. *Proceedings 1942 Convention,* UMWA, pp. 99-105; S. D. Alinsky, *Lewis,* pp. 248-249.

58. UMWJ, February 1, 1942, pp. 5, 12.

59. S. D. Alinsky, *Lewis,* pp. 250-253.

60. NYT, Jan. 19, 1942, p. 1.

61. Joseph C. Goulden, *Meany* (New York, 1972), pp. 90-91; John L. Lewis to Philip Murray, January 23, 1942, Adolph Germer Papers, Box 5, SHSW.

62. J. C. Goulden, *Meany,* p. 90.

63. UMWJ, Feb. 1, 1942, p. 6.

64. Joel Seidman, *American Labor from Defense to Reconversion* (Chicago, 1953), pp. 65-66; Philip Taft, *The A. F. of L. from the Death of Gompers to the Merger* (New York, 1959), p. 222.

65. S. D. Alinsky, *Lewis,* pp. 223-225.

66. Lee Pressman Interview, COHC, pp. 48-49.

67. David McDonald, *Union Man* (New York, 1969), p. 140.

68. Lee Pressman Interview, COHC, pp. 50-53.

69. D. McDonald, pp. 159-160.

70. James Robb Interview, PSULA, p. 25.

71. Lee Pressman Interview, COHC, pp. 60-61.

72. S. D. Alinsky, pp. 233-237.

73. NYT, Mar. 15, 1942, p. 32, Mar. 29, 1942, p. 1; "Statement on Financial Relationship of United Mine Workers of America and Congress of Industrial Organizations," May 26, 1942, Adolph Germer Papers, Box 23, File 58, SHSW.

74. UMWJ, Apr. 15, 1942, p. 4; S. D. Alinsky, p. 257; NYT, Apr. 25, 1942, p. 15.

75. UMWJ, Apr. 15, 1942, pp. 6-7.

76. NYT, May 3, 1942, p. 45, May 4, 1942, p. 8.

77. S. D. Alinsky, pp. 259-273; NYT, May 26, 1942, p. 14, May 27, 1942, p. 12, May 28, 1942, p. 36, May 29, 1942, p. 9.

78. Pete Phillippi to Jack O'Leary, June 22, 1942, John L. Lewis—M.A. File, UMWAA.

79. *Proceedings 1942 Convention,* UMWA, p. 191.

80. S. D. Alinsky, p. 272.

81. "Thirty-Seventh Biennial Convention of United Mine Workers of America," Wieck Papers, Box 13, ALHUA, WSU.

82. *Proceedings 1942 Convention,* UMWA, p. 470.

NOTES TO CHAPTER 18

1. UMWJ, June 15, 1942, p. 20.

2. Telegram, John L. Lewis to Thomas J. Price, July 17, 1942, UMW District 6 Papers, B9-F9, Ohio University.

3. Faber McCloskey to John Brophy, May 11, 1943, John Brophy Papers, A5-10, CUA.

4. *Proceedings 1939 Convention,* CIO, p. 6.

5. UMWJ, June 15, 1942, p. 7.

6. UMWJ, Jan. 1, 1943, p. 11.

7. UMWJ, Mar. 1, 1942, p. 10; UMWJ, Oct. 1, 1942, p. 10; UMWJ, Sept. 1, 1944, p. 8.

8. UMWJ, Mar. 15, 1943, p. 18.

9. UMWJ, Aug. 15, 1943, p. 6.

10. UMWJ, Apr. 15, 1943, p. 11.

11. UMWJ, Apr. 1, 1943, p. 7.

12. *Ibid.*

13. UMWJ, March 15, 1943, p. 3.

14. UMWJ, Feb. 15, 1943, p. 4.

15. Nelson Lichtenstein, "Industrial Unionism Under the No-Strike Pledge: A Study of the CIO During the Second World War" (Ph.D. Dissertation, University of California, Berkeley, 1974), pp. 189-192, 220-221.

16. W. Jett Lauck to John L. Lewis, Feb. 24, 1943, W. Jett Lauck Papers, Collection 4742, Box 360, File "Coal Case—1943," UVL.

17. UMWJ, Mar. 15, 1943, pp. 9, 17.

18. UMWJ, Apr. 1, 1943, p. 7.

19. James A. Wechsler, *Labor Baron* (New York, 1944), p. 3.

20. "Report on Anthracite Coal Strike," Jan. 14, 1943, RG 202, NWLB, Box 165, N.A. For the fullest account of the Anthracite wildcats see J. R. Sperry, "Rebellion within the Ranks: Pennsylvania Anthracite, John L. Lewis, and the Coal Strike of 1943," *Pennsylvania History*, XL, 3 (July 1973), pp. 293-312.

21. John L. Lewis to George W. Taylor, Jan. 13, 1943, and Telegram, John L. Lewis to All Local Unions, Districts 1, 7, and 9, Jan. 15, 1943, RG 202, NWLB, Series 13; UMWJ, Feb. 1, 1943, p. 7.

22. Telegram, Thomas Kennedy to Franklin D. Roosevelt, Jan. 19, 1943, and John L. Lewis to Roosevelt, Jan. 19, 1943, Roosevelt Papers, OF 407B, Box 28, FDRL; "Memorandum," Jan. 21, 1943, RG 202, NWLB, Series 13, N.A; N. Lichtenstein, pp. 449-452; Saul D. Alinsky, *John L. Lewis* (New York, 1949), pp. 282-283.

23. "Statement of Mr. John L. Lewis, President, United Mine Workers of America-CIO [*sic*]," RG 202, NWLB, Series 13, N.A. Statement was published in UMWJ, Feb. 1, 1943, so that Lewis's views circulated widely among the miners.

24. "Memorandum to Mr. Lewis," Feb. 24, 1943, and W. Jett Lauck to John L. Lewis, Mar. 21, 1943. W. Jett Lauck Papers, Collection 4742, Box 360, File "Coal Case—1943," UVL; Faber McCloskey to John Brophy, May 11, 1943, John Brophy Papers, A5-10, CUA.

25. "Memorandum to Mr. Lewis," Feb. 24, 1943, W. Jett Lauck to John L. Lewis, Mar. 21, 1943, and W. Jett Lauck to John L. Lewis, Apr. 4, 1943, all in W. Jett Lauck Papers, Collection 4742, Box 360, File "Coal Case—1943," UVL; Colston E. Warne, "Coal—The First Major Test of the Little Steel Formula," in Colston E. Warne *et al., Yearbook of American Labor*, Vol. 1, *War Labor Policies* (New York, 1945), pp. 279-280.

26. UMWJ, Mar. 15, 1943, pp. 9, 17-21.

27. NYT, Mar. 16, 1943.

28. Warne, p. 281; Thomas C. Clapp, "The Bituminous Coal Strike of 1943" (Ph.D. Dissertation, University of Toledo, 1974), pp. 89-90.

29. "Press Release," Mar. 22, 1943, Roosevelt Papers, FDRL; T. C. Clapp, pp. 92-93.

30. W. Jett Lauck to John L. Lewis, Apr. 2, 1943; Lauck to Lewis, Apr. 4, 1943; and Lauck to Lewis, Apr. 7, 1943, all in W. Jett Lauck Papers, Collection 4742, Box 360, File "Coal Case—1943," UVL.

31. NYT, Apr. 5, 1943, and Apr. 6, 1943.

32. UMWJ, Apr. 15, 1943, p. 4.

33. S. D. Alinsky, pp. 297-298; Proceedings 1944 Convention, UMWA, pp. 142-146.

34. S. D. Alinsky, p. 298.

35. Richard Polenberg, War and Society (Philadelphia, 1972), p. 165.

36. UMWJ, Apr. 1, 1943, p. 6.

37. "Memorandum," Apr. 29, 1943, Roosevelt Papers, PPF 3024, FDRL; Senator Joseph F. Guffey to M. H. McIntyre, Feb. 13, 1942, Roosevelt Papers, PPF 451, FDRL; Franklin D. Roosevelt to James G. Patton, June 28, 1943, Roosevelt Papers, PPF 471, FDRL; R. Polenberg, pp. 163-164; J. A. Wechsler, p. 246.

38. UMWJ, Apr. 1, 1943, p. 8.

39. William H. Davis to President Franklin D. Roosevelt, Apr. 28, 1943, Roosevelt Papers, OF 407-B, FDRL; UMWJ, May 1, 1943, pp. 3-5.

40. S. D. Alinsky, p. 299; C. E. Warne, p. 285; William H. Davis to President Franklin D. Roosevelt, Apr. 28, 1943, Roosevelt Papers, OF 407-B, FDRL.

41. "Press Release," Apr. 29, 1943, Roosevelt Papers, FDRL.

42. S. D. Alinsky, p. 300; UMWJ, May 15, 1943, p. 6.

43. R. Polenberg, p. 164.

44. "Press Release," May 1, 1943, Roosevelt Papers, FDRL.

45. The fullest account of the Lewis-Ickes May 2 meeting is in T. C. Clapp, pp. 145-147. He misdates the conference, however, and at times is confused. Harold Ickes commented on the meeting in "Crisis in Coal," Collier's (September 4, 1943), p. 57. Most likely because of his dispute with the NWLB, he claims that: "I made it clear that I had no power to consider wages and that I would not assume that I had such power." However, it was not until the following day that Roosevelt defined the government's position toward the union in Memorandum, McIntyre to Franklin D. Roosevelt, May 3, 1943, Roosevelt Papers, OF 407-B, Box 29, FDRL.

46. UMWJ, May 15, 1943, p. 3.

47. "Press Release," May 2, 1943, Roosevelt Papers, FDRL.

48. Memorandum, McIntyre to Tully, May 3, 1943, and Memorandum, McIntyre to Franklin D. Roosevelt, March 3, 1943, Roosevelt Papers, OF 407-B, Box 29, FDRL. In a 1942 dispute between the Brotherhood of Locomotive Firemen and Engineers and the Toledo, Peoria, and Western Railroad, the government seized the railroad on March 22, 1942, and then the federal manager, John W. Barrigan, negotiated an accord with the union that the NWLB approved, T. C. Clapp, pp. 148-149.

49. UMWJ, May 15, 1943, pp. 4-5; C. E. Warne, p. 286.

50. Proceedings 1944 Convention, UMWA, pp. 163-165. A. F. of L. and CIO representatives on the NWLB threatened to leave the board along with employers' representatives if Lewis was allowed to circumvent its authority. They were willing to grant the miners a liberal award, but only if Lewis was restrained. Memorandum from Malcolm Ross and Richard Deverall to Harold Ickes, May 17, 1943, Ickes Papers, Secretary of Interior Files, Box 148, L.C.

51. NYT, May 18, 1943.

52. J. A. Wechsler, p. 244; Adolph Germer Diary, Saturday, May 15, 1943, Adolph Germer Papers, Box 25, SHSW.

53. UMWJ, June 1, 1943, pp. 15-17.

54. The most thorough analysis of the NWLB's May 25 Directive Order can be found in T. C. Clapp, pp. 111-121 and 157-162. After an extensive review of the statistical data available to the board, Clapp (p. 121) concludes: "Certainly, had the coal dispute been considered on its own merits, the miners would have qualified for wage increases in accordance with the wartime policy of correcting substandard wages."

55. "In the Matter of Operators Negotiating Committee, Appalachian Joint Conference and Operators Negotiating Committee, Southern Appalachian Joint Wage Conference and United Mine Workers of America, May 25, 1943," RG 202, NWLB, Box 99, N.A.

56. UMWJ, June 1, 1943, pp. 3-5.

57. Ibid.; Proceedings 1944 Convention, UMWA, pp. 168-169; NYT, June 1, 1943.

58. T. C. Clapp, p. 173.

59. Wayne Morse to President Franklin D. Roosevelt, June 2, 1943, Roosevelt Papers, OF 407-B, File "Coal Strike-1943," FDRL.

60. T. C. Clapp, p. 179; UMWJ, June 15, 1943, pp. 14-16; W. Jett Lauck Diary, June 4, 1943, W. Jett Lauck Papers, UVL.

61. UMWJ, June 15, 1943, pp. 14-16.

62. Ibid.; T. C. Clapp, pp. 185-188.

63. N. Lichtenstein, pp. 496-505.

64. Proceedings 1944 Convention, UMWA, pp. 174-181.

65. Proceedings 1944 Convention, UMWA, pp. 179-181.

66. W. Jett Lauck Diary, June 20, 1943, W. Jett Lauck Papers, UVL.

67. "Memorandum of June 21 Coal Conference," Gardner Papers, Box 4, file Coal (1943), Truman Library.

68. "Memorandum of June 22 Coal Conference," Gardner Papers, Box 4, file Coal (1943), Truman Library.

69. UMWJ, July 15, 1943, pp. 3-4.

70. Ibid., p. 8; NYT, June 24, 1943.

71. NYT, June 26, 1943.

72. S. D. Alinsky, pp. 315-316; for statements of rank-and-file discontent with Lewis's handling of the situation, see NYT, June 24, 1943.

73. NYT, July 21, 1943; John L. Lewis to Abe Fortas, June 29, 1943, and "Memorandum of August 27, 1943," by T. J. Thomas, RG 245 D/I, Box 2371, N.A.

74. T. C. Clapp, pp. 206-214. Ickes also tried to modify the administration's interpretation of the punitive provisions of the Smith-Connally act. See Harold Ickes to President Franklin D. Roosevelt, July 28, 1943, and Ickes to William Davis, July 27, 1943, Gardner Papers, Box 4, file Coal (1943), Truman Library.

75. C. E. Warne, p. 293.

76. UMWJ, Aug. 1, 1943, pp. 3-7.

77. Proceedings 1944 Convention, UMWA, pp. 195-205.

78. UMWJ, Oct. 1, 1943, pp. 3-5; Telegram, John L. Lewis to Local Unions in Alabama, District 20, and Indiana, District 11, October 16, 1943, RG 202, NWLB, Series #3, N.A.

79. UMWJ, Sept. 15, 1943, p. 6; UMWJ, Oct. 1, 1943, pp. 8-9; UMWJ, Oct. 15, 1943, p. 5.

80. C. E. Warne, pp. 295-296; Telegram, John L. Lewis to Local Unions in Alabama, District 20, and Indiana, District 11, October 16, 1943, RG 202, NWLB, Series #3, N.A.

81. "Decision In Matter of Illinois Coal Operators Association and the United Mine

Workers of America and District 12, UMWA, October 26, 1943," Roosevelt Papers, OF 407-B, File "Coal Strike—1943," FDRL; C. E. Warne, p. 296.

82. William H. Davis to President Franklin D. Roosevelt, Oct. 28, 1943, Roosevelt Papers, OF 407-B, File "Coal Strike—1943," FDRL.

83. "Press Release, Franklin D. Roosevelt to William Davis, October 29, 1943," Roosevelt Papers, OF 407-B, File "Coal Strike—1943," FDRL.

84. John L. Lewis, "Not Guilty," *Collier's* (July 15, 1944), pp. 12, 49.

85. UMWJ, Nov. 15, 1943, p. 6.

86. W. Jett Lauck Diary, Nov. 4, 1943, W. Jett Lauck Papers, UVL.

87. "Memorandum of Agreement, November 3, 1943," and Harold Ickes to William Davis, Nov. 12, 1943, RG 202, Box 99, File "William Davis, Coal," N.A.; William Davis to Harold Ickes, Nov. 5, 1943, Roosevelt Papers, OF 407-B, File "Coal Strike—1943," FDRL; C. E. Warne, pp. 296-298.

88. C. E. Warne, p. 298.

NOTES TO CHAPTER 19

1. National War Labor Board, Editorial Digest, May 25, 1945, RG 202, Box 165, File "Anthracite Coal, 1945", N.A.; Wellington Roe, *Juggernaut* (Philadelphia, 1948).

2. NYT, Oct. 3, 1946, p. 8, Oct. 26, 1946, p. 1; *New Republic* (November 4, 1946), p. 571. These charges have been most recently revived in Ladislas Farrago, *The Game of the Foxes* (New York, 1971), pp. 351-365. See Ch. 12,   and Ch. 13, for earlier allegations linking Lewis to Nazi diplomacy.

3. John Brophy to Paul and Bea, June 10, 1943, John Brophy Papers, Box A5-10, File "1943, CIO-Lewis," CUA.

4. James B. Patton to Franklin D. Roosevelt, June 19, 1943, Roosevelt Papers, PPF 471, FDRL.

5. Franklin D. Roosevelt to James G. Patton, June 28, 1943, Roosevelt Papers, PPF 471, FDRL.

6. Reprinted in NYT, May 27, 1946, p. 3.

7. Louis Stark, "The Warwick of the House of Labor," NYT Magazine (February 10, 1946), pp. 12, 51.

8. NYT, December 8, 1946, p. 1.

9. Senator Joseph F. Guffey to M. H. McIntyre, February 13, 1942, Roosevelt Papers, PPF 451, FDRL; Memorandum, Franklin D. Roosevelt to Grace Tully, May 10, 1943, including attached unsigned memorandum of April 29, 1943, Roosevelt Papers, PPF 3024, FDRL.

10. Garet Garrett to John L. Lewis, March 29, 1944; Lewis to Garrett, March 31, 1944; Lewis to Herbert Hoover, May 22, 1944; and Memorandum, May 26, 1944, all Herbert Hoover Papers, "Post-Presidency Individual—John L. Lewis," Hoover Library.

11. NYT, Sept. 16, 1944, p. 1.

12. Elliot Janeway, "Trial and Error: John L. Lewis Plays a Lone Hand for High Stakes," *Fortune* (July 1943), pp. 64, 90.

13. Cyrus Eaton to John L. Lewis, Nov. 21, 1944, and Lewis to Eaton, Nov. 24, 1944, JLL-Personal File, 1944, UMWAA.

14. H. L. Derby to John L. Lewis, Nov. 20, 1944, JLL-Personal File, 1944, UMWAA.

15. NYT, Jan. 21, 1944, p. 34; NYT, Jan. 24, 1944, p. 17; Edwin A. Lahey, "The

AFL and Lewis," *New Republic* (Feb. 7, 1944), pp. 172-173; NYT, Apr. 12, 1944, p. 38, NYT, May 1, 1944, p. 3.

16. William Green to John L. Lewis, May 8, 1944, and Lewis to Green, May 8, 1944, Misc. File, UMWAA.

17. Dale Kramer, "John L. Lewis: Last Bid? His Adventures with the Dairy Farmers," *Harper's Magazine* (Aug., 1942), pp. 275-283; James A. Wechsler, *Labor Baron* (New York, 1944), pp. 183-191.

18. W. Roe, p. 195.

19. Edward A. Wieck, "Thirty-Eighth Constitutional Convention of the United Mine Workers of America," Wieck Papers, Collection #89, Box 13, ALHUA, WSU.

20. *Ibid.*, J. A. Wechsler, pp. 78-79.

21. Edward A. Wieck, "Midwest and Eastern Conference on Autonomy and Self-Government, United Mine Workers of America, Cincinnati, Ohio, July 2, 1944," p. 6, Edward A. Wieck Papers, Collection #89, Box 12, ALHUA, WSU; *Newsweek* (September 25, 1944), pp. 68-69.

22. E. A. Wieck, "Midwest and Eastern Conference on Autonomy and Self-Government, United Mine Workers of America, Cincinnati, Ohio, July 2, 1944," pp. 1-2, Edward A. Wieck Papers, Collection #89, Box 12, ALHUA, WSU.

23. *Ibid.*, pp. 2-20.

24. *Ibid.*, pp. 10-12.

25. *Ibid.*, pp. 14-15.

26. NYT, Sept. 13, 1944, p. 13; Edward A. Wieck to Mary van Kleeck, Sept. 11, 1944, Edward A. Wieck Papers, Collection #89, Box 13, ALHUA, WSU.

27. *Proceedings 1944 Convention*, UMWA, pp. 316-337; Edward A. Wieck, "Thirty-Eighth Constitutional Convention of the United Mine Workers of America," Edward A. Wieck Papers, Collection #89, Box 13, ALHUA, WSU.

28. *Ibid.*

29. *Ibid.*

30. *Ibid.*; NYT, May 23, 1948, p. 17.

31. W. Jett Lauck Diary, Feb. 28-Mar. 1, 1945, W. Jett Lauck Papers, UVL.

32. NYT, Apr. 13, 1945, p. 16; UMWJ, Apr. 15, 1945, pp. 3-7; Colston E. Warne, "Industrial Relations in Coal," in Colston E. Warne *et al.*, *Labor in Postwar America* (New York, 1949), pp. 368-370.

33. Editorial Digest, National War Labor Board, RG 202, Box 165, File "Anthracite Coal-1945," N.A.

34. UMWJ, Oct. 1, 1945, p. 3; NYT, Sept. 29, 1945, p. 1; UMWJ, Nov. 1, 1945, p. 5; C. E. Warne, pp. 370-371.

35. UMWJ, Nov. 15, 1945, p. 19; *Time* (Nov. 19, 1945), pp. 21-22.

36. Louis Stark, "The Warwick of the House of Labor," NYT Magazine (Feb. 10, 1946), p. 51.

37. UMWJ, Mar. 1, 1946, p. 4.

38. William Green to John L. Lewis, Dec. 19, 1944; Lewis to Green, Jan. 13, 1945; Green to Lewis, Feb. 9, 1945; Lewis to Green, Feb. 10, 1945; Telegram, Green to Lewis, Feb. 13, 1945; Telegram, Lewis to Green, Feb. 13, 1945; and Lewis to Green, Feb. 14, 1945, all in Misc. File, UMWAA; NYT, Jan. 21, 1945, p. 1.

39. John L. Lewis to William Green, Jan. 12, 1946, and Lewis to Green, Jan. 17, 1946, Misc. File, UMWAA.

40. William Green to John L. Lewis, Feb. 2, 1946, Misc. File, UMWAA; UMWJ, Feb. 15, 1946, p. 3.

41. Rex Lauck, ed., *John L. Lewis and the International Union* (Washington, D.C., 1952), p. 21; Edward A. Wieck, "Thirty-Eighth Constitutional Convention of the United

Mine Workers of America," Edward A. Wieck Papers, Collection #89, Box 13, ALHUA, WSU.

42. NYT, Apr. 10, 1946, p. 18, Apr. 3, 1946, p. 1, Mar. 23, 1946, p. 14.

43. UMWJ, Apr. 15, 1946, p. 5.

44. NYT, Apr. 11, 1946, p. 1.

45. NYT, May 5, 1946, p. 1, May 6, 1946, p. 1.

46. UMWJ, May 15, 1946, p. 3.

47. "Statement by the President, May 16, 1946," Truman Papers, OF 407-B, Box 1159, Truman Library.

48. "Agreement," John W. Gibson Papers, Box 5, File "Labor-coal," Truman Library.

49. UMWJ, July 15, 1946, pp. 3-4.

50. NYT, Sept. 14, 1946, p. 1; UMWJ, Sept. 15, 1946, pp. 3-4; UMWJ, Oct. 1, 1946, pp. 3-4.

51. NYT, September 29, 1946, p. 19; W. Jett Lauck Diary, October 3-6, 1946, Lauch Papers, UVL.

52. John L. Lewis to J. A. Krug, Oct. 21, 1946, Warner Gardner Papers, Box 4, File "Coal (1946-7)," Truman Library.

53. N. H. Collisson to John L. Lewis, Oct. 22, 1946; Telegram, J. A. Krug to Lewis, Oct. 22, 1946; and Lewis to Krug, Oct. 22, 1946, all in RG 245, N.A.; Memorandum, E. D. Boyle to the Under Secretary, Oct. 25, 1946, Clark M. Clifford Papers, Box 3, File "Coal Case #1," Truman Library.

54. Memorandum, by E. D. Doyle, Nov. 16, 1946, Warner Gardner Papers, Box 4, File "Coal (1946-7)," Truman Library.

55. "Minutes of the Meetings of the Coal Mines Administrator, U. S. Department of the Interior, and Representatives of the United Mine Workers of America," Nov. 1, 4, 6, 7, 11, 1946, Warner Gardner Papers, Box 4, File "Coal (1946-7)," Truman Library.

56. Matthew S. Connelly to Ed O'Connell, Nov. 7, 1946, Harry S Truman Papers, OF, Box 935, file 290, Truman Library; *New Republic* (Dec. 16, 1946), pp. 790-791; *U. S. News* (Nov. 29, 1946), p. 52.

57. Memorandum J. A. Krug to President Harry S Truman, Nov. 13, 1946, Clark M. Clifford Papers, Box 3, File "Coal Case #1," Truman Library.

58. "Outline of Testimony, Secretary of the Interior, Nov. 26, 1946," RG 245, N.A.; UMWJ, Nov. 15, 1946, p. 11; J. A. Krug to John L. Lewis, Nov. 14, 1946, Warner Gardner Papers, Box 4, File "Coal (1946-7)," Truman Library.

59. Tris Coffin, "John L's Last Stand," *Nation* (Dec. 7, 1946), pp. 639-641. John L. Lewis to J. A. Krug, Nov. 15, 1946; "Press Release," Nov. 15, 1946; Lewis to Krug, Nov. 15, 1946, and Krug to Lewis, Nov. 15, 1946, all in Warner Gardner Papers, Box 4, File "Coal (1946-7)," Truman Library.

60. Memorandum, re *United States vs. Frank J. Hayes, et al.*, Clark M. Clifford Papers, Box 4, File "Coal Case #3," Truman Library; NYT, Nov. 18, 1946, p. 1.

61. NYT, Nov. 19, 1946, p. 1.

62. *Ibid.*; "1946-Bituminous Coal Strike Chronology," Warner Gardner Papers, Box 4, File "Coal (1946-7)," Truman Library.

63. NYT, Nov. 21, 1946, p. 1, Nov. 22, 1946, p. 1, Nov. 23, 1946, p. 1.

64. Jules Abels, *The Truman Scandals* (Chicago, 1956), p. 177; George G. Moore to John L. Lewis, Nov. 23, 1946, JLL-Personal Files, UMWAA; NYT, Dec. 1, 1946, p. 1.

65. NYT, Nov. 28, 1946, p. 1; W. Roe, p. 189.

66. *Time* (Dec. 16, 1946), pp. 22-24.

67. NYT, Dec. 8, 1946, p. 1.

68. C. E. Warne, pp. 374-379; NYT, Mar. 7, 1947, p. 1; NYT, Mar. 20, 1947, p. 1.

69. *Time* (Dec. 2, 1946), pp. 19-20; *Time* (Dec. 16, 1946), pp. 22-24; NYT, Nov. 26, 1946, p. 1, Nov. 28, 1946, p. 1, Dec. 14, 1946, p. 10.

70. Robert S. Allen and William V. Shannon, *The Truman Merry-go-Round* (New York, 1950), p. 26; Booth Mooney, *The Politicians: 1945-1960* (Philadelphia, 1970), p. 36.

NOTES TO CHAPTER 20

1. NYT, June 10, 1949, p. 1; Oct. 6, 1950, p. 18.

2. *Proceedings 1948 Convention*, UMWA, p. 13.

3. For the political calculations behind Truman's attack on Lewis see Memorandum J. A. Krug to the President, Nov. 13, 1946, Clark M. Clifford Papers, Box 3, File "Coal Case #1," Truman Library.

4. NYT, Sept. 23, 1948, p. 20. For an example of Truman's mindset see text of a speech he wrote, reprinted in Cabell Phillips, *The Truman Presidency* (Baltimore, 1966), p. 116.

5. NYT, Oct. 6, 1950, p. 18.

6. *Testimony of John L. Lewis Before Congressional Committees on Centralia Explosion* (Washington, D.C., Labor's Non-Partisan League, 1947), pp. 10-22.

7. *Ibid.*

8. *Ibid.*; John L. Lewis to Captain N. H. Collisson, Apr. 5, 1947, RG 245, N.A.; Collisson to Lewis, Apr. 5, 1947, Warner Gardner Papers, Box 4, File "Coal (1946-7)," Truman Library; *Proceedings 1948 Convention*, UMWA, pp. 50-57; Walter Millis, ed., *The Forrestal Diaries* (New York, 1951), p. 260.

9. UMWJ, Apr. 1, 1947, pp. 6-7; Josephine Roche to John L. Lewis, Josephine Roche Papers, Box 25, UCL.

10. UMWJ, Apr. 1, 1947, pp. 6-7; NYT, Apr. 23, 1948, p. 18, Mar. 21, 1949, p. 1, Mar. 25, 1949, p. 1; James Boyd file, Josephine Roche Papers, Box 25, UCL; Sam Stavisky, "The Lady who Licked John L. Lewis," *Collier's* (June 4, 1949), pp. 14-15, 68-70; UMWJ, June 15, 1959, pp. 5-7, 13.

11. UMWJ, Mar. 15, 1947, pp. 5-6, 13-21.

12. *Proceedings 1948 Convention*, UMWA, pp. 58-69; NYT, June 3, 1947, p. 5, June 28, 1947, p. 1; UMWJ, July 15, 1947, pp. 3-5.

13. "National Bituminous Coal Wage Agreement of 1947," UMWAA.

14. *Proceedings 1947 Convention*, A. F. of L., pp. 486-493.

15. *Ibid.*

16. "Executive Memorandum," Oct. 21, 1947, Misc. file, UMWAA; NYT, Nov. 2, 1947, p. 20; UMWJ, Nov. 1, 1947, pp. 3-4; NYT, Dec. 13, 1947, p. 1.

17. "Proceedings of International Executive Board Meeting," Dec. 12, 1947, pp. 311-330, Misc. File, UMWAA; *Proceedings 1952 Convention*, UMWA, p. 394.

18. *Proceedings 1952 Convention*, UMWA, pp. 198-200; UMWJ, May 1, 1953, pp. 11-13.

19. "Report to the President on the Labor Dispute in the Bituminous Coal Industry by the Board of Inquiry created by Executive Order No. 9939," Harry S Truman Papers, OF, Box 1159, file 407-B, Truman Library.

20. *Proceedings 1948 Convention*, UMWA, pp. 78-82.

21. *Ibid.*; NYT, Mar. 17, 1948, p. 1.

22. NYT, Mar. 16, 1948, p. 1, Mar. 17, 1948, p. 1.

23. *Proceedings 1948 Convention,* UMWA, pp. 85-86; NYT, Mar. 21, 1948, p. 1.
24. *Proceedings 1948 Convention*, UMWA, p. 87.
25. *Ibid.*, pp. 87-88.
26. *Ibid.*, pp. 89-90.
27. UMWJ, Apr. 15, 1948, p. 10; UMWJ, Apr. 1, 1948, pp. 3, 12; NYT, Mar. 27, 1948, p. 1, Mar. 29, 1948, p. 1, Mar. 31, 1948, p. 1.
28. "Report to the President on the Labor Dispute in the Bituminous Coal Industry by the Board of Inquiry created by Executive Order 9939," Harry S Truman Papers, OF, Box 1159, file 407-B, Truman Library.
29. Harry S Truman to Attorney General Tom C. Clark, Apr. 3, 1948, Harry S Truman Papers, OF, Box 1159, file 407-B, Truman Library; NYT, Apr. 4, 1948, pp. 1, 33-34.
30. UMWJ, Apr. 15, 1948, p. 10.
31. *U.S. News & World Report* (Apr. 23, 1948), pp. 34-35; NYT, Apr. 11, 1948, p. 1.
32. UMWJ, Apr. 15, 1948, p. 3; *Proceedings 1948 Convention,* UMWA, p. 102.
33. NYT, Apr. 21, 1948, p. 1; NYT, Apr. 22, 1948, p. 1; *Proceedings 1948 Convention,* UMWA, p. 103.
34. UMWJ, May 1, 1948, pp. 3-4; NYT, Apr. 22, 1948, p. 1, Apr. 29, 1948, p. 1, Apr. 30, 1948, p. 1.
35. NYT, Apr. 13, 1948, p. 24, Apr. 14, 1948, p. 19, Apr. 17, 1948, p. 8.
36. NYT, Aug. 2, 1949, p. 1, Aug. 19, 1949, p. 1, Aug. 27, 1949, p. 6.
37. *Proceedings 1948 Convention,* UMWA, pp. 104-120; NYT, May 20, 1948, p. 1.
38. *Proceedings 1948 Convention,* UMWA, pp. 120-125; UMWJ, June 1, 1948, pp. 3, 10-11; UMWJ, June 15, 1948, pp. 3-4; NYT, June 5, 1948, p. 1.
39. *Proceedings 1948 Convention,* UMWA, pp 126-143; UMWJ, June 15, 1948, pp. 3-4.
40. UMWJ, July 1, 1948, pp. 3-5; NYT, June 23, 1948, p. 1; *Proceedings 1948 Convention,* UMWA, p. 145; "National Bituminous Coal Wage Agreement of 1948," Misc. File, UMWAA.
41. *Proceedings 1948 Convention,* UMWA, pp. 146-147.
42. Sam H. Shurr and Bruce C. Netschert, *Energy in the American Economy, 1850-1875* (Baltimore, 1960), pp. 74-83.
43. NYT, Apr. 5, 1959, p. 33.
44. For the 1949 fight for pensions in the steel industry see Vincent D. Sweeney, *The United Steelworkers of America* (Pittsburgh, 1956), pp. 81-93.
45. *Proceedings 1952 Convention,* UMWA, pp. 31-42.
46. *Ibid.,* p. 43.
47. UMWJ, June 15, 1949, pp. 3-4.
48. *Proceedings 1952 Convention*, UMWA, pp. 148-150.
49. *Ibid.*, pp. 63-70.
50. NYT, Mar. 5, 1950, VI, p. 1.
51. *Proceedings 1952 Convention,* UMWA, pp. 47-49.
52. *Ibid.*, pp. 49-52, 71; UMWJ, Oct. 1, 1949, pp. 3-4; NYT, July 26, 1949, p. 2, Sept. 17, 1949, p. 1.
53. UMWJ, Oct. 1, 1949, p. 3.
54. UMWJ, Oct. 15, 1949, p. 3.
55. *Proceedings 1952 Convention,* UMWA, pp. 81-83; UMWJ, Nov. 1, 1949, p. 3.
56. *Proceedings 1952 Convention,* UMWA, pp. 90-95; UMWJ, Nov. 15, 1949, pp. 3-4; Cyrus S. Ching to the President, Nov. 16, 1949, Harry S Truman Papers, OF, Box 1159, file 407-B, Truman Library.
57. *Proceedings 1952 Convention,* UMWA, p. 96; NYT, Jan. 8, 1950, IV, p. 10.
58. NYT, Jan. 9, 1950, p. 1; Jan. 12, 1950, p. 1.

59. NYT, Jan. 8, 1950, IV p. 10; Jan. 21, 1950, p. 1, Jan. 26, 1950, p. 1; Josephine Roche to John L. Lewis, Jan. 17, 1950; Roche to Lewis, Jan. 16, 1950; ''Press Release,'' Jan. 13, 1950, Department of the Interior Information Service; and Chicago *Tribune*, Jan. 14, 1950, all in Josephine Roche Papers, Box 25, UCL; *Proceedings 1952 Convention*, UMWA, pp. 98-99.

60. NYT, Jan. 27, 1950, p. 1.

61. President Harry S Truman to George H. Love, John L. Lewis, Harry M. Moses, and Joseph E. Moody, Jan. 31, 1950, Harry S Truman Papers, OF, Box 1159, file 407-B, Truman Library.

62. ''Press Conference, John L. Lewis, February 2, 1950,'' and ''Love Press Conference, February 2, 1950,'' Harry S Truman Papers, OF, Box 1159, file 407-B, Truman Library.

63. John L. Lewis to Harry S Truman, Feb. 4, 1950, and ''White House Press Release, February 4, 1950,'' Harry S Truman Papers, OF, Box 1159, file 407-B, Truman Library.

64. *Proceedings 1952 Convention*, UMWA, pp. 105-116.

65. *Ibid.*, pp. 117-118.

66. *Ibid.*, pp. 118, 125; NYT, Feb. 12, 1950, p. 1, Feb. 18, 1950, p. 1.

67. Josephine Roche to John L. Lewis, Feb. 20, 1950, Josephine Roche Papers, Box 25, UCL; NYT, Feb. 21, 1950, p. 1; *Proceedings 1952 Convention*, UMWA, pp. 123-124; UMWJ, Mar. 1, 1950, pp. 3-4.

68. ''White House Press Release, March 3, 1950,'' Harry S Truman Papers, OF, Box 1159, file 407-B, Truman Library.

69. ''National Bituminous Coal Wage Agreement of 1950,'' UMWAA.

70. *Proceedings 1952 Convention*, UMWA, pp. 126-127.

NOTES TO CHAPTER 21

1. NYT, May 21, 1949, p. 1.

2. UMWJ, Nov. 1, 1949, p. 5.

3. UMWJ, Mar. 15, 1950, p. 7; UMWJ, Apr. 15, 1950, pp. 3-4; UMWJ, Sept. 1, 1950, p. 3; UMWJ, July 1, 1951, pp. 6, 11-13.

4. UMWJ, Mar. 15, 1950, p. 7.

5. NYT, Dec. 22, 1953, p. 1; *Fortune* (Aug., 1954), pp. 48-50.

6. *Fortune* (Aug., 1954), pp. 48-50; David McDonald, *Union Man* (New York, 1969), pp. 241-242; A. H. Raskin, ''John L. Lewis—'A Glorious Anachronism','' NYT Magazine (Feb. 13, 1955), pp. 15, 33-35.

7. UMWJ, Sept. 15, 1955, pp. 3-6.

8. John Owens to James Carey, Nov. 30, 1955, and Carey to John L. Lewis, Nov. 30, 1955, CIO Secretary-Treasurers' Office Collection, #185, Box 34, ALHUA, WSU.

9. Joseph E. Finley, *The Corrupt Kingdom* (New York, 1972), p. 208.

10. *Proceedings 1956 Convention*, UMWA, p. 79.

11. J. E. Finley, p. 170; James Ridgeway, *The Last Play* (New York, 1973), p. 208.

12. *Fortune* (Sept., 1962), p. 102.

13. UMWJ, Feb. 15, 1957, pp. 10-12.

14. J. Ridgeway, pp. 14-19; UMWJ, Feb. 15, 1957, p. 11.

15. UMWJ, Feb. 1, 1951, pp. 3-4; *Proceedings 1954 Convention*, UMWA, pp. 150-154; *Business Week* (Jan. 27, 1951), pp. 112-114.

16. *Proceedings 1952 Convention*, UMWA, pp. 22-51; UMWJ, Oct. 1, 1952, pp. 3-4.

17. *Proceedings 1956 Convention*, UMWA, pp. 51-53.

18. *Ibid.*, pp. 53-59.

19. *Ibid.*, pp. 66-71.

20. *Ibid.*, p. 62.

21. John L. Lewis to Harry Moses, Oct. 21, 1952, Harry S Truman Papers, OF, Box 6159, File 407-B, Truman Library.

22. *Proceedings 1956 Convention,* UMWA, pp. 73-75.

23. *Ibid.*, pp. 77-78.

24. Burt Cochran, *Harry Truman and the Crisis Presidency* (New York, 1973), pp. 342-346.

25. UMWJ, Nov. 15, 1952, pp. 3-4; UMWJ, Dec. 15, 1952, pp. 3-5.

26. *Proceedings 1956 Convention*, UMWA, pp. 112-114.

27. *Ibid.*

28. *Ibid.*, p. 117; UMWJ, Dec. 15, 1952, p. 3.

29. UMWJ, Nov. 1, 1954, p. 5.

30. *Proceedings 1960 Convention,* UMWA, p. 31.

31. UMWJ, Apr. 1, 1958, pp. 3-5; UMWJ, Aug. 1, 1959, pp. 3-4, 14-18.

32. UMWJ, Aug. 15, 1956, pp. 3-4, 6, 10-14.

33. UMWJ, May 15, 1958, pp. 3-4, 10-11; UMWJ, Mar. 1, 1959, pp. 3-4.

34. UMWJ, Nov. 15, 1959, p. 5.

35. *Ibid.*, p. 6.

36. NYT, June 30, 1953, p. 32.

37. Brit Hume, *Death in the Mines* (New York, 1971), p. 27.

38. J. E. Finley, pp. 136-158; Trevor Armbrister, *Act of Vengeance* (New York, 1975), pp. 82-85; Nat Caldwell and Gene S. Graham, "The Strange Romance between John L. Lewis and Cyrus Eaton," *Harper's Magazine* (Dec., 1961), pp. 25-32; T. N. Bethel, *Conspiracy in Coal* (Huntington, West Va., n.d.).

39. T. Armbrister, pp. 82-83.

40. *Ibid.*, p. 85.

41. *Ibid.*, p. 67; J. E. Finley, pp. 144-145.

42. J. E. Finley, pp. 153-154.

43. For Lewis's pre-1950s financial activities see: NYT, Apr. 23, 1949, p. 10; Adolph Germer to Bernard B. Carvicher, June 25, 1925, Adolph Germer Papers, Box 9, SHSW; *Facts for Miners*, Adolph Germer Papers, Box 23, File 57, SHSW; Josephine Roche Papers, Box 25, UCL.

44. NYT, Apr. 17, 1949, p. 78; Washington *Post*, Mar. 11, 1949; *U.S. News & World Report* (June 30, 1950), p. 39; J. E. Finley, p. 198.

45. *U.S. News & World Report* (Sept. 2, 1955), pp. 58-61; *U.S. News & World Report* (June 29, 1956), pp. 58-60; J. E. Finley, pp. 159-163.

46. *Proceedings 1960 Convention,* UMWA, pp. 257-261.

47. *Ibid.*, pp. 257-262.

48. *Ibid.*, pp. 256-258.

49. *Ibid.*, pp. 259-261.

50. NYT, Apr. 17, 1960, p. 7.

51. T. N. Bethel, p. 22; J. E. Finley, p. 162; *Forbes* (May 1, 1956), pp. 17-22.

52. Nat Caldwell and Gene S. Graham, "The Strange Romance between John L. Lewis and Cyrus Eaton," *Harper's Magazine* (Dec., 1961), pp. 29-30.

53. Cyrus Eaton to John L. Lewis, n.d., John L. Lewis G. A. File, 1960-1969, UMWAA.

54. "Statement of John L. Lewis before Subcommittee on Welfare and Pension Funds of the United States Senate Committee on Labor and Public Welfare, Nov. 28, 1955," p. 2. Misc. File, UMWAA.

55. Robert J. Myers, "Experience of the UMWA Welfare and Retirement Fund," *Industrial and Labor Relations Review* (Oct., 1956), pp. 93-100; *Annual Reports, UMWA Welfare and Retirement Fund,* 1954-1958, JLL Papers (microfilm copy), SHSW, Reel 2.

56. Ruth Q. Sun, "Mine Workers Served by Unique Health Plan," *GP* (May, 1953), pp. 89-93; Robert J. Myers, "Further Experience of the UMWA Welfare and Retirement Fund," *Industrial and Labor Relations Review* (July, 1961), pp. 556-562.

57. J. E. Finley, p. 186, UMWJ, July 1, 1957, p. 10.

58. Robert J. Myers, "Experience of the UMWA Welfare and Retirement Fund," *Industrial and Labor Relations Review* (Oct., 1956), p. 96; Washington, D.C. *Time-Herald*, Sept. 8, 1953.

59. R. Q. Sun, p. 91; J. E. Finley, pp. 189-190.

60. J. E. Finley, pp. 190-191.

61. R. Q. Sun, p. 75; *Business Week* (June 14, 1958), p. 30; *Charleston Gazette*, clipping, n.d., Josephine Roche Papers, Box 25, UCL.

62. *Proceedings 1956 Convention*, UMWA, p. 419.

63. UMWJ, June 15, 1956.

64. NYT, Nov. 10, 1952, p. 17; Nov. 22, 1952, p. 24; *Proceedings 1956 Convention*, UMWA, p. 290.

65. NYT, Aug. 25, 1949, p. 26, Sept. 24, 1949, p. 24, Sept. 28, 1949, p. 31, Oct. 5, 1949, p. 25, Oct. 21, 1949, p. 19, Jan. 13, 1950, p. 24.

66. NYT, Feb. 25, 1950, p. 8.

67. John L. Lewis, "Labor and the Domestic Economy: Time for Teamwork," *Vital Speeches* (July, 1953), pp. 634-638.

68. UMWJ, May 15, 1959, p. 7; *Statement of John L. Lewis in Opposition to the Taft-Hartley Act, April 24, 1953,* JLL Papers (microfilm copy), SHSW, Reel 2.

69. UMWJ, May 15, 1959, p. 3.

70. UMWJ, July 1, 1957, p. 10.

71. UMWJ, June 15, 1959, p. 10.

72. T. Armbrister, pp. 303-305.

73. UMWJ, May 15, 1959, p. 8.

74. NYT, Feb. 20, 1947, p. 27; "Certificate," JLL Papers (microfilm copy), SHSW, Reel 2.

75. Washington, D.C. *Evening Star*, June 13, 1948; Washington, D.C. *Evening Star*, Nov. 21, 1956.

76. UMWJ, Jan. 15, 1958, p. 4.

77. UMWJ, Dec. 15, 1959, p. 3.

78. John H. Wollen to John L. Lewis, Dec. 31, 1959, Josephine Roche Papers, Box 25, UCL.

79. Draft, Herbert Hoover to John L. Lewis (December 18, 1959), Herbert Hoover Papers, "Individual-Lewis, John L.," Hoover Library.

NOTES TO CHAPTER 22

1. NYT, Jan. 15, 1960, p. 8.

2. Trevor Armbrister, *Act of Vengeance* (New York, 1975), p. 43; Interview with John Owens, Dec. 5, 1975, Cambridge, Ohio.

3. UMWJ, July 1, 1962, p. 3; Cyrus Eaton to Josephine Roche, Dec. 17, 1962, and Eaton to John L. Lewis, May 15, 1964, Josephine Roche Papers, Box 25, UCL.

4. UMWJ, July 15, 1962, p. 8; Joseph E. Finley, *The Corrupt Kingdom* (New York, 1972), pp. 174-175; NYT, May 20, 1961, p. 21; Memorandum, John Owens to W. A. Boyle, R. O. Lewis, John L. Lewis, Sept. 25, 1963, John L. Lewis Personal, GA File, UMWAA.

5. "Report of the United Mine Workers of America Welfare and Retirement Fund for year ending June 30, 1961," JLL Papers (microfilm copy), SHSW, Reel 2.

6. J. E. Finley, pp. 191-193; R. O. Lewis to John L. Lewis, Mar. 15, 1963, Misc. file, UMWAA; Brit Hume, *Death in the Mines* (New York, 1971), pp. 31-34.

7. J. E. Finley, pp. 193-197; B. Hume, p. 32; Robert J. Myers, "The Mine Workers' Welfare and Retirement Fund: Fifteen Years' Experience," *Industrial and Labor Relations Review* (Jan. 1967), p. 269.

8. J. E. Finley, pp. 191-192; B. Hume, pp. 33-34.

9. J. E. Finley, pp. 34-35; B. Hume, pp. 34-35.

10. "Remarks of Joseph P. Routh, April 3, 1963," JLL Papers (microfilm copy), SHSW, Reel 3.

11. "Remarks of John L. Lewis, April 3, 1963," JLL Papers (microfilm copy), SHSW, Reel 3.

12. *Ibid.*

13. Josephine Roche Papers, Box 25, CUL.

14. UMWJ, July 1, 1969, p. 22.

15. "E. V. Debs File," John L. Lewis—Personal File, UMWAA.

16. John L. Lewis to Frederick A. Colwell, Oct. 12, 1961, John L. Lewis—Personal, M.A. File, UMWAA.

17. UMWJ, June 1, 1964, p. 12; Interview with George DeNucci, Dec. 5, 1975, Columbus, Ohio.

18. UMWJ, Jan. 1, 1964, p. 4.

19. UMWJ, Mar. 1, 1965, pp. 13-14; UMWJ, July 1, 1969, pp. 22-23; UMWJ, June 1, 1964, p. 4; UMWJ, Jan. 1, 1964, p. 4.

20. UMWJ, Jan. 1, 1964, p. 4. John L. Lewis to Josephine Roche, Apr. 27, 1964; Lewis to Randolph C. Downes, Apr. 20, 1959; Lewis to Justin McCarthy, June 23, 1967; Harold Ward to Roche, Feb. 26, 1964; and Rex Lauck to Lewis, Feb. 25, 1964, all in Josephine Roche Papers, Box 25, UCL. Lewis to McCarthy, Feb. 28, 1963, John L. Lewis—Personal File. M.A. 1960-1969, UMWAA.

21. John L. Lewis to Josephine Roche, Aug. 30, 1960, Josephine Roche Papers, Box 25, UCL.

22. Josephine Roche to John L. Lewis, Aug. 19, 1964, Box 25, UCL.

23. Josephine Roche to John L. Lewis, Dec. 22, 1959, Josephine Roche Papers, Box 25, UCL.

24. Cyrus Eaton to John L. Lewis, Dec. 28, 1963, and Eaton to Lewis, Feb. 12, 1968, John L. Lewis—Personal, GA File 1960-1967, UMWAA.

25. John L. Lewis to Thomas D. Lewis, Dec. 8, 1955, John L. Lewis—Personal File, UMWAA.

26. UMWJ, Jan. 15, 1962, p. 5; NYT, Jan. 8, 1962, p. 39.

27. Len DeCaux, *Labor Radical* (Boston, 1970), p. 258.

28. NYT, Mar. 24, 1964, p. 1.

29. B. Hume, pp. 42-43.

30. T. Armbrister, p. 58.

31. J. E. Finley, pp. 280-281.

32. B. Hume, p. 16.

33. NYT, May 23, 1969, p. 20.
34. T. Armbrister, p. 59.
35. *Ibid.*, pp. 58-59, 74-75.
36. NYT, June 13, 1969, p. 47.
37. Saul D. Alinsky, *John L. Lewis* (New York, 1949), p. 372.
38. NYT, June 13, 1969, p. 46.

Sources

Any thorough bibliography of sources, books, and essays that sheds light on John L. Lewis and the American labor movement would be voluminous, owing to his more than five decades of trade-union activity and his significance to recent United States history. What follows, then, does no more than discuss the sources that proved most important in preparing a life of Lewis, offer some insight into our research methods, and note the best of the published literature.

Recently oral history interviews have become quite the rage among biographers, and we must admit that we too used an extensive number of such interviews in preparing the life of John L. Lewis. Yet interviews with acquaintances and associates of Lewis proved simultaneously illuminating and disappointing. Those interviewed personally by the authors either did not know Lewis well enough, their memories had dimmed owing to age, or, for whatever reasons, they preferred to reveal little about Lewis. These factors made such interviews of limited use to us. The interviews recorded by others and collected in university-sponsored oral history collections proved even more treacherous to use. Owing either to inadequate preparation on the part of the interviewer and carelessness or obfuscation on the part of the interviewee, many of the oral history transcripts are replete with contradictions and factual errors, both gross and minor. If we had relied on oral history to develop facts about Lewis, we would have written an inaccurate biography. Only facts that could be verified by other more trustworthy sources were taken from the oral histories. If the oral histories were useful—and indeed they were—their utility lay in the interviewees' characterization of John L. Lewis as a person, their anecdotes, apocryphal stories, and rendering of milieu. Oral history, as generally practiced in this country, excels in providing historical *color* and dramatic tales; it fails to elucidate past events accurately. In short, our characterization of Lewis's personality relies to some extent on oral history; our description and analysis of his career and actions, except for anecdotes, does not.

The same problems beset our correspondence with surviving members of the Lewis family—all from Myrta's side—and individuals born and raised in turn-of-the-century Lucas. In most cases, such correspondence confirmed facts we derived elsewhere or provided information, occasionally quite revealing, available only to family members.

Despite all the limitations we discovered during our travails with oral history, we may have relied on such information too heavily—but not without good reason. What remains in the way of John L. Lewis papers is most noteworthy for its lack of personal correspondence or records. The main body of Lewis papers stored at the State Historical Society of Wisconsin and available on microfilm contains almost *no* family letters. Its most revealing sections include three Lewis travel diaries (largely an expense record), family bills and receipts for antiques and household furnishings, typescripts of Lewis's major public speeches, and an excellent collection of newspaper and magazine clippings. Remarkably, the United Mine Workers Archives contain more personal correspondence than the Lewis private papers. And even then, family letters are rare indeed. Because the union archives had not yet been collated or catalogued when we worked through it, we may have missed items of interest. But it seems clear from the union's records that Lewis preferred to conduct "official" business over the telephone or face-to-face, *not* on paper. He also preferred phone conversations to correspondence with Myrta, and the only surviving letters to his children, grandchildren, and other family members are most notable for their formality and coldness.

The archival materials on Lewis's union and public career are rather better. The papers of Adolph Germer (SHSW), John Brophy (CUA), and William Mitch (PSULA), associates and critics of Lewis in the United Mine Workers and CIO, are filled with correspondence, printed materials, and detailed diaries (for Germer and Brophy) that describe internal struggles in the miners' union and CIO. The John H. Walker Papers (University of Illinois Library) are replete with letters concerning Lewis's rise to power in the UMW and the union's electoral shenanigans from 1916 to 1930. The Edward Wieck and Heber Blankenhorn Papers (ALHUA, WSU) are particularly good on the history of the mine workers and CIO from the 1920s through the 1940s. The Powers Hapgood Papers (Lilly Library, University of Indiana) contains revealing correspondence on UMW politics during the 1920s, especially the role of Communists, the founding of CIO, and Lewis's resignation as CIO president in 1940. In a class by itself are the papers of W. Jett Lauck (Alderson Library, University of Virginia) for he was Lewis's official economic consultant, tax adviser, and something of a friend. Lauck's diaries, in particular, disclose much about Lewis's personal and official behavior during the 1930s.

Three collections are especially important on the founding and early history of the CIO. The AFL Papers (SHSW) and the Executive Council minutes, 1933-1936 (in possession of David Brody), include thousands of pages of material and correspondence concerning the struggle between the industrial union advocates and the "old guard" of the A. F. of L. Katherine Pollack Ellickson's Papers (FDRL, microfilm) include her original handwritten minutes, as well as typed copies, of early CIO executive board meetings that offer rare insight into Lewis's attitudes and strategy, c. 1936-1937. The Sidney Hillman Papers (Amalgamated Clothing Workers of America Archives) are especially good on the founding of CIO, its early activities, and the eventual split between Hillman and Lewis.

The papers and records of federal officials and agencies provide the best sources for the history of Lewis's politics and the relationship among the UMWA, the coal operators, and the federal government. The papers of all the Presidents from Calvin Coolidge through Harry S Truman are filled with items dealing with coal strikes, Lewis's collective-bargaining and strike tactics, and the efforts of the chief executives to temper Lewis's behavior without suffering political damage. Several collections in the National Archives and the Federal Records Center, Suitland, Maryland, also contain similar sorts of material. Record Group 174, the general records of the Department of Labor, are especially rich for the tenures of secretaries William B. Wilson, 1913-1921, and Frances Perkins, 1933-1945. Record Group 60, Department of Justice, has excellent files on the 1919 coal strike and developments in West Virginia during the 1920s. Record Group 280, the files of the United States Mediation and Conciliation Service, are most helpful in tracing the changing pattern of behavior toward Lewis and the UMWA displayed by coal operators. Record Group 9, National Recovery Administration, includes interesting data on public policy concerning unionism in the coal mines, 1933-1935. Record Groups 202 (National War Labor Board) and 245 (Solid Fuels Administration) are the best sources of material on the World War II miners' strikes, Lewis's wartime antics, and federal reactions to the aforementioned.

A word must be said about collections whose contents promised much but disclosed little. The Philip Murray and CIO papers (CUA) were singularly disappointing in substance though voluminous. The same can be said about the Josephine Roche Papers (Western Historical Collections, University of Colorado). Despite Roche's long and close relationship with Lewis, few truly illuminating items appear in the papers currently open for use. Equally disappointing were the papers of Van A. Bittner (West Virginia University Library), Michael Kosik (PSULA), and the CIO secretary treasurer's office (ALUHA, WSU). Other collections that, although not disappointing, provided only scattered fragments of information are cited in the full list of sources consulted.

Among printed sources the most important were the proceedings of the United Mine Workers, the A. F. of L., and the CIO, as well as the *United Mine Workers Journal.* Congressional hearings on coal mining and federal reports also contained considerable amounts of information. Less useful were such industry trade journals as *Coal Age, Coal Trade Bulletin, Black Diamond, American Miner,* and *CIO News.*

PRIMARY SOURCES

1. *Personal Interviews*
   Len DeCaux
   George DeNucci
   David Dubinsky
   Rex Lauck
   John Owens
   Jacob Potofsky
   A. H. Raskin

2. *Lewis Family and Lucas Area Correspondents*
   Mrs. Doris Bell
   Mrs. Herbert Bell
   Mrs. Fern B. Bryden
   Mrs. Albert Halls
   Mrs. Mary MacNamara

3. *Oral History Transcripts*
   A. *Columbia University Oral History Collection*

Major	Minor	
John Brophy	James Carey	Norman Thomas
Cyrus Ching	John Carmody	Stanley Washburn
Gardner Jackson	Marquis Childs	Leo Wolman
Edwin A. Lahey	William H. Davis	
James M. Landis	J. W. Edelman	
Isadore Lubin	Julius Emspak	
Frances Perkins	Morris Ernst	
Lee Pressman	John Frey	
Alfred Staehle	Alfred J. Hayes	
(McGraw-Hill Project)	Nicholas Kelley	
J. David Stern	Arthur Krock	
R. J. Thomas	J. W. Madden	
Florence Thorne	Edward McKinney	
	H. L. Mitchell	
	Edward A. O'Neal	
	William Pollock	
	George Rublee	
	Boris Shiskin	

B. *Pennsylvania State University Oral History Collection*

Major	*Minor*
John W. Chorey	Albert Atallah
David J. McDonald	Ross Atwell
Rt. Rev. Msgr. Charles Rice	Earl Bester
James Robb	John Brownlee
	Hugh Carcella
	Ruben E. Farr
	John Grajciar
	James J. Matles
	George Patterson
	Harold J. Ruttenberg
	Harry Wines
	N. A. Zonarich

C. *Sangamon State University—Coal Mining and Union Activities Project*
Art Gramlich
Myrta Nickey
Joseph Ozanic, Sr.

4. *Manuscript and Archival Collections*

A. *John L. Lewis Records*

John L. Lewis Papers, Microfilm Set, State Historical Society of Wisconsin.
United Mine Workers of America Archives, John L. Lewis Master Alphabetical File, Subject Matter File, Personal File, and Miscellaneous Files.

B. *Records of Labor Leaders and Trade Unions*

A. F. of L. Papers, State Historical Society of Wisconsin.
A. F. of L., Executive Council Minutes, 1933-1936, Microfilm, Possession of Professor David Brody.
Heber Blankenhorn Papers, Archives of Labor History and Urban Affairs, Wayne State University.
Van A. Bittner Papers, West Virginia University Library.
John Brophy Papers, Catholic University of America.
CIO Papers, Catholic University of America.
CIO Secretary Treasurer's Office Records, Archives of Labor History and Urban Affairs, Wayne State University.
Katherine Pollack Ellickson Papers, Franklin D. Roosevelt Library.
John Frey Papers, Library of Congress.
Adolph Germer Papers, State Historical Society of Wisconsin.
Samuel Gompers Letterbooks, Library of Congress.
Powers Hapgood Papers, Lilly Library, Indiana University.
Sidney Hillman Papers, Amalgamated Clothing Workers of America Archives.
Michael Kosik Papers, Pennsylvania State University Labor Archives.
Henry J. Kraus Papers, Archives of Labor History and Urban Affairs, Wayne State University.
Louis Leonard Papers, Pennsylvania State University Labor Archives.
Duncan MacDonald Papers, Illinois State Historical Survey, Springfield.

William Mitch Papers, Pennsylvania State University Labor Archives.
Philip Murray Papers, Catholic University of America.
Harold J. Ruttenberg Papers, Pennsylvania State University Labor Archives.
Steel Workers Organizing Committee-CIO, Pennsylvania State University Labor
    Archives.
Hazel and Bud Simons Papers, Archives of Labor History and Urban Affairs, Wayne
    State University.
United Mine Workers of America, District 6 Papers, Ohio University Archives.
John H. Walker Papers, University of Illinois Library.
Edward A. Wieck Papers, Archives of Labor History and Urban Affairs, Wayne State
    Affairs, Wayne State University.

C. *Public Records and Archives*
  a) *Presidential*
    Calvin Coolidge Papers, Library of Congress.
    Dwight D. Eisenhower Papers, Eisenhower Library, Abilene, Kansas.
    Warren G. Harding Papers, Ohio Historical Society.
    Herbert Hoover Papers, Hoover Library, West Branch, Iowa.
    Franklin D. Roosevelt Papers, Roosevelt Library, Hyde Park, New York.
    Harry S Truman Papers, Truman Library, Independence, Missouri.
    Woodrow Wilson Papers, Library of Congress.
  b) *National Archives*
    Department of Justice, Record Group 60.
    Department of Labor, Record Group 174, Boxes 86-187.
    National Recovery Administration, Record Group 9.
    National War Labor Board, Record Group 202 (also at Federal Records Center,
        Suitland, Maryland).
    Solid Fuels Administration, Record Group 245, Federal Records Center, Suitland,
        Maryland.
    United States Mediation and Conciliation Service, Record Group 280 (also Federal
        Records Center, Suitland, Maryland).

D. *Miscellaneous Collections*
  Justus Collins Papers, West Virginia University Library.
  Clark M. Clifford Papers, Truman Library, Independence, Missouri.
  Warner Gardner Papers, Truman Library, Independence, Missouri.
  Harold L. Ickes Papers, Library of Congress.
  W. Jett Lauck Papers, Alderson Library, University of Virginia.
  Josephine Roche Papers, Western Historical Collections, University of Colorado.

BASIC SECONDARY LITERATURE

A. *The Biographical Void*

Cecil Carnes, *John L. Lewis: Leader of Labor* (New York, 1936), the first of the
biographies is also the poorest. Focused largely on Lewis's public career during the 1920s,
it is a pastiche of newspaper clippings, nonanalytical, and almost hagiographical in its
admiration for Lewis. Carnes also prints false information about the Lewis family that
subsequent biographers simply reprinted.

C. L. Sulzberger's *Sit-Down with John L. Lewis* (New York, 1938), is better than Carnes, provides more analysis, although brief, and is infinitely better written.

James Wechsler, *Labor Baron: A Portrait of John L. Lewis* (New York, 1944), is a powerful indictment of the labor leader. Written in response to Lewis's break with Franklin D. Roosevelt and the World War II coal strikes, Wechsler's book criticizes Lewis for sacrificing both the national interest and the future of the labor movement to his own selfish ambitions. If Wechsler does justice to Lewis's critics and victims, he, too, fails to illuminate his subject's personal life, reprints Carnes' errors, and underestimates Lewis's contribution to the American labor movement. A similar evaluation applies to Wellington Roe's extensive biographic treatment of Lewis in *Juggernaut* (Philadelphia, 1948), written to defend the passage of the Taft-Hartley Act.

Saul D. Alinsky, *John L. Lewis: An Unauthorized Biography* (New York, 1949), is the strangest book of all. Considered by many to be an example of hagiography, Lewis himself considered it inaccurate and misleading. Large sections of the biography reprint verbatim the content of conversations between Lewis and Alinsky. Yet nothing in the surviving Lewis papers suggests that Alinsky and Lewis were close, met often, and engaged in long conversations. Moreover, the Alinsky Papers at the University of Illinois-Congress Circle contain no notes or other evidence that Alinsky used in the preparation of the biography. It is hard to conceive that a man who rejected out-of-hand Alfred A. Knopf's proposal (with a substantial cash advance) that A. J. Liebling prepare a Lewis-sanctioned biography opened his soul to Saul Alinsky. Hence Alinsky's book must be read with great caution.

C. K. McFarland, *Roosevelt, Lewis, and the New Deal, 1933-1940* (Fort Worth, 1970), is simply too insubstantial, skimpily researched, and nonanalytical to be of much use. And Rex Lauck (ed.), *John L. Lewis and The International Union* (Washington, D.C., 1952), is essentially a UMWA "souvenir" publication.

Louis Adamic, *My America, 1928-1938* (New York, 1938), contains, among other essays, perhaps the most perceptive analysis of Lewis's character, ideas, and ambitions.

George M. Korson's children's biography, *John L. Lewis: Young Militant Labor Leader* (Indianapolis, 1970), is interesting for two reasons. First, Lewis chose Korson as official biographer and UMW historian. Second, Lewis spent time with Korson and conversed with him at length. For those reasons, the children's biography, if not factually accurate, describes Lewis's family life, childhood, and adolescence precisely as the subject preferred to remember it or embellish it.

B. *The Mine Workers: An Historical Lacuna*

No solid, scholarly study of the UMWA currently exists. A variety of monographs probe specialized aspects of the coal industry, labor-management relations, and brief periods of union history. The closest version to a synthesis remains McAlester Coleman, *Men and Coal* (New York, 1943), a spritely journalistic account of American coal miners and their struggle to build a union. It is a fast-paced sympathetic treatment of miners and their union and Lewis's stewardship of the UMW that runs from the mid-nineteenth century to the 1943 wartime strike.

If no up-to-date history of national unionism among the mine workers is in print, the situation for the districts and regions is worse. Not a single UMWA district or a geographically homogeneous American coal-mining region is the subject of a book or monograph, scholarly or otherwise.

Knowledge about life and culture among American coal miners in Lewis's lifetime is almost equally bare. Aside from several sterile sociological analyses of coal-mining communities since 1945, we must rely for insight into the miners' way of life on such autobiographies as John Brophy, *A Miner's Life,* edited by John O.H.P. Hall (Madison, Wis., 1964), and Wyndham Mortimer, *Organize! My Life As a Union Man* (Boston, 1971), or Jack Conroy's novel, *The Disinherited* (New York, 1933).

C. *Prosperity, Depression, and New Deal, 1920-1940*

For this period of Lewis's career, many excellent books and essays provide background information. Irving Bernstein's *The Lean Years: A History of the American Worker, 1933-1940* (Boston, 1969), provides the best synthesis of labor history during the interwar years. Bernstein covers working conditions, the evolution of trade unionism, politics, government-labor relations and many other topics in great detail.

The impact of federal government actions on Lewis and the mine workers during the 1920s can best be followed in Robert H. Zieger, *Republicans and Labor, 1919-1929* (Lexington, Ky., 1969), and Ellis Hawley, "Secretary Hoover and the Bituminous Coal Problem, 1921-1928," *Business History Review,* XLII (Autumn, 1968), 247-270.

A series of excellent contemporary books describes the great labor upheaval of the 1930s. Among the best are Edward Levinson, *Labor on the March* (New York, 1956 ed.), written by the *New York Post*'s labor reporter and later publicist for the United Auto Workers; Mary Heaton Vorse, *Labor's New Millions* (New York, 1938), by a left-wing journalist-activist who sympathized openly with the more militant members of CIO; Herbert Harris, *Labor's Civil War* (New York, 1940), by a union sympathizer who understood the causes of the interunion conflicts as well as the justice of the CIO's position yet treated the A. F. of L. fairly; and Robert R. Brooks, *When Labor Organizes* (New Haven, 1938), and *Unions of Their Own Choosing* (New Haven, 1939), more scholarly studies of how new unions emerged in 1936-1937 and the impact of the National Labor Relations Board on trade unionism.

Studies of Franklin D. Roosevelt and the New Deal are too numerous to cite separately and, moreover, most of them devote relatively little space to the labor upheaval. But in order to understand better the political milieu of the 1930s, one should consult James M. Burns, *Roosevelt: The Lion and the Fox* (New York, 1956); William E. Leuchtenberg, *Franklin D. Roosevelt and the New Deal, 1932-1940* (New York, 1963), and Arthur M. Schlesinger, Jr., *The Coming of the New Deal* (Boston, 1959), and *The Politics of Upheaval* (Boston, 1960).

Several long and detailed books analyze the split within the labor movement. The most encyclopaedic and dispassionate of such studies is Walter Galenson, *The CIO Challenge to the AFL: A History of the American Labor Movement, 1935-1941* (Cambridge, Mass., 1960). Equally encyclopaedic but duller is Philip Taft's second volume in his official history of the A. F. of L., *The A. F. of L. from the Death of Gompers to the Merger* (New York, 1959). More stirring and also highly partisan is the history of the CIO written by Trotskyist journalist Art Preis, who covered labor affairs for the Socialist Workers party newspaper, *Labor's Giant Step: Twenty Years of the CIO* (New York, 1964).

Especially revealing insights into John L. Lewis's role and behavior during the 1930s may be found in three narrower, more specialized studies of the period. Sidney Fine, *Sit-Down: The General Motors Strike of 1936-1937* (Ann Arbor, 1969), is a densely detailed description of the most important CIO strike and the best analysis in print of government-labor interaction during the New Deal. Matthew Josephson, *Sidney Hillman: Statesman of American Labor* (New York, 1952), is good on the emergence of CIO, relations between Lewis and Hillman, and Lewis's break with Roosevelt. Len DeCaux, *Labor Radical: From the Wobblies to CIO* (Boston, 1970), presents an exceedingly sympathetic portrait of Lewis and his role in CIO through the eyes and memory of the CIO's first editor-publicist and also a Communist.

Finally, a series of essays and review-essays by David Brody raises the most salient questions concerning the emergence of CIO, the triumph of mass-production unionism, and the role of John L. Lewis: "The Emergence of Mass-Production Unionism," in John Braeman *et. al.* (eds.), *Change and Continuity in Twentieth-Century America* (Columbus, Ohio, 1964); "The Expansion of the American Labor Movement: Institutional Sources of Stimulus and Restraint," in Stephen E. Ambrose (ed.), *Institutions in Modern America* (Baltimore, 1967), pp. 11-36; "Labor and the Great Depression: The Interpretive Prospects," *Labor History*, XIII (Spring, 1972), 231-244; "Radical Labor History and Rank-and-File Militancy," *ibid.*, XVI (Winter, 1975), 117-126.

D. *War, Affluent Society, and Retirement, 1941-1969*

Several young scholars are beginning to correct the lack of historical studies of labor during and immediately following World War II. Still, Joel Seidman's *American Labor from Defense to Reconversion* (Chicago, 1953) remains the best published survey of government wartime agencies and policies, although it is limited by the archival collections available at the time of writing. With the passing of two decades, Nelson Lichtenstein ably exploited a vast range of sources for his excellent "Industrial Unionism Under the No-Strike Pledge: A Study of the CIO During the Second World War" (Ph.D. dissertation, University of California, Berkeley, 1974), which contains valuable information on government policy and Lewis's responses. Thomas C. Clapp, "The Bituminous Coal Strike of 1943" (Ph.D. dissertation, University of Toledo, 1974) is a generally useful—although in places confused—narrative of this critical event. The important January, 1943, anthracite rebellion is treated in J. R. Sperry, "Rebellion Within the Ranks: Pennsylvania Anthracite, John L. Lewis, and the Coal Strike of 1943," *Pennsylvania History*, XL (July, 1973), 293-312.

Few historical studies exist on labor in the late 1940s and 1950s, and in those works that are available Lewis and the UMW are scarcely mentioned because of their isolation from the mainstream of the union movement. Likewise, studies of the Truman Administration treat sparsely the president's feud with Lewis. David McDonald's self-serving autobiography *Union Man* (New York, 1969) provides only a few tidbits on his relations with his former boss. Joseph C. Goulden, *Meany* (New York, 1972) inflates and distorts its subject's disagreements with Lewis in order to make the AFL-CIO president appear as a titantic statesman of the labor movement.

Beginning in the 1960s, a number of "muckraking" books and articles exposed the corruption, mismanagement, and insensitivity of the UMWA. The most able of these is Brit Hume, *Death in the Mines* (New York, 1971), which focuses primarily on the manipulations of the Welfare and Retirement Fund, the problems of black lung disease, and the union's reluctance to demand mine safety. Joseph E. Finley, *The Corrupt Kingdom* (New York, 1972) is an interesting "lawyer's brief" linking the crimes of the Boyle regime to the earlier practices of John L. Lewis. T. N. Bethel's Appalachian Movement Press pamphlet *Conspiracy in Coal* (Huntington, W. Va., n.d.) exposes Lewis's cozy relationship with the big operators in the 1950s and also criticizes the union's financial empire. Finally, several popular books treat the events surrounding Yablonski's murder, the best of which is Treavor Armbrister, *Act of Vengeance* (New York, 1975).

Index

Index